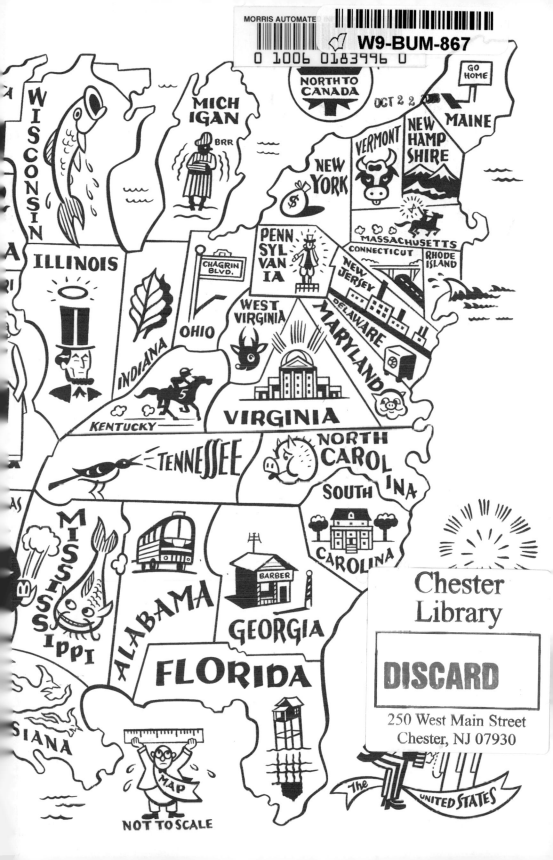

STATE

BY

STATE

Also edited by
Matt Weiland and Sean Wilsey

The Thinking Fan's Guide to the World Cup

An Imprint of HarperCollins*Publishers*

STATE

BY

STATE

A PANORAMIC PORTRAIT
OF AMERICA

EDITED BY

Matt Weiland & Sean Wilsey

HarperCollins books may be purchased for educational, business,
or sales promotional use. For information, please write:
Special Markets Department, HarperCollins Publishers,
10 East 53rd Street, New York, NY 10022.

FIRST EDITION

Book design by Sunil Manchikanti
Insert design by Jennifer Ann Daddio and Sunil Manchikanti

Library of Congress Cataloging-in-Publication Data is
available upon request.

ISBN: 978-0-06-147090-5

08 09 10 11 12   OV/RRD   10 9 8 7 6 5 4 3 2 1

Contents

List of Tables

Preface
Matt Weiland

This book started with a hunch and a conviction. The conviction was the easy part: that despite drive-time radio and the nightly news and the Sunday paper, despite all the books and blog posts, the documentaries and songs, America and the lives lived here remain strangely and surprisingly underdescribed. So many mirrors and yet we know ourselves so poorly! Often it takes a tragedy to remind us so: when residents of the Lower Ninth Ward in New Orleans stand dazed on their rooftops wondering why the flood water came so fast and the drinking water so slow; when coal miners are rescued in West Virginia or entombed in Utah; when the lives of cleaners and brokers, accountants and firemen are memorialized after September 11—who hasn't marvelled at the richness of lives we don't know?

The same is true of the landscape and the past we've lived across it. The topography and climate of America may be the richest in the world, yet what ends up on the page so rarely seems to capture its dynamism, its variety, its intensity. Sure, the deepest canyons and the wettest waterfalls and the curviest roads make cameos in ads for automobiles and soda pop and life insurance; and plenty of stories, fictional and true, are set in the streets and skylines of our principal cities. But what about everywhere else: the half-dead towns too alive to be ghosts, the rusting historical markers buried in the weeds, the anonymous bits of land with their own hidden histories and surprising beauties and grace? There is poetry in the Rand McNally Atlas and wonder in the back rooms and basements of a thousand local archives and historical societies, but all too often it seems trapped there. Somehow we've come to take for granted what our country looks like, what happened here, and what it feels like to live here. Shouldn't we know it all in finer detail?

The hunch was less obvious, but the more we thought about it the more convinced we became of its truth. It was this: that America, for all its bland interstate highways and big-box superstores, retains an essential, deep-grained variety. No one doubts that America is growing more homogeneous with each passing year. Go from one time zone to another and the increasing sameness of everywhere is plain: one city blurs into another; the same architects build the same buildings, the same stores line the same streets, the same songs play on the radio; regional accents fade and everyone seems to be from somewhere else. And yet the fifty states—united by rhetoric and musket nearly 250 years ago, reaffirmed in their unity by rhetoric and rifle a century later, and bound together today as tightly as any confederation on earth—somehow stubbornly resist blending into a single undifferentiated whole.

The fifty states differ in landscape, topography, and weather; in political outlook, cultural preference, and social ideals; in accent, temperament, and sense of humor. It's not just that the West Coast is a world away from the East, that Yankees stick out in the South, or that Blue States and Red States don't see eye to eye. It's deeper than that: The fifty states themselves have individual places in our collective imagination, and they offer their natives a mind-set, even a world-view. For all the talk of identity in American life, the personal fact that defines American lives as much as gender, ethnicity, or class is where you're from, which more than anything means your home state.

Sean Wilsey and I started talking about all this last year, just as I was moving back to America after four years of living abroad. I was hitting the Americana hard: I read *Moby Dick* and *Huck Finn* again, and I gorged on Preston Sturges films and Will Eisner comics and the aching Old Time music that is heavy on banjos and beards. I spent a long Sunday walking down Broadway and a weekend bicycling on the Jersey Shore and a week driving 3,000 miles through the Midwest. I ate a whole lot of pie. I was reveling in what the poet Delmore Schwartz called "the beautiful American word, Sure," and growing obsessed with the vibrancy and individuality of the American states. I told more than one person that I thought the Indian mounds of Ohio were deeply, profoundly fascinating; that the glories of the Nevada desert remain shockingly unsung; that I wanted a long slow bus ride in the wake of Sherman's March through Georgia or along the Great Western Cattle Trail from Texas through Oklahoma and Kansas. I don't know what I was after, exactly, except to experience again some simple American virtues: the essential looseness of American lives, the vitality and variety of American vistas, the cut and jib of American talk.

The more Sean and I talked about it, the more we wanted to know the details—what makes one state different from another? What are each state's particularities and idiosyncrasies, their prejudices and biases, their beauty marks and moles, their cadences and jokes? We knew we couldn't find out everything—who could possibly be comprehensive about their own household, let alone an entire state? But couldn't we put together a book that captures something essential, something fundamental and distinctive about each state? We wanted something broad-minded and good-hearted; something bold, intimate, and funny; something full of personal anecdote and strange characters and hidden truths. What we wanted, we realized, was a road trip in book form. Who better to turn to than our finest novelists and reporters?

Such a project had been done before on a much grander scale: the WPA American Guide series of the Federal Writers' Project in the 1930s. As part of the New Deal, the Federal Writers' Project put more than six thousand American writers, archivists, and researchers back to work, creating a vivid, detailed, and lasting portrait of America at the time. Some of the finest writers in the country worked for the project, including Conrad Aiken, Nelson Algren, Saul Bellow, Arna Bontemps, John Cheever, Jack Conroy, Edward Dahlberg, Ralph Ellison, Zora Neale Hurston, David Ignatow, Meridel LeSueur, Kenneth Rexroth, Wallace Stegner, Studs Terkel, and Richard Wright. The project produced hundreds of books and pamphlets, including guides to dozens of major cities, as well as to interstates and regions (*U.S. 1*; *The Oregon Trail*; *The Arrowhead of Minnesota*; *Here's New England!*). The project also gathered oral histories, slave narratives, recordings of folk songs, and collections of folklore and social history (*The Italians of Omaha*; *The Negro in New York*; *Baseball in Old Chicago*; *Who's Who in the Zoo*).

But the crowning achievement of the Federal Writers' Project was the creation of the state guides. Taking as their mantra "To describe America to Americans," these books documented the forty-eight states of the time in unprecedented detail and with great charm. Each guide ran more than 500 pages and featured original, unsigned essays on a state's history, its literature and art, its architecture and public transportation, its flora and fauna, its industry and agriculture. Many included essays on topics unique to each state as well: on the movie industry in California and dairy farming in Wisconsin; on marine lore in Michigan and tall tales in Oregon; on arts and crafts in Arizona and cuisine in Louisiana; on mining jargon in Nevada and Chinook words in Alaska; on Abraham Lincoln in Illinois and Daniel Boone in Kentucky. Each guide also featured detailed descriptions of that state's major cities and towns; maps and guided tours of each state's principal monuments and attractions; and a section of original photographs, too. (Eudora Welty took photos for the Mississippi guide; Ben Shahn took ones for Ohio.)

It was an extraordinarily ambitious project, guided by the will to describe, by intrepid curiosity, by raw idealism, and by a reinvigorated sense of national pride even at the depths of the Depression. Writers, critics, and historians of the time hailed it as a landmark undertaking. John Steinbeck called the state guides "the most comprehensive account of the United States ever got together . . . by the best writers in America." To Lewis Mumford, they were "the finest contribution to American patriotism that has been made in our generation." And Alfred Kazin said they constituted "an extraordinary epic. . . . Out of the great storehouse of facts behind the guides—geological, geographic, meteorological, ethnological, historical, political, sociological, economic—there emerged an America unexampled in density and regional diversity."

Even President Franklin D. Roosevelt gave the project an encomium, though he wasn't at his fireside chattiest when he said of the guides that they "ably illustrate our national way of life yet at the same time portray variants in local patterns of living and regional development." Still: He was right. The BBC reporter Alistair Cooke was looser lipped when he wrote to the director of the Federal Writers' Project in 1939: "I hope to buy, beg, steal, annex, or 'protect' a complete library of the guides before I die." (He did, and with their model in mind he set off on a cross-country reporting road trip for the BBC in 1941. The result is the recently discovered manuscript published as *The American Home Front, 1941–1942*.)

But for all that, the Federal Writers' Project wasn't perfect. It was wracked by a Red Scare that tagged its underlying ideals and practical commitments as Communist propaganda, and it was riven by an ongoing argument over which writers federal money should be used to support: the most indigent or the most talented. This latter argument was reflected in the fact that some of the guides suffer from leaden prose and read as though they were written by committee—which was often the case. John Cheever, who was an editor on the *WPA Guide to New York City*, bitterly described his job as "twisting into order the sentences written by some incredibly lazy bastards." The WPA Guides were also conceived as guidebooks, which meant that for all their charm and information, they were too anonymous, too stiff, and too formulaic for what Sean and I had in mind.

So though we wanted to make a book inspired by the ideals behind the WPA Guides and the lore and telling details within them, we also wanted something more personal, more eccentric, and more partial. And, lacking the $27 million that the United States government poured into the Federal Writers' Project, we envisioned a single book rather than a thousand, this one featuring a different writer for each of the fifty states. Others over the years have had a similar idea, and we looked to them for inspiration too: the underappreciated journalist John Gunther's monumental *Inside U.S.A.* (1947); the anthology of fiction set in each state called *U.S. Stories* (1949); Neal R. Pierce and Jerry Hagstrom's astoundingly informative *Book of America: Inside Fifty States Today* (1983); the stylish series of pieces on each state that John Leonard edited for *The Nation* in 2002. We also looked to the wry charm of radio programs like Garrison Keillor's *A Prairie Home Companion*, Ira Glass's *This American Life*, and Michael Feldman's *Whad'Ya Know?*, as well as the travel writings of Calvin Trillin, Ian Frazier, and Roy Blount, Jr., and the songwriter Sufjan Stevens's quixotic project to record an album devoted to each of the fifty states.

So one spring day in Manhattan Sean and I huddled in a booth at the Old Town Bar to sort out a plan. First we agreed that we didn't want the pieces to be victory laps for writers known for writing about a particular state: We have loved and learned from—for example—Joan Didion on California, Carl Hiaasen on Florida, Garrison Keillor on Minnesota, and Larry McMurtry on Texas, but you won't find them here. We wanted some pieces by writers native to a particular state, of course, but we also wanted some by newcomers, and others by writers we'd send to states they'd never been to, to get a sense of the place as only a writer with a map and fresh eyes and a deadline can get. Second, we agreed that we didn't want the book to become a kind of beauty contest full of partisan arguments for the superiority of one's own state: We wanted the good, the bad, the ugly. Third, we wanted the book to go beyond personal history—so we sought out and commissioned travel accounts, historical essays, contemporary reportage, and works of oral history. To everyone we said: Tell us a story about your state, the more personal the better, something that captures the essence of the place. Not the kind of story one hears in a musty lecture hall or one reads in the dusty pages of an encyclopedia. The kind of story the enlisted soldier tells his boot-camp bunkmate about back home. The kind of story, wistful and wise, that begins, "Well, I don't know about you, but where I come from . . ."

With a map of America and a list of a couple hundred of our favorite writers before us, we started to seek out writers to tell us something we didn't know. I don't think it does any discredit to the writers here to say that others we asked declined our invitation: John Updike felt his knowledge of the place we asked him to write about was too rooted in the past for the task at hand; Don DeLillo preferred to write about what originated in his own "dim interior"; J. D. Salinger stayed silent. Other responses were disappointing but helpful in stirring our resolve: Richard Ford pointed to the danger of superficiality—quite right, we thought, and one we've strived hard to avoid, always prodding our writers to get out of their own skin, to write about ways their own experience was informed by that of others. Roger Angell was dubious about our hunch: "I would guess that a lot of the strong regionalism that was around in the 1930s has been wiped away, flattened by interstates and TV and by whole generations leaving home as fast as they can." Too true! And all the more reason to plow ahead, we thought, and see what particular, local, remains.

Angell also mentioned that he "remember[ed] the WPA books pretty well. The authors were inflamed by the concept and most of all by being paid money to write." Our authors were inflamed, but whether it was by the concept or the money I'm not sure. Some, it's true, took some convincing. I'm pretty sure we've promised a beer and a bump to every writer in the book. And the carton of frozen orange juice that Sean mailed to William T. Vollmann (uh . . . long story) likely has the Department of Homeland Security on our trail. But the simple truth is that everyone responded with enthusiasm and gusto even without—or anyway before—the juice and whiskey. Three writers even vied for the privilege of writing about New Jersey.

In the end we assembled a mix of novelists, reporters, cartoonists, a cook, a playwright, a filmmaker, and a musician. Their pieces total more than 200,000 words. What would someone who has never been to America make of it from their work? Perhaps she would detect a robust ambivalence about home: the kind of deep and nuanced patriotism, I'd say, that can only come from knowing your country's past and having faith in its future. Perhaps she'd note a prevalence of that singular American trait of buoyancy, an energetic warmth and open-mindedness, as well as a surprising obsession with bumper stickers, Native Americans, and Wal-Mart. And I imagine she'd notice a strong sense of renewal, of the great flux and energy that new waves of immigrants bring (as the pieces about Bosnians in Missouri, Chinese in

Georgia, Mexicans in Iowa, and at least one Ghanaian in Michigan make plain).

But for my part, in reading *State by State*, I'm just glad to have gone to some interesting places. Some are well known, like the Civil War battlefield at Shiloh, Robert Smithson's *Spiral Jetty*, the Alamo, Roswell, the headquarters of the IRS, the parking lot at Mount Rushmore, John James Audubon's house in Hendersonville, Kentucky, and Mark Twain's boyhood home in Hannibal, Missouri. Others are more anonymous but no less significant in their way: a pawnshop in Las Vegas, a roadhouse in Wichita, an S&M club in San Franciso, a diner in Key West.

And I'm glad to have learned something: I now know how to ditch-ski and how to make a good tortilla, how a salmon gets caught, and how a hog has sex (loudly). I know to ask for buttermilk pie in Texas, mint candy in Indiana, a Christmas kringle in Wisconsin, and a traveler in South Carolina. I know who Yoopers, Yup'iks, Sheepeaters, and Slower Lowers are; what frost heaves do; where the largest mass execution on American soil took place; when Michigan acquired its Upper Peninsula; and why there's no such thing as a Massachusettsean.

And I know this: that the complete set of WPA Guides that belonged to Alistair Cooke is in good hands—our writers'. In the middle of commissioning pieces from our fifty writers, Sean bought the set from a bookseller who kindly took a shine to our undertaking. We shipped them off to our contributors to inspire their work, and we hope the great curiosity about America and American lives those magnificent guides evince is evident in their essays.

State by State may not be the "great storehouse of facts" that Kazin declared the WPA Guides to be. But we hope it will, in time, live up to the words that another critic, Malcolm Cowley, once bestowed on the Federal Writers' Project itself: "a rowdy, idealistic, sometimes farcical experiment . . . that refuses to be forgotten."

Introduction: State by State
Sean Wilsey

In the fall of 2002 I set out to drive a 1960 Chevy Apache 10 pickup truck, at 45 mph, from far west Texas to New York City—2,364 miles through desert, suburbs, forests, lake-spattered plains, mountains, farmland, more suburbs, and the Holland Tunnel. A year before this drive the planes had hit the World Trade Center, twenty blocks from my apartment. And in the months before and after that my best friend from childhood had died, my best friend from adolescence had died, my senior-most aunt had died, the man I'd long thought of as a father and my actual father had died. I thought a long slow drive across much of America would allow me to catch up with these losses.

But I wasn't going alone. My traveling companions were an architect named Michael Meredith and a dog named Charlie Chaplin. Michael and I had become friends in Marfa, Texas—the town where the minimalist artist Donald Judd exiled himself in the 1970s from the "glib and harsh" New York art scene—in 2000, when Michael was in town designing a house for Judd's longtime partner, and my wife and I were guests of the Lannan Foundation, each working on a book. Michael left for a teaching job back east, and my wife and I stayed on. That's when I first saw the truck, in front of the post office: boxy, banged up, covered in sky blue house paint, half smashed windshield a lattice of stars and linear cracks, like a flag. A Mexican man in his sixties walked outside with his mail and drove it away. Then I biked around town till I found it parked out by the cemetery. Jesse Santesteban, the owner, showed me where he'd signed the engine compartment like an artist, and said that I could take a closer look. The doors had handmade wooden armrests, and the seatbelts were fashioned of canvas and chain link. An orange shag carpet covered the floorboards. I offered him $1,200, cash. He handed over a green plastic keychain that read LAUGH, LIVE, LOVE, AND BE HAPPY! and warned, "Don't take it over 45 or it'll throw a rod." A friend later explained, "That's a polite way of saying the engine will explode."

My wife and I adopted Charlie around the same time. When we took him back to New York a couple months later, I left the truck, which Jesse agreed to look after. Two years on, Charlie (now quite big) and I flew back in order to try and drive this piece-of-folk-art-cum-deathtrap, which had never gone farther than the nearby town of Pecos, across the country, seeing America slowly, a way almost nobody gets, or wants, to see it.

Driving slow both satisfied and ran contrary to my instinct to flee. And, pleasingly to my mind, it made fun of the two main preoccupations of our entire country: velocity and ease. Not that I didn't appreciate velocity in particular. The will to speed had long been one of my defining characteristics. On a road trip a few years prior I'd tried to set a car's cruise control at 140 miles per hour. Now I would piss off and get passed by everyone, including a guy hauling hay and a wide-load trailer pulling a house. I almost passed a school bus in Arkansas, but, when the sleepy driver spotted me, he floored it.

I would be the slowest person in America.

Marfa is surrounded by one of the few untouched landscapes remaining in the lower 48—a high desert formed in the Permian period and left more or less alone in the 250 million years since. All roads out of town lead across empty yellow grasslands, through blue sage and cactus-covered mountains, where the traveler's only company is the weather. A hailstorm once blackened the sky behind me, caught up, dented my hood, starred my windshield, covering the pavement in ice cubes, and moved on into the distance. At night the stars glowed like phosphorescence in the sea and were as abundant as static on a broken TV.

At 9:00 a.m. on a Wednesday, I honked the horn in front of a small adobe, where Michael had spent the night with some friends. It was a clear sound in the dry desert air. On the phone we'd planned out the trip as follows: always take back roads, eat only in nonchains, never hurry, spend a day in San Antonio meeting a man I'll call Don Harris for whom Michael might design a house (potentially his first to be built), write songs to perform at an open mike in Nashville. Charlie would ride in the bed of the truck, and we would have the cab. I tied his long leash to the truck's roll bar, so he'd know not to jump out.

Michael looked like an architect—thin, with thick glasses, black pants, and a white shirt, the two colors separated by a belt with a brushed steel buckle. He'd met Charlie, but this was his first look at the truck.

"Hello Charles," he said to Charlie, then remarked, "I like the shotgun rack."

"Yeah," I said. "It's also good for keeping umbrellas."

He stared. "*No*, man. *Umbrellas?* What kind of wuss-ass keeps umbrellas in his shotgun rack?"

Before I could answer he noticed the stick shift.

"Oh, shit, I didn't sleep all night because I was worried about that. I can't drive stick."

"What?"

"Sorry, I didn't think it would be a stick shift. It's American. Everything's easy in America."

"It's from 1960."

I figured I could teach him. There was nothing to hit out in the desert. Then he told me we had to be in San Antonio by 9 a.m. the next day to meet Don, his potential client. San Antonio was just under 400 miles away. I'd been thinking we'd reach Del Rio, half the distance, following along the Rio Grande.

"You know we can only go 45."

"What? C'mon—you're joking, right?"

"No. Really. Look at this thing," I said. Michael took in the ancient interior and medieval seatbelts. "Can you call and say that we'll get there around noon?"

"I only have his email. I just told him we'd be there."

"Well," I said, "We'll keep driving till we make it."

Partially out of courtesy, I didn't want to tell him the engine would explode. As Jack Kerouac said about himself and Neal Cassady, his friend and driving companion in *On the Road,* we "tiptoed around each other like heartbreaking new friends."

From the Marfa grasslands, east through the Glass Mountains, we made the town of Alpine, 30-odd miles away, in forty-five minutes. The gas gauge fell by a third. Afraid there wasn't a lot of gas in the next leg we decided to buy two six-gallon jerry cans, along with tools, water, and food.

I should mention here the weird coincidence that we were driving our way through a book I'd never read: John Steinbeck's *Travels With Charley*, wherein—I've now read it—the author and his dog, Charley, lit out on the back roads of America, in the fall of 1960, in a new GM pickup, in order to "rediscover this monster land." Steinbeck is precise and prescient about America, observing that "there will come a time when we can no longer afford our wastefulness—chemical wastes in the rivers, metal wastes everywhere, and atomic wastes buried deep in the earth or sunk in the sea." And in a letter Steinbeck wrote to Adlai Stevenson (quoted in Jay Parini's introduction), he makes the dead-on assessment that as a country we "can stand anything God and Nature throw at us save only plenty. If I wanted to destroy a nation, I would give it too much and I would have it on its knees, miserable, greedy and sick."

But I engaged in no such musing as we made our way east—too absorbed with correcting the steering, an act of constant attention. Around lunch time we'd made it 70 more miles. We stopped outside the town of Marathon and filled up the tank again.

A lean old man touched his cowboy hat, pointed at the truck, and said, "'65?"

Michael replied, "Yep," and the man walked away.

I said, "It's a '60, actually."

Michael said, "Yeah, but why bother correcting somebody? He doesn't care what year it is really, he just wants to feel like he *knows* something—now he feels good."

We were on a slight downhill—a good place to learn stick, so I let Michael drive. The truck got going after a few stalls, and we rolled through the Chihuahuan Desert. Getting cocky, he tried to sneak it up to 50 and I shouted him down as he struggled with the loose steering, veering into the oncoming lane—me scared and hollering "Watch out!"; him apologizing "Sorry, sorry, I got a trick leg!"—until a rank of orange plastic drums, like buoys in the sea of the desert, shunted us to the side of the road. Two border patrol agents asked where we were going.

In this context, Michael in his architect's uniform and me in a skateboard sweatshirt and Kangol cap, I imagined we made no sense as anything other than a gay couple. They walked off to confer, and seemed to be snickering. Eventually they waved us on. I willed Michael not to stall. And he didn't. Instead he threw it in reverse, and we started rolling back toward Marfa.

The agents didn't bother hiding their laughter.

Then Michael stalled. Charlie lost his balance, fell over in the bed, and gave me an aggrieved look. A few minutes later he tried to dive out of the back. I jumped from the cab and somehow caught him before he could hang himself on his leash. He lifted his nose and gave me a gentle tap on the neck. I sat him between Michael and me, and took the wheel.

Charlie was a Catahoula, the state dog of Louisiana, which looks like a spotted wolf, a dingo, or, as a man who spotted him on the street once put it, "one of those wild dogs of Africa." When he was happy, Charlie's eyes—deep, orange, unblinking—laughed, and he opened his mouth, curled back his lips, and nodded his head up and down. He was also conversational and made a lot of noises that definitely weren't barking, growling, or anything canine. Things like: "Wroarowlwolf." "Oohwar." "Rrolf." "Aaahlh!" "Meol." "Wrrp." Going by all the distinct letters I heard him pronounce (a talent shared by Steinbeck's Charley) I was pretty sure I could have taught him to speak a few words in English.

The landscape unfolded, changing only because the light was changing. It seemed we had made no progress. Only my discomfort had progressed. The truck's bench seat had springs that poked most of the way through on the driver's side, and the result of a couple hours sitting on it was searing pain. Adding to the discomfort, Charlie kept subtly shoving me, until my arm was fully extended to reach the Bakelite knob on top of the shifter, my left hip pressed into the door, and he was *at the wheel*.

Michael broke his silence and said, "I found out a couple days ago that I'm one of the six finalists to design a memorial for the victims of the attack on the Pentagon."

It took me a second to realize what he was talking about.

"What? The 9/11 memorial in Washington?"

"Yeah. Right where the plane crashed."

"Wow. What's your design?"

"It's a viewing pedestal. The people who come to remember are the memorial. They're living statues. The idea is to be really small and intimate next to something that is out-of-control big—one of the few manmade objects you can see from outer space. For a memorial it seems better to be modest—it's more likely to be built if it isn't expensive. But I can't believe they picked me as a finalist."

"It's amazing."

"To be able to memorialize something on the same ground where people died is amazing. But I don't know what the victims' families are going to think about my idea. I have to meet with them next week in D.C. And the New York victims' families, too. The New York families also want the New York names in D.C. Of course the D.C. names aren't going to be in New York."

This struck me as an insult to grief. "When do you have to meet the families?"

"Uh." Long pause. "Tuesday."

I told Michael it was impossible.

"Let's just keep driving," he said.

Signs of civilization had begun to appear along the road, indicating our emergence from the landscape of the Paleozoic and into twenty-first century America. A strange tension had been set up, and it would pull at us for the rest of the trip. What would happen to my plans to go slow?

A t around midnight we arrived in San Antonio, pulled up to the Menger Hotel, in Alamo Plaza (next to the Alamo itself), where we were to meet Don, and asked about a room. The answer: no dogs. So we found a motel right beneath I–37. I noticed there was a back entrance, checked in, and while Michael took our stuff inside, I walked Charlie around the neighborhood, then through the back, catching the door before it closed behind a woman in a tight gray business suit. Charlie followed me and sat like a gentleman. She gave him a look of withering contempt.

Had she mistaken Charlie for another, very similar looking, Texas Catahoula, named Smut, then notorious in certain parts of the state for swimming in President George W. Bush's pool, and moreover, when Vladimir Putin came to visit, per an article in the *Dallas Morning News*, "barking and chasing after the president and his visitors"? (The paper also quoted the Westerfields, Bush's neighbors and Smut's owners. Mrs. Westerfield said, "He chased those Russian dignitaries all over that place." Noting that they'd eventually castrated the dog, Mr. Westerfield lamented, "That old boy lost everything because he wouldn't stay off the president's place.")

T he lobby of the Menger Hotel was pillared, balconied, sconce-and-stained-glass-lit, Victorian. Don Harris, a middle-aged man in the midst of all this distinctiveness, was perfectly nondescript. He had a white shirt and a rounded physique that seemed to make the light fall away from him.

Michael said hello and introduced me as a writer. Formalities concluded, Don asked if he could tell us a bit about the city, then started talking, without stopping—delivering a monologue, that was, to me, a coastal American, with a general bias against our landlocked interior, a total revelation about the history, depth, and texture at the heart of the country. He said:

"San Antonio has always seemed to me to be a city out of a Borges story, particularly one with knife fighters, political thugs, and Hispanic-Irish gangsters, like *Death and the Compass*. The past here is so intense that it's also the present, and nothing ever really disappears. The city's always existed with wild Indians, soldiers, priests, *vaqueros*, *pachucos*, socialites, aristocrats, writers, and working people, in a constant mix. Conrad's favorite writer, R. B. Cunninghame Graham, the Scottish lord—the real king of Scotland some say—spent several years in San Antonio, attempting to become a cattle baron, going broke, and then, out of desperation, beginning his writing career with an account of a hanging in Cotulla for the San Antonio *Express*. Stephen Crane wandered around with the Chili Queens in the same plaza where the Comanches would ride into town and receive tribute—pay or the town would be burnt and looted. Till recently it was represented by Congressman Henry B. Gonzalez, the boxer congressman—who flattened another congressman with a single punch, and tried to impeach the first Bush. This lobby is the setting for a scene from *All the Pretty Horses*. John Grady Cole spies on his mother, sitting with 'boots crossed one over the other' (I know *El Cormac* is being reappraised here and there—but he's still bulletproof in Texas). The Gunter—another cattle king hotel—is where Robert Johnson made his first recordings, in 1936, and rock and roll was born. Eisenhower had an office in town, and he was in it on the morning he heard about Pearl Harbor. I don't even think he was a general then. The San Antonio gangster Freddie Carrasco, while in prison at Huntsville, made a suit of armor in the style of Ned Kelly and tried to shoot his way out. This is what I mean when I mention Borges."

Then a brisk walk outside. A few quick turns, and we dodged inside a bar where three gamblers blatantly played cards for money. A drunk shouted "Dammit!" and lurched at nondescript Don, who wove and kept walking toward a glimmer of sunlight at the back. It was a very long bar, terminating at a balcony overlooking the San Antonio River. We stepped out onto it and Don hooked a thumb behind us. "The Esquire Bar, *the lost state of Esquire*. Claimed to be one of the longest bars in Texas. Kind of place that people have *their* booths in. Completely democratic crowd, too, in the social sense: criminal lawyers and their clients, thugs, and socialites."

Later I looked the place up and found it reduced the following customer reviews on *Citysearch*: "Pros: cheap drinks Cons: staff, bathrooms, local Hispanics," and, "Only nefarious locals go here. Not recommended for northerners or passers-by."

Don showed us the courthouse, "machine gunned one morning during the early '70s amidst a ferocious drug war that came to a head with a federal judge's assassination by Woody Harrelson's dad." Then he placed San Antonio in continental context, taking us to the edge of a sleepy square and declaring: "Travis Park, in my view, is where Latin America begins. Everything north of this park, in governance and culture, is English; everything south, all the way to Cape Horn, is Spanish. It's the actual border of the two Americas."

Who *is* he?" I asked Michael over brisket and white bread at Black's BBQ in Lockhart, 72 miles later.

"I don't know. He's just this guy who wrote me and said he wanted to build a house. I don't know!"

I do know now. Don told us he "used to live in the Paradise Valley in Montana with my literary friends Richard Ford and Thomas McGuane." Coincidence provided a coda to our day when I met the writer Richard Ford at a wedding, and I asked him about this.

Ford squinted and said, "Don Harris . . . Don Harris . . ." Then he raised his hands and shouted, "Don Harris is a fugitive from justice! He fled the country to Mexico. I was giving a reading in South Carolina when someone said there was a friend of mine who wanted me to go outside and see him. I said, 'Tell him to come in here,' but they said he wouldn't. I asked his name and they told me 'Esteban De Jesús' and I went outside and it was Don. If he's back in the U.S. now and using his own name he must have resolved his legal troubles. But I'll tell you this, he can't be practicing law—he was disbarred. And don't let your friend build a house for Don Harris!"

In Crockett, Texas (named for Davy Crockett, who supposedly camped there on the way to the Alamo), the next morning, we were so far behind Michael's schedule there was no way we could make the coast without blowing the engine. Our sad room in a seedy motel, still 200 miles deep in Texas, was of the sort Steinbeck, feeling sorry for himself, described as "dirty yellow, the curtains like the underskirts of a slattern."

"Splendor in the Pines" was the Crockett town motto. The reality was gasoline and junk food in the pines. I walked Charlie across a leach field from the L of our hotel, over to a pawnshop (it shared a single prefab building with a feed store), where cheap, sun-bleached acoustic guitars hung in the window.

"Michael," I said when I got back. "There's a pawnshop next door. Let's buy a guitar so we can work out a routine for Nashville."

He replied, distractedly, "OK, yeah. Cool, man."

We ate a breakfast of packaged pound cakes and Sunny Delight, then made for Louisiana, swaying along an empty road that threaded through trees, interrupted by house after house that proved America is poor. I let Michael drive. Entering Shreveport, he ran just-turned-red after just-turned-red, to avoid stopping/stalling, me shouting "Hang onto your ass, Charlie!" as we wrenched around a corner and onto a road north toward Arkansas. Surrounded by Louisiana farmland, we pulled over. This was Charlie's chance to know his native soil. He sniffed around. Michael's cell phone rang. The Pentagon finalists had just been announced that morning in Washington. A reporter from the Albany *Times Union*, the paper Michael had delivered as a boy, wanted to interview him. He talked earnestly as I drove. Then, in Arkansas, we stopped at a gas station, selling unbranded gas, to fill up and to get snacks. A thin, beautifully sulky woman in a housedress, right out of a WPA photograph, was sweeping some concrete around the pumps. Her twin sister was at the register, talking lazily with a sexy blonde in a tube top. They were around our age—early thirties. I asked, trying to flirt, "Can you recommend a healthy snack?" There was a long pause till the counter-working twin replied, in an accent of such deep Arkansan exoticness, a subtle inflection making it clear how unfascinating she found me, "How 'bout some peanut butter and *crackers*?"

As we pulled out of the station Michael said, "They were like sirens."

Half an hour later, when we'd finished our crackers, I realized, "Damn, we forgot to buy a guitar for Nashville!"

"We'll just a-capella it and get booed off stage—with a lot of thigh slappin' and hooting!" Michael declared.

This was what I'd imagined. Why I'd wanted him to come along. We made up a Yankee ballad about southern food and southern accents—how we couldn't resist either one. Title: "I Got the South in My Mouth!" It was a beautiful day for a drive. Sunny. Breeze full of birds. Singing, our voices were bad and scratchy. We both were starting to get colds. As the day progressed we filled the Apache with loaded Kleenex and cough drop wrappers—a major divergence from Steinbeck, who had a camper van on the back of his truck, and filled it with "bourbon, scotch, gin, vermouth, vodka, a medium good brandy, aged applejack, and a case of beer"—then lamented that "if there had been room . . . I would have packed the WPA Guides to the States, all forty-eight volumes of them." Steinbeck could have spent a lot less time getting lost, then depressed, then drunk.

We had pie for dinner (having skipped lunch), after which, Michael's cell ringing with the occasional journalist, I silently drove, and drove, and drove, and drove, the strain on the engine and the torque of our incompatible needs seeming sure to cause some sort of an explosion, till, suddenly, we rounded a corner in a blank part of the map, out of cell range, off all grids that I knew, near the Mississippi border, where a strip of river and two gas stations, plus some fireworks stalls, nothing you could call a town, had nonetheless caused two groups of young men to come into proximity—one shirtless and black and drinking beer, the other shirtless and white and selling Confederate flag patches and 9/11 keepsakes. We filled the tank at a station frequented exclusively by black customers, and looked across a dirt road at a station frequented exclusively by white people. The heavy sound of insects was all around, while harsh stares came from the white gas station at the two Yankees and their wild dog of Africa. Then the whites started to shout at the blacks. When the word, *"Fuck!"* rang out, we fled. No more back roads that night. We made for the interstate.

Coming out of the midnight darkness of St. Francis County, Arkansas, we took I–40 (which runs all the way from California to North Carolina) across the Mississippi River—while endless trucks did the same thing. Twenty miles from the bridge we broke into a column that stretched back as far as we could see. (Turning around, Michael said, "They just keep going *forever.*") East of this juncture is the one single lane section of I–40 coast to coast. Usually it's single lane for only a mile. But that night construction had the highway down to half capacity for more like twenty. The lane was tight, and the looseness of the Apache's steering was magnified by the sensation of driving in a trench—I slowed down to 40, 35, 30, to keep from crashing into guardrails or road workers. Soon we were holding back a flood of trucks. Space opened up in front of us. By mid span on the Hernando de Soto, the bridge that carries I–40 into Memphis, we had nothing but open pavement ahead, while in our wake so many drivers had hit their brakes that the sky was red. I looked in the rear view mirror and saw a screaming trucker. At the same moment he blew his air horn, and contorted his face in rage. A wrathful *BWOOOOOOOOOOOOOOOOOOOLF!*

sound filled my ears and seemed like it was coming straight out of his mouth.

We exited the highway in Lakeland, Tennessee, and Michael said, "That was terrifying. I thought we were going to die." It was a too close encounter with American velocity—the terror of stopping all these trucks from hurtling along at 80, loaded with consumer goods, all the things we need to make life easy.

After checking in to a big Super 8, overlooking the highway, I walked Charlie along something called Huff Puff Road, dropped him in the room then went to check the truck's engine, which looked like it was sweating oil. When I returned Michael was watching TV, Charlie was drinking out of the toilet, and an ad for *Snoop Dogg's Girls Gone Wild* came on. Snoop screwed up his face and framed his gold jewelry-covered chest with his arms; teenagers on streets and beaches flashed their breasts at him. It was mesmerizing. When the ad was over a feeling of loneliness crushed us to sleep.

At Michael's insistence we spent the whole next day on the interstate, needle at 45, sometimes creeping up to 50, steady rain falling. A pool formed in the dents on the hood. In five hours we got to Nashville, ate, and kept going, not even mentioning our plans for an open mike. Hoping to relieve the spring-induced pain in my thigh, I let Michael drive till he almost crashed, and I took over again. Pain or terror—those were my choices. Steinbeck described the interstate as a "wide gash" where the minimum speed "was greater than any I had previously driven," and, "You are bound to the wheel and your eyes to the car ahead and to the rear-view mirror for the car behind and the side mirror for the car or truck about to pass. . . . When we get these thruways across the whole country . . . it will be possible to drive from New York to California without seeing a single thing."

By nightfall in Knoxville I was done. We exited into a deserted downtown. "This is it," I said. "I can't take any more of this. You want to get there on time, just rent a car."

"Shit, man. No," Michael said. We hadn't talked for hours. "We have to do this together."

"What? Sit silently in terror? This thing won't go any faster." Michael was silent. Unable to think of anything else to say, I came out with, "And that's such an *architect's* belt buckle."

Then I got out of the truck with Charlie and walked off.

When I got back Michael said, "OK. I'll get a car. But I don't want the trip to end like this. Let's find a back road and drive as far as we can tonight. I'll get a rental tomorrow."

What followed was the best drive of the trip. Michael took the wheel, and I looked out the window: a hundred miles along an empty road that followed a low ridge line, like a levee through the woods, nothing but trees with slashes of cloud-filtered moonlight coming through their leaves, and shreds of silver river visible beyond their bare trunks.

We ended up in Kingsport, improbably large for a fume-choked industrial city nobody's ever heard of. We checked into an Econo Lodge. Michael went to the room and I took Charlie on a walk. Stumbling along, my dog also looking sick of it all, I was suddenly so weary I thought I might fall asleep standing up. I half noticed something catching the streetlight in some wet grass, and let go of Charlie's leash so he could go investigate. Suddenly he was lying on his back and rolling on it. He *dug in*. Legs straight up in the air, head kicked back, Charlie twisted side-to-side, a look of ecstasy on his smiling face, his eyes pure white. I'd never seen him so fulfilled. I laughed. Here was his inner Smut. When he got up I saw what looked like a huge pork chop with a flap of white chamois on top and a rack of thick rib bones: a dead animal that had gone flat and sunk into the earth. Then the smell hit me—*hard*. Death: *You've been pondering me. Well, hellooooo!*

When Michael and I said good-bye, early the next day, I wished him luck with his memorial. He wished me luck with the rest of the trip, affectionately referred to Charlie as "Charles," and said, "Good call on the belt buckle. I'm gonna get rid of it."

Charlie and I carried on in what smelled like a coffin. Forty minutes later, on a brief stretch of unavoidable interstate, Michael passed us in a tiny silver car and we honked and waved. Then Charlie and I disappeared into the rainy closeness of Virginia and West Virginia, following Route 460, where the two states traded places every few miles. For lunch, on the main street of an old mining town, I went to a pizza place, where there were four tables. I ordered a salad, and the dark-skinned proprietor brought me fresh feta, olives, lettuce, peppers, bread—the homemade meal I'd been wanting the whole trip. After devouring it I asked him where he was from, and he told me Egypt.

I drove seventeen hours without a rest, crossing the Mason Dixon line at 1:00 a.m., at the same time as an Amish buggy with reflective bands Velcroed around its horses' ankles; a quick sleep in Harrisburg, PA, where, beside the banks of the Susquehanna River, hoping to remove the spring that had been boring into my pelvis, I disemboweled the bench seat with a pocket knife; past the Hershey chocolate factory, over toward the Jersey border; across the deep-carved bed of the Delaware River on a gleaming steel bridge, barely wide enough for the truck; another highway gash, and finally we saw the New York skyline. My dog said "Wroarowlwolf!"

M ichael didn't win the contest to design the 9/11 memorial in Washington. He told me, "They're actually really smart at the Pentagon, and they could obviously see through my criticism of the massive war machine." He's now teaching at Harvard, and has a dog of his own.

Charlie died of cancer in 2004, just a few months after the birth of Daphne's and my son. When he saw the baby he gave him one of his gentle taps; wet nose on top of bald head.

I still have the truck. It cheers up everyone who sees it in New York (especially firemen; especially when my wife's at the wheel). I've recently been thinking of driving it back to Texas with my family, a reverse trip that, with our two small children, would definitely mock ease even more than velocity.

THE 50 STATES

ALABAMA

CAPITAL   Montgomery

ENTERED UNION   1819 (22nd)

ORIGIN OF NAME   Possibly from a Choctaw Indian word meaning "thicket-clearers" or "vegetation-gatherers"

NICKNAME   Yellowhammer State

MOTTO   Audemus jura nostra defendere ("We dare defend our rights")

RESIDENTS   Alabamian or Alabaman

U.S. REPRESENTATIVES   7

STATE BIRD   yellowhammer

STATE FLOWER   camellia

STATE TREE   Southern longleaf pine

STATE SONG   "Alabama"

LAND AREA   50,744 sq. mi.

GEOGRAPHIC CENTER   In Chilton Co., 12 mi. SW of Clanton

POPULATION   4,557,808

WHITE   71.1%

BLACK   26.0%

AMERICAN INDIAN   0.5%

ASIAN   0.7%

HISPANIC/LATINO   1.7%

UNDER 18   26.3%

65 AND OVER   13.0%

MEDIAN AGE   35.8

ALABAMA
George Packer

In the summer of 1980, when I was nineteen, I worked as a $600-a-month intern at a government-funded poverty law center in Alabama, renting a matchbox house with two black law students at the crumbling edge of downtown Mobile. It was a record hot summer, at a record high in urban seediness: Mobile, the poor man's New Orleans, was hollowed out by economic stagnation and the white exodus that followed desegregation. Carter was in the White House, the azaleas in Bienville Square were dead, and the sixteen blocks between the house and office offered the comfort of no trees, only the glare of the sun and an assortment of drunks, casual laborers, and petty criminals. My yellow short-sleeved Oxford shirt, too heavy in the humidity, instantly marked me as a carpetbagger, and one morning a razor-thin limping man pursued me block after block, yelling, "Hey! Asshole!" Anomie set in the day I arrived—everything shut down for Memorial Day weekend—and pursued me all the way to my departure in August. At times it grew so intense that the only relief came in cups of mocha-flavored instant International Coffee, from a red-and-white tin, which I bought at a shop downtown and savored as the taste of civilization itself.

The house on St. Francis Street had only one air-conditioner. Carlos, the law student to arrive first, grabbed it, and never let go. Cooled only by an ineffective fan, my room began to incubate turd-sized cockroaches. Carlos, from American University in Washington, despised me on sight. This was upsetting, because I had gone South with the idea of becoming a latter-day soldier in the civil rights struggle. I saw myself, in all modesty, as an heir to Schwerner and Goodman, the two white northerners killed in 1964 outside Philadelphia, Mississippi, with their black movement colleague Chaney. The Mother's Day melee when the Freedom Riders pulled into the Birmingham bus terminal, the fire hoses and K-9 squads in Linn Park, George Wallace standing in the doorway at the University of Alabama to prevent Vivian Malone and James Hood from becoming the first black students to attend—in my mind, all of this had happened the day before yesterday. My backpack carried Robert Coles's study of the psychology of black children during desegregation, *Children of Crisis*, Anne Moody's memoir of growing up black during the civil rights era, *Coming of Age in Mississippi*, and (because I accepted Black Power as a necessary stage of the movement) Eldridge

Cleaver's *Soul on Ice*. But it was hard to sustain my own private freedom ride after I discovered that Carlos kept a personal roll of toilet paper in his bedroom, ferrying it back and forth to the john. So much for black and white together.

That first weekend, before contempt had hardened into hatred, Carlos and I went out to get a bite to eat. A black neighbor saw us round the corner and exclaimed in wonder, "You black and you white but you both walking together!" Confronted with this nightmare tableau of black abjectness, white noblesse, and assumed interracial harmony, Carlos dispatched both the neighbor and me with a strained, sneering laugh. It was little consolation that Raymond, the other housemate, from Rutgers and gay, liked me fine.

Carlos's rejection nagged at me all summer, but my civil rights romance was too strong to be snuffed out. The law center was opening satellite offices in the rural counties north of Mobile Bay, and I spent many days doing advance work by way of Greyhound buses to Monroeville and Evergreen. These were some of the poorest places in America. In Monroe County, which, according to the 1980 census, was 43 percent black, median white family income was $17,600 and median black family income was just over $9,000. Conecuh County was even poorer. I interviewed an old woman with a picture on the wall of her shack showing the two Kennedys and King under the words "The Three Who Set Us Free." She didn't seem very free: There was no indoor plumbing in the shack. The revolution of the early sixties had blown through the bigger cities in Alabama and barely touched these piney backwoods. "We get along just fine with our colored folks," the probate judge of Monroe County told me, sounding like a hundred years of predecessors.

I was looking for something—marches, drama, self-sacrifice, community, history—that now existed only in books. Less than two decades before, when Coles was working as a child psychiatrist amid the upheavals of southern desegregation, a young black civil rights worker told him that he'd joined the movement because "I'll be lucky if I can vote, and be treated better than a dog every time I go to register my car, or try for a driving license, or go to buy something in a store." By 1980, what was left of the movement had migrated behind the closed doors of the courts. The law center was involved in several important civil rights suits, including desegregation and voting rights cases against the Mobile school board and county commission, but these were moving slowly, obscurely, through the legal system. Class-action lawsuits were not what I had in mind that summer. I wanted the sight of headlights in my rearview mirror on a rural road. In fact, the Klan still operated in Mobile, as the country learned just a few months later, in March 1981, when two of its members randomly lynched a nineteen-year-old black youth on a city street. (Eventually they were convicted, and one was electrocuted in the first execution of a white man for the murder of a black man in Alabama since 1913. The United Klans of America was later bankrupted by a civil suit that forced the Alabama chapter to turn over its Tuscaloosa meeting hall to the victim's mother, who used the proceeds to buy her first house.) But the main battle for equality in Alabama and the South was over. I had arrived in time for its ambiguous and incomplete aftermath: superficial civility, de facto segregation, economic inequality, with most of the stirring old words gone stale from sloganeering. As Carlos made clear, laws did not change hearts.

In mid-July, Ronald Reagan was nominated by the Republican convention in Detroit. In a Comfort Inn on the outskirts of Evergreen, the seat of Conecuh County, I watched the Osmonds sing "Together a New Beginning" on TV. "This convention has shown to all America a party united, with positive programs for solving the nation's problems," Reagan told the sea of delegates, "a party ready to build a new consensus with all those across the land who share a community of values embodied in these words: family, work, neighborhood, peace, and freedom." Outside my room, it was well over 100 degrees; the air felt like a swamp.

That summer I was so intent on searching for what had already vanished that I missed the great change taking place in Alabama. The racial backlash was complete, but the state's move to the right was only just beginning. Alabama's history as a bastion of Democratic politics was long, recent, and still showed signs of life. Four years earlier, the state had gone for Carter—the last time it voted for a Democratic presidential candidate. In 1980, Alabama chose Reagan over Carter by only seventeen thousand votes out of almost 1.4 million cast. But that year the politics of cultural conservatism began spreading from the Sun Belt throughout the country, with race one primal theme among many others—God, guns, patriotism, taxes, government, family. The Christian right had emerged as an organized force in politics the year before, with the founding of the Moral Majority. Alabama was about to become the quintessential red state.

Politics in the American South has always been a battle over the meaning of populism. The politician who claims convincingly to speak for the people and against the "elites" (whoever they might be), in the language of ordinary folk, wins the crucial advantage. Even if he loses an election, he secures the title of authenticity. In 1980 in Alabama, populism completed a transformation that had been going on ever since the start of the civil rights movement. The elites—ridiculed from the podium of the Republican convention that summer—became government bureaucrats, privileged do-gooders, unelected judges, out-of-touch academics, meddling outsiders. They were cultural, not economic, elites, and they didn't understand or share the basic values of "authentic" Alabamians. They were too sophisticated for God, too chicken for guns, too intrusive for freedom, too perverse for family. A "real" person was a white man who lived in a new suburb, drove a truck with a religious or pro-gun bumper sticker, listened to Lynyrd Skynyrd, sent his children to a private Christian school, and voted Republican.

This has been the style and content of Southern populism my entire life. It's one of the most powerful forces in American history. It reshaped the country's political map, not just moving the solid South out of the Democratic column and into the Republican camp, but pushing the rest of the country in the same direction. As early as 1974, the historian John Egerton wrote about the "southernization of America," describing it as a cultural phenomenon as well as a political one. It drove George H.W. Bush to pretend to like pork rinds; George W. Bush to campaign at NASCAR racetracks; and the Democrats to nominate sons of the South in five of seven elections from 1976 to 2000. It identifies real Americanism with a Southern accent, an insouciant swagger, a down-home manner, and an undercurrent of violence. It's a white male style.

I was a foreigner in Alabama, but I went there because I had extensive roots. When I was a boy we had spent parts of several summers in Birmingham, where my mother had grown up. Until her death in 1974, my grandmother lived in a rambling Victorian house on Rhodes Circle, canning preserves in her basement and playing a card game called Help Your Neighbor in the front parlor. I had assorted aunts, uncles, and cousins scattered from Albertville to Montgomery. My mother's father, George Huddleston, who died at age ninety, a few months before I was born, and gave me my name, represented Birmingham in Congress from 1915 to 1937. The older of his two sons took the seat from 1955 to 1965. After George Jr.'s death, his widow, my aunt A. J., became a fervent born-again Christian of the charismatic strain.

That summer, I knew nothing about my grandfather other than a handful of family stories told by my mother and aunts and cousins, in which he invariably came off as a remote, stern, just figure, a sort of Old Testament God, with a biting sense of humor who would tolerate no "posturing" or pretense from his much-younger wife and his clan of five children. I remained utterly ignorant of George Huddleston's public life and political career for almost twenty more years. Then I discovered an Alabama that few people today know or remember. It was a state with a secret history: liberalism.

My grandfather came down from Tennessee in 1891, started a law practice in Birmingham, and later ran for Congress. His public career fell between the end of Reconstruction and the beginning of civil rights. In the summer of 1901, Alabama's political leaders drafted a constitution that imposed literacy tests, property qualifications, and poll taxes on the state's voters. Their undisguised intention was to undo the Fifteenth Amendment and disqualify black people from voting (many poor whites were also disenfranchised). With this document the white ruling class took Alabama's blacks out of politics for the next half century, until the Montgomery bus boycott in 1955 began to reverse the crime. In this interval, which coincided with the Populist, Progressive, and New Deal eras, the eternal southern fever of race cooled down and lay dormant for a while. With color removed from politics, Alabama was temporarily free to obsess itself with a different, maybe even more stubborn, problem—class conflict between rich and poor.

The righteous anger of the economically dispossessed became the political fuel of Southern liberals like my grandfather. After winning his congressional seat in 1914 with the vote of Birmingham's white working class and Jefferson County's white farmers, George Huddleston gave a series of speeches that could have been delivered by Eugene Debs: "We are confronted with conditions never before experienced and which are getting worse daily. The wealth of the nation is in the hands of the few and everything is monopolized, resulting in trusts which levy heavy tolls on the masses in the shape of unreasonable and unjust profits . . . I am well versed in the race question which has hung like a dark pall over the South, and being a southerner I know how it feels to have a negro placed alongside of you at your work, but I want to say to you that economical conditions make it more important that you give more consideration to the conditions of your black co-laborer than you do your employer."

My grandfather was not a religious man—like Thomas Jefferson, his faith lay in human reason and popular rule—but what's striking about the language of many other Southern Populists and Progressives was the use of religiosity in the cause of economic equality. The same biblical allusions and Christian moralism deployed against gay rights and abortion in the past quarter century were used a hundred years ago against concentrated wealth. The basic appeal to class over race presented a direct threat to the interests that Alabama's planters and industrialists had tried to enshrine in the constitution of 1901, which, in addition to turning blacks and poor whites into non-citizens, mandated property tax rates so low that they continue to bankrupt the state to this day. When the defenders of Alabama's working people, like my grandfather, raised their voices, the ruling class, known as the Big Mules, fought back hard; their periods out of state power were relatively brief, but they were unable to consolidate their hold as long as they couldn't claim the populist mantle. In the early part of the twentieth century, class and cultural politics in Alabama cut across each other in surprising ways.

One of the strangest decades was the 1920s, when Klansmen put on their robes and returned to prominence, creating a reign of terror for blacks and Catholics. During the same period, on the national level, the Klan began to make the anti-elitist attack on the social engineering of liberals that has been the mainstay of right-wing populism and Republican political discourse for half a century now. In 1926, Hiram Evans, Imperial Wizard and Emperor, used the pages of *North American Review* to sneer at "intellectually mongrelized 'Liberals'," saying, "The average Liberal idea is apparently that those who can produce should carry the unfit, and let the unfit rule them. This aberration would have been impossible, of course, if American Liberalism had kept its feet on the ground. Instead it became wholly academic, lost all touch with the plain people, disowned its instincts and common sense, and lived in a world of pure, high, groundless logic." There's a straight line from Evans's essay to the campaign rhetoric of George Wallace, running for President in 1968, about "pointy-headed bureaucrats who can't park a bicycle straight," to George W. Bush's mockery of Al Gore as a policy wonk and John Kerry as a windsurfer.

But at the same time, during the 1920s, politicians backed by the Klan were Alabama's liberal economic reformers. Governor Bibb Graves, believed to be the Exalted Cyclops of the Montgomery chapter, abolished the system of using state prisoners as conscripted laborers (known as convict lease), raised corporate taxes, and introduced education and health reforms. Hugo Black, a United States senator from 1927 until 1937, when F.D.R. appointed him to the Supreme Court, was a civil liberties and economic liberal who (mainly for opportunistic reasons) was a Klansman in the early 1920s.

For a couple of decades, there was no perceived contradiction in Southern political rhetoric between white supremacy and economic egalitarianism. With the Great Depression and the New Deal, an even more liberal brand of politician came to power in Alabama, holding relatively enlightened views of race. Governor Big Jim Folsom and the state's United States senators, John Bankhead (uncle of Tallulah) and Lister Hill, made Alabama the most politically progressive state in the South during the 1940s. In 1938, Birmingham's Municipal Auditorium hosted the Southern Conference for Human Welfare, an interracial coalition that included Eleanor Roosevelt, Gunnar Myrdal, C. Vann Woodward, and Hugo Black. Its agenda of economic and racial equality represented the high-water mark of Southern liberalism.

In the postwar years, the Democratic party began to take up civil rights for the first time. And Alabama headed toward an inevitable reckoning, based on the iron law of Southern politics: Whatever increases black rights loses white support. When Harry S. Truman integrated the military and passed equal employment legislation, a large number of Southern Democrats decided to bolt the party. They convened in July of 1948 under the banner of the Dixiecrats, at the same Municipal Auditorium in Birmingham where the Southern Conference for Human Welfare had met a decade earlier. Truman was lynched in effigy from the balcony of a nearby posh hotel. The participants at the States Rights Convention included Strom Thurmond, who became the Dixiecrats' presidential nominee that summer, Eugene "Bull" Connor, who would achieve infamy in 1963 by turning the full force of the Birmingham police and fire departments on black children marching for civil rights, the anti-Semite Gerald L. K. Smith, and the authors of the books *The Place of the Negro* and *The Jews Have Got the Atom Bomb*. The rhetoric was hate-filled and paranoid in a way the South hadn't heard before. This wasn't old-fashioned racism, but something new and even more toxic: anti–New Deal, anti-Communist, segregationist, populist. In the eyes of this breakaway faction of Southern Democrats, Social Security and civil rights were conjoined plots on the part of Washington against individual liberty. The nouveau-riche oilman, the doctrinaire libertarian, the purveyor of the Red Terror, and the conspiracy-minded bigot found that they had a political movement in common. Thurmond called the Fair Employment Practices Commission "the nearest thing to communism ever advocated in these United States." The Dixiecrats didn't outlive 1948, but their movement signaled a great shift in American politics. The convention that summer in Birmingham gave rise to Goldwater and Reagan, the modern Republican Party, the Southern strategy, Newt Gingrich, and George W. Bush. It was the end of Southern liberalism and the beginning of the New Right.

Alabama's secret liberal history depended on the disappearance of blacks from public life. My grandfather's political career as a defender of the working man—which ended when he was defeated in 1936, after turning against Roosevelt's New Deal legislation on the grounds that it concentrated too much power in the federal government—was made possible by the accident of its timing. His son was elected to the same seat a few months after *Brown* v. *Board of Education*. Instead of standing up for labor against big business, my uncle signed the Southern Manifesto, repudiating integration, in 1956. Seven years later, in the spring of 1963, when the movement was reaching its climax, he got up on the floor of the House to defend the use of dogs and fire hoses on peaceful, mostly underage, demonstrators in Birmingham. And yet he lost the following year to a more ardent defender of segregation, in the wave of Republican victories that Barry Goldwater's presidential campaign carried across the South after the Civil Rights Act of 1964 (upon signing it, Lyndon Johnson declared to his aide Bill Moyers, "We have just lost the South for a generation").

That was the end of the Huddlestons in public life. After 1964, there was no more room for them in state politics.

The tribe of surviving white liberals in Alabama today is so tiny and embattled that they all know one another personally. Separated by color or philosophy from the state's dominant groups, they are outcasts and oddballs, equal parts Atticus Finch and Boo Radley. They are fiction-writing spinsters, amateur historians, public defenders in small-town courthouses, poli sci professors at Tuscaloosa and Birmingham Southern, civil rights veterans, internal exiles who cannot or will not leave. They drawl apologies in unmistakably local accents to out-of-state visitors for the latest antics of Alabama politicians. They suffer from a commingling of conscience, privilege, and impotence. And a large fraction of them are members of my extended family.

What separates the Huddlestons most dramatically from their home state is not attitudes toward race—these days almost everyone in Alabama claims to be for civil rights—but religion. They are secularists in a state that at times seems to be run as a Christian theocracy. My cousins were particularly embarrassed in the summer of 2001 when Roy Moore, a former kickboxer-turned-cowboy and the chief justice of the Alabama Supreme Court, had a two-and-a-half ton granite monument to the Ten Commandments installed in the court's rotunda in the middle of the night. The stunt became a national story when Chief Justice Moore defied a federal court order to have the monolith removed. He was unseated in 2003 by a state judicial panel.

In 2004, ex-Justice Moore joined the opposition to a proposed amendment to the state constitution that would have removed language mandating racially segregated schools and the discriminatory poll tax from the original 1901 document. Moore argued that the changes would have allowed federal judges to force the state to raise taxes for school improvements—a powerful, if misleading, argument in Alabama. The amendment narrowly lost, and the state constitution remained officially racist.

The Ten Commandments caper and the failure to amend the constitution made Alabama a national showcase for the fringe of the religious right. One of my cousins in Birmingham wrote me during this time to apologize personally on behalf of the state and remind me of our grandfather's contributions to Alabama politics. And yet, in his uncompromising moralism, his conviction that politics is a contest between absolute good and evil, Roy Moore was a slightly freakish descendant of the original Populists. In 1895, an Alabama Populist believed in federal taxation, regulation of corporations, spending on schools, and enfranchisement of blacks (when it wasn't too inconvenient). A century and a little more later, an Alabama populist opposed pretty much all of these. But the style and language remained almost the same, as did the core, supercharged issues: race, religion, taxes.

In the late nineties, I started going back to Alabama in order to write a book about my grandfather and the history of American liberalism. I made a series of visits to Birmingham, and through my aunt A. J. and a handful of local friends I discovered that history had begun to take another strange turn in Alabama. Roy Moore was not the only face of Christian populism there. An interracial movement of conservative evangelicals had picked up the fallen banner of civil rights and given it new colors and patterns, combining the aspiration toward racial equality and social justice with an emphasis on individual sin and redemption. In downtown Birmingham, not far from the site of the old Municipal Auditorium where the Dixiecrats had met, there was an unadorned church called New City. Its members, black and white, were far from being Huddleston liberals (one Sunday, the black pastor subjected his pregnant teenage daughter and her boyfriend to a mortifying public outing and confession from the pulpit). But they worked in the black projects with unwed mothers and drug addicts, and some of the members were beginning to realize that saving one soul at a time in an unjust society was inadequate. One of the church founders, a white evangelical named Tim Ritchie, summed up the dilemma: "Structural change is no good if you don't have change of hearts; change of hearts is no good if you don't have change of structures."

In Alabama, the hardest, ugliest structure is the reactionary constitution of 1901, which has gone unamended for over a century. In 2002, in the spirit of the interracial evangelical movement, a law professor at the University of Alabama named Susan Pace Hamill, a practicing Methodist with a divinity degree, published a book called *The Least of These: Fair Taxes and the Moral Duty of Christians*. In it, she argued that the state's tax code, enshrined in the constitution, under which Alabamians making less than $13,000 pay almost 11 percent of their income in taxes and those making over $229,000 pay barely 4 percent, is immoral and un-Christian.

This was an argument designed to have a chance of being taken seriously in Alabama. One unlikely convert was Governor Bob Riley, a teetotaling conservative Republican of the low-tax, fundamentalist variety from the rural middle of the state. He proposed a referendum that would increase state taxes by $1.2 billion, raising tax rates on the rich and corporations and lowering them for the poor, in order to allow the chronically deficit-ridden state to keep prisons open and improve schools. Riley made his case on New Testament grounds: "According to Christian ethics, we're supposed to love God, love each other, and help take care of the poor. It is immoral to charge somebody making $5,000 an income tax." But the Alabama chapter of the Christian Coalition and most conservative churches opposed the plan, and in September 2003 it was defeated by 2 to 1.

Still, something had changed, as if some Alabamians were beginning to recall the zeal for justice that had animated my grandfather and other men and women of his time. The state's political passions have been historically violent, based in extreme, almost unearthly claims: God's love, God's wrath; white supremacy, universal brotherhood; personal sin, the evil of injustice. Beneath the dominant story of a harsh inequality enforced by police dogs and popular votes, there is a hidden narrative: Alabama's persistent effort at self-correction. Those making the effort usually fail, but they have never entirely disappeared.

My time as a law intern and belated civil rights worker in Mobile in 1980 is now farther away than that summer was from the cataclysms of 1963. Color is the oldest, deepest truth in Alabama, but it ebbs and flows. If we are entering one of its cycles of remission, then there's a chance for this state of believers to find other outlets for the eschatological passions that have brought them so often to the mouth of hell.

ALASKA

CAPITAL   Juneau

ENTERED UNION   1959 (49th)

ORIGIN OF NAME   Corruption of Aleut word meaning
   "great land" or "that which the sea breaks against"

NICKNAME   The Last Frontier or Land of the Midnight Sun

MOTTO   "North to the Future"

RESIDENTS   Alaskan

U.S. REPRESENTATIVES   1

STATE BIRD   willow ptarmigan

STATE FLOWER   forget-me-not

STATE TREE   Sitka spruce

STATE SONG   "Alaska's Flag"

LAND AREA   571,951 sq. mi.

GEOGRAPHIC CENTER   60 mi. NW of Mt. McKinley

POPULATION   663,661

WHITE   69.3%

BLACK   3.5%

AMERICAN INDIAN   15.6%

ASIAN   4.0%

HISPANIC/LATINO   4.1%

UNDER 18   30.4%

65 AND OVER   5.7%

MEDIAN AGE   32.4

ALASKA
Paul Greenberg

Just before I left for Emmonak, a village of 800 people on the west coast of Alaska, an Alaskan fish trader named Jac Gadwill emailed me the following: "Do be prepared for a bit of 'culture shock' here. Wonderful, loving people, but this is the USA's own third world country. Fortunately it also has the finest salmon by far in the world. This is why the Yup'iks (meaning is 'Real People') settled here over 10,000 years ago. We just yesterday shipped kings from here to some of NY's finer restaurants, direct to them, via FedEx." In a later message Jac added, "Once here, worry about nothing. If expectations are not high, we have what passes for a house type bunkhouse with groceries."

No one was waiting for me at the corrugated-metal shed that serves as Emmonak's airport terminal. Two thirtyish bush pilots were passing the morning between flights. A platinum blond Grant Aviation dispatcher offered to call Jac Gadwill for me. "If you're here to write an article, you've got a lot of material," she said picking up the phone. "I really should be journaling." Then, after asking whether I needed to go number one or number two, she directed me to the exit door where, along with one of the bush pilots, I peed off the back stoop.

When I returned, someone who looked like Nick Nolte and my college Russian teacher stood squinting at me.

"You Paul?" Jac Gadwill asked.

"Yeah."

"Got here OK, did you?"

"Yep."

He stared down at the ground for a moment, and then looked up and appraised me with his head cocked at an angle. "Boy, you look good here," he said finally. "You should stay."

We went out to Jac's industrial-sized pickup truck and headed down the gray ooze of a road that led into town. Jac had this to say about his three decades in the Alaska salmon business:

"In the Lower 48, people are sort of arranged. You know when they get out of school what they're gonna do, what they're gonna achieve. In Alaska it's all mixed up. It's like everybody's running even along a mud track. But then all of a sudden someone throws sand under one guy's feet and zoom!

Off he goes. And you're like 'how'd he do that?' Well, I'm kind of that person. A few years back someone threw some sand under my feet and off I went."

Soon we arrived at the "house type bunkhouse" and adjoining office building. A sign hung in front of the office: KWIKPAK FISHERIES, NEQSUKEG-CIKINA

"I asked an elder in a village up the river a ways what the Yup'ik word for 'good fishing' was and that's what he came up with," Jac said. "Well, when I had the sign done up I asked the locals here in Emmo what they thought of it. They just kind of stared and said, 'Something to do with fishing, right?' Turns out the dialect's different in every village. I tell you," Jac said, "This thing is gonna kill me."

"This thing," as Jac likes to call Kwikpak Fisheries, is something both new and old in the ten-thousand-year history of Alaskan man and Alaskan salmon. What makes it old is its basic principle—native people in small boats fishing for wild salmon. What makes it new is the same thing. Kwikpak is the only fishing company in the world that has earned recognition from the Fair Trade Federation. It is native owned and largely native operated, with the exception of Jac Gadwill and an associate who handles the sales end of things in Anchorage. If all goes well, Gadwill and the Yup'ik board of directors hope that these particular native people catching these particular Yukon king salmon will bring to market one of the more extraordinary fish on Earth.

"Why don't you go take a look around town?" Jac told me, heading up the thrown-together staircase leading to his office. "I'm gonna go call Fish and Game and see if we can't get us an opening and get you out fishing. I'll try the sugar-and-honey approach. If that doesn't work, I'll get my Lithuanian blood up."

I'm often confounded by the pointlessness of all the driving that goes on in America. At my family's cabin in northern New York state, cars stream by in a relentless drone down Route 86, even during mud season, when there are no outdoor sports to pursue, no tourists to serve. Where are they going, really?

In Emmonak, our cultural tendency to drive for driving's sake is laid bare, and appears possibly to have its origins in Native American nomadism. Aside from Kwikpak Fisheries, an Ace Hardware, and the post office, there is pretty much nowhere for the town's residents to go. Nor is there anywhere outside of town to go. Alaska is very markedly split 40/60 between south and north. The southern 40 percent has roads, outlet stores, McDonald's, nail salons, psychiatrists, summer houses owned by Californians, and a phone number you can call if you'd like to claim a moose you saw killed on the highway. The northern 60 percent of Alaska has nothing. Seen from above, Emmonak is very clearly in the middle of that nothing. It was explored and abandoned by Russians, barely settled by Americans, and no roads connect it to anything.

And yet, when you walk down the village's abbreviated thoroughfare, you cannot get away from the traffic. There are grandmothers in babushka scarves, fathers with sons riding piggyback, even children clearly under the legal driving age zooming their all-terrain vehicles up and down the road, shouting in the cold, foggy air. Winter's arrival is not totally unwelcome, in large part because the distance you can drive is vastly expanded. It is not unusual to snowmobile 100 miles to shoot a moose.

But I was on foot and the Yup'ik barely noticed me. A woman in the distance called out to a purebred pug that had the same name as my first dog, "Sweetie! Sweetie!" A little farther along, in the yard of a kind of jigsaw puzzle house made of salvaged sky-blue plywood, a man grasped the eye socket of what looked to be a bloody walrus head with his left hand and sawed away at a tusk with his right. "Sweetie! Sweetie!" the voice called out. From the second story of another jigsaw puzzle house a man scolded: "You sleep all day. Good for nothing, you can't even catch fish. Damn Eskimo."

On this day, the salmon situation was making the Yup'ik Nation particularly idle. Everyone was waiting for a handful of mostly white men and women at the Fish and Game Department at the far end of town to determine if enough salmon had escaped into the upper river to allow a commercial opening of the fishery. The Fish and Game Department was still in its "conservative regime," having been rattled when the Yukon king salmon population plummeted several years ago for unknown reasons. The fish's numbers have been slowly inching back up, but this year's escapement goals were not being met, and Fish and Game was proceeding with a degree of caution that was exasperating people like Jac Gadwill.

Seen in the greater context of what has happened around the country, though, it's easy to understand Fish and Game's caution. Twenty years ago, I left college for a while and found a job counting salmon for the Bureau of Land Management in Eugene, Oregon; I figured fisheries management might be something I'd like to do with my life. But during that season in the late 1980s, there were no fish to manage. The Pacific Northwest salmon runs were starting to wink out for good at that time, just as they had winked out 200 years ago in my home rivers back east. During my three months of salmon counting, I sighted one lone fish. Stories like this make Alaska seem like a wise old man sitting on a far northern perch overlooking the destruction that humanity has wrought. Today only Alaska has enough salmon to support a serious commercial fishery. The millions of fish that return to spawn each year in Alaskan rivers are a beautiful and profitable spectacle. Fish and Game is desperate not to screw it up.

At the same time, Fish and Game must manage another population on the Yukon: Yup'ik Eskimos. Which is why they will allow "subsistence openings" during which the Yup'ik can catch salmon for their personal consumption. Only if the amount of salmon in the river exceeds both the escapement and subsistence goals does Fish and Game allow a commercial opening. And when a commercial opening takes place, the Yup'ik can sell what they've caught to Kwikpak Fisheries.

When I had finished my tour of Emmonak and returned to the office, Jac Gadwill shushed me with a finger while he listened to the radio. A woman with a flat, Midwestern accent droned out the bad news.

"At this time Fish and Game will not be opening the commercial king salmon fishery. There will be a subsistence opening *only* in the Y–1 and Y–2 sections of the river from 12 to 6 p.m."

Jac slumped in his chair. He took a long drag on his cigarette and exhaled with a smoky cough. "No milk and cookies for Fish and Game."

He pushed a button on an intercom.

"Sweetheart," he said, "can you see if Ray and Francine are around? I want to get Paul here out on the river."

Jac then handed me some orange rubber overalls and a thick, very comfortable pair of wool socks, and wished me good fishing.

Ray Waska, Jr.'s, face looks pinned back by the wind as his open metal skiff roars through the channels of the Yukon Delta. A giant outboard engine propels the skiff, and it is unclear if Ray is smiling or if the wind itself is whipping up the corners of his mouth. Sitting next to him is his wife Francine in camo gear, and at the bow of the boat is their teenage son, Rudy. Their three-year-old daughter, Kaylie, wearing pink, racing-style sunglasses and a matching pink jacket, is crouched between Francine's knees. Their five other children are at the grandparents' fish camp, hidden away in the channels some twenty or thirty miles up river. When I ask Francine if she plans on having more children, she tells me, "Ray and I kinda want twenty."

If e. e. cummings had wished to retire to a place where the world was truly puddle-luscious, then the Yukon Delta would have been a good choice. Minnesota boasts of being "the land of 10,000 lakes." Alaska has more than three million, and it seems a good number of them are potholes and broken-off oxbows that surround the Yukon. There is so much of everything— sky, wind, water, and the clouds of mosquitoes that make a stinging space helmet around your head the second the boat slows down under ten miles per hour.

How the Yup'ik find their way amidst this shifting matrix of bald shoreline and brown water is any white man's guess. Hardly a tree or rock marks the way and, as with any truly natural delta, the landform is semi-permanent, sinking or rising at the whim of the river. And yet, there is never a hesitation in the forward momentum of our boat. Turns are made with unquestionable assurance until all of a sudden the engine cuts out, and Rudy rushes to the front to start paying out net line. We are subsistence fishing.

Once we are set up and anchored there is nothing to do. The net hangs vertically in a sixty-yard-long, surface-to-bottom curtain blocking passage in a small section of the river. The mesh openings in our gill net are big enough to accommodate the head and shoulders of a salmon. If a fish swims into the net, it will be stopped midway through. If it tries to back out, it will find its gills ensnared in the mesh. A few more thrashes and its fins will be caught.

The buoys strung along the top of the net start to twitch. Having only seen one wild salmon in my life, I rise in my seat. Ray and Rudy barely notice. Fish and Game has set a six-inch mesh size on the nets today—the size that will ensnare the gills of the more common (and ten times less valu-able) chum salmon. The kings have heads that are bigger than the allowed mesh size, and they should be able to bounce off unharmed if they hit the net. If it's just chums coming in, the thinking goes, you might as well fill the net before you haul.

But haul we finally do. After just four hand-over-fist pulls on the net, the first three salmon are in the boat.

"Chums," Ray says, the native way, clipping the consonant cluster at the end so that it almost sounds like "chumps." It's a little like factory work. Haul, haul, salmon, salmon, flop, flop. But just as things start to seem commonplace, Ray tenses. He pushes his son out of the way, makes one last haul, and *thwap!* A much bigger, more beautiful salmon lies on the deck. It has accidentally snared itself in a net meant for chums, its lower jaw wrapped three times around the twine.

"King," Ray says, the faintest trace of excitement in his voice.

The fish is three feet long and around thirty pounds—twice as big as the chums, with a steel-colored head. Since Fish and Game has declared a subsistence opening only, the king cannot be sold to Kwikpak. But nobody has said anything about barter. We pull anchor and blast our way down river. The wind is starting to penetrate my rubber overalls. The only part of my body that is warm is my feet, stowed snugly in Jac Gadwill's socks.

Around a bend and the boat slows again. A mosquito helmet forms around each of our heads. Rising up above us is a massive cargo ship, the *Olitok*. We pull up next to the ship and bang on the hull. Some prior communication has evidently taken place, for a few moments later the ship's cook appears on deck carrying two ten-pound packages of frozen chicken parts. Francine stands and smiles. Yellow Styrofoam backing. Plastic wrap. A bar code sticker that says $19.99. Francine appraises the package.

"Gee," she says, "I hope this doesn't have freezer burn."

Ray nods his head to the cook and reaches down into a cooler. With one huge haul he grabs the king salmon and throws it up onto the deck where it lands steely and shimmering in the watery sunlight.

A pause.

"Holy shit!" says the cook. He looks down at it, shuffles his feet, and glances at the frozen chicken he's traded in return.

"Hold on a sec," he says. He slips a hand into the gill plate of the salmon, drops the fish, picks it up again, and disappears into the galley. He returns in a moment with two packages of frozen ground chuck.

"Gee thanks," says Francine. She looks at it again and turns to me. "Do you think these have freezer burn?"

Ray's mother, Laurie, and I sit under a four-legged corrugated-metal canopy on a hill overlooking a football field–sized clearing that is the Waska family fish camp. A dog named Romanoff spins and barks. Dozens of grandchildren, some directly related, some adopted, run around in the grass and mud. Jac Gadwill jokes that the sharing of children is so common among the Yup'ik that some families may have accidentally adopted their own.

Using a fan-shaped *ulok* fashioned from an old circular-saw blade, Laurie starts to break down the 400 pounds of salmon we've caught over the last two days. She makes a slit on either side of the fish's anal fin and then runs the blade down the length of the spine. The fillets are smooth and flawless.

When I give it a go, I am extremely conscious of her staring at me. In this subsistence environment I am trying to fillet as close to the bone as possible. Laurie frowns at what I've done and takes the *ulok* away from me.

"Too much meat," she says.

"I was trying not to waste."

"Too much meat," she repeats.

"That one's pretty good, isn't it?" I say, holding up my second fish.

"It'll dry," she says. She stares down at the pink-orange mess of meat and bones that has accumulated at our feet. We are literally up to our ankles in lox.

"In the old days," Laurie says, "nothing went to waste. We used to dry the heads and feed 'em to the sled dogs in winter." She looks at me struggling with my third salmon and softens. "My mother tried to teach me how to make boots out of seal skin. She used whale muscle to make the thread. It took forever. I told her I wasn't going to do it! And she said, 'If you don't learn, your children will never have boots!'" Laurie lets out a big laugh. Her teeth are speckled with gold fillings. "I never did learn," she says.

We continue cutting in silence. As we're getting ready to go up to dinner, a skiff pulls up to the dock. A woman is at the wheel and she wears a bright red-and-white Grant Aviation jacket. Laurie's mouth drops open as she rises and waves.

"Oh, thank God," she says, half to herself.

The new arrival comes down the gangplank to the fish camp. The Waskas' youngest daughter, Roberta, is a big-shouldered girl, with a loud and pleasant laugh. The Waskas seem to give her a wide berth.

Inside the neat blue house, a wood stove burning, we all sit down to the salmon Ray Waska, Sr., has grilled. He has used a native recipe that involves a fair amount of Lowry's Seasoning Salt. Ketchup is served with the meal. Roberta squeezes in next to me on the bench.

A beer would go well with the meal. But it's illegal to possess alcohol of any kind in Yup'ik territory. A fifth of Jack Daniel's goes for $150 on the black market. With no toast possible to mark the presence of a guest from far away, Ray Sr. talks in general terms.

"We're happy to have you here, Paul. It's a shame you can't stay longer. See more of our people."

"I'd like that."

"Next time you come," Ray Sr. says, "you need to go up river a way. See the real Eskimos. We're all mixed blood around here. But up there you'll see the real classic Eskimo look. Little nose, round face."

I look at Ray Sr. and see a man with a little nose and a round face.

"But all people are the same," he says. "That's what I believe, anyway."

The conversation continues along these lines. Differences are described between peoples. I am told how the dog Romanoff got his name—he was born in the village of Romanoff, a settlement founded and abandoned by Russians. Finally, Roberta, bored by the conversation she's heard too many times, turns to me.

"Wanna go outside and see my brother's grave?" she says.

"Okay."

Roberta lights up a cigarette and blows smoke out of the corner of her mouth. Her big Grant Aviation jacket makes her look like a pilot and makes me feel like a stewardess. She stubs out the cigarette and I follow her into the woods. There is a tidy grave with a cross in an arrangement that reminds me of the graves of the rural Orthodox in provincial Russia. She lights up another cigarette.

"So are you working for Grant Aviation?"

"Naw," Roberta says. "I mean, I used to."

"Got tired of it?"

A pause, a foot shuffle, and then, "Actually, I just got out of being incarcerated."

"Where?"

"Oh, over in Bethel."

"Yeah?"

"Yeah. A girl started a fight with me and I had to finish it."

"At least you won."

She gives me a wink. "Also, my friend got caught selling alcohol."

Crises are shared in the Yup'ik Nation, and while I was out at the Waskas a pickup truck in the town of St. Mary's went off the road and two of the teenagers inside were killed.

"Now there's gonna be eight suicides," Jac Gadwill told me the day after I'd returned from the fish camp. He looked as if he had not slept. It was unclear if it was the deaths that had kept him up or the Arctic summer sun, pouring in the windows of the bunkhouse all night long. "It's true," Jac said. "You'll see."

We are seated aboard a tiny airplane, clouds gathering in the sky above.

The same pilot I had peed off the back stoop with starts up the plane. The readout on the navigation system says, NO USABLE POSITION. DEAD RECKONING ON.

As soon as the plane leaves the ground, Jac falls asleep. En route to comfort the parents of the dead teenagers in St. Mary's, we stop in the village of Kotlik, one of Kwikpak's smaller satellite fishing stations. Jac awakes and sprints out of the plane the moment we come to a halt. We hop on two waiting ATVs. Jac has instituted an electronic time card system that he believes will make paying the Yup'ik more efficient. But the people in Kotlik haven't been able to get the system going, and our visit is evidently going to be a bit of a dressing down.

Kotlik is even more isolated than Emmonak, but you can see where this roadless outpost could soon become Emmonak-sized with all its associated traffic problems. Bare heating pipes that lead off a central generator sprout into prongs along a tundra boardwalk that edges each house. Some of the prongs dead end and are clearly meant to one day connect to houses that have not yet been built. My ATV driver, just back from Iraq (he liked it *a lot*!) remembers that when he was a child, berries could be gathered in springtime off the side of the boardwalk. Now, the town has grown beyond his recognition and a haul of many miles into the bush is required if berries are to be gathered in any number.

We pull up to a new loading dock at the side of the river. Jac points to an older, dilapidated dock nearby. "I built that one out of scraps a few years ago. Got weathered in for three days while I was doing it. Slept on the floor of that trailer. No food."

He looks around and squints toward a field in the distance. "Now we got it so we can get a Herc in here and fly it out to Seattle with twenty thousand pounds of fresh kings. Get it to New York in a day."

Soon we are back on the airplane headed toward St. Mary's. The cloud ceiling has fallen considerably, and Jac peers through the windscreen at the dull landscape ahead.

"We ain't gonna make it," he says.

"We might make it," the pilot says, and dips the plane down into a patch of smoother air.

Jac lowers his head and mutters, "We ain't gonna make it."

Suddenly he looks inexpressibly tired. A tiredness that seems to seep out of his bones and into mine. For a while Jac thought he was in his mid to late fifties, but recently, at the Boston Seafood Show, a colleague who had known him for most of his many years as an Alaska fish trader added things up and pointed out that he must be sixty.

"Do you really need to do all this?" I ask him.

"I tell ya," Jac says, "I made a million dollars in a day once. Other times, I say I came to Alaska with $600 in my pocket and it's taken me twenty years to make back my $600." Then a pause. "But no, I guess I did all right in the end. I guess I'm kind of doing it for this," he says pointing at his heart. "See, I'm a Catholic and I kinda think that people when they end their life should have done something worthwhile." He grows silent and looks out the window, and then mutters, "But this thing is all-consuming."

"I'm sorry, folks," the pilot says. "We aren't gonna make it."

"Knew it," Jac says under his breath.

The plane banks low and hard. We sit in silence until the now-familiar town of Emmonak comes back into view. "Better to be here than halfway from there," Jac says.

Back in the airport shed the Grant Aviation flight schedule has been completely upended and we learn that my flight to Anchorage left hours before it was supposed to. But after a quick conversation, and a wink from Jac, the platinum blond dispatcher reroutes me via Bethel.

I gather up my bags and make my way toward a waiting airplane. Jac reaches out and unexpectedly gives me a massive hug.

"Damn, I tell you, Paul," he says, shaking his head, "you look good here. You could make the cut. I could mentor you."

I feel a strange flutter in my heart and laugh. I shake Jac's hand and climb aboard the plane. We take off abruptly, as all small planes do—a comforting feeling of control you don't have aboard the big jets. A feeling that makes me think, as we pass over the harsh rock mountains that separate the Yukon flood plain from the civilization to the south, *In a pinch, I could do it. I could fly this plane.*

ARIZONA

CAPITAL   Phoenix

ENTERED UNION   1912 (48th)

ORIGIN OF NAME   Possibly from the O'odham Indian word for "little spring"

NICKNAME   Grand Canyon State

MOTTO   Ditat Deus ("God enriches")

RESIDENTS   Arizonan or Arizonian

U.S. REPRESENTATIVES   8

STATE BIRD   cactus wren

STATE FLOWER   flower of saguaro cactus

STATE TREE   palo verde

STATE SONG   "Arizona"

LAND AREA   113,635 sq. mi.

GEOGRAPHIC CENTER   In Yavapai Co., 55 mi. ESE of Prescott

POPULATION   5,939,292

WHITE   75.5%

BLACK   3.1%

AMERICAN INDIAN   5.0%

ASIAN   1.8%

HISPANIC/LATINO   25.3%

UNDER 18   26.6%

65 AND OVER   13.0%

MEDIAN AGE   34.2

ARIZONA
Lydia Millet

I was living in the West Village, walking to work in the Flatiron building, and a couple of months past my thirtieth birthday when I decided, almost overnight, to quit my comfortable job and leave New York City for the desert.

At first I hedged my bets, both claiming and believing I planned to return a couple of months later after a brief hiatus. I had lived in the Southwest for a short time after college and felt enchanted by the landscape; Tucson was home to my favorite conservation group, a rabble-rousing, litigious bunch whose activist founder would shortly be written up in *The New Yorker* as a cross between St. Francis of Assisi and Jesse James. I figured I'd volunteer there.

It would be a temporary stint; my boyfriend of seven years was still in our shared apartment on 11th Street, a couple of blocks from the Hudson River, and I loved him. New York was a city I knew well and was fond of. Most of my closest friends lived there—all those who didn't live in LA, anyway—as well as, seemingly, ninety-five percent of the writers in America and their agents and publishers and the momentous, entertaining hubbub of a driven, self-important arts culture. I had worked hard throughout my twenties, even back to my teens, to become a novelist who was part of that culture.

But just a few days after I got to the desert, on impulse, I bought a house.

Enormous, thirty-foot saguaro cacti stood guard around the house with their multiple skyward-pointing arms and noisy bird holes; there were washes where small rivers ran through the sand in monsoon season, groves of palo verde trees with velvety green bark and shimmering yellow flowers, prickly pear and barrel cactus, creosote bushes. To the west, east, and south were jagged mountain ranges called the Sky Islands, sharp, purple-red volcanic peaks with the white domes of massive observatory telescopes glittering in the sun. The valley was called Avra and was dotted with ancient petroglyph sites, many still unstudied by archaeologists; it had been lived in by Indians for millennia and was still home to reservations. Foxes, coyotes, and roadrunners wandered beneath my windows, wild boar-like animals called javelinas came through the yard in herds at dusk and dawn, and there was an occasional bobcat sighting. Florid sunsets with towering clouds were inscribed on a vast and open sky, and at night the absence of city light made visible hundreds of thousands of stars.

The house itself, though I saw potential in it, was a scar on the face of the land. Built of army-surplus plywood, riddled with termites, floored in wretched, peeling linoleum the color of dried blood, and inhabited by pack rats, bark scorpions, black widows, and even Western diamondback rattlesnakes, it was not a standard impulse-buy for a city girl who could barely stand to plunge her own toilet. It lay forty minutes from Tucson on the edge of a national park; set well back from a dirt road, it was a kind of slapdash shack on a fifteen-acre parcel of lush Sonoran desert.

The insult to the land that was my house was replicated and magnified throughout the rest of the manmade environs, whose other dwellings were often even more derelict and ugly, mostly single- or doublewide trailers. Some functioned as meth labs, others housed Harley drivers and off-roading enthusiasts who kept rusting buses and Airstreams in their yards and revved their engines ceaselessly on weekend afternoons, then drove around in circles on barren lots littered with trash. Mailboxes were painted in camouflage, bashed in on the sides, or housed in cinderblock fortifications, possibly suggesting a reluctance on the part of my neighbors to open their arms to the outside world. Driveways were marked with NO TRESPASSING or KEEP OUT! signs, guarded by barking or even vicious dogs, and hung with chains.

The only place to buy food without making the half-hour drive through the rolling hills of the park to the city's outskirts was an establishment called the Minit Market, a convenience store/gas station about five minutes' drive away that sells cigarettes, Wonder Bread, Twinkies, energy drinks, and a small refrigerator's worth of wilting iceberg lettuce. It is frequented by crowds of emaciated, sun-worn guys in jacked-up trucks, their acid-wash girlfriends, and snaggletooth kids with half-open mouths and scarily vacant faces—some, and sometimes all, of the above smelling from afar of nicotine or alcohol. Almost exclusively, the clientele was rough, ragged, dissipated, and incurious. Once, on a smoking jag, I tried to buy cigarettes from a cashier who couldn't read enough to tell the difference between Camel and Marlboro.

I was no stranger to small towns; I had lived in small-town Georgia, small-town North Carolina, small towns in southern Germany and France. This wasn't a small-town thing, and it wasn't just poverty either: The valley's median income is only a couple of thousand dollars below the national average. It was something else, I felt, something more: an exaggeration. It was the canteen from *Star Wars*, minus diversity.

Yet nearly a decade later I still live in that house. I'm married to that activist. And I never want to leave.

This is a place where the horrible meets the divine. In that way it seems more American than any of the progressive, multicultural cities I've called home in the past—America being, to me, an outrageous collision of beauty and tawdriness, willful ignorance and avid exploration, boundless permission and angry violation.

Where I live is less than an hour from the border with Mexico, in a sage-green desert studded with dramatic peaks and valleys, but Arizona is far more varied than this. It's also high Alpine meadows with tundra, vast forests of ponderosa pine, the canyon cliff dwellings of the Anasazi, the Grand Canyon, the Petrified Forest, the Painted Desert, and the stark, Mars-evoking red buttes of Monument Valley in the Navajo Nation that occupies the northeast corner of the state, where so many SUV commercials are set. It's rivers like the San Pedro, sometime home to almost half the bird species in the country, and grasslands like those at Buenos Aires National Wildlife Refuge, where the last of the North American jaguars have recently been seen.

But no litany of sights can get to why I feel compelled to live here. I was never a nature girl, growing up, though I always loved animals; I didn't hike or camp until very recently. I always lived in cities. And I'm not a hermit either, in fact I'm an extrovert who actively misses her absent friends. Yet despite this I choose to make my life in the middle of what my closest friends and siblings think is nowhere. When they visit, some of them are indifferent to the landscape, others like or even love it, but in the end they're either bored or depressed by the situation's ruralness. I have to admit: many times, even in Tucson itself—a city of over half a million with plenty going on—I feel at a loss for the dense intellectual cover of places like New York, Boston, or Chicago.

And on a practical level the isolation of the valley is inconvenient. Every weekday, for instance, I have to drive my little girl through the national park, over a steep mountain pass, and into town for preschool, because there's nothing out here. By the time we get back, at least in the so-called winter months, the sun is low in the sky, and as I drive along the meandering, hilly park roads I have to swerve to avoid centipedes, desert tortoises, ringtails, and other animals that emerge from their burrows in the day's waning hours and seem to offer themselves as roadkill.

This commute will likely continue for the next fifteen years.

There's also the strange distress I feel when I go to the gas station. Because it's the only place around to buy stuff, locals flock there, and the Minit Market begins to play the role of social hub. The society it depicts is grim. All the clichés of hell apply; it's a blight of a place. Hard to say whether it's the Fifth Circle, full of the sullen, the slothful, and those tormented by rage, or the Seventh, where dwell the violent against man and blasphemers of God. (It's definitely not the Sixth: No one here seems passionate enough to be a heretic.) It's not that the customers are uniformly poor—many drive rigs worth sixty or seventy thousand dollars, tricked-out, enormous trucks I could never afford even if I cared to—but there's no denying that those Valley residents who are poor do tend to show up here. The Minit selects out for those who won't or can't make the drive into town, where superior shopping options are available. And there's a certain texture to the custom, a quality both miserable and self-righteous, brimming with pent-up aggression and hostility while at the same time passive and despairing. And white. Very, very white. Tucson itself is more than 40 percent Latino, but out where we live there's hardly anyone Hispanic.

Popular T-shirts worn by Minit Market patrons say more than a physical description of them could. The commonest shirts bear product endorsements: Corona, Bud Ice, Coors, Miller Lite, Joe Camel, Metallica, Playboy, and the American flag. There are also attitude shirts, of course. One I ran into most recently proclaimed THE ONLY JOB I NEED IS A BLOWJOB.

Under the Minit's fluorescent tubes are illuminated some of the starkest artifacts of bottom-barrel culture: flashy, metallic lottery tickets, lighters and lighter cases emblazoned with naked vixen and fast cars, many varieties of smokeless tobacco and condoms, packets of magical energy pills promising vigor and youthfulness, aisle upon aisle of pastel-colored foods that will outlive us all. Behind the counter, employees tend to be haggard, pasty, and greasy-haired, with slashes of black eyeliner or blue eyeshadow liberally applied. It's always women working these low-paid jobs, some old, some young, all beaten-down looking. Even at Subway, also housed in the building and with a more rapid staff turnover, there are very few men and never one over twenty.

All of us in Picture Rocks live near the national park, yet the Minit doesn't draw much tourist car traffic; most of the trucks, ORVs, and motorcycles cramming the lot on an average Saturday afternoon have local plates.

But we're also on a well-known biking route, and packs of healthy, tanned cyclists often descend on the Minit on weekends in their expensive, Day-glo gear and helmets, looking as foreign as a legion of itinerant Frenchmen. They hydrate quickly and hop on their bikes again, clearly anxious to get back on the road.

It's true that the Minit isn't the only establishment located at the "four-way," as we locals call it. There's also a produce stand run by a guy named Kermit, known for his friendliness and eerie imitations of cat sounds, which amuse and mystify my daughter, and sometimes a lady who sells pies from a van. Across the street is a bar called the Wagon Wheel, complete with a large antique example of same on the dusty façade. And a little ways down is a family-owned hardware store manned by a clan that likes to boast of their prowess at vermin-killing. (Triumphantly massacred vermin I have personally heard about from clan members include Sonoran desert, a.k.a Colorado River, toads, which barely eke out a living in this arid place and are visible only around monsoon time; snakes, including but by no means limited to those that are venomous; and small antelope squirrels that look just like chipmunks.) These places are powerful in their own right, but the Minit is a far more populous locale, always with lines at the cash registers, always bustling, the center of it all.

At first I tried to embrace the Minit. Clearly I was the interloper. Unlike most of the natives, some of whom were descended from families that had worked the nearby open-pit copper mines, I had a postsecondary education, was a refugee from the Big Apple, and owned a house bought with money inherited from my mother. I didn't want to be a class warfare cliché with my dismissal of all those Kools and Kid Rock CDs and necklaces bearing the flowery, gold-washed words ANGEL/SLUT. I told myself I could reach an accommodation with these items. I tried to develop a companionable familiarity with them; I referred to the store fondly as the Mullet Market, started drinking four-packs of Red Bull, and sometimes stood in the parking lot for long periods doing nothing but smoking, quaffing my Bull, and leaning against the faded hood of my pickup watching traffic. Though not an Avra Valley native, I figured, I could at least show solidarity with the lifestyle.

Still, as the weeks and months passed the Minit's stultifying effect became undeniable. Every time I talked to someone else waiting in line at the register—at the Minit, you always have to wait—I felt a sense of either horror or oppression settling over me, suffocating my intention to be open-minded. Whether it was the Hummer driver inveighing against the cyclists who dared to slow him down, the woman with psoriasis who pulled her whining son by the ear and spat on the floor, or the stooped old guy who told me while paging through a tabloid that the Olsen twins, then thirteen years old, were lying sluts but great pieces of ass, there was always something in the Minit that set my teeth against it. And frankly, it didn't take more than five or ten of these monolithic encounters to seal the deal.

The arrogant middle-classer looks at bottom-barrel culture and deems it vile, its proponents inferior. The condescending liberal is similarly repulsed by the language and leanings of that culture, but ascribes its proponents' tastes to their environment: the dropout rate, deadbeat dads, the corrosive influences of drugs and alcohol, the motorhead lifestyle, television. It's an uncomfortable position: on the one hand, you don't want to be a pig; on the other, you don't want to be a sucker.

Then too, my yuppie inclinations were rising stubbornly to the surface. When I started trail-running and stopped smoking, I felt the parking lot no longer welcomed me. Without a cigarette dangling from my lips, I failed entirely to fit in, lost whatever pretensions I might have had to a hardscrabble jadedness.

And when I traded in my cheap, beat-up truck for a perky little Prius, the breakup was final.

The Minit ethos dominates the valley. Big trucks with massive light bars and reactionary bumper stickers roar by, beer bottles and cigarettes flying out the driver's-side windows; men on my own street hone their shooting skills in their front yards; and park rangers' vehicles, sheriff's cars, and Border Patrol vans are common sights clustered together on the side of the road, mostly collaring DUIs and the poachers who steal wildlife from the park—snakes and lizards are targets, as well as saguaros. College graduates are in a small minority, and news readers are few and far between. It's a forty-minute commute to the average job in Tucson, which makes the settlements here a strange hybrid of rural outpost and suburb.

Regular shoppers who can't afford to buy the gas to get into town often enough for groceries sustain their families on the inventory of the Minit, the Wagon Wheel, and—over the past couple of years at least—Kermit's produce stand. Nestled among the soft hills and purple mountains is a significant meth-manufacturing industry, spawning bad behavior and periodic sudden fires. The public elementary school suffers such a high rate of absenteeism that it's in danger of being shut down; also it seems to have a small evangelical church attached to it. The valley boasts dangerous back-country routes followed by illegal immigrants coming up from the border. And there's a high rate of violent and property crime. Burglaries are frequent— we've had more than one.

My house is sixteen miles from the city limits, with rolling parkland and a mountain range in between; nationally our zip code is best known as the home of a world-renowned desert zoo, with half a million visitors a year, whose stated mission is to "encourage people to live in harmony with nature." And sure, there are a few people around here who try to do just that. But far more people are doing exactly what they want: to rip it all up. They want to widen the slow, rolling roads, make them straighter and bigger and faster. They want to raze the vegetation around their houses—vegetation that will not grow back in our lifetimes—and pave their driveways and yards. They buy their houses on quiet dirt roads but instantly want to lay down asphalt: when a couple of our neighbors moved in, they went door to door right away circulating a petition to pave the road. They made their rounds in a hulking F350, which sat empty and idling loudly in our driveway while the man stood at my door talking.

Newcomers divert the natural washes off their property by building large concrete dams—without, of course, the permits technically required under obscure federal statutes like the Clean Water Act. They ride their off-road vehicles into the nearby national monument—on the other side of the valley from the park—tearing up the fragile sand-and-shrub ecosystems and killing off tortoises, birds, and other animals. Kids under ten years old drive their ORVs to the Minit on weekends, sharing the road, when they're not veering off it onto the dusty shoulder at high speeds, with cars going sixty miles an hour.

Our neighbors rip the ancient cactus out of their yards with large earth-moving machines because cactuses have spines, and they don't want those; they prefer to plant orange trees, oleander, and bougainvillea. They slap down cheap tract houses on earth denuded and packed down by cattle grazing, making the doublewides that came before them look like marvels of restraint; they build garages bigger than their homes and then plop down prefab sheds the size of airplane hangars in the backyard to house their motorized thrillcraft. More and more of the breathtaking desert is quickly converted to its opposite, joining in hideousness the flattened, weedy patches of agricultural land formerly used to grow cotton, the ragged cones of mine tailings spotting the flatlands, a municipal airport where hang-gliders alight, and at the northern end of the valley a giant, polluting cement plant.

It would be far too much to ask that people live here because they love it. That would be, in fact, to assume free choice was operant in their ending up in this place, as it was for me, with the benefit of a nest egg from my family's farm and a livelihood that allows telecommuting; that would be to assume a kind of perfect society. (Many of the new homeowners obviously did come here by choice, in fact, among them plenty of middle-class retirees; but there are also longer-term residents who seem to be here chiefly because they can't get out.) None of the ripping up, none of the "custom homes" that are anything but custom or the drivers who run over rabbits and quail on purpose should surprise me. This is simply what happens at the tail end of the American frontier, at the last gasp of water's engineered abundance, in the final moment of hopeful expansion before the crash. This is business as usual outside the hugely sprawling, ephemeral cities of the West.

But it does surprise me, or more accurately, it hurts. All of the ravening, the sad ache of its waste, occurs side-by-side with the peaks of the beautiful park, the canyons and arroyos, the saguaro and ironwood groves. The animals that live here and have existed, in some cases, for twenty million years. When the storms come, in August, we can sometimes see seven different lightning storms at once from the balcony of my house, massive cloud banks receding across the valley into the mountains—the Waterman range, the Silverbells, the sacred peak called Baboquivari. We've watched mass migrations of tarantulas and caterpillars move across the valley, by the tens of thousands. At night, the Milky Way streaks overhead; I can stand in the yard and gaze up at its soft infinitude as a mild breeze moves the branches of the palo verdes and bats flit through the warm air.

I know my presence here is no boon to the place. It would do far better without all of us—without me, self-conscious and trying to walk softly; without my harder-living compatriots; without the ugly hubbub of all of us bringing our litter and noise and concrete to paradise. But I can't help myself. This, to me, is the closest I've ever come to the eternal and the sublime; this valley tells me that when it's time for me to die I don't need to be afraid. I can die happy, because the world is stunning and the sky will go on forever.

ARKANSAS

CAPITAL Little Rock

ENTERED UNION 1836 (25th)

ORIGIN OF NAME From the Quapaw Indians' word "acansa" meaning "downstream"

NICKNAME The Natural State

MOTTO Regnat populus ("The people rule")

RESIDENTS Arkansan or Arkansawyer

U.S. REPRESENTATIVES 4

STATE BIRD mockingbird

STATE FLOWER apple blossom

STATE TREE pine

STATE SONG "Arkansas"

LAND AREA 52,068 sq. mi.

GEOGRAPHIC CENTER In Pulaski Co., 12 mi. SW of Little Rock

POPULATION 2,779,154

WHITE 80.0%

BLACK 15.7%

AMERICAN INDIAN 0.7%

ASIAN 0.8%

HISPANIC/LATINO 3.2%

UNDER 18 25.4%

65 AND OVER 14.0%

MEDIAN AGE 36.0

ARKANSAS
Kevin Brockmeier

They appeared in the spring of 1991, suddenly and in great numbers, like dandelions colonizing a meadow: thousands of green bumper stickers with white letters reading "Speak Up for Decency." At first, no one was quite sure where they came from. You would glimpse one in a Kroger parking lot, then a second pulling out of a Super Stop, then a third pausing to make a left at a stoplight. The fourth, fifth, sixth, and seventh you would notice as you drove to work or school the next morning, and the eighth through the seventeenth as you drove back home. There was one in every cluster of cars, it seemed. They were impossible to miss.

It was not long before a response emerged: thousands of yellow bumper stickers, designed according to the same template, but this time reading "Speak Up for Liberty." Soon you found as many of these on the road as you did of the originals. Car for car there were probably a few more Decency supporters in the city, but sticker for sticker the two were running at a dead heat, since some cars sported multiple Liberty stickers—it wasn't remarkable to see as many as a dozen papered across the back of a van—while most of the cars with Decency stickers featured only one.

I was eighteen when all of this took place, a senior at Parkview High School, Little Rock, Arkansas's arts and science magnet. It was a place where the Liberties far outnumbered the Decencies, a haven for dancers, actors, painters, misfits, hipsters, skaters, straight edgers, band geeks, boys with makeup and girls without. We were the only school in the city (very probably in the state) with a preoperative transsexual in the student body. One of my friends wore a cape and a beret to class most days and was never once beaten up. Even at Parkview, though, you could find the occasional Decency in the parking lot, on a pickup truck or an El Camino, nestled far back by the bus roundabout.

It appeared—though who had noticed it before?—that they were engaged in a kind of combat, Liberty and Decency, or at least that they were preparing for engagement, like two duelists marking out their paces. In Arkansas, it seemed that this was simply the way of things: We were always preparing for engagement, without ever quite entering the fray. We were a conservative state with a predominantly Democratic legislature. We were home to both Tony Alamo of Tony Alamo Christian Ministries and St. Janor

Hypercleats of the Church of the Subgenius. Throughout the eighties, we had voted in large numbers for Ronald Reagan and George H. W. Bush, yet we were readying the stage to send our young liberal governor to the White House. As a people, we were not so much divided as we were emphatically self-abnegating. The bumper stickers were merely the latest symptom of this disorder. And although they never became a subject of widespread debate in the halls of my high school, as they did in the editorial pages of our competing state newspapers, the *Arkansas Democrat* and the *Arkansas Gazette*, there were glancing references made to them all the time. I remember overhearing conversations about where you could buy the bumper stickers and who was behind them, how you could rearrange the letters, along with jokes about Speaking Up for Potpourri, Speaking Up for Tennessee, Speaking Up for Retirees.

Nobody knew exactly how the dispute had originated. At least I didn't. If it seemed one week that half the people in the city were speaking up for decency and the next week that the other half were speaking up for liberty, well, that was no more mysterious than the process by which everyone suddenly began listening to the same album or using the latest piece of slang— which is to say profoundly mysterious, but not particularly exceptional.

I have since learned the broad outlines of the story: how the "Speak Up for Decency" campaign was initiated by members of Fellowship Bible Church, one of Little Rock's largest and most influential nondenominational evangelical congregations, in response to what they perceived as the superabundance of violence and sexual promiscuity in the media; how among the targets of the campaign was *Spectrum Weekly*, a local alternative newspaper that carried 900 numbers and gay personal ads in its back pages; and how *Spectrum*'s marketing and circulation director initiated the "Speak Up for Liberty" campaign after someone began badgering the paper's advertisers and emptying its distribution racks.

My friends and I had heard of Fellowship Bible Church, and we had read *Spectrum*, but at the time we knew none of these intricacies. We could certainly see that the Decency backers and the Liberty backers were arrayed on opposite sides of a conflict, though, and we were able to intuit the fault lines—roughly, that:

The Decencies were religious (though there was nothing innately religious about decency).

The Liberties were secular (though there was nothing innately secular about liberty).

The Decencies were symbolically if not actually concentrated in West

Little Rock, the new-growth area of the city, with all the most recent chain stores and restaurants.

The Liberties were symbolically if not actually concentrated in Hillcrest, the old-left neighborhood of the city, with all the little cafés and boutiques.

The Decencies were bothered by profanity, homosexuality, and the bullying immodesty of American culture.

The Liberties were bothered by repression, censorship, and the bullying sanctimony of American culture.

The Decencies had, around 1988, been at least slightly irritated by Scorsese's *The Last Temptation of Christ*, but resisted the provocation to see it.

The Liberties had, around 1988, been at least slightly irritated by Scorsese's *The Last Temptation of Christ*, but resisted the provocation to skip it.

The Decencies would, around 1996, attach "Promise Keepers: I ♥ My Wife" stickers to their cars.

The Liberties would, around 1996, find it amusing to contemplate replacing the little red ♥s on the "Promise Keepers" stickers with little black ♣s.

The Decencies placed their confidence in early mornings, good manners, the 1950s, and the family as a nurturing ground for children.

The Liberties placed their confidence in late nights, outspokenness, the 1960s, and the family as a nurturing ground for adults.

At heart, the Decencies distrusted where we were going.

At heart, the Liberties distrusted where we had been.

Both the Decencies and the Liberties held that they themselves were best defined by where they placed their confidence. Both the Decencies and the Liberties held that their opponents were best defined by what they distrusted. And, of course, both the Decencies and the Liberties believed in the bumper sticker as a platform for social engagement.

The bumper sticker could be put to other uses, and I had seen that done many times before: the bumper sticker as advertisement ("Support Rice-Growers"), the bumper sticker as inside joke ("No Roger, No Rerun, No Rent"), the bumper sticker as boast ("My Child Is an Honor Student at Carver Elementary"), the bumper sticker as a token of personality ("I'd Rather Be Fishing"), the bumper sticker as self-amused kiss-off ("Yes, as a Matter of Fact, I Do Own the Whole Damn Road"). It took a particular kind of person to politicize the bumper sticker, though it's possible that the Decency stickers had only been retroactively politicized by the Liberty stickers; I'm sure that at least some of the people who displayed them had failed to realize they were choosing sides in a debate.

For a while, I thought the stickers might be part of a national campaign, like the ones that appeared every four years just before a presidential race. I had owned such a sticker when I was eleven, a black "Fritz Busters" sticker with a caricature of Walter Mondale inside the *Ghostbusters* logo, which I liked not because I was a Ronald Reagan fan but because I was a *Ghostbusters* fan. It turned out, though, that the Decency stickers were a purely local phenomenon, the Liberty stickers a purely local response.

As the weeks went by, the dispute showed no signs of abating. More and more stickers appeared on the backs of Little Rock's cars. Fewer and fewer people were unaware of them. The letters in the editorial pages of the *Arkansas Democrat* and the *Arkansas Gazette* (respectively—and, once more, symbolically if not actually—Little Rock's Decency paper and Little Rock's Liberty paper) became more frequent and more vociferous:

> Some religious leaders use censorship to keep the truth from their followers and others. Teachers cannot teach if they must try to please the censors. Some censors even try to change history.
>
> —A. W. Taylor, *Arkansas Democrat*, January 5, 1991

> Look at us in 1991. Pornography allowed under the guise of free speech. The big three TV bigmouths busy presenting mind-boggling bias as news.
>
> —Rod A. Porter, *Arkansas Democrat*, January 31, 1991

> Wake up! There was and is no Jesus, just as there was no Adam, no Moses, no Apostles. Human beings created the gods of religion, not the other way around, and if they did not, if there is a God like the Jews and Christians believe, then every sin and everything evil is his crime, not ours, because he invented them! So don't try to save me, I'm not lost!
>
> —Pablo Rodriguez-Santiago, *Arkansas Gazette*, March 10, 1991

> We are so deceived and desensitized to demonic array that we're turning into another Sodom and Gomorrah. . . . There's a new television show called "Dinosaur." It shows children talking back to parents and has sex and crime. It's something Satan has thrown into the eyes of our children and we parents are responsible for our children's time.
>
> —Sonny Tobin, *Arkansas Gazette*, May 25, 1991

It continued like this for months, the two factions shouting each other down on the letters pages as their bumper stickers fought for supremacy over the tails of the city's cars. Back and forth they went, through the summer and into the fall.

There was an incursion of Liberty.

There was a backlash of Decency.

There was a counterstroke of Liberty.

There was a retaliation of Decency.

There was a brief hiccup of Tolerance, I am told, but I was away from home and I missed it.

In August of 1991, when I left Little Rock for college, both Decency and Liberty were nearly ubiquitous. By 1997, when I returned home, they had begun to vanish from the automotive landscape. The Liberties lingered a bit longer than the Decencies—not, I would guess, out of any particular depth of conviction, but simply because the class of drivers likely to advertise Liberty on their bumpers were not as wealthy and therefore more apt to own six-year-old cars than the class of drivers likely to advertise Decency. This was recently made plain to me when, in an effort to remind myself what the original "Speak Up for Decency" stickers looked like, I spent a few minutes coasting through the parking lot of Fellowship Bible Church during Sunday services and was greeted by row after row of Saturn Skys, Mitsubishi Eclipses, and Land Rover LR2s, all with wet-looking factory glosses of color. I tried a few other churches in the same neighborhood, the Church of Christ on Rodney Parham, the Immanuel Baptist on Shackleford, and the First Baptist on Pleasant Valley, all without success. Finally I was able to track one of the stickers down outside a Wal-Mart in Southwest Little Rock, where used cars go to live out their retirement years. Could it be, I wondered, that all our disagreements are destined to end this way, blanching out and wearing away at the edges, handed along from one generation to the next until their original meaning has been all but lost and they have been replaced by new disagreements, or by the old disagreements in new guises, each in its turn following the slow passage from faith to commerce?

Today Fellowship Bible Church has grown out of its acreage, *Spectrum* has been replaced by the *Little Rock Free Press*, and very few of the stickers remain on the road. Most of those that do are peeling and barely legible. I saw no more than five or six, distributed as you might expect, in the spring of 2004, when Bush/Cheney and Kerry/Edwards stickers began appearing suddenly and in great numbers, like mushrooms feeding off a decaying forest, in the back windshields of the city's cars and SUVs. (It's almost always windshields these days rather than bumpers, though I don't know why; I suppose there are fashions in sticker placement, as in everything.)

It has been several years since the last flickering trace of the dispute crossed my gaze. I was exiting the highway behind an old Plymouth K-car, its frame dented and its paint faded with age, a fixer-upper, I imagined, donated by some well-intentioned father to the cause of his son's adolescence. The sticker below the license plate was a one-off letterpress creation, the kind you used to be able to design for yourself at the state fair in the days before cheap home laser printers. It read, "Speak Up for Puberty."

Here, finally, was a cause we could all support.

CALIFORNIA

CAPITAL Sacramento

ENTERED UNION 1850 (31st)

ORIGIN OF NAME From a book, Las Sergas de Esplandián, by Garcia Ordóñez de Montalvo, c. 1500

NICKNAME Golden State

MOTTO Eureka! ("I Have Found It!")

RESIDENTS Californian

U.S. REPRESENTATIVES 53

STATE BIRD California valley quail

STATE FLOWER golden poppy

STATE TREE California redwoods (*Sequoia sempervirens* and *Sequoiadendron giganteum*)

STATE SONG "I Love You, California"

LAND AREA 155,959 sq. mi.

GEOGRAPHIC CENTER In Madera Co., 38 mi. E of Madera

POPULATION 36,132,147

WHITE 59.5%

BLACK 6.7%

AMERICAN INDIAN 1.0%

ASIAN 10.9%

HISPANIC/LATINO 32.4%

UNDER 18 27.3%

65 AND OVER 10.6%

MEDIAN AGE 33.3

CALIFORNIA
William T. Vollmann

It says something about our changing America that once upon a time, an art-friendly governmental organization commissioned one volume about each of our fifty states; whereas this book, inspired by the WPA's example, has been commercially published and allows each state only a few thousand words. Fortunately, mass culture, with its big box warehouses of the landscape, language, and mind itself, has already destroyed so many differences between states that there is less to say anyhow. Of course the ambiance of Florida still varies from that of Montana, Hawaii's from Alaska's, but aren't their television programs the same? Accordingly, I dare to hope that a generation or two from now, if a sequel to this sequel comes out, its writers will have life even easier.

My home state has met its own losses during this ongoing destruction of differences. Who believes in the "California dream" anymore?

In conquistador times, the dream was that California was an island of Amazons. With equal lust, missionaries envisioned it as an empire of saved souls and slave labor. Meanwhile vast ranches named themselves upon the land, their devout and secular respective owners dreaming Biblical dreams of cattle increase; at this time California's principal export was hides. Seized by the United States of America, California now began to incarnate a dream of gold. Once Everyman's surface deposits played out, the dream, disseminated in great measure by the railroads, took on a character of agrarian luxuriance. Los Angeles's orange groves thickened; boosters began to speak of "Tropical California," and citrus soon became a gorgeous golden infection. Other phrases of the day were "ease," "salubriousness," "reclamation," meaning the transformation of the land from a supposedly waste state (you see, it had been wasted by Indians, who were rapidly dispossessed, enslaved, or exterminated for the greater good) into homesteads, and that epitome of Americanism, "self-sufficiency." As a twentieth-century song insisted, it never rains in California; hence the inhabitants of that sunshiny paradise began to addict themselves to irrigation. In such audacious projects as the settlement of the Imperial Valley's desert, self-sufficiency required reclamation at taxpayers' expense; and the more people came to California, the more water was needed, whose financing required either more public money, as for instance in the construction of Hoover Dam, or else new land sales—which meant buyers, who needed more water. Meanwhile, oil wells came and mostly went in southern California, industrializing and urbanizing their surroundings. More jobs meant still more people. And always danced the dream that California was somehow special: the living would be gracious in the grapefruit-scented sea breezes of everlasting summer. Ever more homesteads became corporate farms; highways crawled with cars, so we built freeways and kept building them; city air turned brown. Although the poorly paid and often ghastly labor of migrant workers continued to be more or less hidden, at least until César Chávez commenced his marches, fasts, and boycotts, quite visibly enough the urban ghettos stood out on California's flesh like sores. In Nathanael West's *The Day of the Locust*, the dream had already become a nightmare parody, tricked out with the desperate lust of the masses to drug themselves with a glimpse of any Hollywood celebrity; spiced with the rage of those who had believed the brochures and now discovered that exchanging Pittsburgh or Cedar Rapids for a scrap of California real estate had not made their lives wonderful. The California I know is in part the land of long commutes, unaffordable homes, Superfund toxic waste sites, overburdened public services, bad schools (except for the rich), increasing crime—in short, the land of reality.

All the same, it is still true that in California, one will find the highest number both of endemic species and of total species in the United States. And many subspecies of my own general sort of life form occupy interesting niches in the socioeconomic bio-region called California.

I was born here, and I have lived most of my life here. I like the unassuming informality (when was the last time I had to wear a suit?), the tolerant, or, if you prefer, the blasé anonymity (who cares if that woman is sticking her tongue in another woman's mouth?), and even the superficiality. Most of my fellow Californians seem to be from somewhere else. In the grimy old brick towns of the East, I sometimes feel that people have grown up history-stained. Boston, Providence, Salem, Rochester, these places are alien to me, for winters, rains, and ancient violence blotch their walls. In California, where the future promises continued sunniness, most of what I see is new: big box stores, mini-malls, armies of cookie-cutter houses where there used to be fields and wetlands. Drive-ins take too long; I order a drive-*through*'s burger, living the California dream.

A certain California creek I know is a green secret, rich in willows and tamarisks through which one must fight to see the white-foamed brown water spilling through the tender grass. Ants, flies, butterflies, and lizards live there. And if I take five steps back, past the rock with the petroglyphs on it, I'm once again in a desert, and before me runs the most unassuming G-string of green in a rocky gulley.

Meanwhile, the 104,000 irrigated acres of Palo Verde have made green fields out of the Colorado River's western shore for a span as narrow in time as is that desert creek in space—not much more than a century.

And on a still larger scale is California itself, whose desert places have been made green in thousands of places—and whose marshes have been drained, whose lakes have been polluted, whose mountains and forests have been dynamited here and there, whose water table sinks and sinks.

In the middle of the twentieth century, California was America's number one cantaloupe producer (346,000 tons), and number two grapefruit producer (137,000 tons). The California of Steinbeck's novels is fundamentally agricultural. *In Dubious Battle* revolves around a fruit pickers' strike. *East of Eden* and *Of Mice and Men* are both set in the California ranch country. *The Grapes of Wrath* deals with Okies' vision of California as a farmer's paradise—and with the actuality, namely that they find themselves locked out of those farms. Just as Mishima's *Sea of Fertility* tetralogy was named after an airless wasteland on the moon, so California's abundance often appears in a disturbing arid perspective, should one only take a few steps back.

Across the street from Los Angeles's Central Library, descending from the vertically grooved Bank of America tower, is a winding staircase whose two lanes are divided by a high channel of silver-white water spilling down cement-walled rocky concretions. The water swivels gracefully down a canyon of skyscrapers, trees, and shrubs, ending in a fountain, a flower stand, and a café in number 633, some of whose windows boast tapering upside-down reflections of the Citigroup Building, which in turn offers from its horizontal black window-stripes a lovely basketworks, namely the concrete waffle-grid on the library reflected and distorted.

Get in a car (since this is Los Angeles; this is California), and roll past the brown corduroy cube of the International School of Languages, the lovely white filigree of the Torah Center, then Pico Cleaners, Eliass Kosher Market, the detached single-story commercial cubes on the six-lane wideness of Pico Boulevard. Here as in so many California cities the evening "rush" of cars means that cars don't move at all; cars wait so patiently and gleamingly to make the long gentle curve of Highway 71 and thereby enter the shade of olive-grassed hills.

All this was desert once. Someday it will surely be desert again. Meanwhile, Los Angeles irrigates its concrete and asphalt garden at the expense of, among other places, the Owens Valley, which from Westgard Pass appears pale yellow-green, slightly lush. As one comes down into the Owens Valley it flattens out and so do its colors: pastel with dust, snow, clouds, and bluish-green veins of trees faded white and blue in an old Mediterranean travel poster. The grayish-green fields or desert (hard to distinguish from a distance) now begins to show white abrasions; and the greenish-gray gets grayer, resolving into sagebrush. The rich brown windings of Owens Creek once became Owens River, then Owens Lake. Owens Lake is a dust bowl now, thanks to the thirst of Los Angeles.

But don't say the past is gone in California! In Santa Monica, which of course belongs to Los Angeles, the old Packard showroom on Wilshire Boulevard (now a Mercedes-Benz dealership) reflects in its window the phony Spanish curvy red roof tiles of the bagel place; and above the huge panes in which this reflection appears, the elaborate metalwork resembles the frilly scales of the palm tree in front, and then there are flesh-colored wriggles around the white archway. Nowadays this edifice likewise possesses a faux Spanish roof, there on wide Wilshire Boulevard, seventeen-odd blocks from the sea.

D rive on; so much more of California than I can tell you is about driving nowadays! You can roll from Los Angeles north to Sacramento on Interstate 5 (which, as a matter of fact, runs all the way from Mexico to Canada), seeing not much else but dry mountains, flat fields, and urban sprawl, glittering monster trucks and shining four-doors rolling down wide ways between narrow green strips. This route exaggerates the ruination of my home state. From the freeway it is especially easy to believe that, say, Stockton stretches hideously east and west, like the worst of Los Angeles. But if you do turn, say, east, you will pass through vineyards, dark green fields of tall corn, rolling reddish-green fields speckled with dappled cows, walnut orchards, one of which is enclosed in a long white fence. Pass the Poppy Ranch, and here in yellow grass is a double-doored metal gate, with a rusty star inset in each door. Presently you will enter Calaveras County, which is literally the County of Skulls. In Wallace, I remember the beautiful California look of blond grass and live oaks; on Highway 29 I look down into live oak valleys fringed by blond grass and a few clouds. The grass now begins to be tinted with wetter olive hues. In place of that faux Spanish roof in Santa Monica I find the old two-story store façades of Angels Camp. Crossing the lake bridge into Tuolumne County (three vultures in the cloudy sky), I inspect the genuine original replica of Mark Twain's cabin with its truly-o original chimney, the whole fenced off absurdly and surrounded, respectfully but noticeably, by houses. If I chose, I could take that as a metonym of my poor California. But in Sonora, once settled by Mexicans and named after their state, now the county seat of our American republic, California may still be called the evening sunlight on oak leaves, which are still green in mid-September, and down below me the amplified referee calls a football game. Meanwhile, the Tuolumne County Courthouse (cornerstone laid in 1898) stands silent, its copper double doors locked well and studded with copper stars. Looking inside, I can see inlaid marble tile. Atop the building's pillared white crown rides a weathervane.

Here in Sonora I will sleep; and in the morning, sitting on the balcony of the Gunn House Motor Lodge, which was built by Mexican laborers for, of all people, Dr. Gunn, I will look across the tiny pool and over the white roses, above the fence and across the parking lot to the steep, densely treed hill, some of whose leaves are finally going yellow. Two windows of an old house will peer out at me through the branches, like the eyes of a face with unkempt bangs.

The Lodge, you may be assured, is guaranteed historic by its own sign, and within the room, in a band around the walls, one finds the epitome of vulgar American gentility: a shelf of classics, with globes and model sailboats tucked in; and because the management, or their decorators, or more likely the company that the decorators went to, trusted that none of us looks closely, much less reads, it turns out that there are only a dozen titles: *The Iliad, Oliver Twist, War and Peace,* etcetera, which, like that globe and model sailboat, simply repeat, round and round, with real doors and windows cut out of them—American, I said, not merely Californian; for in spite of her faux Spanish roofs, California retains her mania for newness, which requires unhypocritical obliteration.

Above Sonora, Highway 109 arrives in high pine forest, supplying such metropoli as Confidence (population 50), then Sugar Pine (150 souls), not to mention Mi-Wuk Village, the town I went to see in hopes of discovering a plaque, a museum of Indian artifacts, or some assertion of California history. I bought a bag of ice at the steep-roofed Mi-Wuk Market, which also sold chains for various makes of cars. The clerk said two dollars and seventy-five cents. I asked him where the hiking was, and he said to go to Pinecrest Lake, not here. I asked him whether this had been a Miwok settlement, and he said that he guessed it had been. I asked whether he knew what had happened to the Miwoks, and he said that he did not. ("I think that some developer named the town," explained the park ranger up the road. "I don't know. All the streets have Indian names. There's really not much around here.")—And so I rolled on out of Mi-Wuk Village, which had the usual Sierra look: a trifle gloomy, with a scattering of prefabricated edifices on either side of the highway, then pines behind and around, casting everything into dark monotony.

Not far below Sonora lies Jamestown's lovely white church with its boarded-up windows, a yellow-grassed bluff and blue sky behind; then there are bulls and cows on a green field, and still more cattle beneath a tree on a yellow field; next comes Chinese Camp, whose rock-knives and live oaks rise out of the hot blond grass, and this town is far smaller than Mi-Wuk Village. In the grocery-tavern where one can buy bad replicas of Indian moccasins for a nice cheap price, there is a man who wears camouflage fatigues and who speaks in what I take to be an Australian accent. I asked him if any of the five thousand Chinese who founded the town had stayed, and he replied that they had not—because it was a *camp*, see. He said that it had been unsafe to be a non-Caucasian gold miner in those nineteenth-century days, so when the construction of the transcontinental railroad offered them a chance to escape the vigilantes and make a fixed wage, the Chinese all packed up. This was something like the tale of Sonora, whose Mexican miners had been run out after the Americans assessed them a special tax, then marched on their camp, bearing guns and flags. I asked the man in camouflage whether he had found any Chinese artifacts, and he replied that he had discovered opium pipes, opium bottles, and marbles made of grayish clay.

A trifle farther down, just past the gated homes of Copper Hills, you will find Copperopolis, which once upon a time was the West's principal source of, yes, copper. An ancient A-frame structure, which must have been a works of some kind, broods over a hillock of broken rocks streaked blue and green. A rusty cylinder with a pointed top lies a few steps away. It resembles the tip of a giant's pencil; I could have hidden half my body inside. At the base of the hill, a live oak grows out of a roofless stone room. And now I am already back on the main road, where the two-story Old Corner Saloon wears its own helpfully "historic" sign: The upper floor was once a whorehouse.

And then one rides down Highway 4, out of Copperopolis and down through wet olive grass under the cloudy sky until a more beautiful view of the Central Valley than I could ever have imagined appears below me: a vast, reddish-orange flatness, with shadows and trees, and gulleyed a little, like the plains of Wyoming. Here comes the town of Farmington, where inside Lagorio's Grill & Bar some women were laughing and some men in biker T-shirts were drinking cheap beer, and since my sweetheart wanted something nonalcoholic to drink, I stood up at the bar with her and waited until it was our turn and then we waited some more because we were not regulars. When the barmaid came, I said to my sweetheart: "I wonder if they have orange juice," to which the barmaid replied: "While you're wondering, I'll go serve some customers."

Two men were drinking beer. The closest one said that he and his friend were voyaging from bar to bar. Perhaps because it was noon on a Saturday, they were still sitting up straight; they were not yet drooping like the leaves of a walnut tree. Somebody ordered a hamburger with American cheese, and the closest man said: "What other kind of cheese is there? Don't give me that *wetback* cheese!"

His friend said to the barmaid: "I'll have a burger. You'll be the bun."

And the regulars went on with their steely bantering happiness, while a family sat eating burgers and a young boy in a hooded sweatshirt wandered through the darkness; and when the barmaid brought our lunch she called me honey.

Mr. Sean Wilsey, who commissioned this essay, expressed concern that I might not have sufficiently emphasized (a) the positive and (b) the Pacific Coast, so I humbly requested some expense money and set off to re-admire one of my favorite places, the Point Reyes National Seashore, which frequently wins that pleasant cliché *pristine*. Unfortunately, just then a freighter bumped into the Bay Bridge, and out came 58,000 gallons of heavy fuel oil. Four days later, black clots had already begun to wash up at Point Reyes. "On the surface, it would appear that we did everything by the book in this case as far as responding," said Coast Guard Commandant Adm. Thad Allen, thereby informing me that everything was A-OK. A week after the accident, I set off to inspect that surface, motoring along Sir Francis Drake Boulevard, and meeting congregations of redwoods along the way. "I love these tunnels of trees," said my sweetheart; for it was so shady and sweet with the foliage down by the river, with the cedar smell and the ferns; then we ducked back into the gray green dry country. There was a shaggy yellow-orange willow in Olema, after which we achieved the slightly grander metropolis of Point Reyes Station, where California struts her stuff for tourist money; the handwoven scarves have been helpfully tagged "wearable art," and you can look through the big window at the Cowgirl Creamery to see people kneading the curds of their artisanal cheese. After lunching at an organic diner, we passed a dried-out marsh on Highway 1, then came out into the Point Reyes National Seashore, whose scent of fog, trees, and dirt differed strikingly from the mountain smell around Sonora. The air cooled. Walking through the Bishop pines, which grow nowhere except along the coasts of California and Mexico, we touched a bush with white feather-seeds like dandelions. Some three-leafed brambles had gone whimsically crimson. Ahead lay the Pacific like a hardening of the sky. The white sun rested on that blue sea far down below the piney raspberry hills.

At first, Limantour Beach seemed the same as ever, but, as in that creepy science-fiction classic *On the Beach*, not everything was right. Beside a shining piece of kelp lay a black blob of something the size of my forefinger, something that smelled like asphalt and was sickeningly soft. A few paces beyond, a clump of kelp looked burned; actually its tentacles were black with oil. The shore was marked by translucent dead jellyfish every fifty or a hundred yards. For some reason the flies disdained them in favor of the oiled black kelp, which seemed disgustingly hairy, like a magnified insect leg. Now here lay a blob as large as three fingers.

Sometimes the blobs were strangely attractive, as when they resembled obsidian; and I remember a lovely, gleaming-black ribbon of kelp. Then came a mat of black kelp like a bird's nest, and more dead jellyfish. Sometimes a blob might be the size of a luxury steak, black and sticky; then it was usually an oiled dead jellyfish. Dig into it with a stick, and the tissue separated. But these manifestations, though ubiquitous, were not densely arrayed; and they occurred in conjunction with the Dutch blue sky and the dunes with the yellow-green grass.

A single sea bird, black with oil, skittered and dove. The other birds appeared untouched. Soon my sweetheart and I had black fingers from holding hands.

We looked out, as most human beings do, looking out, as we all do, at the horizon. Then we drove back to Olema, passing through stands of Bishop pines, where the late afternoon was tinged as if with sea light.

The next morning, parting from the fat sticky evergreen cones of Olema, we headed in the direction of Stinson Beach, and the highway wound in and out of what could have been Sonora foothills. Then that signature California landscape gave way to another: green darkness decorated by the pale vertical stripes of eucalyptus trunks.

The low flat blueness of Bolinas Lagoon smelled of mud and salt. A white heron stood ankle-deep in the water, very still, with its beak out, and the shadow beneath it resembled a gravestone. Shimmering stripes of blue and brown bedecked the water, and the horizon was a line of trees protruding from a cloud bank. Wandering through the green reeds, I could discover no petroleum spoor. Waterfowl squeaked overhead in flocks. White ducks floated on the trembling water, occupying both sides of the boundary between blank blueness and reflected trees. My sweetheart showed me a tree-hive she had found the last time she was there. Even this late in the season, a few bees were humming in and out. We came to another place where the ducks were as thick as pebbles. An egret waded with large yet deliberate steps, its head seeming all the tinier atop its long, long neck. I took out my pocketknife and slit open one of the jade green stalks of fennel and rubbed it on my face before giving my sweetheart a surprise kiss. Then as we approached that flotilla of ducks we began to find big black globs of oil on the grass. So we left that place, passing a great blue heron that stood at the edge of a grass-island, staring down into a channel, no doubt watching for lunch. Passing a concretion called Seadrift, whose ugly edifices were partially redeemed by bamboo and passionflower behind some of its fences, we drove through Stinson Beach and then followed the highway up the steep dry grass-hills at the edge of the Pacific.

Before long we were in Sausalito, a tourist trap possessed of the same superficial pleasantness as Carmel: art galleries, restaurants, and shops that sold those expensively conformist items which one buys not for oneself but to fulfill some dreary gift-giving obligation. To remind me that this was California, a façade informed me of the existence of a NUTRITIONIST STRUCTURAL INTEGRATIONIST CRANIOPATH, and then another building announced itself as MySpaEvent.com. I always enjoy Sausalito regardless, because it commands such a fine view of the Bay, with Angel Island not more than a mile or two across the water, and the Berkeley hills shining blue-green beyond the Bay Bridge, and Alcatraz resembling a white neoclassical city from this angle, and, best of all, my favorite city, San Francisco, which was a platter of porcelain cups, pitchers, and saltshakers upon a tray of fog. Speaking of which, it was past noon, and there was a restaurant where I sometimes liked to watch San Francisco over a salad or a Bloody Mary. So we sat on the deck with the Bay so warm blue and ripply. My sweetheart decided that she could probably swim as far as Angel Island. And a blond California girl in a sundress sat beside her boyfriend, gazing at the bobbing boats. As we ate our lunch the fog slipped across San Francisco until only the tip of the Transamerica Pyramid was left. Then the city was utterly gone; and by the time we got our dessert it had come back again. Our waiter remarked that he could no longer walk his dog in the park at Point Isabel over in Richmond, because the beach there was so slicked over that the authorities had closed it. Indeed, after lunch we strolled along the sea-edge and found black globs on this or that rock. A warning notice from the Audubon Society advised us to leave contaminated birds alone, and to avoid stepping in the oil and thereby spreading it. So we drove out of Sausalito, and paid our five-dollar toll to cross the Golden Gate Bridge, whose pillars faded off into the fog, and an ovoid blur of the Presidio peering out at us from a mousehole of clear air. Then we were in San Francisco.

San Francisco is my favorite American city, in part because it houses multitudes of secret worlds; and so, solely to please Mr. Wilsey, and certainly not out of any proclivities of my own, I put on my lipstick and earrings, while my sweetheart, who now stood nude in the lovely wig I had bought her, told me to close my eyes until she was ready to surprise me with her new outfit, a dominatrix costume. You see, we were off to spend more expense money at a certain S&M club and dungeon whose workshop that night addressed a question of considerable interest to any loving couple: What are the most effective ways to inflict fear and spicy physical stimulation upon a submissive, employing hot and sharp objects as needed? The truth is that I will always remain proud to be a Californian. I have the right to act in any consensual way that I choose; so does anyone else. In Sacramento, I might go duck hunting; in the Sierras, I could hike on my own terms; so, in San Francisco, I watched the nude submissive getting taped and lashed to the padded table, with an absorbent gauze pad beneath her buttocks and a mask over her face. Submissives, by the way, are also called bottoms, and dominants are tops. This bottom's top was not her lover, they told us later, but someone with whom she liked to play these extreme games, sometimes for four or five hours at a time. The top, a middle-aged woman in camouflage pants, pegged out the bottom's labia and nailed them into the table. She began sharpening a knife. Then she began to demand, interrogate, threaten. She made the bottom hold a little bell in her left hand. I knew that that was the safety device: If the bottom were to shake it or drop it, then it would ring and the session would stop.

What happened next—the breast-slapping, the playing with the chopped liver, the forced pistol-sucking, the hammering all around her, the screaming—was slightly horrifying to me at first; and every now and then the top would do something between the other woman's legs so that her mouth would open and she would loudly moan. On a folding chair not far from me sat a beautiful black dominant with long blond hair. Her submissive was a dreamy white boy with glasses who sat on the floor just in front of her, with his head against her knees. At the scariest parts she caressed his head a little absently. Near them sat two gray-haired, Rubenesque women, one of whom watched the performance smiling, with her head on the other's shoulder.

"I want to see some *blood*," the top was saying, and she stabbed any number of syringes into the bottom's breasts, leaving them in so that she could laughingly twang them back and forth. The bottom moaned. The room stank of sweat. Now the top was tenderly kneading her breast, all the while shocking her with an electric wand; wherever she directed the spark, she had deposited a piece of flash cotton, which instantly flamed, then went out. Much of what she was doing to the bottom was mental; the bottom later said that she believed she was getting pierced at those moments, when actually not any mark was left.

"Oh, you're bleeding real nice!" the top said. Chuckling, she imitated her submissive's moans. The audience smiled happily. Then at last she was doing something between the bottom's legs, something that must have been very painful since the woman was screaming, arching her back and contorting her face like a mother in labor; finally her head rose up from the table—and when it was all over I learned from her that I had not at all understood what I had been looking at, that she had been climaxing then and evidently had climaxed on at least one of the earlier occasions when I had thought her to be in physical agony. After she was unmasked and untied, she stood up smiling. The top gave her a gift-wrapped present, and then the two women kissed each other on the lips. They spoke to us about each other with affection, gratitude, and respect. They wanted to know what the audience thought, and smiled when the audience said that they were *hot*. That was another time that I felt thankful to be a Californian, which is to say a believer in the right of any adult to act upon her preferences beyond the point of extremity as long as whatever she does remains consensual.

San Francisco, like other American cities, utilizes various invisibles—for instance, the Salvadoran day laborer Alex, who for ten dollars spoke to me in a mixture of English and Spanish, the latter translated by my sweetheart. I asked him how his life was here, and he said: "Very difficult, especially in the winter. It's very cold; there's little work. You can go all day without getting any work. Sometimes you go four or five days without any work."

"How much do you need each day to pay your living expenses?"

"Maybe 100," he said, and when he broke down his costs I learned that his calculations, like those of so many poor people, did not add up, for he said: "I pay $450 a month in rent, twenty a day for food. Sometimes I eat some hamburger, fast food. I have no cooking facilities. For transportation sometimes somebody give me a ride. For bus, fifty cents."

He had six siblings—"Just one with my mother and five with my father." His daughter was in El Salvador and his wife in Pennsylvania. "Wife" was the word he used, but later he said: "My daughter's mother, I don't consider her my wife."

He said that he had crossed the border legally, which may or may not have been true. I asked what it was like for those who crossed illegally, and he said: "Some people think of it as an adventure but they put their lives in danger because there's delinquency in the borders of both countries, so people lose their lives or get assaulted. I have a lot of friends who have had to beg to get food at the border."

"How well do the people from El Salvador and the people from Mexico get along?"

"There's quite a bit of conflict at this corner. Some people get more work and some people get less work. The depression of not getting work makes them hate the people who do get it. Sometimes people come to blows. It's a difference between the countries. In general, my friends who are from El Salvador speak better English and have better transportation. So they come across better with employers."

I asked how the day laborers regarded the rest of us with easy lives. He said: "Sometimes they think that this can't go on, that those rich people's money will run out. The ones at the corner would like to be like them and have their money."

Once upon a time, California's missionaries dreamed of saved souls and slave labor. Perhaps some souls have in fact been saved to enjoy their lives in leisure. As for others such as Alex, they maintain me in my middle-class salvation.

California's traffic creeps and farts. Alex stands on the corner. And not far from Mi-wuk Village (closer even than that well-recommended Pinecrest Lake), one can walk a trail high over the Stanislaus River, which is sometimes a transparent brown with many whirlpools through which the rock can be seen; and at other times the river is white with rapids. The morning smells like pine and honey; and the reality of Freeway California is curtained behind many evergreen hands drooping down into sweet-smelling ferns that have refused to relinquish summer. A cedar log, rotting into orange powder, is moist to the touch; deer dung is turning back into dirt and has already taken on dirt's clean smell.

Sitting beneath an overhang of Sierra rock, listening to the river, I believe in John Muir's wild California. Flying from Sacramento to Los Angeles, I look out the scratched oval window and rejoice at the lack of human spoor in the mountains below me. In the redwood forests near the Oregon border and the foggy flower-meadows around Point Reyes, my illusion of tranquil purity is restored. I love my darling California so much that I would believe in any sweetness.

COLORADO

CAPITAL   Denver

ENTERED UNION   1876 (38th)

ORIGIN OF NAME   From the Spanish for "ruddy" or "red"

NICKNAME   Centennial State

MOTTO   Nil sine Numine ("Nothing without Providence")

RESIDENTS   Coloradan or Coloradoan

U.S. REPRESENTATIVES   7

STATE BIRD   lark bunting

STATE FLOWER   Rocky Mountain columbine

STATE TREE   Colorado blue spruce

STATE SONG   "Where the Columbines Grow"

LAND AREA   103,717 sq. mi.

GEOGRAPHIC CENTER   In Park Co., 30 mi. NW of Pikes Peak

POPULATION   4,665,177

WHITE   82.8%

BLACK   3.8%

AMERICAN INDIAN   1.0%

ASIAN   2.2%

HISPANIC/LATINO   17.1%

UNDER 18   25.6%

65 AND OVER   9.7%

MEDIAN AGE   34.3

COLORADO
Benjamin Kunkel

Of all the boxy Western states, Colorado and Wyoming are the boxiest—almost perfect rectangles—and when I was a kid and wanted an idea of my state I could do no better than to picture a box of Neapolitan ice cream. Just as a block of such ice cream is divided into three equal portions of strawberry, chocolate, and vanilla, Colorado consists of a high semi-arid plateau in the western third of the state; the heaped summits of the southern Rockies in the center; and in the east the plains rolling away toward Kansas. It's mostly the mountainous central part of the state, however, that people have in mind when they think of the place, and as it happens it was there in the real *Coloradan* part of Colorado that I grew up. At first we lived in a cabin my parents had built up Salt Creek, outside the town of Eagle, with the help of other long-haired recent transplants—it was part of that movement of hippies "back to the land." And once I was of an age to walk around the world unattended, I don't believe I had any trouble understanding why my parents had been drawn to this land in particular, or why adults should pronounce the word *Colorado* with a certain inflection of romance and pride.

The mountain to one side of Salt Creek fanned up in sheets of sun-scoured red sandstone dotted with pinion and juniper trees; sometimes, in a patch of overlapping snow and shadow, you saw a cactus too. The mountain opposite was a different world entirely, since it faced north and conserved its water in the shade: a somber looming mass thick with spruce and fir. The first of the beautiful ordinary things I remember are the creek gabbling away in its bed and the smell of rained-on sage bringing out an unsuspected sweetness from the land: thoughts of water in a dry place. But the thinness and dryness of the air on clear days—as of something brittle that would never break—was also thrilling, and what I liked doing on days like that was to clamber up the red mountain, which always offered some new place to be discovered among its troughs of brilliant dirt and tilted spines.

So it wasn't necessary to grow up and go away to recognize the beauty of the place, something anyone can see, native or not, visiting or having come to stay. A friend from New York took a road trip with me, one fall, through the San Juan Mountains, down along the Million Dollar Highway, and re-marked one afternoon when we'd stopped the car to get out and look: "Your state kicks the ass of anybody else's state." The opinion is arguable, but not on a clear day in the San Juans when the leaves have turned.

Jean Stafford, probably the best writer Colorado has so far produced, described the state's atmosphere better than anyone: "The violent violet peaks stood out against a sky of cruel, infuriated blue, and the snows at timberline shone like sun-struck mirrors." In the same story, a red canoe gleams "in the pure light like a bright, immaculate wound." I don't know why this language of hurt should attach to alpine Colorado, or why, in the best-known version of the traditional song, the man of constant sorrow ("I seen trouble all my days") should be bound for Colorado ("where I was born and partly raised"). Unless I do know why: The pure light and gin-clear air can't be matched by your life. They will only put a hurt look into your eyes, whether you stay or go.

Not that nowhere else in America has clear light and thin air—but unlike other such places Colorado isn't frigidly cold, or bone dry, and most of its tall mountains aren't even overwhelming. The peaks of the southern Rockies generally start from so high a base that they don't tower away from you; their summits are almost companionable, in spite of their location in the sky. This means that alpine Colorado doesn't repel or begrudge habitation in the way of most alpine places; and faces of red sandstone flood many a cold valley with a fictitious sensation of warmth. The warmth can be quite real, too, in a state as far south as Virginia, at least until the sun passes behind a cloud and leaves the air, with no memory for scent, moisture, or temperature, as cold as if the sun had never shone.

The combination of thin air and thick geology is a lesson in the brevity and virtual unreality of our own time, and may even supply the reason why so many schools of American Buddhists have established centers and retreats here. Of course the shopping malls strung along the highways and the stack-a-shack condos (as I remember my father calling them when they first appeared in the Eagle Valley) propose their own lesson in nonattachment, being so recently built beneath durable mountains, and never built to last.

For as long as I can remember I have had a sense of the shallowness and impermanence of American settlement in Colorado. My father comes from Oregon, my mother from Massachusetts, and they met as undergraduates at the University of Colorado, where my father had gone on a skiing scholarship and my mother had gone, I think, because unlike her siblings she didn't want to become a banker or remain a Catholic. They settled up

Salt Creek in 1971, and, in a reversal of the more usual order, my father's parents followed them there. My parents' friends were amateur beekeepers, gardeners, cabinet makers, guitarists, and our more immediate neighbors likewise seemed to be making things up as they went along. One had a field full of junk cars, many children, and a drinking problem; he was always driving off the road. Another ran the local airfield and kept a mountain lion for a pet; when he and his wife divorced later on, she married an arms dealer and moved to Istanbul.

There was nothing else I knew—we didn't have a TV—but even so I could tell our life was new and rare and unsponsored by tradition. Perhaps I sensed how far from north shore Massachusetts my mother felt, living in a narrow mountain valley and raising three kids in a cabin heated by a stove; when she took me fishing and I caught a fish, she had no idea what to do with it. Everything was improvisation, with the thrill and risk the word implies. My father the former English major, with no training as a land surveyor, started a surveying company when he and his partner both chipped in $20 to open a bank account. And life up Salt Creek acquired a real enough frontier air on at least those occasions when a pack rat ventured out from the wall in the living room and my father picked up his .22 rifle to shoot it, a practice that could be unsettling to guests but which mostly impressed me as a display of good aim. No doubt precisely because we lived eight miles from town, and the town of Eagle was so rudimentary in those days, my parents didn't want us to grow up uncivilized, and not only insisted that we wear pants to the dinner table but drilled us there in good manners.

I never thought we would stay up Salt Creek forever. It was plainly in the nature of mountain valleys, with their gray abandoned barns and garden plots being reabsorbed into the land, that you left them one day. And yet when we moved away to the enormous metropolis of Glenwood Springs (population 5,000), I felt the loss of my red mountain more intensely, it seems, than any loss since, never mind the compensatory facts of having a bike and a town to ride it in.

G lenwood Springs is named for the natural hot springs that emerge, smelling of sulfur, near the junction of the Colorado and the Roaring Fork rivers, and as a spa town centered around a huge outdoor pool Glenwood has always attracted more than its share of quacks and people in need of a cure. In 1887, this meant that the gunfighter Doc Holliday repaired to Glenwood when he fell ill with TB; his grave is a local landmark. In Willa

Cather's *A Lost Lady*, a visit to the town revives for a time the failing spirits of lovely, tragic Mrs. Forrester: "Last winter I was with the Dalzells at Glenwood Springs for three weeks," she says, "and I was surprised at myself. I could dance all night and not feel tired." From the early 1980s, I recall a high incidence of New Age religion, born-again Christianity, health kicks, diet fads, even spoon-bending. My mother went no further in the direction of Reagan-era self-reinvention than to get a perm and begin doing aerobics, though her connections in the exercise world meant that when the movie *Breakin'* (1984) caused me and some friends to develop a mania for breakdancing, she was able to recruit a dance teacher from the community college to give us pale mountain children classes in moonwalking, head-spinning, and the worm.

Along with the religious fashions and lifestyle improvisation of the adult world, there were also divorces and bankruptcies—and when one of the partners with whom my father had invested in real estate went bankrupt and needed some cash, our family returned to Eagle to take up residence in the vacation house the man had built while he was flush. Our own finances were all right because my father had started a software company in tiny Eagle, of all places; he'd learned to fly a small plane and this enabled him to deal with clients throughout the West. In the fields just below our new house we kept horses and experimented for a time with grazing cattle. My mother began teaching aerobics herself. And when I admired my parents, it was for their adaptability to new circumstances, and when I disapproved of them it was essentially for the same reason: I told myself they didn't know what they were doing.

It may have been that I set about convincing them to let me go back east to boarding school because I had the notion that somewhere in America people did things more or less correctly and by the book. And at school in New Hampshire I did meet kids from places like New England, the South, even California, where evidently they had more in the way of traditions and customs than we did in Eagle. These people and their parents knew or pretended to know how to speak and dress, possessed a common store of cultural knowledge, often observed the rites of some religion, and vacationed in the same places year after year. It took me some time to grasp the source of all this assurance: These families belonged to a far more clearly articulated class structure than mine had in Colorado. Then I began to miss the western indifference if not to money then at least to status and prestige. I was far from indifferent to those things myself, and feeling that it sounded better to come from Colorado in general rather than Eagle in particular, "Colorado" became where I said I was from, with the result that after enough repetitions of this claim I was able to convince myself that I really was somehow derived from the state at large.

To come from Colorado may make you especially aware of what a strange signifier a state is, meaning hardly anything at the same time that it means a great deal. Culturally, economically, and historically, the western plateau and the eastern plains don't have much in common, and even the mountainous middle section of the state is literally split in two, by the Continental Divide. If such a territory existed in Europe or Asia, the people on the western slope of the mountains would speak one language and the people on the eastern slope another; in South America, they'd at least fly different flags. Even in the western United States, where borders are mostly ruler-straight, the north-south-running state lines (since North America is a continent of north-south-running mountain chains) often fall roughly alongside the spine of the mountains. None of Colorado's borders, however, corresponds to any natural fact, so that, even more than other states, Colorado has to secure its existence mostly in the mind.

It's as difficult to say what the idea of the state is as to deny its existence, though certainly it has something to do with beauty, purity, and independence. To every Coloradan I know, in any case, that romantic place-name *Colorado* signifies much more than simply that the first Spanish missionaries noticed the red color of a big river flush with spring runoff. Two in particular of the Spanish also noticed one evening while lost in a spring blizzard— or so the legend goes—that the high mountain looming before them was impressed with a cruciform snowfield starkly distinct from the surrounding face of rock, a snowfield so miraculously centered on the northeast face of the peak and so proportional to the cross of the Roman church that the lost Spaniards can hardly be blamed for taking this glimpse of what is still called the Mount of the Holy Cross for a sign that their journey was blessed; and perhaps contemporary Coloradans can likewise be forgiven for loading a mere administrative rectangle with romantic ideas.

Colorado gains many more residents than it loses every year, especially in and around the cities along the Front Range, at the base of the Rockies, and it would seem that especially since the late 1960s, when the image of California began to darken, Colorado has taken on some of California's role as an American promised land of natural beauty, affordable real estate, and a brand-new chance. Denver Broncos fans will recall that when the great quarterback John Elway was drafted by Baltimore in 1983, he insisted on being traded to a West Coast team, and then seemed to consider this condition satisfactorily met when he ended up in the landlocked city of Denver: an attitude expressive of the sense that Colorado was somehow a new shore of American possibility. And Colorado—a state, like California, first settled by Americans in a gold rush—has acquired or else always possessed much of the Californian endowment of promise and terror.

Severance from history is probably the deepest tradition of the state. I was nineteen before I knew to ascribe the thinness of the human presence on the land to the fact that Colorado had rid itself more completely of Indians than any other Western state or territory: no small distinction. Today, in all the large extent of Colorado—eighth biggest of the states—there is only the slightest sliver of a reservation, and Indians, in my childhood, were not the real if marginal presence they are in New Mexico, Arizona, or Montana; they were just gone. My idea of the state—it is still the prevailing idea—was a slide-show succession of prospectors, cattlemen, downhill skiers: romantic individualists. I didn't know that the tin-pan prospectors had been swiftly replaced by gigantic concerns like the Colorado Fuel & Iron Corporation, property of the Rockefellers. The coal strike called against this company by the United Mine Workers in September 1913 came to a head in April of the next year when the National Guard machine-gunned an encampment of striking workers and their families, killing seventeen people, ten of them children: a scandal that ninety years ago would have been the best-known political fact about Colorado. I never heard of the Ludlow Massacre while growing up. The state to this day remains an open-shop.

People think of early Coloradans as rugged Protestants lighting out for the territory and forget the earlier career of this idea. By 1924 the KKK dominated both parties in the statehouse; the Governor was a Klansman and so was one Senator. The Klan in Colorado, with relatively few blacks or Jews to persecute, directed its energies mostly against Catholics and Orthodox Christians, those Greeks, Italians, Mexicans, and Serbs, in other words, who formed the largest portion of the organized working class. And this would seem to be the ugly side of that feeling of purity the mountain air can inspire in you—that such a beautiful place is especially vulnerable to being spoiled by the presence of the wrong people. Lately the most prominent Coloradan in national politics is the nativist Congressman Tom Tancredo (grandson of two Italian immigrants), who has proposed the deportation of every unauthorized immigrant in the country and floated the idea that in response to any future Islamist terror in the US, the government might do well to "take out" Mecca.

In the 150 years since the Pike's Peak gold rush, people have come to Colorado to be among the first ones here. They have settled, by the millions, along the Front Range in order to be alone with nature and with others of their kind. Today at the foot of Pike's Peak spreads the agglomeration of strip malls and suburbs known as Colorado Springs, North American headquarters of both the Christian Right and (in the suburb of Manitou Springs) the New Age witchcraft movement. And this is only the beginning of the enclave character promoted by the mountains. Besides Buddhists, Wiccans, hippies, and evangelicals, there are also communities consecrated to winter sports and to Mormonism. But what the geography of the mountains really fosters, in present-day America, is a translation of class stratification into literal terms of altitude. The rich live at high altitude, where they enjoy unobstructed views of snow-covered peaks, the cleanly green glitter of aspen trees, and what Fitzgerald (adjusted for inflation) called the consoling proximity of multi-millionaires. With every hundred-foot drop in elevation, property values decline, along with the moisture content of the soil, until a valley has broadened out into a semi-arid scrubland where workers in the so-called service industry plant their trailers among the sagebrush and low tan hills.

A few years ago, when my parents found that the Eagle Valley had filled up with housing developments and shopping centers, they moved away to the south fork of the White River, up against the Flat Tops Wilderness and twenty-two miles from the nearest town of Meeker. So they went back to the land a second time, now with a satellite TV and Internet subscription. My father put in a landing strip at the bottom of the driveway. My mother, who had seemed like such a sociable person, turned out to be satisfied writing emails to her friends and far-flung children, and taking long hikes with my father and their dogs. And the hikes you can take on the south fork are truly something, with deer and elk, foxes, ermine, and pheasants, even the occasional black bear or mountain lion, slipping through the stands of spruce and aspen and ponderosa pine, while the blank sound of the river unfurls itself continuously in the distance below.

We forget that before the nineteenth century mountains were not what they are today: they were wild, waste places, difficult when not impossible to live on or to cultivate, and they weren't considered beautiful. In the days before, say, the Louisiana Purchase (in which Jefferson acquired for the United States a corner of what's now Colorado), if an ordinary American were asked to explain why some places on earth were mountains and others were not, he would probably have replied, in line with the physico-theology of the day, that such inhospitable land must have been cursed or simply abandoned by God. And even if he didn't believe in such explanations, the cultural hangover from them would have prevented him from regarding mountain landscapes as picturesque. It took Romanticism in philosophy and the arts, with its creed of individual spiritual growth and its love of wildness and of solitude, to bring about a revaluation of mountains. Then their barrenness became their purity, and their quality of abandonment a symbol of spiritual independence—a fundamental shift in perceptions that at length became the second nature of the ordinary person, especially once supplemented by a geological understanding of how mountains form. Today not even the fundamentalists of Colorado Springs ascribe the existence of mountains to eruptions of God's temper.

Colorado has been one of America's proving grounds of romantic individualism, and lately has come to illustrate the contradictions of romanticism as a mass phenomenon. The contradictions are inevitable when everyone seeks seclusion in the same pristine spots; there goes their seclusion and pristineness. So you move on to another valley and renew the process you have just fled, or you remain in your large house on its small lawn of scorched grass, and resent your neighbors for spoiling your view as you spoil theirs. In theory, it would be possible to build dense townships and small cities in the mountains, thus concentrating in one place a population that is after all united, if in anything, by its attraction to intact landscapes. In practice, even a still-small town like Eagle is an amorphous spill of suburbs and commercial parks spreading out from a disused old downtown. And that, too, might be fine—everyone might consider sprawl perfectly fine—if most Coloradans didn't still long for the old uncluttered land, and feel that it was everyone but themselves and their like-minded friends who was a blight on the face of nature.

The other contradiction of mass romanticism in Colorado comes from the geology of the state itself: coal, natural gas, and oil shale, all of which Colorado has in abundance. There in the mountains my parents have created the happiest picture of married life in one's sixties that I know, but by the time I reach their age I doubt whether oil will be so plentiful and cheap that it will be possible to fly a small plane from a landing strip at the bottom of your driveway, or drive twenty or forty or sixty miles to go grocery shopping. And if these things do remain possible, it may be because Colorado's Piceance Basin, not far west of my parent's home, and Colorado's Roane Plateau, not far south, have been so intensively mined and drilled for their respective reserves of oil shale and natural gas that the area will be unrecognizable. The land Coloradans cherish, land they came for or have stayed for, will turn out to have been loved not wisely but too well, as the burning of fossil fuels generally spells the end of a stable climate (perhaps including a stable ski season), and provokes a series of droughts that a dry part of the country with a population growing by almost 2 percent a year would seem unlikely to endure with special grace. It's hard to predict what will happen to Colorado, and to the country from which it is hardly divided by its set of perpendicular lines, but it seems clear enough by now that you can't have a population of many millions pursuing a lifestyle devoted to seclusion, mobility, and the picturesque without undermining those same things. Already that cruciform snowfield first seen as a Roman cross by the pair of lost Spanish missionaries tends to melt away and disappear for longer and longer portions of each year.

CONNECTICUT

CAPITAL   Hartford

ENTERED UNION   1788 (5th)

ORIGIN OF NAME   From an Indian word, Quinnehtukqut, meaning "beside the long tidal river"

NICKNAMES   Constitution State or Nutmeg State

MOTTO   Qui transtulit sustinet ("He who transplanted still sustains")

RESIDENTS   Connecticuter or Nutmegger

U.S. REPRESENTATIVES   5

STATE BIRD   American robin

STATE FLOWER   mountain laurel

STATE TREE   white oak

STATE SONG   "Yankee Doodle"

LAND AREA   4,844 sq. mi.

GEOGRAPHIC CENTER   In Hartford Co., at East Berlin

POPULATION   3,510,297

WHITE   81.6%

BLACK   9.1%

AMERICAN INDIAN   0.3%

ASIAN   2.4%

HISPANIC/LATINO   9.4%

UNDER 18   24.7%

65 AND OVER   13.8%

MEDIAN AGE   37.4

CONNECTICUT
Rick Moody

Connecticut is a state that's hard to love, but which I love anyhow, as one often loves what wounds—if only for the familiarity. It's a state where almost nothing is made, where the affluence of the state as a whole is in marked contrast to the deprivation and desperation of the cities. A state where a veneer of propriety is belied by the acting-out behavior of citizens and politicians alike. A state where the preeminent approaches to life are rectitude and hypocrisy. A state of marshes, of estuaries, of farms that are no longer farmed. A state that you *drive through*, on the way to somewhere else, somewhere better. A white state, whose cities are black. A state well known for WASPs that is now largely kept up by Latinos. A state that does almost nothing first or best, but which did once, indisputably, build the finest roadway in the land.

To enter the Merritt Parkway from the west, you do so from the Hutchinson River Parkway, which itself runs from the marshes of Co-Op City, in the Bronx, all the way to the Connecticut line. The Hutch is a pretty drive, but these days the last few miles are divided by ugly, industrial cement lane dividers that I've been told have one purpose only: to protect against multi-vehicle crashes featuring that monstrosity of postmodernity, the sport utility vehicle.

But in this way you are carried onto the Merritt, onto 37.5 miles of verdant, hilly, narrow limited-access road that is now designated a National Scenic Byway. The Merritt, naturally, has avoided ugly, functional cement lane dividers. The Merritt, in all but a very few places, is never less than verdant, always quaint, always old-fashioned. It suggests a Connecticut of myth, a green and pleasant respite from the high velocity of city life.

When this suburban artery appears in my dreams, as it often does, what I see are its forested passages and rolling hills, which were neither cut nor filled during the laborious construction process, begun in 1938, well before the interstate highway boom of the late forties and fifties. Recently, however, the parallel one hundred and fifty feet of green space that runs alongside the Merritt, procured back at the time of the original land acquisition, has come to the attention of the Department of Traffic planners, who'd love to get their hands on it in order to add some more lanes. The state is chipping away at every feature of the Merritt's original design. There's even legislation afoot to permit *longer* vehicles to drive on the Merritt, thus ending the passenger-cars-only rule that has been on the books since the parkway was first opened. What's to become of this beautiful and iconic roadway? And what becomes of the old idea of Connecticut if the Connecticut that was once visible from the parkway no longer exists?

I moved out of state in 1975, when I went off to boarding school in New Hampshire. My mother, whose father had lived in Pelham, New York, moved back there herself. My father bought an apartment in Manhattan, and a house on Fishers Island, a possession of New York State that, according to legend, became New York State territory in a trade for Greenwich, Connecticut. Ever since my father bought that house I have been driving back and forth *across* Connecticut, almost always on the Merritt, to the Fishers Island Ferry Terminal in New London. To do so, I drive to the very end of the parkway, at the Housatonic River bridge. In the old days, this was a steel grid bridge, and it was very slippery. On the way across the Housatonic, then as now, you could see the Sikorsky helicopter factory, major supplier to the Pentagon (they build the Black Hawk helicopter, among other models), and one of the state's largest remaining businesses.

In the thirty years since I moved away, I have watched Connecticut pave itself over, bit by bit, town by town. The legendary New York City suburbs of Fairfield County, where I was raised, grow ever more like the metropolitan sections of New Jersey, full of McMansions and subdivisions. This despite the former importance of zoning to the development of Connecticut. I've watched the phenomenon of American Indian gambling pavilions in the eastern part of the state, and I've watched the further dilapidation of the cities, as one local politician after another is carted away to the penitentiary.

Exit 28, among the first of several exits in Greenwich (where the Merritt begins), takes you off the parkway at Round Hill Road. That's the street on which you will find, nestled among the estates, the legendary Round Hill Club, golfing destination of choice in Fairfield County and a summer spot for relaxation for the affluent of Greenwich when they're not summering on Nantucket or Martha's Vineyard. Greenwich has the highest per capita income ($99,300) in the county that has the highest per capita income in the state that has the highest per capita income in the country. When I was growing up, Greenwich had a strange, sinister allure. It was the place where all the power and glamour concentrated themselves. Its winding, leafy streets concealed houses owned by tennis players, musicians, captains of industry, and, as you know from the Martha Moxley narrative, a brace of distantly related Kennedys. All the kids seemed to go to Greenwich Country Day. They wore a lot of corduroy.

In boarding school I met a lot of kids from Greenwich. Among them a young woman I'll call Fiona (the other names here are also changed), whose family were regulars at the Round Hill Club. Her dad worked in finance. Her mom was an heiress. Both her parents had rather bad drinking problems. One day after graduation, though I had only a learner's permit, I made off with my mother's Olds Cutlass Supreme and drove from Pelham to Greenwich to locate Fiona. I took my brother and stepbrother with me. We had all been drinking. I believe we drank the whole way to Greenwich.

By dead reckoning I turned a certain corner and found Fiona's familial manse, just off the parkway. We got out of the car with the inflated self-regard of desperados. After I rang the doorbell and called out, Fiona turned up before us. Her mother stood at the far side of the turnaround in the driveway to watch suspiciously. Eventually, we were invited to go swimming in their pool, which, like everything else about the property was *large*. Something was wrong, and Fiona and her mother seemed to be arguing, and so ultimately we interlopers left, as precipitously as we had come. We took the interstate back to Pelham, and I scraped the Olds on the side of the garage door and didn't tell my mother about it. This episode seems to me now to reek of Connecticut, to reek of the melancholy, desperation, and drunkenness that lie below the pristine surfaces of the richest county in the richest state.

But it's just the beginning. Five years later, I met Fiona again at a dance recital. She'd been to a school out West that specialized in modern dance, and for her M.F.A. she was about to apply to a similar program at Tisch School of the Arts in New York. She was a lesbian. With a very bad drinking problem. I had one too. We were imperfect for each other. Especially since there was a girlfriend with whom she lived.

Soon, it was Fiona and I who were living together, except that we were both sleeping around on the side and drinking a lot. In the interval, her parents had divorced. Occasionally we went to the Round Hill Club to visit with Fiona's dad. Her mom, in exile from the country club set, was showing signs of what turned out to be a very bad case of anorexia. In Fiona's family, problems of this sort ran on the distaff line.

After the divorce, her mom got a little rental unit in Greenwich, not far off the Merritt. Fiona and I were now not only drinking a lot but consuming (to our subsequent regret) an abundance of cocaine.

One morning, Fiona said: "No one's heard from my mother for three days." We didn't panic at first. It was just one of those things that wasn't out of the realm of possibility. Barely concealed addictions, her eating disorder, these made for a fair amount of undependability. It was a day or two later that Fiona got the call. Her mother had been found dead in her rental in Greenwich. Diet aids had apparently helped to engender sudden heart failure in her late forties.

The Merritt Parkway arcs around a manmade pond in Greenwich, created as a by-product of parkway construction. It once had a few picnic tables for those who intended to watch the Sunday drivers. The road then passes through Stamford. I'm leaving out the Stamford exit that heads downtown, because almost everyone in Connecticut wishes that the state had no cities, that its cities were relocated elsewhere. The Connecticut cities are hives of civic corruption (Bridgeport, Waterbury), or else are simply being emptied (Hartford, New London) because of an almost total absence of industry. These cities are well known for their criminal activity, for their gangs, for their political corruption, and for draining the state coffers of its tax monies. The Merritt avoids these cities almost entirely and so manages to preserve its stylized beauty. In fact, probably what the Merritt Parkway does, by avoiding the cities, and connecting instead the affluent villages of the state of Connecticut with the megalopolis to its south, is promote a notion of the bedroom community. The suburbs of Connecticut are the institutional model for suburbs everywhere else. Brookline, Massachusetts; Grosse Point, Michigan; Oak Park, Illinois—they all follow a model developed in Westchester and Fairfield counties—the satellites of wealth and power that orbit around New York City, the first great city of the New World. These suburbs, made possible by commuter railroads and limited-access roadways, were founded on notions that, through the dissemination of Connecticut, would work everywhere: Build good public (and private) schools, zone relentlessly, drive out minorities.

Stamford, at Exit 34 (where Route 104 runs into the city center), is where the people of color of Connecticut landed during LBJ's Great Society.

(The same neighborhood now houses numerous corporations, or divisions thereof: Conair, Pitney Bowes, MXEnergy, Time Warner Cable, etc., bent on avoiding the taxation in the city of New York.) Of this and other fiscally challenged metropolises, you can get a better idea from I–95, which visits them all. Exit 34, Long Ridge Road, like its relative at Exit 35, High Ridge Road, gives access to the north side of Stamford, where we moved when we were, relatively speaking, poor. I was nine years old, my brother was seven, my sister twelve. This was after my parents divorced, and my mother, as happened in those days, got custody. There was a rule about her not moving farther than fifty miles away. My father stayed in Darien (Exit 37) where we'd lived before the separation. We set ourselves up in Stamford, in 1970, and I started that fall at Northeast Elementary School.

For a number of reasons, Northeast was completely different from school in Darien. For example: Jewish kids! I didn't even know what *Jewish* meant.

Two boys who lived on my street, Bruce and Steve, both of them Jewish, wore their hair longer than we were allowed to, and sported bell-bottoms of a particularly unrepentant variety. Though my mother was always trying to dress me like I would be an accountant when I grew up, they made some efforts to befriend me.

Both were well informed in sexual matters. Despite the disintegration of my own family, which had more than a little to do with extra-marital nonsense, I knew nothing about sex. Bruce and Steve filled me in with torrents of specifics and with exhibits, beginning, for example, with Bruce's mother's vibrator. Or was it her dildo? We also saw her prescription for birth control pills. A further lesson involved an explanation of the burden of menstruation.

Later in life, when I was at the Jewish Museum for a literary event, I ran into Bruce, after thirty or more years. And it was he who had, in fact, become an accountant.

Another friend at Exit 35, or thereabouts, was an African American kid named Hampton. Hampton was funny, imperturbable, athletic, gregarious. I liked him a lot. However, as with the Jewish kids, I knew nothing about African-American kids. I was dimly aware that difference was important, or at least that conflict adhered to this idea of difference. But I didn't know what I was supposed to do about it. Did I have a responsibility? Should I have known that I came from a part of the world that was racially, ethnically, and religiously homogenous, as a lot of Connecticut still is, and that because of this I needed to make an effort to show some respect? One day Hampton asked me if I would come over to his house to play, and I *froze*. In Darien, I'd gone to visit a friend and found detritus everywhere, newspapers piled high, dishes with food encrusted all over the place, empty bottles, trash. Later, I understood that this friend's parents had fallen out of life somehow. With drink probably. At the time I couldn't understand how anyone could live there and not experience family life as a kind of imprisonment.

Somehow I wrongly associated that situation with Hampton's invitation. When I didn't respond, his mother called my mother. I think it was Hampton's birthday. Somehow I wriggled out of the invitation. After that, Hampton had a suspicious look in his eyes when he saw me.

The distance between Exit 35 and Exit 37 isn't more than five or six miles, but it's probably the single stretch of pavement that I know best in memory and imagination.

It's easy to re-create the setting: in my father's Firebird we made this journey, back and forth from Stamford to Darien, where my dad lived in the house we'd occupied before the divorce. Ironwood Lane. Probably a drive of no more than twenty minutes, but it seems longer. It seems in memory that I'm always in someone's car, making this voyage of visitation. There is no place that more reminds me of the end of my parents' marriage than this stretch of pavement.

What did I see on these Merritt Parkway journeys? Although George Dunkelberger's stunning art deco overpasses begin right at King Road, in Greenwich, it's the ones you go under near New Canaan that feel memorable to me, like the Lapham Road overpass with its fleur-de-lis details, and the Comstock Hill Road overpass just before Norwalk that features an Indian relief sculpture by Edward Ferrari (who worked on many of Dunkelberger's bridges).

In 1971 or 1972 the landscaping on the Merritt, which was part of its initial charm, had not yet lapsed into woody overgrowth. In the later seventies, the various agencies in charge of the parkway decided that landscaping was too expensive (which is almost always what happens when government attempts oversight of the beautiful), and so the many local flowering plants that lined the road were allowed to die unreplaced. I can remember that bygone landscaping only dimly, because my memories are layered over with innumerable adult trips.

Eventually, we came to Exit 37. If you travel south here, upon disembarking from the Merritt, you arrive in Darien, where I lived until I was nine, and where my father lived for a good five years longer, in the house where we left him. They filmed the original *Stepford Wives* here. Well, they filmed one sequence at Darien's Good Wives Shopping Center, anyway, the name of which must have seemed too good to be true. My sister claimed her bicycle was in one shot. This was a badge of honor. We lived a couple of miles from the Good Wives Shopping Center, and everywhere around us were fancy houses with big lawns and lots of kids.

Not long after we arrived, we met the family across Ironwood Lane from us, the Dawsons. As in my own family, the Dawson progeny numbered three. There was a girl my older sister's age; a second daughter my own age; and then a boy, a couple years younger than my younger brother. We got very close with these Dawsons. They were either over at our house, or we were at theirs, throughout the late sixties. Mrs. Dawson was a bombshell. Mr. Dawson was, I suppose, charismatic. He'd been a professional tennis player for a while. He knew Stan Smith. He always had tickets for the U.S. Open. There were a lot of cocktail parties, featuring Dawsons, Moodys, and various groups of neighbors.

My mother fell in love with Mr. Dawson. And then my father fell reactively into some similar relationship with Mrs. Dawson. Soon both couples divorced. By the time I was living in Stamford (and, later, in New Canaan, Exit 37), my father and Mrs. Dawson were seeing one another from across Ironwood Lane. At the same time, my mother was dating Mr. Dawson, who'd bought a farm just outside Redding (Exit 44). This was a big seventies mess, a Connecticut mess, but the worst part of it was we all loved these Dawson kids. We believed, for a time, that my mother and Mr. Dawson would marry. Which would make the Dawsons our step-siblings! In which case, why was I spending so much time trying to get Laurie Dawson, the middle daughter, to kiss me and to take off her clothes? She was going to be my stepsister! In fact, it was possible she was going to be my stepsister *twice over!*

Exit 38 is where the Merritt Parkway ended after the first phase of its construction was completed in 1938. This exit is technically in Norwalk, which in the early seventies was the lower middle-class town in Fairfield County. My father's parents lived there during the period I'm describing (1968–1975). Among the other prejudices that were harbored in my family was the prejudice that lower middle-class towns were homely and cheap. And so we used to drive through Norwalk at Christmastime to look at its garish Christmas displays. We laughed derisively. That my grandparents felt comfortable in Norwalk, however, hints at the class anxieties roiling beneath the surface of my family, as in the state generally.

Exit 38 also leads to a neighborhood at the edge of New Canaan called Silvermine. There's an art school there, and some colonial houses, and, of course, the world famous psychiatric facility called Silver Hill, where both Michael Jackson and Philip Roth allegedly did some work on their respective addictions. This neighborhood is where I lived with my mother and brother after we left Stamford. (My sister had gone off to school.) I guess New Canaan was considered a better fit for us kids. The schools were better than in Stamford, or so it was said. I went to East School in the sixth grade, where I briefly served as class president, and was, actually, kind of popular for a minute (despite the fact that I was having recurrent anxiety problems and throwing up a lot). After sixth grade, I went to Saxe Junior High School (just down the street from where they filmed some of *The Ice Storm*, based on my novel about these years), which was the middle school for the entirety of New Canaan. A lot of kids went to the private or parochial schools (like my New Canaan coeval, Ann Coulter, the quintessential model of a good New Canaan girl). But the majority of us went to Saxe, the good kids and the bad kids, the rich kids and the less rich kids, the black kids (such as there were of them), the Asian kids, the special ed kids, those new to town, and those whose families had been there for generations.

While I was beginning at junior high school, my mother was breaking up with Mr. Dawson. Apparently he had found some new inamorata. My mother went into a long fit of despond, which coincided with the beginning of my own troubles.

The junior high years were definitively *the worst years of my life.* Part of this had to do with the physical threats that were my daily fare. Since I didn't go through puberty until I'd already left New Canaan, and was scrawny anyway, I was a frequent target of extortionists. Probably it was not as bad for me as for many others. The threats of bodily harm were rarely carried out.

I don't know why homophobia inevitably seems to be the single most important community-building principle of middle school life, but that's how it was at my school. Saxe wasn't overtly racist or anti-Semitic, probably because it was so homogenous. But it sure was homophobic. *Faggot* was the most frequently used epithet at Saxe. All social outcasts were *fags*—whether or not they had anything resembling same-sex libidinous cathections. A guy in town who'd been some kind of pedophile, name of Putnam, was so legendary among my fellow junior high students that a *putt* (short *u* sound) became shorthand for fag, in our circles, and thereby the worst slander of all. Fags were bad at gym, fags were good at school, especially in really faggy subjects like English or Math, fags were bad at shop, fags liked art or theater, fags didn't have any girlfriends or weren't going steady with anyone, and some fags didn't even know what all this stuff meant.

It certainly was a nickname used on me a lot, *fag*, and it didn't help that I *was* trying to have sex with a lot of my guy friends at the time. I would have loved a goat to know what love was and was eager to explore bodies with anyone, any age, any race, any sex. Anyone who slept over at my house got a shy solicitation. I was turned down by a lot of friends, but some of them, boys and girls, were willing to experiment a little bit. This was my way of working out my parents' spectacularly obvious and faithless inclinations as far as seventies *Love, American Style* sexuality went. My parents never kissed in public, nor expressed much, if any, affection for one another, but they seemed to have sexual adventures with great abandon, marriage being no inhibitor of availability. Perhaps it's not surprising that I too had my double life, in which I was the earnest straight-A student while at the same time, whenever the opportunity arose, I was trying to get my friends to take off their clothes and *hold me*. Some of these friends were football players, hockey players, guys who were, theoretically, not *fags*.

There was no way this was going to end well.

The last section of the Merritt Parkway was finished between 1939 and 1940. Probably the Merritt Parkway was completed as quickly as it was because the country was, consciously or unconsciously, preparing for wartime. If so, it's appropriate that the parkway terminates right beside Sikorsky, the Black Hawk helicopter manufacturer. But before the Merritt terminates at Exit 52, we need to pause at Exit 44, which leads off toward Redding. When I was a kid this part of Connecticut was still genuine farm country. The farm where Mr. Dawson spent his weekends was up this way, for example. We followed tortuous roads in and around forests and reservoirs, until we arrived there, to loiter in his barn, playing in the straw.

I remember the last trip we made up this way. I remember the oldest Dawson girl allowed that she was interested in and contemplating some assignation with the eldest boy of Mr. Dawson's new girlfriend. I remember a wanton, decadent vibe to the get-together. My mother skulked around the premises like some evolutionary throwback, a housewife among swingers, like she didn't know how *not* to be there. I couldn't figure the whole thing out. Was the visit meant to be for our benefit?

The middle Dawson, Laurie, my former love interest, had as hard a time as I did with all of this. I heard variously, in the years after, about her suicide attempts, her cocaine addiction, her marriage and divorce. Back in our era of turmoil, she had an ominous psychosomatic cough that never seemed to get better, coming and going with disturbing regularity. Everyone tried to persuade her simply to *behave*, as though persuasion would work.

In 2001, she and I were back in touch briefly. She was living outside Washington, D.C., and I was meant to be there in September on business. We arranged to meet for dinner in Georgetown. I'd enjoyed talking on the phone with Laurie occasionally, but once I actually saw her, in the lobby of my hotel, I was uncomfortable about the whole encounter. For Laurie, this was not going to be a light, tragicomic conversation about the uncivilized Connecticut we once knew. For her, all of this hypocrisy and mendacity was dangerous and fresh. As we talked over dinner, she came up with ever more horrible stories: a certain man on our street had beaten his wife regularly, a certain man was so alcoholic that he lost his seat on the Stock Exchange and bought a liquor store at the shopping center, and so on. Everywhere was deceit, despair, and grim secrets. Her eyes burned with a need to *get even.*

When dinner was over, I confess I was happy to get away. I felt guilty for being so happy, for feeling relieved. But this is just the truth of things sometimes. Sometimes sweeping away the past occasions a feeling of liberation. Was that what I felt, giddily returning to my hotel room?

That dinner took place on September 10, 2001. Next morning, after I was evacuated from the National Endowment for the Arts (where my business had taken me), and while trying to manage a call on the hotel telephone to my wife, who worked downtown in New York City, the one message that did reach me was from Laurie Dawson. She'd been at Reagan National Airport right as the plane struck the Pentagon. She was there as the airport was emptied by the authorities. On foot, she headed for downtown D.C., but along the way, in a crowd of other evacuees, she'd fallen down an embankment and sprained a knee and a shoulder. She was in a hotel, she said, badly injured, and very scared. When I went to look in on her, full of foreboding, her hotel had Secret Service in front of it. Perhaps there was a Saudi prince inside? You had to present identification just to get to the concierge. Laurie came downstairs on crutches, completely distraught. She had a hundred theories about the implications of that day, and she lurched from one to another. But no matter what she said what she seemed to mean was that she'd never gotten over Connecticut.

DELAWARE

CAPITAL Dover

ENTERED UNION 1787 (1st)

ORIGIN OF NAME From Delaware River and Bay; named in turn for Sir Thomas West, Baron De La Warr

NICKNAMES Diamond State, First State, or Small Wonder

MOTTO "Liberty and independence"

RESIDENTS Delawarean

U.S. REPRESENTATIVES 1

STATE BIRD blue hen chicken

STATE FLOWER peach blossom

STATE TREE American holly

STATE SONG "Our Delaware"

LAND AREA 1,954 sq. mi.

GEOGRAPHIC CENTER In Kent Co., 11 mi. S of Dover

POPULATION 843,524

WHITE 74.6%

BLACK 19.2%

AMERICAN INDIAN 0.3%

ASIAN 2.1%

HISPANIC/LATINO 4.8%

UNDER 18 24.8

65 AND OVER 13.0

MEDIAN AGE 36.0

DELAWARE
Craig Taylor

"We've got good watermelons down south because of the sandy soil," the Butcher Shop Assistant says from behind the counter at Moore's Quality Meats in Laurel, Delaware. It's a bright autumn day and Laurel shimmers in the sun. When asked about the state of Delaware today, the Butcher Shop Assistant tells me about good soil, good produce, and what it's like to be a small strip on a large map. One of her relatives ran into people in California who had never heard of the place. Delaware? Nope.

Laurel is located down south in what's known as "Lower," the agricultural part of the state. It is home to what the Butcher Shop Assistant says is "like, four million chickens. We have a lot of them around here." At Moore's, they sell hot country sausage, stay open seven days a week, and engage in conversations with the customers that stretch on and on.

"The upper part of Delaware is city-like," says her co-worker. "I know we're small but there's a big difference between the two parts. The way people do things, people's attitudes. It's all separated by the canal."

"She's studying."

"I'm studying to be a veterinarian."

"Which is a bit strange seeing as you work in a butcher shop," says the Butcher Shop Assistant.

"Which is a bit strange, I guess," says her co-worker.

"She's not a vegetarian neither."

The co-worker shrugs.

"People make fun of the way we talk. People from northern Delaware."

"I go across the canal," says the Butcher Shop Assistant, "and I go up to New York, and they don't know why I'm speaking so slow."

"To the northerners we're 'Slower Lower'."

"But I was down in Georgia for six years," the Butcher Shop Assistant continues. "They made fun of the way I talked there too. They thought I was fast-talking down there. We're right in the middle. Of everything."

The Retiree came out to live in Rehoboth Beach, on the Delaware coast, from D.C. "I moved out here before all the gays came, too. It's a big gay town now. There's no problems here with gay living, but they want to build a gays-only housing development in Rehoboth. What if I wanted to live there? What if I told them I thought gay meant happy, because it did mean happy at one point?"

There is a gathering for greyhound owners scheduled this weekend and both beach towns, Dewey and Rehoboth, have dogs with thin faces prowling the streets at the end of short leashes. The motel signs read GREYHOUNDS WELCOME and on the boardwalk members of the fire department operate an animatronic puppy. The Retiree is wearing shorts with palm trees stitched on the legs. The heat is stifling so he chills Jujubes in his fridge and then carries them in his pockets to beat Indian summer. They feel to him like cold pebbles, he says. The tourists swarm around him in Rehoboth on weekends, shuffling past on the boardwalk. There are minivans parked illegally on patches of grass near his house, stuffed with purchases from the outlet stores just outside town.

"They come from everywhere to get away from their sales tax," says the Retiree. "The sales tax is our weapon. We're small. Small like a thumb and useful like a thumb. Can you imagine this country without thumbs? We have a purpose and we make things a damn of a lot easier for the rest of the USA."

Just outside St. Georges, the Chesapeake and Delaware Canal flows quietly in the sunlight, a speedboat cutting up the still water as it disappears toward the coast. The canal is thirty-five feet deep and fourteen miles long, cutting rural from industrial, chicken farmer from credit card maker. Construction began in earnest in 1824 after a first initiative failed eighteen years earlier due to lack of funds.

On this day the water is free of industry. The container ships that eventually took over from the schooners, the barges, tugs, and propeller steamers are nowhere to be seen. Long gone is any hint of the dirty industrial slog of thousands of Irishmen who were paid less than a dollar a day to keep the soft slides of the surrounding marshlands in place during the construction. Thanks to them there are still Cretaceous fossils and reptile bones littering the dredge spoils. Another recreational boat passes and its wake leaves waves lapping at the pebbles on the edge of this watery line.

Why is Wilmington the way it is?" The Bookseller is an amiable guy with sandy hair and a touch of a drawl. He grew up in Wilmington, just outside the city, still on the tramline, though the trams had wheels by then. He has run the shop with his wife for thirty-one years. "Why is Delaware the way it is? You've got to go back to 1968, to the Martin Luther King assassination riots here. Some areas were burned.

"I was at my brother's gas station at the time. There was a curfew. Everybody got in their houses. We were right across the street from the firehouse so we were staying open to feed the fire trucks that were using Route 40 to go into the city. They were letting things burn pretty much, but just in case, we were prepared. All of a sudden here come the National Guard trucks coming toward the city from our little airbase where they were headquartered. Here they are coming up Maryland Avenue and I'm seeing these guys in the back of some deuce and a half trucks, the old military trucks with the hoops on top, and I know some of them. They've got guns in their hands. I'm thinking, Oh my God, we're in trouble now.

"The problem was we had a governor from below the canal who had no idea what the city was like. Those Guards should have been pulled back and pulled out within weeks. It went on for over a year. He left them in. He was afraid to make that move. He had no understanding of the city. To him this was the wild jungles of Watts, LA, and he had these National Guard troops stationed on the corners for a year. What's business going to do? It just ruined Wilmington. That was probably the seminal moment for Wilmington itself as a city. It has never recovered from it."

At around five in the afternoon, the Tenth Street bus shelter in Caesar Rodney Square in Wilmington is placid and full of tired faces and wilted shopping bags. There are pinpoint cracks in each of the shelter's windows. The Two Mothers are sitting in the King Street shelter, wrestling their strollers down, cracking open juice containers, jiggling sleeping children. An iPod headphone dangles from one's collar, sending out tinny beats. There are no buses in sight.

"So as not to be the thing, is what I'm saying, you know what I'm saying? New York is the thing. We're not the thing," says one of the Mothers.

"To be close to the *things* but not to be, like, the thing itself," says the other.

Across the road light is falling on the Bank of America building. These are the few blocks of power, hemming in Caesar Rodney Square.

"No one's like, *Delaware, oh that's the thing.*"

"But we can squirt into New York, into Philly. Everything is either twenty minutes or two hours away from Delaware."

"There's nothing in between."

A bus arrives. Passengers grab their plastic shopping bags and sway toward the exit. Outside, a couple of men are throwing empty beer cans at the trash.

"All these streets round here clear out at five o'clock. It's like, the white people head toward those parking lots. Black people come down to take the bus."

"It takes them twenty minutes to get home."

"Yeah, it takes us two hours."

The Lawyer in Wilmington says he only gives deep background. It is Delaware after all: Everyone knows everyone. "The thing with Delaware is that we're receptive. We're receptive to change the law to accommodate business trends. For example, when the LLC, the limited liability corporation, came into being, many corporations said we like the LLC better. We want to move toward that. Delaware was at the cutting edge of adjusting laws so that INC could move to an LLC, an LLC to an INC, partnership to an LLC, an LLP—limited liability partnership—to an LLLP, a limited liability limited partnership. In other words, we're very in tune with the modern problems a corporate identity must deal with and we are willing to change the laws to accommodate the practical problems that corporations face.

"We have a court of chancery, which is a court of equity, which is guided by the law but, more so, it's guided by hundreds of years of precedence. What do corporations want? They want stability. They want to know that they're not going to get a rogue judge. There's no jury. In some very very minor cases, there can be a jury, but 99.99999 percent of the time there's no jury. They want to know they have a business judge, a business expert, an arbitrator, if you will, who is an expert on business practices and can quickly find out what's going on and get to the bottom of it. And also corporations know when they make a contract, 200 years of history are standing behind it. The stability is what can't be replicated.

"We are like the maitre d'. We're welcoming to business. *You want this? I'll take care of you. You want the best seat? I'll take care of you.*"

A row of four Sports Fans sit at the bar in Newark, upstate Delaware, the college town. They're wearing check shirts and black belts. Their cell phones are holstered. The baseball players on the television look like angry horses swatting away pests. Flies are visible in the close-ups of their faces, swirling about in the evening air. The New York Yankees' Alex Rodriguez keeps fouling balls off and then strikes out with a runner in scoring position.

"Look at those flies," the Yankee Fan says. He's scratching his arm. "It's like *The Birds* out there. My skin is crawling." No one wears a hat from a Delaware team. Everyone in Delaware has elsewhere allegiance. There are a few Red Sox hats, a little love for the Yankees, a lot for Philly.

"No allegiance means any allegiance," says the Sports Fan who has just untucked his dress shirt, disappeared the tie, and is now sprinkling flavored seasoning on the melted cheese of the crispy fries. "What's happening to baseball players? They all seem to be named, like, Bronson Sardinha," he says. "They all seem to be named Coco Crisp."

"Fuck the Yankees," someone says.

"Fuck Cleveland," someone says.

"Fuck baseball," says a female voice. She's blond and perched over a glass of red wine with a thin disc of liquid at the bottom.

Later in the evening Sports Fans troop to the bathroom, one at a time. "At least there's the Delaware Smash," says a guy at the urinal. "It's our only pro team. They're a tennis team. They're going to do real well. It's all we've got." He dries his hands under tacked-up copies of the *News Journal* with a story on bodies from Iraq being flown back to Dover. "But come on, you know . . . a tennis team?"

They say Delaware's boring because they don't have enough stuff here," says the Entrepreneur. She's sitting in her church in downtown Wilmington. She was saved when she was sixteen. She's now twenty-four. The sign outside the church reads EXTREME FAITH!!! EXTREME POWER!!! EXTREME PRAISE!!! EXTREME PRESENCE!!!

"It's enough stuff for me. There's a lot of banks here. It's good for entrepreneurs like me. I want to start a program, a nonprofit organization, and start up a shelter and things like that. I want to start a coffee shop, that's what I want to start. I'm not a real coffee drinker, so maybe I can add something the other shops don't have besides just hot chocolate and tea. Christians, you know, they need someplace where they can just fellowship together. There's Brew-haha and Starbucks but I don't really feel them, you know what I mean?

"So what else is there to do here? I see people fishing on the Brandywine and I say, What're you going to do with those fish? They're fishing and crabbing. I don't know if you can catch anything in there but if you can I wouldn't suggest you eat it. This is the Chemical State. Always. You hear about the du Ponts?!"

Route 9 crosses the canal and curves east toward the Delaware River and then off down the coast. The commercial traffic is sparse. On the weekend holiday bikers streak past on shiny Harleys. Outside Delaware City, the Two Fishermen sit in the reeds next to the road behind the metal barrier with empty Corona bottles littered around their feet. White string leads out into the water. They've tied chicken to the string to catch the crabs. There are already more than twenty clacking in the battered red-and-white cooler.

"Mucho caliente, mucho sol and we catch more crabs," says Fisherman Uno. He works at the Champion factory in Wilmington but his boss lives south of the canal and tells him where to lay his line.

"We don't worry," says Fisherman Dos.

"All the fish is good," says Fisherman Uno. "All the crabs is good. Healthy, good. When we get the sun it's even better."

Across the highway, across the rough water of the Delaware, the towers of the Hope Creek Nuclear Generating Station rise up.

The State Senator and her partner are sharing dinner with the Bookseller and the Bookseller's Wife. There is a prepared mushroom salad, pizza with fig and homemade cornmeal crust. The Bookseller rode his bicycle from the shop in Wilmington to this ring of suburbs. "Did you notice our solar panels?" he says. "We're on the grid."

"In Delaware," the Bookseller's Wife says, after the food has been passed. "We are very, very friendly to banks."

"Oh boy. Here we go."

"That's Governor Pete du Pont's contribution to the state's economy," she says. "We're basically the onshore version of the Cayman Islands. Legitimized usury is what we've got."

"Do we have any usury laws at all?" the Bookseller asks.

The State Senator finishes a bite. "There used to be a cap on the interest banks and lending institutions could charge," the State Senator says. "When Pete du Pont did the banking bill to attract banks to come here they repealed the cap."

"And that was debated for what, an hour at most?" The Bookseller answers his own questions. "Pretty much. It was just thrown out there."

"Now Sears can charge 25 percent interest."

"And then their gross profits are taxed at unbelievably low percentages," says the Bookseller's Wife. "We as a business in Delaware pay 8.7 percent gross tax. But banks—it's a graduated thing—the bulk of their profits are taxed at 1.7 percent."

"Each industry has a different rate," says the State Senator. "When I asked why the rates were different the answer was: We don't know. Grocery stores, which have one of the lowest profit margins at something like 1.2 percent profit, have one of the highest percentages. You look at banks and some of the real high-end profits . . ."

"Most banks are taxed at 1.7 percent," says the Bookseller's Wife.

The State Senator continues: "It really does have to do with who the lobbyists are as to what rate you're going to pay. If you have an effective lobby, then the law gets amended to lower the taxes in that particular industry."

"It's called corporate extortion," says the Bookseller's Wife.

"Don't get her started," says the Bookseller.

"When the banking bill passed there seemed to be this culture of get rid of dirty industry," says the State Senator. "We want clean banks. They brought all of these clean banks in who paid minimum wage to the vast majority of their employees and paid no health care benefits. So they're nice and clean but in the meantime all these good manufacturing jobs, Electric Hose and Rubber and all those places, folded up their tents and left. GM and Chrysler were the last of the really good manufacturing jobs."

The Bookseller's Wife nods. "Now they're going after the bio-tech sector because that's another clean, white-collar industry. We gave AstraZeneca how much money?"

"Four-point-something million," says the Bookseller.

"Corporate welfare," adds the State Senator.

The Bookseller goes on: "We gave Wal-Mart $1.4 million to bring their distribution center into Smyrna. Here are the richest people in the world. We gave 1.4 million to them."

"Look what we gave to Bank of America," says the State Senator. "Was it $17 million? I was the only person who voted against it. I said why are we giving Bank of America $17 million? They took over MBNA."

"Oh, they had sweetheart deals," says the Bookseller's Wife. "One after another."

"Don't get her started," says the Bookseller.

"The city gave them a $4.5-million piece of property for nothing," says the State Senator.

"No property taxes," says the Bookseller's Wife.

"It's jobs," says the Bookseller.

"When MBNA sold out to Bank of America they started making noises saying, 'We've already got a headquarters down in Texas. We might just move our operations down there,'" the State Senator continues. "So Delaware started to grovel. One of the ways we grovelled was to say, 'Here's a $17 million tax cut if you'll stay.' They never promised anything in return for that. In fact, they've cut how many thousand jobs? So they've stuck it to us even with their $17 million welfare check."

"They all do it," says the Bookseller's Wife. What's left of the corn-crust pizza has cooled.

"No politician wants to be against jobs," says the Bookseller. "No one wants to go out on lost jobs."

In the storefront church in Wilmington, the Evangelist's cell phone vibrates against a table. Someone on the other end is buying a car and the Evangelist asks, "Is God showing you a two-door or a four-door? Don't settle for something little."

She has recently moved to Delaware from rural New York. Her revelations, she says, have been awesome. They have far outweighed the struggles with divorce and car repossession in her own life. "I came here from a community in the country," she says. "A country mouse to a city mouse, mostly all white people to all black people. Not that it's a problem—I love black people but I think they still hold that yoke of bondage of hatred toward white people. My heart breaks for them for what we did to them. I can relate to them because I moved into an almost all black area with the church. I can relate to how they must feel being a minority. I think I feel like Rosa Parks going OK, now I know what it feels like trying to get accepted because of my skin color. I've actually had two people look at me because of my skin color when they shook my hand. It made me feel uncomfortable but I just felt like, OK God, you're showing me something and this is how they feel. I didn't reject them. I was pleasant to them.

"I grew up in a high school where there were no black people, in a grade school where there were none, so it's totally different for me. But I don't look at blacks any different than I look at Mexicans, Chinese, Japanese. I don't look at anyone as if they were different. It's the world we live in.

"When I moved to Wilmington I didn't think they'd accept me. I said 'God, they're black.' He said, 'I know. I made 'em.' I thought, wow, I just got rebuked from the Lord. My girlfriends were like, 'Are you sure you heard from God?' He spoke to me for two weeks through dreams and through impressions. He spoke to me to come to Delaware. He kept giving me Deuteronomy 11, which is 'Cross over the river Jordan and if you obey and heed my voice then all these blessings will come upon you.' So I chose to come."

The Former Governor is now ninety-one but his mind is sharp. He sits near the window of his house in a suburb of Wilmington looking at the expanse of trees in the backyard. He was the fair-haired boy early in his career as a chemist at DuPont but the relationship soured. He says DuPont brought in the company psychiatrist to comment on his stability after he challenged their hiring policy toward blacks. His favorite political cartoons hang in the hall. On one he rides an elephant, defending the coastline from a frowning barrel of oil.

"We have a Chesapeake and Delaware Canal, which hooks the Delaware to Chesapeake Bay," he says. "The modern bridge is quite fancy but the old one is a big arch, a narrow bridge with traffic each way. If you go up there and look south, you see wide open spaces and great marshland. There are places that have become national refuges. I'd always go visit those places and look over toward New Jersey and out toward Spain. There's a lot of bird life in that area.

"My nine-year-old got me interested in birds. He'd go out in the woods in the morning before the sun came up to see what birds sang first. One morning I went with him to see what the hell he was doing and he got me interested. His older brother got interested so I'd take those two boys and we'd go up and down the Delaware coast. We'd move down along the Delaware River, going in and out from the river, into the forest along the way and down to southern Delaware. We'd have dinner down in Maryland at night, get up early in the morning, and come back a different route. I got to know that coast. I walked over nearly all of it.

"Just before I became governor in 1969 it became apparent the major battle that was developing was that coast. Thirteen international oil companies and major transportation companies, including one owned by George H.W. Bush, wanted to develop. Shell had detailed plans to build a large refinery on the five thousand acres they owned in the choice places along the Delaware Bay. People organized to fight them. The argument went all the way up through our state supreme court. The state supreme court gave permission to Shell to go ahead and build the plant. That's when I became governor. I felt teed off. One of the key things I was going to do was stop this plan to industrialize the area. It wasn't important just to Delaware.

"Up north of here is refinery after refinery. There are all kinds of petro-chemical complexes. We have one of them in Delaware City. That was done long before I was governor. We used to use it as an example: You want that Delaware City thing to march on down the coast? That's exactly what would have happened. It was an outstanding place for oil companies. Deep water, the oil coming in direct from overseas, absolutely open land. The outlets for the oil were there since we're close to the East Coast markets. But I said to the state we had to have a big debate. We have two opportunities for our coast zone. We can leave it as it is for fishing and hunting and boating and swimming and just lying out in the sun. Or we can participate in the world's most rapid and largest industrializations. We can't do both. They're incompatible. I favor the former but let's have a big debate. All the business community, including the DuPont company, didn't say very much. Then I declared a moratorium—no more building in these areas until we decide what we're going to do. That's when all hell broke loose. I got called down to Washington by the Secretary of Commerce, Maurice Stans, who later got in trouble over the Watergate problem. He said to me in his huge office, 'These twenty-five men sitting here with us have been working for ten years on this project to develop this Delaware coast. This is so fundamentally important to our country.' He got up, walked over to me, pointed his finger, and said, 'Governor, you're being disloyal to your country.' I jumped up and said, 'Hell no, I'm being loyal to future generations.'

"By this time these oil companies had all hired law firms in Delaware and they started really to beat on me. All the unions were upset. How irritated were the unions? The electrical workers union was celebrating its sixtieth anniversary and asked the governor to come and make some comments. It was a great big room, round tables, ten people at each one, except right below the podium was a table for ten with nobody seated there. I wondered what the hell that was for.

"The president got up to introduce me and said, 'He's the one who blocked all these jobs for us down there.' The crowd booed me and booed me. I got up to make my few remarks and they got up and booed me even harder and then there was a blast of trumpets in the back of the room and in came my opponent for election with nine of his people. The whole crowd jumped up and applauded and those ten marched down and sat at that table right in front of me. That's hard politics.

"We had a real knock-down, drag-out battle and we got our bill through the legislature by one vote. The final vote, the records show, was won by more than one vote but the real battle was over an amendment that the oil companies had written. So we won that battle. One vote.

"When little Delaware started to take on these oil companies, which were a damn problem all over the world, environmental groups in other parts of the world kept watching what was happening in Delaware. The National Audubon Society and the Sierra Club were all watching what was happening here in little Delaware. A month after I signed that bill into law the World Wildlife Fund had its big convention in New York City at the Waldorf-Astoria. They gave me their gold medal and when Prince Bernard of the Netherlands presented that medal he said, 'This is the first time in the world any community had won such a battle against the oil companies.'

"Over this item I lost my bid for reelection. The business community worked against me. The very community that played a role in me getting elected. After all, I came from the DuPont company. But I felt comfortable. I was right. I had the conviction, see? Damn do-gooder, they called me. I used to say to groups: 'Put all the people in the world in three piles. The do-nothingers over here, the do-badders over there, and the do-gooders.' I know what pile I want to be in."

I went to Massachusetts at thirteen," says the Hotel Handyman in down-town Wilmington. He's seventeen, soft-spoken, and ever present in the building. His hair is pulled back into a tidy ponytail. He painted the walls of the hotel for free as an intern. He fills in at the front desk when they need him. He does dishes in the kitchen when they call out his name. "I was surprised by Massachusetts back then. The streets were longer, the air was different. You get this creamy air in Massachusetts. Some states have got rich air. You get that misty air feeling in Pennsylvania. The air here, people get accustomed to it. Some say pollution, I don't believe it.

"The taxes were different in Massachusetts. I didn't feel too comfortable. Here something is five dollars—cheap. There it'll be $5.15, or something. It'll be $6.18. I'm like, huh? I'm like, I'm going back to Wilmington. I'm going to buy a Big Mac in Wilmington.

"Here's my phrase: 'Wilmington always has a hold on you.' You may leave but you come back. You live a sweeter life here. I've lived here all my seventeen years. Mom moved from Puerto Rico. She'd heard about it from foreigners. People on vacation said they were from Wilmington. My dad went to college and spent thirty-four years at DuPont. Those were his golden years. They gave him good work. Dad got a house, got everything going. I thought about DuPont, but they said they wanted a degree or a high-school diploma. I'm getting that. I'm a GED—in Delaware they call it a Good Enough Diploma.

"I do maintenance but I'm also doing music. The music's about putting Delaware on the map. It's about telling it as it is here, about the parties but about the place economically as well. You've got Westside on 4th Street. That's the Hispanic street. They pervade over there. Riverside—guys trying to be big shots. Northside—they rap about how fresh they are. It's about making money. You hear people say I can get money by hustling. Sure, you can make money by hustling but here you get more money from work because it's more secure. We got big banks here. We've got people here rapping about a stable job. If anyone it'll be me rapping about sales tax. If I'm rich I would not move out because of taxes, see? I wouldn't have to.

"I've got a lot more motivation these days," the Hotel Handyman says. "Because I've got a baby on the way. I can't wait to hold that baby. I've been saving money like crazy. I got a bank account now. It's hard for a seventeen-year-old to get a bank account in other states. In Delaware I got an account like no problem. It's smooth. The management is nice. I met my girl at elementary school and I've been with her on and off since we were ten. She's been by my side. At first I was like, a baby? Man. But now I'm saving. I'm looking toward the light."

FLORIDA

CAPITAL Tallahassee

ENTERED UNION 1845 (27th)

ORIGIN OF NAME From the Spanish Pascua Florida, meaning "Feast of Flowers" (Easter)

NICKNAME Sunshine State

MOTTO "In God We Trust"

RESIDENTS Floridian or Floridan

U.S. REPRESENTATIVES 25

STATE BIRD mockingbird

STATE FLOWER orange blossom

STATE TREE sabal (or cabbage) palm

STATE SONG "Suwannee River"

LAND AREA 53,927 sq. mi.

GEOGRAPHIC CENTER In Hernando Co., 12 mi. NNW of Brooksville

POPULATION 17,789,864

WHITE 78.0%

BLACK 14.6%

AMERICAN INDIAN 0.3%

ASIAN 1.7%

HISPANIC/LATINO 16.8%

UNDER 18 22.8%

65 AND OVER 17.6%

MEDIAN AGE 38.7

FLORIDA
Joshua Ferris

We came down to Florida from Danville, Illinois, in 1985 on the matrimonial whim of my mother and stepfather. She had three kids, the youngest just over a year old, while he'd been a bachelor for half a dozen years.
Freeze-frame on the two of them feeding each other wedding cake, then cut
to a U-Haul without air conditioning and the white Volkswagen behind it
leaving small-town USA for Key West, where Dennis had been hired by
the Florida Department of Law Enforcement to work narcotics. They are
still married today, but I believe the full impact of what he'd done hit him
for the first time only when we made that trip together full of bicker and
demands, the hot wind blasting through the open windows of our U-Haul.
We did not know much about bladder control and my stepfather is a man
who likes to drive straight through.

Anyone who knows Dennis knows he is law enforcement through and
through, but before hitting US 1, where the massive stucco seashell warehouses, the fishing resorts, and roadside bars of the Florida Keys begin, I
knew so little about him that it would not have come as a surprise if he had
stopped at a Texaco, emerged from the men's room with newly dyed hair,
and returning to the U-Haul told me to call him Breaker.

We knew nothing about Florida living. One of our first hurricanes
taught us that quickly enough. You know the shaky-camera footage of
palms bent in half by the wind and street signs pulled out of the ground
and water coming fast down the street. We watched such a show from our
front windows. When it was over, my sister and brother and I went out and
played in floodwaters three feet deep. We swam in the street as if it were a
swimming pool. The storm had passed and an eerie stillness had taken hold
of the air. I couldn't make sense of the charged but breathless atmospherics
as the bruised skies hovered overhead like the end of days. Calm prevailed
absolutely. My mother supervised while we played and swam in those dubious waters. No one joined us. Not a soul emerged from the neighboring
houses to assess the damage or sigh with relief. We continued to play when
the rain and wind started up again. Finally, a man came out of his house and
shouted across the street to my mom.

"You know it's the eye, right?"

"The eye?"

"Of the hurricane."

She hurried us inside just as another two hours of battering winds and swift waters out of the Caribbean resumed their assault.

Our house on Cudjoe Key was elevated on stilts to protect against such flooding. It was essentially a three-bedroom apartment pitched twenty feet in the air. I was spellbound at first sight of it, a typical frame house magically elevated into the treetops. And our backyard terminated with a canal that ran out to the bay. To give a rural boy his own body of water is to give him the grace necessary, at least in part, to forgive the adults responsible for relocating him. The canal was unwalled and tree lined, fifteen feet deep and sludge bottomed, the water amber colored and scummy with white flotsam, really ugly. I jumped in every day. I didn't care that jellyfish stung my body up and down. Standing at the boat ramp, I fished the canal and caught snapper and grouper and an evil-looking mother called the toadfish I didn't even bother taking off the hook. When I caught a toadfish I just cut the line. I would have tossed the whole pole in before touching a toadfish. I canoed out to the bay. I snorkeled practically the entire coast of the Gulf of Mexico. I paddled under the bridge and later when I had saved enough to buy a small motorboat I raced across the blue shallows. I camped in historic forts. Dennis knew members of the Coast Guard who ferried us seventy miles west to the Dry Tortugas, where we stayed three days, parched from lack of planning and eaten alive by no-see-ums. My friend Michael Jones and I once saw in the distance a blue shark thrashing hard in the sand after the tide had receded; it was bigger than our eight-foot canoe. Michael jumped into the water to drag the canoe toward the shark because he thought in the shallows that was faster than paddling, and we were just dense and wild enough to think we could land an agitated shark from a canoe with line and reel. I sailed on schooners and I swam with dolphins. I tickled lobster out of holes regardless of eels. I came eye to eye with a man-sized barracuda in water so clear I could count its teeth. With my friends I egged cars on US 1 and then dove into the canals to elude the drivers who stopped to chase after us.

But water leisure 24/7 bored me after a while and I began to mow lawns and pull weeds on behalf of any paying neighbor for three bucks an hour. I collected about twenty clients up and down Cudjoe Key. Some jobs were deathly boring and others were bizarre. My stepbrother and I helped a guy build a private beach on his ocean-front property one summer. He was a cheap bastard who paid us only a buck-fifty an hour to do the *Cool Hand Luke* labor of shoveling massive quantities of sand from the truck down to his denuded yard and gradually into the water. He thought it would sink and stay, but within three months his quixotic dream had been washed out to sea along with a major investment in sand and Tiki lights and our two months of accumulated buck fifties. You can't make a beach where the ocean doesn't want one.

I started working at a Godfather's Pizza franchise a few months later. My mom knew the manager. Law enforcement has a hierarchy of its own and includes a code of snobbery. Probation and Parole is often snubbed as chump change in the penal circles, but my mother had taken a job there and she did it with diligence and commitment. Her Volkswagen Jetta was so well known in Bahama Village, a few blocks off Duval where the drugs flow—it's a short step in Key West from the vendors selling Panama hats made of palm leaves to the vendors selling crack in the daylight—that she couldn't park down there without having her tires slashed. Her reputation was such among the criminati of Key West that when Judge Fowler went easy and sentenced someone to house arrest, if they knew anything they'd ask, "You gonna make Patty Haley my probation officer?" And when he said he might, they said, "Then just send me to prison."

Almost all of her community controlees worked the tourist trade. As part of her job she had to stop in their places of employment to make sure they were where they said they'd be, and in that way she got to know the area restaurant managers and owners. I was paid under the table at God-father's to wash dishes on the weekends. By the time a district manager down from Miami paid an unexpected visit, I was preparing ingredients and making the pizzas. So among other violations, the DM found an eleven-year-old pulling pies out of the oven, which we did with a pair of slip-joint pliers. The franchise closed soon after. It's now a scuba shop.

Next I worked at The Galley Grill on Summerland Key, one mile-marker east of Cudjoe. Before my shift started, I swept and mopped the floor for an additional five bucks and then I did the dishes in the kitchen next to a bulky ex-hockey fanatic turned biker named Charlie who didn't appreciate my company. He came and went on a Harley and kept his long hair in bandannas. He tolerated me enough to teach me how to properly peel and fillet a shrimp and how to cook a killer scampi.

The owners of The Galley Grill were a married couple. I remember little about them. They, too, paid me under the table. I was in love with their middle daughter who worked nights as a waitress. When she came into the kitchen with dirty dishes I tried looking down her blouse as she bent to the sink and my success rate was high because she wore loose clothes with no bra, which is pretty standard dress code for the Keys.

The walk to The Galley Grill from our house was a mile of mangroves along a steep dropoff from US 1 so that as I walked along I could hardly see the passing cars. I stumbled on a man once taking advantage of this obscurity to masturbate in his car. I startled him as I approached and he startled me. I saw a flash of some pornographic rag as he frantically tried to zip up. I started running and he gunned the car and roared up the slope.

Eventually the daily drive into Key West became too taxing on my mom and Dennis and we moved off Cudjoe, which put The Galley Grill out of reach and I had to quit. But living on the island itself expanded my options. I started working for a place called The Eatery, which had a popular breakfast buffet. We ate there after church sometimes, depending on how well we'd endured the sermon.

What had been a beachhead hosting a steamship pier in the Gulf of Mexico was by 1985 the setting for a breakfast hotspot for tourists at the southern end of Duval. By then the beach had been reduced by condos and hotels to a small strip of sand that hardly deserved an official name, nevertheless called South Beach. Diners happily looked upon this sandbox and thought it paradise.

The Eatery's owners were a husband and wife named Bill and Gail. Bill had a bulbous gut on a very skinny frame, so bulbous and independent of the rest of his body it seemed he should be able to detach it and set it on the counter next to the cash register. He was rumored to be an alcoholic and never let anyone touch the till, nor did he ever say hello when I arrived on weekend mornings. I showed up at seven and he just looked at me with his full-moon eyes and the darker half-moon bags under them. I went in back, put on an apron, and took a broom out to the flagstones in front of the restaurant. Overnight the sand had drifted up and the departing tide left a curvy line of brackish seaweed on the beach. The light was still dim at seven and so I might find two beach bums not yet run off by Bill, having sex under a palm. I'd hardly sweep the flagstones for watching them; I was twelve and that was the Big Show. But half the time as the light came up I'd discover it was just two men and lose interest. When I came in from sweeping, Bill sent me out for *café con leche* some Cubans sold out of a shack down the street.

When he warmed up to me, Bill showed me his Taser gun. The two blue electric pincers looked innocuous enough, but their terrible sound when triggered implied the worst possible death. "Know what this is?" he asked. "Know how many times I've been broken into? More than forty times. Count that," he demanded. "Forty." If he caught someone breaking in again, his plan was to torture and kill them. "This isn't the half of what I'd use," he said ominously.

During tourist season the morning rush at The Eatery ended around two in the afternoon. Then the waitresses sat for the first time in six hours in a small covey of two-tops half partitioned by latticework. They smoked and counted their tips, stacks of ones a foot high and much smaller stacks of fives and tens.

Hazel was an old hippie with a bitter edge and wicked laugh who used to describe her acid trips to me. She looked her age, which was probably forty, but a hard, used forty, the sort of forty that says no dental insurance, terrible luck with men, estranged children, and dogs waiting for her at home. She taught me over and above anything else that a long drag on a Camel at the waitress station can make heading back to the dining room with a coffee pot somehow bearable. I visited her at home once for a reason I can no longer remember and found her sunbathing on a cheap chaise longue, and while I was not attracted to her much, my pubescent urges begged her to seduce me.

Rhonda was more maternal. She called me sweetie or honey and offered a world-weary smile that seemed to strive for something grander. Her body was plumply huggable. It had an expansiveness that seemed to invite anyone in need to nuzzle her bosom in a nonsexual way. I never had any Hazel-like fantasies about Rhonda. A small mole, red as a ruby, was set in the curve of her cheek. She was alone in providing for her two young kids.

Billy Ray was the only waiter. He could not have weighed more than a hundred pounds and ten of that was mustache. He was rumored to be dying of AIDS. When he came out of the closet, he turned around and burned the closet. He sexually harassed me, as it can only be described, in an over-the-top, John Waters sort of way, with lewd innuendo and outright propositions, but then he did this sort of thing to everyone, including Rhonda and Hazel and even Bill, who responded only by staring in silent revulsion. This taught me pity. Billy Ray told crude jokes about fags. This taught me tolerance.

The Eatery buffet included orange juice dispensed from a large plastic container and sometimes the spigot would clog up with pulp. Billy Ray would take the container into the kitchen, set it down on the stainless steel counter, and say to me in a high-pitched Southern accent, "Now normally you suck, Josh, you suck, but for this little problem you have to blow, you have to BLOW!" He'd bend and put his lips over the spigot and blow hard into the container to dislodge the pulp and his breath would bubble up through the juice. Then he'd walk back out into the dining room and return the orange juice to its place beside the dry cereal.

To watch the three of them pull their massive wads of cash from their aprons and Ball jars after their shifts died down and stack them upon the two-tops was to consider them the wealthiest people in the world, just filthy with cold hard cash, when in reality they had rent and debt and bills and kids and who knows what periodic addictions, and they had all these things in a paradise of free living where they could never afford to buy a piece of land. I worked for spending money and came home to a fridge full of groceries and a free bedroom. They worked to see themselves into next week.

Working the dishes at The Eatery there were always two of us, me and a second dishwasher, usually a drifter, a drunk, or an addict momentarily collected, precariously employed, and looking like hell, looking craven or used or dying. One of us took the bin dishes coming in from the dining room and the other the pots and pans. The pots and pans were a dog's life, man, really shit work for how the grits would fry like an epoxy to the bottoms and the peach cobbler on the buffet table would harden around the edges under the heat lamps and everything needed a Brillo pad. Everything needed to soak for twelve hours, but the line cook was screaming for it all after only half an hour and I'd have to put the bin dishes on hold and join the drunk at the industrial sinks and we'd work side by side while the bins kept coming from the two bus-boys, both named Richard, both forty and on parole, screaming at me because the buffet plates were running low and there were no more forks and the line of tourists waiting to be seated was out the door. So then I'd return to the bin dishes and try to bury myself out. Each bin was a cold coffee soup of plates and silverware and buffet foods—scrambled eggs and sausage ends and soggy napkins and biscuit mush. I'd run a load of just forks and then a load of just plates and then just forks again while the bins continued to stream in, the line cook continued to holler, the tourists continued to line up, and life, already winning, beat the drunk at the pots and pans down another notch, strengthening his conviction that his lot was all misery and his place in the workforce a folly of destiny he was better to deny. There was never any guarantee that any dishwasher on staff would still be on staff when I came in the following weekend.

I learned the word jailbait from the first of many line cooks employed by The Eatery, a middle-aged man I knew for so short a period of time all his features have turned foggy. I remember only his eager, creepy smile. I thought jailbait a magical word. I knew what "jail" meant and I knew what "bait" meant but that you could combine the two to form a compound word with an elusive meaning made language a dynamic and mysterious thing.

The line cook had written the word on a napkin and placed it in one of the bins and when the bin made its way back to me I read the note. It said, "You know what jailbait is?" I was naïve enough to think I was getting a vocabulary lesson. "What's jailbait?" I asked him. "You are," he said. Over the next couple of weekends there were other notes on other napkins.

This was not Billy Ray's innocuous flamboyance. This was something sinister and uncomfortable. Dennis drove down with me and we sat with Bill and when I came in the next weekend the line cook was gone. I had not meant for anyone to get fired.

"Don't feel bad," said David, the breakfast cook. "It's not the first thing he's done."

Later, when I started cooking lunch for The Eatery, David and I spent time together over the enormous grill. He spoke gently. While I prepared lunch he scrambled huge quantities of eggs for the breakfast buffet. Gradually a drop of sweat appeared at the tip of his pointy nose, and as the eggs turned curdy in consistency, the drop quivered and fell.

I knew only one thing about David: Both of his parents had died in a plane crash when he was very young. He was rumored to be gay but because it never came up it didn't matter any more or less than the brute fact of my raging puberty. He got annoyed at others from time to time, but with me he was infinitely patient. I remember him cracking an egg in each hand into a five-gallon bucket. He had to fill three five-gallon buckets, fifteen pounds of yokes and whites, every afternoon in anticipation of the following morning's buffet. He wore his hair in a Mohawk and sometimes I would arrive after a week of school to find the Mohawk dyed some shocking Pantone. He had crooked teeth and smoked with the timid poise of a teenage girl. When something tickled him, he laughed, but his laugh was soundless.

When I wasn't working, I attended middle school. Sugarloaf Middle School is home of the Hammerhead Sharks, and with friends I got up to the usual mischief. I also started to take school seriously. One day we were given the assignment to write an essay on the importance of environmental protection. The topic was "Why We Should Save the Salt Ponds." I didn't know what a salt pond was. I began my essay by asking, "Does Key West really need another T-shirt shop?"

I thought I was being punished when some time later I was called down to the principal's office. Instead, Principal Martinez told me I had won the contest. I didn't remember the essay and never knew it was part of any contest. My prize was a canoe trip through the salt ponds with Jimmy Buffett, mayor of Margaritaville and the contest sponsor.

I was driven to Jimmy Buffett's house by one of his handlers in a circuitous manner, as if I were a journalist and Jimmy a terrorist in deep cover. Jimmy's exact residence was a closely held secret on the island and it didn't matter that I didn't know the man from Luciano Pavarotti. When I arrived, Jimmy was exceptionally warm and kind. We went out back to his canal and stepped down into the canoe. A Jamaican with dreadlocks sat in back and paddled. Jimmy explained what I was about to see and why it was important to preserve it. And the salt ponds were exquisitely beautiful: essentially a series of winding mangrove rivulets, dark as secret tunnels, barely wider than the canoe and overhung with lush vegetation. It was like my own private *Goonies*. Jimmy and the Jamaican took turns naming plants and birds and cracking jokes.

For all the beauty of the salt ponds, however, the most exciting part of the boat ride was over before we left Jimmy's canal. We had canoed past beautiful house after beautiful house with elaborate docks and boats up on lifts. I was watching them go by when I noticed her sunbathing on her deck. She was nineteen or twenty-five or thirty. It didn't matter. She had removed her bikini top to let the sun worship her. This was a much more priceless thing for me to see than a stupid old salt pond. I clamped my eyes down on her and didn't let go. She didn't flinch as we floated by—too quickly, too quickly! When she was out of sight I turned to Jimmy, who had spotted her too. I blushed at being caught, but he put me right at my ease. In the middle of a body of water, drifting down a canal on a canoe, he said, "I have to get out in this neighborhood more often."

Soon after that they filled in the salt ponds and put up condominiums and a mall.

Early Jimmy Buffett could have easily sung the story of one of the dishwashers I split duties with at The Eatery. He was a wiry drunk named Snake, presumably on account of the coat of tattoos he wore like a second skin. His arms were thin as flagpoles and when he scrubbed at a pot the biceps came out like lanyard rope. We got along, probably because he was willing to answer my questions. I wanted to know about girls, jail, tattoos, and anything he could tell me that might clue me in on how a life could come to be his. What he wanted to talk about, in the same spirit and tone I now hear friends talk about their newborns, was rum.

I convinced Snake to (1) buy rum for the two of us, (2) shelter me in his apartment while I drank it, and (3) do #1 and #2 despite my age (twelve), his prior convictions (many), and his awareness of what my parents did for a living. How I did this rested entirely on my willingness to put up the money for the rum.

"How much does rum cost?" I asked.

"The rum I like costs three bucks."

After work, I gave Snake five dollars and we met up on a street corner and walked to his apartment. It was a one-room efficiency with no TV, sofa, chairs, pictures, or coffee table. It was decorated exclusively with camel-colored carpet. His only possession was a sink full of dirty dishes. He cleaned two glasses and brought out the ice and poured us two rum and Cokes and we sat drinking against the wall under a window with a beat-up blind.

"Where do you sleep, Snake?"

"Right here," he said.

I took my first sip. I was expecting what came in a Coppertone bottle, if Coppertone tasted good—something buttery and summery and as delicious as he described. It was more like something to lubricate a metallic squeak.

"I don't like it."

"I can tell by your face."

"How can you like this?"

"It's an acquired taste."

"I think I'm going to go now."

"You promised, now," he said.

"They'll never know," I reassured him for the fifth or sixth time. "I'll never tell."

I left Snake sitting on the carpet with his feet crossed, holding an icy tumbler full of very weak Coke.

I'm surprised you weren't kidnapped and raped," my mother said to me recently.

"But you were the one who got me the jobs," I said. "You made them possible."

"I don't think I'd let you do it today."

"Why did you let me then?"

"He was law enforcement, I was probation. We knew everybody. What was going to happen to you? It was Key West. Nobody cared."

"Why did I want to work?" I asked her.

"You wanted things. We couldn't afford them, so you went out and got them yourself."

At twelve, I wanted cologne and a waterbed.

"Are you going to write about this?" she asked.

"Do you remember coming into The Eatery on Sunday mornings after church, when I'd be working?"

"Yeah. I remember."

"What did you think of that?"

"I guess I thought it was neat. You were learning about life," she said. "I probably should have been arrested."

For most people, Florida is the place of spring break and white-sand beaches and the promise of sunshine. It evokes visions of cottonheads throwing bocce balls in retirement communities and airboats skating across six inches of water in the Everglades. In Miami, the parties; in Orlando, the theme parks.

But few know about the Flora-Bama bar, located on the border between Florida and Alabama, an area known as the Redneck Riviera. The Flora-Bama sponsors a yearly mullet toss. For a fifteen-dollar entry fee, you have the chance to stand in a ten-foot circle in Alabama and throw a dead mullet across the state line into Florida, no sand on the mullet allowed. Throwing the mullet the farthest wins you a specially designed mullet trophy.

In Naples, Florida, where the gators and panthers of Alligator Alley live just beyond the ever-multiplying strip malls and big box retailers, you can shop at both Master Bait and Tackle *and* Not Just Futons and Barstools.

In Casselberry, you can watch a naked production of *Macbeth* at Club Juana.

You can experience ersatz nostalgia in Seaside and manufactured happiness in Celebration.

In Pensacola, I have witnessed the charismatics floundering on the floor and speaking in tongues during the popular Brownstone Revival, where ex-felons travel all the way from Canada and Alaska to feel the living spirit of Christ in sweaty ceremonies that last till dawn.

In Estero, I have visited the Koreshan State Historic Site, where Cyrus Teed founded a New Jerusalem in 1894, promoting the celibacy that would eventually doom his followers and positing that the universe hangs inside the hollow sphere of the earth.

But for all that, this will always be Florida to me:

One night at The Eatery, I put the chairs up on the tables and swept and mopped the floor and then I gave the bathrooms a scrub down, a hellish job, and when I came out, everyone else had finished for the night. Billy Ray and Rhonda and I walked out together. I don't know why I was working the night shift except to say that it was probably summer and I took any shift they would give me, and I can't say why Rhonda and Billy Ray were working the same shift unless they were pulling doubles because they needed the money, and I can't say why they had agreed to drive me home.

We walked out silent and tired and before we had stepped off the sandy flagstones onto Duval Street, Billy Ray had lit a joint and, without exchanging a word, passed it to Rhonda, who took a hit and passed it back. It was the first time I'd seen anyone smoke pot, and after all the household propaganda leveled against it by the narcotics agent and the probation officer—like "Smoke pot and you could be paralyzed for life" and "Smoke pot and the next thing you'll be doing is crack cocaine. Is that what you want, to be a crackhead?"—Rhonda and Billy Ray were lucky I did not start screaming in the streets. Crime, crime! Pot smokers! Instead I went along. They were giving me a ride. We were quiet and tired. I watched them pass the joint again, a silent communion. We got in Billy Ray's Chevy Nova with its rusted bodywork and shredded upholstery and only by some elaborate pedal voodoo did he manage to turn over the engine. We erupted in a cartoon of exhaust. He backed out just as Don McLean's "American Pie" came on the radio. You will think, "I know that song. That song has been played on TV and in movies and on oldies stations *ad nauseam*." And maybe you will think, "I would be fine never hearing that song again," or maybe even "I hate that awful saccharine song," but it was not like that. They turned up the radio the second the song came on and I remember the feeling of unbelievable good fortune that swept the car. "American Pie" was like some lost key to the kingdom. It was my first time hearing it. Why did the song sound so familiar, almost primal? By the end I was singing the chorus along with them.

> *Bye-Bye, Miss American Pie*
> *drove my Chevy to the levee*
> *but the levee was dry*

I would soon leave Key West and never see them again. Snake was fired during the week for too many no-shows and I never got a chance to say goodbye. The night cook who I have not mentioned but who introduced me to jazz disappeared into the oblivion of addiction. Puberty came and went for me, as did high school and college and my twenties. Bill and Gail sold The Eatery. I recently made a few inquiries and learned they have divorced.

The Eatery has changed hands many times since I worked there and is now called the Duval Street Beach Club, one more layer of commercial palimpsest on an island that had been all mangrove and sapodilla and tamarind. I returned for my wedding and had breakfast at the Duval Street Beach Club but there was no buffet, no line of tourists, no Rhonda or Hazel or Billy Ray and no soundless laugh from David. They are as gone as that Godfather's franchise and the salt ponds.

The song lasted five minutes, just long enough for the drive down Flagler. The windows were open and the weather was pleasant and the two people sitting in front passed the joint back and forth as they sang along. They knew every word. It no longer mattered how tired the day had made them. We rumbled along. They sang out the window. Don McLean never sang his song like that. It has not been sung the same way since. I don't think they would remember this now, if they are still alive. It was just a song and a ride and another night for them. But for me it was the beginning of life.

GEORGIA

CAPITAL Atlanta

ENTERED UNION 1788 (4th)

ORIGIN OF NAME In honor of George II of England

NICKNAMES Peach State or Empire State of the South

MOTTO "Wisdom, justice, and moderation"

RESIDENTS Georgian

U.S. REPRESENTATIVES 13

STATE BIRD brown thrasher

STATE FLOWER Cherokee rose

STATE TREE live oak

STATE SONG "Georgia on My Mind"

LAND AREA 57,906 sq. mi.

GEOGRAPHIC CENTER In Twiggs Co., 18 mi. SE of
   Macon

POPULATION 9,072,576

WHITE 65.1%

BLACK 28.7%

AMERICAN INDIAN 0.3%

ASIAN 2.1%

HISPANIC/LATINO 5.3%

UNDER 18 26.5%

65 AND OVER 9.6%

MEDIAN AGE 33.4

GEORGIA

Ha Jin

I don't have a hometown. I grew up a People's Liberation Army brat, moving around with my father. I can say I am a northerner, since my first twenty-six years were spent in the northeast of China, but that is the most I can associate myself with a place.

For a long time I couldn't understand why Alyosha, the youngest of the Karamazov brothers in Dostoevsky's novel, speaks so passionately about the wholesomeness and sacredness of good childhood memories. I got into the habit of asking people I knew, especially middle-aged and older Chinese women, about their happy childhood memories. Some of them would shake their heads, unable to recall a single one. That made me wonder how anyone could love a place without any good memories of it, despite its being one's hometown or native land.

I do have two or three happy childhood memories, which still bind me emotionally to northeastern China. But Georgia, for which I am full of affectionate memories, is different. It is the place where I had my first home, and learned how to live and work as a writer.

Many Chinese prefer Georgia to other parts of America because the climate is similar to that of their home provinces south of the Yangtze River. In the 1990s, so many Asian and other immigrants moved to the Atlanta area that new elementary and middle schools were built throughout the northeastern suburbs, and trailer classrooms were commonplace.

I moved to Georgia in the summer of 1993 to take a job at Emory University. In the beginning I lived in an apartment in Atlanta, with my wife and ten-year-old son, but soon we found that houses were quite affordable in some of the suburbs, and the schools were safer and better. So we bought a small home in Lilburn, fifteen miles east of the city. The house was a solid brick ranch on a third of an acre of sloping land, with a ten-acre lake at the back. At first sight, somehow, I felt the house had good *feng shui*, though I had never been interested in that occult system. The lake was inhabited by a lot of waterfowl: Canada geese, mallards, Russian swans, domestic ducks. Sometimes an angler or two would fish on the opposite shore; they caught bass, bullheads, perch, carp. Adding to the feeling of home was the fact that about half a mile east of our house flowed a brook named Yellow River. But, of course, Georgia was nothing like China. We were the only Asian family in the subdivision; another family was black, and a third was mixed race, black and Filipino; the rest of the thirty-odd households were white. But our neighbors were friendly. The day after we had moved in, a vase of orange dahlias appeared on our doormat with a note that read, "Welcome to the neighborhood—Mrs. Locke." The author of the note was a widow of seventy living alone a few houses down the street. The flowers touched us. Soon word spread that a doctor's family had moved into the subdivision. A few people, after learning of my employment at Emory, asked me if I was a doctor. Put to it, I said, "I'm a doctor who doesn't make money."

We paid $84,000 for our home, which had three small bedrooms, two bathrooms, a half-finished basement, and a carport. With few exceptions, my colleagues all lived in bigger houses closer to Emory. We bought such a modest place because I wasn't sure if I could hold my job for long, and didn't want to take out a big mortgage. I was hired to teach poetry writing, which was a position I felt I had gotten by luck. I had never attended a poetry workshop and had no idea how to fulfill my role as a poet in residence. Poets in other parts of the country often asked me, "Who's the poet at Emory?" They could not imagine it was me. I felt I might lose my job at any time. Once, I even blurted out to my boss, Frank Manley, a tall, flat-shouldered man in his early sixties, who was the director of our creative writing program, "I will stay in Georgia even if I don't get tenure."

"Why?" He smiled, narrowing his eyes.

"Because life is easier down here."

"Indeed it is."

Frank drove a pickup truck and owned a small farm, where he didn't grow anything. He went there every week just to write.

My misgivings about my job security were not totally unfounded. Later Frank revealed that some people in our department had doubted my qualifications. As a friend, he always stuck up for me. When I was naturalized in the fall of 1997, he went to the department the next morning and told everybody that I had become a citizen. He must have believed that my brand-new citizenship would add to my qualifications.

But the main reason I planned to live in Georgia, even if I lost my job, was not the easy life. It was that I loved my house, the first real home I had ever had. In my backyard the land stretched two hundred feet to the waterside. Soon after we had moved in, we noticed that when it rained the lake would rise and submerge the shore. The result was severe erosion, and I began to fear that we might eventually lose a good part of the yard. To stop this, I started to gather rocks and lay them down along the waterside.

At the time, fire hydrants were being installed in the neighborhood, and boulders were dug out and left beside the road. I would collect them with a hand truck. It was hard work, and usually I could only ship back one at a time. Some weighed more than a hundred pounds. If a boulder was too big, I would try to break it with a sledgehammer. Whenever I took a rest from writing or reading, I would set out with my hand truck, wearing cowhide gloves, work boots, and a Chicago Bulls cap. Sometimes I would bring a pickaxe to dig out the ones that were still half buried. The work involved my family, too. If my son came across a sizable rock, he would tell me so that I could go fetch it. If a load was too heavy, my wife would give me a hand. It took us almost two months to finish the rock bank, which was about 150 feet long and came up a foot above the water. I enjoyed the labor very much, because, at last, on this tiny piece of land, I could arrange my own nest. The happy experience inspired poetry, and I wrote my first poem set in the state, "Lilburn, Georgia," in which I imagined that the result of this labor would last forever.

Our rock bank impressed the neighbors so much that a few families around the lake soon started building imitations. The soil erosion must have bedeviled them for years, as some of them had used wood boards to stop it, but in vain. Now they saw my way as a permanent solution.

"Smart idea, man," observed a neighbor as I was removing mud from my boots with a twig. He was a small man called Harold with graying whiskers. He waved at the lakeside. "But a tough job."

Harold worked at the General Motors plant in Doraville. Unlike the other neighbors, he wouldn't bother about his shore.

By then the roadside construction was over, so the other homeowners had to buy rocks for their projects. Truckloads of granite were shipped to their yards, and soon their watersides turned bluish. My shore was variegated brown, built of scavenged boulders and mismatched rocks. To everyone's amazement, these small new banks not only stopped the erosion but also brightened the appearance of the lake, especially when viewed from the opposite shore.

Back in China, I had been a college instructor and had never had decent housing; my wife and I had lived in a room in a dorm belonging to a food research institute where my father worked after he retired from the army. That confining experience instilled in us an obsession with houses. Even though we had just bought ours, we kept looking at others. At the time, the whole of Georgia had only four million inhabitants and there was plenty of land. Home construction was going on everywhere, even in the wintertime. Once a week my wife and I would drive around and look at new homes. "Those are cheap," she would say about a group of frame houses with wood siding. To us, a brick house was always superior to a wood one. We inspected the materials used for the homes and discovered that the blood-red Georgian bricks were harder and heavier than those made in the Northeast, thanks to the native red clay.

We would also go inside some of the houses, since they were never locked. What is the good of that? we often wondered about the cathedral-ceilinged living rooms. What a waste of space. Instead of such a big fancy room, it would be much better to have two extra bedrooms upstairs. I couldn't figure out why the first floors were supported by plywood box girders and the second floors by solid wood. My wife, a mathematician, said the plywood box girders were actually stronger, but I was not convinced. Most of the houses, priced under $200,000, were well built, with four bedrooms, a large living room, a two-car garage, and a brick façade. Some people purchased their own lots and customized their mansions. Even those usually cost less than $250,000.

On the way back to our house we would stop at one or two farmers' markets, which sold all kinds of produce. This was the first time I ever saw fingered citrons, donut peaches, purslanes, sea mushrooms, amaranth, wild chives, and even cactus pads for sale. Near our neighborhood, on Lawrenceville Highway, there was a small Cherokee farmers' market, selling mainly local produce, and we often went there to buy boiled peanuts and green corn, fresh and hot from the pot. Nearby were other small shops: a family-owned hardware store, a barbecue shack, a one man barbershop. When there was no hair to cut, the barber, a taciturn, stalwart figure, would sit in a chair outside the door, smoking a pipe and watching traffic. I liked shopping at those small stores, whose owners, while handing back change, would say, "Appreciate your business, sir. Come back again."

Another obsession that had grown out of my childhood privation was bibliomania. Soon after I came to the United States, as a graduate student, in 1985, I decided to bring back to China a personal library, partly because I had never had access to a public library growing up. So I began buying books, and in two years I had collected more than forty boxes. Having no room for them in the small apartment where my wife and I had landed in Somerville, Massachusetts, I persuaded my landlord to rent me, for sixty-five dollars a month, an attic storage room. But after the Tiananmen massacre, my wife and I decided to stay in the United States, and my project for a personal library was abandoned. We didn't even know where we would live in the future, so my wife urged me to get rid of the books. I took a few boxes to local stores and libraries, but nobody wanted them. They were too specialized. Who among general readers could read Pindar's *Victory Songs* in the Greek or Akhmatova's *Complete Poems* in the Russian? I couldn't (and still cannot), but I dreamed of someday having the leisure to learn the languages. No way out, I began to throw my library away, two or three boxes a week. For a long time afterward I felt as miserable as if I were ill.

Even so, I didn't stop collecting books. By 1993, I had two dozen boxes, most of which I stored in a garage and later took to Georgia with me.

Now that we had our own house and I was teaching full time, my bibliomania raged beyond bounds. I bought bookshelves and set them up—more than a dozen against two walls in the living room, six in my study, five in the pantry. New books were expensive; still, I bought a lot of them for my teaching and writing. The public libraries in Gwinnett County had an odd custom of discarding any book that had not been checked out for a year. They would ship these books to a warehouse on Five Forks Trickum Road (which connects the old mail-stop Five Forks and the Mountain Park area, formerly known as Trickum) and hold an annual sale, letting them go for a dime a copy. The first time I went to the book sale I bought four boxes.

On my way to work, a sixteen-mile drive, I would pass five Goodwill stores, all run by churches, and each the size of a supermarket. They all had book sections. I never came across a yard sale or garage sale in Georgia. Instead, people would donate what they could no longer use to Goodwill. They had sections for furniture, clothing, appliances, books, toys, artworks, even jewelry. I would stop at one or two of those stores on my way home and search through the stacks of books. Over the years I got many windfalls, among them *The Word Finder*, the best reference book for English collocations but long out of print, and first editions of *For Whom the Bell Tolls*, *The Heart of the Matter*, and *Beloved*. I cared more about usefulness than rarity, so a useful book, bought for a quarter, would thrill me more than a first edition.

My wife often complained that I was cluttering our house, but I simply couldn't stop building my library. I told her I needed the books for teaching.

Churches were a major power in Georgia. Advertisements for Bible studies were everywhere. Some of them were just a large portrait of Jesus Christ, occasionally with words on them, such as, "What Have You Told Others About Me?" or, "Come, Now Is the Time to Follow My Path." Every week, seminarians in black suits and ties would show up at our door to read out a few verses from the New Testament and try to convert us. Some of them were black teenage boys. They would carry the Bible and say, "Can I share some of our Lord's words with you, sir?" I would listen to them read, but couldn't yield to their persuasions.

On my way to work, I would also pass two Christian bookstores, both of which carried thousands of titles, including various concordances to the major translations of the Bible. My friend Bruce Covey managed a religious bookstore on the Emory campus, which was part of a chain owned by the Methodist church. He agreed to help me find work at one of these Methodist bookstores if I was denied tenure.

The Bible was vital to my writing in those years. I was isolated, and had to figure out how to proceed as a writer. As an English professor, I dared not ask my colleagues about English usage, styles, and idioms; and I wouldn't share my writing with others, afraid it might be marred by solecisms. I had to learn to be self-sufficient. I began to dip into the Bible, and found that the prose differed from version to version, stylistically. I liked the fluidity of the New International Version, the rigor of the New King James Version, the lucidity of Today's English Version, the freshness of the New Century Version. I also bought the exhaustive concordances to the major versions of the Bible—well-bound tomes, eleven by nine inches in size, each more than a thousand pages thick. Whenever I was unsure of a phrase or a collocation, I would look it up in the concordances to see how it was used in the Scriptures.

Every day when I was at work on my second short story collection, *Under the Red Flag*, I read the New International Version of the Bible, which, as a supreme model of neutral English, contributed to the fluidity of the prose in that collection. I sent the manuscript to the University of Georgia Press, in 1996, and it won the Flannery O'Connor Prize for Short Fiction. Soon after being informed of the award, I received the edited manuscript from Charles East, an accomplished short story writer and the series editor. He had written two and a half pages of suggestions for changes and corrections. I felt so embarrassed that I called him to apologize, saying I had done my best to polish the manuscript and was sorry there were still so many things to be fixed.

He chuckled. "To tell you the truth, this is the first time I've given less than ten pages of suggestions for a book in the series." For me that was a turning point, as I realized that I could produce a presentable book manuscript on my own. This step toward self-sufficiency came because my life in Georgia had made me turn to the Bible.

In retrospect, my nine years in Georgia were crucial to me as a beginning writer. Isolation forced me to be detached and to concentrate, and kept my mind sensitive to things around me. Every day, when taking a break from writing, I would stroll alone around the lake with a cane to keep away aggressive dogs. The subdivision had no sidewalks, so I always walked on the left-hand side of the streets, facing traffic. Occasionally I would stop to watch some older men fishing on the opposite shore. Some of them were Eastern European immigrants and couldn't speak a word of English. On weekdays the neighborhood was very quiet, as children had gone to school and their parents to work, and I ambled alone. Many ideas and plans for my later books were thought out on those walks, and many confusions were clarified after long reflections. Before moving to Georgia, I had never understood why Robert Bly once said that poets needed loneliness to nourish their art. Now, in this small town in the Peach State, I had finally learned to be alone and accept solitude as my working condition.

I no longer live there now. Since 2002 I've been back in Massachusetts. But not long ago my wife and I drove down to our first real home. To our dismay, our former neighborhood had changed, becoming subdued, as if in a torpor; even the waterfowl in the lake were no longer loud and lusty, and the water was greenish, not as clear as before. Perhaps there had been a long drought, or perhaps our feelings for this place had changed. Deep down I felt as if there was a barrier between me and that little piece of land where we had once lived. We stood at the lakeside for a long time, gazing from a distance at the rock bank, the tall maples and sweet gums, the clumps of elephant ears, and the sloping backyard planted with two half circles of monkey grass. All of it had once belonged to us, but now the place felt drab and exhausted. Maybe this was due, in part, to the Wal-Mart that had recently opened nearby. With the appearance of the big department store, many small businesses had disappeared—the one-man barbershop, the family-owned hardware store, the barbecue shack, the Cherokee farmers' market, even one of the Goodwill stores, all were gone.

I realized that we might have left our former abode in time. For my family, home can be built anywhere.

HAWAII

CAPITAL Honolulu (on O'ahu)

ENTERED UNION 1959 (50th)

ORIGIN OF NAME Uncertain. The islands may have been named by Hawai'i Loa, their traditional discoverer. Or they may have been named after Hawai'i or Hawaiki, the traditional home of the Polynesians.

NICKNAME Aloha State

MOTTO Ua Mau ke Ea o ka 'Āina i ka Pono ("The life of the land is perpetuated in righteousness")

RESIDENTS Hawaiian, also *kama 'āina* (native-born nonethnic Hawaiian), and *malihini* (newcomer)

U.S. REPRESENTATIVES 2

STATE BIRD nēnē (Hawaiian goose)

STATE FLOWER hibiscus (yellow)

STATE TREE kukui (candlenut)

STATE SONG "Hawai'i Pono'i"

LAND AREA 6,423 sq. mi.

GEOGRAPHIC CENTER Between islands of Hawai'i and Maui

POPULATION 1,275,194

WHITE 24.3%

BLACK 1.8%

AMERICAN INDIAN 0.3%

ASIAN 41.6%;

NATIVE HAWAIIAN AND OTHER PACIFIC ISLANDER 9.4%

HISPANIC/LATINO 7.2%

UNDER 18 24.4%

65 AND OVER 13.3%

MEDIAN AGE 36.2

HAWAII
Tara Bray Smith

I could see it when I looked west from Polihale beach at sunset, curtained by golden–pink clouds: the forbidden island. Eighteen miles across the Kaulakahi Channel from Kaua'i, seventeen miles long and six wide, dry, low-lying, and—except for the Native Hawaiians who lived there and the Robinson brothers who owned it—completely off-limits to visitors. The island of Ni'ihau was forbidden, the Robinsons owned it, and they were my cousins. Sort of. My mother was the wayward daughter of a plantation family that both hated and prided itself on being *haole*—white—and once-important, and while we still had some land, it was on the dry, west side of Kaua'i, without a good beach. So we claimed other families as our own. The Robinsons were cousins through marriage. My mother must have told me this, and I repeated it as often as I could.

Once I told a teacher's aide. We were on a school bus, on a field trip to Salt Pond, which was dry and historical but had nice sand. (Hawaiians made *'alae*, red sea salt, here, the kind that Cook traded iron for when he first anchored off nearby Waimea in 1778.)

"I'm related to the Robinsons, you know."

Not eve n a teacher—a teacher's aide. I remember her as bored, long haired, not attached to me or to anything else on the bus. She pretended not to hear.

"They're my cousins."

Bragging is *shame*: the Hawaiian equivalent of losing face, probably brought over by Japanese sugar workers in the 1880s, along with *sashimi* and taking one's slippers off outside the house. Calling the Robinsons relatives was no small claim. Hawaii at the end of its plantation era was a provincial place, and Kaua'i, where I lived, was even smaller, dominated by the names of missionary families that had, as the old joke went, come to do good and ended up doing well. But although my great-grandparents lived on a plantation in Waimea, sugar was almost finished by the time I grew up ("the unions!") and my family, Norwegians who'd arrived in the late 1800s, had gotten in the game late and could only secure a lease on their sugar acreage. Real "children of the land"—*kama'aina*—were supposed to breakfast barefoot at the Outrigger and own a sailing canoe. Only my grandmother was a member of the club, and none of us kids had a tab.

Maybe the Robinsons did; I don't know. They kept to themselves. "Ni'ihau leans back firmly," the saying goes, a reference to its position furthest west in the chain of Hawaiian islands, and also to its historic isolation. Only 600 people lived on the island in 1864, when Elizabeth McHutcheson Sinclair, a Scottish emigrant by way of New Zealand, bought it from the Hawaiian crown for $10,000 in gold. The family was severely private. Even the Native Hawaiians who lived on Ni'ihau weren't supposed to talk: "The Ni'ihau people . . . are, legally, our guests," Keith Robinson, heir of Elizabeth Sinclair, wrote in a 1997 op-ed in the *Honolulu Star-Bulletin*:

> Unlike tenants, they pay no rent and there are no formal contractual obligations. For private reasons of our own, we have for decades given those guests free but revocable privileges that are probably far greater than those allowed by any other landowner in America. They are given free housing. They also have unlimited supplies of free mutton and pork, and beef is available to them at prices far below what the general public pays. . . . They have free hunting, fishing, camping, and sightseeing access to every part of a relatively unspoiled private island—probably the only place in all Hawai'i and maybe even the entire United States where this occurs. We have carefully maintained the privacy of their community, and also have not permitted the kind of immigration and settlement that has submerged and destroyed the Hawaiian language and culture everywhere else in Hawai'i. . . . To put it bluntly, I don't know any other landowner anywhere in the United States who does nearly as much for guests as we do.

Today Ni'ihau is the largest private island in the world. Around 150 people officially live there, though the actual population is smaller. (Many Ni'ihau families reside on the west side of Kaua'i, in the town of Kekaha, or on O'ahu, in the beachside communities of Wai'anae and Nanakuli, where Ni'ihau's most famous son, singer Israel Kamakawiwo'ole, grew up.) All, except for Keith and Bruce Robinson, Ni'ihau's heirs, are of nearly pure Hawaiian descent, and the island is off-limits to visitors beyond the state-mandated access to shoreline. It is a seclusion that has lasted almost a hundred years, since Aubrey Robinson, a nephew of the original owner, prohibited steamboats from landing in 1915, and it is a striking, if not disturbing, arrangement. The residents of Ni'ihau agree to follow a sober, moral lifestyle as defined by the family (no drinking, cigarette smoking, or taking drugs).

They agree not to talk—about the land, the Robinsons, or the radar first installed on the island in the 1940s as part of what has become the Pacific Missile Range Facility at Barking Sands on Kaua'i, testing ground for America's expanding missile defense program. Ni'ihauans rely on the Robinsons' boat, barge, and helicopter to get to Kaua'i, sometimes paying for their air travel by bartering valuable Ni'ihau shell *lei*, jewelry made from the island's abundant and tiny *kahelelani* shells. (The barge comes once a week, depending on weather, to bring food, supplies, and water—the island collects less than seven inches a year—while the helicopter travels several times a week for tourist trips and as necessary for medical emergencies.) Up until the early 1940s Ni'ihau was isolated enough not to know when Pearl Harbor was bombed, though O'ahu is less than two hundred miles away. This allowed for a strange bit of history known as the Ni'ihau incident, whereby a Japanese fighter pilot named Shigenori Nishikaichi, heading back toward his aircraft carrier from the attack on Pearl Harbor, crash landed on the island, proceeding, with the help of two of Ni'ihau's four Japanese residents, to take the entire island hostage. Aylmer Robinson, Aubrey's son, was on Kaua'i at the time. A group of Hawaiians, led by a heroic man named Bene Kanahele, eventually killed the Japanese pilot, despite the fact that Kanahele had been shot and that the pilot was in possession of the island's only gun. Kanahele's companion, a woman named Aunty 'Ela, smashed the head of one of Nishikaichi's accomplices with a rock, killing him. The third Japanese man committed suicide. It has been theorized that the report of the Ni'ihau incident led, in part, to the American internment of Japanese under Roosevelt, though Hawai'i's *Nissei*, for the most part, were not interned, as they were needed for labor on the sugar plantations.

"Life on Ni'ihau isn't like it is on any other of the Hawaiian Islands," Elama Kanahele recalls in a collection of oral histories, *Aloha Niihau*. "There is no hospital on Ni'ihau and no doctor. We leave everything up to God, even our very lives." The island has no running water, no telephones (cell phones are not allowed, though Kaua'i's towers often yield a signal), no Internet; power is provided by generators and solar panels, and houses in Pu'uwai village—the word *pu'uwai* means heart—are often lit by gas lamps at night. Only the Robinsons have indoor plumbing. The sheep and cattle ranch that provided employment for generations has closed; a few Hawaiians are involved in the special ops training that the military sometimes runs on the island, but most subsist on government money. While the Robinsons run their helicopter tours weekly, and occasionally host two-day hunting safaris, Ni'ihauans only rarely interact with visitors, and then usually only to sell shell *lei*. Since there is no money on the island, tourists must pay the helicopter's pilot. The Robinsons later distribute the proceeds as goods.

A rare resident lives past sixty; there is still one part-Japanese man who is somewhere around eighty-five. Though Ni'ihauans are American citizens, with Social Security numbers, birth certificates, and passports—if they choose—they are also residents of a private island. If they leave, they may not be able to return. About half of every generation stays, maybe less. Since there are, at most, a hundred or so people who reside on Ni'ihau at any one time, in fifty years the island will probably be empty, denuded by the starving wild boar, sheep, and cattle that are descended from Mother Sinclair's original stable.

Or not. Maybe it will become a state park. Perhaps it will be developed. Ni'ihau is quiet and beautiful and "unspoiled," if unspoiled means no hotels or timeshares or big box stores, though plastic washes up here as it does everywhere. (The garbage dump of the world, a nearby vortex of currents called the North Pacific Gyre, is estimated to contain concentrations of plastic *greater than three million pieces per square kilometer.*) The island's fate is entirely in the Robinsons' hands, but since both Bruce and Keith are in their sixties, it would be more accurate to say that it is in the hands of Bruce's children. Two from a first marriage live on the mainland. Four are half-Hawaiian by a Ni'ihau woman. They live mostly on Kaua'i.

So Ni'ihau is the Hawai'i of Hawai'i, or was, back when telling someone you were from Hawai'i made their eyes glassy. I have been to the island twice, the first time with my father, in 1980, when I was ten. We were guests of an adventurous Aussie named Doug Arnott, who, on the pretext of diving in the underwater crater of nearby Lehua Rock, swung us close to the island's southern end, just outside the reef, where he encouraged my father and me and another couple to swim in to have a look around.

Maybe we spent an hour there. The day was so crammed with the classic features of adventure (Doug carried a spear gun when we went snorkeling, in case of sharks) that I have a hard time remembering what the experience actually felt like. We beachcombed. We found a human skull—many skulls, actually. The Ni'ihauans buried their dead in the dunes near the beach, my father told me, and I remember particularly a child's skull, small as a grapefruit. Did I reach for it? To touch a bone, especially a Hawaiian one, disturbs its *mana*, the life force Hawaiians believe inhabits all things.

Over the crest of another small dune, the couple farther ahead gathered lobsters from the reef. My father and I searched for Japanese green-glass fishing floats. We were trespassers, where we were was forbidden, nearly magical in its isolation, *yet I was related*.

When there was a shout from the couple—"The Hawaiians are coming! The Hawaiians are coming!"—my father did not wait for me. He took the only pair of fins, ran into the water, and started swimming back to the boat, an eighth of a mile offshore. I followed him, of course. Today I would have been terrified: not of the Hawaiians, though the fear in that shout was real, but of the ocean. Sharks had gathered under the boat while we were on shore; the Australian had been cleaning fish we'd caught off Lehua Rock, and the blood had attracted them.

Onboard, we watched "the Hawaiians" in their Vietnam-era Jeep, probably the only car on the island. We had trespassed on their land. Did they think of it as their land? I seem to remember having the sense that their protectiveness was also a form of servitude. They were guarding their property, but also guarding it for someone else. But there they were in the Jeep and, yes, there was the rifle. I saw it through binoculars. I may have asked if they could shoot us from there. No, Doug didn't imagine they could. The way back to Kaua'i was so rough that he wore a motorcycle helmet to protect himself from the crashing waves. The rest of us crouched along the sides of the boat, hunkering under towels, life jackets on.

Hawai'i is America's last state. Growing up there, I liked to think I was as special as the tourists seemed to think I was. The need for this grew as I left, went to college in New Hampshire, and learned that not only did no one really think of us, but also their surprise and delight at my being from Hawai'i was based on a misapprehension of what it was actually like there. The ads had worked. People thought it was paradise. Which of course it was. I cavorted under waterfalls that splashed onto beaches; I saw live volcanoes erupt; I ate bananas, mangoes, and coconuts that I picked out of trees. But Paul Theroux was right when he observed that Hawai'i—"where senior prom was the social event of the year"—reminded him of a Midwestern state, with its delight in high-school football, *American Idol*, and Wal-Mart. We are special and we are just a regular old state, like Ohio (which I used to make fun of—something to do with sunburns) or North Dakota (which I could not even picture). This is a familiar feeling to an American. Are we really just another country in the world, like Paraguay and Mauritania? Of course not. We are a country, yes, but a little more equal.

The private fiefdom that is Ni'ihau encapsulates the problem of all of Hawai'i. When the U.S. acquired the archipelago it acquired its sugar tit, its holiday spot, and the best natural harbor east of Sydney, today able to berth the entire U.S. Pacific Fleet, the largest naval command in the world. "The Hawaiian pear is now fully ripe, and this is the golden hour of the United States to pluck it," John L. Stevens, U.S. minister to Hawai'i, famously wrote on the occasion of Queen Lili'uokalani's overthrow and imprisonment by a sugar-backed junta of white, mostly American, businessmen and politicians in 1893. A year later, a troubled Democratic President Cleveland would write: "Thus it appears that Hawai'i was taken possession of by the United States forces without the consent or wish of the government of the islands, or of anybody else so far as shown, except the United States Minister." But Republican McKinley replaced Cleveland in 1896 and, two years later, the annexation of Cuba, the Philippines, and Guam drew Hawai'i firmly into the fold. It remained a territory for more than sixty years. America had become an empire.

At Camp Smith, up on Halawa Heights overlooking Pearl Harbor, sits the headquarters of PACOM, the biggest unified military command center in the history of the world. Over 60 percent of the Earth's surface, from California to Africa, the Arctic to the Antarctic, and 50 percent of its population—China, North Korea, South Korea, Japan, India, and Russia, as well as their armed forces—is monitored, patrolled, and surveilled by the U.S. Pacific Command. Between now and 2010, 60 percent of America's attack submarine fleet will move from Norfolk, Virginia, and Groton, Connecticut, to here. It's China we're preparing for, of course. This in addition to 7.4 million tourists in 2005, a record. When I drive the upper road from Kona to Waimea on the southernmost Big Island, a road I drove every day to school in ninth grade, rounding the bend under the old Greenwell property I swear I can see LA emerging from the lava plains. The golf courses are greening the black patch by patch, and around them will come the timeshares and housing developments, which need gas stations and Safeways and stoplights. By the ocean, the super-rich live on their private turquoise bays: Microsoft's Paul Allen, Dell's Michael Dell. They've opened the gate down at Kua Bay and made it a public park. I like this. It's beautiful. There are turtles in the water. But man, it's crowded.

Last year I went back to Ni'ihau. I am not sure why: some combination of curiosity and self-reflexive fascination. These were (sort of) my people, this was (not really) my 'aina, my land. Or maybe I wanted to get to the bottom of things but I was too ashamed to ask. So I went on one of the tourist helicopter flights to the same beach my father and I snuck onto back in 1980. It cost $275 per person, including lunch. I went with my ex-stepmother, Debbie. My father had died surfing the year before; if he were alive maybe I would have gone with him.

The trip was uneventful: a beautiful beach that might have been anywhere in Hawai'i, with the junk-a-lunk concrete block sun shelter, the sheep skull perched on a rock, the long dunes, the lava rock tide pools, and the sunbleached plastic trash—though the sand, I found, was deeper and the water did seem cleaner. The sun was very hot; the island was dry and covered with mesquite. I found a perfect cowry. I found 'opihi, the black-and-white cone-shaped limpet good for eating. I lay in the sand and covered myself, and fell asleep when the clouds came. I thought about my father. I didn't even try to imagine what life was like here. It felt impossible—though this, too, seems like a failure of empathy. We ate lunch and got ready to leave. No one came down to the landing to trade shell *lei* that day, but Mr. and Mrs. Teixeira, our traveling companions from Las Vegas, did find the skeleton of a dolphin in a tide pool. Mostly I liked the ride there and back, over land that I knew. The Robinsons still own almost 45,000 acres in Makaweli and Olokele Valley on Kaua'i's west side, six thousand of which is planted in sugar, some of the last in the state. There's a plan to build an ethanol plant there now. My great-great-grandfather's plantation used to be just down the road.

"All these kids nowadays have no idea what it smells like," Debbie said as we approached, and it's true. Burning sugar fields smell like caramel, but processing is mustier, with notes of rotten fruit and spit-up; to us it's familiar and country.

The one time I saw a Robinson in the flesh was at a family lu'au in 1998. A great-great-great-uncle had married the original settler's daughter, it turned out. Keith Robinson was as I had pictured him, a tough, ascetic man, with a faded cotton shirt and a defined jaw—a kind of human version of one of the pale blue, two-cent Missionary stamps, sent between Hawai'i and New England in the 1850s and considered among the most valuable in the world. My memory dresses him in *palaka*, the checkered cloth the plantation stores sold. Sun-speckled and graying, he showed us the flowers he was trying to seed, a personal project to bring back from near-extinction many of the endemics that had almost perished in the never-ending stream of foreign plants and animals that come to Hawai'i, making these islands the home of the largest number of endangered species in the United States. On a tray lay a wilted white hibiscus with a scarlet stamen, *Koki'o ke'oke'o*, or *Hibiscus waimeae*, more delicate than the military-red hibiscus often associated with the state. He passed the tray around. It was twilight. He told us to smell it. It's one of the few hibiscuses that has a fragrance, he said. In Eden nothing must have smelled very strong.

Next to it was a red flower, also wilted, but larger: the *Kokia cookei*. It was the last we'd see of the plant, he told us, one of the rarest in the world. At the time, he had been working on propagating it and other Hawaiian endemics at an undisclosed location, far up in Olokele Valley. I have seen the *Kokia cookei* just that once, but I know the *Koki'o ke'oke'o*; I have several of its cousins on my porch in Germany, where I live now, distantly related to this species that found its way to the most isolated group of islands in the world, dropped its seeds, and stayed. Endemic, from there and nowhere else. Like its more common cousins, the *Koki'o ke'oke'o* lives for exactly one day, doesn't close until afternoon, and then, on or off the stem, in or out of water, it dies.

IDAHO

CAPITAL Boise

ENTERED UNION 1890 (43rd)

ORIGIN OF NAME An invented name whose meaning is
   unknown; possibly derived from a Shoshonean greeting
   meaning "good morning"

NICKNAME Gem State

MOTTO Esto perpetua ("It is forever")

RESIDENTS Idahoan

U.S. REPRESENTATIVES 2

STATE BIRD mountain bluebird

STATE FLOWER syringa

STATE TREE white pine

STATE SONG "Here We Have Idaho"

LAND AREA 82,747 sq. mi.

GEOGRAPHIC CENTER In Custer Co., at Custer,
   SW of Challis

POPULATION 1,429,096

WHITE 91.0%

BLACK 0.4%

AMERICAN INDIAN 1.4%

ASIAN 0.9%

HISPANIC/LATINO 7.9%

UNDER 18 28.5%

65 AND OVER 11.3%

MEDIAN AGE 33.2

IDAHO
Anthony Doerr

Winter in the mountains of central Idaho and the snow has let up. A slim horn of moon hangs in the gap between two peaks. I zip up my sleeping bag, pull on mittens.

It's maybe twenty degrees. The lake I'm camped beside is just beginning to freeze—paper-thin sheets of ice are interlocking above the shallows. The clouds have peeled away. The sky travels through a long spectrum of purples.

Everything seems poised to become something else. Silhouettes of trees on the ridgelines might become men; boulders might stand and stretch and slink away. I am at 7,800 feet, five miles from a road, forty miles from a town, and yet here come whispers, six or seven syllables, carrying across the water.

I blink into the dimness. My heart roars. The lake I'm camped beside is still. The mountains glow. Nothing. No one.

Welcome to Idaho. We have ten major rivers, eighteen ski resorts, and fifteen people per square mile. We have hidden valleys where the wind pours through seams of aspens and makes a sound in the leaves exactly like the sound of rain falling on a pond. We have forests where the growing season is so short that fifty-year-old trees are only four feet tall, and get so rimed with ice in January that they look like gardens of oversized, glittering cauliflower. We also have an escalating methamphetamine crisis, looming water disputes, massive agribusiness feedlots, and hour-long lines to eat dinner at The Cheesecake Factory.

Forget tourist brochures, forget airbrushed photos of sunsets, forget travel magazine spreads of fly-fishermen at dawn casting into a smoking bend of Silver Creek. Idaho is bigger than eighty Rhode Islands and most of its boundaries are entirely arbitrary. Some parts get hardly any snow and some get eight feet. Vast stretches of the state are arid and yet inside these borders are almost 16,000 miles of rivers.

In January you can stand in a polo shirt outside a Starbucks in Boise and call somebody in Madagascar on a cellular telephone while 150 miles away a mountain goat stands on a mountaintop in the River of No Return looking down over an unbroken desert of snow twenty feet deep. Nothing I will ever write could do this place justice.

A mong the quantities of peoples and tribes who have traveled, slept, and died in the topographical anomaly that is presently called Idaho, among the twelve thousand years of their successive, unknowable generations, the great bulk of them marking time in ways we would only vaguely understand, was a small group of people who lived in the sprawling mountains surrounding the Salmon River.

They've been known by lots of names: Tukudeka, Sheepeaters, Toyani, Snakes, Arrow Makers. There probably weren't ever more than a couple of thousand of them. They lived in caves, in clefts in the rocks, and in wickiups made of sticks. They wore snowshoes in winter, and their furs were expertly tanned. Sometimes, supposedly, they hunted while wearing the decapitated heads of animals. Their bows, painstakingly crafted by heating and laminating sections of sheep horn, were renowned: One witness describes one of these bows sending an obsidian-tipped arrow through a nine-inch pine tree at a distance of fifteen paces.

That any human beings raised children in this rugged, shattered country, so close to timberline, stupefies me. In winter, the temperature rarely climbs above freezing and it's not uncommon for trees to snap in the cold. Summer is no picnic, either: not with bears and cougars, thunderstorms and forest fires; not with insects rising from the meadows in huge, throbbing clouds.

These people, these Tukudeka, have been called hermits, skulkers, and scavengers. A party of explorers who encountered them in 1819 described them as "truly wild men of the mountains . . . dressed in sheepskin garments, living among rocks in caves." The 1937 *WPA Guide to Idaho* called them "wily and treacherous, though cowardly."

I'd call them old-school, bad-ass. Intrepid. Remarkable. I'd say they were more involved in the natural world than any of us could ever hope to be.

A whirlwind history: In 1805, when Sacagawea led Lewis and Clark into what is now called Idaho, the explorers found legions of beavers. Back in Europe, top hats made of felt were getting unreasonably popular. And guess which kind of animal fur makes the best hat felt?

For the next forty years, fur trappers slew Idaho's animals by the hundreds of thousands. In one season in the 1830s, the Hudson's Bay Company recorded taking eighty thousand beavers from the Snake River.

On the heels of trappers were missionaries, and on the heels of missionaries were settlers. By the mid 1840s, by the time fashionable Europeans preferred hats made of silk, the Snake River had become a "fur desert" and an east-west highway called the Oregon Trail had been established.

One by one, the people whose ancestors had been hunting, fishing, and digging up roots in this country for centuries were displaced, excluded, or eliminated. By the middle of the nineteenth century, of Idaho's original tribes, only the Tukudeka, with their hunting dogs and rabbit-skin blankets and year-round snows, could have remained fairly isolated.

But in 1862, prospectors found gold in the Boise Basin. Dozens of strikes were made. Boomtowns sprouted like mushrooms. Soon gold-seekers were working up every creek in every mountain range, no matter how inaccessible.

Meanwhile diseases carried by domestic sheep were decimating native herds of bighorn. Smallpox was doing the same to native humans. Survivors were being relocated systematically. When they resisted, they were forced off their land.

It's a familiar story: emigrants, eager to let livestock graze the camas meadows, depicted native people as bloodthirsty terrorists. Native people, hungry, desperate, watching cows and hogs chew up roots their families depended on for generations, said they were only protecting their way of life.

The summer of 1877 saw the Nez Percé War. The summer of 1878 saw the Bannock War. Subduing troublesome Indians became an American machinery unto itself. Military careers depended on it. Merchants in Boise were said to dread the prospects of a peaceful summer.

By the beginning of 1879, the Tukudeka had been decimated by illness, their primary source of food was vanishing, and their ancient hunting grounds had been invaded by armed prospectors. How many Tukudeka could have been left, maybe thirty or forty families? They still dressed in hides, wove baskets, and cooked in clay pots. They still fitted their weapons with stone points. They were, perhaps, the last Native Americans in the contiguous United States to live in a way their ancestors would immediately recognize.

And yet they had to know what was coming. In February of 1879, five Chinese miners were found murdered in an abandoned town twenty-three miles north of present-day Stanley. Not long afterward, two white ranchers were found dead on the south fork of the Salmon River. In both instances, the Tukudeka, accused of harboring renegades from previous Indian wars, were blamed. Settlers roared for protection.

So on the last day of May, Troop G, First Cavalry, soldiers of the United States Army, rode out from Boise to hunt down the last free-roaming native people in Idaho. The cavalcade did not have an easy time of it. Swollen creeks swept away mules and horses. They were assailed by lightning, snow, and hail; their animals were plagued by wood ticks and mosquitoes. Seemingly every day a mule pitched off a precipice and tumbled hundreds of feet into a rocky drainage.

It wasn't until mid-August, 79 days after leaving Boise, that the soldiers in Troop G saw any real traces of their quarry: several empty wickiups, one of which had some firewood stacked beside it.

Two days later, reinforced by several dozen mounted infantrymen, they climbed to a diamond-shaped expanse of sawgrass and sagebrush, hemmed in by mountains, that is now a backcountry airstrip called Soldier Bar. There, at the base of a rocky slope, their scouts found a hastily evacuated camp. There were 10 wickiups, buckskin, beads, blankets, pots, and pans.

Among the cavalrymen of Troop G was a private named Edgar Hoffner, a novel-reading, pipe-smoking cavalryman who kept a daily diary. "We turned our horses out after getting to this camp, to await developments," he wrote. "Gathered up every thing that we could find and consigned it to the flames."

So casual! So nonchalant! How do things get to the point where a person would think so little of burning the possessions of eight or nine families?

When you look for evil in an individual person, though, you'll almost never find it. In his diary, Hoffner is often funny, often wistful. He misses home; he gets in snowball fights with other soldiers; he pines "for a cottage by the sea, for a cabin in the wood." When he has no food, he says he eats "wind pudding" for supper. Indeed, when he's not burning the possessions of Tukudeka families, Private Hoffner behaves much as any of my friends might in similar circumstances, if my friends were better with horses and significantly tougher about missing meals. He is kind to his fellow soldiers; he manages to keep a sense of humor in any weather.

And what about the settlers who demanded the Tukudeka be brought in? Isn't it folly to judge them, too? They lived deep in snowed-in valleys in houses they had built by hand: purlin roofs, log walls, cold decanting through cracks and knotholes. The wind-wracked faces of big mountains stared down at them all day. And maybe once a year some utterly foreign man emerged from the snows in animal furs with a few possessions tied to the back of a dog? Surely that'd be enough to make any of us sleep with a shotgun under the bed.

All their lives they'd pumped each other full of terrible stories: Indians were attacking wagon trains and burning children in front of their mothers; Indians were ruthless and inhuman assassins. By the late nineteenth century, the Tukudeka were probably more legend than reality, anyway; they were yetis, sylphs, bogeymen. Anything happened—a rancher was murdered, a horse was stolen, a pie disappeared off a windowsill—and who were you going to blame?

It's snowing; it's freezing cold; you wrap your sleeping children in blankets and listen to the wind pour off the mountains. You think: The winter, the darkness, the fastness beyond my front door—it's populated.

On the morning of August 20, 1879, squads of cavalrymen started up the steep inclines surrounding Soldier Bar. Twenty men stayed behind with the pack train as a rear guard. By the time the riders were five miles away, they heard gunfire. They sprinted back, many on foot, as the slopes were too steep for horses. There had been an ambush. One of the men in the rear guard was shot through both legs and soon died.

That night the soldiers went to sleep in the grass at intervals of ten feet, clothes on, carbines loaded.

"The hostiles," wrote Private Hoffner, "have signal fires on the mountains on two sides of us."

More and more lately, I am haunted by that night. Twin fires burn on the mountainsides. Six dozen cavalrymen—panicky, keyed up, pissed off—lay down to sleep in the grass. They had just buried a comrade and they were nearly out of food.

Above them on the rocky slopes, maybe forty or fifty Tukudeka—toddlers, adolescents, women, men—tried to keep the babies quiet. They were among the last of their people, among the last free native people in the entire United States. The Civil War was over, Edison had invented the phonograph, and these people were still living outside, still making their homes in what any of us would call the middle of nowhere.

Maybe they were scared; maybe they were furious; maybe they were resigned. Probably they were hungry. Probably there were some refugee Bannocks or Nez Percé with them, men who had so far avoided the reservation, men who had rifles, men who had known little in their lives besides deracination and subjugation.

It'd be another couple of hours until dawn. If it was clear, the Milky Way would have been huge and dazzling, a sleeve of light draped across the sky. And in all that immensity, there was *nowhere* for the Tukudeka to go, no retreat, no quarter, the world had left them behind, somehow they had become strange and wrong, scattered amongst the hills, and everything was on the line: their idioms, their legends, their ancestors, their kids.

Maybe they slept; maybe one or two managed to forget their situation long enough to whisper to each other and smile, before the crystalline night reasserted itself and their aches and injuries came back and they were reminded again of the soldiers camped in the field below, bent on chasing them down.

One hundred and twenty-eight years later, I'm camped beside an alpine lake in December, not terribly far from Soldier Bar. For me nothing is more compelling in this country than the night skies: On winter nights the stars flicker white and red and blue, twisting and glittering in their places. In the same moment they can seem both astonishingly close and impossibly far away. This is not typically comforting: You feel the size of the Earth beneath your back, which is massive enough to hold all of its cities and oceans and creatures in the sway of its gravity, and on the far side of the Earth is the sun, 300,000 times more massive than the Earth, and slowly your thoughts begin to bump up against the enormity of the Milky Way, in which our entire solar system is merely a mote.

I close my eyes; I think of the brook trout in the lake beside me, quick and sleek, little sleeves of muscle suspended in the black water, their fins and bellies fringed with orange, their backs aswarm with patterns. The snowy peaks gleam in the moonlight. In a few days this lake will be frozen over, and I wonder if the fish turn up their eyes, if they watch the lights traveling through the sky, if they sense that this could be the last time they will be able to see them.

There are claims the Tukudeka may have been a distinct cultural group for one thousand years. Some of the sites they used suggest a cultural continuity that stretches back as far as eight thousand years. But by August 1879, there were only a few families left, trying to get some sleep among the rocks.

A December night in 2007. An August night in 1879. Between me and them stretches an abyss, the automobile and the airplane, penicillin and the microchip, plastic furniture and space travel. Did the Tukudeka understand how fragile memory can be? Did they bury their memories on the hillsides around them, hoping someday someone might return to dig them back up?

"The conquest of the earth," wrote Joseph Conrad, "which mostly means the taking it away from those who have a different complexion or slightly flatter noses than ourselves, is not a pretty thing when you look into it too much."

Territory and gold, civilization versus wilderness, Rome versus the barbarians. Out of the history of Idaho come the whispers of the Tukudeka; comes Private Edgar Hoffner with his tobacco and rifle; come the relentless brooms of progress.

Fifty-one Native Americans from that area eventually surrendered to the United States Army in October of 1879. The following year, they were moved to the Fort Hall reservation, a good 200 miles from the Salmon River country. Whoever remained in the folds of the mountains might have hidden there another ten years. But the Indian Wars were over, and the last of Idaho's tribes had been relocated.

The Northern Pacific laid rails across the panhandle in 1882 and the Union Pacific sewed up the southern part of the Territory in 1884. In 1890, Idaho became a state.

Even to neighboring tribes, some historians say, the Tukudeka had seemed like druids, gnomes, elves. They were blamed for bad luck and big storms and lost objects. They were the Old Way, the hard way, the unknowable. They lived a life that was hard to believe.

Sometimes, in the winter, I stop at an intersection in Boise and watch the sleet coming down in slow sheets, raking across the foothills, all browns and whites, the cars splashing past around me—even the trees looking miserable, dormant, waiting, uncomfortable—and I think: Thank God I don't have to sleep outside tonight.

And Idaho? Many of the places the Tukudeka knew are still here: cold green forks of rivers and here-and-there copses of cottonwoods and great broken slopes of volcanic scree aglow with lichen, and clouds like vast men-of-war dragging tentacles of rain across the ridgelines. Idaho still has the most roadless land in the Lower 48 and the largest single designated wilderness area, too. We have two gorges deeper than the Grand Canyon. We have sagebrush prowled by skinny foxes with the pilfered eggs of songbirds clamped gingerly in their teeth, and whole hillsides skittering with grasshoppers the color of straw.

Every life here, no matter how sequestered, no matter how impounded, is still informed by the land, for better or worse. And that for me is what Idaho continues to be about, this territory, this state, this country, the stripe of the Milky Way printed across a velvet sky, and the silhouettes of mountains strobing in and out of view during lightning storms.

I live here because, even if I only have one afternoon, a few hours between obligations, I can ride a bike up into the hills above Boise, into cooler, more watered places, where wildflowers color the hillsides and the remains of old burns are still plain—the great blackened skeletons of sentinel ponderosa, granite blocks half-tumbled on the hillsides, spring creeks carving through the gulches. After twenty minutes of pedaling, the city of Boise will be far enough below that its features will have faded and become a wide green blur, bedded between mountain ranges, a haze over it, maybe the first evening lights winking on.

The history of our planet is one of absolutely relentless change. Everything—mammoths, short-faced bears, western camels—eventually goes extinct. For about two million years, every August, tens of thousands of salmon poured into the rivers of Idaho. Redfish Lake, 900 miles from the Pacific, supposedly turned crimson with sockeyes. Last summer, only four fish made it back, and they were born in a hatchery. And there's no reason to think it won't happen to us, too; that, someday, some final band of humans will build signal fires among the rocks, and look down at who or whatever has come to finish us off.

The country the Tukudeka lived in, craggy, hazardous, hammered by snow, near-holy in its beauty, is still here. A person can go see the Sawtooth Mountains and the Salmon River and even hike to Soldier Bar, where Private Hoffner helped bury his comrade, and where some of the last free Tukudeka rested among the rocks; and there are even less-traveled places, like the Lost River Range, or the Lemhi Mountains, which are about as far as you can get nowadays, in the Lower 48, from anybody.

A person can still go into the country and find a few ghosts, some pictographs, a stone hunting blind, a stick or two from a forgotten sheep trap.

"You people of low lands," wrote Private Hoffner in 1878, "have no idea how loud thunder can roar or how bright flashing the lightning is on the mountain tops."

A person can still walk into the mountains and stare up at the welter of stars.

ILLINOIS

CAPITAL   Springfield

ENTERED UNION   1818 (21st)

ORIGIN OF NAME   Algonquin for "tribe of superior men"

NICKNAME   Prairie State

MOTTO   "State sovereignty, national union"

RESIDENTS   Illinoisian

U.S. REPRESENTATIVES   19

STATE BIRD   cardinal

STATE FLOWER   violet

STATE TREE   white oak

STATE SONG   "Illinois"

LAND AREA   55,584 sq. mi.

GEOGRAPHIC CENTER   In Logan Co., 28 mi. NE of
  Springfield

POPULATION   12,763,371

WHITE   73.5%

BLACK   15.1%

AMERICAN INDIAN   0.2%

ASIAN   3.4%

HISPANIC/LATINO   12.3%

UNDER 18   26.1%

65 AND OVER   12.1%

MEDIAN AGE   34.7

ILLINOIS
Dave Eggers

The slogan on all license plates in Illinois, for as long as anyone can remember, has been *Land of Lincoln*. Everyone in Illinois and all sensible people elsewhere believe it to be the best license-plate slogan of all the states in our union. The closest runner-up would be New Hampshire's fiery *Live Free or Die*, but that slogan scares children. A license-plate slogan shouldn't scare children and shouldn't include the words "or die." A license-plate slogan shouldn't encourage death in the face of curtailed personal liberties. A license-plate slogan should, without threats or hysterics, evoke the moral essence and scenic grandeur of a state, and if possible it should be alliterative and should mention everyone's favorite president. The slogan on the 9.6 million registered vehicles in the state of Illinois does all those things, and sets the tone for all conduct, personal and public, in the state, and guides and inspires all of our plans and pursuits. It is the best of all license-plate slogans. Is Illinois, therefore, the best of all states? This has been often argued and often proved. Through the course of this essay, many examples of the first-ness of Illinois will be offered into evidence— the state is first in everything from snacks to bombs—but perhaps no endorsement is more important than Lincoln's own: He himself believed Illinois best.

He was born in the Kentucky wilderness, raised in a log cabin with a dirt floor, and by the time he was a teenager, he was ready for better things. His father, a pioneer broken by the early death of his wife (whom Abraham called his *angel mother*), brought his new wife and family to Indiana for a spell and then to Illinois, where his gangly son would grow into a man, would reinvent himself and soon the nation.

They settled close to the center of Illinois, in Macon County, and there the future president's father set up a homestead near the north bank of the Sangamon River. Thomas Lincoln was accustomed to putting his strapping son to work, and so set him on building a fence around the fifteen acres. Abe split dozens of logs to form the barrier, and though this task was onerous, it was not without benefits: When he ran for president decades later, his party, the Republicans, needing a nickname as catchy as "Tippecanoe and Tyler Too," and "Old Hickory," dubbed him "The Rail Splitter." Someone even painted a Harlequin-style portrait of Lincoln, his foot on a rail, hammer high overhead, and shirt agape. It was to be the one and only time sex appeal was used to sell the concept of Abraham Lincoln.

When he wasn't working on the farm, he was reading—constantly reading books and newspapers, educating himself about politics, law, and the world, and after just a few months in Illinois, he was inspired to give his first political speech. The site was Renshaw's store in Decatur, then a village of less than a dozen cabins, and the subject was the future of Illinois. As the legend goes, there were a few local candidates in the shop, holding a debate, and Lincoln's teenaged buddies asked Abe to demand some beverages for the audience—a standard thing at the time, apparently. Abe stepped forward, and instead of demanding lemonade for all or else, he gave a moving soliloquy about the potential of the Sangamon River to bring wealth to the region. If they could encourage trade to swing into the state via the Mississippi, into which the Sangamon flowed, then prosperity would ensue. All who saw him speak were impressed, and his name was linked even then with the residents' ideas of a better future for their pioneer land. Shortly after that Lincoln left home for good, pursuing a half-dozen careers—carpenter, store clerk, post master, surveyor, soldier—before finally settling on the law. But his first love was the river, and a few months after his speech at Renshaw's, he set about becoming a steamboat man. He took a job on a flatboat headed down the Mississippi to New Orleans. He was eighteen and his life as an independent and self-made man had begun.

While on the subject of water and gumption and Illlinois being first among states, it has to be pointed out that Chicago opened the nation's first aquarium, in 1893; that puts us at Number One in fish and oceanography and all related pursuits. Just a few years before that, Illinoisians invented the skyscraper. We were first, erecting the Home Insurance Building in 1885, the first of the so-called Chicago School's contributions to urban architecture. That innovative structure, the first steel-framed building, set the high standard for architectural courage and discerning taste that has been key in Chicago's having the reputation, forever after, for the best high-rise architecture in the nation. Home to Louis Sullivan, Ludwig Mies van der Rohe, the John Hancock, the gorgeous Gothic at 35 Wacker, and now Millennium Park's Gehry and Kapoor—Chicago would be No. 1 even without the Sears Tower. At 1,730 feet the Sears was the tallest in the world when it was built and remains today the tallest building in the United States. If one discounts, and one should, the inelegant towers of Dubai and Taipei that are now by some voodoo measurement "taller" than the Sears, ours remains the highest structure on the planet.

Lincoln also was tall. Six-foot-four or so, he was almost freakish in an age where the average height was well under six feet. He made an immediate impression in New Salem, a tiny town along the Sangamon just west of Decatur. Founded just two years before his arrival in 1831, Lincoln settled in the town almost by accident. A flatboat he was manning became stuck in the river astride the town, and he and the boat's crew had to unload it before it sank. The whole town watched as he worked with two men to save the provisions aboard. Seeing his strength and ingenuity, he was offered a job on the spot, at Offut's general store, and that's where he stayed, more or less, for the next six years. It was in cozy New Salem where he was encouraged, where he continued to educate himself, and where the locals bolstered his confidence such that he ran for office just a year after arriving in the town. He was twenty-three. He described himself as "an uneducated, penniless boy," and his contemporaries were quick to point out that he "had nothing, only plenty of friends." He didn't win that first time out, but he did collect 277 of the 300 votes cast in his own precinct, and he would be sent up the ballot at the next available opportunity.

He was elected in 1834, and went to Vandalia, then the state capital, in a new suit he bought with sixty borrowed dollars. (It was the first proper suit he ever owned, and even then it looked funny. For years, even at his famed speech at New York's Cooper Union, he would catch grief for his poor sartorial sense. It could be that nothing short of a miracle would look right on such a strangely shaped man.) When the legislature was not in session, Lincoln struggled to make ends meet; the salary for a state senator was meager. But as always, his friends helped him find a way They found him a job as a surveyor, and this gave him the opportunity to see ever-more of the beautiful state he represented. In his spare time, he educated himself in the law. Without any formal training—all this time he'd had only one year of proper education—he passed the bar. Eventually he traveled downriver, riding a horse lent by a friend, to live in Springfield, now the state's capital, and to practice law. Very soon his firm was considered one of the best in the state (let's assume it was the best), and if Lincoln was Number One in Illinois, it would follow that Lincoln was therefore the Number One self-educated attorney in the country.

That do-it-yourself spirit infuses *The Adventures of Augie March*, Illinoisian Saul Bellow's breathless, rollicking novel about a young man emerging from the slums of Chicago to make his way upward and outward in the world. It begins: "I am an American, Chicago born—Chicago, that somber city—and go at things as I have taught myself, free-style, and will make the record in my own way . . ." This beginning could describe any number of innovators, like Lincoln, who struck forth from Illinois, from Chicago. The state's contributions to the arts are vast, from jazz (Miles Davis, Herbie Hancock, Benny Goodman all were born there), the blues (Muddy Waters, Howlin' Wolf, Willie Dixon, Buddy Guy, Junior Wells all made a home there) to theater (Steppenwolf) to comedy (Second City), there is something unique about the place: It's big enough to challenge and buttress the bold, but it's small enough to nurture with skepticism—but not cynicism—the fragile nature of the avant-garde.

It follows, then, that Chicago would be where Oprah Winfrey would get her start. Born in rural Mississippi to a young unmarried mother, Winfrey eventually maneuvered—free-style, if you will—into a job co-anchoring the evening news at nineteen years old. That was in Tennessee, but she was noticed in Chicago, and in 1983 was brought north and given a job hosting the low-rated morning show *AM Chicago*. Through a combination of her great empathy and quick wit, her program was soon immensely popular, was renamed the *Oprah Winfrey Show*, and within a few years was being broadcast nationally. Taking advice from Roger Ebert, another product of Illinois and in our lifetime the Number One plainspoken explainer and champion of film, Winfrey signed a syndication deal that gave her control over her show and allowed her to reap the benefits of her work. Because she started in Chicago and, like Lincoln, chose to remain in the state that embraced her, Winfrey has for over two decades brought in approximately all of Illinois's tax revenue.

And because Winfrey has led the most readers to the greatest number of books in contemporary times, Illinois is the most important state in terms of reading, sales of books, and the resurgence of book clubs and quantity of people who have recently read *Anna Karenina* and *Middlesex* (by now-Chicagoan Jeffrey Eugenides). Not surprisingly, Chicago is home to the largest public library system in the world, with more than two million volumes—all of them better than the books held in other cities' libraries. This overwhelming evidence of a civic commitment to literacy led directly to Illinois ranking first in the number of Nobel Prize–winning American authors. We have two: Bellow (Chicago), and Ernest Hemingway (Oak Park).

The list of Number Ones is endless and will be touched on only. Illinois is Number One in snack foods, as the place where Cracker Jack was introduced (at the Chicago World's Fair, 1893); where the most cookies were ever produced in one year (Oreos, Nabisco, Chicago, 1996); and where "I Wish I Were an Oscar Mayer Wiener" was written, in 1963, by Richard Trentlage from Fox River Grove, who was responding to an open contest for a new hot dog jingle. It was Illinois that brought the world McDonald's and Dairy Queen, and Chicago that produced the confectioner Walt Disney. We have for decades produced the most pumpkins, considered by tastemakers the Number One fruit in the world, and have produced the two best sports teams of the modern era, the 1985 Bears, and the 1995 Bulls. It goes without saying that Illinois is Number One in places where Michael Jordan played, and where Scottie Pippen often played better. It is Number One in places Walter Payton goosestepped and talked in his strange falsetto, and Number One in all things Ditka, Singletary, Fencik, Perry, and Dent. It is Number One in number of mayors named Daley. Number One in corn production (or probably close to number one), and ethanol production (almost definitely). Number One, definitively, in birthplace of essential bands of the 1970s: REO Speedwagon (of Champaign-Urbana); Styx (of Chicago); Cheap Trick (Rockford). Number One in settings for John Hughes movies (*Sixteen Candles, The Breakfast Club, Home Alone, Home Alone II, Ferris Bueller's Day Off*, among others). We have the Number One most beautiful and charming baseball park in the country, Wrigley Field, and we also have its opposite, the Number One most timidly designed and charmless ballpark, Cellular Park, which looks far worse than it sounds. That park's team, the White Sox, has fans that hail from any one of suburbs made possible through permutations of the following seven words: River, Lake, Ridge, Stream, Woods, Forest, and Park (452).

Illinois—the most in the world—ranks first in the frequency with which its name is mispronounced. No one seems to make the mistake of pronouncing the *s* in Arkansas, but far too many do so with our *s*—including Ron Zook, coach of the University of Illinois football team, who did so at the rally welcoming his arrival to the school in 2004. There was great suspicion about him for some time, until he brought the team to the 2007 Rose Bowl, which would have been fine had he not forgotten to continue coaching after the game had begun. But about the mispronunciation: This tendency led some to suggest legislation that would make pronouncing the *s* a crime. The proposed law would impose the following penalties on mispronouncers:

> First offense: $50,000 fine
> Second offense: Vocal cord scraping
> Third offense: Vocal cord adjustment
> Fourth offense: Execution

That may seem extreme, but Illinois, a low-lying and uncomplicated land, has long been home to towering and passionate iconclasts. Take the abolitionist Elijah Lovejoy. A Presbyterian minister, he settled in Alton, in the southwestern portion of the state, and there he began to publish the *Alton Observer*, a Puritan newspaper full of soaring rhetoric exalting his God and denouncing all vice and weakness. Eventually he turned his attention to slavery, and found his life's purpose in doing all he could in print to bring the abomination to an end. And though he found many people who agreed with him, many southern Illinoisians, being geographically so close to slave states and being themselves connected by blood and tradition to the South, were not so keen to have a rabble-rouser living and agitating in their midst. They asked him to stop publishing anti-slavery screeds. He continued to do so. Then they asked again, and then they threatened. Nothing dissuaded him, so mobs destroyed his press. He bought another press and resumed. They destroyed this press, too. He bought another one, and continued with his work until a mob beset him on November 7, 1837, and he was killed while defending his press and his family, rifle in hand. His death was a martyr's end, and accordingly, disciples continued the work he'd begun. In his honor Benjamin Lundy published the *Genius of Universal Emancipation*—easily the best-named of all abolitionist (or any other) papers—and that led to the less-grandly-named *Genius of Liberty*, which gave way to the *Western Citizen*, no doubt an important periodical but with a name that puts in mind land-usage laws in Idaho.

Alton was one of a number of towns, most of them south of the suburb-ring encircling Chicago, which have long been immortalized as settings of the most famous set of debates in American history, those between Lincoln and his pint-sized adversary, Stephen Douglas. Charleston, Quincy, Galesburg, Freeport, Ottawa, Alton—we know their names chiefly because a great fight was fought in these town squares and parks, that, in Lincoln's own words, represented "the eternal struggle between these two principles—right and wrong—throughout the world. They are the two principles that have stood face to face from the beginning of time; and will ever continue to struggle. The one is the common right of humanity and the other the divine right of kings." The two debated slavery and the freedom of men throughout 1858, and it was in part Lincoln's oratory that vaulted him into the presidency two years later.

When the struggle over slavery gave way to the Civil War, it was not just Lincoln who directed, via Illinois, the course of history. Ulysses Grant, yet another man self-made of our state, emerged from Galena, on our western edge, where he had been hired as a leather-worker. A heavy drinker whose family had largely given up on him, Grant seemed destined to a life of binges and brokenheartedness. But by the time the war came around, he was sober enough to think his experience as a soldier might prove useful to the war effort. The Union army was disorganized, for sure, and badly needed a man like him, well trained and stalwart. He rose quickly, from a command in Cairo (pronounced, for no good reason, Kay-ro) to command of the northern armies, to victory for them and the nation.

Not to underline the obvious, but if we assume that the Civil War was the most important war in our country's history, and Illinois was the most important state involved in that conflict, then it follows that Illinois is the most important to the history of the country, most essential to the Union being held together against all odds and most indispensible to the country's resurrection and continued existence. Had our forebears not elected Lincoln, had they not nurtured him and provided for him a sturdy foundation from which to launch his presidential hopes, he would not have been elected to that office, and instead the country would have been stuck with some lesser light, who would have preferred the dissolution of the Union and god knows what other wrongheaded stew of appeasement and compromise. Suffice it to say that the country would have had to live, for years or decades more, under the wretched shadow of the atrocity that was slavery. Illinois gave America Abraham Lincoln, a man who was at once humble, morally unshakeable, courageous, and preposterously eloquent.

Speaking of Barack Obama, he is of course an Illinoisian. He may have spent some time in Hawaii, but he is an Illinoisian in all ways that matter, and is heir to Lincoln in more facets than one. Like Lincoln, he is thin. Like Lincoln, he can deliver a speech. Like Lincoln, he has a wry sense of humor and has the savvy to know when to use it. Like Lincoln, he inspires crowds with his oratory and feels at home around people, all people, all the time. He is comfortable, for example, around Dick Durbin, the other senator from Illinois, a man less magnetic than Obama but no less steadfast and true. In the mold of his predecessor Paul Simon, Durbin looks like a suburban bank manager but he is bold and brave: he voted against the war in Iraq, is frequently called the most liberal member of the Senate, and consistently gets an F from the NRA, god bless him. Durbin is fan and friend to Obama, erstwhile opponent of Hillary Rodham Clinton, yet another proud product of this great state. She was born in Chicago and raised in Park Ridge, a close and comfortable suburb of the city, by conservative parents who instilled in her the importance of hard work and allegiance to conservative values. As a young woman, she worked for and voted for Barry Goldwater, and came to her senses before the election of his heir, Ronald Reagan, yet another favorite son of the state—or at least of its downstate denizens.

Though often thought of as a Californian, Reagan grew up in a way that says everything about the small-town essence of most of Illinois. His family spent time in tiny Tampico and finally settled in Dixon, both towns in the northwest part of the state. In Dixon young Reagan attended high school, worked as a lifeguard—he saved seventy-seven lives—and starred in plays and sports, in various roles and with varying reviews. He attended Eureka College and afterward began a career as a radio announcer, specializing in baseball play-by-play. While calling games for the Cubs, Reagan traveled to California, where he took a screen test, which led to his career as an actor. The rest was the rest, whatever you want to make of it.

In any case, Reagan, too, was made in Lincoln's image: Like Lincoln he was tall and could ride a horse. Like Lincoln he came from a small town that loved him and filled him with confidence, and grounded his thinking and hardened his sense of right and wrong. And like Lincoln, his every utterance is now used (or twisted) to serve any given side of any given issue. He is the Republican party's most beloved figure—they've given up claiming Lincoln, let's hope—and while Abe won the Civil War, Reagan won the Cold War, with the help of yet another product of Illinois innovation, the atomic bomb.

It was under the bleachers of the University of Chicago's football field that the first atomic chain reaction was initiated. This was courtesy of Enrico Fermi and Leo Szilard, and led to the bomb, which led to the deaths of hundreds of thousands of Japanese innocents, and to the end of WWII. Illinois was thereafter home to the first commercial nuclear reactor, Unit 1 at Commonwealth Edison's Dresden Power Station, and to this day Illinois maintains far more nuclear power plants (eleven) than any other state. Few people know this, including most residents of the state.

It's possible, too, that Illinois ranks first in contradictions, in self-delusions, in strange dichotomies. It contains both the biggest city in the Midwest, and some of the most intensely rural areas in the country. It contains the most dependably Democratic counties (Cook, home of the Daley machines) and some of the most stubbornly Republican (much of downstate). Chicago, for its part, has been host to some of the greatest strides in civil rights, and yet remains one of the most segregated cities in the world. For much of the twentieth century, in fact, Illinois was Number One in urban segregation. The segregation, evidenced by the almost entirely white north side of the city and the almost entirely African-American south side, was so extreme that sociologists had to invent a new term, *hypersegregation*, to describe it. The South Side was home for many years to the horribly misguided experiment in public housing, the Robert Taylor Homes, which the comics artist Chris Ware (a Chicagoan) once referred to as "black people boxes."

The Robert Taylor Homes, named after an African-American activist and Chicago Housing Authority official, comprised twenty-eight wretchedly designed buildings, all of them identical, that stretched in a straight line almost three miles down the south side of the city. At their most densely occupied, the buildings housed twenty-seven thousand people, all of them poor, all but a few African-American. Planned, ostensibly, to provide affordable housing to those receiving public assistance, the development included virtually no trees, grass, public amenities, or anything approaching humane standards of living. Though many prominent figures emerged from the RTHs, including baseball star Kirby Puckett and Massachusetts governor Deval Patrick, for most residents the buildings were unrivaled in their hopelessness, and standing in the shadow of the city's constant neglect, they were overrun by drugs and gangs. Thankfully, the city came to its senses after a mere forty-five years, and the homes, every last one of them, were destroyed between 2005 and 2007, to make way for Legends South, a mixed-income community of low-rise buildings.

Just south of where the Robert Taylor Homes stood, the urban bustle of Chicago gives way, quickly and decisively, to rural country of unrivaled flatness and quiet. Nowhere else does a massive city dissolve so conclusively—drive south from Chicago for twelve minutes and you'll see the flattest, most rural country imaginable. For much of its 56,650 square miles, the flatness of the state seems plain weird. The land is without contour and the roads are straight. On I–57, one can drive for hours without feeling even the gentlest slope, or having to turn one's car even a few degrees in any direction. This makes possible the most incredible feats while driving, including reading, shaving, sandwich-making, outfit-changing, and flossing. Every student living in the north of the state and attending college downstate, in Champaign-Urbana, for example, knows of these possibilities, even though none would ever attempt them, knowing them to be dangerous.

But this is lovely country. It's the Midwest, after all, for all of its curses and blessings. And as sophisticated as so many Illinoisians try to be, and as quickly as so many of them attempt to leave the state once of age, nearly all of them are quick to claim themselves as Midwesterners first and foremost. "I guess it's the Midwesterner in me," they say, to explain, for instance, their reluctance, once installed in a more cosmopolitan and jaded place, to join in experiments involving pipes, ropes, candles, or gerbils. "We don't do that in the Midwest," they say, and here they're thinking about those drives down I-57, passing grain silos and Stuckey's, when they're thankful for the plainness of the land and the moral sense of its people—most of them, anyway—and their disinclination to overthink a simple concept, like stopping for someone who's run out of gas.

For instance, you may be driving downstate some day. You may be driving from your former home in the far north of the state, past Chicago, past its ridiculously beautiful Loop, the lake—we haven't mentioned the Lake!—past the now-cleaner Chicago River cutting perfectly through the city, all the bridges carrying people over, and you'll keep driving south, past the city, past where the Robert Taylor Homes stood, and onward down the state. You will be driving down to Champaign-Urbana, where you went to school, and after the hours of flat unturning road, once within twenty minutes of the twin cities, you will notice that you are running out of gas. How is this possible? Twenty years with a driver's license, having made this drive 100 or more times, and you run out of gas on I-57 in January. The temperature will be no degrees, and the wind chill will be 18 below zero. And you will be wearing a windbreaker.

But you are in the Midwest. This means that you will stand outside your car, your bones so cold that all you can say is "Oh my god oh my god oh my god" in rapid succession while dancing in place, but you will not stand for long. Every car will stop. Every car. The first few will be full of dogs and will be going the wrong way, so you will allow them to continue along. The third will be full of a mom and dad and two kids and two teens, and they will have the windows open. You will get inside, the car riding so low with the weight that a speed bump will send you all to the ceiling. And with the windows open—why are the windows open?—it will still, somehow, be warm inside.

The couple's kids are eight and eleven and seventeen, and the teenaged daughter, white, has with her her boyfriend, African-American. He will be more comfortable with the parents than the teenage daughter, who sulks as a matter of nature. The kids and teens will be sitting on each other's laps, laughing about it, tickling each other, while you sit with them, on the left side of the backseat, apologizing for running out of gas in the middle of the day, on such an impossibly cold day. They'll laugh and laugh about that, and then quickly go back into what they were all talking about before picking you up—whether they should go to St. Louis that weekend to see the Arch—just about forgetting that you're there at all (so routine is it to pick up frozen strangers). They'll drop you off at the gas station, and you'll tell them not to wait, and they'll head out, off to take the daughter's boy-friend to a job interview. After you fill your red jerry can with a gallon of gas, you'll step out onto the road again—oh my god oh my god the cold, it's irrational and mean as a snake—and it will take maybe fifteen seconds before a trucker sees you, nods for you to jump into the cab, and will drive you back to your car, two miles down the road. The whole thing will take twenty minutes. This experience, which you had in various forms four other times while attending college downstate—because your '81 Rabbit's gas meter didn't work so well—means that Illinois is Number One, for you at least, in terms of its sense of goodness, plain goodness that makes you happy to be from there, and from nowhere else, because where would you or anyone be without its uncomplicated virtue, its contrast of the horse sense of its flatlands and the progressive-pushing-forth done up north? The land, you have to admit, makes you sappy. The land makes you proud. You're a wuss for loving that land, Land of Lincoln, as you do. But you do.

INDIANA

CAPITAL   Indianapolis

ENTERED UNION   1816 (19th)

ORIGIN OF NAME   Meaning "land of Indians"

NICKNAME   Hoosier State

MOTTO   "The Crossroads of America"

RESIDENTS   Indianan, Indianian, or Hoosier

U.S. REPRESENTATIVES   9

STATE BIRD   cardinal

STATE FLOWER   peony

STATE TREE   tulip tree

STATE SONG   "On the Banks of the Wabash, Far Away"

LAND AREA   35,867 sq. mi.

GEOGRAPHIC CENTER   In Boone Co., 14 mi. NNW of Indianapolis

POPULATION   6,271,973

WHITE   88.6%

BLACK   8.4%

AMERICAN INDIAN   0.3%

ASIAN   1.0%

HISPANIC/LATINO   3.5%

UNDER 18   25.9%

65 AND OVER   12.4%

MEDIAN AGE   35.2

INDIANA
Susan Choi

Last summer, I flew home to Indiana. The day I landed, in August, was the midpoint of a historic heat wave. My father picked me up at the South Bend Regional Airport with an unopened quart of milk, an unopened quart of orange juice, an unopened box of granola cereal, a half-pound of smoked German-style bologna, an unopened jar of brown deli mustard, six slices of rye bread, two nectarines, two pears, and absolutely no ice, not a single cube of it, packed in a cooler in the back of his Volvo. I'd told him I hoped to start our car trip as soon as I got there. He took me literally. He lives fifteen minutes from the airport, but we didn't even swing by his house. His overnight bag was in the back of the car with the cooler.

I'd said I had to be there for my work, but I'd really come back to see him. Four months earlier, I'd turned in my third novel, and once again, although the book was fiction, I'd plundered my poor father's life for material. This time I really had gone too far. Even my mother thought so. "Has your father read this?" was the first thing she demanded after I sent her the manuscript. At the time of that call, in June, I wasn't sure. Now, in August, I still wasn't sure. In between, in July, my father had been to New York, but all he'd said about the book was that he hadn't yet finished it.

And so a week after he left, I called and said I had to visit Indiana for the piece I was writing, and then I'd booked a ticket, fretful with my actual purpose, to see if he was angry with me. With him it had always been easiest to talk in the car or while drinking. I was eight months pregnant, so I proposed that we drive around Indiana for a couple of days. We'd see the sights he'd never seen in his forty-odd years living there, or that I'd never seen even though I'd been born there, almost forty years before. He agreed with delight, and for the rest of the month mailed me guidebooks and maps, all the while never uttering a word about the book I had written.

Until my parents split up, in 1979, the three of us lived in a subdivision of South Bend called Miami Trails, after one of the many no-longer-indigenous tribes of the region. In some ways, we felt like frontier's people. Our ranch-style houses had been built for us on lots that were cleared for the purpose, and while I lived there, the rest of the nearby woods were chopped down and made into lawns. In summer we kids would run wild long after our bedtimes, scaling heaps of dirt from the freshly dug foundations, and jumping into the unfinished holes. (And once, in the case of Dana Mickel—whose name now surprisingly blooms in my mind from the tombs of long-lost memory—gouging a main artery, so that an ambulance came.) All that churned dirt yielded Indian beads: minute, white, cylindrical, unevenly scored, less like the makings of man than the droppings of ancient insects.

But in every other way Miami Trails was tame and bland. Every house had a station wagon in the driveway and a skinny tree from the nursery ailing in the front yard. All the mothers stayed home, and all the dads were like my best friend Dawn's dad, who was a salesman for Procter & Gamble. My father alone was anomalous. The other adults on the block were Dana's Mom, or Lizzie's Dad, or, in cases of thin acquaintanceship, Mr. Booker, but my father, a Korean-born professor of math at the local university, was only "Dr. Choi." My parents, when referred to jointly, were "Vivian and Dr. Choi."

I've always shared that impression: of my father as different, a short-term and uncomfortable tenant in Indiana. After my parents split and my mother and I moved to Texas, my father's ongoing residence in Indiana seemed at best improvisational, at worst unlikely survival against terrible odds. Yet the first stop on our itinerary was my father's suggestion, and a place about which he was clearly excited: the town of Rolling Prairie, briefly the site of a progressive institution called the Interlaken School. The school had long since been razed, but my father wanted to go there anyway, because the sculptor Isamu Noguchi attended Interlaken for one month in 1918, at the age of thirteen. Noguchi's white American mother had sent him there from Japan, after his Japanese father rejected him.

My father has long carried on a romance with Noguchi, who apparently arrived in Indiana at thirteen all alone, with little more than a bag of esoteric carpentry tools. My father had turned up in Rolling Prairie on a recon mission, to find the school before my visit, with little more than its name. He found it by interviewing daylight drinkers at a skeevy-looking roadhouse. Most of the men hunched along the dim bar had no idea what he was talking about, but one of them thought it had been beside a pond called Silver Lake, on the grounds of the Apostolic School of Rolling Prairie.

Now my father directed me into Apostolic's parking lot, and we glimpsed Silver Lake in the distance. But he was far more eager to introduce me to the man from the roadhouse. "Turn down here," he insisted, gesturing me out of Apostolic's driveway and into that of a trim little house just a few hundred yards down the road. The man who emerged from beneath an aluminum carport looked at us blankly, but my father still made for him, one hand extended. "Hello!" he said. "Do you remember? I came and asked you about Interlaken?"

"Oh, yeah," the man recalled in a savoring way, as if reliving that diverting incident.

Mr. Galloway turned out to be seventy-seven, and as we stood in his driveway he announced that he had lived in the house for fifty-five of those years. The house had flowerbeds on all sides and a thriving rose garden in front, with a scarecrow in the form of a grandly dressed lady in long gloves and a big floppy hat. There were also many pairs of antlers mounted over the doors. Mr. Galloway's pickup truck, gleaming brightly beneath the aluminum carport, bore decals reading "National Wild Turkey Federation," "National Rifle Association," and "Pheasants Forever."

In his more than half-century here, Mr. Galloway had ambled the margins of Silver Lake untold times, and it was on one of those walks, years ago, that he came upon a fountain pen inscribed "Interlaken." It was a rare find, in his opinion. Back then any boy who lost a pen from his pocket would try hard to reclaim it. "I've found pennies out there too, but nothing larger. Anything larger you'd look for, just as hard as you'd look for a pen." I expected him to produce the artifact for us, but instead he bent his beneficent gaze on me, gigantically pregnant in the shimmering heat. He'd been one of twelve children, he told us, "and none of us died!"

"She's writing about Indiana," my father explained. For the sake of appearances, I took out a notebook and recorded the spelling of Mr. Galloway's name.

"A book?" Mr. Galloway practically twinkled.

"No, an essay . . ."

When we thanked him, and wished him a good day, he invited us to come any time. "We'll always find something to talk about," he predicted.

"A nice man," my father said, beaming with satisfaction as we drove away.

Apart from my first two books, which he read with a diligence not necessarily compatible with enjoyment, my father has never been much of a reader of fiction, at least not since his college days in the late 1950s, when he attended the University of the South on a church-sponsored scholarship after emigrating from postwar Korea. It was entirely in the interests of manipulating our conversation toward my book that I'd conceived of our road trip as a sort of Hoosier literary tour.

"The writer Theodore Dreiser is from Terre Haute," I announced, as we headed west from Rolling Prairie to Michigan City, where we planned to turn south. "Dreiser's novel *Sister Carrie* was published in 1900, and was very controversial; he's considered the *ur*-American Realist, which seems to mean that his work is depressing." I was prepared to lecture like this for a while.

"Dreiser," my father interrupted thoughtfully. "Your grandpa translated him into Korean. *An American Tragedy*. The one with Elizabeth Taylor."

Although I've spent half my life pumping my father for information about my grandfather, a well-known literary scholar in Korea from the thirties through his death in the sixties, this was news to me. I'd only recently been astonished to learn that my grandfather was the first translator of Joyce's *Portrait of the Artist as a Young Man* into Japanese. "Was he a fan of Dreiser's?"

"Oh, I think he just did it to make some quick money."

I did the math. Dreiser's *An American Tragedy* had been the basis for *A Place in the Sun*, the hugely successful 1951 movie starring Montgomery Clift, Shelley Winters, and Elizabeth Taylor. For that translation to have been lucrative, my grandfather must have done it after the movie's release, and also probably after the Korean War ceasefire, in 1953. My father had left Korea in 1955, not to return in his father's lifetime. I wondered if my grandfather had still been working on Dreiser when they said their good-byes.

But I didn't really want to go to Terre Haute, which seemed to feel as scornful toward Dreiser as he'd felt toward it. There was no Dreiser House or Dreiser Museum. Instead I was headed for Brookston, where the writer William Gass lived very briefly, and to which he refers in the opening lines of *In the Heart of the Heart of the Country*. "Gass is a writer more important to writers than readers," I claimed, probably inaccurately. Here was a place for my father to bring up my writing, but he was keen to hear all about Gass.

The road south from Michigan City to Brookston is Route 421, and on it we tumbled abruptly from strip malls to beauty. Our two lanes cleaved corn and soybeans. Our progress was interrupted almost metronomically by identically sized but distinct little towns. Later, when I looked at the map, I confirmed what I'd felt in my feet: Towns made me brake an average of every eight miles, as if four miles were the maximum distance all farmers are willing to go to replenish their needs at the general store. And yet, for their master-plan spacing, the towns were all different. Sometimes the road pierced the town like a string through a bead. Other times there was only an off-center junction, and then you glimpsed the town, like Wanatah, hiding itself on the far side of fields.

This was how Gass felt, I thought, when he wrote of Brookston,

> So I have sailed the seas and come . . .
> to B . . .
> a small town fastened to a field in Indiana.

But by the time we were approaching Brookston the evenly spaced towns were shabbier and shabbier, and Brookston itself was so dreary we didn't even stop. I'd imagined us eating our lunch in some shaded town square, but there was nothing like that in Brookston, not even the "library given by Carnegie" that Gass wrote about.

My father had picked me up at the airport at noon; now it was past three, and we were starving. The only patch of green the map showed in the region was eight miles down the road, at the Tippecanoe Battlefield Memorial, the site of the rout by William Henry Harrison of the forces of the Prophet, the brother of Tecumseh, in 1811. Apparently the battle was a fatal blow to the short-lived Indian Confederacy that attempted to beat back the white man; Harrison did so well for white men that when he ran for President with John Tyler in 1840 his campaign slogan was "Tippecanoe and Tyler too."

I learned most of this from a couple of plaques, hot as cattle brands in the withering sun. In the relative cool of the Memorial's gift shop I noticed, as I often notice at places commemorating the removal of the red man from his ancestral lands, a preponderance of dream-catchers and squaw dolls and stuffed wolves. I'd lost track of my father since using the rest room, but when I told the overweight white woman at the gift shop register that I was looking for an older gentleman, she let me know she wasn't easily fooled: "I haven't noticed anyone like THAT." I spotted my father outside, wandering dazed from flagpole to commemorative rock, and rushed to intercept him. We ate the bologna and rye bread in the terrible heat beneath a gazebo, as wasps drifted overhead. Afterwards, driving through Lafayette, a truck passed us decorated with a bumper sticker explaining that "MARRIAGE = [a stick figure of a man] + [a stick figure of a woman]."

"I'd like to go to Crawfordsville," my father announced, indicating its place on the map. "Ezra Pound lived there once."

"Really? Pound lived there? How'd you learn that?"

"I just read it somewhere."

In Crawfordsville we were both impressed by Wabash College, a cluster of jewels in a green velvet case. Handsome brick buildings faced one another across an oval driveway, beneath giant shade trees. Wabash College is all male, and one hundred years ago a young Ezra Pound was fired from his teaching position there for hosting "an actress" in his rooms. Pound proceeded to move to Europe, and grow fond of Mussolini, and eventually got himself returned to this country and indicted for treason. Leaving the College to rejoin Main Street, we saw a handsome building of caramel-colored stone: CARNEGIE LIBRARY.

"Hey!" I exclaimed. "Gass stole Crawfordsville's library, and gave it to Brookston!" Creative license, I might have gone on to muse. For some reason I didn't. Then we were quiet as we left the little town where Pound was once young and wild, before his disgrace.

Ever since I was in my mid-twenties—the same age as my father when he left Korea—and began writing seriously, I've been fixated on my father. I've been obsessed with his past and his soul, his misadventures and regrets. I've used him as a fiction cornucopia, which has meant, I've increasingly feared, that I've made him a mere object. But it's equally true that he's put himself into this role. Time and again, he's let me "interview" him; when he's read the results, distorted by "creative license," he's never complained. Even more, time and again, he's broached the thorniest subjects himself. Noguchi and Pound; an Asian boy deprived of his father and a literary titan brought low by unpopular politics: There's a reason the lives of these men cast a spell on my father. He keeps cracking open his Pandora's box of unspeakable subjects, the same subjects that drove him from Korea a half-century back, and that stranded him here in the heart of the heart of the country.

My grandfather, the translator of Dreiser and Joyce, was also one of the most despised intellectuals Korea produced in the past century. I learned this not from my father, of course, but from other Koreans, and from professors of Korean literature, for whom my grandfather is a towering figure and a very big problem—Korea's own Pound. Like Pound, my grandfather was a conspicuous apologist for a despicable regime, in his case, the occupying Japanese on the Korean peninsula. He either believed, or was believed to believe, that Koreans were racially inferior to Japanese. He either believed, or was believed to believe, that Korea's best hopes for the future lay in subsuming herself to the Japanese empire.

The question of whether he really believed all these things is unanswerable, and perhaps this explains my father's ambivalence toward both countries. I've heard my father speak Japanese, which he learned as a boy, and I've also heard him claim (untruthfully) he's forgotten Korean. We trekked to Chicago for Japanese noodles when I was a kid, yet my father has called Japanese culture derivative. He assiduously avoided other Koreans my whole childhood, and then served as president of South Bend's Korean Association in the late 1990s, once enough Koreans had arrived to associate. I've heard him say things about Koreans that could get him punched in the face.

And that evening in Bloomington, where we were staying the night, my father dithered in front of an Italian restaurant, a Greek restaurant, a Mexican restaurant, a Thai restaurant, and a Turkish restaurant before admitting that what he wanted was what he always wants, Japanese food. Once we arrived at what we were told was the best of Bloomington's several Japanese restaurants, my father wanted some obscure item of traditional *Korean* home cooking that wouldn't have been on the menu even if this had been a Korean restaurant. Not for the first time I asked myself: how had my father gotten by in Indiana for almost forty years? And how could he fight the old battle, between Japan and Korea, even here in the cornfed Midwest?

Of course the waitress in the Japanese place was Korean. She drew us a meticulous map to a Korean homestyle restaurant nearby where, miraculously, my father could get just the dish he was hankering for.

"We'll go tomorrow," my father decided.

M y plan for the next day was simple. I wanted to drive down to the toe of Indiana to see a town called New Harmony, the site of serial utopian experiments of international renown. The WPA Guide puts it irresistibly when it calls New Harmony one of "the world aristocracy of villages that have made history." The road we set out on from Bloomington was multilane and ugly, but with a distinction that has also made history: the creamy gray strata of Indiana limestone exposed by its roadcuts. Indiana limestone is some of the best in the world, cladding some of the most iconic buildings in the country, including the Pentagon and the Empire State Building. But soon we left that highway for US 50. Then we were winding through intimate countryside, in and out of dappled woods.

Rounding a bend I had to brake suddenly. An Amish wagon was moving slowly down the road, drawn by clop-clopping horses. Bearded patriarch, smooth-faced teenage boy, and a little boy, not more than eight. All in black pants and vests, and long shirtsleeves that weren't white but a rich royal blue; golden straw hats on their heads. They stared at us with no emotion discernible on their breathtaking faces as we carefully passed them. For many minutes after I was transfixed by the memory of their uncommon physical beauty: the nut brown of their skin, their lean bodies, their royal blue shirtsleeves. My father was less impressed. "They lead healthy lives," he pointed out.

It was on this pastoral, secretive road that we brought up my grandfather again—or, rather, my father's family's sufferings, which were caused by his father's disgrace. "One time," my father remembered, "when things were very bad," he caught a glimpse of his mother undressed and realized she was starving. Not long after, my father's oldest sister, who was nineteen or so, ran away, and my grandfather was shattered, and obsessed for the rest of his life with locating his daughter.

"But wouldn't any parent be obsessed with finding any lost child?" I asked.

My father carried on, ignoring my question. "And I said, 'Goddamn this situation!' My sister showed the way," he recalled. "I said, 'I'll follow her.' "

We had entered Martin County, famed for its beauty, and indeed it was beautiful, deeply forested, with dapples of sun making lace of the slow little road, but I could scarcely take it in because now my father was sobbing.

When he finally started speaking again, he skipped to the day at least fifteen years later, just after my parents had wed in Ann Arbor, when my grandfather called from Korea to say the sister was found. She, too, had wound up in the Midwest—in Manhattan, Kansas, the widow of a GI she'd met in Japan. When my father was reunited with her, she seemed sorry my mother existed: "I finally find my family," my father quoted her saying, "and it turns out you're married."

What did *that* mean? I asked. But this question, like so many regarding his family, did not rate an answer. The atmosphere of revelation had dissolved. Even the road had lost charm. It had flattened and spread, become more of a highway, in response to the changing terrain. The horizon had gone far away, to accommodate mile after mile of soybeans and corn.

New Harmony was an enigma. Down its quaint nineteenth-century streets we passed storybook houses, all flawlessly preserved, and all bolted and locked. An empty parking lot at the margin of town was attached to a huge modern structure resembling a heap of ice-cube trays. The entrance was hidden in back; parts still seemed to be under construction.

The building called itself the Athenaeum, promising learning to all, but demanded money—to see what?—if you wanted to get past its entirely average gift shop.

"What happens here?" I asked the overly made-up woman at the register.

"This is where *the past meets the present*," she informed me, with scorn.

"I mean, is this a library, or a museum, or something?"

"This is *the Athenaeum*," she seethed. "Designed by Richard Meier!"

There wasn't even a gazebo where we could eat lunch. Speeding back to Bloomington, we passed gigantic insectoid farm machines stalking over the fields like the invaders in *War of the Worlds.* The radio told us that in Princeton, which we'd passed through a few hours before, three coal miners had died in a shaft. A passing truck's bumper sticker announced that IF MARY HAD BEEN PRO-CHOICE THERE WOULDN'T BE CHRISTMAS!

"You know," my father said, "something interesting has happened. I was talking to the chair of our department, and he's asked if I can commit to keep teaching another five years."

"You're seventy . . . something," I objected.

"Well, of course, if I'm not feeling well or anything like that, it's no hard obligation."

"But you'd been thinking of retiring!" I reminded him. "Maybe coming East."

"Oh, I still want to do that," my father said vaguely. "Next time you visit you should bring Dexter," he added after a moment, referring to my three-year-old son. "I've made a very nice garden at my house. I think he would like it."

We found the Korean homestyle restaurant in a tiny, dilapidated strip mall, and almost from the instant we arrived things went south. The whole trip I'd expected some moment of static between my father and a more typical Indianan. Instead the moment came here, between my father and a ponytailed Korean-American girl. I'd just put our things on a table when my father wheeled away from the counter. "Let's get out of here," he snarled.

"What? Don't they have what you want?"

The problem wasn't that they lacked the dish we'd come for, but that they lacked beer. "I can't serve liquor," the girl explained, almost in tears. "I'm only sixteen." Her mother, the cook, was partly visible through the door to a small bare-bones kitchen. A younger boy, perhaps ten, was perched at a back table, toiling over his homework.

I persuaded my father to stay, and we received our food on plastic trays from the wary girl. The food was the sort you can only get some place like that—authentic and good. But my father, swiftly clearing his plate, began to sound his theme about how all Koreans care for is money, opening restaurants and such to get rich.

"You think these people are rich?"

Then I added, more gently, "Dad, if you weren't Korean yourself, some of the things that you say would be . . . really a problem."

"I don't mean badly," he said, unperturbed.

The next day was the last of our trip, and I'd found the narrowest and most winding road yet. The corn came right up to the shoulder and loomed over the roof of the car. We turned constant right angles, as if along the borders of one patch of property after another. PRAY TO END ABORTION begged a sign in a well-tended yard. "So," I began awkwardly. My father had unearthed the difficult subject, but it was up to me now to say more. That year he'd brought up yesterday—the year his sister was found, the first year of my parents' tempestuous marriage—was the very same year I'd so freely portrayed in my book. The one time my mother ever confided in me about it she stopped herself midway and said, in horror, "You're not going to *write* about this?" My father and I had never touched on these things. I'd never known if he knew what I knew.

"Honey," he said before I could continue. "I've been wanting to say something to you. It's about your new book."

"Oh, Dad!" I said, about to weep, or beg forgiveness, or lecture him on the nature of fiction.

"It is a masterpiece," he declared, in a tone of combat.

"You—"

"Please don't argue! I mean to use this word. The book's a *goddamn masterpiece.*"

My whole adult life all I've done is tell stories about my father—privately and publicly, in my mind and in print—and all I've done is to get him dead wrong. The stranger in a strange land: dead wrong. The private, prideful, prickly man who would fly off the handle when he read my portrayal: dead wrong. It occurred to me, for the very first time, that maybe he liked my work *because* I got him so wrong. Because I've peopled the world with so many inaccurate versions of him, and in a mischievous way, this feels to him like the freedom of living multiple lives. But even now I was probably getting him wrong yet again.

North of Indianapolis it was US 31—that desolate, ruler-straight highway—that took us back home. This was the dreary Indiana of my childhood. Four lanes splitting the fields. The occasional single light tossed on its wire by the wind, blinking yellow for caution. So I shouldn't have been startled when my father turned on a side road just inside the South Bend city limits and I found myself plunged in the past.

Miami Trails: slightly shrunken but in most ways unchanged. My father drove past the incline where, learning to ride my bike, I lost control and smashed into a hedge. And then he drove us—slowly, but never touching the brake—past our old house, where we lived before he and my mother split up. There were all the once-spindly trees, the Douglas firs and dogwoods and poplars that my father put in, and beside which he used to photograph me, to see who would grow faster. The trees had won.

"Should I go back?" he asked, as we rounded a corner and the house slipped away.

"No," I said. How could Indiana be so sleepy, or so socially conservative, or so economically depressed, or whatever the hell it was that let that house lurk there, unchanged apart from the trees, so that it could leap forth and bludgeon my heart? Of course, everything else had been transformed. A few miles south of South Bend, before my father had taken the wheel, we'd gone on another detour, through the farm town of Bremen. My father had remembered a favorite hard candy of his, a candy that all through my childhood was always in his coat pocket, or strewn in his otherwise empty desk drawers. He'd probably been reminded of it because I'd resurrected this very same candy for use in my book. I had it as "a particular off-brand hard peppermint, football-shaped with a red and green stripe." "Exactly," my father agreed. But I'd assumed they were a cruddy generic my father bought because they came cheaper than Starlight Mints. Now he told me they were in fact a local specialty, which he prized for their exceptional flavor. So I was dead wrong again.

"They used to make them here in Bremen," my father said, increasingly excited. "There used to be a little shop. Let's go and see."

Once, all the mint for Wrigley's Spearmint Gum was grown in and around South Bend, and Bremen's mint crop was especially famous. Bremen was known as Mint City, and as we came into town some surviving businesses—"Mint City Motors"—attested to this fact. But all we saw were soybeans. I turned again, on SR 331, for the last leg from Bremen to South Bend. But at the sight of a small grocery store my father stopped me. "Pull in here! So I can ask some stupid question!"

Sweat-stained and rumpled, his face half-concealed by an old baseball cap, my seventy-something Korean father made a beeline for a slow-moving white woman crossing the parking lot, while I braced myself for her baffled repulse of his question.

"Oh, *yes*," I heard her exclaim. And for several minutes, on the steaming blacktop, my father and the woman stood spinning the shared web of memory.

"And they were *excellent* candies," said my father.

"And don't you remember?" said the woman. "When the air smelled like mint?"

IOWA

CAPITAL   Des Moines

ENTERED UNION   1846 (29th)

ORIGIN OF NAME   Probably from an Indian word
   meaning "this is the place" or "the beautiful land"

NICKNAME   Hawkeye State

MOTTO   "Our liberties we prize and
   our rights we will maintain"

RESIDENTS   Iowan

U.S. REPRESENTATIVES   5

STATE BIRD   eastern goldfinch

STATE FLOWER   wild rose

STATE TREE   oak

STATE SONG   "Song of Iowa"

LAND AREA   55,869 sq. mi.

GEOGRAPHIC CENTER   In Story Co., 5 mi. NE of Ames

POPULATION   2,966,334

WHITE   93.9%

BLACK   2.1%

AMERICAN INDIAN   0.3%

ASIAN   1.3%

HISPANIC/LATINO   2.8%

UNDER 18   25.1%

65 AND OVER   14.9%

MEDIAN AGE   36.6

IOWA
Dagoberto Gilb

What do I visualize when I think of Iowa except, like everyone, a cartoon image of it: corn and pigs and big farmers who eat hearty American food. I'm on a flight out of Dallas-Fort Worth to Des Moines, on a regional ER4 jet, a 50-seater, and I've got the single side on row 12, the emergency exit, with extra legroom. The two-seat side on my right is empty up to the last minute, when a huge, healthy man moves into it before take-off. He has to be six-five easy, 250 minimum, but I wouldn't call him fat. He smiles at me like we're onto it like a stash, us big guys. He reads a newspaper slowly, the not very taxing *USA Today*, but at least he's reading. What I see are his hands. Oversized, wrinkled and thickened by work. Up a few rows is another Iowan, a man so huge I can't see how he isn't making the plane dip. I'm used to flights out of shorter cultures.

When we land, I call my friend Mando, who is due to pick me up. *"El aguila ha tortillado,"* I tell him, joking. We always stuff those bad words into a tortilla. *"I'll be there in ten, tortillero,"* he answers me. As I stand and move to the aisle, out of nowhere an older woman appears two rows ahead on the two-seat side. She is staring at me like she overheard. I didn't see her before because, seated, her head was behind the headrest, hidden. *Con una cara morena*, a dark face classic of historic Mexico, she would make a perfect tourist painting. She isn't much higher than the headrest now either, standing. We file out into the airport corridor, signs with arrows from the ceilings. She is ahead of me, walking slow, looking side to side, others looping around her. It seems she is waiting for me to catch up. *"¿Vas a la mochila?"* she asks me. I assume she means the baggage area, so I tell her to just follow me. *"¿A la mochila?"* she asks again. She's frightened about getting lost, because a couple of times we've had to curve around people and make a turn. Yes, straight ahead, it's a walk, it's usually a long walk in airports, it's more in front of us, and we're going there, I have baggage too, I have a suitcase. This appeases her, she's walking faster, I'm walking slower, we travel side by side. It's a blazing summer from below Dallas and above Iowa and to the east and west, it's too warm even inside, and she is wearing a thin pink sweater over her flowery black dress that seems to bury her shoes. Her *trenza*, her black and gray braid, reaches below the middle of her back.

She's from Guadalajara, and it's her first time in the United States.

She's still tense. Thinking maybe it was immigration or customs lines she's worrying about, I tell her that she passed through that once, when she went through Dallas—thinking maybe this is a worry. And she's never been on an escalator. I have to show her. I want to hold her hand, but don't want to be too forward. I have to tell her when to step when we get to the bottom. Her hop is like a five-year-old's, and when we make the final turn, the aluminum baggage claim area visible, I practically can't keep up with her. As we reach it, right then walking through the glass doors is her family, probably her son's, her daughter-in-law, a granddaughter the oldest and most shy to see her, a grandson maybe ten, and a newborn. They all hug and then she is holding the baby grandchild, and she and the women step off to the side, while the father and son, in sports shorts and American football jerseys and sneakers, both with buzzcuts, wait near me as the suitcases circle.

T his is about the tortilla. This is about corn grown in Iowa. This is about the people who are in the *campos* of Iowa picking the vegetables and walking the cornfields. Those people are Mexican people. They are of the culture where hand-ground *masa* was first patted into tortillas and, because of that, it is said that the physical body of any Mexicano is at least half-corn. They are from the civilization that worshipped the corn plant as a god—in some regions, such as what became known as Guatemala, the God, the image of God—and they are from the soil and nation where this corn we all have learned to eat and to feed as grain for healthy livestock was first developed and harvested five thousand years ago. They are the people who now are driven here, because even corn, and the tortilla, is going up in price even more since the '90s NAFTA treaty, and subsidized corn in the United States is cheaper to import, while its demand increases its value to the corporate farmers in Mexico. Because corn has become an ethanol fuel industry, its hybrid grain is even more highly sought.

But in Mexico, the ordinary *milpas*—cornfields—are shrinking in size, and those people who traditionally worked them can't make enough to survive in their villages. So they are leaving, like animals in a drought, going to the big cities to find jobs, and they are crossing the border into the U.S. because that is where most jobs are. They come to Iowa because they will be hired and work in meat-packing plants cheaply, hard, and they work in the fields cheaply, and hard. And as they walk *las milpas* in Iowa to do as their culture has done for thousands of years, anti-immigration ideologues bash them for spoiling what they see as a field of dreams as clean and pure as Iowa butter, as nostalgic as baseball, as all-American as Kevin Costner.

How to make a commercial tortilla: There are fifteen fifty-five gallon drums, and every night the corn soaks four to five hours, bubbling under fifteen burners, and they are stirred with paddles like a rowboat's oars. After a while, using a can of a measured size, lime is scooped out of sacks, mixed in, and stirred and stirred. A foam like from the ocean rises, which means it is working, breaking down the corn so it is healthy to eat. Then the corn rests a few hours. While it is still warm, tin buckets with holes in the bottom drain the water and remove the corn so it can be ground in the *molino*, where stones turn it into *masa*. Now a ball the size of a watermelon, it is fed between twin rollers that flatten it and onto a conveyer where it is cut. This raw tortilla falls onto a traveling grill, cooking one side, then is flipped to another for grilling on its other side, until it drops onto one more belt which drops it onto a cooked stack. There women count the tortillas onto waxed paper. They wrap up this counted pile, flip over the package— in, say, Corpus Christi, Texas, it might read Charro Tortillas—and stack them in a box for delivery.

Here in Iowa in mid-July, the leaves of cornstalks are waxy, veined, like a narrow palm, and the two sides of each leaf peel and fall away from its spine as they grow out—water can funnel right into that crease like halved paper, run down the stalk, drench the shallow roots—until they are long enough to droop delicately, tenderly, at their end points. Their stalks are bamboo thin and knuckled and already as tall as I am. I can see through them to a light casting through, like a mist. It's the blue sky, blue as an imagined heaven, blue that isn't only sky but is this earth, as close as the tallest green stalks and leaves touching it, and it is, noticeably, more blue because it rests on top of the cornfield.

Blocks to the east of the golden domes of the Iowa State Capitol Building in Des Moines is the most Mexican neighborhood in the city. A few years ago this wasn't so. Now when you drive on E. 14th, you see a street whose appeal is to people who need transportation to and from jobs, the used car and truck dealers, auto repair shops, parts houses, tire stores, and corner stores with the cheapest gas prices, and, alongside hamburger joints and diners, *taquerías*. The Mexican businesses bear names that are tourist recognizable and famed—Aztec, Los Pinos, Fiesta Cancún, El Tequilero. The newest market, La Tapitia is doing so well that the area around it has expanded into a mall. Today it is busy inside, lots of employees and check-out stands, these shoppers wanting Mexican products—beans, rice, and fideos, cheeses, dried *chiles* in bulk and packaged, spices, sauces and *moles*, cooking oils, crackers and cookies, meat and poultry cut their style, still-hot *carnitas* and *chicharron*, fruits and vegetables we Americans know well and also those like yucca and prickly pear and *guayaba*, and coconut, and sliced white bread, and stacks and stacks of tortillas. I want corn tortillas and buy a couple of packages listing the preservative-free three ingredients only—lime, corn, water—and a *paleta* of watermelon *con chile*.

On the way out, in that small entry and exit room that all markets have now for throwaway papers and bulletin boards and charcoal and hand-shopping carts there are two stacks of scissored slips from an Eagle Eye Detasseling, one hot orange, another a fluorescent green, looking for workers to "walk the cornfields" and take off the *espigas*, the tassles. It goes on, *El trabajo empezara por el 10 de julio. Venga a la orientación el lunes 2 de Julio a las 6 de la tarde atras de La Tienda Favorita* says the green one, while the orange one, also with a date, adds the word *seguro*, "safe," to its *HAY TRABAJO* heading, making clear that this is a contractor who will hire people who have immigration documents and those who don't, though. That July date already past, I go to La Tienda Favorita, a small, unintimidating Mexican meat market in the heart of this downtown community, to see if anyone there might know something. The owner and his son say maybe they were there one morning, but they don't remember exactly, clearly not something standing in their minds as important or noticeable. On a counter near the local Latino newspaper, another clipped slip, that green, with another line of information in bold font: *necesito 30 trabajadores para la espiga*.

I walk over to the capitol. Capitols are the cathedrals of government, teaching us hallowed doctrine and belief and history. Iowa's United States story began in 1803 when President Thomas Jefferson bought it from the French—part of the Louisiana Purchase—and began distinguishing a state history in 1846. On a stairway wall between the first and second floors of the capitol building Iowa represents its philosophical genesis in a five-panel mural by artist Edwin Blashfield called "Westward": A family of pioneers are traveling west in a covered wagon, a prairie schooner. Angels floating behind them carry a steam engine and an electric dynamo, while the angels in front have baskets of seeds to drop. The angel nearest to the front holds a large book open at the middle, pointing it like a headlight, yet also meant to be seen by anyone ahead of them, as though it were a sacred and irrefutable commandment, both proof and inspiration.

A few miles away, at the Iowa Corn Promotion Board offices, a generous information coordinator gives me a lesson on the differences between field corn and edible corn (how each silk thread we see when we husk is like an umbilical cord to each individual kernel on the cob), and the names of each (sweet, pop, flint, dent, flour, broom, waxymaize, pod). Also there is the latest biogenetic corn, or what some call "frankencorn"—she chuckles at that, dismissing the criticism. It's only good, only the latest change in corn that has always been cross-fertilized. Just as some are developed to be more drought resistant, others to bear more kernels or to mature in shorter growing seasons for different altitudes, these are genetically altered to be immune to, for instance, certain pesticides or soil fungi. Corn, which evolved from the wild *teocinte* of Central Mexico, she explains, has always been cross-fertilized by hand (and Monarch butterflies) and has evolved for the times and the region. What does she say about the history of *maiz* being sacred, a god in early Mexico? She has no idea why it was worshipped.

On University Avenue, only some blocks from Drake University, it's dinnertime at a lunch truck. Silver like an Airstream and hooked up like one too, it is moored on this empty lot, aluminum poles and thin rope and white plastic roof making a cabana-like porch on the order window, wooden picnic benches under it. The food is Mexican, not overstuffed TexMex, so the *tacos al pastor* are on traditionally small corn tortillas, delicate, with a slice of avocado and with a wedge or two of *limón*. I get a bottle of pineapple Jarritos soda and sit at a table next to a man wearing an LA Dodgers baseball cap. I open the conversation by mentioning the white paint splattered all over his clothes, asking if he's a painter. He does everything, he says. He works on a *rancho* not far from here, the *rancho* that belongs to the man who runs the local hospital. He does everything on it, not just paint: He works the yard, tends the pool, takes care of the horses—which they don't ride. He's all by himself out there, he says. An estate, I think, not a ranch. He's from Michoacán, from the city of Morelia, and he'll have been here three years in August. Two more years, he tells me, and he'll go home. Doesn't everyone say that? Yes, but he means it. He's lonely. He wants to go home. Why does he do it? To better his family. They are there, waiting for him. I pause, finally ask if he knows any farmer, anyone hiring workers for *las milpas*. Oh yes, he is sure these jobs are around. He suggests a market around the corner. He says there will be ads in the Spanish newspapers they sell there. My eyes go down the street his words direct me to. I have to remind myself that this is Iowa.

M y own manifest destiny comes as a message left on my answering machine back in Texas, and it's through Proteus, a migrant farmworkers
outreach program, that I will find a farmer's cornfields. Reluctant to really
dial anybody's number at six in the morning, I do anyway. On the other end
of the line, it sounds more like wide-awake noon, voices and voices beyond
the one confirming, saying *Come on.* My directions are 80 east, 218 south, 22
east . . . I can't miss it.

Interstate 80: So many cars are new or almost new, all freshly washed,
and the trucks—eighteen-wheelers, FedEx, UPS, Wal-Mart—they too are
washed clean. They travel an uncluttered and unlittered highway that feels
much more lane-roomy than it really is. Iowa this July is more a hobbitland
of unwild, luxuriant green. It seems all the land is planted—soybean is
the other big crop—but it is the cornfields that dominate their fields both
flat and contoured up hills in curved and squared lines, like vast, groomed
Versailles gardens.

On the two-lane 22, a sheriff pulls me over for driving a too slow 30
mph through an intersection. Sir, I saw the eighteen-wheeler in my rearview
mirror, and that's why I didn't slow down more, because I'm afraid I'm going
to miss my turn. . . . When it seemed like I'd gone too far a few miles farther, I pull over beside a man and woman, Iowans from head to toe except
they're speaking Spanish, and she directs me across the road, right at the
sign, Bell's Melons. I should've seen it myself maybe half a block back up
the road.

I go through the warehouse to get to the office, passing twelve-foot
stacks of empty pallets on the vast, empty cement floor, only one loaded
with boxes of vegetables. It's being plastic wrapped off a spool by a couple
of men in overalls who don't speak Spanish, watched by a couple of men
who do. Inside the small office, women are handling clipboards and pencils
and answering phones ringing from every corner. Terri Bell, with her reading glasses in heavy use and a handful of colored markers, exasperated yet
kind, is organizing time sheets and grocery lists of what's still needed for
the *campesinos'* lunches. Her husband Tom, he's the one who comes for
me. Wiry and quick, he tells me right away that I'll have to follow him
around. The men—H2A workers, meaning they have papers and are hired
temporarily—arrived on buses from Monterrey, Mexico, last night, and this
is their first full day here. Tom is all movement, and even as he's on the
phone he hands me the same cream *gorra*, hat that he gives these men—it
reads SYNGENTA across it, the international seed corporation—and a red
bandanna with his own business name and its logo, a basket with three ears

of shucked ripe corn standing tall. On the way to the fields in his red Chevy 4x4, he tells me he pays $500 for their round-trip, and he's hired around 450 workers from early July to early August. He pays $9.95 an hour, charges $11.20 a day for food. They work the cornfields, and also pick beans, cucumbers, watermelon—to name a few. Why not illegals? It's not worth the risk. Why not Americans? He can't find them.

We drive on a paved road behind and parallel to the highway, a neighborhood of what once were one- or two-bedroom workers' homes, now squeezed in by two or three trailer homes mounted on cement foundations. We stop at what is like a compound, outside the kitchen-slash-mess hall add-on to a brick schoolhouse—a banner over the stoves and grills reads SUPER COCINA LOS AMIGOS. People are packing ice chests of lunches and counting how many meals go in each, getting the numbers right. As Tom sorts out a problem with the ice machine's outdoor run-off hose, I head over to a picnic bench where a group of men, young and older, are sitting. Beyond them, on an open field, a few men kick around a soccer ball. They all go eyes up and quiet once I'm close, like I bear bad news. Instead, I find out that they are all from Durango. Have they done this work before? Half of them say no. The one who seems the eldest, a straw hat, dark skin weathered, says he's done it most of his life. How did he find out about this, in Iowa? Just heard. But how, exactly? They look around at one another, nobody sure what to say. Do you hear about it . . . like, maybe you would gossip? They laugh at that. One heard it from this one next to him, he's the one who told that one, thus. Isn't Durango a long trip from Monterrey? They all shrug, the questions making them self-conscious. You just took a bus there? They say yes and nod, are now smiling at me. They took a bus to Monterrey, they signed some papers, and a bus brought them here.

The school building is where Tom Bell went to elementary school. Now it's been converted into a bunkhouse for his workers—all men, only men. At the top of the first stairs in, there are old couches and a TV set up in the corner—a *novela* is playing—and then we pass through a small room, maybe fifteen or twenty bunk beds, all just built of fresh cut 2x4 and 2x6. Like a dad pleased by his son's expensive college graduation, Tom shows me how much he's transformed the school: Where we stand used to be above the gym floor, where you could watch a game, and down below was where the courts were. Down below now are maybe 100 more bunk beds, all occupied. Clothes are already hanging off them, a few have already washed underwear and socks and laid them out to dry on the head and foot boards. In a far corner, another lounge area of old couches, a TV up high, that same *novela*. The showers are gym-like, the sink for hands and face and teeth and probably rinsing underwear is a room-length trough with a dozen or so faucets. The walls and ceilings show the new remodel, all the new studs exposed, sheathed by pressed-wood, low-grade ply. Windows are open. A fan is mounted up high to blow in more air. Iowa? Right now it looks and sounds and—the kitchen is right next to this big space—smells like it's Mexico.

Tom doesn't speak a word of Spanish. What does he think about all these people here? He loves these people and he's proud to do them right, he says. He owns a condo in Manzanillo. When all this gets done, in the winter, he and his wife relax there for a month. He loves it.

Becky is my ride to a cornfield being walked—it's known by a field number, the digits as natural and recognizable to them as a pet's name. Her blue pickup is loaded with iced sodas and a chest of *lonches*, and she wants to know why it has to be her who takes me and she isn't entirely joking. She's a big Iowa woman, a '60s grown-up, born and raised not far away, rooted to the driver's seat. Her tattoos barely visible under the browned sunburn of her fleshy upper arms, she also works biker gatherings and just retired from the clerical staff at the university. It's a few ranch roads to where we go, a route that crosses the rich Iowa River and leads to Muscatine. Talking about the men bunking in the school, she says she cannot imagine the raunch of it—sweat and dirty socks, snores, farts from those beans. Who'd be able to stand all of these men? she asks. Then again she might, she tells me after a pause, smiling dirty-minded.

We pull onto a dirt farm road where dust rises from behind like bad smoke rings and stop alongside the cornfield, near the rented yellow school bus that transports the workers. Tom's son is there to wave at us from his pickup—he's on the phone, as busy as his dad. It is lunch time, and men too short to be seen inside the tall corn jungle begin to emerge. No factory whistle, and it's not like a construction site either, where it's a certain hour and everyone stops everything. Mostly in pairs, the *campesinos* exit slowly, unrushed, from the world of *zurcos*, rows, bandannas under their hats to wrap their necks, bandannas and dark glasses masking their faces—a few have mosquito netting too—and long sleeved shirts and gloves covering their arms an hands. Each has a *mochilla*—a daybag or a plastic store bag to carry an extra shirt or rain poncho or some rubber boots and their own personal valuables—slung over their back or in hand. On their belts is a rubber clip for a soda bottle full of water. The gloves and bottle clip are gifts from Bell's Detasseling. They get their *lonches* from the ice chests—a *caldo* of pork, pineapple, and bell pepper, a fresh jalapeño, tortillas still warm in foil. A few men go inside to sit on the soft seats there. A few sit against a side of the bus, in a slant of shade. I go over to three who rest at the back, to the water igloo, taking their time before they eat.

I tell them how they all look like Sub-Comandante Marcos coming out from the jungle. After a moment to absorb my joke, they look at each other until they finally grin. They are from Monterrey, young, though one must be closer to thirty than the other two. None of them have crossed the U.S.-Mexico border before now. Only one of them has worked in agriculture previously, but this isn't hard work except for the hours—though it isn't so hot yet, even with the long-sleeved shirts that they have to wear, the fields aren't too muddy, the mosquitos aren't too bad. Jobs are hard to find in Mexico. The youngest one talks about working in garages and restaurants. There is a lot of danger to do other things. The older one says how running *movidas* might seem good for a little bit, but it's not worth the trouble. This work is good for them, even if it's only a month. We are looking at the sky, more Hollywood than Iowa, the clouds too white, too flawlessly shaded gray to be believed, too beautiful. The older one asks about me and I tell them how I was born in Los Angeles and worked construction and now live in Texas. Even through their mirror glasses, I see their eyes go starry. I mention El Paso and the capital, Austin, and how in Dallas . . . and how in Houston . . . and it's as though I am speaking of mythical lands. I gesture to the east and tell them over there is where Chicago is, very close. The youngest one jokes how fast they could get there. The other two aren't even considering it, though the third, a quiet one, takes a couple of steps in that direction to see that much closer. This is good for now, the older says. It's what they have. After a pause, the younger one returns, sincerely, *asi es la vida.*

We drive to another field, more masked *campesinos* breaking through the corn jungle rows unexcitedly, unhurried, to take lunch. The conversations are muted. Music they like and don't, other places they've been. Muted, like they are faraway. On this field the crew chief has them leave their *mochila* at the beginning of each row until they come in for lunch, and all but three have been picked up. When most have finished eating, two of the stragglers appear and nod, pleased, about where to find the lunches. Twenty minutes later, the last one, Oscar, unmasked, finally comes out just as these other two go back to work. He's eighteen, maybe twenty-one, and unlike all the others I've seen so far he is overweight in that soft manner of a good boy from El Paso or San Antonio, playing too many video games, sitting in front of a TV with sodas, candies, Doritos. He is tired but also much more—lost, miserable, mom-sick—and he can barely speak, though he does: a thank you when he is told where he will find his *lonche*. When he is done eating—maybe he does take an entire half hour, but certainly no more than that—he ends his lunchbreak in the same self-absorbed, unself-conscious way he began, stepping back, like his feet hurt, to a line of *zurcos* where the others have been out of sight for some time already.

The rows of these *milpas* have been mowed earlier so that they are all of an even height. They are arranged so that one male plant from one seed will pollinate at least the two females, grown from a different seed, on either side of it, so that the layout is four rows of females, a male row, four female, a male, and so on. The leaves of the first male stalk are sprayed a Day-Glo orange—the men must know which it is because its *aspigas*, its tassles, are the only ones that must be left untouched: It is their pollen that will reach the female silks below that will grow the kernels on the cob, a new, third seed that will be harvested. Though corn carries with it both male and female parts, what the *campesinos* are doing is castrating the ones in the rows of four, yanking off their male parts. On a first pass, men pull this shaft out of its stalk, the one blooming an unpollinating tassle, from its node, effectively castrating the plant, leaving the *cañajote* beneath. The tassle pops out easily, a juiced, fleshy pop that sounds like cracking a knuckle, and is dropped onto the dirt of the *zurco*. After a second pass through, there is yet another pass, this one crosswise, made by a more seasoned *chequeador*, a checker, who looks for misses. Wrapped in the same leaf husk as the ripen female corn on the cob we know, peeled away it looks much like young rye or wheat, only deep green, and huskier. When left to bloom, the sun on it, the green becomes more golden, the yellowish pollen sticky, though not as sticky as the white female silks waiting beneath. The field has to be a 99.7 to 99.8 percent detasseled for the crop to germinate the exact corn seed that is hoped for.

Five thousand years of walking *las milpas* in Mexico, the descendents of those people are now in Iowa, walking the cornfields, attending to this cross-fertilization work considered spiritual way back then. Iowa's Mexicans are only a little more aware of corn's history than those in Iowa are. It's as though the migration of the Mexican deity itself has finally summoned its native worshippers to tend to it, populating the soil it grows in. I ask Becky: Ten, fifteen years ago it would have been high-school and college boys and girls from towns here. It was not only a summer ritual, but a good income for the summer. Now you have to hire as many as you can because only half stay with it. They are too hot. They are too sunburned. One doesn't want to work past 2 p.m., another says she can't. One wants to rest a day because he got too tired the day before. Or it's the weekend. Or it was just the weekend and now he wants to sleep in. One has to babysit on certain days, and then maybe the next just doesn't feel like showing up at all. And then there's the other, smaller issues. If someone's litter from lunch gets left behind, for instance, you ask one to pick it up. It's not mine, is the answer. Pick it up anyway. It's not mine. OK, but pick it up anyway. I didn't leave that. Just pick it up! There is no litter in these *campos*, and these *mexicanos* are always polite and they work until they are told it is time to stop. There are a lot more cornfields than there used to be, and there wouldn't be enough Iowa people around who could work the fields even if.

To be at the school buses at 4:30 a.m. you have to get up and go to them earlier. It's dark then, the rising sun in the east an ember of blue light so pure it calms all in its sight, the only nature visible except when a stray head- and taillight flash by on its sizzling highway. The buses idling, the *campesinos* with *mochila* hung on shoulder, hats on, and work IDs looped around their neck, find their way inside the bus they are assigned. So effortless and still, it's almost like nature itself. A couple of men greet me when those men have gone, walking out of the kitchen with Styrofoam coffee cups steaming. The first one is named Raúl and he's originally from Big Spring, Texas. Been here for so many years now he's for Iowa football and thinks this year they'll beat Texas. He works as a translator, and he tells me it's the best job he's ever had. When his wife and two teenage children drive up in a pickup—they're working for the Bells too—he introduces them all to me, switching into English. His wife is a native Iowan, he met her when he'd first come up here for work. His children, sleepy as they are, are nothing but polite. They are Iowans.

When they take off, Alejandro, the man Tom Bell probably counts on the most, comes over. Alex is what they call him. This is his fifth year here. He is employed at least a month before the other workers and at least a month after, always the longest. When three men pile out of the bunkhouse at 5 a.m., it's him who is shaking his head at them—he told everyone 4:30, and now there's no ride until 6:30. They wait over on the school steps. Alejandro is from Nayarit, which is on the Pacific Ocean side of Mexico, a long way from a bus depot in Monterrey. He's picked everything, he tells me proudly, every fruit and every vegetable. Just before he came here, he'd been working in a sugar cane factory back home. This is a good job, he says.

He'll come back as often as he can. Tom Bell treats him well, treats them all well. What happens when someone can't take it, can't make it out there? It happens, and they find something around the grounds for them to do. It all works out.

It is dawn now, blue-gray, more people, more talk, no more indoor lights needed. Alejandro yells over to those guys sitting. He tells them they can get a ride in a pickup that just pulled up, that it's going to their field, to not forget to check in with their crew chief. Six-feet five-inches high, Alejandro is as tall and lean as the healthiest Iowa cornstalk, as native of Mexico to *maiz*, and he is right in the middle of the field of dreams.

KANSAS

CAPITAL   Topeka

ENTERED UNION   1861 (34th)

ORIGIN OF NAME   From a Sioux word meaning "people of
the south wind"

NICKNAMES   Sunflower State or Jayhawk State

MOTTO   Ad astra per aspera ("To the stars through difficulties")

RESIDENTS   Kansan

U.S. REPRESENTATIVES   4

STATE BIRD   western meadowlark

STATE FLOWER   sunflower

STATE TREE   cottonwood

STATE SONG   "Home on the Range"

LAND AREA   81,815 sq. mi.

GEOGRAPHIC CENTER   In Barton Co., 15 mi. NE of
Great Bend

POPULATION   2,744,687

WHITE   86.1%

BLACK   5.7%

AMERICAN INDIAN   0.9%

ASIAN   1.7%

HISPANIC/LATINO   7.0%

UNDER 18   26.5%

65 AND OVER   13.3%

MEDIAN AGE   35.2

KANSAS
Jim Lewis

I want to tell you a story about Kansas, or rather, to tell you a story that Kansas once told about me. This was in Wichita, at a place called the Coyote Club, a roadhouse out on the north side of town just before the fields began, with a big gravel parking lot outside, and beyond it a set of railroad tracks that carried freight up through little towns like Sedgwick and Walton and Peabody, to Topeka, before turning north-west for the Nebraska border. The club had first opened in 1935, and it had gone through several names—the Hobble-De-Hoy, the Country Castle—before becoming the Coyote Club.

There were bullet holes in the stone walls beside the front door; I heard several different stories about how they got there. Inside, there was a main dance floor big enough for a couple of hundred people, and a short, messy bar with scores of 8x10 publicity photos in frames on the wall above it: punk bands, blues bands, crooners, whoever happened to be passing through town and needed a place to play. It was summer. I made a midnight call to a friend of mine in New York from a phone in the club manager's office and said something like, "This place is unbelievable. What am I doing here?"

Let's say there are two separate and distinct places called Kansas, or two ideas of the same place. I'm sure there are more than two; I'm sure there are as many as there are people who live there, or have visited, or have ever thought about the place. But there are at least these two. One is, for lack of a better word, the real Kansas, where people live and work, and go to school, buy car insurance, check the weather report, fight with their families, weigh their produce at the supermarket—live pretty much as people live anywhere, allowing for the distinctions of local culture, climate, tradition, and the like.

The other Kansas is the Kansas of the Mind. This Kansas is mythical, even exotic, precisely because it represents a kind of zero degree America, the heart of the heart of the country: a land of great wide plains and endless fields of grass, long winds, girls in old cowboy boots. If you grew up, as I did, in New York and London, visiting this Kansas is like *The Wizard of Oz* in reverse, where one passes from the daily drudge of the Emerald City, with its glassy canyons and cartoonish personalities, into a fantastic world of empty landscapes, battered buildings, imminent weather, nice people, and very long drives. I was twenty-five when I ended up there.

It happened like this, and just about this quickly: I was doing graduate work in philosophy at Columbia, and teaching the Core "Great Books" Curriculum to undergraduates. One weekend I met a girl from Texas, and on Monday she went home. We talked on the phone for a few weeks, and then made plans to spend a month together in Austin, but by the time I got down there she had changed her mind, and decided she didn't want me around after all. I got drunk at nine in the morning and took a Greyhound to Houston; that night I went to a place called the Hey Hey Club to see a friend of mine, who was playing bass for an R&B singer and sax-player named Johnny Reno. Backstage after the show, Reno took me aside. He was a thin, dapper man in his mid-thirties, a showman; they had just finished their set and his face was shining. "I hear you've been having some trouble with a girl," he said. I confirmed that I had. "Why don't you come on the road with us for a few weeks?" he said.

A note here. I've received more kindnesses in my life than I can possibly have deserved; at moments when unhappiness or trouble, in its various forms, has threatened to overtake me, there's often been a someone nearby who's offered me, through no motivation other than sympathy or generosity, a way out. Reno was one of those people, and so were the men in his band. I had nothing to do and no place to go, no money, and I had just been dismissed by a woman I cared about. I was deadweight, along for the ride, and aside from George, the bass player, I was a stranger to them. But they took me in, they shared their bus with me, their motel rooms, their jokes, and, on those nights when Reno would call me up on stage during the band's encore, to bash on a guitar while we tore through a couple of Roy Orbison songs, they shared their stage. George, Billy, Michael, and Reno himself: they rescued me, they were good to me, all they wanted was for me to enjoy myself; and I surely did.

We went to Fort Worth and stayed at Reno's house for a few days, and then started up through Oklahoma, Kansas, and Nebraska, and down through Missouri and Arkansas. I might as well say that we drank a lot, and snorted a lot of crystal meth, and we went barreling over the Great Plains in Reno's bus, stopping at night to load equipment into some club, play a couple of sets, crash in a motel room, and then begin again the next morning. Oklahoma City, Kansas City, Omaha, Little Rock: The names were as perfumed and mythic to me as Paris or Athens or Tunisia would have been; but I had been to Paris and Athens and Tunisia, to Cologne and to

Cambridge. I had never been to Texarkana, or Shreveport, let alone to those long flat spaces in between. I took a camera with me and shot off a couple of rolls. Almost every picture shows the same thing, and they all look like abstractions: the blue above meeting the greenish-brown below, and nothing in between.

Freedom, room to move, a place in time. We'd stop at a gas station in the middle of nowhere to fill up, and emerge from the bus to stretch our legs and stare dazedly down a hundred miles of flat highway, and I would think the same things other people think when they get onto the Plains: I can do anything here. No one can find me. There's nothing to bump into, nothing to break, there are no surprises when you can see the next car coming from miles away. The days unfold on an endless playing field.

When we got to Wichita one Saturday night, there were high-school kids cruising up and down the main drag, shouting things from car to car, and generally whooping it up. They really did that: It was like arriving in New York for the first time—say, after growing up in Wichita—and discovering that everyone really is either Italian, Hasidic, or gay. I couldn't have been more delighted to see it. We loaded the band's equipment into the Coyote Club, and went back to the Holiday Inn for a nap.

Then back to the club, and another new, essential thing. I had spent much of my youth in nightclubs: Max's Kansas City and CB's in high school, and later Hurrah and the Mudd Club, Tier 3, the Roxy, the Paradise Garage—New York's vast and shifting world after hours. I'd seen drag shows at the Escuelita, drank warm beer at an anarchist club in an abandoned building in the East End of London. But I'd never seen a hundred guys in gimme caps mixing with a hundred girls in tight Wranglers, while outside a miles-long freight train passed. This was their weekend, and this was what they did with it; they paid a little money, got a loud hot show from Reno and his band, flirted, danced, drank, made a night for themselves. I did pretty much the same, and I learned something along the way.

It happened like this. I'd noticed a girl when we first came in: long-legged and very lovely, with long, straight brown hair and perfect pale skin, she was about my age and her eyes were glittering with mischief. She looked upon the Coyote Club and all the people there with some mixture of exasperation and amusement; she knew them, she was fond of them, but she seemed just a little too glamorous for the place, and she wore an expression that suggested that she'd had it with all this, and she'd be gone if she could just figure out where to go, and how to get there. A little later, I was standing halfway between the bar and the entrance to the club when she sidled up to me, and opened up a conversation by saying, in a smart, musical voice, "Didn't I work on your pickup truck this afternoon?" I looked at her—she was just about to smile—and I replied, in all seriousness and sincerity, "No, I don't think so. I'm not from here." And she laughed.

Reader, a rube in reverse is a rube nonetheless. I hadn't realized she was kidding; it never occurred to me that everything about me made it perfectly plain that I wasn't from there.

In itself this is not unusual. I have a tendency, fortunately or not, to believe that I'm invisible even when the facts would indicate otherwise. I've wandered blithely through the slums of Karachi, with no more sense of myself than it took to notice that everyone seemed very polite. On the sidewalk in Shigatse, in southern Tibet, I made a joke to a companion about my quest to document the yeti, that mythical creature, oversized, pale, and unusually hairy, only to realize, some hours later, that people were staring because that was me, exactly—that I was it: the Abominable Snowman. In the Congo, children in little villages would jump up and down, point and shout *muzungu!*, while I vaguely wondered why they identified the photographer I was traveling with, who was Vietnamese, as a "white man." You see what I mean.

The composition of the world is such that these little self-recognitions, when they finally occur, usually mean noticing that I'm white, or western, or American; but not in Kansas, no—it was the first place I had ever been where it was obvious, at least to everyone else, that I was swarthy, eastern, and vaguely foreign. I went into the Coyote Club dressed, as far as I can recollect it, like a Jewish Johnny Thunders (this was twenty years ago, when I could get away with that sort of thing). I thought of Kansas as exotic, but it wasn't until the girl laughed that I realized that Kansas thought of me that way, too.

There are two things that I need to stress here. The first is that when I say it was Kansas that first taught me that I'm not exactly white, I don't mean that I felt black: I'm not, and I didn't, and I wouldn't presume to speak for someone who was black, or Mexican, or Indian, or know what they might feel when in the Midwest. Perhaps what I felt is better described as a vague sense of my own ethnicity. Now that I live in Texas I feel it surprisingly often: Every few months someone will say to me, with startling frankness, "You're not from here, are you?" I heard it from a check-out girl, who blurted the question out as I was loading up my groceries; I heard it from a contractor who was working on my house. I heard it from a Mexican woman who stood beside me in the take-out line of a restaurant (though under most circumstances, she would probably describe me as Anglo: the ironies ripple across the language). Usually, it means something like, "You're nose is bigger than most people's around here,"—which it is—or, "You stand differently: You're wound a little tighter than we are"—which I am. These are facts, and every so often someone decides there's no point in ignoring them.

The second thing I want to make clear is that there was nothing sinister in the experience, nothing offensive intended, and no offense taken. I didn't feel objectified, or debased, or despised, or ostracized, or unwelcome. There in the Coyote Club, and this is the point, everyone was looking for some fun, including me, and everyone found it. The curiosity that was brought to bear, the amusement, the desire to get out of your same old ways and into something new: that was mutual, and not just harmless but a boon.

The girl who approached me: her name was Emmy, she worked at the car rental desk at Wichita Airport, and she was all around adorable. We went to her house and talked for a while, then back to my room on the twenty-first floor of the Holiday Inn—about as high up off the floor of Wichita as you could get, with an illuminated minor league baseball stadium lying down below, beyond that, the lights of the city, and beyond that, Kansas in all directions into the darkness. I left Wichita the next morning (Emmy woke up to see me off, then went back to bed, to luxuriate under the protection of a check-out time that was still some hours away), a little bit smarter, happier, and more bold.

I said something at the start here about the Kansas of the Mind, but the reverse is true as well. The mind is a kind of Kansas, or mine is anyway. Or my memories are: For one thing, I seldom go there, so however near they may be, they remain somehow far away. They are vast and green, and both perfectly plain and inescapably mysterious; there are heat patches along the way that create shimmering, hallucinatory reflections, and tornados in the distance. There are pretty girls, loud music, jokes that it sometimes takes me a while to get. I'm different there, different than I am here and now— smaller, in some obscure way, and always astounded by the feeling of freedom—and different than everybody else as well. In the Kansas that is my memory, I'm not yet me, but not quite another, either. As I say, I don't go there often, but I don't need to; I know that it'll be waiting for me whenever I get around to revisiting, and I know, because this is the point of such places, that it will be exactly the same.

KENTUCKY

CAPITAL Frankfort

ENTERED UNION 1792 (15th)

ORIGIN OF NAME From an Iroquoian word Ken-tah-te meaning "land of tomorrow" or "dark or bloody ground," or "meadow land"

NICKNAME Bluegrass State

MOTTO "United we stand, divided we fall"

RESIDENTS Kentuckian

U.S. REPRESENTATIVES 6

STATE BIRD Kentucky cardinal

STATE FLOWER goldenrod

STATE TREE tulip poplar

STATE SONG "My Old Kentucky Home"

LAND AREA 39,728 sq. mi.

GEOGRAPHIC CENTER In Marion Co., 3 mi. NNW of Lebanon

POPULATION 4,173,405

WHITE 90.1%

BLACK 7.3%

AMERICAN INDIAN 0.2%

ASIAN 0.7%

HISPANIC/LATINO 1.5%

UNDER 18 24.6%

65 AND OVER 12.5%

MEDIAN AGE 35.9

KENTUCKY
John Jeremiah Sullivan

The Commonwealth of Kentucky is shaped like an alligator's head. It is also shaped like the Commonwealth of Virginia, as if the latter were advancing westward by generation of adult clones. In a way this is so. The southern borders of these states are keyed to the same horizontal projection—one surveyed by the frontier planter William Byrd in 1728—while the rivers forming their northern extents fall back just opposite each other from the eastern and western flanks of the Appalachian massif. There's a mirroring there. In 1818 one of the few people able to mount even a semi-coherent accounting of the ancient processes responsible for it neared Louisville aboard a long covered flatboat that following local custom he called an ark. It was summer. He was traveling down the Ohio, on the alligator's eye. He'd convinced a couple of booksellers in Pittsburgh to advance him $100 for a new and more accurate map of the river's tributaries. That was mostly a way to earn travel money on his part, which is fine, because in the end they refused to publish what he wrote. He was thirty-two, not famous but known in scientific circles, mainly for his work on Sicilian fishes. In Sicily, which was held by the British, one did not want to sound too French, so he went by his matronymic, Schmaltz. Since coming to Kentucky however he had resumed the name of Constantine Rafinesque.

"Who is Rafinesque, and what is his character?" once asked John Jacob Astor. The context of the question is not given. Rafinesque himself could get dizzy before the complexity of the answer. "Versatility of talents and of professions," he wrote, "is not uncommon in America; but those which I have exhibited . . . may appear to exceed belief: and yet it is a positive fact that in knowledge I have been a Botanist, Naturalist, Geologist, Geographer, Historian, Poet, Philosopher, Philologist, Economist, Philanthropist. . . ."

The first thing one notices about this oft-quoted self-description is its ostentation, with hints of insanity. The second is that it's woefully incomplete. Rafinesque, who is cursorily named by Darwin in *On the Origin of Species* as a forerunner in the study of evolution, in fact came closer than anyone else to grasping natural selection in the decades before that book was published. He came up with the name *Taino* for the islanders whom Columbus met. He is hailed as "the father of American myriapodology" (the study of many-legged bugs). He was the first person to understand dust, that much of it comes from the atmosphere. He invented the word "malacology" (the study of mollusks). In 1831 he contacted a philosophical club in New York, proposing the establishment of a "Congress of Peaceful Nations." He'd already written an open letter to the Cherokee warning them that they would soon be forcefully moved to the West, a full decade before it happened. These examples are chosen at random.

Those river arks only moved downstream. The owners broke them and sold the lumber when they'd made their destinations. They were floating islands, often lashed together (as during Rafinesque's trip) into caravans. An 1810 account says they were shaped like "parallelograms." Some were seventy feet long. You lived in a cabin or out on deck, other times in a tent, with an open cooking fire. There were animals. To go ashore and come back, which you could do whenever you wanted, you took your own, smaller boat, kept tied to the gunwale. The arks went slow when the water was slow, fast when it was fast, and crashed when it was very fast. This distinctly American mode of travel sufficed throughout the interior for a century and is now so gone we struggle to reconstitute its crudest details. It has no Twain. Rafinesque liked the arks because he could botanize as they drifted. He felt the vegetable pulse of the continent shuddering down its veins. The green world whispered to him. He tells us in a short, hectic, wounded memoir, written near the end, precisely what it said. "You are a conqueror."

The New World had a way of never being new. I don't mean the Native Americans. That part is obvious. But in European terms, somebody was always already there. The first person De Soto met in Florida spoke Spanish. In fact, was a Spaniard! Is it the Plymouth voyage or one of the Jamestown voyages that had on it a group of Indians coming back from a visit to London? These days everyone knows not even Columbus made a "discovery"; the Vikings beat him by a half-millennium. Just so Rafinesque, that first time he crossed the Kentucky mountains, had a whole prior American career, an earlier act. From 1802 to 1805 he'd crisscrossed New England, been in the fields and at the high tables, patronized as something of a boy genius—he was just nineteen when he first arrived, on the pretense of apprenticing to a mercantile firm, though he instantly vanished into the woods—and squinted at by a few who noted his "mania" for discovery. It was said he attempted to rename and reclassify the first common weed he spotted on American soil.

Nonetheless influential persons encouraged Rafinesque. Benjamin Rush, a Declaration signer and the first great American physician, offered him an apprenticeship in his practice, medicine and botany being closer together then. Rafinesque refused. His destiny had been revealed to him and did not lie in the city. At the time, Jefferson's Corps of Discovery was in the Far West. Later expeditions might look to the South, at Louisiana and Arkansas, or toward "the Apalachian mountains, the least known of all our mountains, and which," said Rafinesque, "I pant to explore." He was taken to meet Jefferson, and they corresponded. The earth, which Rafinesque believed was an "organized animal rolling in space," had arranged for him to be present and correctly positioned at this moment, just as a continent of taxonomically pristine vastnesses offered itself to science. He would gladly, he wrote to *messr. le président*, serve as official Corps naturalist, being supremely and, although it gave him no pleasure to say so, uniquely qualified for the role.

Jefferson either never received or else neglected the letter. He thought of Lewis and Clark's expedition as primarily a military thing and would never have forced a socially indifferent French polymath on the "nine young men from Kentucky." Instead he sent Lewis himself to Philadelphia and had him tutored by the savants. Rafinesque, who was in the city and had secretly allowed himself to credit a claim that he'd soon be asked to join the mission, must have seethed. He watched another man's body step into his future and occupy his moment. The things we'd know if they'd sent Rafinesque to the Pacific! His fevered interest in Indian languages alone—almost without parallel for his day. Even as it was, even on his own, he somehow talked the War Department into sending out vocabulary questionnaires to all of its Indian agents. One sees these mentioned with great esteem by linguists who have no idea Rafinesque was behind them.

A mission of discovery would have molded and disciplined him as a researcher. For once he'd have known the weight of a duty as large as his own self-regard. Every person of learning on the East Coast and in the European capitals would have waited on his findings regarding the flora and fauna and tribes. The western mountains. He'd have been forced to anticipate broad scrutiny, to adapt and refine the radically advanced system of natural classification he was beginning to contemplate, for he had already begun to peel away slightly from the "indelicate" and arbitrary sexual system of Linnaeus, his great master and guide. No choice but to go methodically, to keep to what he could see—the number of specimens alone would dictate that.

He chafed when he heard no reply and sailed for Sicily, muttering as always that they hadn't been ready for him here, wherever. This is how it was with Rafinesque, always too quick to take offense, too antsy—untouchable in the field, certainly, but never able to *sit*. His departure was lamented in the press. Yet he left, and with, it has to be admitted, a certain petulance.

Three days after his ship weighed anchor one of his friends in Philadelphia intercepted a letter from Jefferson. A new expedition was forming. This one would seek the Red River. If Rafinesque were still interested, a place could be made. It was as far as I know an unprecedented provision on Jefferson's part, made expressly with Rafinesque in mind. Jefferson had seen very well what he was in the room with when they met. Now Rafinesque's embarrassed friends had to reply with the news. "Unfortunately, Sir, . . ."

I'm not sure America ever completely forgave Rafinesque for this betrayal, this weakness of faith. By "America" I mean the land. It had called him. He had not come. He went to Sicily instead.

There he married the blonde Josephine Vacarro. They had a son and daughter. It's said he produced a much-admired brandy vintage without ever tasting a single drop, so strong was his loathing for spirituous liquors, so instinctive his understanding of chemical behavior. The sharpest detail from the Sicilian years is hidden in the journals of William Swainson, a towering English naturalist of the early nineteenth century who worked for a few years on Italian fishes and met with Rafinesque. Swainson conceded the brilliance but complained like everyone about the lack of meticulousness, in preserving specimens, for instance. He says Rafinesque used to walk down to the fish markets near his house, where the fishermen knew to put aside anything weird for him. He found many new species this way, one while Swainson was with him. Yet although Swainson begged him to dry and keep the fish properly after he'd finished drawing and naming it, Rafinesque insisted on eating it. He lived well. He got involved in some sort of medical business and made loads of money. He paid litter-bearers to carry him through the hills, laughing that in Sicily only a beggar walks. The men slept in the meadows while he herborized. A decade passed.

When Rafinesque returned to North America—of course he did; destiny can't be eluded, only perverted—he went to find John James Audubon. He asked for the great man in Louisville, but they told him Audubon had gone deeper, into the forest, to Hendersonville, where he'd opened a general store. Rafinesque longed to see his new paintings of western birds, not yet published but already famous among the learned. He knew Audubon liked to incorporate local flora into his pictures and was sure he'd find new species of plants there, hidden, as it were, even from Audubon himself. As great naturalists who worked for money in an age of gentlemen herborizers there would have been immediate sympathy. In childhood, both had been driven by revolutionary violence to flee relatively happy Francophone homes, Rafinesque's in Marseilles and Audubon's in Haiti.

Audubon was out walking when he noticed the boatmen staring at something by the landing. It's through his eyes, which so little escaped, that we see Rafinesque again, almost, in "a long loose coat of yellow nankeen, much the worse of the many rubs it had got in its time and stained all over with the juice of plants, hung loosely about him like a sack. A waistcoat of the same, with enormous pockets, and buttoned up to the chin, reached below over a pair of tight pantaloons. . . . His beard was as long as I have known my own to be during . . . peregrinations, and his lank black hair hung loosely over his shoulder."

Their first meeting was a potentially grotesque slow-motion pileup of awkwardnesses from which they emerged smiling together in perfect good humor. Rafinesque stooped like a peddler under a gigantic bundle of dried plants strapped to his back. He walked up to Audubon "with a rapid step" and asked where one could find Audubon. Audubon said, "I am the man." Rafinesque did a little dance and rubbed his hands. Then he gave Audubon a letter of introduction from some heavyweight back East. Audubon read it and asked, "May I see the fish?" What fish? "This says I'm being sent an odd fish." It seems I am the fish! Audubon stammered, but Rafinesque laughed.

Audubon offered to send servants for the luggage, but the traveler carried only his "pack of weeds" or as Audubon calls them elsewhere, "his grasses." Rafinesque's other things rose in the unexplained gigantic pockets and included mainly the notebook bound in oiled leather, linen for pressing plants, and a broad umbrella. He walked on the ground now. In fact he refused to ride any of the many horses he was offered, saying all botanists ought to walk, to stay close to the earth.

There are those who'd make Rafinesque's entire eight-year Kentucky period coincident with the onset of mental degeneration. And it was: *and his genius grew*. His genius grew as his errors and embarrassments multiplied. This is what maddened about him and always will. He won't reconcile.

Consider: It's at this time that Rafinesque begins planning his masterpiece, *Ichthylogia Ohiensis*, the posthumous rediscovery of which will spark the rehabilitation of his standing in the late nineteenth century. Yet it's on this same trip to Kentucky that the seeds of his academic shame are gathered, for along the river he's confronted with the Mounds, those rain-smoothed earthen monuments raised on the landscape by hundreds of generations of Native American builders. "They struck me with astonishment and induced me to study," Rafinesque says. He calls them "earthy remains" and notes how swiftly they're falling to the plough, "and will be obliterated ere long." There are a few places left in Kentucky, mostly on family farms, where you can see them as Rafinesque did, geometric land sculptures covered with grass, half in the field and half in the forest. Rafinesque declares it "high time that these monuments should all be accurately surveyed" and undertakes the work himself. But the book he produces, *The American Nations*, is worthless, an interminable pseudo-scholarly unfolding of his theories on the origin of New World societies, which he contends sprang from a voyage of Mediterranean *ür*-colonizers, the Atalantes. On and on, lineages of chiefs, names, dates, for thousands of years, information that would change everything, had Rafinesque actually possessed it, had he not somehow himself been able to sit there and endure the sheer tedium of inventing it. And then, not content with fraud, he descends to forgery, cooking up an entire migration saga for the Lenape Indian tribe, one that corroborates to a striking extent his ideas about prehistory. He writes of having received, in Kentucky, a set of "curiously carved" wooden sticks, the markings on which consumed him for years, until finally he completed his great decipherment. The sticks themselves disappeared, a tragedy, but at least the translation survived. This was the famous *Walam Olum*, which obsessed the pharmaceutical tycoon Eli Lilly his whole adult life and is still taken for real in corners of the scholarly world, though it was definitively revealed to be a hoax by the Lenape scholar David M. Oestreicher in 1994.

Ethnographically speaking the *Walam Olum* is probably worthless, too. There was only one true writing system in the pre-Columbian Americas, the Mayan. As it happens, Rafinesque is today considered the "prime mover" in the eventual decipherment of the Mayan glyphs, making him the only thinker in history ever to have both successfully unlocked the secrets of one ancient language and at least half-deviously attempted to counterfeit the existence of another. But it's the lovely and disorientingly modern poetry the *Walam Olum*'s verses become when unburdened of scholarly expectation I wish to honor. The *Walam Olum* is in fact a great nineteenth-century American poem. Written in the 1820s or early '30s and purporting to date from the dawn of time, it's not a translation but a divination, performed in a state of at least partial madness by someone for whom English was a fourth or fifth language.

It freezes was there, it snows was
there, it is cold was there.
To possess mild coldness and much
game, they go to the northerly plain, to
hunt cattle they go.
To be strong and to be rich the comers
Divided into tillers and hunters.
The most strong, the most good, the
most holy, the hunters they are.
And the hunters spread themselves,
becoming northerlings, easterlings,
southerlings, westerlings.

Rafinesque's virtues are often misplaced in this way. You can't ever trust him or even listen to him about his own work. He doesn't understand it. He never had time to understand it. Is his forged enthnographic artifact a great original poem? Well, his "great poem," *The World: Or, Instability*, is sadly inept and simpy, but its long train of self-explanatory endnotes, predating *The Waste Land* by a hundred years, ranks among his finest writings. It's there he fantasizes about hot-air balloons with sails and steam power and shaped like "a boat or spindle, a fish or a bird." It's there he calls for an end to enclosures, a return to the commons. "I hate the sight of fences like the Indians!" he says. It's Rafinesque the stylist, among all the souls he contained, whom we should get to know. Like Conrad or Isak Dinesen, he made the subtle offness of his foreign inflection work for him in English, finding effects concealed from native speakers. Warning would-be field workers he wrote, "You may travel over an unhealthy region or in a sickly season, you may fall sick on the road and become helpless, unless you be very careful."

Rafinesque and Audubon spent three weeks together. All Americans ought to read, in Audubon's *Ornithological Biography*, his chapter on their idyll in Hendersonville; it's our Gauguin and Van Gogh, with kinder madness. Audubon says, "I observed some degree of impatience in his request to be allowed at once to see what I had." At the house, "I opened my portfolios and laid them before him." Rafinesque gives criticisms, "which were of the greatest advantage to me," says Audubon, "for, being well acquainted with books as well as with nature, he was well fitted to give me advice." Audubon even got Rafinesque to drink brandy, though he did it only by scaring him into arrhythmia, leading him on a snipe hunt in a miles-thick canebrake where it got dark and stormed and a young bear brushed them, and the canes popped in the suffocating humidity like guns, and "the withered particles of leaves and bark attached to the cane stuck to our clothes." Like scales. Now they were the fishes! Audubon had hunted with Boone and chuckled at such adventures. Rafinesque had shot a bird once and never got over the "cruelty."

Safely home they sat up over cold meat. "I listened to him with as much delight as TELEMACHUS could have listened to MENTOR," Audubon says. It was hot, and they put the window open. The candle drew bugs. We have then Messers. RAFINESQUE and AUDUBON at the table by the open window in the middle of the night in 1818, in Kentucky, a state whose name the natives have for some reason always wanted to mean "dark and bloody ground" but that probably means "meadow land," and they are joking in English and French about bugs, on a night of summer weather all central Kentuckians know, of thunderstorms that have suddenly given onto a mysteriously invigorating late humidity. Gazing down on the forest that surrounds these two like a starless ocean, you'd assume they were the loneliest people on earth, but in fact they're at rare ease, and inside the cone of their little flame, it's Paris. Audubon grabs a big beetle and bets it can carry a candlestick on its back. Says Rafinesque, "I should like to see the experiment made."

> It was made, and the insect moved about, dragging its burden so as to make the candlestick change its position as if by magic, until coming upon the edge of the table, it dropped on the floor, took to wing, and made its escape.

Before dawn Audubon woke to uproar. Hurtling through Rafinesque's door he found the smaller man leaping naked in the dark, holding the neck of Audubon's Stradivarius, which he'd bashed to splinters trying to stun small bats. These had come to eat bugs by his still-burning candle. Rafinesque was "convinced they belonged to 'a new species,'" but they turned out to be common pips.

Some days later, out of possible embarrassment over this incident, Rafinesque vanished at evening without a word. He rejoined the ark. "We were perfectly reconciled to his oddities," Audubon says, "and hoped that his sojourn might be of long duration." Rafinesque barely mentions the visit in his own memoir and says it lasted three days.

As Rafinesque wrote in *The World*: "Fare-thee-well truly glorious earthly genius."

LOUISIANA

CAPITAL   Baton Rouge

ENTERED UNION   1812 (18th)

ORIGIN OF NAME   In honor of Louis XIV of France

NICKNAME   Pelican State

MOTTO   "Union, justice, and confidence"

RESIDENTS   Louisianan or Louisianian

U.S. REPRESENTATIVES   7

STATE FLOWER   magnolia

STATE BIRD   eastern brown pelican

STATE TREE   bald cypress

STATE SONGS   "Give Me Louisiana" and "You Are My Sunshine"

LAND AREA   43,562 sq. mi.

GEOGRAPHIC CENTER   In Avoyelles Parish, 3 mi. SE of Marksville

POPULATION   4,523,628

WHITE   63.9%

BLACK   32.5%

AMERICAN INDIAN   0.6%

ASIAN   1.2%

HISPANIC/LATINO   2.4%

UNDER 18   27.3%

65 AND OVER   11.6%

MEDIAN AGE   34.0

LOUISIANA
Joshua Clark

"At the age of four, I saw the little girl in our house. She was always turning all the faucets on. My parents would be having sex and she'd turn the light on. She just thought it was funny."

A smile inflates Cari Roy's cheeks almost to caricature, vanquishing the wrinkles from around her eyes, her glare exuding an easy energy. A crystal ball lies on her dining room table between us. She keeps it just for fun, says she doesn't need such instruments.

"You'd be hard-pressed to go into any building in New Orleans and not find spirits. This town is soaked with them. Fifteen thousand people died in one summer from yellow fever. Where do you think all those bodies went? We didn't have enough cemeteries. We're living on bodies."

Roy first ventured from psychic to ghost-hunter when the novelist Anne Rice brought her in to investigate her properties, and since then Roy has become a sort of spiritual guru in New Orleans.

"Katrina woke the dead. It woke up people who had died in the last flood. Those impressions overlapped like crazy with the new spirits. It was a psychic cluster fuck, like throwing gasoline on a paranormal fire. It was the closest thing I've experienced to the paranormal in sci-fi films. I mean, the *amount* of dead. All walking around in a daze. They too were evacuating from the storm, panic stricken, running in terror."

Roy had front-row seats. She lives here on the boundary between the Upper Ninth Ward, which stayed dry through the storm's aftermath, and the Lower Ninth Ward, which went underwater. The lavender shutters on her double shotgun house seem to melt into the air as the day dies outside.

"Some spirits just can't come to terms with the fact that they no longer have a grasp on life, that they no longer *control* it. Like a junkie, they still want their fix. When I came back after the storm, there was a dead woman wandering around my block searching for her family. Using my little psychic short radio waves, I eventually found her family just outside of town. I sent her there. She was really, really pissed. She always hated the suburbs."

Like many, Roy claims water is geologically conducive to spirits. And the Big Easy is built on swamp around the deepest part of the most powerful river in the world. Partly due to this unique ecosystem, through three centuries New Orleans has seen more than its fair share of suffering. And yet it could be argued the town has always put a smile on the face of death. Like those old Mardi Gras masks, the city balances the tear in its eye with a grin on its lips. New Orleanians love their dead as much as they do the living. Death here is dragged into the light, just as it is into blinding limestone tombs beside the interstate during rush hour.

"They especially hold onto dead people in the Ninth Ward," says Roy. "Spirits love this. Would you go somewhere people don't pay any attention to you?"

Through her open door she gazes across the street at the Industrial Canal levee, its darkness partially eclipsing the twilit horizon. This side was lucky. It was the other that finally gave way to a twenty-foot wall of water. "Hell, since the storm, we're all still walking around here half dead."

I do a different type of ghost tour," says Randy Ping, one of New Orleans's most respected ghost tour guides. "I don't do the usual *'Here's the house where the spirits are so unhappy!'* I don't believe in any of that shit at *all*."

I've brought Ping to a coffee shop courtyard to meet Jeff Dwyer, a clinical specialist in cardiology and ghost-hunter from California. I first met Dwyer three years ago while he was in New Orleans researching his third ghost-hunting book. "Ghost aren't like fallen leaves," Dwyer told me that morning in the Lower Ninth Ward. "They can't be blown away by wind or washed away by floods. These catastrophes often infuse them with new energy, making them more active and easier to discover. And renovation is the best time to find ghosts. There's often activity when their home's being disturbed."

Ping shifts his black boots alongside Dwyer's white Reeboks. He is easily half Dwyer's age, his dyed black hair tucked into a long pony tail, a cigarette hovering between long-nailed fingers and silver rings. "I think that people who have a strong belief in the supernatural should go have an MRI done," Ping says. "It was in *Scientific American* a few years ago, they have a neurological disorder."

"Really?" Dwyer says, smiling. "Well, I guess I should have the lab give me an MRI when I get back."

Ping stubs his cigarette out. He is not joking, nor is he specifically criticizing Dwyer. "There's plenty of old buildings down here in New Orleans with their fair share of creaky boards and old timbers and bad air conditioning and plumbing," Ping says, "and some jackass turns on a faucet and it doesn't come on right away and he forgets about it and an hour later it turns on automatically when the water pressure's back up and he exclaims, 'The place is haunted!' You know—real freaking *morons*."

Dwyer maintains a clinical, detached expression. "I think there is a direct correlation between the level of education here and the number of ghost stories," Ping says, smoke and words pouring through his teeth, where he bites a fresh cigarette. "It's hard in America to find a less literate society than New Orleans. People need to find a way to remember certain historical events. Add a ghost to a story and it makes it good enough for the kids to remember."

"And you conduct ghost tours?" Dwyer asks.

"I moved here from Oklahoma to find ghosts. I have gone to every single one of these places—ones that are supposed to be so incredibly haunted. Not once have I *ever* seen *anything* that gives me *any* belief at all that there is *any*thing supernatural going on."

"I've never tried to convince anyone into accepting my experiences, or my beliefs," says Dwyer.

"It's not about beliefs, it's about facts for me," Ping says. "Ghost stories are the only stories I loved when I was a kid. They're very important. Just like the Bible or any other mythology. But what's important is that people give these stories a life of their own, that people know *why* things happen that inspire the legends."

"What I love is that ghost stories often take us outside history texts, into the unknown histories of ordinary people, everyday lives," Dwyer says. "It opens our eyes to the realities experienced by people we can relate to. I have always held a fascination with the day-to-day existence of people who lived a hundred years ago or more. I wonder where they would get a drink of cold water in August. Or what you might spend all your time looking at if you were a little girl my daughter's age, feeling that your death is coming from some plague, or a fire or flood, a hurricane, then to be so quickly forgotten when it passes."

Ping nods, sucks down the last of his coffee, and says, "The ghost is secondary."

"So why don't you just do history tours?"

"We've tried it. People won't go on them," Ping says. "You can't sell history here."

It's 3 a.m. and my girlfriend is sitting up in my bed screaming hell at me and I'm too afraid to open my eyes. I might see what she sees. She says there's five of them, all men. One of them is standing on my bedside table over me, she says, his head bobbing back and forth, pupils all white, laughing soundlessly. I keep telling her she's dreaming. She tells me the one by the foot of the bed is fat, so fat the buttons on his shirt have burst. She buries her head into my shoulder, swears she's wide awake. And I still can't open my eyes. They're wearing prison uniforms, she says, with big black-and-white stripes. Their ankles chained to each other. One is pointing, shouting at her. "Go away! Get out of here!" she keeps screaming. I hold her with one arm, the other fumbling blindly for the lamp switch. Light! They're gone, she says. I open my eyes.

I sleep with the lights on for the next month. For weeks she hears chains dragging over the floor of our rooms in the oldest apartment building in America. But I don't. And I still haven't seen a ghost. Not ever. Instead I often lie in bed ashamed of my gutless instincts, how I wouldn't open my eyes that night, blowing my one chance to see—or just as importantly, *not* to see—a ghost.

I've had psychics in my apartment describe white fluffy spirit dogs that follow me around, the kid who likes to sit on my washing machine, an enraged lover who murdered his spouses and wants to murder me. None of it matches anything in my real world. I've worked the graveyard shift in supposedly haunted bars and the only zombies I've seen are the sunken ones hunched in a dark corner, endlessly shoving their paychecks into video poker machines.

But I hope. I hear the strange tapping on my dresser some nights, the dozens of little voices speaking to me in that second before sleep when my rational mind has quit. Sometimes I tell them to just shut up and get in bed with me, go to sleep, dammit.

Tagging along with people who could see ghosts is fine, but I want to see them too. And so much for the one-man shows, I'm going to get myself a full team, science and gadgets—electromagnetic field readers, electronic voice phenomena recorders, cameras, infrared, thermometers, barometers, the works. But none of the paranormal organizations within Louisiana is willing to brave the Ninth Ward. The largest balks—"You want us to bring $10,000 worth of equipment into *that* neighborhood?!"—despite never having set foot there.

After months of research, it seems the National Paranormal Society, based in Miami, each member boasting over ten years experience in paranormal investigation, is the most capable, organized, and, if such a thing can exist, legitimate.

After several emails, Rich Valdes, president of the National Paranormal

Society, calls me back. None of his team has ever been to Louisiana. Perfect. I tell him I have a futon and plenty of floor space, and two months later they drive the fifteen hours from Miami.

A church-going Christian and home-studied demonologist, Valdes is a big bear of a man—half teddy, half grizzly—with the slit eyes of a pit bull, the obligatory shaved head and goatee of a nightclub bouncer, and a mortal fear of clowns and frogs. By contrast, Angel—Pagan practitioner, Reiki master, and the team's "medium"—seems a gentle giant. He uses psychometry: the alleged ability to obtain information about a person or event by touching a related object. Olga, the field analyst, is a bleached platinum blonde, with little vampire canine teeth, the tiniest bit of eyeliner on her eyelids to set off her angelic face in all its paleness, and bits of a DISCIPLINE back tattoo, from her days in the Marines, peeking out from her tank top.

Olga handles the scientific, Rich the historical, and Angel the metaphysical. Like doctors, they diagnose hauntings from symptoms. There are three types of ghosts: apparition, residual haunt, and an actual haunting. They boast about all the simple explanations they've found to debunk supposed hauntings, and they show me proof of their greatest catches, like a child's voice crying, "Save our souls," caught on tape in the middle of an abandoned cemetery at night.

I brief the team about the city, the affected areas, specific homes of the deceased. But first Angel leaves the apartment. He always goes into a case cold. This way only when his spiritual findings align with the historical and scientific ones are they credible. The metaphysical confirmed by the physical. When he returns, Angel asks me to stand in front of a window, facing away from him. Without telling me what he's doing, he stands five feet behind me and manages to push me forward into the window, then I watch him manipulate divining rods with trembling hands.

Angel got his start helping his grandmother with an exorcism in Puerto Rico at the age of thirteen. He tries to remove the fear people often have of their deceased loved ones. "I've never charged money," he says. "I was given this gift for free, so it's not my right to charge others for it." He recalls a run-in with O. J. Simpson in the Miami Home Depot where he works—"He stayed far away from me." He remembers seeing the numbers 911 continuously but not knowing what they meant before the towers fell and later discovering that some of the hijackers had learned to fly planes just down the street from him; a little girl's ghost waking him up, telling him to get out, minutes before he would have been trapped in his apartment by a fire downstairs; the Creole woman singing in the courtyard beside us on our way to the Ninth Ward.

"I see body bags all over the floor," says Angel, an hour later, standing in the center of a gutted Baptist church, their video cameras' lights and flashes hardly making a dent in the cavernous darkness. "I can hear them praying. Someone is saying, 'I was here. Nobody found my body.' "

It's midnight in the Lower Ninth. We're scouting. The farther we crawl into the mangled houses, the path to the bathroom, to the kitchen, the bedrooms, a few pictures laid out on an overturned sofa, the more we feel what was once a home. The human things are still here, the viscera of other peoples' material lives splayed beneath our dirty sneakers. I find Rich standing in the middle of a dark street, staring lost into block after block after block that once contained homes, chest-high weeds surrounding the concrete slabs of their foundations. "I'm embarrassed to be an American right now," he says. "This is bullshit. Just absolute *bullshit*."

Like the rest of Miami, they suffered Hurricane Andrew in 1992. But only now do they understand the vast difference between tidal surge and flooding, between natural disasters and manmade ones.

"Ummmm, guys . . . " Olga mutters. "I think we're getting carjacked." And so we are.

We spend the next few days visiting sites where people died from Katrina's aftermath.

Some had made the news, but most hadn't even warranted an obituary. Angel touches each house, tells us the age and sex of the deceased, but there's only residual energy left—like an analog recording, a fingerprint, nothing sentient. Until one afternoon we find a house with 1 DEAD IN ATTIC still spray-painted in yellow across its door. Angel leans onto the side of the house, head bowed, his arms resting upon an open window sill, hands inside the dark. "He's holding my hand right now," he whispers. "Feel how cold it is right here, inside the sill."

Olga and I shove in the back door. I've long since dismissed any guilt over trespassing into these abandoned properties. On the contrary, I feel it's criminal to leave these spaces unexplored, untold, and that they've remained that way for too long already. We find a firm route through the sagging, shattered belly of the gutted house. Flashes and beeps kill the dark and the silence as Rich and Olga take pictures. The EMF meter chirps wildly in my hands, then stops. "I'm getting a D initial," Angel says. "Daryl." He stands in the center of the house, looking up into the exposed attic. "This spirit, he's asking me, 'Can you show me how to get out?'"

We return to the house that night. "I call on you Gabriel, archangel of light, to illuminate the path for this lost soul!" Angel cries. He claps once, louder than I've ever heard a clap. A second later there is a loud swooshing sound, like something shooting out the window. "Did you hear that?" Olga asks. Rich says it went right beside his ear.

Two hours later we're watching the footage in a booth at the back of drag queen show while they sip on sodas. The shots taken while Angel was supposedly talking to the ghost reveal an "orb," a hazy bubble of light the size of a baseball, about two feet in front of his eyes, directly in his line of sight.

The next day, after visiting the tomb of New Orleans's most famed voodoo priestess and the temple of the most famed live one, we're in a booth at the back of Flanagan's Pub. The morning after Katrina, plywood over the bar's front door reads, WE WILL NOT DIE SOBER! Randy Ping joins us for lunch and quickly echoes his earlier sentiments with Jeff Dwyer: "Never in twenty years have I ever seen anything I couldn't explain scientifically."

The supernatural, as I'm learning, is a bit like faith or God or love—proving it scientifically can get sticky. Sensitives like Angel and Jeff Dwyer argue that you just have to be able to open yourself enough to absorb the proof all around us. And indeed, when your eyes and ears (and nose and fingers) are completely open to signs, they seem to be everywhere. But are you simply choosing a few convenient needles from the billion-needle haystack of sensory input that humans receive every second?

"We will not ever incorporate any Katrina ghost stories into our tour," Ping says. "It is too recent. And it is a large event. And there's still some people who believe that their missing relative is going to be found. I don't want to be the person who has to go and tell them they're dead. I think it would be so improper for anyone to tell a ghost story about it for at least 100 years, and that's our promise."

He relates a horrific, true story of slaves being tortured and experimented on just down the street, in 1834, and how it was kept alive by a ghost story that began 100 years later. "This city wanted to ignore it. The polite white society was so humiliated by it, because it flew in the face of everything they said they represented and the laws protecting slaves, the Code Noir, here was supposed to be saying."

"Like Katrina," says Olga.

On the National Paranormal Society's last night in town we venture back into the Lower Ninth, this time searching for life rather than death, a more daunting task. And there it is, a lone FEMA trailer sitting just a block from where the levee breached.

We hear the trailer door unlatch, then slam shut. A man, fiftyish, graying hair and goatee, a good six feet in T-shirt and slacks, comes strutting around the corner, walks right through us, and lobs a small brown bag full of something into the chest-high weeds across the street. "Just feeding the cats," he says.

He shakes our hands with a wet palm, says his name is Robert Green, tells us to come inside, his momentum hunching him forward. We follow him into the cramped trailer strewn with papers, a printer taking up the bulk of his kitchen table. The place is hot from a turkey he's cooking.

"We went to the Superdome the day before the storm," he says, eyes still burning with hope beneath heavy lids, his drooping eyelids a side effect of the asthma medication he now takes because of the formaldehyde in the trailer. "It was worse than a football game, the lines were so long. My mother couldn't take standing up outside. So then we came back home. We were afraid of trees falling. But we didn't think we'd have to face a barge coming through the levee wall.

"This is before the storm even hit. Barely light enough for us to see. We were fighting water at four in the morning. Five minutes to get into the attic. Then I fell through the ceiling, cut my hand. Water was so filthy I had to get surgery three days later in Houston. We floated on the roof of our house two blocks. My mother fell in, she drowned. But we resuscitated her. Then the hurricane hits.

"This one here's my granddaughter, Nai Nai," he says, handing us a photo. "My daughter, her mother, lived down the street, but she already had her hands full, so I took care of Nai Nai, raised her in my house like a daughter. I pulled her up out of the attic, put her on the roof, and when I turned around, she fell in the water. I know when she was in the water, she expected me to stick my hands in and pull her out. That'll haunt me for a while."

Green says he can swim in a pool, but wasn't going to be able to in the dirty, flowing water. And at three, Nai Nai was simply too young. "When my baby fell in the water I screamed, 'Jesus! Jesus! Jesus!' and then I stopped yelling because I couldn't blame Him anymore."

Only later would Angel tell me it was at this moment that he heard Green's mother say, "As soon as you stopped calling His name, He picked her up."

"Then my mother died," Green says.

He lifts a small wooden cross off his VCR. A picture of his granddaughter Nai Nai is taped to it. "Sometimes she knocks this cross off the TV. And I'll say Nai Nai, quit cutting up up there!

"I don't feel that they're unsettled souls. I feel like they're here, but they're watching over us. This is home for them. As long as there's rebuilding, they out guarding their home. Everybody's content. My granddaughter's content. She's happy with the way things are going. That's one reason I'm here all by myself and I don't feel scared. That's the reason I can talk about them and I don't cry in the corner after you all leave. And I don't want to lose my pain, because my pain is actually what made me who I am today, strong enough to take what I'm going through now."

He walks us outside, where a folding table is propped lengthwise against his trailer, scrawled wide with black marker. It begins, WE JUST WANT OUR COUNTRY TO LOVE US AS MUCH AS WE LOVE OUR COUNTRY. "Yeah, one night I was watching *Rambo 2*, and he said that," says Green. "And then the song at the end was pretty good and I wrote this line from it right here, see—THE STRENGTH OF OUR COUNTRY BELONGS TO US."

I've never seen a place look so weak as he walks the path his house took down the street, shows us where it snagged on an elm beneath the water, before the water again tore it loose, rammed it into another tree, then kept going until it hit a truck and finally another house.

"My other grandkids are doing really well in Houston. When the time comes and I can build my house, they'll come back. I fought like hell to get back to this spot where we were. This is home. I'm not afraid to be here at nighttime. This is still where we grew up. I used to play football in the streets. My son grew up playing football in the streets. Me and my granddaughters, we would take a walk in the nighttime, check out the sun setting, tell them about the stars. Used to walk around the block every day and say hi to my elderly neighbors. This is where we all felt comfortable. Here. This is the spot. I found my mother's body here on December 29. It was four months to the day after the storm. We could smell her from 100 feet away. It was not bloated. All her hair was gone off her head, but all her organs were inside."

I remember that Halloween night just weeks after the storm. I snuck between Humvee patrols through the shards of this neighborhood, right by this very spot, into the last region of New Orleans off limits, feeling the little ghosts watching me, begging them to take my hand, but none would show themselves.

"From here I could see her skull," says Green, standing in the weeds. "And see the clothes she had on that day. I used to help her dress every day, so I recognized her clothing. I said, 'There's momma's body right there.' Simple as that. Her lower jawbone fell out. So the next day I had to come back to this spot and find her jaw, her dentures, brought them to the coroner and then he released the body to us.

"We buried my granddaughter first because her sister kept making deals that 'I won't worry about no Christmas presents if you bring my sister back.' So I felt we should put her to rest like that. She would have been four years old. . . . Now it's quiet like this. It'll be quiet like this for a long time."

He turns to Angel, asks him, "So, you feel anything?"

"I can see the houses still standing," says Angel.

"I never saw the houses gone," says Green.

Later, Angel stands in the center of the Lower Ninth smiling, seeing houses still standing where now lay only concrete slabs. Lawns where there are now chest-high weeds. People where now live only insects. "There's nothing to say to Green," he says. "He knows it all already."

We walk to the final resting place of a house in which ten people perished, four blocks from Green's trailer. "The family ranged from a five-year-old to someone in their seventies," Angel says. "William, Yvonne, Miss Clara are three names. I can hear buildings crashing into each other. The sound was horrible. Like a monster coming through here. They keep reliving it."

After his team returns to Miami, I spend days trying to verify these names, but anyone who might have known them is gone, and I can find no record of the survivors anywhere in the United States.

I try to verify other names of the storm's victims that Angel conjured. But every search is fruitless. There's no trace left of them. The only people within eye's reach of the 1 DEAD IN ATTIC house are four Hondurans, non-English-speaking residents who came here after the storm to help rebuild. I comb through the phone book, calling all the names that could be related to the ones Angel came up with, but all their numbers in the pre-Katrina phone books are disconnected now, and the names are gone from the new books.

On the first day I met him, when we walked by the spot, Angel claimed a man was shot on a specific corner in Jackson Square ten years ago. Buckling over with pain, he cried that he felt the bullet enter his own chest.

But no one I talk to remembers this tragedy, even in such a public place, so long before the one which reset the clocks here. The police department's homicide division tells me they lost all their records in the flooding. A spokeswoman dismisses it, saying, "There's been a murder on almost every corner in New Orleans by now."

The city's record, its contemporary histories, the lives of so many of its people, are mostly lost, washed away. Only the ghosts remain.

MAINE

CAPITAL   Augusta

ENTERED UNION   1820 (23rd)

ORIGIN OF NAME   First used to distinguish the mainland from the
offshore islands. Possibly meant as a compliment to Henrietta
Maria, queen of Charles I of England, who owned the province
of Mayne in France.

NICKNAME   Pine Tree State

MOTTO   Dirigo ("I lead")

RESIDENTS   Mainer

U.S. REPRESENTATIVES   2

STATE BIRD   chickadee

STATE FLOWER   white pine cone and tassel

STATE TREE   white pine tree

STATE SONG   "State of Maine Song"

LAND AREA   30,862 sq. mi.

GEOGRAPHIC CENTER   In Piscataquis Co., 18 mi. N of Dover-Foxcroft

POPULATION   1,321,505

WHITE   96.9%

BLACK   0.5%

AMERICAN INDIAN   0.6%

ASIAN   0.7%

HISPANIC/LATINO   0.7%

UNDER 18   23.6%

65 AND OVER   14.4%

MEDIAN AGE   38.6

MAINE
Heidi Julavits

By the time this essay is published I will already be in hiding, probably in a midsized Sunbelt city, living under a pseudonym, and receiving no packages. Maine, a Libertarian-minded, keep-to-your-own-business kind of state, does not take kindly to written assessments, possibly because to write about the place is to say "I am an authority," and nobody, by Maine standards, is more deserving of a beat-down—or of persecution, or expulsion—than an authority. When my husband and I ask our neighbor, a professional boat-builder and former electrician, if he can lend some advice about boat-building and wiring, he'll first demur that he knows nothing in the slightest about boat-building and wiring. Of boat-building—like three-million-dollar, ninety-foot yachts he says, "Anybody can do it." Because authority holds such little weight, there is no zoning in our town, which means there are no building permits, which means you could, as my husband often jokingly threatened to do, erect a brownstone in your back field. Civilians rule in rural Maine, thus it's best not to incite the civilians by writing about them.

But here I am, writing about them, an act of inexcusable treason since I am, if you subscribe to the legal definition, a "Mainer," with a folder of convincing documentation that includes a birth certificate and a failed driving test from the Portland DMV. I'll admit that my authority, already questionable, suffers innate limitations because I'm a certain kind of Mainer—Averagely Seaworthy First-Generation Over-Educated Urban Coastal pretty much describes my brand of nativeness. I can tie a bowline, I know a nun from a bell from a can, and a harbor seal from a lobster pot, but I know squat about the daily life trials facing the lake-and-mountain set. I didn't portage a canoe until I was eighteen (and living in New Hampshire); I didn't sight my first official moose until I was in my thirties. But because my Maine is the basis of the Maine cued in the minds of the non-Maine public when they hear the word "Maine," I'm inclined to issue a cultural correction, even a doomed one. I've spent a lifetime bristling at the *Murder She Wrote* doddery quaint clapboard nonsense that passes as Maine in the cultural vernacular. Maine, according to this vernacular, is a state filled with people possessed of great, garbled wisdom who eat lobster like it's bologna and die in ironic drowning accidents.

But non-natives—"From Aways" in native parlance—aren't the only ones indulging in gross acts of distortion. Maine's state slogan, recently changed from "Vacationland" to "The Way Life Should Be," represents one of the boldest moves in the annals of intentional misrepresentation, depending on your notion of ideal living conditions. There are more obese people in Maine than in any other New England state. In Maine, it's illegal to bait bears with donuts and then shoot them (presumably, people, and bears, should be less fat because of this law). Maine has more cat owners than any other state. Maine's drug of choice is coffee brandy. If you want to grow your own food, which an astonishing number of people in Maine feel compelled to do, you have 122 days to accomplish this between frosts. The annual mean temperature on the coast, where I live four months per year, is 46 degrees (40 degrees up north). If you spend a year in Maine, you'll enjoy 128 days of rain, 48 days of fog, and 17 days of snow. The only state poorer than Maine in 2005, the year of Hurricane Katrina, was Louisiana. Meaning, the only state worse off financially was a state that suffered the most crippling natural disaster in the history of this country. In Maine, meanwhile, 2005 was business as usual—just a lot of fat people hanging out in the rain with their cats, drinking coffee brandy and trying, without cheating, to kill a bear.

It should come as no surprise that such an elite group would be extremely cautious, if not downright parsimonious, when extending membership privileges to others. And once they've hopped the cement walls that encircle the Maine border, people discover the state's population divided into two categories—Natives and From Aways. Easy stuff on first inspection. Either you were born here or you were not. But From Away is a highly relative term, applicable to anyone who didn't grow up in the place where you are standing at that very moment. Taken to its logical extreme, everyone is a From Away— i.e., everyone who isn't You is a From Away—but Mainers don't tend to get so Hegelian about it. Instead, they invoke the town line or the water boundary that separates you from the people who graciously took you in, like a family that loves to flash before you on a nightly basis your adoption papers. Take, for example, an obituary oft-cited by a friend when trying to convey, to the average tourist, just how far away they are from the place they're currently visiting. According to this obituary, a woman had lived her entire ninety-plus years, save the first three weeks she was alive, on a remote island. She was known in her tiny community, in which she had clocked nearly a century marked primarily by winter, as the Woman From Away. I suffer similarly. I was born in Portland, Maine. I left the state when I was eighteen and returned at the age of thirty-three. My husband and I bought a house in a town three hours northeast of Portland. Thus I am a From Away in my home state.

The easy thing about being a From Away, however, is that your community has extremely low expectations for you. You're meant to screw up regularly at great cost to your homeowner's insurance, because such screwups are entertaining and an excellent way to warm the hearts of even the most indifferent natives. We proved highly entertaining. We showed up and promptly burst our pipes, ruining a room that had, based on the plaster and lathe we had to chunk into garbage bags, not been touched in nearly 200 years. In other words, we were the stupidest people in almost 200 years to live in this house. We were welcomed throughout the land. Months later I went into the bookstore twelve miles away, and the clerk said to me, "Aren't you the person with the burst pipe?" Our tale of successful integration assumed some chilling misshapes in the coming year; a woman whose mother lives in D.C. said she'd heard from another woman in D.C. who was friends with the woman who used to own our house that our house had burned down. I panicked before realizing this was just another variation on the Welcome You Delightful Idiot story.

I'm glad I didn't have to burn my house down to be embraced as the know-nothing I was, but some people have gone to nearly that extreme. Take, for example, Auslander. Auslander showed up from a city and knew too much. He had big plans for the town, including a low-income housing project, a ferry, maybe even a university. Then he put the ashes from his woodstove in a plastic bag and left them on his barn floor. The barn caught fire, the volunteers were called. We weren't in Maine at the time; two weeks later we drove up for a visit. A neighbor came by to say hello. "Did you hear about Auslander's barn?" he asked. We decided to take a walk, get some brisk Maine air. Halfway to town a friend stopped in his truck. "Did you hear about Auslander's barn?" he asked. Later another friend called. "Did you hear about Auslander's barn?" she asked. There was a Schadenfreude-y undertone to this news, but it also had the sweet enthusiasm of a birth announcement. Auslander had finally arrived.

Here's what you will talk about over dinner: You will talk about firewood. You will talk about the benefits of in-floor heating, and the R-value of your new insulation, and whether or not you should pre-buy your furnace oil. You will talk about unconventional uses for your Shop-Vac, such as catching bats or chugging loose the antique vegetable clog in your graywater pipe. You will talk about unconventional uses for your table saw, such as slicing homemade bread. You will talk about pouring dye in your toilet during the wintertime so that the effluent pattern will be marked in pink on the snow in your backyard, usually not in the desired fan shape but in a single graven line, suggesting that your leachfield's kaput. You will talk about septic mounds and how to landscape them—someone will probably mention the lady who put a bocce court on top of hers and how it's impossible to grow grass on hardpack without a few truckloads of superdirt. You'll talk about the mother of four who left her husband for the piano teacher, the psycho guy who poisoned the well of a lesbian sandwich maker, the erotic outsider art produced by your plumber, the maybe-pedophile at the local zendo, whether you'd rather live next door to alpacas or miniature horses, whether so-and-so's grandmother really did meet the actual spider that inspired E. B. White to write *Charlotte's Web*, if the From Away who bought the general store is gay and if this means there will be snazzier food for sale, whether the furry carcass left on your porch by a coyote was once a bird, a rabbit, or a vole, if you should cut your house in two and move it, in pieces, further away from the road, if you want to invest in a quarter of a cow or half a pig, why you should never buy a boat, why you definitely should or definitely should not use blown-in insulation, whether or not it is symbolic that your carpenter's favorite movie is *Fitzcarraldo*, when the winter will end, when the rain will end, when the fog will end.

Stano was just Stan until Gitano came along and he and Gitano got into it. (Note: What follows is accurate only to the degree that the gossip surrounding the battle between Gitano and Stano can be considered accurate. I'd put the accuracy percentage at about 82; I'd also posit that the composite story resulting from a collective effort at storytelling is, in fact, a kind of contemporary fable, true in its generalities if fanciful in its specifics.) Gitano is some kind of Vet who did time in various slammers for, rumors variously have it, drugs, drinking, sexual misdemeanors, or some criminal cocktail of the three. This is his second act in our town—his first act concluded abruptly when he started hanging around with the lobstermen's teenage daughters, misdemeanoring them maybe, and the lobstermen ran him off. He signaled his peaceful return with a rock cairn—an impressive stack of round granite rocks that he balanced, one atop the other, across from the general store.

But peaceful his return was possibly not. Depending on whom you ask, Gitano has psychologically imprisoned an old lady who, conveniently, had no husband nor heirs to challenge this hostile (or not, depending) take-over. He lives with her in her antique Cape and does odd jobs—really fucking odd jobs—like painting a two-story-high whale breaching under a rainbow on the side of her barn, and painting her entire house a yellow that's a number of shades harder on the eye than a New York taxi cab, and installing triangular second-floor dormers that strongly vibe Buckminster Fuller. Stan, a nervous sort of guy who thinks the world is out to get him—and it is—owns the inn and restaurant directly next to Gitano's house. Stan took issue with the house's lurid paint color, but the whale, painted in a style one might best call Hippie Van Acid Trip, put Stan over the very thin edge he travels daily. He got into it with Gitano, and Gitano got into it with him. Gitano wrote a sign, aimed at Stan's customers, that read FOR THE AMOUNT OF MONEY YOU'RE SPENDING ON DINNER YOU COULD FEED A STARVING FAMILY FOR A MONTH. For sale beneath the sign was a table full of sad seedlings. Stan tried to get Gitano kicked out of town again on a general nuisance charge; in retaliation, Gitano ran for town selectman. He lost.

Somewhere in the midst of all this, Gitano lashed out at his other neighbor, a sweet woman with a green thumb. He called this woman a fucking cunt and painted on the side of his house that faced her kitchen window the words GO HOME, which might seem a strange message to send to a person inside her own house, but the woman spends half the year in Florida. Stan, meanwhile, decided to go after Gitano on an aesthetic violation. Appealing to the summer people, i.e., people with a bit more invested in the notion that their Vacationland remain the way life should be, i.e., easier on the eye and absent powerfully ugly houses, he asked that they demand Gitano repaint his Cape and lose the whale. This did not work. One of the most respected longtime From Aways pointed out that other From Aways, tackier McMansion-building From Aways, were threatening to move to our town from "the Island," i.e., Mount Desert Island, on which there was no more McMansion land available. Those people, he said, would take one look at Gitano's house and invest their money elsewhere. *Fucking cunt*, that house says to all who look upon it. *Go home.*

Doctors tend to be extraneous professionals in a place where sickness is ignored and pain is not often felt. My neighbor, when helping us quarter our felled maple crushed his thumb in the motorized wood splitter, remarked tonelessly "That smarts," wrapped his thumb in a handkerchief, and went to work. If you bring your sick child to the doctor, she will say

"Yup, she's sick," and send you home without a prescription. If you accidentally drop your baby on her head, the doctor will tell you about the time
her baby ended up pinioned between the jaws of a wolfhound. Many people
give birth to their children at home, including doctors. If you have a baby in
the hospital, they will likely not offer you painkillers; if pressed, they will
offer you a drug that dates back to the 1980s. Many people do not vaccinate
their children; if you ask what will happen if that child wants to go to college and must produce an immunization record, they will say "I'm hoping
she'll apprentice."

To decode: To treat pain or sickness would be to acknowledge that pain
and sickness exist, and to acknowledge that pain and sickness exist would
be to admit that we might be vulnerable to pain and sickness. This works
as an emotional-physical management principle except when it really does
not. People, as people do everywhere, particularly in cold climates braced by
high levels of alcohol and stoicism, kill themselves. There was the farmer
who went down to the shore and shot himself on the same rock where his
own father had shot himself a few decades previous. There was the couple
that committed couple suicide. Apparently one person was dying, one person
was tired of living. They dealt with the problem alone and definitively. Their
deaths made a poetically self-reliant Mainer sort of sense.

What was confusing about the farmer was this: He killed himself
during the warm months. If you've ever spent a winter in Maine, metaphorical suicide is often invoked during the weeks of oppressive cold and dark (in
Portland, on New Year's Day, the sun rises at 7:14 a.m. and sets at 4:14 p.m.)
Which makes a summer suicide tragically perplexing. You survived the
worst and now you kill yourself? But now I can better conceive of a summer
suicide. In late June, when summer hasn't even kicked in and already the
days are getting shorter, I am seized by a kind of epic desperation. On these
days I am reminded of doing drugs, and reach instead for my decanter of
coffee brandy. I am reminded of when, after doing drugs on a semi-regular
basis, your terror of the come-down creeps closer and closer to the apex of
your druggy glory, until the moment when you're nearing your happiest is
also the moment most tinged with terror and apprehension because you're
about to begin the long descent. If you had to pull the plug, maybe the perfect ending place is on the upswing.

Before the Iraq War, the American flags Martha Stewartizing the porch of
every white Maine farmhouse were about as indicative of their owners'

politics as a hanging plant. Then the U.S. invaded Iraq, and flag symbolism narrowed sharply from Generic Yankee to Pro-War Patriot. Most of the flags came down, but those that stayed up conveyed something very unmistakable. A flag dialogue ensued. A man began sticking white flags in his front lawn, flags like those little flags that mark an invisible fence, one flag for each dead American soldier. The town selectmen voted to hang American flags on the electrical poles leading into town, using money from the town budget for the project and neglecting to ask permission of the electric company. Sounding in from the margins were the rainbow flags, often in windsock form, that fluttered from mailboxes marking dirt driveways disappearing into the woods. Mostly these flags were employed in the Generic Cultural Diversity Tolerance sense. Yes, some were specifically flown as war protest flags, but the off-the-gridders who mount these flags tend to consider all governmental acts, even presumably benign ones, suspect. The rainbow represents a disapproval of the First World so consummate that the war is just a fraction of the American shit pie they're fake-cheerfully rejecting. Also, none of them are gay.

The Libertarian Mainer impulse is to live and let live: which usually translates to think whatever you want, I won't deign to derail you—but since people have started dying in a distant place, this permissive attitude toward belief diversity has closed ranks. The first Fourth of July following the invasion of Iraq, a woman marched in our tiny town parade wearing a rubber George Bush mask and two giant bloody rubber hands. People booed her. For reasons possibly unrelated, she does not live in our town anymore. Military tanks and fire engines dominated the following year's Independence Day parade. At the public elementary school, the principal decided to expose the kids to the religions of the world, and some people got upset because he was teaching the kids neutrally about Islam. The worry ran that the principal was humanizing Muslims and thus secretly suggesting the kids have sympathy for the enemy. This was read as a double-secret ploy to encourage them to go forever soft on the very people who were terrorizing democracy. For reasons possibly unrelated, the principal does not live in our town anymore.

Fortunately, our town enjoys an annual group catharsis, a night during which we are all terrorized equally, and by our own kind, as a gentle reminder that evil often comes from within. On Hell Night, July 3 of every year, teenagers drive around town "collecting" items from other people's property. Lawn chairs. Street signs. Inn signs. Boats. Cars. Docks. (The savvier folks see this as a door-to-door Dumpster opportunity, and leave out their old boats and cars and docks for collection.) These items are dragged through town and artfully arranged, much like Gitano's rock cairns, in a gravity-defying pile in front of the general store. In the wee hours of the evening, the teenagers build a fire and drink beer and look at the pile. In the wee hours of the morning, the oldsters drink coffee and look at the pile. At around 6 a.m., a guy with a truck so banged up it looks like it best belongs on the pile arrives to dismantle the pile. This is where the looking gets good—a very old man in a very old truck picking up a very old truck with the jaws of his antique crane, and dropping that very old truck onto the back of his very old truck, which also holds a very old boat and a very old piece of dock. Soon all that's left of the pile is a macabre-looking oil stain on the asphalt. The watchers disperse, only to reconvene in the same spot a few hours later to wave at the tanks and the fire engines and the schoolchildren dressed as blueberries.

In summation: Mainers are, according to me, completely in keeping with the brisk, stoic, suffer-no-fools Yankee stereotype. And though my secret intent is expose the uncongenial heart of this place that the world thinks it loves to visit, I suspect this essay, for which I have sacrificed my statehood, will have the opposite effect. Ironically, it's the innately hostile quality of the state and its inhabitants that makes the place the Vacationland it undeniably is. Because who doesn't want the bullshit cut clear through by an ice storm? Who doesn't want to feel that they're missing something, or that they're being excluded from something, or that the boat left without them? and is never coming back? What I'm talking about is the reason so many artists and painters and potters and Utopianists and loners and off-the-gridders and *Fitzcarraldo*-loving carpenters fantasize about living in Maine, and why so many of those bleak dreamers actually do live there. It's why these people, when they visit, say, California, wish to have their souls removed so that they'll be the kind of person who can live in a sunny, warm, easy-weathered place, free of metaphysical dread. Never is it clearer that my moment-by-moment existence is eluding me than when I'm in Maine. *Go Home* is the mantra I hear in my own head as I'm looking out the windows of my own eyes and I'm as home as I can possibly physically get. The cold months pass too slowly, and I'm wishing to be elsewhere. The warm months pass so quickly that they're impossible to savor without a great deal of grief and regret thrown in to keep me healthily distant from my joy, which will soon evaporate. Always I am at a remove from myself. I am my own From Away and so, no matter where I hide, I am as native a Mainer as they come.

MARYLAND

CAPITAL   Annapolis

ENTERED UNION   1788 (7th)

ORIGIN OF NAME   In honor of Henrietta Maria, queen of Charles I of England

NICKNAMES   Free State or Old Line State

MOTTO   Fatti maschii, parole femine ("Manly deeds, womanly words")

RESIDENTS   Marylander

U.S. REPRESENTATIVES   8

STATE BIRD   Baltimore oriole

STATE FLOWER   black-eyed Susan

STATE TREE   white oak

STATE SONG   "Maryland! My Maryland!"

LAND AREA   9,774 sq. mi.

GEOGRAPHIC CENTER   In Prince George's Co., 4 1/2 mi. NW of Davidsonville

POPULATION   5,600,388

WHITE   64.0%

BLACK   27.9%

AMERICAN INDIAN   0.3%

ASIAN   4.0%

HISPANIC/LATINO   4.3%

UNDER 18   25.6%

65 AND OVER   11.3%

MEDIAN AGE   36.0

MARYLAND
Myla Goldberg

My childhood was spent in Laurel, Maryland, in a development named Montpelier after the erstwhile plantation on whose acreage it sat. It was a late-sixties era Levitt & Sons community—one of the last built by the veritable inventors of twentieth-century suburbia. Four floor plans and their mirror images were arranged along four square miles of lawns and curving lanes to create the semblance of diversity, blocks of two-story homes enlivened by the occasional ranch. No address was without a bucolic or poetic appellation like Fernwood Turn, Cedarbrook Lane, or Mt. Pleasant Drive—though the only genuinely descriptive name, and this from a purely demographic standpoint, was Ivory Pass. I liked the place best during the impressive blizzards of the 1970s when those lanes and drives became impassable for days and towering piles of shoveled snow obscured my view of everything, making it easier to pretend I was elsewhere. The whole point of a suburb, after all, is its proximity to somewhere else. From Montpelier it was about a half-hour drive to Washington, D.C., or Baltimore. It was an even shorter commute to the federal agencies located in and around Laurel itself, not all of which were keen on being identified. Growing up, I was told to say that my father worked for the government. If pressed, I could specify the Department of Defense. These were the Cold War days when NSA stood for No Such Agency, when my father's fifteen-minute commute with his Carter-era carpool ended at an unmarked exit.

I spent a good portion of my childhood seeking escape. If I searched hard enough, I was certain I'd discover territory I alternately thought of as the wilderness or the country. One of my earliest forays involved hiking along the drainage ditch that ran behind some of the neighboring houses in the hope it would lead to a river or a lake, preferably one that had yet to be named. When that failed, I took to my bike. Near the edge of Montpelier I found a prairie—a seemingly endless ribbon of high grass—that would have better facilitated Laura Ingalls Wilder fantasies without the skeletal power lines that sutured its length from horizon to horizon. Upon mustering the courage to cross the commercial street that marked the beginning of the nonresidential world, I discovered a curving, wooded back road edged with wildflowers. One unmarked turn-off ended at a complex of anonymous buildings guarded by a man in a sentry booth, whose singular contribution to my historic expedition was the directive "Turn the bicycle around and exit the premises" repeated with military-industrial insistence until I took his advice. I kept to the main road after that, which was exhilaratingly devoid of curbs, houses, and manicured lawns and which delivered me to a land of unpremeditated foliage, unmowed grass, and the occasional barn. I pedaled past Poultry Road, Entomology Road, and Biocontrol Road in a state of unbounded derring-do. I had not seen a single car since leaving Montpelier, and thought I might have been the only living thing until I discovered pigs—actual pigs!—snuffling in and out of low cinderblock outbuildings. Never mind that their hutches were marked with the letters USDA and the words RESEARCH ANIMAL SERVICES, SWINE UNIT, or that I had passed signs that read NO TRESPASSING/GOVERNMENT PROPERTY. The day was an idyll spent gazing at animal life, picking fist-sized bouquets of wildflowers, and exploring the untrammeled woods that stretched on either side of the road for ten feet before the appearance of fences topped with barbed wire.

Meager as my version of the country may have been, the other alternative to suburbia was too daunting to even attempt. What I knew of the city came from being driven south on the Baltimore-Washington Parkway by my father to visit the Hirshhorn and the National Air and Space Museum and north for shopping excursions with my mother to spend my allowance on stickers and candy at Baltimore's Inner Harbor. My childhood impressions of Baltimore were limited almost solely to this waterside shopping mall, the rest of the city existing in my suburban consciousness as a bastion of poverty and crime, a notion reinforced by momentary glimpses of liquor stores and people with bad teeth on the occasion a wrong turn was taken to or from shopping. My impression of Washington, D.C, as a safer place was, in retrospect, a function of my parents' assiduous efforts to keep to its northwest quadrant—except for the summer months when we would bring home bushels of live crabs from the D.C. Fish Market (an isolated destination point in the anathema that was southeast portion of the city). In addition to weekend museum trips and seasonal crab forays, we would spend each Fourth of July at the Washington Monument along with the rest of the greater metropolitan area, suffering through monumental lines to use the bathroom and then lying on the lawn to watch fireworks explode over the National Mall. The city was a hodgepodge of isolated, seemingly unrelated locales that required cars and adults to reach, and that sometimes necessitated peeing in the shrubs that fronted the main headquarters of the Internal Revenue Service. My young imagination required something less logistically complicated, something that could be conjured from a few experimental pigs and some roadside trees.

As it turns out, my childhood expeditions were only off by about forty miles. Seventeen of Maryland's twenty-two counties belong to the country, but Prince George's County—where I grew up—composes part of the state's non-rural nexus. Picturing Maryland as a gun pointing west, I lived in the suburban portion of its trigger, along with most of the state's population. This area lies sandwiched between the rural areas that form Maryland's barrel and handle. The result is our national red-state/blue-state division writ in miniature. Montgomery County—a neighboring trigger-county twenty miles south of Baltimore—recently approved a school sex-ed curriculum that includes homosexuality, while forty miles north of Baltimore, Cecil County parents recently protested the adoption of a biology textbook that didn't include creationism. Someone driving north from Washington, D.C., to Philadelphia on Interstate 95 will traverse these cultural poles in about ninety minutes.

As a trigger-dweller, it was easy to forget about my handle and barrel neighbors. The voice of P. G. County tends to be the voice of the state. Rural Maryland—whose population overwhelmingly votes Republican and speaks in Southern accents—hasn't influenced a Presidential election in 100 years. In fifth grade, my incipient sense of state pride depended upon Maryland's Northern-ness. I—it was made clear—was a Yankee. Maryland, after all, fought for the Union in the Civil War. I accepted this as unquestioningly as state bird, flower, and flag and in the spirit of self-satisfaction with which it was taught, as if I and my eleven-year-old classmates and our teacher, Mrs. Henley—in addition to belonging to one of five states in the nation that had voted against Reagan in 1980—had personally contributed to Maryland's having chosen the correct side of American history over a century before any of us had been born. Even now, having lived in New York City for over ten years, Yankee is still a word I apply to myself without once thinking of baseball. My self-identification is such that I smiled smugly when, at the turn of the millennium, Georgia fell into conflict over the Confederate trappings of its state flag. Georgia's foibles seemed so alien, so distant. Then I learned about Maryland's state song.

I must have learned its title along with the oriole and the black-eyed Susan. I thought I had somehow forgotten the words until I looked them up and realized that my memory was not the problem. There's a reason Mrs. Henley didn't opt for a class sing-along. The following are excerpts from "Maryland! My Maryland!" meant to be sung to the tune of "Oh Christmas Tree":

The despot's heel is on thy shore,
Maryland! My Maryland.
His torch is at the temple door,
Maryland! My Maryland...
She is not dead, nor deaf, nor dumb—
Huzza! She spurns the Northern scum!
She breathes! She burns! She'll come! She'll come!
Maryland! My Maryland!

This catchy little defamation of Abraham Lincoln and exhortation to join the Confederacy was penned in 1861. Its author, James Ryder Randall, was a Maryland-born poet. He was inspired to such heights of martial grandiloquence by the death of a friend during the riots that occurred when Southern sympathizers attacked Union troops marching through Baltimore on their way to defend Washington, D.C.—which signified a major gap in my lifelong understanding of Maryland's historical loyalties. For while it is true that Maryland voted to remain in the Union, this only occured after Lincoln—in a historically unprecedented act of executive privilege—suspended *habeas corpus*. What enabled a twenty-first century president to establish Guantanamo allowed a nineteenth century one to imprison nine Maryland legislators with Southern sympathies who—had they been permitted to remain in elected office—would have tipped the state legislature in favor of Maryland's secession from the Union. Growing up in a town bordered by covert federal agencies, in a neighborhood where people tended not to talk about what they did for a living, perhaps it is apt that I grew up with a similarly selective understanding of my state's past. I don't blame Mrs. Henley for my incomplete education: she was probably as embarrassed as I was to learn the truth. "Maryland! My Maryland!" was not adopted as the state song until 1939—over seventy years after Randall's verses should have been a quaint historical footnote. Right around the time I was tracing a picture of an orange-and-black bird into my fifth-grade notebook, a state senator from Montgomery County received a death threat for introducing a bill that advocated the state song's retirement.

My life-long sense of kinship with those north of the Mason-Dixon Line was the last casualty of my civil re-education. I recently learned that my born-and-bred Bostonian friends don't think of themselves as Yankees. In New England, there was no Us and Them: the nearest battlefield was over 400 miles away. In Maryland, battle lines divided homes and back-yards. About ninety minutes west of Laurel, Interstate 270, Marylanders fought and died for both armies at the Battle of Antietam, where over three thousand Union and Confederate soldiers were killed and twenty thousand wounded. Almost 150 years later we still feel the need to pick sides. The state's flag nicely encapsulates our cultural schizophrenia. Instead of the default blue-with-something-slapped-down-in-the-middle, it is divided into four diagonally-symmetrical sections. A slanted yellow-and-black checkerboard fills the upper right and lower left quadrants, an op-art red-and-white cross inhabits the upper left and lower right. Though the design derives from the shield in the coat of arms of Maryland's colonial founder, only the yellow-and-black checkerboard was originally associated with the state. The red-and-white cross was adopted by Maryland's secessionists, who flew the cross as a banner and wore it when they joined the Confederate Army so that their bodies would be shipped back to the right place. When the state flag appeared in the decades after the Civil War, the joining of these two patterns was meant to represent reconciliation, but the cross and checkerboard have no colors in common, no shared shapes.

Since I left Maryland, housing integration has invalidated Montpelier's Ivory Pass and the National Security Agency has posted an exit ramp off the Baltimore-Washington Parkway that reads NSA. The wooded road that provided my escape from suburbia has been widened, its trees knocked down to accommodate a bedroom community whose streets have names like Sumner Grove, but the pastoral quiet of Poultry Road remains uncompromised and the pigs are still there, snuffling. The state song remains the same. If you happen to be driving through Cecil County on Interstate 95, look for the Confederate flag. Originally, it was flown from a flagpole in a yard overlooking the highway just south of the Perryville exit. Recently, perhaps inspired by Randall's unrelenting poesy, its owner mounted it—pole and all—atop an industrial cherry-picker, allowing the thing to attain a height that surpasses the length of the torch-wielding arm of the Statue of Liberty.

> Thou wilt not yield the Vandal toll,
> Maryland! My Maryland.
> Thou wilt not crook to his control,
> Maryland! My Maryland.
> Better the fire upon thee roll, Better the blade, the shot, the bowl
> Than crucifixion of the soul,
> Maryland! My Maryland!

MASSACHUSETTS

CAPITAL   Boston

ENTERED UNION   1788 (6th)

ORIGIN OF NAME   From the Massachusett tribe of
   Native Americans, meaning "at or about the great hill"

NICKNAMES   Bay State or Old Colony State

MOTTO   Ense petit placidam sub libertate quietem ("By the
   sword we seek peace, but peace only under liberty")

RESIDENTS   Bay Stater

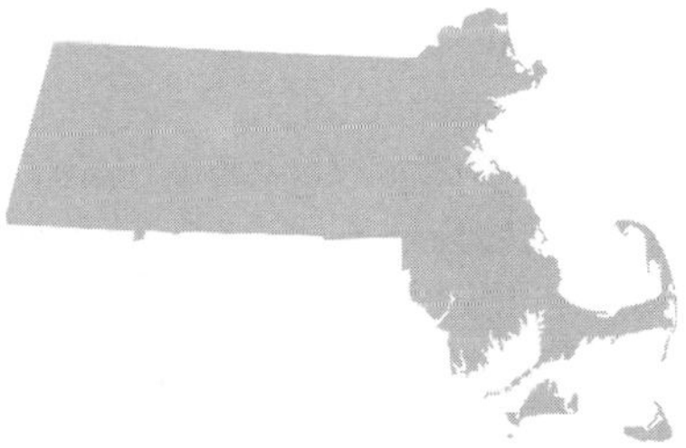

U.S. REPRESENTATIVES   10

STATE BIRD   chickadee

STATE FLOWER   mayflower

STATE TREE   American elm

STATE SONG   "All Hail to Massachusetts"

LAND AREA   7,840 sq. mi.

GEOGRAPHIC CENTER   In the town of Rutland in Worcester Co.

POPULATION   6,398,743

WHITE   84.5%

BLACK   5.4%

AMERICAN INDIAN   0.2%

ASIAN   3.8%

HISPANIC/LATINO   6.8%

UNDER 18   23.6%

65 AND OVER   13.5%

MEDIAN AGE   36.5

MASSACHUSETTS
John Hodgman

In the west, the state is as straight and uncomplicated as a flag, its little valleys sheltering what passes for our farm belt. The center gives way to the semicircle of former paper mill towns and textile mill towns crowding up to the capital. And then we are on the eastern shores, ragged and tangled in history, the Maine-like hump of the North Shore stretching down and curving up into the weird withered arm of Cape Cod, where the Pilgrims landed and started the whole thing.

The effect is such that, if you look at a map of Massachusetts and squint your eyes, you might imagine you are looking at the nation itself, only with no Texas, and a horribly deformed Florida. You might be tempted to believe that the whole country shaped itself in Massachusetts's honor. Certainly many in Massachusetts have believed so.

From its beginning, Massachusetts was self-importantly aware of its own self-importance, its special place in the history of our country. Outlining the divine mission of the colony he helped to found, Puritan John Endicott would call it the "Bulwark Against the Kingdom of the Anti-Christ." I still call it that today—it's better than the "Bay State."

Liberty, as they say, was cradled here, largely in the Green Dragon Tavern, where Sam Adams (Brewer, Patriot) roused his friends to dump East India tea into Boston harbor and blame it on the Indians. The first shot of the Revolution was fired in Concord, and the first American Army was raised in Cambridge. Massachusetts offered the first state constitution, and it served as model for the rest of the country. And in my own lifetime, it was Massachusetts that gave birth to the first gourmet food shop that served only pudding, and, yes, it was called "Pudding It First."

After independence, however, something changed. Massachusetts became unnecessary. Its farming population left for the newly opened west. Its trading fortunes foundered, giving way to textile and paper mills and small factories. For a while we were making half the nation's shoes—and many of those were made by children! So don't say we couldn't compete!

But as the mills were shuttered throughout the twentieth century, so Massachusetts's influence on the nation waned. Quincy was once known as the City of Presidents. Specifically, the City of Two Presidents: John Adams, and then, by astonishing coincidence, John *Quincy* Adams. Later, the Massachusetts Presidential Spawning tanks would also produce Calvin Coolidge, a Vermonter who took up residence in the great lesbian town of Northampton; and then, of course, JFK would arise from Brookline. But now the very idea that a national leader might come from Massachusetts is routinely and cruelly rebuffed. No matter how absurdly patrician, nebbishy, or Mormon they may seem.

So when you are growing up there it is difficult to escape the impression that you are lingering too long in a story that has long been over.

The Pilgrims came in 1620, of course, but they were looking for Virginia. Tired of dying on the open sea, they decided to settle Plymouth and die on land for a while. A Native American named Samoset welcomed them to what was, like it or not, their new home. And with the aid and friendship of the Wampanoags, and their chief, Massasoit, they stopped dying, started farming, and invented Thanksgiving.

But this new land was not any kind of melting pot.

By 1630, the Puritans had come and settled the lumpy isthmus we now call Boston. As you know, the Puritans left England, angrily, because (a) they were dissatisfied with Elizabethan accommodation of Catholicism, and (b) they thought they knew everything. Dissent was not tolerated within the Massachusetts Bay Colony, and that is why Roger Williams, who thought the Puritans should actually compensate the Indians for their land, had to leave, and founded Rhode Island; and that is why Thomas Hooker, who thought even those people who didn't go to church should be able to vote, had to leave, and founded Connecticut. You could do that sort of thing then: just go ahead and form a new state. And so all of New England was built on the long lasting foundation of an absolute inability to be near anyone different.*

It continued this way in Massachusetts, over many long and lonely winters. Towns would gather by necessity around a central green and turn their backs on one another. We would sit by the fire and brood and make brooms and bridles and such, and since familiarity among neighbors was scarce, we

---

*What happened to the Wampanoags? In 1676, Massasoit's son, Metacon, got the crazy idea that the Europeans would eventually kill all the Native Americans. Who knows what goes through people's minds? In any case, he began to raise an army to prevent this from happening, but he was betrayed. Forced into battle before he was ready, he was swiftly routed, and his people were slaughtered. It is a story that vibrates with tragedy, and that profoundly changed the trajectory of Massachusetts history and, arguably, the history of the whole country. Did you notice I put it in a footnote? That's our little joke.

would instead, through sheer Yankee ingenuity, breed contempt from *unfamiliarity*. The result of this contempt: an ironic "commonwealth" of closely knit groups of isolationists.

I guess that I am from Massachusetts. But I never felt at home there, and, really, no one ever does.

There are Texans and there are Minnesotans and even Californians, though that is a state as geographically and culturally motley as the entire eastern seaboard. But no one calls himself a "Massachusettsean," in part because it is impossible to say, and in part because ours is a tradition of exclusion.

Often, now, when I tell people I am from Massachusetts, they ask me: Why don't you have an accent? This happens especially when I tell them, as I often do, that I park my car in Harvard Yard.

That is when I have to explain to them that *that* accent—the one they know from *Cheers* and *The Departed*, with its flinty dropped r's and inexplicably fancy-pants long a's, is specifically a Boston Irish accent, primarily South Boston, but ranging throughout the working class suburbs where things were once built or made.

And then I must explain that even though my father came from the paper mill town of Fitchburg and still says "ahhnt" for "aunt," he switched vocal gears into a kind of upper middle-class neutral when he left to go to college, just like my mom did when she left *her* working class neighborhood in Philadelphia.

I cannot even imitate that accent, I tell them.

But by then, they are looking at me doubtfully, like I am lying about being from Massachusetts. They are looking at me as though I come from no place at all.

Another reason I did not feel at home was because I do not like sports. As I write this, the New England Patriots have just lost the Super Bowl. I am very glad of this development. (I can write this, because I am now in New York. And I am wearing a suit of armor.)

Boston has much to offer any visitor. There is of course a fine symphony orchestra, world-famous universities, and the Mother Church of Christian Science, which has a truly boss reflecting pool. However, if you do not like sports, Boston does not have much to offer you. The local sports teams—which I am told are the Baseball Red Sox, the Football Patriots, the Basketball Celtics, the Hockey Bears, and of course the famous Boston Lobsters of the World Team Tennis League—are an obsession.

When a game is on, it will be broadcast in every bar, home, and taxi cab. I once frequented an eccentric coffeehouse in a small town in western Massachusetts. It hosted literary readings and served vegetarian food and a small selection of wines. I loved it. It had a small TV that showed only a closed circuit feed of the baby eagles that had recently been hatched at a local bird sanctuary (which seemed perfectly reasonable to me). Unless there was a Red Sox game on, in which case, *sports would actually preempt baby eagles.*

In the finest restaurant the waiter will be checking the scores and passing news of the game between the busboy in the kitchen and the Harvard professor at the table. The professor will tell you that, in a city largely stratified by class, race, and ethnicity, sports erases all those distinctions and reminds us of our common humanity and re-ties, season by season, the frayed threads that hold our community together. He will probably be wearing a baseball hat as he says it, one of those good-quality, fitted jobs. He will be an ass. And if you tell this professor that you don't happen to like sports, he will ask what is wrong with you. And then he will punch you in the face.

For most of my growing up, I could tolerate this, for, despite the occasional basketball championship, the sports teams were all losers. Famously, cursedly, the Boston Red Sox would lose again and again and again, and this made sense to me.

For sadness, grievance, anger, and frustration: This is what really pleases the Bostonian and inspires him. When Oliver Wendell Holmes dubbed Boston the "Hub of the Universe" in the mid-nineteenth century, it was already a mean joke. Boston's cultural and financial dominance of the country had long since fled to the wheel's new center, hated New York. And the Boston I grew up in reveled in its first-class status as a second-class city. Even someone who does not like sports (me) must appreciate the poetry of it: what better expression of self-loathing than to hate *The Yankees.*

But oh, there was a time when we were at the center of things.

Consider the Seven Years' War. I know you often do. 1756–1763. Unable to properly farm its own rocky land or manufacture its own goods, Boston built a merchant empire of clipper ships. We bought sugar and molasses from the French Caribbean, completely ignoring the fact that our own mother country was in the midst of a great naval war with France.

Completely ignoring the fact that by our commerce we were funding the French army that was, in fact, raiding our own little towns in the western hills. Because who cares about them? We made that sugar into rum, and we aged it in Medford and we traded that in turn to Africa for slaves, which we then sold to the South for money to buy more sugar and molasses.

This is known as the "Triangle Trade," though you may know it as "Massholism."

We were rescued from that prosperity by the Sugar Act of 1764. It was the first of many coercive taxes levied on us by England that sought to prevent Boston from making the enormous fortunes in enemy goods and human trafficking to which we had become accustomed. Naturally, this made us angry. It drove us to rebellion. It was not until we were oppressed, outnumbered, and, in 1770, massacred, that we were *ourselves* again: bitter, angry, and, accidentally, good.

So that is why I am glad the Patriots lost. Not because of Schadenfreude.* Because I already feel an outsider in Boston when we're losing. When we're winning, I do not recognize it at all. I do not understand a Boston triumphant, for what city would that be? Dallas? Is that what we want?

I f you are looking for a place to eat in Boston, may I recommend the Downtown Café on LaGrange Street?† This is a restaurant I worked in one summer when I was in college.

It was located near Boston's "Combat Zone," the small downtown cluster of adult bookstores and strip clubs where this once-Puritan town imprisoned its sin. But by the time I worked there, in the early nineties, sin had escaped. Video, and soon the Internet, would render the Combat Zone unneeded, and it was already largely abandoned.

As far as I could tell we were the only operating business on our block of LaGrange, apart from a dusty looking haberdashery, which, by my guess, opened roughly once per decade. The Downtown was a small place—maybe six tables, with salmon-colored tablecloths—serving primarily a gay clientele.

The owner and chef was an enormous Rasputin-looking gay man named Dan who cooked in the tiny open kitchen, usually while yelling. He always kept the back door open behind him as he worked. A little white ghost of a stray cat lived in the vacant lot there, and he would feed her every day. While prepping for an evening's shift, once, he heard her yowling furiously.

*Attention jocks: That means "pleasure taken in someone else's misfortune."
†With the one small caveat that it, in fact, does not exist anymore.

"That tom cat has got at her," he said gleefully, while cutting up chicken. Another long, painful, coital scream echoed in. "She loves it!"

The sole waiter was another gay man named Luigi, who was nicknamed "Wege." I know it was spelled that way because he had each letter tattooed on the fingers of his right hand, between the first and second knuckles. He was short and tough. His day job was at the pawnshop a few blocks down, and he looked exactly like a gay, middle-aged man who worked in a pawnshop and was not about to take anything from anybody anymore.

And then there was me, in the back, washing dishes. I was not gay, though I am sure they never believed it, because I did not like sports and why else would I be there?

The answer: A friend of mine had worked there and had gotten me the job, and I liked being paid in cash, and I liked eating for free. And also, it was like a secret society. As far as I could tell, the restaurant had never advertised or been covered in the press, and there was no foot traffic on our deserted block. During the dinner hour the place would slowly fill with those in the know, calling to Dan as they entered, hugging him.

Sometimes I had to make deliveries. Dan had gotten a concession to make bar snacks for a nearby comedy club in the theater district. And so, from time to time he'd make up a plate of extremely greasy chicken fingers and have me run across Boylston Street, through a parking lot, to the club. A waitress would take the chicken fingers out to the patrons. I'd wait there, and listen to the comic, and watch the young Bostonians laugh at the jokes. For some reason, I remember them all wearing pastel yellow polo shirts. Even the girls.

After a few minutes, the waitress would bring the chicken fingers back on their now-soggy paper plate.

"They thought they were gross," she would tell me. And I would walk them back over to the Downtown, and present them to Dan, who would suggest different ways they could fuck themselves.

As the night got later (and in Boston, the night never gets particularly late: the subway system, known as the "T," stops running at 12:30 a.m., for why would anyone want to be out later than that?), the strippers would come in and so would the strange young men who manned the peepshow booths. They came to gossip and get a little foul-mouthed, Rasputiney love from Dan. I'd be told to get the industrial-size vat of intensely yellow vanilla ice cream down from the freezer shelf and he would make them all milkshakes. LaGrange Street was deathly quiet and barely lit.

And even though I didn't belong there, I felt in good company there, among the non-sports fans in the gay restaurant that, despite Boston's large and thriving gay community, still nestled up next to the Combat Zone as if out of some unconscious sense of shame.

Then we'd close up, and Dan would hand me some extra money to give Wege a ride home. He lived in South Boston with his elderly mother. I don't remember what we talked about on those rides. I remember thinking that South Boston seemed like an unusual place for a gay man with an Italian name to live, no matter how tough he was or how many tattoos he had on his fingers. I remember him opening the car door, 2 a.m. blinking on the dashboard clock, and looking carefully up and down the street before walking to his door.

One night I sat with Dan and had a soda as he counted the night's receipts. Another bunch of chicken fingers had come back, and business wasn't good. He was in a bad mood. We got to talking about the woman who had worked there before me—the friend who had gotten me the job.

"She's got her head in the clouds," he said.

He told me that he had fired her, even though she had said she quit. I don't know who was telling the truth.

"She still lives at home," he said. "She's still a baby, still thinks daddy's going to take care of her." Then he looked at me seriously. "At some point, you have to throw your parents out of the house."

I have spent a lot of years trying to figure out what that weird, upside-down, sentence was supposed to mean. Now I appreciate it as the answer to an essentially Massachusettsean dilemma: It's how you leave home when you just can't bear to leave home.

In the mid-1800s some other non-sports fans and fancy-pantses got together, mostly in Concord, MA, and called themselves the Transcendentalists.

Ralph Waldo Emerson is perhaps the most famous of these freethinkers. Emerson said there is a "wise silence" inside all of us, and in it, a kind of divinity—an intuitive personal spirituality, that when we are attuned to it, makes all of reality an echo of our soul. Or something. No one really knew what he was talking about. But he enchanted a fairly large group of writers and intellectuals, among them Henry David Thoreau, a local Concordian school teacher and neck-bearded misanthrope and, occasionally, Emerson's gardener. Disenchanted with civilization, Thoreau built a cabin in the woods to ponder nature and silence and to play the flute a lot (not a euphemism).

But not every Transcendentalist wanted to live alone in a cabin. And so the movement established special communities in which they could build a perfect world.

The most famous of these was the agricultural commune of Brook Farm, in Roxbury, MA, where Emerson and Nathaniel Hawthorne dwelled for a time. But there was also Fruitlands in Cambridge, and outside our borders the Oneida community in New York. Emerson wrote, "not a reading man but has a draft of a new community in his waistcoat pocket."

And while Brookline, founded 1705, predated all of these experiments by almost 150 years, by the time I was raised in it, it was clearly an exercise in Utopia.

Brookline is a large, affluent town surrounded on three sides by Boston, but never quite a part of it. Here was a town of beautiful homes, graciously arranged on broad streets and dotted with green parks and little ponds and grand ideals . . . where the wealthy championed rent control; where the whites bussed blacks to Brookline High School (modestly known on its letterhead as *"The* High School") and then offered them a ride home!; where indeed all of the children were well educated at good public schools that taught sex education and Marxist theories and *One Hundred Years of Solitude*.

When, during the 1988 presidential debates, Michael Dukakis, a Brookliner, was asked how he would respond if his wife was raped, he surprised a nation by responding mildly that he actually wouldn't take the rapist by the neck and strap him into the electric chair and stab forks into his eyes until he was dead. But Brookline was not surprised. We nodded, for he was our neighbor, and he had clearly transcended such base emotions as vengeance.

In the mid-seventies, at least, Brookline was a place where a young married couple from working-class Fitchburg and working-class Philadelphia with one child could scrape together the money to buy not only a home, but a home with sixteen rooms, in a beautiful neighborhood, surrounded by doctors and heirs to department store fortunes. And there the three could wander in that gigantic house, sixteen gigantic rooms away from everything else in the world, the child completely unaware that this was in any way unusual.

My parents were not alone. Most in Brookline were rootless. Boston University and Boston College students were inhaled into its streets each fall and exhaled back to the nation every summer. My friend John Lin's mother came to school every Chinese New Year with great greasy paper bags of homemade shrimp toast. My next-door neighbor's father grew up in Denmark and made his own bread and put actual candles on his Christmas tree. And I made my friends and my world among the professors' kids and the children of divorce who traveled to Brookline like pilgrims.

Every summer during college, I would work at the Coolidge Corner Movie Theater, a beautiful old cinema from the 1920s famous for its double features of art films and samurai movies. I saw *Annie Hall* there when I was nine years old. And that's what I did instead of playing soccer. Coolidge Corner is Brookline's commercial hub, home to the famed S.S. Pierce Building, which in turn once housed that great and noble failed experiment in single-subject retailing, "Pudding It First."

I had been working at the Coolidge since high school, and it was a very pleasant job. The primary responsibilities were selling tickets to the art films, directing patrons to the theater, making popcorn, melting butter, and then nothing. While it did not pay much, it offered hour upon hour of glorious nothing: the kind of perfect balance between work and wise silence that the Brook Farmers could only have dreamed of.

This nothing might be spent sitting on the blue bench on the street, reading and watching the slow river of Harvard Street roll by, a parade of childhood friends and local eccentrics (the skirted man, the bearded woman). Or visiting friends at other nearby merchants—the young English majors at the bookstore, or Jay at the record store, or the woman at the Coffee Connection who would eventually become my wife—and getting free things from them, knowing that I had the power to admit them gratis to *Wings of Desire* in return, in the spirit of perfect cooperation.

My favorite place in the theater was the old-fashioned glass ticket booth. I would lock myself in, cramped up at the knees by the ticket machine, everything smelling of oil and metal and cigarette smoke. I would watch Brookline, and contemplate, and hatch my scheme. When I was done with college, I would move back, and get all my friends to move back, and everything would be the same, forever. I would form my own utopia . . . my own home . . . amazingly, impossibly, right in my own hometown.

I certainly had a lot of time to dream of that utopia in that booth, my cabin in the woods, because I really wasn't selling a whole lot of tickets. I dreamed it watching the record store close, and the Coffee Connection close. I dreamed it as friends who were moving away came and said good-bye and kissed the glass that separated me from the world. I dreamed it as I watched two women march before the theater, chanting in thick Russian accents:

"Help keep this theater from demolishing," because it had been sold, and its future was uncertain. I dreamed it watching the Brookline sky, so wide and liquid blue, not a building over six stories high in sight, turn purple and dark. I watched the time pass, and I hated every minute of it.

The Brook Farm community failed in 1847. It had always struggled financially, and then things grew difficult when, a few years earlier, its founder became enamored of Charles Fourier and his very specific idea of communal living.

Very specifically, his idea was that everyone should live in the same building, called a Phalanstery, which would house workshops, living quarters, dining halls, libraries, salons—everything that life might offer under the same enormous, enormous roof. And, really, why would anyone not want to live that way—a whole life, from work to study to sex, in a single ship-like building, adrift in a wilderness? They were building the Phalanstery when it caught fire and burned down. For some reason, they didn't try building it again. No one came back to utopia after that, not even its founder.

I live in New York City now, largely because the woman who would become my wife told me she was moving here. We've been here for thirteen years, and I have not regretted my betrayal, though I do not call myself a "New Yorker."

You may be surprised to learn, though, that I still live part time in Massachusetts. I certainly was surprised to learn it.

Here is what happened.

About twenty years ago, my parents sold the sixteen-room house, and as you might guess, this gave them enough capital for two normal houses and a college education for me. They found one normal house in the eastern end of Brookline, the very last block of the town before Boston, right in the shadow of Fenway Park, if you can believe it, because I guess they had a sense of humor.

The other was a small, 1970s-era junk-modern cabin with a sloping roof and unfinished solar heating system in the hills of western Massachusetts.

The house is at the northern end of the Pioneer Valley, a cluster of little towns and farms and closed mills that follow the twining routes of the Connecticut River and I–91, north from Springfield, through Northampton and Deerfield and Greenfield all the way up to Vermont. There are cornfields and dairy farms and incongruous fields of shade tobacco for cigar wrappers, the leaves still dried in long, beat-up shacks that hug the road. And for every field, there's a fall: Turner's Falls, Miller's Falls, Shelburne Falls, etc., because surrounding the river are high, rolling hills cut through with swift little rivers that used to power all sorts of mills.

We had been coming out to the Hill Towns for years. My mother had a good friend who had grown up in Greenfield, named Jackie, and from time to time we would spend weekends with her in her little three-room house that hung over the North River at the end of a then-unnamed road. Jackie got her mail by walking across a condemned bridge to go to the general store. On one side of her house was a barely marked path cutting steeply down to the river, its banks of solid rocks cut over millennia into "potholes," natural round basins full of dark water and little flies. On the other side of the house were her only neighbors, a family who seemed to collect stray dogs and snowmobiles.

I am not trying to give you the impression that this was charming. Rather, I mean to say that as beautiful as the area was, and as much fun as I had there, it was all tinged by the reasonable fear that I was going to fall off a bridge, be bit by a dog, lose my footing on a hill, crack my head open on a slippery rock, and drown. This was not the Berkshires, with its quaint inns and twilight picnics where you would listen to the Boston Symphony Orchestra while eating pasta salad on a soft lawn surrounded by fireflies. This was a cluster of anxious, struggling little towns full of failed and failing businesses, badly constructed houses, and people sitting outside them, staring at you as you drove by.

An hour south, the traveler will find Northampton and Amherst—former homes of Calvin Coolidge and Emily Dickinson. These two prosperous towns host five intensely liberal liberal arts colleges, including Hampshire, which has granted at least one degree, I happen to know, in stand-up comedy. But up here, this was what those college kids called "Massatucky," which is cruel and unfair to both Massachusetts and Kentucky, but you get the picture.

There was an organic market in Shelburne Falls, though, and a store selling middle-aged hippie jewelry and intricate blown-glass sculptures that looked like little planets. From time to time, Jackie would ruefully comment that the area was being invaded by New Yorkers, buying up weekend homes and studio space on the cheap. But I never saw any evidence of it, and even as a teenager I thought she was insane. Why would someone from New York drive four hours to come here for the weekend? Didn't New York have its own depressed former mill towns to visit?

It made more sense that the hills would be invaded by moneyed folk just two hours away, from Brookline, for example. And so my mother decided to look for a place there. She wanted a house by a river, like Jackie's, but since you can't build on the river anymore, those are hard to come by. Instead she bought the junk-modern cabin on the side of a hill next to what had been a pond, until the beavers dammed it up into a bog. She and my dad would spend weekends there. And I would visit with the woman who was now my wife. And some years later, my mother died, and not long after, Jackie died as well. (That's how it goes with cancer; if you don't know it yet, you will eventually.) My dad had lost interest in the place, or could not bear it any more. And I once again found myself with a home in Massachusetts.

It was not a very good or big house, and at nights the bugs came up from the bog fiercely. But we were not rich, and the night stars were bright and dazzling and free. We had children, and we began carting them up there for the better part of the summer out of the feeling that they would benefit from the opportunity to run around in a space larger than a living room.

The area has come up in the world somewhat, largely on the back of scented candles. Surely the traveler is familiar with Yankee Candle, with its massive compound of candles, housewares, and year-round Christmas supplies in Deerfield—"The Scenter of the Universe?" We spent a couple of school vacations and hot summers there, in relatively pleasant but absolute and unremitting isolation, enjoying it to some degree; to some degree wondering what we were doing.

The time came though, not long ago, when our two children were growing larger, and the house was growing more junky than ever, and the sentimental pleasure of keeping up my mother's failed colony in the hills was beginning to wear off. We were about to give up and sell it, when something happened.

Our neighbor came over. It was amazing. He just walked across the street, Samoset-like, to say: "Welcome, strangers." He had his daughter with him, a year older than my own. He and his wife were locals, but they had just bought the land across the street and built a house there. I told him I hadn't even noticed. By then our two daughters were playing. I stood there, not knowing what to do.

"Would you like a ginger ale?" I said.

And he said yes, and luckily I had some ginger ale, and for the first time in the dozen years my mother and I had had the house, we had company.

I explained to him that we were probably going to move, because the house was too small and falling apart. We watched our daughters playing. And he said, "Did I mention I build and renovate houses?"

Then another thing happened. Looking for Internet access, I found myself in a used bookstore thirty minutes south, by yet another little river, in a converted grist mill. They had free wireless there, and a café. The café had been started by a young couple, she from Amherst, he from Texas. They both had nose rings and big ideas about having readings and concerts in the café, and selling vegetarian food and carefully selected wines.

But just to be clear, they were not assholes. They were lovely and smart, and they sold "Cowboy Coffee" with the grounds left in the bottom. Every time someone bought a cup and finished it, they would take a Polaroid and put it on the wall. I looked around and saw dozens and dozens of young people, old people, locals, college kids, Massholes and Massatuckians and dozens more, all holding up their empty cups, grinning through the caffeine haze, initiated into their own little coffee utopia.

"I would like to have some of that coffee," I said. "I would like to be on that wall."

"OK," said the young couple.

And I drank it, and it was terrible. And then I had my picture taken. I was a New Yorker now, and I had invaded. But I felt more at home in Massachusetts than ever.

"What is that television show?" I asked, pointing to a tiny TV.

"We have a closed circuit link to the baby eagles that have just been hatched at the local bird sanctuary," they said.

"That sounds perfectly reasonable," I said.

"That is," they said, "unless there is a Red Sox game on."

And I stopped and I thought about it for a moment. And then I said, "That sounds perfectly reasonable, too."

MICHIGAN

CAPITAL Lansing

ENTERED UNION 1837 (26th)

ORIGIN OF NAME From an Indian word meaning "great or large lake"

NICKNAME Wolverine State or Great Lake State

MOTTO Si quaeris peninsulam amoenam circumspice ("If you seek a pleasant peninsula, look around you")

RESIDENTS Michigander

U.S. REPRESENTATIVES 15

STATE BIRD robin

STATE FLOWER apple blossom

STATE TREE white pine

STATE SONG "My Michigan" and "Michigan, My Michigan"

LAND AREA 56,804 sq. mi.

GEOGRAPHIC CENTER In Wexford Co., 5 mi. NNW of Cadillac

POPULATION 10,120,860

WHITE 80.2%

BLACK 14.2%

AMERICAN INDIAN 0.6%

ASIAN 1.8%

HISPANIC/LATINO 3.3%

UNDER 18 26.1%

65 AND OVER 12.3%

MEDIAN AGE 35.5

MICHIGAN
Mohammed Naseehu Ali

In October of 1988, my parents—as if to punish me for some egregious offense deserving of banishment—took me, their first son, to the airport in Accra, Ghana's capital city, and put me on a Boeing 747 bound for America. The departure hall, with its malfunctioning cooling system and creaky ceiling fans that only recycled trapped heat, was just as hot and humid as outside. When my flight was announced for boarding, the horde of family members who came to bid me good-bye huddled in a corner, and with hands and heads facing the heavens, prayed for my protection and well-being in America. My destination was Interlochen, a small northern Michigan town of 3,500 people. Six hundred of them were temporary residents of the Interlochen Arts Academy, where I was enrolled to begin my sophomore year of high school.

It was the first time I had left Ghana and the comfort of Hausa-Islamic culture, which, as a way of strengthening kinship and religious cohesion, emphasized doing everything—from praying and eating to traveling—in the company of other Muslims. I made my way alone across the ocean, first to New York, then to Detroit, and finally to Traverse City, at the northern tip of Michigan. As I headed west, everything got whiter: Of the four hundred or so passengers on the flight from Ghana, more than three-quarters were black. By the time we had crossed the Atlantic and I had switched to a smaller plane to Detroit, the percentage of black and white was roughly fifty-fifty. On the final leg of the trip, I was the only black person on the plane.

During the layover in Detroit, I headed for the payphone. An uncle had given me a roll of U.S. quarters and implored me to call him upon arrival or in case of emergency. I was excited to tell him I was here, in America! Also, I was supposed to use some of the quarters to call and notify school authorities that I was on my way—since all efforts to reach the admission's office through Ghana Telecom had proven futile in the week before my departure. But not knowing how to use a payphone—and with a new immigrant's timidity barring me from mustering the nerve to ask how—I bungled my way and somehow lost all but four of the quarters. I couldn't understand the fast-paced American accent of the phone's automated operator, and I was never sure exactly when to put in the coins—before or during or after conversation. It felt like playing a slot machine on which you could only lose. I boarded my third flight of the day without reaching my uncle.

Finally, almost exactly twenty-four hours after I had left West Africa, the puddle jumper that flew me gingerly over the lakes, marshlands, and deep pine forests of northern Michigan taxied onto the tarmac of the airport in Traverse City, known as the Cherry Capital Airport. Though my own research had warned me of the cold temperatures in northern Michigan, I realized during the short walk from the plane to the airport building that no amount of reading could have prepared anyone for such drastic climate change. Up to my arrival I had not experienced temperature below sixty degrees, and therefore wasn't equipped with the biological or mental thermal gauge to be able to tell what cold—real cold—meant. I was wearing a *fugu* robe, a matching pair of loose pants, and a Hausa embroidered hat. I couldn't have been more climatically out of place than a polar bear that suddenly finds itself in the middle of the West African bush.

I'd watched plenty of American movies, though, so I confidently assumed that every airport in America was the size of a small city. But there I was in an airport even smaller than the one in Accra. I had anxiously noted the absence of any other black person in the airport when we landed, and double-takes from other passengers were making me nervous. Within fifteen minutes of the propeller plane's landing, the long, rectangular hall that served as arrival and departure halls was all but deserted. Of the handful of people remaining, I was the only passenger—the others were airline and airport employees. The baggage handler, who also served as airport custodian, began locking the doors and windows, and prepared to close the airport for the night. Perhaps my parents' decision to send me off to a boarding school in the woods of northern Michigan was a punishment after all.

Beginning to panic, I headed to the airport's phone booth, where I was almost sure the four quarters I had left would meet the same fate as the ones I had lost in Detroit. Just then a lady dressed in full airline employee accoutrement—white shirt, multi-colored scarf, and pressed, navy trousers—approached.

"Hello," she said, warmly but with a hitch in her voice. She seemed kind but a little bewildered, which I took to be her reaction to the elaborate hand-stitched Ghanaian outfit I had on.

"Hello," I said in a thick, Johnny-just-drop, Ghanaian-accented English.

"The airport will be closing in a few minutes. . . . Do you need any assistance with transportation or anything?"

I was so nervous I could only stammer: "I am going to Inta-low-chin. . . ."

She gave me a puzzled look. "Inta-low-chin?"

"Yes, Inta-low-chin Arts Academy," I blurted out, thinking God help me, I may be in the wrong town altogether.

"Oh, you mean Interlochen, the arts camp!"

I couldn't even pronounce the one word I needed most to know.

Michigan's name is derived from the original French settlers' bastardization of the Ojibwe tribe term, *Mishigami*, meaning "large water" or "large lake." It is the only bi-peninsular state in the United States; it has the longest freshwater shoreline in the world, and the second longest total shoreline in the continental United States next to Alaska. After California and Florida, there are more recreational boats in Michigan than anywhere in America. Bounded by four of the five Great Lakes (Lake Erie, Lake Huron, Lake Michigan, and Lake Superior), and with hundreds of little lakes dotted all over the state, a person in Michigan is never more than six miles from a natural water source.

All of this aquatic abundance has yielded the state's moniker as the Great Lakes State. But some still call Michigan the Wolverine State, a nickname it earned during the state's little-known spat with Ohio. The Toledo War (1835–1836) was a bloodless boundary dispute between the then territory of Michigan and adjoining Ohio over a 468-square-mile region along their border, now known as the Toledo Strip. Under a compromise resolution adopted by Congress in December 1836, Michigan surrendered the land in exchange for its statehood and approximately three-quarters of the Upper Peninsula.

Owing to its shape, the Lower Peninsula is dubbed "the mitten," which explains the strange but universal phenomenon in Michigan of residents pointing to the corresponding spot on the back of one's left hand when asked where in the state he or she comes from. The Upper Peninsula, which is separated from the Lower Peninsula by the Straits of Mackinac, a five-mile channel that joins Lake Huron to Lake Michigan, is known as the U.P. Hence its residents are called "Yoopers." (I have always wondered why the residents of the Lower Peninsula are not therefore called "Loopers.")

An individual from Michigan is called a "Michigander" and has what I have observed to be a perpetual fixation with the weather. The reason for this is simple: They have lots and lots of it—snowstorms, thunderstorms, long daylight hours, extreme heat during the summers, and even tornadoes. The northern part of the Lower Peninsula and the entire Upper Peninsula has an even more severe climate: warm, humid but shorter summers and long, cold to very cold winters. My high school lies just below the cuticle of the imaginary pinkie of the five fingers hidden inside the proverbial mitten—the coldest part of the state.

People in the U.P. and the northernmost parts of the mitten start preparing for winter as early as August. Some parts of the state average high temperatures below freezing from December through February, and this continues into early March in the far northern parts. During the late fall through the middle of February, the state is frequently subjected to heavy "lake effect" snow, which is created when the cold air that passes over the relatively warm waters of the Great Lakes picks up moisture and heat, then eventually drops the moisture in the form of snow when the air reaches the downwind shore. The state receives a good amount of precipitation throughout the year, averaging from 30 to 40 inches per year. For this, at least, I was prepared: In southeastern Ghana, annual rainfall hovers well above 80 inches.

Most Michiganders I came in contact with were unconditionally generous, always willing to give a helping hand to someone in need; and they did so with patience and an amazing grace that was reminiscent of the traditions of my Hausa culture, which placed the generous treatment of sojourners very high on its list of morals and ethics. Examples of such generosity from Michiganders were evident to me in the first days of my arrival. From the airline lady who kept the airport open for a school official to show up, to the Academy's van driver who, knowing that the cafeteria would be closed by the time we arrived on campus, stopped at a gas station and bought me a slice of pizza and a can of "pop" (Michiganese for soda), to my residence hall's housemother, who knocked on my door early in the morning carrying blankets and warm sheets for me. Overnight the housemaster had phoned to tell her that the "African student had arrived, but he didn't bring any blankets or sheets."

Soon after my arrival in Michigan, it became apparent that I would need somewhere to go to during the many short, interspersed holidays in the school's academic year. My Ghanaian school was only a forty-five-minute drive from my home. Moreover, the educational system in Ghana tolerated very little holiday making, considering it a distraction. I spent my first Thanksgiving at the house of a fellow student from Cleveland, Ohio, and I lived with my campus housemother's family during the Christmas holidays.

Not long after that, a woman who worked in the admissions office all but adopted me into her family. She and her husband and two daughters offered me the spare room in their house and told me I was welcome to stay with them during school breaks, weekends, or whenever I simply needed a break from campus life.

The family lived in Kingsley, a village of less than one thousand people south of Traverse City. Until my arrival, no black person had ever lived there. My host father was a hulk of a man, standing well over six feet and weighing a hefty 280 pounds; and yet he was as nimble and graceful as a gazelle on the improvised basketball court in front of our car garage, where we often played our lopsided one-on-one games. His demeanor and personality could be summed up in two words: gentle giant. He could be very funny, but he said little most of the time. He was a Republican who owned several guns, and he spoke often about racial injustice and inequality in America, especially about the plight of American Indians.

As a way of telling the direction of the East, my father had instructed me before I left Africa that I look for the direction of my shadow at midday, and that wherever it pointed was East, where Muslims face to pray. The problem with this unscientific yet time-tested and effective method of navigation in Michigan is that I didn't see any sun for the first three or four days after my arrival. By mid-October fall weather in northern Michigan is usually well under way, which means it could be cloudy, dreary, and sunless for days. Luckily, Islamic teaching allows one, when in doubt or in a foreign land, to face anywhere to pray until he or she is able to determine the actual direction of Kaaba, the holy black mosque in Mecca.

In general, Michiganders have a live-and-let-live attitude about life, with a deep sense of religiosity and a strong kinship to family and friends. Open-minded and curious about other people's beliefs and cultures, the Michiganders I know are more listeners than preachers. In my three years of living in the midst of a Christian family, no one ever talked to me about Christianity or tried to impress upon me its virtues. Instead, they respected my beliefs and religious practices, and were awed by my determination to pray five times daily despite the geographical and climatic challenges I faced. Muslims are instructed to rid their minds, hearts, and environments of any distraction when they stand to pray before Allah. And even though I never mentioned this to my host family, they somehow figured it out on their own. Anytime I went up to my room to pray, my host mother would turn down the volume of the television set and my younger sister would shut the door to her room, from where rock or country music always blasted.

Michigan's long winters and rugged, wild environment are responsible for creating what I observed to be the three distinct types of Michiganders: there is the *Poet*, who spends lots of time observing nature and writing about it; the *Outdoorsman*, men and/or women who engage the elements through skiing, ice-fishing, and hunting through the sullen months of winter; and the *Sports Fanatic*, the ordinary Michigander who passes endless hours watching sports on television.

Michiganders' poetic sensibility may seem unlikely, but there is a long tradition—especially in northern Michigan—of writing about topography and landscape there. After all, this is what Hemingway did in the Nick Adams stories, which capture his childhood summers in northern Michigan. Modern Michigan writers, such as Jim Harrison, Michael Delp, Judith Minty, Jack Driscoll, and Jack Ridl, describe the state's freshwater landscapes and its pine forests and the animals hidden in them, and meditate on the intense effect of nature on Michiganders.

The Michigander's great love of the outdoors I found difficult to fathom at first. Given the state's miserably cold, rainy, and snowy climate, you'd think its people would be perpetual indoor dwellers. But in fact the average Michigander is devoted to skiing, ice-fishing, fishing, boating, camping, mushroom hunting, and deer hunting—pretty much everything that can be done outdoors. Michiganders even love two-tracking—the freezing practice of buddies armed with a twelve-pack of beer driving a truck slowly through the woods while they drink, gaze at deer, and shoot the shit, if not shoot any deer. While two-tracking, it is common for folks to park their truck in the bushes to allow for an oncoming two-tracking vehicle to pass (this is how the sport got its name), and also to park when clusters of morel mushrooms are spotted, which can be picked and taken home for dinner.

The state of Michigan's Department of Natural Resource offers hunting licenses for all kinds of animals: from bear, elk, and caribou to turkeys, ducks, and geese. But by far the most popular animal to hunt is the deer. During the combined archery and firearms deer hunting season in October and November, residents from all walks of life and from every part of the state head into the woods in their four-wheelers, hoping to bring home some venison. One year my host dad brought home two bucks, one shot with his bow and arrow and the other with his gun. Watching an animal being skinned wasn't something new to me; I knew how to do it by the time I was eleven. The Feast of Sacrifice—one of the two major festivals in the Muslim world—is celebrated to mark the end of the Islamic calendar and also the end of pilgrimage season to the holy lands of Mecca and Medina. And each year throughout my upbringing in Ghana, I watched as dozens of goats, sheep, and cows were slaughtered in our compound in sacrifice to Allah, in return for His eternal blessing. So the sight of my host father, hunkered in our garage, his blood-smeared hands pulling on the entrails of the carcass, made me even more comfortable with my newfound family. For me it was also a eureka! moment of sorts, at the discovery that, after all, white folks were no different from blacks or Muslims when it came to blood-letting as a means of appeasing hunger, tradition, the gods, or Allah himself.

Most of all, Michiganders are fanatical in their support for their local sports teams, from high school and college to professional, and spend untold hours during the long winter months watching football, basketball, ice hockey, and car racing. During the Thanksgiving and Christmas holidays, my host mother, father, and sisters and I would pack ourselves into two cars and drive to this aunt or uncle's or that grandpa or grandma's house, where various branches of the family would congregate. The men, including the boys, would gravitate toward the living room, where the television was invariably set to one college football game or another. I came to suspect that, for the men, one of the main reasons they enjoyed the bi-annual gatherings was that it offered them the opportunity to wax poetic and brag to each other about their new ski gadgets, fishing gear, and rifles. It was also an opportunity for people to show their allegiance to their preferred teams, which was mostly decided by the colleges their sons or daughters had attended, were attending, or planned to attend after high school.

The most dominant sports rivalry in Michigan involves the Spartans and the Wolverines, the football teams of Michigan State University and University of Michigan respectively. Branches of the large extended family would arrive at these family gatherings donned in winter coats, hats, mittens, and socks, sometimes with towels and duffel bags in tow, sometimes even undergarments emblazoned with the colors and logos of the team they rooted for, to jeer those who rooted for other teams or to maintain their pride if their team was losing. The color and battle lines were always clearly drawn at these friendly family reunions. Either you wore green (Spartans) or you wore blue (Wolverines), and you arrived prepared to taunt each other's family's team's lackluster performance in previous games. An uncle whose son had long ago graduated from Michigan State would never let go of his bitterness and anger—which had sometimes kept him quiet and sullen all evening—because of the stranglehold Michigan had maintained for so many years on the neck of Michigan State. Yet at the end of each family gathering, it was the fraternity and sorority of the various men and women who married into each other's families that won the day, and not the bitter, agonizing sports rivalry, something that had become a mere ritual, and like all rituals, an emotional and psychological therapy to its participants.

My three-year stay in northern Michigan changed my life and made me what I am. For one thing, I came to the conclusion that I wanted to continue living in areas that have lots of snow, hence my decision to attend Bennington College . . . in Vermont. And the quiet solace of pristine snowfall during the winter months and the long, bright, and cheerful summer days played a big role in making a dedicated writer out of me. No environment could have been more fertile for my imagination and ideas than the natural wonderland that is northern Michigan.

The connection between my host family and my African family has taken genuine and strong root over the years. My two daughters call my host mother "Grandma Michigan" and their biological grandmother "Grandma Ghana." Their "Grandpa Michigan," I am sad to say, lost a battle with cancer a few years ago, but he lives on in our memory, and I will always be grateful for all that he gave me.

I now live far from Michigan, in New York City, where snowfalls are scant and dirty, and certainly not the kind that inspires a writer to type away. And I have lost whatever little of that distinctive Michigan accent— what one website devoted to Michigan lore described as "a little bit Fargo, a little bit nasal Chicago, and a little bit Canada"—that I picked up during my years in the state. But I still see myself as a Michigander. When anyone asks me where I'm from, I say: Michigan. My questioner typically does a double take and asks, "But where are you *really* from?" To which I say again: *Michigan.* I am a Michigander now, or perhaps better yet, an Afrigander.

MINNESOTA

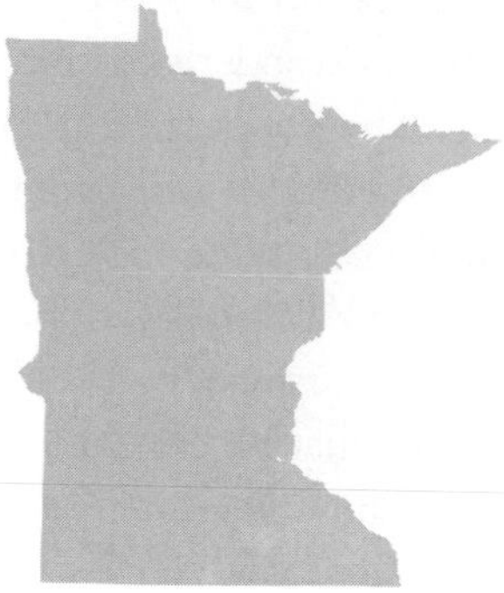

CAPITAL St. Paul

ENTERED UNION 1858 (32nd)

ORIGIN OF NAME From a Dakota Indian word
  meaning "sky-tinted water"

NICKNAMES North Star State, Gopher State,
  or Land of 10,000 Lakes

MOTTO L'Étoile du Nord ("The North Star")

RESIDENTS Minnesotan

U.S. REPRESENTATIVES 8

STATE BIRD common loon (also called great northern diver)

STATE FLOWER lady slipper

STATE TREE red (or Norway) pine

STATE SONG "Hail Minnesota"

LAND AREA 79,610 sq. mi.

GEOGRAPHIC CENTER In Crow Wing Co., 10 mi. SW of Brainerd

POPULATION 5,132,799

WHITE 89.4%

BLACK 3.5%

AMERICAN INDIAN 1.1%

ASIAN 2.9%

HISPANIC/LATINO 2.9%

UNDER 18 26.2%

65 AND OVER 12.1%

MEDIAN AGE 35.4

MINNESOTA
Philip Connors

The last time I was in Minneapolis in summer, I went with family and friends to a Minnesota Twins game at that aesthetic mistake known as the Hubert H. Humphrey Metrodome. We loitered outside the stadium in the light of early evening, delaying our entry into the marshmallow atmosphere of the Humpty Dome until the last possible minute before first pitch. My friend Mark sidled up to join the line at the sweet corn stand. "Look!" he whispered, pointing to the man in front of him. "It's Garrison Keillor." Sure enough, there was the state bard, ordering his pregame snack. As Keillor paid, took his roasted corn, and stepped away, Mark stepped up . . . only to be told by the corn girl that she was plum out. Garrison Keillor had walked with the last ear.

What can anyone say about Minnesota in the face of thirty years and perhaps a thousand performances of *A Prairie Home Companion?* Keillor's excavation of Scandinavian mores, his probing of Catholic versus Lutheran sensibilities, his tweaks of our taciturn and cool-headed nature—no other state has ceded the duties of its myth-making to one person with such a wide reach. I feel a little like Mark did that day: as if I'm standing in line at the sweet corn stand of the Minnesota soul, only to find that Garrison Keillor has been here already and cleaned the joint out.

I spent twenty-two of my first twenty-three years in Minnesota, but I now live in New Mexico—culturally, if not quite geographically, about as far from Minnesota as possible without leaving the country. Yet even in the Mexican-American borderlands we exiles from the North Country have a way of finding each other. I've become friendly with two fellow Minnesotans here, and they both remind me of the ways of our home state. One is the only friend I've made in the last ten years who bothers to remember my birthday. That's typical of Minnesotans. We remember. We send the card or the gift. We do the little things that keep a hum of continuity about our lives.

I met my other Minnesota friend, Ron, at a little place that serves New Mexican wine. I was tending bar; Ron was having a drink with his wife. His chiselled Nordic face and my nasal voice gave us away, and we struck up a quick friendship. Now we play cribbage a couple of times a week when the bar is slow in the afternoon. Ron calls it his therapy, and he's only half joking. His wife has Alzheimer's with progressive dementia, and she's always there with him in the bar. I don't look askance or make a fuss when she curses him or punches him in the shoulder.

"Okay, dear, we'll be all right," he says in a soothing voice as the blows rain down. That he hasn't institutionalized her makes him, in some people's eyes, something of a saint, and therefore true to the culture that raised him: Minnesotans are in it for the long haul. We do the little things even when life refuses to hum smoothly along. That he takes her out drinking nearly every day, an activity that seems to exacerbate her confusion, makes him something more complicated, and he's the first to admit that lunch and dinner and drinks on the town are far cheaper than a bill from—as he always puts it—the funny farm.

Our parsimony—financial and emotional—can, of course, border on the callous. This is a side of ourselves we acknowledge best in our jokes. Take this one, for example:

Ole died. His wife Lena went to the local paper to pay for an obituary notice. The ad manager, after offering his condolences, asked Lena what she'd like to say about Ole.

"Just put, 'Ole died.'" said Lena.

"That's it? Just 'Ole died'? Surely, there must be something more you'd like to say about him. If it's money you're concerned about, I should tell you the first five words are free."

Lena pondered this a moment and said, "OK, say, 'Ole died. Boat for sale.'"

Like many of the mythologies of Minnesota, such jokes have a ring of truth about them. But from a distance, out here on the northern edge of the Chihuahuan Desert, it's easier to see how much of it all is willfully simplified. Take our relationship with water, which on the face of it appears to be simple love and appreciation: "Land of 10,000 Lakes" is one of Minnesota's nicknames. (There are really as many as 16,000 lakes, depending on how you define them, but—well, we don't like to boast, you know.) Before the arrival of white settlers in the nineteenth century, the state was covered by a profusion of swamps, sloughs, and "prairie potholes," lakes too small to be judged of any value. A legacy of the Wisconsin Glaciation of only 12,000 years ago, when a great ice sheet covered most of the state, these wetlands were a refuge for migratory birds, as well as insurance against flooding and runoff. They were also an impediment to the agrarian designs of early homesteaders, who set about draining them in a frenzy of dredging and ditch digging. By 1920, 79 miles of ditches and nearly 500 miles of underground tile drained close to 45,000 acres of land in the county where I grew up. By the 1960s, farmers had drained 11.7 million acres statewide—nearly a quarter of the state's total land mass. In other words, water—which our state enshrines as something almost holy—had been the object of a relentless war.

The Minnesota of mythology is a rural, even pastoral place, where neighbors help neighbors and everyone's fortunes are tied to the weather and the market price of corn and beans. In truth, rural Minnesota has been in decline for more than half a century—for almost half its meager existence. Founded along the tentacles of the railroad companies, who platted towns and named the streets before they had inhabitants, the small towns of rural Minnesota are a fading relic of a previous century. Sixty percent of the state's population now lives in Minneapolis or St. Paul or their surrounding suburbs. More than 100 acres of farmland, on average, are consumed every day by suburban sprawl. The days of thriving little villages, each with its own ethnicity—Danes in Tyler, Germans in Sanborn, Belgians in Ghent, Icelanders in Minneota—are over, and with them has gone some of the charm and weirdness of the old Minnesota.

We cling to one myth above all, though—the myth that we possess an elusive quality called "Minnesota Nice," which sounds like it was coined by the state tourism board. It can be read as a shorter way of saying, "If you can't say something nice, don't say anything at all." I've always found that attitude severely limiting—too often a recipe not for Minnesota Nice but for Minnesota Passive-Aggressive. Shame, it seems to me, forms the foundation of Minnesota Nice, and shame internalized can come out looking awfully warped. Our shame originates in poverty, in the squalid conditions our Northern European ancestors fled in search of a life with dignity. Many of them made good on that chance in Minnesota in the face of locusts, prairie fires, bad weather, isolation, and a hundred other challenges we can no longer imagine. To speak ill of them—to speak ill of anyone   is to mock their dignity, the thing they earned to our lasting benefit. They arrived in the New World wanting to be left the hell alone to do their work. In return for that courtesy they'd leave you alone too.

I grew up on a farm in southwest Minnesota, near Currie, a town which then had about 350 people and now, according to the most recent census, has just 225. It seemed to me that any history worth knowing was within my reach. My great-grandfather, descendant of French-Canadian Catholics, lived just down the road, and I would often ask him to tell me about the time he saw the first motorcar coming over the hill from the town of Dovray, home of the summer celebration "Uff-Da Days." Pioneer cabins were preserved at Lake Shetek, within a ten-minute drive of our farm, and although there were plaques and monuments that made mention of certain bloody incidents from the past, no great emphasis was placed on them. History, for me, began in 1887, when my great-great-grandfather Dositheus Gervais first came to the Des Moines River country.

The original homestead lay a mile to the west of my bedroom. Its two yard lights twinkled after dark low on the horizon. My great-grandfather lived all his life there. He saw both that very first motorcar and the last train to come barreling out of the East. My grandmother and her siblings retrieved corncobs from the pigpens to burn in the stove and warm the house during the Depression. I came of age in the bosom of traditions that felt somehow eternal. We held late-summer pig roasts. We were regulars at 4-H club meetings. Church attendance was non-negotiable, as was respect for all manner of Jell-O salad cuisine.

In truth, that way of life, which felt timeless to my child's mind, was barely more than a century old, and its establishment required a great deal of butchery. All through the early half of the nineteenth century, settlers came in droves to Minnesota, pushing the native Dakota from their ancestral hunting grounds. One treaty followed on another, opening land to the newly arriving settlers. By the 1850s the remaining Dakota—those who'd survived the white man's whiskey, whooping cough, and cholera—were confined to a twenty-mile-wide reservation along the Minnesota River. In 1850 there were 6,000 whites in the entire Minnesota Territory. By 1856 there were 200,000. The buffalo were dwindling, near extinction. Game of all kinds was increasingly sparse. The Dakota relied, in large measure, on annual payments from the government, payments ratified by Congress to pay for the ceded treaty land. Sometimes these payments didn't arrive. When they did, they often went straight to unscrupulous traders who held the Dakota in permanent debt.

In 1862, with the Civil War already becoming a drain on the national treasury, the annuity payment was late in coming by months. The Dakota, many of them starving, pleaded with the agency traders to release food stores and keep them alive on credit. The traders refused. One said, "So far as I am concerned, if they are hungry, let them eat grass or their own dung."

What resulted was called, depending on your point of view, the Sioux Uprising, the Sioux Outbreak, the Dakota War, or the Dakota Conflict. The one thing you can't call it is Minnesota Nice. It began on Sunday, August 17, 1862—the same day the annuity payment finally left St. Paul on a wagon train, two kegs of gold coins worth $71,000.

The fighting went on for six weeks. At least 500 soldiers and white settlers were killed, though perhaps many more. The scale of the Dakota dead has never been accurately counted, although nearly two thousand were imprisoned over that winter near what would one day become the Mall of America, in Bloomington, a suburb of Minneapolis. Typical, perhaps, of our unsentimental nature that we would one day build a shrine to commerce on the site of what was once a concentration camp.

Eventually those who survived the camp were shipped out to Nebraska and South Dakota. Meanwhile, more than 300 Dakota prisoners were convicted of murder and rape by military tribunals and sentenced to death by hanging. President Abraham Lincoln reviewed the trial transcripts and commuted all but thirty-nine of the death sentences. One of the thirty-nine was spared at the last minute. The remaining thirty-eight Dakota men constitute the largest mass execution on a single day in American history. The *WPA Guide to Minnesota*, in its entry on Mankato, records the scene in that town on the day after Christmas, 1862:

> The day of execution was bitterly cold. Large throngs of people, among them many armed men, milled through the streets. Every vantage point for the hanging had been appropriated hours before. Two thousand Minnesota troops had been moved to the scene to prevent disorder, but no violence was attempted.
>
> Thirty-eight Indians were hanged simultaneously from a single gallows. They asked that the chains, by which they were bound in pairs, be removed so they might walk to the platform in a single file. This was done, and, singing an Indian war song, each placed the rope around his own neck and continued singing while the cap was adjusted over his eyes. At the appointed time, W. H. Dooley, whose entire family had been massacred at Lake Shetek, cut the 2-inch scaffolding rope, and the entire number dropped to their death.
>
> With this multiple hanging, the largest legal wholesale execution that has ever taken place in the United States, came the

end of Indian worries to the residents of Mankato. A granite marker commemorating the hanging stands on the site of the execution, on the northwest corner of Front and Main Sts.

Mankato is southwestern Minnesota's leading metropolis. . . .

One can't help but admire that smooth transition from the largest mass execution in American history to the boosterism of Mankato's bright and shining status as "southwestern Minnesota's leading metropolis," with nothing but a granite monument between. *If you can't say something nice . . .*

A few years ago I went back home to see how my father's cousins were faring as small farmers in the twenty-first century. They were the fourth generation to plow the glacial till of southwestern Minnesota. My father's own stab at farming, beginning in 1973 on a quarter section of rented land, lasted eleven years, until the bank told him: Enough. Yet his cousins had survived—thrived, even—and I wondered how and why.

A number of possible explanations presented themselves. They'd inherited land outright, whereas my father had been forced to rent. Skyrocketing interest rates, coupled with a dip in commodity prices, had squeezed out the marginal operators. My father had borrowed money at the wrong time, and with a complete lack of collateral. When the loan officers came calling, he had nothing to offer in sacrifice to their demand that he pay up or get out.

My father's first cousins eked through the lean years, aided by the generation ahead of them, my father's uncles, who'd built enough goodwill and capital to help their sons stave off repossession. Not so my father. His link to farming came through his mother, not his father, so he started with nothing. A maternal lineage, rather than a paternal one, had doomed him from the start, as perhaps it would have any serf or sharecropper anywhere the world over.

What was shocking were the rewards my father's cousins had gathered in the intervening couple of decades. They farmed now on thousands of acres, not hundreds. They drove fancy pickup trucks, owned lakefront property and second homes. A simple Internet search offered the truth of where their riches had come from: good ol' Uncle Sam. Recently I clicked again on a database of farm subsidy payments, and found that five of my father's first cousins had been paid, all told, $3 million between 1995 and 2005—and that on top of whatever they'd earned outright for the sale of their corn and soybeans. They worked hard, certainly. They'd saved and scrimped through the lean years. They were good and honorable yeomen, and now they'd come through to their great reward: a prime place at the trough of the welfare state. All that corn syrup guzzled down the gullets of America's overweight children, all that beef inefficiently fattened on cheap feed, all that ethanol being distilled in heartland refineries: all of it underwritten by as wasteful a government program as now exists this side of the defense industry. In the last ten years, the federal government has paid $131 million in subsidies and disaster insurance in just the county where I grew up. Corn is subsidized to keep it cheap, and the subsidies encourage overproduction, which encourages a scramble for ever more ways to use corn, and thus bigger subsidies—the perfect feedback loop of government welfare.

Of course I couldn't say that to them. They preferred the old story, in which they remained the true heirs of Ole Rölvaag's *Giants in the Earth*—the great novel of pioneering on the northern plains—and I was still, almost against my will, Minnesota Nice.

Now, on those rare occasions when I'm home again, I'm invariably seized by the itch to drive. Out the window endless fields of corn and soybeans scroll by, the rigid, right-angled geometry of Midwestern grain farming, here and there pockmarked by strange little remnant sloughs and swamps and lakes ringed with cattails and reeds. The horizon is treeless but for the occasional wind row of ash and elm planted in the Dust Bowl years, to stop the soil from blowing away entirely. Half the wind rows mark working farms. The other half stand watch over houses and buildings the color of ash in their abandonment, machinery rusting in the weeds. There are other Minnesotas, of course—the wilderness of the northern Boundary Waters, where travel is limited to foot and canoe; the Mississippi River country of the east, where bluffs rise hundreds of feet above the river's breadth—but this is my Minnesota, manufactured from an old American dream and haunted now by failure.

Just off old Highway 30, I come upon what remains of my first and truest home in the world. A lone silo and quonset hut stand just south of the highway, gray and forlorn against the bright blue sky. I pull into the lane and park the car next to a field of waist-high corn. The house and garage, the grove of trees, the granary, the chicken coop, the hayloft and pumphouse and corn crib—all are gone, burned to ash and plowed into the earth for a few more acres of tillable land.

I wander the quarter section a while, but the sheer geometric monotony imposed by a cornfield on the playground of my childhood blocks my access to the past. Only later, as I return via the back roads to my parents' house, a rooster's tail of gravel dust rising behind the car, do I begin to see it whole again. I remember that just east of the house, in a bare patch of earth next to the grove, my brother and I had practiced farming in miniature from the age of five. We gathered seeds spilled from the planter, or snuck handfuls from the bags stacked in the granary, and then we dug little rows in the dirt. We tucked the seeds in the furrow and covered them with a thin layer of soil. Within days we had little corn plants poking toward the sunlight. For a month or so we sprayed our little field with the garden hose, imitating summer storms; with our tractors we tilled between the rows to keep the weeds at bay. I see us again in our childhood naïveté, practicing for the agricultural artistry of adulthood, practicing for a future that, for reasons beyond our control, would not be ours.

And then, before I get carried away in sentimentality, I tell myself it was a piece of luck, that failure. It set me free to make a failure of myself in other ways. Without that original failure perhaps I'd still be there, picking rocks in springtime, wheeling back and forth through the corn in a giant combine on a few hundred acres of someone else's land, playing out the final chapter in the old dream as I listened to Garrison Keillor on the radio and daydreamed about the ways I could spend my government check.

The books in the WPA's American Guide series, the inspiration for State by State, *contain hundreds of photographs that show daily life as it was in America during the 1930s and '40s: oil wells on the front lawn of the Oklahoma capitol building, a dog lying on the rug of a Vermont public library, a woman with her mouth full of pie. In the same spirit we asked the fifty writers in* State by State *to each choose a single image—a personal snapshot, a found photograph, an unknown (or sometimes a well-known) painting—that captured something essential about their respective states today. Their selections follow; the captions are the writers' own.*

JON ROWLEY

ALASKA   Chum salmon, set to dry at the Waska's camp on the Yukon River. Salted rather than smoked, the finished product is usually eaten unheated and straight up. But it's also good in a soup. *—Paul Greenberg*

ARIZONA   A storm that descended suddenly on our backyard, and turned afternoon into sunset. *—Lydia Millet*

An orange crate label from **CALIFORNIA**: the land of beauty and perfection. *—William T. Vollmann*

RIGHT: **COLORADO**   Photo taken by my sister Erin on the south fork of the White River, while on a hike with our parents. —*Benjamin Kunkel*

BELOW: **CONNECTICUT** The Merritt Parkway as rendered by another Connecticut resident (Exit 48), the accomplished contemporary painter Maureen Gallace. —*Rick Moody*

ERIN KUNKEL

COURTESY 303 GALLERY

OPPOSITE PAGE:

TOP: **DELAWARE**   The cooling tower of a New Jersey power plant rises up across Delaware Bay from Augustine Beach. —*Craig Taylor*

MIDDLE: **HAWAII**   From the quiet southern end of Waikiki. I like to think Fitzgerald was imagining this spot when Tom Buchanan asks Daisy if she ever loved him, "Not at Kapiolani? . . . Not that day I carried you down from the Punch Bowl to keep your shoes dry?" Today more than 30,000 hotel rooms line the two-mile strand. —*Tara Bray Smith*

BOTTOM: **IOWA**   *Maiz* en Iowa. —*Dagoberto Gilb*

TOP: **KANSAS** On Highway 81, just south of the Nebraska border, we came upon an abandoned farmhouse that had been colonized by a pack of semi-feral but surprisingly amiable pigs. —*Jim Lewis*

RIGHT: **LOUISIANA** Katrina images have all but become cliché now, but, for me, this one says everything about America and the drowning of New Orleans—a Minnesota girl whose Lutheran high school class spent their spring break trying to save homes in the Ninth Ward. —*Joshua Clark*

BELOW: **MARYLAND** This is what Maryland tastes like. All blue crabs are seasoned with this stuff, which is made exclusively in-state. —*Myla Goldberg*

ABOVE: The people of **MASSACHUSETTS**.
—*John Hodgman*

RIGHT: **MISSOURI**   Bosnian coffee is available at Eerya Market on Gravois Street in St. Louis . . . and also, Bosnian laundry soap, though why one would need it remains a mystery.
—*Jacki Lyden*

ERTANA KOLENOVIC

BELOW: **MONTANA**   A Shakespeare in the Parks performance in Plains. The town's population, according to the 2000 census, is 1,126. —*Sarah Vowell*

MONTANA SHAKESPEARE IN THE PARKS

RIGHT: **NEVADA** The Neon Boneyard in Las Vegas, where old marquees go to die. —*Charles Bock*

ABOVE: **NEW MEXICO** Francis took this photo, staring back at our footprints in the gypsum dunes at White Sands. —*Ellery Washington*

RIGHT: **NEW YORK** Welcoming visitors since 300,000,000 B.C.E. This is my brother Tom in 1957. —*Jonathan Franzen*

TOP LEFT: **OREGON**   Michael Brophy's painting showing Portland, the city that timber built, as it rose from the forest. By the time I got to it, Portland looked like the first panel of this three-part story. —*Joe Sacco*

TOP RIGHT: **PENNSYLVANIA**   My birthplace is green—the same prelapsarian shade that European poets and philosophers invoked when they first gazed across the Atlantic and envisioned Eden in the virgin New World forests. —*Andrea Lee*

ABOVE: **SOUTH CAROLINA**   Church can happen pretty much anywhere (and everywhere) in South Carolina, as it does here outside Columbia, reminding us how great a sacrifice it was for Jesus to give up heaven for earth. —*Jack Hitt*

ABOVE: **SOUTH DAKOTA**   How disappointing it is to visit Mount Rushmore in person. It is neither more nor less than the image we have been seeing of it all our lives. —*Saïd Sayrafiezadeh*

LEFT: **TENNESSEE**   My friend Debbie took this picture of her daughter Sarah on Nashville's Bicentennial Mall. Sarah is slightly more fluid of movement, and more beautiful, than the water itself. — *Ann Patchett*

WASHINGTON There is a point in the lives of all Washingtonians when they first travel outside their home state and realize that not all trees look like this. —*Carrie Brownstein*

WEST VIRGINIA In the '50s and '60s, jewelry was more demure, but girls are girls: a 1980s Rose Red and Snow White taste West Virginia strawberries. —*Jayne Anne Phillips*

WISCONSIN Of the 14,000 lakes in Wisconsin, this shoreline is part of the one I know best: Lake Owen. —*Daphne Beal*

WORLD'S HIGHEST STANDARD OF LIVING

There's no way like the *American Way*

General Outdoor Adv Co

ABOVE: **ARKANSAS** Little Rock is a place of many bridges. This one, the latest to open, crosses the Arkansas River above the Murray Lock and Dam, and was winkingly christened the "Big Dam Bridge." —*Kevin Brockmeier*

ABOVE: **ALABAMA** Whenever racial passions die down, the battle turns to the injustices of class. —*George Packer*

ABOVE: **FLORIDA** The singer Jimmy Buffett and me in Key West, sometime around 1986. At ten you don't know Jimmy Buffett from Warren Buffett. But if I could do it all over again, I'd ask him to sing "In the Shelter" for me, his best song. —*Joshua Ferris*

LEFT: **GEORGIA** A solid brick ranch in Lilburn—the first real home I ever had. —*Ha Jin*

ROBERT L. SEGAL

IDAHO A couple of years ago, my friend Geoff and I found a 3-wood and an ammo box full of golf balls at the summit of Idaho's highest peak, Mount Borah (12,655 feet), in the Lost River range. Here's Geoff clubbing one to kingdom come. No, they weren't biodegradable, but we only hit two, I promise. —*Anthony Doerr*

ILLINOIS This is a mural in Wicker Park, very close to the 826 Chicago tutoring center. The big Illinoisians are there—Oprah, Obama, Lincoln. —*Dave Eggers*

CHRIS P. JOHNSON

NOAA

INDIANA The tornado was my childhood bogeyman: nothing terrified more. The double funnel that touched down near my hometown of South Bend was the most intense of the Palm Sunday tornado outbreak of April 11, 1965, the worst in U.S. history. —*Susan Choi*

KENTUCKY Half the Mount Horeb Circle, an "Adena Sacred Circle" in Central Kentucky, from about the time of Christ. In slow-motion film of water drops, there's a frame where you see this shape. —*John Jeremiah Sullivan*

Insult with a Smile: the Sirens of **MAINE** welcome you. —*Heidi Julavits*

MINNESOTA Small-town bars and country taverns like this one, near Lake Shetek, remain attractive places to warm up after a day of snowmobiling. —*Philip Connors*

MICHIGAN Water, water everywhere! With 11,000 inland lakes and four Great Lakes touching the shores of the state, Michiganders are attracted to the natural water sources that surround them the same way the geese are to the lake shores. —*Mohammed Naseem Ali*

MISSISSIPPI My wife and I will be buried in pine boxes here in the cemetery where lies William Faulkner and many of our older friends. —*Barry Hannah*

NEW HAMPSHIRE Shaker Quarters, East Canterbury, New Hampshire. I came across the beguilingly plain diaries of Brother Irving Greenwood, who arrived here as an orphan in 1886. He loved mechanical objects and riding a bicycle around the grounds in the evenings before supper. —*Will Blythe*

NEBRASKA   The virile sower of seeds atop the state capitol in Lincoln is ever poised to fling. —*Alexander Payne*

NEW JERSEY   Bayway Refinery: Smells like teen spirit. —*Anthony Bourdain*

LEFT: **NORTH CAROLINA**   The pig that lives atop Crook's Corner, a famous and favorite eatery in Chapel Hill. —*Randall Kenan*

BELOW: **NORTH DAKOTA**   Messages along the major highways seem to come out of nowhere, giving you a little nudge from beyond, as if God were a gentle second-grade teacher. —*Louise Erdrich*

LISA KLAUSNER

LEFT: **OHIO** answers to many gods, some of whom enjoy playing with big trucks. This pylon was one of four Gods of Industry guarding the entrances to the Lorain-Carnegie Bridge in downtown Cleveland. They all scared me to death. —*Susan Orlean*

BELOW: **OKLAHOMA** has more interior shoreline than almost any other state. And, in Tulsa, beautiful sunsets you can see from both the rich and the poor sides of town. —*S. E. Hinton*

JOSEPH J. MCGOVERN, JR., RHODE ISLAND
OFFICE OF LIBRARY & INFORMATION SERVICES

RHODE ISLAND: The Kingston Free Library (1775–76). On the upper floor I took ballet and recorder lessons, and also performed, at age twelve, in a production of *Free to Be You and Me.* —*Jhumpa Lahiri*

LEFT: **TEXAS** Big Tex, the icon of the Texas State Fair, standing beneath the big Texas sky. He is 52 feet tall and wears size 70 boots, a 75 gallon hat, a size 100 180/181 shirt and 284W/185L XXXXXL jeans. —*Cristina Henríquez*

RIGHT: **UTAH** *Spiral Jetty,* Robert Smithson's entropic wonder. —*David Rakoff*

WYATT SEIPP

VERMONT Are these hills alive, or what? This was taken up on Danby Mountain, and captures Vermont's rolling, oblique, canted, stratified terrain at its 3D finest. The 1D ridgeline is also a fine example of the subtle yet provocative Green Mountain silhouette. —*Alison Bechdel*

VIRGINIA Burial party collecting bones and skulls a year after the battle of Cold Harbor, Virginia, where the Union Army incurred seven thousand casualties on June 3, 1864. Confederate losses are unknown. —*Tony Horwitz*

WYOMING Skating over wild ice beneath the Tetons: Because we have to ski or snowshoe to get to the lake and it's bitterly cold and only a few hardy souls attempt the trip, there is a secret, fresh quality to the activity, like humans only just got here. —*Alexandra Fuller*

MISSISSIPPI

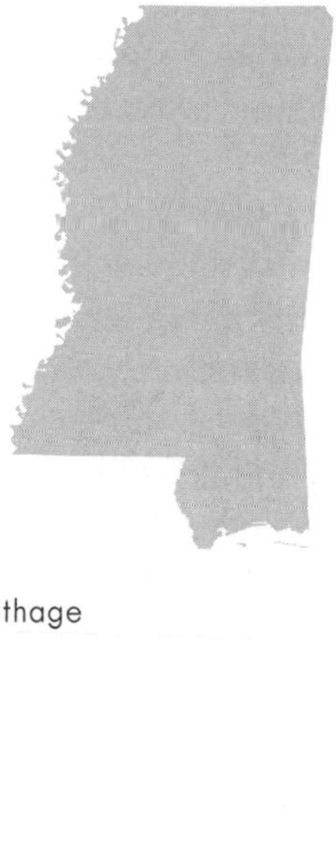

CAPITAL Jackson

ENTERED UNION 1817 (20th)

ORIGIN OF NAME From an Indian word meaning
"Father of Waters"

NICKNAME Magnolia State

MOTTO Virtute et armis ("By valor and arms")

RESIDENTS Mississippian

U.S. REPRESENTATIVES 4

STATE BIRD mockingbird

STATE FLOWER flower or bloom of the magnolia or
evergreen magnolia

STATE TREE magnolia

STATE SONG "Go, Mississippi"

LAND AREA 46,907 sq. mi.

GEOGRAPHIC CENTER In Leake Co., 9 mi. WNW of Carthage

POPULATION 2,921,088

WHITE 61.4%

BLACK 36.3%

AMERICAN INDIAN 0.4%

ASIAN 0.7%

HISPANIC/LATINO 1.4%

UNDER 18 27.3%

65 AND OVER 12.1%

MEDIAN AGE 33.8

MISSISSIPPI
Barry Hannah

For me, Mississippi has been a sweet experience of surpassing natural beauty and smart, gentle, talented gals and pals. At one time I thought I'd never return to my home state or town, Clinton, because of the horrors inflicted on black folks when I was growing up and worsening during my college years at a small Baptist college I was forced into by my mother, a loving but ultragodly woman. She had dedicated her life to the Lord after, as she told it, she prayed to God and asked Him to spare her from fatal asthma. He did, in Clinton, Mississippi, just after World War II. My father was driving the family to Arizona to save her from Pascagoula, where both of my parents worked during the war years at Ingalls Shipyard, a dredged harbor that has launched many nuclear submarines. It's got palm trees and sea, but it's deadly for breathing problems.

Now, whatdayaknow, at age sixty-five I have deadly breathing problems myself, but caused by cigarettes and aggravated, I think, by chemotherapy. I have Non-Hodgkins lymphoma and will die of it in seven years or so if I respond to treatment. Disease is boring and for me, crammed with wrath, I have to fight every day. My lung condition has improved by constant chewing of Nicorette gum and having several near smokeless days. I feel better than I have in years. My wrath came almost wholly from being unable to visit and fish our glorious inland seas, Sardis, Endi, and Granada reservoirs, close at hand. I've accumulated enough fishing equipment to last several families a decade of fishing, some of it dating back to when my children were young and we had deep sport together.

Seven years ago, after almost dying of pneumonia—low immunity from chemo—completely sober and off everything but Tylenol, I had a deep dream of the physical Christ while I was in the hospital. He had the lean strong body of a workingman and in a wheaten robe was holding out his arms to me. In this dream I said, "I've not paid enough attention to you." He was silent, but I awoke in front of my wife Susan, weeping and saying over and over, "I've seen Christ and your father, who was a saint!" This was exactly what that dream gave me and I've repeated it *ad absurdum* in writing and speech, because it was a dream realer than a dream, and I did not lie. I was astounded. Mozart was playing on a little jambox Susan had brought from home. It put me at home and gave me courage, although I was weak as a kitten and afflicted by intense pain all over, having lost thirty-five pounds in two weeks.

The doctors gave up on my chances but I had excellent medical care and somehow I survived. In my town, Oxford, you have brilliant gentle folks all around you, and fast friends, along with the sweet beauty of big oaks, magnolias, the mansions on Lamar Street, and broad avenues hugged by sycamores, river birches, dogwoods, Japanese maples, hickories, poplars, and Bradford pear trees, those of the famous chandelier look. Of course I've left out a horde of protesting plants—ash, pecans, and giant pines.

I hesitate writing this because our town is growing too fast and slick for us geezers, who puke at almost everything new and at the robotic developments whacking down much of our greenscape. McMansions close together called Wellfleet or something, for godsake, phony "Suthren" culture everywhere. I've had a home in Oxford for twenty-five years and do not encourage anybody to come here. Let them think that we are vicious and tacky racists with nothing to show for our culture but Elvis and the great bluesmen of the Delta, which is just an hour from here. How's this?—there's even a treeless tract of an enclave with a writers' theme. It's got a Faulkner, Welty, Tennessee Williams, Larry Brown, and, yes, a Barry Hannah house. Do I have legal recourse? I don't know, I've been so disgusted by this shithead development that I haven't explored the law. The company is flattering, the actuality snake oil and carpetbagging scum. Or charm, as you wish.

I fished in Larry Brown's lake, which had good crappie, Florida bass, and catfish in it. (Brown's posthumously published novel is called *The Miracle of Catfish*.) We chatted many times on his pier. Larry was great with his hands. He was finishing a solar-powered writing cabin on the south side of the lake when death by heart attack took him, a young fifty-three years of age. As Charles Bukowski says in one of his poems, "When death comes for him / It ought to be ashamed." From almost zero resources except the books his mother got him at the lending library in Memphis and Yocona and Tula, Larry made himself a brilliant artist who knew his time would be short, with heart disease on his father's side killing his pa at forty-nine, I think. His father was also a haunted WWII vet, bad to drink. Larry had 120 rejections before the *Mississippi Review*, a precious organ out of Southern Mississippi University, guided by Frederick Barthelme and Rie Fortenberry, took a short story. Then Shannon Ravenel of Algonquin Books discovered him and served as his exquisite editor and publisher in that fine house begun by Louis Rubin in North Carolina.

Larry was the kind of scrappy and bright Lafayette County denizen that brought me back to my home state and Oxford twenty-five years ago, and though I've been several other places—Montana, Iowa, etc.—to make a living, I've known where my true home was since one night in 1982 in the Hoka Theater and Cafe, where you could watch movies as you ate delicious sandwiches and salads. It was an old warehouse with a tin roof. A huge storm suddenly boiled up, the rain coming thick and heavy on the tin roof. The best song in the world to me. Outdoors the raging weather, King Lear raving mad and walking the heath out there while you're dry, warm, safe. I'm home, baby, my heart said. The Hoka was operated by my friend of equal age, Ron Shapiro, a Jew from St. Louis who may come nearer to the example of Christ than any Christian I know. He exults in the happiness of others, and travels widely on a constant mission to find love and music. I believe the Hoka was the only bohemian/hippie eatery/moviehouse in Mississippi.

The Hoka was where I heard my first reggae, Bob Marley, and talked through the night to writers Willie Morris and his guests William Styron and David Halberstam (RIP to all three gentlemen), and historians, painters, and sculptors, with our whiskey brown bagged and sometimes taken in our good coffee. It's where I met Susan, my wife of twenty-one years now, blond and handsome like Grace Kelly, by god. I was coming down from a two-week drunk that began on the train to New Orleans and the Tulane/ Ole Miss game, which I never saw, winding up on the eastern shore of Mobile around Magnolia Springs, from which I was driven some eight hours to Oxford by a loyal old student from my U of Alabama days. I was wearing bathing trunks and a Harris tweed jacket with tennis shoes. Maybe my legs were good but I know they were skinny. I was blithely eating salad with my hands when I saw her. I proposed immediately on conditions she have a boat and a covered garage. Jim Dees, a friend staunchly for twenty-five years now, interceded for me, telling Susan I was a really good fellow and not always like this.

See? That's Mississippi—helpers and gracious pals and gals.

This is what heaven is, and you can get through poverty and barely middle-class funds with this help. People love you and stick, baby.

Oxford has a cosmopolitan population and an Episcopal tolerance. *Laissez-faire* and *roulez les bons temps*, both. Folks leave you alone or gather quickly to help you or engage in meaningful conversation. The university helps this condition, but the homefolks of the town have their own culture, flowing naturally from each to each as does the help of each other and the "much obliged" mode runs the rural South. You receive constant aid and cheer from easygoing well-wishers all over the place, white and black and international. In fact, for Oxford's 150-year celebration I wrote a poem in which I called the place the "United Nations with catfish on its breath."

Catfish is a major industry throughout Mississippi, especially since cotton went bust along with much private farming. This is a sad development in the Delta, which looks like Egypt after a neutron bomb. Many shut-up stores and mansions all over, all gone with a newer wind. Casinos held the local employment somewhat, but not enough. Viking Range Corporation has taken over the chore of revitalizing a whole big town, Greenwood. They've brought in a fine hotel, a bookstore, and a bakery in the high-end range. Morgan Freeman, the brilliant actor, lives in Charlestown and owns restaurants and a blues club called Ground Zero in Clarksdale, along with his pal Bill Luckett. Their philanthropy is staggering. Freeman and his wife have given air conditioners to tropically hot schools, large gifts to hospitals, and have sponsored wonderful programs in the arts all over the Delta. A pilot and a master sailor in addition to his acting, Freeman is a genius who would stand an excellent chance of being governor of Mississippi, although when I queried him on this topic he said he had zero ambitions that way.

But Mississippi has changed hugely. Its aristocrats are black—Freeman, B.B. King of Indianola, the late Muddy Waters, and the others who picked up a guitar and sang, rocking the Delta, Memphis, then the world.

It is the green and the water that I recall from having grown up in this state that always seems to need rescuing from something—ice storms, teen pregnancy, illiteracy, black-on-black murder, along with the usual interracial atrocities and appalling cruelties matching those of every other state. My youth was blessed by visits to my cousins, aunt, and uncles at Roosevelt State Park in Scott County, about mid-state, where the CCC and WPA crews of the Roosevelt era had made cabins, roads, a big lodge with dinery and kitchens, and clearings for campers around the exquisite lush banks and pebbled spillways full of freshwater mussels and beavers. Roosevelt State Park and its lake promised a child the world as I knew it, the world at its best. Big bass and bluegill filled the water, and fishing as you waded in the cool water was an unforgettable ecstasy. My Uncle Slim owned the family record, I believe, with a seven- or eight-pound black bass. He fished all his life, as I have. If you got hot, you took to the clear cool water, diving off the many piers or off the low or ten-foot-high spring boards. My cousin Ted was an expert diver and swimmer. I was adequate. He could bop to the jukebox in the lodge at age nine when rock and roll was breaking out—the Coasters, Little Anthony, Fats Domino, then Elvis in '56. Old military armaments marked one area of the park, tanks and howitzers and a .20 caliber cannon with shield. You got in these machines and relived the mythology of the War, in which we lost Uncle Bootsy in a B-24 making toward Rommel in North Africa. Bootsy went MIA—the hardest cruelty on loved ones— and I will never forget my mother's sobbing for years over her handsome baby brother, a captain at twenty-three. But we kids were ready to whip the Nazis, Japs, or whoever all over again inside those tanks and behind the artillery pieces in Roosevelt Park. My Aunt Bertha set a fine table of fish or game for Slim and her four boys. She was a woman of beauty and intelligence, but also blessed with the rare gift of silence until something important must be said.

Yes, we were living in apartheid with blacks, nearly half the population of the state then, before the exodus up North or to Los Angeles for jobs and better treatment. But we young were oblivious, thinking the black folks were happy with their lot. *Listen to their happy music on the jukebox!* we thought. And our "maid" seemed mostly happy, as she cooked, ironed, and ran the place, truly.

Then came the atrocities of the Klan when we were in late high school and college. My parents were gentle segregationists, giving much in food and Christmas and Thanksgiving baskets to poor blacks. But then a Jewish client of my father, a life insurance salesman, was the near victim of a bomb on his porch one night. The perpetrators were a man and woman who the FBI and Meridian police shot dead. The woman had been a lovely classmate of mine at Mississippi College, a girl named Cathy with gorgeous legs, from circus people in Miami. She was under the sway of a deeply racist professor at the college, Dr. Caskey, who was our neighbor in Clinton. She taught at an elementary school in Jackson, and indeed taught my niece there. On the nights when her husband was away she rode with the Klan.

I read the newspaper account and could not believe it. I had wanted her deeply but my shyness kept me from saying a word to her. She was a campus beauty.

Later, 1964, came the three civil rights boys killed by the Klan with the collusion of the Philadelphia, Mississippi, police. I wanted out of this stinking, nasty, cowardly state, with its seg scoundrel of a governor, Ross Barnett, who caused the 1962 Ole Miss riot. All the white Baptists backed him or stayed mute. I went off to grad school with a bitter vow never to come near this rot again. (Some of the old race killers are just now being retried and sent to prison.)

But Oxford, the rolling hills, the verdant explosions of everything near, its nearby waters—rivers and inland seas—drew me back. I'm a man happy in his home. My wife and I will be buried in pine boxes here in the cemetery where lies William Faulkner and many of our older friends. I'm lucky in my work, too. Writing books seems a redundant pointless chore when I'm low or depressed. But then I live a few years among my friends old and new here, and I go back to the notebooks and the typewriter as happy about the prospect as I was at age eighteen.

MISSOURI

CAPITAL   Jefferson City

ENTERED UNION   1821 (24th)

ORIGIN OF NAME   Named after the Missouri tribe whose name means "town of the large canoes"

NICKNAME   Show-me State

MOTTO   Salus populi suprema lex esto ("The welfare of the people shall be the supreme law")

RESIDENTS   Missourian

U.S. REPRESENTATIVES   9

STATE FLOWER   hawthorn

STATE BIRD   bluebird

STATE TREE   flowering dogwood

STATE SONG   "Missouri Waltz"

LAND AREA   68,886 sq. mi.

GEOGRAPHIC CENTER   In Miller Co., 20 mi. SW of Jefferson City

POPULATION   5,800,310

WHITE   84.9%

BLACK   11.2%

AMERICAN INDIAN   0.4%

ASIAN   1.1%

HISPANIC/LATINO   2.1%

UNDER 18   25.5%

65 AND OVER   13.5%

MEDIAN AGE   36.1

MISSOURI
Jacki Lyden

I first came to St. Louis in 1985, as a young NPR reporter, there to chronicle the city's struggle to stagger back to life. Union Station, a ninety-year-old masterpiece that local residents claimed saw more traffic during WWII than Kennedy Airport on any given day, had just been refurbished for $176 million. An enterprising loft developer, Leon Strauss of the Pantheon Corporation, complained to me in a story I did that "the sense of abandonment in St. Louis is so profound, so uniquely 'St. Louisian,' that we're able to take over 100 acres of the Central West End without a single newspaper or radio station asking a question about it." Indeed, when Pantheon held a party to open its lofts, which I attended, almost no one came, despite panoramic views of the Mississippi and prices of $625 a month for 1,000 square feet.

Once the fourth-largest city in the United States, St. Louis was a ghost of its former glory. It was as if all the descendants of its pioneers had kept going west, no longer full of adventure but frightened urban refugees, turning their backs on the city as fast as their forebears had come. On the north side of the city, which was mostly black, there were fifteen thousand public housing units for fifty thousand people who couldn't afford rent or mortgages. Only the architectural grand dames were left to mourn the suburban flight: Union Station, the Forest Park hotel, and the beaux-arts glory of the West End, and its grand, founding-family mansions. These places were the last homage to the era of the steamboat, the fur traders, and the explorers. Elsewhere the city was ghostly, and the spookiness was captured at the time by the photographer Joel Meyerowitz, whose photos showed a forlorn St. Louis, gray and devoid of hope, with a lone inhabitant here and there skulking outside a shuttered bar. Though the soaring Saarinen arch at the western edge of the Mississippi River was beautiful, a 630-foot stainless steel masterpiece, it seemed like a mocking tombstone for a great but dead city, like Carthage.

Since then, refugees of religious and ethnic persecution have helped make St. Louis grow again, just as they did in the nineteenth century. Meet the Bosnian refugees, the biggest wave of immigrants to the city since the Italians came in the early part of the twentieth century. St. Louis is now home to approximately fifty thousand Bosnians—the biggest Bosnian population outside Bosnia itself. Most of them arrived between 1997 and 2003—the period of the official U.S. Bosnian resettlement program. That was part of an era when the State Department was aggressive about relocating war refugees, unlike today, when they are mired in red tape and sandbagged by the Department of Homeland Security. Bosnian Muslims, who had been uprooted by ethnic cleansing in the Balkan war, filed affidavits to sponsor friends and relatives. Through enterprise and pluck, they made the city their own. St. Louis is their unofficial capital, and their unofficial spokesman is named Sukrija "Suki" Dzidzovic. He is the St. Louis pioneer of today, a link to the era of resourcefulness and possibility. It's a pity he didn't arrive by raft, like Huck Finn and Tom Sawyer. But like Samuel Clemens, that son of the Mississippi, Suki is a newspaper man.

I went back to St. Louis last fall to meet him. When he picked me up at the St. Louis airport, I tried to open with a few pleasantries about my early trips to St. Louis and what a sad place it was back then. He cut me off.

"My life is not so simple as yours," he said, before I'd even uncapped a pen and pulled out a notebook. We were in his SUV, which doubles as a communication center: the Dell laptop with Internet card that lets him follow news articles from Bosnia on the go. He and his wife Mirsada can edit their newspaper while driving, and they do.

Suki, as everyone calls him, is a former captain in the Yugoslav Peoples Army under Tito. He was born in 1957 in a village on the Adriatic coast, and he grew up in Sarajevo. It was never easy for Muslims to rise as officers in Tito's army, or gain entry into the military school which honed him. He is a lean and handsome man, graying and finely featured with a barely contained energy, and it is easy to imagine him in command. In fact, it is hard to imagine him not in command.

Suki is the founder and publisher of *Sabah*, the only Bosnian newspaper printed outside of Bosnia in the world. Or so Suki claims. He speaks with the confidence of Dale Carnegie, Charles Atlas, and Donald Trump. By all accounts his newspaper is the voice of the 300,000-strong Bosnian diaspora in America. "*Sabah*" means dawn, and for Suki, life has dawned again. He came to St. Louis in 2005, following other Bosnians. Missouri is his own private Manifest Destiny, and he intends to conquer it.

"My life has three distinct parts," he said, veering out onto I–70. I searched for the seat belt as he careened from lane to lane, smoking and taking phone calls and swearing at the GPS lady. "The first, special military prep school called Rajlovac, for the training of elite officers. I don't like but 100 percent there is employed after graduating and they hate the Muslim officers. Second part, to Sarajevo. I was under siege in Sarajevo for three and one-half years. Third part of life, I am here, St. Louis. Write that. This is interesting for you."

And then he floored it. He hates to go less than the speed limit. He's been known to tempt cops, with some success, to give him tickets.

"I like to break the rules," he says. "I feel bad when I comply with them, when things are too normal. This gonna show you what I mean. I was in D.C., speed limit is 60 mph. There was police car in middle lane and people in front of me didn't like to pass him. I pass police car and look at him and he look at me. He put his lights on. My wife turned to me and said, 'You are crazy'. I say, I am individual. Here is supposed to be country of individuals."

Mirsada Dzidzovic, who has the dark look and sexy exoticism of a flamenco dancer, is Suki's layout editor. They have also been married since 1977. In ten years of working on *Sabah* together, they've never missed a newspaper deadline. Their daughter Ertana is *Sabah*'s advertising manager; her husband is the sports editor.

Suki publishes 20,000 papers weekly. Ertana told me proudly: "Don't think we are just 20,000 papers. It changes hands four times. That means it is read by 80,000 people." They threw a huge party for the ten-year anniversary of the paper in September 2007 in St. Louis. The Bosnian ambassador in Washington attended. The president of Bosnia flew in from Sarajevo.

In 1851, St. Louis had more immigrants than any other city in the country. Some 43 percent of the city was foreign born. A woman I know named Anne Taussig, herself a fourth-generation St. Louisian whose great-grandfather came from Prague, read me the following statistic: "Between 1840 and 1860, the city recorded tenfold growth, from 16,000 to 160,000, as a result of its strategic position on the Mississippi. The newly built cross-country railroad added to the thousands." In the end, of course, the railroads killed those wedding-cake paddle-wheelers. And though St. Louis put on a grand show with the World's Fair of 1904, by the mid-twentieth century the city's population had gone into freefall, sliding from being the fourth largest city in the United States to the eighteenth largest today.

Enter the Bosnians. They are largely responsible for boosting the city's population four years in a row for the first time in a half-century. Most of the Bosnians now in the St. Louis area—as many as 80 percent of them, in fact—emigrated first to some other part of the United States. That means St. Louis is beating out many other communities where they originally emigrated, most likely due to the lower costs of living in St. Louis. There are twenty-five Bosnian "settlements" in the United States in all, from San Francisco to Tampa. Why St. Louis? "The city had everything they needed," says Anna Crosslin, the president of the International Institute of St. Louis, which started bidding on contracts to bring Bosnians to the city in 1995. They succeeded. The IISTL is a former settlement house dating back to 1920. Crosslin's father is Japanese and she was born in Japan. But she's been a St. Louisian for three decades now. She says "it was a dance" with the State Department to get Bosnians to St. Louis. There were already many Mexican immigrants in St. Louis, and people from Burundi and Somalia. But most of them are unskilled laborers; the Bosnians brought skills.

"We had plentiful jobs. We had a welcoming attitude. And most of all, we had an affordable place to live." True enough, but surely the fact that the Bosnians are white has made their middle-class mainlining a bit easier, too? "I would say being white hasn't helped them and hasn't hurt them," says Crosslin, slowly. "They are educated, highly educated."

Suki is much more blunt. "Missourians would rather have Bosnian workers than blacks"—but that, in his judgment, is because the Bosnians work very hard and take pride in what they've done for the city. If there is prejudice helping them, he says, it is an American phenomenon, not the Bosnians. His wife, Mirsada, puts it this way: "The reasons Missourians trust us is that we didn't come here to lie, we came here to tell the truth, and even in Bosnia, a lot of the truth is prohibited. But here we have no discrimination and no jealousy. And that's why we can live here and buy houses."

"The truth is," says Taussig, "we were thrilled to see all these immigrants—not just the Bosnians—take up the slack because I don't know who would have taken up the slack. They didn't know one neighborhood from another, though they've learned. And sometimes they inculcate *our* prejudices. They're the new economic base of the city." And she adds: "The Bosnians—I think they have all those classic, core, American values in terms of wanting to be ambitious for their families, wanting a good safe place of opportunity for themselves, and to raise their families and be successful and be wealthy."

Mayor Francis Slay cannot say enough good things about them. "The Bosnians truly seem to enjoy being here," he told me. "They're industrious. They're hardworking. They have created their own chamber of commerce, erected the first minaret, held festivals, increased the tax base, and added to the spice of the city." It's an American success story.

When Suki was a boy in military school in Sarajevo, he read Mark Twain's *Tom Sawyer.* He was twelve or so, about the same age as Tom. His memory of the exact details of *Tom Sawyer* were hazy after almost forty years, but he remembered the hiding in a cave, the sense of heroism for a young boy, the liberation of a slave, and being part of something important. "It was a story to show boys they could be something positive," he says.

Like Twain, Suki was born excited, full of the sense of doing something grand and important. But it seemed Mark Twain and his fictional avatar would have little to do with Suki's life. Ask him about his boyhood school days, though, and he still has the school schedule memorized. And it's clear he loved it:

"Up at 5:30 for exercise for half an hour, winter or summer, we're out there bare chested doing our exercises. Then, 6 a.m., breakfast line. At 7:30, classes, 2:30, lunch, 3:30 to 4 p.m., sports, 4 to 8, mandatory study. Make sure the book is in front of you. Somewhere in there is half an hour for the news, we watch all together. Eight p.m. to 9 p.m., dinner. Nine to 9:30, play accordion, 9:30 to 10 p.m., clean everything. At 10 p.m., lights out."

His specialty was military electronics. He learned to defuse bombs: "French Durandal, English cluster bombs BL755. Any type of NATO armaments." He also learned about every battle important to the Yugoslav People's Army, from the Battle of Kosovo to World War II. And he learned about chemical and biological weapons.

"Interesting part of my story," continues Suki. We had gone perhaps three miles from the airport and I already had writer's cramp. Biographically speaking, we were still in the 1980s—just when I was floundering around Missouri, covering the Times Beach dioxin spill without a biohazard suit, and Suki was in Belgrade in a soldier's uniform.

"My love was actually photography; not military. Military is my head, not my heart. During my work in Belgrade I developed interest in photo labs and custom color. But it was very difficult to find the chemicals in Communist country." He pronounces the *ch* in chemicals. "As military officer, I can't just go to Italy or Germany so I sent my wife. I enrolled her in the photo school. I send her just for cover. I took the pictures. Little by little, my photos become more professional."

Suki married Mirsada when he was nineteen and she was eighteen, and they lived a good life in Belgrade. But they were both homesick for Sarajevo;

and Suki could not get the military to discharge him. Then came 1991, and "something incredible. They discharged me. Said 'Go.' No interviews, normally takes like five years to get out. They knew the siege was coming, and I was Muslim."

When he and Mirsada and their two kids—they have another girl, Arijana, now twenty—returned to Sarajevo, the streets were already blockaded and the atmosphere ominous. Little by little, the city was tightening up: barricades, checkpoints, people demanding to see papers, military planes swooping overhead. In March, 1992, he heard shots around 3 or 4 in the morning. Looking out the window, he saw people already falling in the street. He saw Bosnian defenders, running around, "playing like it was cowboys, firing at everything."

"I called to them. I said, 'Hey, guys, I'm a former military officer. Can I help you?' They asked me if I had a gun. I told them I'd turned mine in. 'Then fuck you,' they said."

He got pretty much the same reaction the next day at the main Bosnian military base. The city wasn't being bombed from the sky, and an aerial demolition expert wasn't really needed. (He did eventually disassemble a Valencia X cluster bomb with 147 bomblets in it.)

"But information, this, I knew, they would need." He got permission to organize a newspaper, *ISTO*, which stood for Information Coverage for Territorial Defense. Bosnian journalists contributed to it and they, his former staff sergeants, big-name journalists now in Sarajevo, still write for him at *Sabah*. But back then, Suki was just a deputy press officer in the Bosnian army. And a photographer.

"I took pictures. I organized the first photo exhibit under the siege, called 'Stop the Barbarism.'" And often, he says, he passed his pictures to Western photographers who passed the photos off as their own, trading him for food and rolls of film. When the electricity went out, he turned a car into a giant enlarger by using its battery and putting the lens where the light should be. When he ran out of film, he cut up movie reel film. But it was too high a contrast.

Soon, Sarajevo was hell. The family house was right on the frontlines. They were starving. Mirsada, whose English is rougher than her husband's, tried to describe to me what they ate. I wasn't following. We looked at weeds on the Internet. It turned out that they were eating stinging nettles, which she said she had made into pies.

Suki cheated death several times. Once a bullet meant for him went through his windshield and lodged in the headrest of his front seat, an inch or two from his head. On another occasion, Mirsada looked out a window and saw six children playing in a cherry tree. A moment later, artillery cut them to shreds.

The family hung on until the day a sniper shot through the window into Ertana's chair. Suki, Mirsada, and the girls fled the next day, through the tunnel the Bosnians had dug under the Sarajevo airport. Six months later, after a period of living in Germany, they arrived in New York. Suki had two brothers there; one was a hairdresser, Gigi, and the other a building superintendent, Lazlo. He borrowed a set of car keys from Lazlo, and drove, he said, listening to jazz, going as fast as he felt like driving "until I had driven off the map." He found himself on the tip of Long Island. He spoke no English. An agent at a gas station drew him a picture, and that's how he knew where he was.

Coming to America from a Communist country, says Suki, was like landing on the moon. With his excellent technical skills—chemistry, physics, engineering, electronics—Suki found work in New York as a darkroom technician, boiler repairman, and building superintendent. The last was an especially good job, because it gave them free housing and a bit of time. But he was restless. He learned English. Mirsada was miserable, cleaning houses and crying. One day, while Suki was at a soccer game watching a Bosnian team clobber a local club, he thought it was a sad thing that only twenty or thirty people had seen the game. On the way home, he stopped at a Queens electronics store and asked for credit to buy a computer, printer, and scanner. He had fifty bucks in his pocket.

"Can I see your license?" the salesman inquired.

"Don't want to drive," Suki snapped. "Want equipment."

The salesman returned with a credit card for $1,800.

"This doesn't buy me even one piece of what I want," Suki barked. "Give me credit for all of it or I take nothing." So the technical works at *Sabah* were acquired. You can get a lot of work done when you are a building superintendent at 109th and Broadway, your apartment is free, your wife is away, and your kids are in school. He charged $1.50 a copy, same price as he charges today.

But his fellow Bosnians let him down: after 300 copies, he couldn't give it away. The press run ran a minimum of a thousand issues, so he subsidized the paper. For years. He worked the same way as he does today: all the time.

In 2005, when a famous Bosnian author touring America invited Suki to accompany him to St. Louis, Suki jumped at the chance. He couldn't believe his eyes.

"St. Louis, after New York, was like being let out of prison," he said. He packed up his family and moved, buying two homes in the old German neighborhood of Bevo Mill, one for his daughter Ertana and her husband (the sports editor) and the other one for Mirsada and himself. Bevo Mill was in transition; older folks were dying off and their kids had left. Now, says Suki, "we are winding back the clock." Or rather, he says, "the clock is going to be set again." We headed to Gbrics restaurant for a plate of sausages called *cepac*.

Gravois Street (pronounced *grah-voize*) is the main thoroughfare of Bevo Mill, which has a restaurant of the same name started by the Anheuser-Busch company, with a windmill on it. On Gravois Street there are now many Bosnian establishments, including the Eerya Market, where you can get Bosnian flour, chocolate, wine, honey—even Bosnian laundry detergent. Some of the women say their husbands have PTSD from the war, so the wives learn the language and work as everything from accountants to hair-dressers. The men drive trucks. So far, only about 1,000 of the Bosnians here are United States citizens. But more become citizens each day. Missouri politicians know the community is here, and come courting.

Suki did something else other immigrant forebears have done: Everywhere he went, he proselytized about the virtues of Missouri, and more people began to come. In Flushing, Queens, says Suki, you get 1,300 or 1,400 square feet for $290,000. Here, one can buy a four-bedroom house with three bathrooms for that money. Suki claims that when he left New York, 50 percent of the Bosnian community came with him to Missouri. I have no way of knowing if this is true.

"When I left," he said, "they had no more representation."

The last time I saw Hannibal, Missouri, was in 1993, when I was reporting on an epic flood that would eclipse thousands of miles of farmland from Iowa to Tennessee. It looked like the forty-dayer out of the Book of Genesis. Hannibal itself saw seventy square miles of farmland go underwater—in a single day. At the time, Suki was under siege in Sarajevo.

As Suki and I approached it, through gorgeous fields and bronzed woodlands, the river played off in the distance, and Suki talked about the time he and Mirsada answered an ad for farm help. They thought it might be nice to live in the country. Because he was Bosnian, he said, he was hired almost over the phone. When he got there and realized he would have to operate farm machinery, he blanched. No way!

As we laughed, I read a sign: ETERNITY IS LIKE MONEY IN THE BANK: WHERE ARE YOU GOING TO SPEND IT?

"Hell," said Suki. He talks politics. He doesn't like the Dayton Accords, thinks Bosnia gave up too much. He talks America. "Branson is great. I love it. I love Silver Dollar City, Ozarks, and the lakes. Whereas Phoenix is ashtray on a table. But for me, best place in country is San Diego. I love old downtown, old-fashioned restaurants, mellow urban scene."

His voice trails off. There are more church signs. The Mississippi riverbank has attracted religious evangelism since the beginning of American exploration. Twain's own father was of a stern religious bent. When we enter Hannibal, it seems both sunlit and depressed, still the place Mark Twain described as "a white town drowsing." A man wearing bib overalls strolls out of Kay's Diner and Truck Stop as if he has all the time in the world.

"Now," says Suki, surveying the scene and looking at me with a wicked grin, "I'm going to kill you."

"Why?"

"Because I like action. And I am going to be bored. Also, I think I am luckier than Mark Twain. When I come to America, I come to New York. And he has to start from nowhere."

Hannibal's dilemma is the same as a hundred towns along the Mississippi: how can a once-thriving river town forge a new identity in a country that has largely turned its back on its greatest waterway? I point out the old courthouse. Marion and Ralls County had so many civic matters once, it built two courthouses. A stunning federal building on Main Street, a former post office hewn out of limestone, was for sale for only a half-million. I point out the way the city sits nestled between two bluffs. And we make our way to the Mark Twain Boyhood Home & Museum. There are, one must admit, far too many businesses in Hannibal using the name Mark Twain, from a ready-mix concrete company to a counseling center. But then, I'm not trying to make a living in Hannibal.

The Mark Twain Boyhood Home & Museum's curator, Henry Sweets, runs Suki and me through the early chapters of Twain's life. Sweets mentions the terrifying financial instability brought about by Twain's father, Judge John Clemens, who died before Twain was twelve. After leaving school for an apprenticeship, young Sam Clemens went to work for his older brother

Orion as a printer. The two started a paper, the *Hannibal Journal*, and in 1853, Clemens was writing an occasional column called "The Rambler" about goings-on about town. After a fire in their printing shop, the brothers were forced to move the printing press into the house.

Henry Sweets shows Suki a typical type box of the time, and how you would have to arrange all that moveable type with a justifying stick. Suki looks wan at the thought.

Henry takes us to the tidy white clapboard house on Hill Street where Twain lived after coming to Hannibal. As many as eighty thousand visitors a year come here from all over the world. (The log book at the museum's Interpretive Center proves it—fifty-seven separate countries in 2007, from Australia to Ukraine.) But on this quiet day, it is just us in a small house with period furniture. What really gets Suki's attention is the tiny stove in the Clemens's parlor.

"Just like a sheet metal one I made from cans of peppers in Sarajevo," he says, "in which we could burn the furniture when we were under siege."

Finally, Henry Sweets takes us to a beautiful overlook called Lovers Leap, where it seemed some boys had come to harm. There is also a story about a town forebear who suspended his daughter in a crystal casket after she had died, inside a local cave. Clemens had lots of great anecdotal material before he ever got out on the Mississippi.

After the tour, Suki and I stop at the Jumping Frog Cafe for a home-made lunch, and look at a copy of the *Hannibal Journal*. One of Clemens's "The Rambler" columns from 1853 mentions a girl Sam is obviously smitten with—and he doesn't sound much like Mark Twain—

> *Love Concealed*
> *To Miss Katie of H—!*
> *Oh, thou will never know how fond a love*
> *This heart could have had for thee—*

Suki says a girl in Bosnia sent him a letter after reading *Tom Sawyer.* "Dear Editor," the letter began, "I am a Bosnian girl who has never seen the sea. But I believe that the sea exists because I live in my imagination a lot. As a writer, even if someone has never seen the occasion, you can give them a good opportunity to dream."

"I mean, try to imagine this city without Mark Twain," says Suki, as we got back into the car. "This person whose town did not support him and his brother and buy their newspaper so they went broke. This would just be a rest stop on the highway, maybe not even that, if not for Mark Twain.

It would be in fragments. But now, look at all these businesses: Huck's Taxi, Mark Twain Hotel, Mark Twain Restaurant. Twain's name got passed to their children and grandchildren." (And that's only the places named for Twain, Tom, and Huck. There's also Becky Thatcher stuff. But not too many establishments named for the fleeing slave, Jim.)

"My newspaper exists because I'm selling ads, but do you think it is Bosnian community that supports me the most? No. It's the Americans. They're the ones who advertise; the Bosnian community thinks all they need is word of mouth. There are maybe 200 or 300 small business owners in Bosnia's St. Louis community. They read the paper and pass it on. But the Americans. They advertise. Maybe if the Bosnian community understood what I'm trying to do, they would be more appreciative. I have not raised my price from the beginning because I'm trying to hold them together. Right now," he says, "only six out of the paper's fifty-two pages are in English, but some day will be 100 percent English.

"And maybe someday in Bevo Mill it is Sabah Restaurant, Sabah Taxi, Sabah Hotel."

And then he floored it all the way back to St. Louis.

MONTANA

CAPITAL   Helena

ENTERED UNION   1889 (41st)

ORIGIN OF NAME   From the Spanish for "mountain"

NICKNAME   Treasure State

MOTTO   Oro y plata ("Gold and silver")

RESIDENTS   Montanan

U.S. REPRESENTATIVES   1

STATE BIRD   Western meadowlark

STATE FLOWER   bitterroot

STATE TREE   ponderosa pine

STATE SONG   "Montana"

LAND AREA   145,552 sq. mi.

GEOGRAPHIC CENTER   In Fergus Co., 11 mi. W of
   Lewistown

POPULATION   935,670

WHITE   90.6%

BLACK   0.3%

AMERICAN INDIAN   6.2%

ASIAN   0.5%

HISPANIC/LATINO   2.0%

UNDER 18   25.5%

65 AND OVER   13.4%

MEDIAN AGE   37.5

MONTANA
Sarah Vowell

The tallest mountain in Montana is former Senate Majority Leader Mike Mansfield's tiny tombstone in Arlington National Cemetery. Could Granite Peak in the Beartooth Mountains usher through the Civil Rights Act and get eighteen-year-olds the right to vote?

The license plates say *Big Sky Country* for a reason but if you really want to learn something about the pink-blue light in winter, go inside, pull off your melting boots, and look at *January Afternoon in the Gallatin Valley*, a Russell Chatham lithograph from 2004. The thin, flat strip of snowy ground is upstaged entirely by an ample stretch of glowing air.

Lewis and Clark Caverns' ceiling drips with the strange beauty of stalactites but it can't be as strange or as beautiful as the films of Missoula's David Lynch, not that the candlelight tours of the caverns at Christmastime aren't recommended. The formations in the caverns were made by something called "hydrostatic pressure" but the best word people can come up with to describe Lynch's work is "Lynchian."

The bald eagles are worth a look-see but so is the YouTube footage of airborne, Butte-born Evel Knievel in flight. Has a bald eagle ever jumped the fountains at Caesar's Palace, cleared the Snake River Canyon, and/or bounded over fourteen Greyhounds—on a motorcycle?

It's thrilling to find out what Montana is like; but it is not entirely dull to find out what Montanans have done. There have never been that many people in the state so the men and women who are here have always tended to stick out. To wit:

Every September mountain man John Colter is honored in the seven-mile "John Colter Run," a cross-country race at Missouri Headwaters State Park. Colter, a member of the Lewis and Clark Expedition, was the first white man to see what would become Yellowstone National Park in 1807. Colter was a trapper, and he and his partner were collecting beaver pelts in 1809 on the hunting grounds of the Blackfoot tribe. Captured by the Blackfoot, Colter's buddy was executed. Rather than do the same to Colter, his captors, just for fun, stripped him naked and told him to run for his life so they could hunt him down. He was barefoot, running fast and far, killing the only Blackfoot who caught up to him with said Blackfoot's own spear. The last 200 yards of the course in the John Colter Run require participants to wade across the Gallatin River in honor of the way Colter escaped the Blackfoot—by diving into the Jefferson River and hiding under a log. (Unlike John Colter, participants in the John Colter run are allowed to wear shoes.)

Three of your more famous names in American history—George Armstrong Custer, Crazy Horse, and Sitting Bull—came to what is now Little Bighorn National Monument near the town of Crow Agency on June 25, 1876. But they're not necessarily the participants in that lopsided skirmish the visitor to the battlefield remembers most vividly. Here, the Seventh Cavalry's tombstones are laid out willy-nilly, the men buried where they fell. None of that Gettysburg grid here—no neat parallel rows. This is more pathetic, more existential, a bloody game of Pick Up Sticks. At the end of the trail, the grave markers end. Or so you think, until you look up, across a ravine and see the lone tombstone of some poor soul who almost got away. He didn't though. He's the one a visitor can't forget.

The population of Montana is small enough to send one measly legislator to the House of Representatives. For nine terms, that congressman was Evel Knievel's first cousin, Pat Williams. After Knievel's death, Williams wrote in the *Bozeman Daily Chronicle* that one time, in the 1960s, he ran into his cousin at Nick's Bar in Butte. Williams recalled:

> I pushed through to the bar and, putting my arm around Knievel's shoulder, I retrieved a newspaper clipping from my wallet, kidding him about the headline: "Knievel to Jump Grand Canyon." He smiled, reached for his own wallet and took out his newspaper clipping with a headline that read "Pat Williams to Run for Legislature."

One of Williams's predecessors, Jeanette Rankin of Missoula, was the first woman elected to the United States House of Representatives and the only member of Congress to vote against the United States entering both World War I and World War II. "I want to stand behind my country," she said in 1916, "but I cannot vote for war." After Pearl Harbor, the House of Representatives voted 388–1 to declare war in 1941; Rankin was the lone dissenter. "War is evil," she said during the Vietnam War, leading the Jeanette Rankin Brigade in a 1968 protest to Capitol Hill at the age of eighty-seven.

Maybe Montana's most lasting legislative gift to the American republic is the Seventeenth Amendment to the United States Constitution, mandating the popular election of senators. That's because in 1899 millionaire William Andrews Clark bought himself a seat in the United States Senate by bribing the Montana State Legislature. (One recipient scored $30,000 for his trouble, which isn't that much less than the present-day Montana median household income.) Clark's example, and that of a couple of similarly public-minded senators, stirred the groundswell for a popular vote. Clark was one of the most talented money-makers of the Gilded Age, which is saying something. At the time of his death, in 1925, he was worth more than $200 million. He deserted the Confederate Army in 1863 and came to Montana Territory for a gold rush in Bannack but soon made more money selling supplies such as eggs to other miners than his claim paid out. From there, he went into banking, railroads, newspapers, and, most notably, mining, becoming one of the three "Copper Kings" of Montana. A tiny supply stop for his railroad between Salt Lake City and Los Angeles turned into Las Vegas, which is why they named that county Clark after him.

If there is one thing all Montanans have in common, other than a disdain for speed limits and a thing for huckleberries, it is a love of William Shakespeare. Thanks to Shakespeare in the Parks, a traveling summer program headquartered at Montana State University since 1973, you don't have to be some city slicker from Billings or Great Falls to enjoy fine Elizabethan entertainment. Nope, you can pile the family and its lawn chairs into the pickup and enjoy *Merry Wives of Windsor* at the Dahl Memorial Lawn in Ekalaka, or take in *Comedy of Errors* at the Fire Hall Park in Wolf Point. Sometimes, according to Shakespeare in the Parks alumnus Bill Pullman, "the outdoors becomes a framing audiovisual that can add a lot of suspense to a plot. When a big thundercloud stacks up high and dark behind the mountains in Chico Hot Springs, you can add a glance in its direction when you are talking about your character being in danger." A Montanan could have seen—for free—almost all of Shakespeare's comedies, a tragedy or three, and the odd Molière, without ever leaving Whitefish. An ex-Montanan could be at the movies in Chicago and, spotting a bit player in a hospital bed in the Sandra Bullock vehicle *While You Were Sleeping*, spill her popcorn while elbowing her friend and exclaiming, "Oh my God! That's Thomas Q. Morris, my family's favorite Shakespearean!" Pullman recalls that audiences in "isolated towns . . . really felt compelled to think about the stories and the characters from Shakespeare. They weren't going to the performance to just say they went or for the sheer entertainment. They wanted to think about how a character in the play might be like some parts dealer they had known or how chance can bring calamity in short order."

Amble alongside the junior scientists and their parents enjoying the Hall of Horns and Teeth at Montana State University's Museum of the Rockies and you can't help but wonder which kid will end up a sunburned scientist someday in the Badlands of Eastern Montana unearthing prehistoric fossils. The museum's curator of paleontology, Jack Horner, was six years old when he dug up a dinosaur bone in his backyard in Shelby. A dyslexic who flunked out of college only to become one of the least pasty recipients of a MacArthur genius grant and the model for the paleontologist in *Jurassic Park*, he discovered the first dinosaur eggs in the western hemisphere, the first dinosaur embryos, and evidence that dinosaurs cared for their young. Asked once if it was lonely to grow up in an isolated place like Montana, he answered, "I actually like sparseness, the emptiness, and I don't find it a bit lonely. How can you be lonely in any ecosystem?"

So ponder the ponderosa pine, but don't forget to read *A River Runs Through It* by Norman "these stories have trees in them" Maclean. Remember that the wind blows through downtown Livingston long and lonesome but so does everything Gary Cooper never said. Know that there's nothing more optimistic than springtime in Paradise Valley, but if you need year-round renewal memorize this line from a Richard Hugo poem set in Philipsburg so you have it handy for life's little cold snaps: "The car that brought you here still runs."

NEBRASKA

CAPITAL Lincoln

ENTERED UNION 1867 (37th)

ORIGIN OF NAME From an Oto Indian word meaning "flat water"

NICKNAMES Cornhusker State or Beef State

MOTTO "Equality before the law"

U.S. REPRESENTATIVES 3

STATE BIRD Western meadowlark

STATE FLOWER goldenrod

STATE TREE cottonwood

STATE SONG "Beautiful Nebraska"

LAND AREA 76,872 sq. mi.

GEOGRAPHIC CENTER In Custer Co., 10 mi. NW of Broken Bow

RESIDENTS Nebraskan

POPULATION 1,758,787

WHITE 89.6%

BLACK 4.0%

AMERICAN INDIAN 0.9%

ASIAN 1.3%

HISPANIC/LATINO 5.5%

UNDER 18 26.3%

65 AND OVER 13.6%

MEDIAN AGE 35.3

NEBRASKA
Alexander Payne

The WPA's *Nebraska: A Guide to the Cornhusker State* begins this way and is a good place to start: "The traveler crossing Nebraska gets an impression of broad fields, deep skies, wind, and sunlight; clouds racing over prairie swells; herds of cattle grazing on the sandhills; red barns and white farmhouses surrounded by fields of tasseling corn and ripening wheat; windmills and wire fences; and men and women who take their living from the soil."

That the first words invoke the traveler rather than the Nebraskan himself captures how Americans have been thinking about the place for over 200 years—as somewhere to travel through, not to. A response we Nebraskans often hear when we say where we're from is, "Oh, I drove through Nebraska once. Boy, that state goes on and on." A kid from San José down the hall from me at Stanford could remember Nebraska only as the place his family bought a new car after they totaled theirs hitting a deer. (That happens a lot, by the way.) For Jack Kerouac "it was perfectly legitimate to go 110 and talk and have all the Nebraska towns—Ogallala, Gothenburg, Kearney, Grand Island, Columbus—unreel with dreamlike rapidity as we roared ahead. . . ." People generally have just a few other associations with the state, if any—Mutual of Omaha, corn, beef, and football.

Americans have been saying about Nebraska, "Boy, that state goes on and on," since well before the automobile was invented. Settlement of the West long preceded that of the Middle West, and what is now Nebraska lay smack in the middle of the trip. It was, apparently still is, a hard slog across that seemingly endless prairie described by early travelers as a sort of desert. (How often do I still hear "cultural desert?") After the initial explorers—Lewis and Clark, Zebulon Pike, and Stephen Long—came the Oregon Trail, the Mormon Trail, the 49ers, the Pony Express, the Transcontinental railroad, the Lincoln Highway, and finally Interstate 80. Now with aviation it's called a "fly-over state." Even birds see Nebraska like this, as each spring hundreds of thousands of migrating sandhill cranes, ducks, and geese famously converge on the Platte River before continuing on. Writer Mari Sandoz called our home "that long flat state that sets between me and any place I want to go." In fact, you're probably just skimming through this chapter on your way to Nevada.

One could not imagine the WPA Guides to Maine or Montana or Missouri or even next-door-neighbor Iowa beginning with the words "the traveler crossing . . ." although people certainly cross those states too. There is something about Nebraska's nature as a place to be traversed rather than as a destination to be reached that has both kept our state sparsely populated and deprived us of a readily grasped identity—even, to a degree, among ourselves. Perhaps it's no coincidence that "plain" and "plain" are the same word.

But startling, strange, and beautiful things happen on those plains, as suggested by the WPA Guide's immediate mention of "skies, wind, and sunlight." We Nebraskans marvel at the big sky, the stunning sunsets, the dazzling electrical storms, the vivid fall hues. But we also contend with hideous freezes, stifling humidity, and catastrophes of nature that make one wonder constantly what sort of people the Indians and pioneers were to have managed out there in the open, utterly exposed—and not so very long ago. Along with the blizzards, prairie fires, floods, tornados, and droughts, there was the practically biblical plague of grasshoppers in the 1870s that obscured sunlight, destroyed all crops, and even stopped trains by making wheels spin uselessly on their crushed bodies. A survivor of the great 1888 blizzard that killed over 100 people wrote, "for a number of years I used to meet people in Omaha who had parts of ears, fingers or toes missing." One day during the 1934 drought, rain struck a dust storm, and a rancher saw geese covered in mud fall to the ground. I grew up a modern city boy, yet my own destiny was altered when in 1975 a tornado that ripped through the center of Omaha blew the roof off my junior high and sent me to a Jesuit school I'd never planned on attending.

Again from the seventy-year-old WPA Guide: "It is this determination to remain on the land, this never-ending struggle of human strength and will against natural forces that characterizes the Nebraskan temperament. Nebraskans are practical in temper—a trait growing out of their continual struggle for life."

"Practical?" What a bland word to refer to the character of our citizenry. But it is true, and it leads me to think about another term often used to describe Nebraskans—conservative. If Nebraskans default, as the overwhelming majority do, to conservatism—political and otherwise—it is not of the type endemic to financial fat-cats, jingoists, haters of the other and of the poor, NRA yahoos, or kooky Evangelicals. It is rather the conservatism born of self-starting, self-reliant individuals—Indians, waves of Germans, Czechs, Swedes—who literally carved their houses out of the ground, broke their backs against the plow, fought the elements, and had little time or patience for those who fell by the wayside. Nebraska was described by explorer Stephen Long in the 1820s as "wholly unfit for cultivation, and . . . uninhabitable by a people depending upon agriculture for their subsistence," but it was beaten into submission, particularly after the Homestead Act of 1862, by austere, frank, no-nonsense, stern, *practical* people. An English settler wrote home in 1870, "If any man has plenty of money, nerves of steel, a constitution warranted to withstand all climates, and . . . an 'India rubber conscience,' he may do well out here. Anyone not possessing these qualities had better stay away." The failure rate among pioneers was extremely high.

It's the conservatism of strong-willed people of modest means who frown upon luxury and ostentation, and this is behind the ethos one finds there today. Omaha, for example, is a prosperous city with many millionaires, but you'd never know it. Unlike Americans on the coasts who flaunt even what they do not have, Nebraskans would never wish to appear—bend over backwards not to appear—better than anyone else or to possess more than what they seemingly need. The state motto is "Equality before the law," but one could add "Equality before others." People are surprised to learn that Warren Buffett still lives in the same middle-class house he bought in 1958 for $31,500, but to us it's perfectly normal—textbook Nebraska. (My parents bought our house, two blocks away, in 1956. They still live there too.) It's common in Omaha for millionaires to hang out with pals of modest means, and the disparity in status is never an issue; it's almost as though we insist it not be an issue. And when people in Nebraska meet for the first time, the question "What do you do?" appears not early but late in a conversation, if at all. It would be in poor taste to appear as if you're judging a person by class, occupation, or bank account; besides, it's personal. Nebraska is also a place where a wealthy citizen might readily stop to help an illegal immigrant push a stalled car out of the street.

Politically, Nebraskans are Republicans to such an extreme that President Clinton did not even set foot in the state until a month before leaving office, and since the WPA Guide was published in 1939, the only Democrat to carry a presidential election there was Lyndon Johnson. Yet Nebraskans are Republicans of a generally fair-minded, plain-speaking, egalitarian sort. During the ugly, fractious partisanship that has so characterized American politics in the last decade, and despite some of my own opinions, I found myself sharing in little of the knee-jerk Republican-bashing I often heard around me; I had, after all, grown up in Nebraska, where people are reasonable and respectful of the opinions of others even in disagreement, and where open confrontation is discouraged—I have my views, but I'd never want them to appear better than your views. We've had more than our share of dull, rigid politicians, but as the WPA Guide points out, "That Nebraskans are practical in temper . . . has been shown frequently by their choice of leaders regardless of caste or political label. The man and the actions are what count. Influenced by the industrial development of the East and by the independence and individualism of the West, Nebraska seems to follow a middle course of liberalism rooted in the soil."

It's the ultra-Republican state that in my lifetime has sent two Democratic senators to Washington at once, hosted the first and so-far only gubernatorial race between two women (the Republican won), and as of this writing has in the Senate one "maverick" Bush-bashing Republican and one conservative Democrat. Going back a few years, Nebraska was the site of the 1892 Progressive Party convention; the home of William Jennings Bryan, the three-time Democratic presidential candidate; and the state that sent Senator George W. Norris, the man FDR called the "perfect, gentle knight of American progressive ideals," to Washington for nearly forty years. Nebraska produced Ike's Attorney General Herbert Brownell, who promoted early civil rights legislation, and JFK's speechwriter Ted Sorensen. And since 1934, it's the only state in the union with only one legislative house—the Unicameral—conceived by an early advocate as a way to decrease partisanship and "to save time, talk and money." Perhaps it's telling that my father is a lifelong Republican, my mother a lifelong Democrat.

I was flattered to be asked to write this entry on Nebraska not only because of the company of such prominent fellow writers but also because I'm a WPA hobbyist with a moderately extensive collection of WPA literature. Yet I was a little sheepish about accepting because I was born and raised in Omaha, and asking an Omahan to write about Nebraska is a little like asking a New Yorker to write about the United States. Like New York, Omaha is the metropolis perched on a far eastern border whose citizens are often ignorant of and spiritually distanced from the country stretching westward, and like New York, Omaha has more in common with other cities its own size than with the geographical area that surrounds it. One can extend this analogy further still. As Washington, D.C., is to New York, Lincoln—the more genteel and provincial capital city to the south, named for a president and conjured practically out of nowhere in order to decentralize power—is to Omaha. And as in the United States as a whole, Nebraska's west lies in a different time zone, is geographically distinct, and looks to a different metropolis—Denver—as its locus of culture, transportation, and shopping. But since roughly a third of all Nebraskans are Omahans, it's not unreasonable to single out my city for discussion, and as a film director who has shot three feature films there, I've spent a lot of time observing it and thinking about it.

In contrast with the more sober agrarian and ranching nature of the rest of the state, Omaha evolved as a rough-and-tumble boomtown anchored in one main industry—transportation. Sitting on the bank of the Missouri River and not far from the Platte, it was perfectly situated to receive steamboats and stagecoaches, outfit travelers, handle freight.

Then, as the natural fulcrum-point between East and West, Omaha was selected as the headquarters of the Union Pacific Railroad. This more than anything else was responsible for transforming what was in the 1850s a sleepy territorial capital of 2,000 people into a bustling regional city of 100,000 four decades later. As a place to process and transport all manner of goods, late nineteenth-century Omaha exploded with factories, mills, breweries, grain elevators, smelters, construction, and the livestock markets and packing houses that drew thousands upon thousands of immigrant Europeans. The Mexicans and Central Americans thronging historically ethnic South Omaha today are but the latest wave of largely Catholic immigrants finding work in meat-packing, construction, and manufacture.

The sedate, white-collar city of today betrays few traces of the Wild West origins that survived into the first decades of the last century—saloons, gambling houses, bordellos, street brawls, political bosses, and old-school prejudice. When my grandfather arrived in Omaha in 1912, he quickly changed his name from Nikolaos Papadopoulos to Nicholas Payne not only as a natural way to assimilate, but also because, just a few years earlier, an anti-Greek riot in South Omaha had forced most Greeks to flee the city. Given my Anglo-Saxon surname, people are often surprised to learn of my true ancestry, but in Nebraska one finds many "secret Greeks," with names like Peterson and Mitchell. In 1919 Omaha history was sadly marked by the lynching, shooting, burning, and dragging through the streets of a black man accused of raping a white woman; the mayor who tried to stop it was nearly lynched as well, and the county courthouse was torched in the process.

Omaha's different now, and the same. Probably as a deliberate repudiation of its "immoral" past, gambling is prohibited in the city, as are real strip clubs (the girls have to wear pasties). But casinos and strippers are right across the bridge in Council Bluffs, Iowa. There are no more lynchings, but there was an anti-immigrant demonstration in front of the Mexican consulate in 2006, and Omaha's black population is one of the most segregated and impoverished of any city's in the nation.

Omaha is different but still the same in lovely ways, too. It's a wealthy, highly "livable" city with successful large corporations, low unemployment, terrific public schools, nice houses and trees, restaurants filled to capacity, a thriving arts and music scene, even a new cinematheque. Visitors are startled by how cool and modern Omaha seems to be, and in the last five years in particular it has ripened into a city sweet with livability. If Minneapolis is the Seattle of the Midwest, then I contend Omaha has become its Portland. Unlike previous generations, my own included, who couldn't wait to get the hell out of that cow town, young people today like it, want to stay, and those attending university in other states return earlier and in greater numbers. In Omaha you don't feel the rumble beneath your feet the way you do in a big city; you can be calm, hear your own thoughts, get your work done. You can still run a string of errands—buy a gift at the mall, drop off your laundry, pick up a prescription, grab lunch, stop by and say a quick hello to a friend—in forty-five minutes, and despite Omaha's massive sprawl, you can still, bizarrely, get *anywhere* in under twenty minutes. I once heard Warren Buffett say that if he lived in New York, he'd get too many ideas in a day, but he only needs one and the time to follow through on it.

Omaha has been able to absorb influences both cosmopolitan and homogenizing without losing its essence. Omaha is still Omaha, perhaps even more than ever. Journalist Robert D. Kaplan, in his 1999 book *An Empire Wilderness*, contrasted it favorably to St. Louis, which he thought had lost its sense of a center, a soul. When Starbucks came to Omaha just six years ago, opening its first store, in typically predatory fashion, a few doors down from a locally owned coffeehouse called the Village Grinder, patronage of the latter increased. No nationally owned franchise business has been granted a lease in The Old Market, downtown Omaha's restaurant and boutique district and the most popular tourist destination in the entire state. We put great value on the local—Omahans support other Omahans, both in town and in the diaspora.

I have lived for years in California, spent long periods in New York, Europe, and South America, but I return constantly to Omaha for work, family, and friendship. Recently I purchased a condo downtown that I plan on owning for the rest of my life. People talk about Sedona, Arizona, as possessing some magical nexus of power, but I think they're talking about Omaha. For some reason the city exercises tremendous gravitational pull over its offspring. One friend, a lawyer and author, lived for years in San Francisco but returned to Omaha, he told me, "to be woven more deeply into the fabric of life." By way of example, he noted the difference between merely hearing of the birth of an old friend's child from afar and being there to go visit during the first week. More poignantly, he spoke of what it's like to hear of the death of a childhood friend's parent. "When I was living in San Francisco, it wouldn't have occurred to me to come back for the funeral. Now that I'm here, I go. That alone has been a huge thing in connecting to my friends, to this place, to my younger self. Those people raised me as much as my own parents." Such sentiments are not unique to Omaha—they can be said of anyone's hometown—but I feel them the way he does, and I know we have our own uniquely flavored version of them in Omaha.

Not long ago, I was in a dispute involving the construction company I'd hired to build the interior of my condo and the developer who had converted the 1929 Art Deco hotel that houses it. The issue involved leaks in the roof and exterior walls that had been revealed during recent rains, and we needed urgently to assign responsibility and seal the roof and façade before dry walling confirmed. Two friends from New York happened to be present to listen in on the discussion among the contractor, the developer, and me, and they told me later it was like hearing a different language. What had struck them was the tone of utter politeness and respect that would make one think there was no dispute at all. No one had begun a sentence with "You goddamned well better . . ." or "I'm going to sue you if you don't . . ." My friends had barely been able to discern when the pleasantries had finished and the true discussion had commenced. Of course it helped that the three of us in dispute were about the same age and had attended the same high school, but business is conducted in Omaha utterly differently from how it might be conducted in New York. It's not just about remaining "nice," although that is part of it: pushiness backfires here. The best way I could explain it to my friends—and I was articulating this even to myself for the first time—was that in Omaha we tend not to doubt the good intentions or innate sense of fairness of others; all we need do is discuss what plainly needs to be done and remind them gently, even indirectly, of their duties. At the same time, and with no contradiction, Omahans are among the frankest people I've ever met.

It's that unique flavor of the Midwest in general and Omaha in particular that I've been trying to capture on film, because I find it so different from the America I see in movies, and because it's so deeply in my heart. I've been interested in trying to observe how human frustrations play out within a culture of niceness and seeming normalcy. I don't think I've yet succeeded, but I'll keep trying. Researching and writing this essay has been yet another stab at it, too. Maybe we Nebraskans feel a little like the travelers—we pass through the state our entire lives without ever quite grasping it. All we know is that Nebraska is at once the middle of nowhere and the center of the universe.

NEVADA

CAPITAL Carson City

ENTERED UNION 1864 (36th)

ORIGIN OF NAME From the Spanish for "snowcapped"

MOTTO "All for Our Country"

NICKNAMES Sagebrush State, Silver State, or Battle Born State

RESIDENTS Nevadan, Nevadian

U.S. REPRESENTATIVES 3

STATE BIRD mountain bluebird

STATE FLOWER sagebrush

STATE TREE single-leaf pinon and bristlecone pine

STATE SONG "Home Means Nevada"

LAND AREA 109,826 sq. mi.

GEOGRAPHIC CENTER In Lander Co., 26 mi. SE of Austin

POPULATION 2,414,807

WHITE 75.2%

BLACK 6.8%

AMERICAN INDIAN 1.3%

ASIAN 4.5%

HISPANIC/LATINO 19.7%

UNDER 18 25.6%

65 AND OVER 11.0%

MEDIAN AGE 35.0

NEVADA
Charles Bock

There's a picture of me in the back of my parents' pawnshop. It must have been taken during the seventies, because I'm not ten years old. Wearing a black knockoff Adidas sweatsuit, I'm surrounded by racks of record players, eight tracks, golf clubs, and typewriters. I'm half turned, looking toward my father, who is holding the camera. In front of me, a long flat cardboard box is jammed with rows of booklets, which are stuffed with pawn tickets. I spent untold afternoons in the back of that store, numerically organizing the tickets and stapling them into the correct books. Sometimes, when I finished with one book, I'd count and roll quarters. It's a Polaroid photo, most likely taken from a hocked camera whose owner had never come back to redeem his ticket.

My parents were far from any clichéd image of pawnbrokers. As soon as you walked into the shop, my dad—a lanky guy with a thickening middle, bright brown eyes, and black hair receding at his temples—greeted you with a kind smile. I see him making small talk while writing up a loan, bringing up the previous night's ballgame, or rolling out one of his favorite groan-worthy jokes, *Hey, do you know who likes cats? No? Mrs. Katz.* In the mid-sixties, he and Mom left the East Coast, following her parents who'd moved to the warmer climate of Vegas from New York City after Mom's mom got cancer. Dad then spent ten years trying to write plays and short stories while dealing craps at different casinos. He once had a screenplay that supposedly was going to be developed into a movie starring Burgess Meredith. Mom taught grade school and tried to sell Tupperware over the phone. They got into pawnbroking because my grandfather—a dice-throwing, trifecta-betting, mathematical genius—had his own pawnshop on Fremont Street, the gambling and tourist mecca of downtown Las Vegas. The struggle of being pawnbrokers became more appealing to my folks than the struggle of trying to make ends meet on their crappy salaries while raising four children. When I was eight or so, Gramps guaranteed the loan that allowed Mom and Dad to take over a struggling downtown pawnshop of their own.

Fremont Street was the heart of the city. Originally a Mormon missionary outpost, Las Vegas was essentially born as a town in 1905, when the completion of the train station prompted the building of shops and the sale of 1,200 lots to private citizens—all downtown. The city, which was officially recognized by the state legislature in 1911, was built from Fremont Street outward. Even in the late nineteen seventies, downtown Las Vegas was just as much a destination as the Strip. Sure, the Strip had huge hotels like Caesar's Palace, The Riviera, The Dunes, and The Sands. Some were clustered together, but for the most part, each resort was an island unto itself, a quarter mile from anything, with long swaths of hard desert between hotels. By contrast, downtown was like the French Quarter: a small and defined area, every place within walking distance. And just as Bourbon Street was lined with one bar after another for partiers to stumble between, Fremont Street was similarly packed with casinos. You couldn't come up with five locations on the planet more ideal for a pawnshop.

Here's how the biz works. You bring in your watch—say it's eighteen-carat gold, and you need a loan on it. You'd like to get five hundred for it. My dad weighs it and discovers the weight is a little light. It's not the greatest make or brand. When you bought that watch three years ago, you paid five hundred. You tell my dad you should get five hundred. Maybe you get pissed. You have all sorts of financial pressures on you and you need that money, so maybe you shout and call my dad a dirty Jew. Maybe not. I don't know you. But let's say you hold back the epithets, and are smooth in your negotiations, and have some luck to boot. Let's also say your watch is actually worth a damn: you get a loan for two, maybe two-fifty. You sign a ticket agreeing to a monthly compounded interest rate of eight percent. Your $250 loan would cost you $270, if you wanted to get the watch out during that first month. Your watch would cost you $291.60 the second month; $314.93 the third. Pawnshops make most of their money on the interest which has accrued when people redeem tickets for their goods. Your ticket says you have six months to redeem your watch. After six months, if you haven't come back, the shop owns the watch—that is, unless you call and explain your difficulties and ask them to hold on for another month. Most will then hold the watch. My parents do that, most likely, my dad wishing you well and sounding positive and trying to make you feel good (*It'll be here waiting for you, don't worry*). This having been said, at a certain point—figure the end of that seventh month—time's up; that watch is going out in a display window.

Making a living this way is methodical, tooth-pulling work; at John's Loan and Jewelry, my parents—neither of whom is named John—toiled for ten hours a day, three hundred and sixty days a year, my mother haggling with locals who needed to hock their goods to help pay their electric bill, my dad dealing with the couple who brought in the family television in order to get baby formula. Here's a former UNLV basketball star turned casino security guard, bringing back in, for the ninth time, the watch he got when the team made it to the regional finals of the NCAA tournament. Here are young lovers looking for wedding bands on the cheap. Thais and Filipinos on international gaming junkets. Drunks on the tail end of holiday benders. Tourists wandering down the showcases, bleary and angry and worn out, busting my parents' chops about how much some item is worth. Or ripened gamblers, who've suffered hard dry runs and are still in the grip of gambling fever, maybe they *live* in the grip, and need to exchange this diamond bracelet for cash, no, not to fill the tank with gas, not to drive back home to California—these are the ones who sign their pawn ticket and receive their bread and go right back in for another run at the craps table.

And there I am, ten years old, emerging from the back of the store, slamming down a wooden security gate. To an electronic chime, I head out the front door into the July heat, darting in between tourists, down Fremont Street, running underneath vents that blow cool air during hundred-degree days and beckon pedestrians into a casino's comfortable darkness. A giant mosaic of the queen of hearts stares up at me from the sidewalk; golden flecks sparkle beneath my every step. The famous winking cowboy sign, Vegas Vic, looms ahead, moving its right arm, pointing toward the Pioneer casino. As Vic's recorded voice booms, *Howdy pardner, welcome to downtown Las Vegas*, I check the time and temperature on the digital clock atop the Mint, and run the block and a half to visit my grandfather—if he doesn't have customers, he'll do magic tricks for me. Or maybe I head over to the liquor store at the Horseshoe for candy and soda and then sneak into their casino, avoiding the security guards so I can stare at the million dollars displayed in a giant horseshoe.

As I circle home again, I read the silk-screened messages on the T-shirts in the windows of souvenir shops—"I lost my [graphic of donkey] in Las Vegas!" and "Greetings from Lost Wages, Nevada!" Outside some of the smaller, nickel-and-dime joints, women in skimpy outfits hand out fun books with coupons for free shrimp cocktails, twenty-five-cent hot dogs, and a five-dollar blackjack bet where you only have to pay two dollars. Usually I'll get my parents lunch from McDonald's—it's about three blocks closer than the coffee shop where I sometimes play pinball. I'm often the shortest person waiting in line there. Along with burgers and fries, I always bring back two large coffees, black, and make sure to ask for cream packets for my mom. Then I head back, balancing the bags of food, the coffees, and my large Coke on the little cardboard tray.

People ask what's it like growing up in Vegas. And later, once I'd been away, I started to realize that life in Vegas is not the norm, most junior high school girls aren't taking Stripping 101 as a required course. Ha. I kid. Except most fifth graders *don't* have a teacher who regularly hocks his gold necklaces with your parents. And, at the time, Las Vegas—specifically the happenings inside John's Loan and Jewelry, that little box of a storefront on Third Street, half a block from Fremont, tucked neatly between the Tiger Room strip club and a six-floor parking structure where prostitutes sometimes worked—*that* was the world I knew.

When I was in seventh grade, Dad lost his lease and had to pay for the construction of a new store, on First, next to another pawnshop, Stoney's. Where the old John's Loan had been directly across the street from the Golden Nugget's front entrance, the new shop—a square bunker of cinderblock and cement—was across the street from the Nugget's backside, by their employee entrance. Still, my parents made the best of it. After all, this space had parking, and they could send any jerk they didn't want to deal with next door (naturally Stoney's did the same thing to them). Eventually the space on the other side of Stoney's became available, and my dad put a liquor store there. Later, Dad split the liquor store in half, opening a men's clothing shop. In keeping with his sense of humor, he put a humongous stuffed gorilla in the front window and dressed it in a Hawaiian shirt. The clientele of casino workers who needed Sansabelt slacks and alterations seemed to get a kick out of this.

By the time I was fourteen, in 1983 or so, my father had gotten his neighbors to go in with him on a new stucco façade and the neon sobriquet *PAWNSHOP PLAZA*; my brothers—Yale and Anthony—had gotten their driver's licenses. Each afternoon, one of them was responsible for bringing me and my twelve-year-old sister downtown after school.

On a typical fall day, Anthony had football practice and Crystal had some rhetoric competition or drama club, so Yale and I would arrive at around 4:30 on the Mint clock. Before heading into the pawnshop, we'd grab sodas and chocolate at the liquor store. Then after receiving a hearty *"Hey, hey, there they are,"* from my dad, we'd settle in the back of John's, try to ignore his occasional and well-meaning pop-ins, and leaf through the sports and entertainment pages of the out-of-town newspapers that Dad had already read through. My father stocked these papers in the liquor store because the hardcore gamblers over at Leroy's—where all the point spreads got calculated—believed that local sports coverage from other cities would give them tips on teams that might help their bets.

At five, *All Things Considered* echoed through stereo speakers—a sign that closing time was approaching. While my parents finished up with whoever had raced in to beat the clock and get their jewelry out of hock, Yale and I hit the front windows, clapping together the small felt boxes that held all the rings for sale. We also emptied the showcases, stacking the trays of necklaces, watches, charms, and bracelets, and depositing everything in the huge walk-in safe.

When there weren't any tourists hanging around, looking at goods they had no intention of buying, Dad would let Mom go early; she'd head off to unwind in a casino while we locked up the store and activated the alarms. Fifteen minutes later, we'd find her at a nickel slot machine, cracking a roll of nickels against the edge of the metal payout tray. All around us would be the sounds of coins rushing into steel tins, that sudden metallic rainfall. I wanted so badly to sneak a play at a slot machine, to be old enough—or brave enough—to try. But I was too afraid of what my parents would do if they found out.

Once we scooped up Mom, all of us would head to the coffee shop inside the Vegas Club. Even more than the steak and seafood place at the California Hotel, the Vegas Club's coffee shop was my favorite place to eat downtown—its walls were covered with autographed photos and memorabilia from sports legends, and the paper placemats were lined with the dimensions of all the major league parks. As at most of the downtown restaurants, the waitstaff knew my parents—a lot of the waiters were customers at the pawnshop. They called my dad John, and my mom Mrs. John. Prime rib specials ($5.95 with a salad and a baked potato) were our usual.

"The city pawn unit keeps calling about the serial numbers for that gun," Mom might say, once she'd gotten a refill of coffee. "I keep telling them we don't have it."

"Someone must have complained," Dad would answer, exhaustion in his voice. He'd break apart a roll, slather on butter.

"They should do me a favor," Mom said, "and drop dead."

"Can we talk about anything else?" asked Yale.

The majority of downtown hotels had been established by men who became the heads of Vegas's big gambling families—Benny Binion (Horseshoe), Sam Boyd (the Mint), Jackie Gaughan (Vegas Club and Plaza Hotel). Like them, my dad dreamed big. Just as the Four Queens had been named for the four daughters of the casino's original owner, my dad, in honor of his kids, named his liquor store Four Aces. By the early eighties, however, the downtown casino owners had become complacent, milking the properties for every cent they could get without reinvesting. By contrast, my father, for all his affable nature and warm smiles, still had ambitions. The business was his shot, so he was always planning, coming up with something that would make things just a little better for the stores—which meant better for us. He slaved to get the liquor shop a license for video poker games. For a short while, the shop even sold microwaved breakfast sandwiches, which my dad gamely named Egg McBagels.

But gradually we realized that Dad wasn't the only one downtown with ambition. During midnight movies and late-night rebroadcasts of UNLV basketball, between the extemporized commercials with the motor-mouthed guy in a referee's outfit who eventually got to the point about the midnight menu over at the Castaways and the constant barrage about Jai Lai, the world's fastest game ("only at the MGM"), you can bet on it, someone new started popping up. Tall. Tailored suits. Subdued pompadour of black hair. His name was Steve Wynn.

Wynn was the new owner and president of the Golden Nugget. In one commercial for his "new" Nugget, he appeared with Wayne Newton. In another, he walked Sinatra through the lobby and up to a master suite, explaining all the improvements he had in store for this hotel, only to get treated like a bellboy at the end. The commercials were always understated, with sly humor. As a kicker, Wynn would promise: *The Golden Nugget: We're going to make Las Vegas famous.*

Wynn once explained his agenda in an interview. "I always wanted to build beautiful hotels. Places that were better than the outside world." In 1984, he set to work on the Golden Nugget. Down came the giant bright-yellow rock that was lit with hundreds of bulbs on the corner of Fremont and First. Then the hotel was repainted, this time a gleaming and classy white. A luxurious pool, which took about six months to install, boasted a fancy lagoon area, exotic deck chairs, strategic mist nozzles, and a glass partition, so that on your way to the casino or the hotel front desk you could watch the sunbathers and swimmers. The Golden Nugget's renovation also involved palm trees and a big white brick wall to delineate exactly where that outside world ended and Wynn's fantasy began. The wall also happened to be just high enough to prevent any of the hotel guests from spotting *PAWNSHOP PLAZA* just across the way.

My dad looked out at that wall and stewed. Soon, true to his entrepreneurial spirit, he'd rented out a small orange and yellow hot-air balloon—maybe ten feet by ten feet. My dad had a sign printed up for John's Loan and Jewelry, which he attached to the balloon. The balloon master—i.e. the retired airline pilot who owned the thing—then attached the balloon to the top of the pawnshop with a series of strong hooks and ropes. Dad's multicolored balloon floated above the store, clearly visible beyond the Golden Nugget's palm trees and wall. An automatic pump kept the balloon inflated twenty-four hours a day, and a small electric interior light illuminated it at night.

If you prompt my father enough, he might tell you about the time Steve Wynn stormed down from his penthouse office and entered the pawnshop. Perhaps he exaggerated the tale. Perhaps he told me not to write about it —"I don't want to be sued," he might have said. So I have to tell you that in a fictional alternative universe, a created place where there are no lawsuits, Wynn might have thrust his finger into my dad's face. "I'm going to get rid of you," he might have threatened. "How much do you want to bet that you're not going to be here this time next year?"

As it turned out, neither my father nor Steve Wynn was going anywhere anytime soon. Outside of the Nugget's high brick wall, Fremont Street still had its own gritty spirit, and that spirit was never more in evidence than it was every December 31. In preparation for the long night ahead, Dad would have ordered twenty-five to thirty thousand dollars worth of beer and champagne. He'd take a nap early in the day but by three o'clock he'd be standing in the middle of the liquor store, waving his arms and directing traffic.

First we'd empty the T-shirt bins and clear out anything that could be stolen (travel sundries, souvenir dice clocks), making a big empty space out of the central floor area. All soda was removed from the coolers and replaced with beer. Metal tubs were placed at strategic points along the floor, then filled with hundreds of pounds of ice, more beer, and ten-dollar champagne. Finally, Crystal, Yale, Anthony, and all of the senior citizens and former customers who worked at the liquor store would put on glittery party hats — you can't work at a downtown Vegas liquor store on New Year's Eve without your glittery party hat.

Long before seven, when the cops put up barriers and Fremont Street closed to traffic, the parking lots were overflowing. The store was already busy, the first wave stopping in for their pre-celebration libations. An Omaha housewife in an evening gown bought whiskey, which she poured into a silver flask; college kids in plaid shirts and backward baseball caps bought 40s of malt liquor and twelve-packs of Bud; a raucous Hispanic couple—she in a skimpy party dress, he in a slick leather trench—stood on line to buy a few bottles of champagne. Happy. Polite. Enthusiastic. Rowdy. Waiting. Ready to cut loose. Getting their party on.

New Year's rockin' Eve, as the ageless Dick Clark called it, was broadcast live from downtown Las Vegas, Nevada. Almost one and a half tons of custom-made fireworks were deployed, shot from the top of the Union Plaza Hotel, in a choreographed celebration—er, make that celebrations. The first, for the East Coast feed at nine, featured a countdown—*three, two, one*—and a fireworks show that was less a practice run than an excuse to take the party up a level, to count and whoop and cheer, to whirl noisemakers and pop corks and make out with strangers while two hundred cops circulated, passing out plastic cups to replace any open bottles they saw. Tens of thousands of people annually crammed into the mouth of Fremont Street. Revelers barely had space to stand. People killed time from the fake countdown to the real one, then killed brain cells from the real countdown until they blacked out. Think Times Square without the frostbite. Think Mardi Gras without the midnight shutdown. Think *Caligula* without a declaration of war on the sea.

If you were partying downtown that night and wanted alcohol, the Four Aces Liquor Emporium was the closest place to get it. From eight p.m. until past two in the morning, our store was packed five deep around every cash register. My dad wore four jackets at once and would circulate, visiting each register for the take, then jamming his pockets with money. When all four coats were stuffed, Dad would run to the safe in the back room and dump out one pocket at a time. Meanwhile, "girls would just come up and hit on you," according to my incredulous brother, Anthony. "The funnest thing of all time," Yale, his twin, called the yearly event. My sister, then a blue-haired punk, also worked a cash register each year. She called the celebrations "as good a party as there could possibly be," with guys constantly trying to pick her up, and she being at an age when, "honestly, that was kind of cool."

By the late eighties, however, big changes were underway. In case you haven't heard, tourists don't tend to arrive in Las Vegas by train anymore. Now, to get to downtown from McCarran International Airport, a person has to pass the Strip. Driving in from California—the source of Vegas's major road traffic—you also hit the Strip before downtown. Of course, the city had been evolving for years, with large and swanky resorts like Caesar's Palace and the Riviera becoming entrenched power brokers, but Steve Wynn, fresh off his success at turning around the Golden Nugget, pushed everything forward at warp speed, providing the blueprint for the future: spectacles, where the full experience was more important than gambling alone. The Mirage and then Treasure Island were financed by Michael Milken's junk bonds to the tune of a reported $530 million. The former boasted a rainforest in the middle of the casino. It had white tigers on display behind glass partitions. From one angle, the flourishes came off as classy. From another, they were ridiculous.

Meanwhile, downtown became a haven for penny-ante grinds and quickie tour packages. Maybe once a month AlarmCo called in the middle of the night. My bleary-eyed father would drive down, check on the latest break-in attempt, and call in with an update *(Yeah. It looks like they tried to climb in through the vents)*. Barbed wire soon went up on the roof. Each morning someone hosed down the area behind the liquor store to get rid of the piss and stench and trash left by derelicts My mom had to call to pester the garbagemen into coming by and emptying the Dumpster—*We pay taxes don't we? Don't we have the right to have our trash picked up?* My dad dutifully shooed away beggars, as well as the poor schmucks who hadn't been able to unload their goods in the store and tried to sell them right on the sidewalk.

I remember being seventeen, waiting at a traffic light after helping to close up the shop, when a guy ran from across the street, up to the driver's side window of my junky Cougar. "Hey man, you need some smoke? You need anything?" This was literally across the street from my parents' store.

I also remember a December visit back from the fancy private college that my parents' toil in the pawnshop had paid for. Across the table from me in the coffee shop of the Vegas Club, my mother and father slumped in their seats, hungry and beat, just trying to hang on until the food came. Meanwhile the waiters could not have cared less. Forget knowing my parents by name, they didn't even know where our dinners were, and they didn't give a damn. I remember looking down at those placemats—still the ones with the ballparks around the edges—and realizing that years had passed since any major league baseball had been played in Toronto's Exhibition Stadium or Atlanta's Fulton County Stadium. When the food finally came, it was glazed, leathery, inedible. The whole experience was a slap in the face; no, actually, it was like watching my mother and father get slapped in the face. This was their life, and I was helpless to do anything about it.

Eventually, there was a bureaucratic answer to downtown's urban free-fall: "The Fremont Street Experience." Fremont Street became an open-air pedestrian mall, closed permanently to vehicular traffic. A long, light-weight metal roof was built, arcing over the street, with a digital screen on its underside—the same kind they have at sporting events, only running five blocks. Starting at nightfall, animated shows ran above the heads of gawking pedestrians—I recall a series of jets flying down the length of the street, trailing an American flag. Part of the renovations shut off traffic for side streets as well, including the side street that was home to my parents' shops.

When Vegas Vic needed repairing—his mechanical arm had stopped moving, his voice was garbled—the execs who ran the Fremont Street Experience told the Pioneer's owner, *Too bad, we can't have anything get in the way of our animated light show, sorry.* Even worse, stores that had been on Fremont for decades—including a jeweler, a luggage store, and the Coronet Drug on the corner of Fourth—places whose owners had invested their livelihoods in downtown and were relying on its renovation, were condemned as urban blight. The city confiscated properties, paid the owners a paltry sum and relocated them, whether they wanted to move or not.

My parents were terrified. It wasn't hard for my dad to envision the property being gift-wrapped and handed to his nemesis, Steve Wynn. But Wynn, as it turned out had other plans. Rather than taking over downtown, he was withdrawing from it all together.

On December 30, 1993, the *Review-Journal* had a story about the fact that, because of a gang fight and shooting the previous year, the fireworks show on Fremont Street had been cancelled. Instead, fireworks would be shot off on the Strip, from Wynn's Treasure Island. Some city officials had called all the small downtown businesses, promising that even without the fireworks, there would still be crowds, and my dad had convinced himself this was true. Brimming with anticipatory energy, he spent that afternoon directing traffic like he always did. And like always, the postcard stands were cleared, the sodas replaced, the tubs filled with ice and alcohol. I see him passing out the party hats. I see him looking at the store's entrance, waiting for the celebration to begin. I cannot spend too much time thinking about this, because, eventually, I'll get to his mouth slowly going slack, those brown eyes going fluid, my dad looking old, shocked, realizing just what was about to happen.

The Horseshoe, its million dollars on display, its liquor and magazine store in the rear, is now gone. The Mint is gone. Most of the famous neon signs that I grew up with—the Dunes, the Sands, that giant Golden Nugget façade—rest in something called the Neon Boneyard; if you want to see them, you can arrange a special tour. And the echo of coins falling on steel is absent from all the casinos now, replaced by weird electric tones and computerized tickets that track your winnings.

As far as downtown is concerned, well, one of the new plans for its renovation involves turning a few streets into a bar and nightclub district. There are also rumblings from a scene of artists and hipsters who have discovered the dilapidated grandeur of this historic neighborhood. And there's a crazy plan involving some sort of massive stadium. What I know for sure: the city just paid $3,600 a pop for twenty-two bronze medallions to commemorate historic facts about "old" Vegas, which were set up along the east end of Fremont Street. Somehow, a number of the facts were wrong. When the mayor was told about it, he told reporters, "I'm hoping people on the Fremont East are half-lit, and could care less what the markers say."

That tells you what you need to know about downtown. Except for this.

In 2007, the owner of the land beneath John's Loan apologized to my dad, as if by selling the property and getting out he'd given up the fight. We still had ten years on the lease, but it was a moot point. Turns out, the newest owners of the Golden Nugget—the third, I believe, since Steve Wynn sold the place—were actually decent and agreeable. The first time their lawyers visited, my dad, seventy-two and sporting a pair of unreliable hearing aids, charmed them with a few jokes.

These days, that giant gorilla from the clothing store is perched in the living room of the house where I grew up, sitting on the plastic-covered sofa that was once my grandmother's. Half of the liquor store stock is three blocks north of Fremont, in the back of my grandfather's old store, which my mom still runs. The pawnshop my dad built, the place I once knew as well as I knew anything on this planet, has been bulldozed. Now it's the construction site for a convention center.

As for Vegas, well, Las Vegas—by which I mean the collective residential area, not what's inside the city limits—has exploded in all directions, suburbs now reaching beyond the confines of the Vegas Valley and into the surrounding mountains. The latest trend is luxury high-rises; even as the housing market takes its epic dive, a real estate web page shows fifty different projects—condos and apartments—springing up on the Strip and in other prime locations, with some one-bedrooms going for a million dollars. Vegas's former combination of populism, individualism, and good dirty fun, which had once been the city's bedrock, is long gone. Instead so many people come here merely to take part in—to play roles in—the spectacle. Sex and sin for high rollers and well-dressed frat kids, the snobbish pretension that masquerades as status, name droppers and VIP champagne table service and whatever billion-dollar resort is opening this year—that's what matters. Media reports commonly point out that Vegas makes more revenue nowadays through service than through gambling. Steve Wynn ends up being a visionary.

And there's no point in complaining. We all know this is where things are heading, not just in this city, not just in this state; nobody who matters would keep things stagnant, even if they could. Still, each time I return to my hometown, I am amazed anew. The sprawl. The scope. I guess that officially makes me an old fuck. Fine. But it's still overwhelming. Whenever I am back here, I spend a fair amount of time driving around, and while I'm flipping between shitty rock radio stations, I'll catch myself recognizing a few stores that are still in the same places they were in my childhood: the McDonald's where my brother's best friend from high school worked; the KFC that went up when I was in eighth grade. Fast food restaurants are marks of permanence in this place.

But people in Vegas still sometimes need cash in a hurry. And it can still be found on the Strip, at its northernmost point, across the street from the Sahara Hotel & Casino in a large shopping plaza. If you visit, you'll find a stand-alone McDonald's, a sports memorabilia store, Chinese and Indian restaurants, and a massage parlor. And you'll also discover that John's Loan and Jewelry is still going strong. My brothers handle most of the business nowadays. But if you stop in, ask for my dad. Tell him Charlie sent you.

NEW HAMPSHIRE

CAPITAL   Concord

ENTERED UNION   1788 (9th)

ORIGIN OF NAME   From the English county of Hampshire

MOTTO   "Live Free or Die"

NICKNAME   Granite State

RESIDENTS   New Hampshirite

U.S. REPRESENTATIVES   2

STATE BIRD   purple finch

STATE FLOWER   purple lilac

STATE TREE   white birch

STATE SONG   "Old New Hampshire" and "New Hampshire, My New Hampshire"

LAND AREA   8,968 sq. mi.

GEOGRAPHIC CENTER   In Belknap Co., 3 mi. E of Ashland

POPULATION   1,309,940

WHITE   96.0%

BLACK   0.7%

AMERICAN INDIAN   0.2%

ASIAN   1.3%

HISPANIC/LATINO   1.7%

UNDER 18   25.0%

65 AND OVER   12.0%

MEDIAN AGE   37.1

NEW HAMPSHIRE
Will Blythe

This journey to New Hampshire starts in my hometown of New York City on a gray, winter day when, adrift in an ocean of narcissism, I am in an increasingly churlish mood. For instance, everyone I know has their own blog. They list their favorite books, movies, songs, friends, bowel movements. One person has 363 friends!

By comparison, I am friendless, and in this epoch, at least, a misanthrope. Though perhaps a drifting, dreamy one, prone to staring at maps and wondering if there might be some other place more conducive to a snaggle-toothed cur. A place where the residents enjoy a sort of bemused relation with themselves. Where they have souls rather than psyches, vegetable gardens rather than blogs. Where they look askance at the act of self-promotion. Where they are sly, tough bastards, undaunted by bad weather.

As for these blog people . . . they groom their sites as intently as suburbanites (or their Mexican yardmen) whack the weeds that grow hard against their curbsides. They post videos of themselves, pictures worthy of a magazine. They tint their skin tones, adjust the background colors, and project themselves into a glamour that everyone can achieve these days. So now—thank you, Photoshop!—we have another democratic anxiety that technology has gifted us.

Not only am I misanthropic, I'm too lazy and despairing for such image-maintenace. The blog people . . . advertising themselves as if they were cans of soup. . . . I like cans of soup, but people who advertise themselves like cans of soup unsettle me. What do they want?

For all I know, I am probably a narcissist myself. The evidence (first person confession) suggests as much. And hell is one narcissist having to listen to another; worse—many others! If Montaigne had been alive today, would he have been a blogger?

And yet, I am tired, tired, tired, sick to death of myself. Sick to death of self in general, sick of all your cute, yapping selves, too. Bored with my stories. Disheartened by my voice. Disgusted even with the sly, tactical self-deprecation that I use to cover my tracks. So much self, so little time. . . . The clamor of Me, Me, Me All the Doodah Day. In the words of a former boss, I am living alone in bad company.

I want a richer silence. I want to be away from my ordinary self. Older remedies, even fear . . . all the antidotes to the small self. I want to disappear into history. Instead, I go to New Hampshire.

A s a traveler here, I have no lineage from which to be descended, no stories of family and local customs. I am passing through. And at this moment what I have is that familiar American sensation produced as you drive a stretch of new highway and the roadside blurs by at top speed. I drive fastest when I have nowhere in particular to go. The gnarled New Hampshire landscape— beat-up hills, homely third- and fourth-growth trees, and rocks, so many rocks that it looks as if the clouds above the state opened up and rained stones for thousands of years—thrums past me. Ah, the stony soil of New England, metaphorical stock of preachers and writers. In the winter, anyway, there's something dirge-like about this country. But I understand . . . the sense of a grudging landscape . . . resistant to man's designs in the same way the soul refuses to submit, whip it though you may. . . . I really do understand this . . . just because it's an old, unoriginal metaphor doesn't make it wrong.

I had gone to New Hampshire once before, on assignment for *Playboy* in the spring of 2007 to cover the haphazard presidential campaign of John Edwards. To the North Country I went, into the White Mountains. In theory, it was spring. But the trees were still bare. Snow clung to woodlots, mountainsides, road margins. Ice sharded the streams.

After winding past grand hotels from the nineteenth century and pop-and-pop bed-and-breakfasts run by gay couples from the twenty-first, I came to the Grand Summit Hotel in Bartlett, where the Carroll County Democrats were hosting their annual Grover Cleveland Dinner, with John Edwards scheduled to speak that night in the White Tail Deer Room. A man dressed as the former president Grover Cleveland (who turned out to be Cleveland's grandson, and a radio personality) waited outside the banquet, chewing on a cigar, and asked, "Is my fly open?" No one answered.

His name was George Cleveland. He told me that he was an Obama man because Obama had Hawaiian roots and that his grandfather had been very popular in Hawaii for having supported the monarchy there.

When they found out I was writing for *Playboy*, the Edwards staffers— anxious young functionaries, swelled with pride at their proximity to a potential President—treated me as if I were suffering from the Ebola virus, giving me wide berth.

The Democrats of Carroll County reacted in one of three ways to my affiliation. They either laughed in embarrassment, told me I was a lucky guy and asked which of the Playmates I had met, or winced and moved quickly across the ballroom, where they eyed me warily the rest of the night. When I moved toward them, notebook in hand, they moved away—a game of hide-and-seek in plain view.

One local politician with whom I had enjoyed an earlier conversation steered his wife my way. "This is the writer from *Playboy*," he told her. To me, he said, "She says I can buy *Playboy* if I'm in it."

"As long as he's not nude," his wife said.

"Oh, I don't think your readers are ready for that," he said.

Apparently, you can learn a lot about the citizens of a state by their attitude toward *Playboy*. In New York, I was just a magazine writer. In New Hampshire, I was—perversely and glamorously—a belated representative of the Sexual Revolution. I have always suspected that people who find nudity an incitement of any sort probably have the best sex lives (conservative Baptist preachers, for instance) but there are some things that even an inadvertent scholar of New Hampshire does not need to know about its citizens.

Good People of New Hampshire, keep at least a few of your secrets to yourselves.

Like the candidates for President, the Devil, too, has apparently spent a lot of time barnstorming in New Hampshire, to mixed effect. They drove him out of Massachusetts, those prigs, and he had to go somewhere and New Hampshire was just next door and it was wilder and there were new businesses cropping up and wherever there is money, there is the Devil who has started up more franchises than Ray Kroc.

In 1692, the Puritan minister Cotton Mather looked out from his pulpit in the Second Church in Boston and saw a New England being overrun by the Devil. He delivered a fast-day sermon called "The horatory and necessary address to a Country now Extraordinarily Alarum'd by the Wrath of the Devil," which was later published in his collection, *The Wonders of the Invisible World*.

"Let us now make a Good and a Right use, of the Prodigious *Descent*, which the *Devil*, in *Great Wrath*, is at this day making upon our Land," Mather told his congregation. "*The Walls of the whole World are broken down!*"

That February, the first accusations of witchcraft had emerged out of Salem, Massachusetts. The trials were finally suspended in October by command of the royal governor. In the following months, nineteen men and women had gone to the gallows for witchcraft. One man who refused to plea had been put to death under heavy stones. Mather had cautiously endorsed the actions of the court trying the accused.

Having whipped New England into a witch-hunting frenzy, Mather eventually suffered second thoughts, although as is so often the case, they arrived too late—five years too late. In his diary, Mather divulged his anxiety that God would find him lacking "for my not appearing with *Vigor* enough to stop the proceedings of the Judges, when the Inextricable Storm from the *Invisible World* assaulted the Country."

As I drive into the New Hampshire night, I feel as if I am penetrating into this Invisible World. I relate to the witches going to their doom, to the preachers sending them. I imagine being pressed to death under heavy stones. In this year of our Lord, 2008, the Walls of the whole World are still broken down. What else is new?

The trees, the broken farms, the rocky land whirr past. There are terrors greater than anonymity, that quicken one . . . the stone descending, the bones cracking . . . blogs, ha!

As Cotton Mather's belatedly vexed conscience suggests, a seventeenth-century woman accused of witchcraft in Massachusetts or Connecticut stood an excellent chance of being executed. Nearly fifty women were hanged. Anne Hibbens was hanged in Boston after a neighbor had accused her of *knowing that people were talking about her.* Mary Parsons of Springfield went to the gallows after the Devil climbed into bed with her in the form of her dead child, whom she so wanted to see again. *She received it into her bed that night and so entered into covenant with Satan.*

But in New Hampshire, or what now constitutes that state, only one woman was ever convicted of witchcraft—Goody Cole. (The Goody stands for Goodwife, which along with Goodhusband, was a common form of address among Puritans at the time, and to the extent that the Puritans were social levelers of a sort, the New England equivalent of Comrade.) In 1656, Cole was accused of bewitching her neighbor's children and cattle. Local residents reported that she had appeared as a dog, a cat, and an eagle. She had also been seen sitting at the table with the Devil, who manifested himself as a black dwarf with a red cap. Cole was also blamed for the loss of a fishing vessel with all hands aboard at Rivermouth.

Found guilty of witchcraft, she was whipped and thrown into jail in

Boston, where she endured fifteen years of imprisonment before being allowed to return to Hampton, where she lived in a kind of banishment in a hut provided for her by the town and continued to be regarded as a witch.

At the public library in Hampton where I discover these facts, the kids, wearing their polar fleece, text-messaging, and doing their homework, call each other "dude." Do they call each other "dude" in the Invisible World?

I ask the waitress at nearby Lamie's Inn (fireplace, old couples eating at three o'clock in the afternoon) what she knows about Goody Cole.

"She's the witch, right? We have a room named after her. When the silverware is crossed, we joke around, 'Oh, she's here.'"

Down the menu, there's a Goody Cole Chicken Sandwich. This strikes me as a tragic, possibly emblematic fall—from a feared witch to a chicken sandwich.

Hanging outside the bar is the front page of the *Manchester Union* of August 26, 1938, announcing a ceremony that occurred the day before in Hampton, vindicating the memory of Goody Cole. The town's selectmen burned copies of the accusations made against her at the trial and mixed them with soil from land she was said to have inhabited.

Attending the ceremony from Hollywood, California, was Mrs. Harry Houdini, the magician's widow. She said that she believed Harry would thank everyone for this and proposed that Halloween be devoted to the exoneration of other falsely accused witches.

I'm looking for ghost-traces. . . . Back on the road I go, heading north from the coast. The highway is my conduit into some other world, and like a dime-store medium, I pick up vibrations from the surrounding landscape. Or maybe the vibrations are from tires that haven't been rotated in a long time. I take inspiration from the words of the poet Donald Hall, a New Hampshire resident who lives at Eagle Pond Farm under the shadow of Mt. Kearsage. He writes that "we do not require ancestors in order to connect, joyously, with a place and a culture." He sees all around him "emigrants from other places who belong more preciously to this place than most old-timers do." Maybe as a traveler, I'm like the mistress to a great man; my nocturnal privileges allow me to know things the good wife can only dream.

In 1904, after twenty years in Europe, Henry James returned to America and went to Chocorua, New Hampshire, to visit his brother, William, who owned a summer place in the White Mountains. William had discouraged his brother's return to the States, warning him of American "vocalization," "the Shocks in general," and the citizenry's propensity to eat boiled eggs with butter for breakfast. But Henry wrote to William that he wanted to see the eggs. "I want to see everything," he added.

In the White Mountains, however, he found himself bothered by the "sallow, saturnine" locals, driving carts and teams. They dressed poorly, they spoke badly. In *The American Scene*, an impressionistic to the point of vaporish record of his travels, James recounts the visit of a local North Country rustic to the front door of a summer person. The nineteenth century marked the advent of the summer person in New Hampshire. He "makes it a condition of *any* intercourse that he be received at the front door," James writes of the local. When the lady of the house appears, the local asks, "Are you the woman of the house?" He has a message, he tells her, from "the washerlady."

James ascribes great importance to this, detecting a breach of etiquette suggestive of a general loss of "forms" in America. I admire James's writing—he is the master of the endless parenthetical and his syntax snakes around itself like the endless ruminations of the terminally stoned. (I like this.) And *The American Scene* is a great repository of place-spirit. But his distaste for this New Hampshire man at the front door makes my democratic, Scotch-Irish heart rise in revolt. That errand-man is one of *my* people. My people turn wry, then truculent in the face of authority. We presume ourselves at least your equal. And we resent the implication that you might think otherwise.

How does this go on century after century? Can such predilections really be in the genes? Even when it comes to architecture . . . in Portsmouth, for example, I am surrounded by handsome Anglican structures made of brick. Elegant, enduring. And there's new high-tech industry down here in the southern part of the state, spreading out from Boston and surroundings. Lots of glass, unorthodox designs. But I couldn't wait to get out into the back country, to the rustic, the austere, the unvarnished. Laconic, democratic buildings, wooden planks, hewed beams, sagging barns. The plain style of those making do.

In my glancing encounters with the people of New Hampshire, I am reminded of the inhabitants of my native North Carolina. They evince that same paradoxical pride in one's modesty, the vanity scraped away like snow from the roads. This can result in an amusing contest in which everyone tries to outdo each other in not being too big for their britches. At worst, such humility becomes its opposite—a perverse and monstrous vainglory.

Where in the South we had the disaster of slavery to darken our souls to this day, New Hampshire has its winters—icy breeding grounds for cabin fevers of paranoia and meanness, for gloom and self-accusation. Lay the long nights and frigid days atop the Puritan conviction that men and women are worthless sinners in the eyes of an angry God, mix in poverty, and you have a recipe for the making of complicated worms.

New Hampshire reminds me of North Carolina in another way— that of a place that derives its identity at least in part by its opposition to another place. This the South continues to do with the North. (Nearly a century and a half after the Civil War, "Yankee" is still a derisory term in the former Confederacy, while for the rest of the country it hardly exists, unless we are talking about baseball, in which it is once again naturally a term of derision, and in New England most especially.) What the North is to the South, Massachusetts is to New Hampshire. A theocracy—once of Puritanism, now of right-thinking (Puritanism 2.0)—versus a land of secessionists. These days, we might throw in Vermont as well, that northern suburb of New York City, with its twee self-righteousness and propensity for expensive whole-grain breads. In that sense, New Hampshire is surrounded by pointy-heads who can't fix a furnace or grow a cabbage.

But historically, it was Massachusetts that exerted a near tyrannical sway in the region. New Hampshire was the wilderness next door, to which the rebels against Puritan authoritarians (ironically, themselves rebels against English oppression) could light out for territory. And New Hampshire's wilderness was genuine—not a pond, for God's sake, a few miles from town. Thoreau, bless his transcendental heart, only went so far into the wild as to be able to return for supper in Concord at Ralph Waldo Emerson's house. A railroad passed by mere yards from his cabin.

The real wilderness swallows a man's shouts. The silence of isolation vibrates in the heart like an arrow shot from the dark woods. Leaves a man talking to himself, to the trees and the rocks. Which is about the time that the landscape starts talking back.

It talks to me tonight as I cross the state, heading west. The roads are empty, the summer people long gone, back to Boston, Providence, New York. Snow swirls in the headlights. Everybody left is a native now.

A waiter I met at the Grover Cleveland Dinner told me that he had 200 years worth of relatives buried in the local graveyard. He just wanted to make enough money to keep living in this place. These days, such a stubborn attachment to home seems downright oppositional.

A New England graveyard had to be moved. One of the occupants had been buried for seventy years. His grand-nephews, themselves ancient, had been asked for permission to move the coffin. One refused for a long time before consenting but declined to attend the exhumation. The other brother attended. Afterwards, they spoke about it.

"Did they?"

"Yep."

"Were you thar?"

"Yep."

"How was the box?"

"Purty nigh gone."

"Coffin?"

"Sorta mouldy."

"D'ja look in?"

"Yep."

"How was Uncle John?"

"Kinda poorly."

When I stop at a gas station to ask if I am on the right road to Meriden, the attendant actually says, "Yep." In that moment, I know how a biologist feels, rediscovering a species long thought extinct. I had encountered a native "Yep" still surviving in the wild as civilization encroached on all sides.

One of the shocking things about going to a new place renowned for certain qualities is to discover that the new place really does possess those qualities. That in New Hampshire, for instance, people in conversation really do tend toward the dry and laconic. It's not just like some Bob Newhart TV show set in a New England inn where the locals dole out sly commentary on the goofy things outsiders do. TV actually got this from New England. What New England does when it gets this back from TV, I don't know, though I wonder if watching such images of yourself results in a tendency to exaggerate your regional characteristics in the interest of higher visibility.

New York, for instance, is a great place for Southerners to really pour on the Southernness, to drawl as if they'd been aged in a barrel of bourbon.

In rural New Hampshire, there is a tendency to use words sparingly, as if the supply might run out by spring. This laconicism is sometimes caricatured as countryspeak, the inarticulate parsimony of rubes and red-necks. It strikes me instead as part of a culture of conservation, of saving. A poor person in the sticks never knows when he might need a part from that rusting car in his front yard. Words in New Hampshire are car parts. Words are tools, worn by usage, carefully maintained, stored nightly in barns and sheds. Words are not for show (an excess of self-display is contrary to the spirit of farming and Puritan effacement); they're for milking, cut-ting firewood, digging (how else would one get down to understatement?). Words are vegetables from the garden, canned and put up in root cellars and kitchen cabinets, to be rationed out over the course of a long winter. Words should approach as closely as possible the condition of silence, honesty being nearly mute.

Yep.

How happy Chris, the Mazda man on Route 4 who sells me a new tire, is to present me with a bill that is even less than originally estimated! He appreciates unexpected economies. He recommends certain brands of tires. We talk passionately about the tires. I had never had such a feeling about tires.

And such a cheap tire! Only $99! He had thought it was going to cost me $125. The soul delights in thrift. Especially when it comes to replacing a flat tire. Is this a New Hampshire thing? Or is it just Chris, the cheerful Mazda man?

The rhapsodists of the American road strike me as a little long in the tooth these days, all those superannuated Kerouacs hung up on that endless spool of a book. Fortunately for Neal Cassady and company, they never had to drive across the country via the Interstate. *On the Interstate* just doesn't have the same ring.

And yet, how restorative to my love of the open road have been the back highways of New Hampshire! I could be driving through 1948. Those old-fashioned, curving blue ribbons wrapping the landscape like a Christmas gift. Buckled and potholed from winter, they're still beautiful, these roads, tended with alacrity by local crews. Donald Hall has written that "social welfare is magnanimous in New Hampshire only when you are a road."

In New Hampshire, local road signs warn of "frost heaves." These befuddled me the first time I saw them. They appear written in a runic tongue, Old English or Norse. There are so many ways to interpret these signs (such a New Hampshire thing—the wry joke that comes gradually at the outlier's expense, but only after the outlier has moved on). Did they mean that frost will heave—a simple declaration of fact? If so, I appreciate being told this. Are they historical markers for a person named Frost Heaves? Unlikely, though I would like to have met the man so named. Or are they simply bumps in the road, caused by the expanding and contracting of winter highways? After wattling over a corrugation of frost heaves on my way up to Canterbury, I can tell you that frost heaves in New Hampshire = the average unmarked road in New York City. And given the choice, my car and I would rather trundle over frost heaves.

A t the old Shaker settlement outside of Canterbury, it becomes apparent that there are at least forty varieties of silence. The snowbanks glisten in the declining light. The wind sweeps across the hill. The ear strains to catch something inaudible. A door bangs as one of the staff leaves for the day. There are no Shakers left here or anywhere. Only curators of Shakerdom.

The last Shaker at Canterbury died in the 1990s, the curator tells me. "Sister Something or Other, I can't quite recall her name. She was in her nineties. We're moving the administrative offices across the road," he says, eager to be on his way.

They let me stay to wander the farm.

I peer into windows, the old glass wavery as a mirage. Antique machines, belts, workbenches, all askew, as if the Shakers hadn't died off but left in a hurry, migrating to some other, more rectilinear universe. I had expected everything to be tidier, more Shaker.

I n Concord, I had come across the diaries of Irving Elmer Greenwood, a former member of this village. He arrived from Providence, Rhode Island, in the care of his grandmother on September 18, 1886, nearly ten years old. His mother had died of consumption four years earlier, his father hadn't wanted him. After his grandmother dropped him off, she returned to Providence.

The Shakers took him in. Their motto was "We make you kindly welcome." They'd lived on and farmed this land since the 1780s, when a local farmer had converted to the religion and donated this hilltop property. In those early days, the Shakers had practiced prayer, marching, and vigorous movement—hence their name.

But by the time that Greenwood was deposited at Canterbury, the marching and vigorous movement had given way to just prayer and singing. And as always, work. At fifteen, Greenwood began to work full-time, tending cows, cutting firewood, tilling the soil. He drove horse teams and learned how to run the saw mill. He loved mechanical things, how to operate and fix them. Another Shaker slogan: "Hands to work, hearts to God."

In 1895, another Canterbury Village boy's father gave him a bicycle, and he allowed Greenwood to ride it among the buildings in the early evening before supper. Irving was nineteen years old. Two years later, at twenty-one, he signed a covenant with the Shakers to become a Brother in the community.

Chastity was required of the Shakers, and if his diaries are any indication, this did not seem an untenable proposition for Greenwood. He did love plays and musicals, however, and avidly took them in on occasional business trips to cities such as Boston. He was not unworldly.

He lived a quiet, good life, and helped bring electricity, telephones, and cars to the Shakers at Canterbury. A typical entry, this of January 16, 1911, reads: "Put in a light at the Office & wire a rheostat at Office & put in a plug for a machine at Sisters' Shop." Greenwood's illuminations would appear to have been of this world, and yet, how they pleased him.

On February 25, 1922, he set up in the Brethren's Shop a Westinghouse Radiophone, as it was called, along with a Magnavox speaker that looked like a horn of plenty. The radio cost $232. He and his friend Arthur were able to tune in to a concert. A couple of days later, five Shaker Sisters were invited to listen to the new radio but with the "weather inclement, results [were] slight."

He died on June 19, 1939, sixty-two years old, leaving the plain notations of his diaries as a more than forty-year record of weather and work, of ice and snow and sweet summers, of planting and harvesting. The Shakers wanted to build a Heaven on Earth. Gentle utopians living on top of a hill. All gone now.

Here on this ancient hillside, I think: Maybe they got out just in time. They were interested in building barns, not reputations. Even if Brother Irving Elmer Greenwood had 363 friends, he would not have advertised this peculiar fact. I doubt he would have counted his friends at all. He counted chickens, cows, snowstorms, vegetables.

Dusk is fast approaching. The wind swirls. Snow crowds the Dwelling House in gust-sculpted waves. The rooms darken and the window glass reflects my face, angular and haunted. The old world—the Shakers' world—is invisible.

But in the bluing light, I detect emanations, faint as ancient radio signals from Brother Irving Elmer Greenwood's Westinghouse with the Magnavox trumpet. I don't know where they're coming from—inside the house, inside me? Or what they are. Or whether they will last. But they are coming.

I feel for a moment, in spite of everything, delivered. Here in this old place, I strain to listen.

NEW JERSEY

CAPITAL   Trenton

ENTERED UNION   1787 (3rd)

ORIGIN OF NAME   From the Channel Isle of Jersey

MOTTO   "Liberty and prosperity"

NICKNAME   Garden State

RESIDENTS   New Jerseyite or New Jerseyan

U.S. REPRESENTATIVES   13

STATE BIRD   eastern goldfinch

STATE FLOWER   purple violet

STATE TREE   red oak

STATE SONG   no official song

LAND AREA   7,417 sq. mi.

GEOGRAPHIC CENTER   In Mercer Co., 5 mi. SE of
   Trenton

POPULATION   8,717,925

WHITE   72.6%

BLACK   13.6%

AMERICAN INDIAN   0.2%

ASIAN   5.7%

HISPANIC/LATINO   13.3%

UNDER 18   24.8%

65 AND OVER   13.2%

MEDIAN AGE   36.7

NEW JERSEY
Anthony Bourdain

Some New Jersey residents enthusiastically—if briefly—tried, a few years back, to get Bruce Springsteen's "Born to Run" named as the official state song. A choice both appropriate and wildly, hilariously inappropriate had it come to pass. Sure, Bruce was, and likely remains, New Jersey's most famous product, our proudest citizen, our bard, our voice—the one guy big enough to say he was from Jersey and even tell you what exit and stand tall while doing it. But the song was about getting the fuck out of Jersey. While it might have been really cool to hear the lines "It's a death trap, a suicide rap" sung by thousands of people at Giants Stadium, I don't know what kind of message that would send. Or, actually, I do know. It would suggest that we're rooting for the wrong team. That we kind of suck—and that, regardless, we celebrate that state.

Even the existence of our version of Bigfoot, our very own legendary state monster, the "Jersey Devil," must be tempered by the knowledge that it was described in the 1946 WPA *Guide to New Jersey* as being "cloven hooved, long-tailed, with the head of a collie dog, the face of a horse, the body of a kangaroo, the wings of a bat and the disposition of a lamb." Which makes it sound no more threatening than a kind of flying Lassie.

Even Frank Sinatra, another native Jerseyite, was scarier than that.

New Jersey, even now when the whole country looks like Jersey, is still, anachronistically, a punchline.

But then—within the imposed borders of childhood—it was a little green world. Tree-lined streets, and eccentric backyards—each one different. Some had flagstone paths that led in mysterious patterns toward hidden gardens, stagnant carp ponds, rotting tree houses, the occasional creek. There seemed always to be a lawn mower going somewhere in the distance and someone coughing in the next house over. It smelled, in summertime, like cut grass—and coffee, from the Savarin Coffee factory, roasting beans in the next town. Once in a while there were other smells, of fermenting things in the marshes and land fills of what we called "the swamps" (actually the northern reaches of the more fragrant-sounding Meadowlands)—and even more sinister odors from the refineries along the Turnpike. Sometimes, the smells were just awful. A sulfurous, rotten egg odor that made the jokes we made about Bayonne and the "Garbage State Parkway" and all those people who lived closer to the factories not so funny anymore. In fact, I wonder if the inferiority complex that Jerseyites famously acquire when meeting New Yorkers has its roots in a vestigial awareness that we come from a state that smells.

Leonia, New Jersey, was a middle-class bedroom community about ten minutes from "the Bridge"—the bridge being the George Washington. That proximity to midtown Manhattan, a trip of about twenty minutes under optimal driving conditions, shaped all of us who lived in New York City's shadow. It defined us, from birth, as the "others." The "bridge and tunnel" crowd, yet without the bragging rights of, say, Brooklyn, or even Queens. We were always close but not ever, ever, "there."

It was the suburbs, but not quite John Cheever territory. Though, for a while, my parents and their friends would get together on summer nights and play croquet—before adjourning to sip martinis and smoke filtered cigarettes. I think that was because they read John Cheever. But all our backyards were too sloped, lumpy, and untended for croquet. As far as I was aware, no one in our world had a tennis court, much less a pool, or had affairs with each other, or committed suicide. That kind of ennui was beyond our means. My father commuted by bus. When I was a small child he was a salesman in the audio department of Willoughby's Camera store in midtown during the days. At night, he was a floor manager at Sam Goody's in the Garden State Plaza.

My friends' parents were commercial artists, college professors, unsuccessful actors, mid-level advertising executives. Everybody seemed to have pretty much the same amount of money. We all vacationed for a week or two a year in the same place: "Down the shore," on Long Beach Island, where about ten or more families would rent or share cottages and bungalows in close proximity. The parents would hang out and the kids would play together. New Jersey summers smelled of beach grass. You had to get up close to smell it, lie down in it, but I did a fair amount of that; either playing with plastic army men or hide and seek as a small boy, or, somewhat later, incompetently prodding the nether regions of equally inept girls. The two-family houses or single-family cottages with outdoor showers and crushed seashell driveways smelled musty when we'd first arrive—happier after a few days: of suntan oil and salt air, sun-bleached wood, the sea, the floors tracked with sand.

When the exterminator truck, spraying for mosquitoes, would come down the block, making a slow U-turn at the beach end, belching white, chromosome-damaging fog from its tank, all the kids would spill out of their houses to chase along in its wake.

There was miniature golf, drive-in movies at Manahawken, an amusement "village" with the obligatory "pirate ship" and "ye olde waffle shop." There were thrill rides and clam bars, fish houses where breaded, deep-fried things were dunked and made golden by the ton. Tumbletown was a field of trampolines in the enticingly named yet somehow forlorn Surf City—a community of five-and-dimes selling inflatable rafts, cheap plastic flip flops, sweatshirts, and the comic books we all needed to survive. There were townie bars, smelling of stale beer, and the shabby, inevitable motels and efficiencies of another time. I was—and remain—curiously fascinated with such places, one time dream destinations with names like the Mermaid, the Neptune, Spindrift, Bide-A-Wee, Ric's Shore Club, the Rip Tide, Sea Spray, and so on; their names in aquamarine neon, the odd letter missing like a lost tooth. (I don't remember, specifically, any of these names. But I'm sure they existed.)

Barnegat Light was crowded, working class, with numbered streets, each ending at the beach, lined tightly on both sides with houses.

The towns of Loveladies and Harvey Cedars, next door, had relatively vast empty spaces between modern, beach-fantasy dune residences with porthole windows, swimming pools, and decks on stilts. We didn't know anyone who lived in such places. They might as well have been moon-men in their enormous, slowly migrating sand-ships—which, when the hurricanes came, would often end up in the bay.

But we knew the squeak of sand against the ear, when half asleep on a beach towel. The comforting rumble of Atlantic waves, breaking against the jetties, the pleasures of stolen cigarettes, steamer clams dripping butter, summer corn, funnel cakes, and finger-fucking.

Was I happy?

I must have been.

In Leonia, some houses were shabbier than others, but there were comfortable constants. By and large, adults seemed smart. Working in, and living so close to Manhattan, we shared the same tastes, lived the same life of the mind as our neighbors. This meant hard-bound copies of *Horizon* and *American Heritage* magazines. Big, brainy libraries with the serious writers of the day heavily represented: Tennessee Williams, Albee, Updike, Bellow. Lush picture books. Naughty stuff like *The Olympia Reader*, Henry Miller, *Lolita* (of course). It meant film night at my house, when my father would come home with two projectors and two films: an action film for the kids upstairs, and *The Treasure of the Sierra Madre* or a Bergman film for the parents downstairs. There was music. There were always books. For the kids, there were *Classic Illustrated Comics*, molded plastic army men, and the *Johnson Smith Catalogue*.

It was the perfect match, really. Bergen County, New Jersey, with its wooded areas, swamps, rubbish dumps—and easily transversed backyards—and the *Johnson Smith Catalogue*—the veritable motherload, the Source, and inspiration—for generations of juvenile delinquents. Antique long before we were born, the same, timeless advertisements for the *Catalogue* beckoned us from the backs of our comics as they had those who came before, summoning us to a tantalizing smorgasbord of destructive behaviors: arson, peeping, sabotage, vandalism, humiliation of our peers, every variety of vicious prank, urging us to acts that today would be called terrorism. Fantastically realistic plastic vomit, itching powder, various foul-smelling substances, magic tricks, these were only some of the "come on." Within the ancient pages of the *Catalogue*, one found smoke powder for bombs, wrist rockets, waterproof fuses. What could one do with those? It didn't take long to figure out. And the lurid pictures of the guy with the X-ray glasses, gaping, tongue out at a female colleague? Apparently, spying on women without their consent was something every red-blooded kid who didn't want sand kicked in his face (like the other ubiquitous ads of the days' comic books) did.

Add illegal fireworks—the gateway drug for aspiring fuck-ups—and one evil brainiac (every neighborhood has one) and you've got a recipe for fun.

Which is to say, Leonia was a paradise. So much to choose from. Up the steep hills at the top of the town was a few-acre wooded area called Highwood Hills, where we could run wild, build forts, pick trash, and set off fireworks. In the opposite direction, below the abandoned rail station, were the vast "swamps," where we could detonate more serious explosives, perpetrate relatively harmless acts of arson, and wallow in the chocolate pudding-like mud that, on reflection, was no doubt loaded with heavy metals . . .

My local brainiac was Steven—a lonely kid who lived down the block. We never saw his parents. Steven knew how to build motorcycles out of lawn mower engines and pilfered frames. He taught me and my friends how to make rockets by painstakingly jamming match heads into drilled-out CO_2 cartridges, packing them in tight, priming them with a waterproof fuse from the *Johnson Smith Catalogue* (natch), and launching them from homemade mortars made from copper pipe. Molotov cocktails, pipe bombs, presented no challenge to Steven. Rubber cement, we learned after much experimentation, made a wonderful substitute for napalm. But gasoline thickened with dishwashing detergent was cheaper, available in volume, and closer to the real thing. Fireworks culture—a sort of prequel/training ground for the drug culture ahead—consumed all of us. In fact, many of the same disaffected young men with unsavory family connections who made the trip to Chinatown or had someone do it for them, went on to supply the recreational substances of our teens. But until that time, it was all about the juvenile delinquent's hierarchy of desire: firecrackers and cherry bombs and yes . . . yes(!!) ash-cans!! . . . and the legendary ("So powerful one a them blew Tommy Precoppio's brother's hand clear off!! It's a quarter stick a dynamite!!") M–80. We discussed the various properties of these pyrotechnical devices with the same breathless tones we would later employ paging through the *Physician's Desk Reference*. ("Oooh . . . Parest 400's!! Black Beauties!! Nice!!") We started with the routine melting of molded plastic army men and the burning and immolating of other toys, but quickly graduated to burning and blowing up vast tracts of Meadowland. I shudder now to remember the "test chamber" I built in my cellar, out of an old milk delivery box lined with insulation material. I'd actually light fireworks, often inside bottles or jars, drop them into the box, and sit on the lid, thrilled by the powerful but muffled THUD, the lid hopping and bowing out beneath me. It's a fucking Jersey miracle I didn't get my young ass and nut-sack full of shrapnel.

There were consequences if you fucked up too bad—as when Steven eventually burned down the grammar school. There were two options for "troubled" or "incorrigible" children: "Juvie" (Juvenile Hall) or the "Pines," Bergen Pines Psychiatric Hospital. No small number of my little friends spent time in one or the other. Steven certainly did. He topped his midnight strike on the grammar school by (it is said) killing his father. I have fond memories of him: awkward, bespectacled (of course), with a bowl haircut, a seemingly empty Tony Perkins Victorian house that smelled of cabbage and sinister Eastern European foods, old clothes—and an instinctive desire to burn down the world that predated by decades the Sex Pistols and the Dead Boys. He was a magnet for blame. If anything burned down or exploded anywhere in the town—even of natural causes—the cops always visited Steven first. Saint-like, he bore all our sins on his shoulders.

There were, however, no consequences for anyone, it appeared, once I changed schools. When I was in fourth grade a relative died, leaving my family just enough money to pack me and my brother off to private school in the larger and much wealthier Englewood. Whereas Leonia had taught me that if you blow up the wrong thing at the wrong time—or break the wrong window—you could end up in Juvie, Englewood quickly taught me that one could—with the right absentee parents—careen thoughtlessly through life without a care. Smash the new car? No problem. Hit and run? Oopsy daisy! Assault? Off to "Non-Traditional" school for you, young man! My new friends all had tennis courts—and, seemingly, no parents. They lived in vast, luxurious empty houses, manned only by expressionless maids and Sherry-sipping nannies. Unused swimming pools, antiques-filled living rooms, cellar rec rooms where anything was permitted. My new friends smelled of nothing but fresh laundry, soap, and money—with the occasional background whiff of marijuana and cigarettes. The few from my town who carpooled from Leonia to school with me, I only now noticed, smelled of bacon and the cooking odors of normal family kitchens. To my eternal, burning shame, I dropped them soon after realizing this. It remains, very likely, even all these years later, the very worst thing I have ever done.

Life in my new school opened up, initially, a larger world. My new friends, as soon as they turned seventeen, got cars, of course. I never owned one myself, I was a passenger for my teenage years. And though cars meant we could expand our horizons exponentially, I think, in some ways, they shrunk.

The car became a living room, moving in predictable patterns up and down New Jersey's routes, highways, parkways, and interstates. We cruised, endlessly, movement a destination unto itself, smoking weed and looking out the windows with fear, contempt, and bemusement. Any sense of superiority we might have felt was tempered by the gnawing certainty that it would soon be us on the other side of the glass. The passing used car lots and furniture stores of Route 17. The diners and malls of Route 4. The tree-lined darkness of the Palisades Interstate. The high speed, multi-laned Route 80, that, somewhere after Paterson, tempted one to just keep going. There were favorite parks (Alison Park in Englewood, North Bridge Park in Fort Lee) in which to hang out. Favorite eateries (Hiram's and the Plaza Diner in Fort Lee, IHOP in Teaneck, Jann's in Paterson, Wolfie's in Paramus). And, of course, the neglected rumpus rooms of a friend's absent or alcoholic parents—semi-psychedelic drug dens, usually decorated with carpet remnants, found objects, souvenirs from older siblings' trips to Morocco, Day-Glo posters. There would be a bong, or a chillum, or a Turkish water pipe—and a drum head to clean seeds. There would be a can of Ozium to kill the smell. A stereo and record collection, invariably including the Allman Brothers' *Eat a Peach* or *At Fillmore East* and *Dark Side of the Moon*— this was obligatory. If hallucinogens were involved, King Crimson might be added to the mix.

We became a transient, loosely associated conglomeration of tribes, coming together only for school and the occasional house party. One tribe to a vehicle, always moving mindlessly, instinctively, like sharks—in search of drugs or food or escape from boredom. A few tribes might converge, briefly, in parking lots, garages, cellars, a disused athletic field, but good would rarely come of it. And our hunting grounds always ended at "the Bridge." Across that, one was on one's own.

A normal New Jersey childhood.

Watching any of a hundred films over the decades since, I realize, maybe the whole world looks like New Jersey when you're young. The predictable arc of alienated teens in suburbia. Looking back, I try to distinguish what was uniquely New Jersey about my childhood? What didn't look like every other Linklater, Spielberg, Kevin Smith film? The joke is over, really.

I realized this on a book tour a while back, waking up in Austin or Minneapolis or St. Louis, at yet another anonymous chain hotel. Not knowing where I was, I threw open the drapes and looked out the window, desperate for orientation. Where was I? How much longer did I have to go? Beneath me, an endless and grimly predictable sequence of Victoria's Secret superstore, McDonald's, the Gap, P. F. Chang's, T. G. I. Friday's, Chili's, Home Depot. Mall after mall separated only by a strip mall or mini mall, stretching out to the horizon, where another glass-covered cityscape clustered perhaps around a shopping district. I could have been anywhere. I could have been in New Jersey.

NEW MEXICO

CAPITAL   Santa Fe

ENTERED UNION   1912 (47th)

ORIGIN OF NAME   From Mexico, "place of Mexitli," an Aztec god or leader

NICKNAME   Land of Enchantment

MOTTO   Crescit eundo ("It grows as it goes")

RESIDENTS   New Mexican

U.S. REPRESENTATIVES   3

STATE BIRD   roadrunner

STATE FLOWER   yucca

STATE TREE   pinyon

STATE SONG   "O Fair New Mexico"

LAND AREA   121,356 sq. mi.

GEOGRAPHIC CENTER   In Torrance Co., 12 mi. SSW of Willard

POPULATION   1,928,384

WHITE   66.8%

BLACK   1.9%

AMERICAN INDIAN   9.5%

ASIAN   1.1%

HISPANIC/LATINO   42.1%

UNDER 18   28.0%

65 AND OVER   11.7%

MEDIAN AGE   34.6

NEW MEXICO
Ellery Washington

Shortly after my tenth birthday I was nearly struck by lightning. It was mid-May, 1975, and I was watching my two older brothers and their teenaged friends attempt vague impersonations of Art Williams and Kareem Abdul-Jabbar on the tar-paved basketball courts behind Saint Bernadette's Church in Albuquerque. The afternoon had been warm and dry, the temperature around seventy-five degrees. Typical central New Mexico weather. By a quarter past five, when my brothers and I had finished our after-school chores and regrouped with the others at the courts, the once-bright blue sky was shaded with darker, rust-tinged hues.

In Albuquerque, violent flash floods and sudden lightning storms were commonplace in the spring. Our parents warned us never to play in the long, flood-prone arroyos, and always to keep an eye out for sudden changes in the sky. That afternoon, however, my attention was so fixed on my brothers' game that I'd ignored the rapidly growing thunderclouds. Even if I'd noticed them, I would never have returned home alone; I was much too infatuated with my brothers to ever leave an event where they actually tolerated my presence. Besides, until that moment, the mortal danger posed by flash floods and lightning strikes was entirely anecdotal—we'd even walked half a mile through an unpaved arroyo on our way to play ball that day.

Then, suddenly, the hair on my head stiffened, I was momentarily blinded by an intense flash of blue-white light, and a thundering crackle filled the entire court. We were stunned. Awed senseless.

When my sight returned, I looked up toward the clouds. They weren't drifting directly overhead, as I'd expected them to be, but instead had settled in two wide columns that reached down to the base of the Sandia Mountains, some five miles away. Off in the distance, ranks of electromagnetic bolts played a beautifully menacing game of flashes and strikes, exchanging frequent charges between the denser masses of humidity. The fact that a single charge had broken with the others to strike the ground less than ten feet from me only reinforced its significance—there was no mistaking it, the strike had been an act of God. My eldest brother was the first to speak. "Man!" he shouted. "That was so *bad*!"

Then, all at once, everyone started talking.

"How did you stay so cool, little man?"

"Maybe little man's not so little after all!"

"Wonder what the others will say when they hear about this!"

My brothers and their friends had mistaken my paralytic shock for stolid strength, a quality they'd never imagined existed beneath my timidity.

I had always been awkward—too skinny, overly polite, bookishly shy. To make matters worse, I was one of only three black kids at Collet Park Elementary, my family the only black family in our upper middle-class, largely white and Hispanic neighborhood. As first-generation black New Mexicans, we played no part in the state's celebrated *tricultural* heritage: Spanish, Indian, and Anglo. And while in urban centers across the country African-Americans were taking to the streets, my mother was at home sewing her own dashikis and teaching us the Black History lessons we weren't being taught in school. I felt completely outside, isolated, until that fortuitous strike.

In the New Mexico of my childhood, plaster statues of the Virgin Mary cried actual tears, mud from pits in dying mining towns healed the afflicted, and the face of Jesus appeared on a white flour tortilla, each miracle inspiring passionate pilgrimages to places like Chimayo, Lake Arthur, and various villages throughout the state. Such stories were frequently featured on the evening news—lending them media-bolstered credibility—simply because of the stir they caused in the local population. Moreover, in many rural communities, centuries of cultural mixing between New Mexico's highly dramatic form of Hispanic Catholicism and Navajo, Hopi, Ute, and Acoma religious rites had created an almost South American sense of mystical realism in everyday life. Even in Albuquerque, even in a scientific family, I was susceptible to the tales of a wrathful Christian god and vengeful Indian ghosts—to hear the neighborhood teenagers tell it, our entire block had been built over a desecrated burial site, putting our families at risk of being tomahawked to pieces by dead Apache warriors every night.

The frequency of lightning storms meant most kids I knew already had a lightning story. But, unlike mine, their stories were usually apocryphal, or at best second-hand: a cousin Steve or Carlos who was nearly struck coming out of the post office with his mother, or an Uncle Diego or Mike who was struck through a keyhole at his machine shop, or a friend of a friend whose vicious mutt had survived three successive bolts before he finally rolled over and died. Now, at sleepovers, before moving on to frightful tales of the *La Jirona* ghost sightings, I was invited to tell my lightning story. Kids I didn't even know ran up to me on the playground to inquire about the life-threatening bolt. I was suddenly *in*. The only thing that could have made me more popular would have been to survive a direct strike.

My parents moved to Albuquerque from Chicago in 1965, the year I was born, after my father was recruited for an engineering post at Sandia Laboratories. Founded in 1949, Sandia opened six years after the Los Alamos Research Center. Sandia's original emphasis was on ordnance engineering—turning the nuclear physics packages created by Los Alamos and Lawrence Livermore National Laboratories into deployable weapons. Following the first atomic bomb test, at the Trinity Site in 1945, and the subsequent end of the Second World War, New Mexico emerged as a leader in nuclear, solar, and geothermal energy research and development. Meanwhile, Albuquerque—located on a wide swath of land between the Sandia and Jemez mountains, divided into east and west by a frequently dry strip of the Rio Grande River—grew from an estimated thirty-five thousand inhabitants, in 1940, to nearly a quarter of a million by 1974, and Sandia Laboratories became one of state's largest employers. We were in the middle of the Cold War; my father, like many of my friends' fathers, was employed as a high-level-security "engineer" at the Labs, the specific tasks he performed classified top secret.

As I passed from childhood into adolescence and learned more about New Mexico's recent history, the superstitions that had plagued and animated my childhood were replaced by a sense of foreboding related to my father's work and the secrecy that surrounded it. My teenage years were filled with rumors of hidden missile silos in the mountains behind our house, rumors that my father played some role in stocking them. Rumors that these missiles put us, in insignificant Albuquerque, on the front line of a nuclear strike. I no longer looked out for lightning; instead I looked up and wondered when a barrage of nuclear warheads would come raining down on us.

Fortunately, I had friends like Gregg, whose father also worked at Sandia. We did our best to diffuse our doomsday apprehensions by making light of the situation. We became avid Cold War spy movie fans, imagined our pocket-protector-wearing parents playing glamorous roles in intricate plots to prevent the Soviets from destroying the free world. We took pleasure in believing that our phones were tapped: We were important enough to have our privacy invaded by the federal government! At school, we shared humorous stories about the convoluted explanations our fathers offered to describe—all the while trying to cover up—exactly what they did at work. A typical dinnertime conversation between Gregg and his father, reported the following day at lunch, went something like this:

> **GREGG'S FATHER:** "Well, hmm . . . I guess you could say I design very specific electronic mechanisms that measure the existence of—well, the levels of, actually—certain radioactive particles in the atmosphere . . . well, not dwelling in the atmosphere, but particles that can get into the atmosphere, by which I mean to say the air, or possibly the water—yes, they can get into the water, too—under, um . . . well, under *certain* conditions, as they don't naturally exist, these radioactive particles I mean, either in the air or in the water . . . but *certain* conditions that might suddenly be present under extraordinary circumstances . . . or rather a sudden and unpredictable circumstance created by human interference . . ."

> **GREGG:** "You mean, like, if the Russians dropped a nuclear bomb on us?"

> **GREGG'S FATHER:** (*a long pause*) "Have you finished your homework yet?"

Still, as much as Gregg and I delighted in our fathers' squirming to avoid revealing secrets they were legally forbidden to tell—*under threat of committing treason*—there were moments when we couldn't escape the weight of our scientific legacy. The day my tenth-grade history teacher gave a lecture on the terrors of Hiroshima, for instance, I wondered if she even realized the guilt and anguish she provoked in many of us, children of parents who worked on mysterious government projects that, we were convinced, might one day perpetuate similar devastation.

In the spring of 2003, my father and I had breakfast at the original Perea's on Juan Tabo (my father's choice), where we often ate when I was in town. I was living in France with my boyfriend Francis but had flown back to New York for several weeks, having arranged my work on a film project there to overlap with a large-scale protest against the war in Iraq. I'd added a New Mexico leg to the journey to visit my parents, now divorced.

Perea's prided itself on its green chili sauce—which in New Mexico is simply called "green chili"—and boasted some of the hottest in the city. As an extra bonus, the morning waitress had a good memory and knew what we wanted even before we ordered: two *huevos rancheros*, my father's with extra green chili and mine with the milder red chili on the side. When she arrived with our plates, I poured a few cursory drops of the red on my eggs and then scraped half of the black beans away from my tortilla. My father grinned at this but said nothing. At sixty-two, he is still a vibrant man, his general air a good-natured, if paradoxical, mix of intensity and lightness. He scooped up a forkful of tortilla, beans, and eggs, dripping with green chili, and aimed it toward his mouth.

"So how long are you in town for?" he asked.

"Only a few days," I said, reaching for a glass of water. "Francis is meeting me here tomorrow. We'll stay at Mom's place for the night, then we're off to visit the Caverns."

My father looked up from his plate. A lightly veiled cringe ticked across his face, then he quickly changed the subject. Knowing the extent to which he disapproved of my being gay, it was difficult for me to talk about Francis. And I completely avoided mentioning my strong feelings about the war. Since 9/11, my father had become increasingly conservative, an avid supporter of the preemptive military strikes that I opposed.

So we talked about food—namely, the fact that many small restaurants like Perea's had recently closed, making it harder to find really hot chili. We talked about my father's latest fishing trip in the Jemez Mountains; he always preferred New Mexico's heavily pined mountain ranges to its arid plains. And I watched as he became light again, describing the trout he'd caught at Fenton Lake. All the while, I could barely touch my plate—the *huevos* were much too spicy, even watered down—and I realized I'd been away from New Mexico for too long. I'd forgotten how to feign indifference when confronted by such a vast array of muzzled topics.

The trip to Carlsbad wasn't my idea—I was flat out against it—but Francis insisted. Only weeks into the Iraq War, the country was in the midst of a conservative swing that included a spike in hate crimes, a broad mistrust of strangers, and a pointed hostility towards Francis's compatriots, the French. Under these circumstances, I had what felt like a natural—and growing— fear of traveling as a gay black man, in a biracial, bi-national relationship, *with a snail-eating, beaujolais-swigging frog, no less*, through any culturally homogeneous rural setting, even in my home state. Central and northern New Mexico, which include Albuquerque, Santa Fe, Taos, and Los Alamos, have long been safe havens for scientists, artists, hippies, and aimless drifters of various types (Francis and I had visited these regions on his two previous trips). I was unsure, however, of how benevolent southern New Mexicans were when it came to outsiders. Twenty-odd years had passed since I'd last seen the Carlsbad Caverns and I wanted to go back, but it clearly wasn't the time.

Yet when I expressed my apprehensions to Francis, he merely recited another of the interesting facts he'd learned on the Internet while still in France.

"I read," he replied, "that Carlsbad has 109 caves, including the deepest in the Western Hemisphere. Over 490 meters."

Our starting point was my mother's flat, adobe-style house in Kachina Hills—an upscale, Indian-themed subdivision sprawled at the foot of the Sandia Mountains. Francis and I would take I–40 east to Highway 283, leading down towards Roswell and Carlsbad, then head on to the Carlsbad Caverns National Park. Two hundred seventy-five miles. Approximately four and a half hours. On the eve of our departure, my mother, Francis, and I were up late, chatting about the proposed route south, when Francis suddenly realized that he'd forgotten to buy a digital camera before leaving Paris. "Don't worry," my mother said, "the Wal-Mart on Eubank and Central is open twenty-four hours."

"You're kidding?" I said, unable to believe Albuquerque actually needed twenty-four-hour Wal-Mart service.

"You never know," my mother said dryly, "when the government might declare *code red*. In which case we can still get duct tape in the middle of the night."

The next morning we were on the road at six-thirty. Though I was glad to be reunited with Francis, I was tired and still apprehensive about the trip. Our midnight excursion to Wal-Mart had lasted well over an hour because Francis had become obsessed with finding the perfect digital device to take pictures inside the Caverns, in case there was only limited artificial light. Now, on the open road, I was driving and he was clicking away under the bright New Mexico sky. Many of those first photos show abandoned gas stations, crumbling adobe houses, empty roadside diners, and the distant convergence of two pastel planes: mesa and sky. Others show a twenty-two-year-old Hispanic waitress with an exhausted smile, a tribe of four elderly drunks sitting on the porch of an abandoned motel lounge. Three children jumping in a puddle of stagnant water and me looking slightly sullen, staring out toward the distant horizon.

Driving south of Albuquerque, through small desert towns with names like Encino, Ramon, and Vaughn, I was reminded that my childhood had been contained inside an economically secure bubble, afforded me by my father's membership in the scientific elite. New Mexico consistently ranks as one of the poorest states in the nation. And as we neared Roswell, I felt surprisingly relieved.

Roswell is a clean, quiet town of approximately forty-five thousand inhabitants. Although a center for irrigation farming, ranching, dairy, and petroleum production, it is best known for the so-called Roswell Incident, named after a supposed UFO crash nearby in 1947, and the subsequent rumors of alien visitation. The original sighting was most likely linked to government high-altitude experiments that were being conducted in the region at the time. On Main Street, Francis and I were greeted by a billboard of two big-headed waif-bodied aliens. We drove past several alien parking lots, the UFO museum, the Alien Zone Cosmic Ice Cream Parlor, the Alien Resistance Headquarters. The memory stick in Francis's new camera was already full and he needed a replacement, so we once more pulled into a Wal-Mart, where the sign welcomed both "Humans and Alien Beings."

The store was cluttered with alien paraphernalia: alien balloons, watches, sunglasses, toilet plungers, towels, umbrellas—the works. Francis paid for his new memory stick and quickly inserted it inside the camera.

"Wasn't that a military academy we passed along the road?" he asked.

"The New Mexico Military Institute."

"I don't understand," he said. As a reflex to the current resentment aimed at the French, Francis had become increasingly condescending when discussing American idiosyncrasies. "Institutes," he continued. "Intelligent people everywhere. Your father, for instance—*scientists* . . . How can so many people in this country believe in *that*!" He pointed his camera at a six-foot, cardboard cutout of one of the ubiquitous, big-headed aliens, this one aiming a blue deionization gun directly at us.

Had Francis asked me that same question a month later, I might have explained my theory that the entire Roswell myth is quintessentially New Mexican, a convergence of superstitious temperament and scientific secrecy. At the time, however, I was too embarrassed to respond. Instead, I shrugged, suggested we backtrack to try a scoop of green Cosmic Ice Cream—it was approaching noon, getting hot—and hurried back out to the car.

We arrived at the Carlsbad Caverns at one-thirty. We were too late to take one of the ranger-guided tours that lead down the longer, more difficult paths: into Spider Cave, perhaps, which would have involved some crawling, or Slaughter Canyon Cave, or The Hall of the White Giants. But we were still in time to take a self-guided tour, leading directly down into the Big Room, the word's largest underground chamber. Entering the cave's enormous limestone mouth, I felt a surge of excitement, just as I had as a child. Unfortunately, I also felt a childish need to prove myself to Francis. As much geographical distance as I'd put between me and my home state— from attending college in California to living in France—I was experiencing a defensive kind of local patriotism in response to the poverty and weirdness Francis and I had witnessed thus far.

"A stalagmite," I explained enthusiastically, "from the Greek *stalagma*, meaning 'drip' or 'drop', is a mineral deposit—like that one there—that rises from the floor of a cave. They're created by dripping mineral solutions and calcium deposits. The formation on the ceiling there, just above it, is called a stalactite. Columns are formed when stalagmites and stalactites meet." I'd learned these classifications from a cave guide when I was six years old, during my first visit to the Caverns.

"Yes," Francis said, responding to my short lesson in Greek. "I read about cave formations on the Internet."

I felt slightly deflated. But the Big Room was more impressive than I'd remembered, with its undulating columns and curving walls. The limestone formations all around us, like grounded clouds, provoked visions of castles, giants, women, and beasts, all glistening with the faint mist that clung to the air throughout the cave. Above our heads, thousands of icicle-like stalactites hung, their watery white sheaths dripping cool water into the dark pools below. The Big Room's natural grandeur dwarfed that of any manmade interior I'd ever seen—including, as I made a point of telling Francis, Notre-Dame and the Hall of Mirrors at Versailles.

Francis and I surfaced from the Big Room by elevator. We'd taken seats in the concrete amphitheater facing the Caverns' natural entrance and were waiting for sunset, the hour at which a fluttering black mass of Mexican free-tail bats was due to exit the caves, when the woman sitting in front of Francis began talking about the war.

"Our son is in the Air Force," the woman said, speaking to the entire group of early retirement aged couples that surrounded us. The languid manner in which she employed the word *air*—two breathless syllables— betrayed a distinct Southern bent. "And he says we have enough *miss-iles* over there to end this thing in a few short weeks."

The woman's words jogged a dormant image I had of the White Sands National Monument, which was only an hour away: a glimpse of the smooth white dunes rising in the distance, and a military patrolman telling my father to turn the car in the opposite direction because the government was currently conducting missile tests. I'd never been back.

I tapped Francis on the shoulder. "We should go to White Sands," I said.

He snapped a picture of a black bird flying overhead. *"Pourquoi pas?"*

The man sitting next to the woman touched her arm. "Don't worry," he said. "He'll be back soon."

"I'm not," the woman replied, with forced conviction. "Not worried at all."

The bats' frenzied exodus impressed Francis more than me. There were fewer bats than I'd expected, maybe due to seasonal breeding habits. The sunset, however, was sufficiently dramatic: a darkening envelope of crimson and burnt orange that slowly folded into the deep blues of night, sealing off the once endless horizon.

The next day, on US 70 West, ten miles from the entrance to the White Sands National Monument, I was stopped by the New Mexico Highway Patrol. History, it seemed, was repeating itself. Unlike my father decades before, however, I was speeding. Francis had warned me several times about the degrees by which the speedometer had continued to climb, but we were in *my* country, in *my* state, and I was feeling a cocky sense of entitlement, having been culturally redeemed from the folly of Roswell by the majesty of the Carlsbad Caverns. Unfortunately, Francis had no compunction about saying I told you so. Not only did he say it, repeatedly—*"Je t'ai dit, hein. Je t'ai dit"*—but he punctuated each repetition with curt puffs of air pushed forward through pursed lips, an infuriatingly French expression of annoyance. Though we hadn't experienced a single unpleasant incident since we'd started our trip, I was nervous and cautioned Francis against speaking French in front of the approaching officer.

"Driver's license and insurance, please." The patrolman made the request without the slightest hint of hostility, which prompted me to ask, before driving all the way to the Monument entrance, if the grounds were actually open that day. "It's clear," the patrolman said. "There haven't been missile tests in over a week."

As the officer sped off in his patrol car, Francis decided it was, once again, safe to speak. "How often does the government test missiles here?" he asked.

"I don't know."

"As long as they're not testing now."

"If they were, they wouldn't let us enter the grounds."

Francis hadn't envisioned the need to factor government missile tests into our travel itinerary. He was quiet for a moment, then, suddenly invigorated by an imagined proximity to danger, he quickly unfolded the map. "While we're at it," he said, "let's visit Trinity."

Set deep in the Tularosa Basin, the White Sands National Monument is the largest gypsum dune field on the planet, covering 275 miles. During the Ice Age, Lake Otero covered much of the Tularosa Basin. When Otero dried out, it left a large flat area of selenite crystals, which is now the Alkali Flat. Unlike dunes made of quartz-based sand crystals, the gypsum doesn't readily convert the sun's heat, and can be walked on barefoot even in the warmest summer months. Weathering and erosion continually break the crystals into sand-sized grains, which are carried by the prevailing winds from the southwest, forming white dunes, and the dunes are constantly changing shape.

According to old Indian lore, however, the restlessness of the dunes is explained by the legend of Pavla Blanca, Mañuela—the ghost of the Great White Sands—whose beloved, the conquistador Hernando de Luna, was killed in 1540 by Apaches at the edge of the great white desert. Hernando's body was never found. Forever after, it is said, Mañuela's spirit arrives nightly in her white wedding gown, whipping the sand into wraith-like eddies as she desperately searches for her lost lover.

Five miles into the Monument, I parked the car on a narrow strip of road that cut directly through a wide white dune. According to the ranger at the entrance, the roads had been cleared of sand that morning, following a particularly acute windstorm the night before. Francis and I walked a mile or so along one of the marked trails leading away from the road before abandoning the trail altogether and wandering freely across the dunes. It was early afternoon, hot, not a cloud in the sky, and we were completely alone. In Francis's pictures, the dunes surrounding us might easily be taken for tall drifts of pure white snow—a barren winterscape somewhere in the frozen north—save for the fact that in several of these photos I'm standing in front of the dunes, barefoot, wearing dark sunglasses, jeans, and a T-shirt.

As we wandered over the dunes, I recounted what I remembered about the Legend of Pavla Blanca. "Obviously Pavla Blanca—the way the dunes dramatically change their form—is caused by the evening winds, but the old Indians still insist it's Mañuela." I was afraid I'd made the tale sound like a cheesy Céline Dion song, but Francis seemed genuinely moved. *"Très joli,"* he said, *"vraiment."*

A white lizard scurried across our path, and Francis followed it with his camera toward a cluster of spiky yucca plants. Meanwhile, I hiked over a nearby dune and settled at its base, burying my feet in the tepid sand. From where I sat there was nothing left to hear or smell, nothing to see except the smooth white crests and the dark blue line where white sand met bright blue sky. I took my sunglasses off, closed my eyes, and leaned back against the dune. I'd nearly fallen asleep when I heard Francis's voice overhead.

"Should we continue on now?" he said. "To Trinity."

I didn't know how long I'd been lying in the sand, but my face was tender, starting to burn. Opening my eyes and staring upward, I was temporarily blinded by the bright desert sun hovering directly behind Francis's face. I put my sunglasses back on.

Less than thirty minutes away, evidence of the first atomic bomb test awaited us. Arguably, Trinity was the reason my parents had come to New Mexico, the reason I was born here, the reason so many of my adolescent anxieties had taken the shape that they had. With my back pressed against the sand, it occurred to me that the present political climate of suspicion and secrecy had tapped into my Cold War fears, exaggerating my current apprehensions, both real and imaginary. Maybe actually seeing the Trinity Site would neutralize my resurrected fears.

But as I stared across the open desert, all I wanted was to remain right there, peacefully intoxicated by the arid skies and pure white sand. I wanted to forget that I was an atomic generation New Mexican. I wanted to stop wondering whether or not there were missiles hidden in the mountains behind my mother's house and somehow go back to being the ten-year-old boy whose social destiny was saved by a bolt of lightning, an intervention beyond his control. I wanted simply to *believe*—to believe that if I was patient enough to wait in the desert until sunset, I might catch a glimpse of the white-robed Mañuela, sweeping across the dunes.

Francis and I were both silent for a moment. Then I smiled. Who was I trying to fool? I was my father's son. I stood and reached for my shoes.

"On y va?" Francis said, encouragingly.

"Sure," I said, brushing the sand from my pants. "Why not?"

NEW YORK

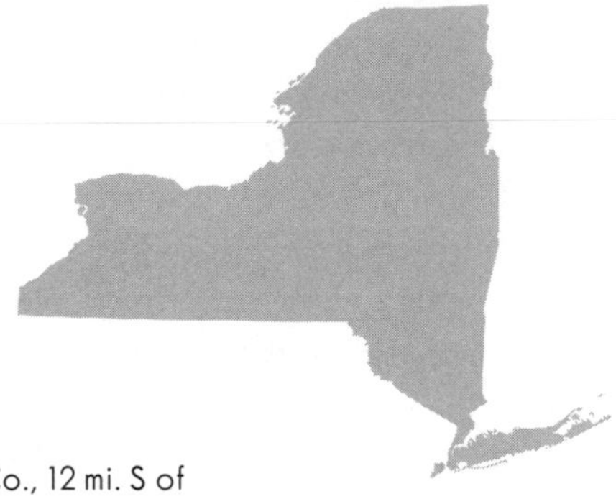

CAPITAL   Albany

ENTERED UNION   1788 (11th)

ORIGIN OF NAME   In honor of the Duke of York

NICKNAME   Empire State

MOTTO   Excelsior ("Ever upward")

RESIDENTS   New Yorker

U.S. REPRESENTATIVES   29

STATE BIRD   bluebird

STATE FLOWER   rose

STATE TREE   sugar maple

STATE SONG   "I Love New York"

LAND AREA   47,214 sq. mi.

GEOGRAPHIC CENTER   In Madison Co., 12 mi. S of
Oneida and 26 mi. SW of Utica

POPULATION   19,254,630

WHITE   67.9%

BLACK   15.9%

AMERICAN INDIAN   0.4%

ASIAN   5.5%

HISPANIC/LATINO   15.1%

UNDER 18   24.7%

65 AND OVER   12.9%

MEDIAN AGE   35.9

NEW YORK
Jonathan Franzen

This interview took place in December, 2007, on the Upper East Side of Manhattan, near the homes of Mayor Mike Bloomberg and then-Governor Eliot Spitzer.

NEW YORK STATE'S PUBLICIST: I am so, so sorry! Everything is late this morning, our former *President* dropped in unexpectedly, as he often does, and our dear little state can never seem to say no to Bill! But I *promise* you you'll get your full half hour with her, even if it means rebooking the entire afternoon. You're lovely to be so patient with us.

JF: We said an hour, though.

NEW YORK STATE'S PUBLICIST: Yes. Yes.

JF: Nine o'clock to ten o'clock is what I wrote down here.

NEW YORK STATE'S PUBLICIST: Yes. And this is for a, uh, travel guide?

JF: Anthology. The fifty states. Which, given that it's inspired by the old WPA Guides, and given that the WPA was the brainchild of the greatest president New York ever produced, I really don't think she wants to end up being the shortest chapter of.

NEW YORK STATE'S PUBLICIST: Right, although, ha ha, she's also the busiest of the fifty, so there may be a certain logic to keeping things brief. If what you're telling me now is that she's just going to be part of some fifty-state cattle call . . . I didn't quite realize . . .

JF: I'm pretty sure I said—

NEW YORK STATE'S PUBLICIST: And it definitely has to be fifty. There's no way it could be, like, five? A Top Five States of the Union kind of thing? Or even a Top Ten? I'm just thinking, you know, to clear out some of the small fry. Or maybe, if you absolutely have to have all fifty, then maybe do it as an appendix? Like: Here are the Top Ten Most Important States, and then here, at the back, in the appendix, are some other states that, you know, exist. Is that conceivably an option?

JF: Sadly, no. But maybe we should reschedule for some other day. When she's not so busy.

NEW YORK STATE'S PUBLICIST: Frankly, Jon, every day is like this. It just gets worse and worse. And since I am *promising* you your full half hour with her today, I think you'd be well advised to take it. However, I do see your point about length—assuming you really are determined to include the small fry. And what I would therefore love to do is show you some amazing new pictures that she's been having taken of herself. It's a program she set up with one of her foundations. Twenty of the world's top art photographers are creating some of the most intimate glimpses that anybody has ever had of an American state. Really different, really special. I don't want to tell you how to do your job. But if I were you? I'd be thinking about twenty-four pages of unique, world-class photography, followed by an intensely personal little interview in which our nation's greatest state reveals her greatest secret passion. Which is . . . the arts! I mean, *that* is New York State. Because, yes, obviously, she's beautiful, she's rich, she's powerful, she's glamorous, she knows *everybody*, she's had the most amazing life journey. But in her secret innermost soul? It's all about the arts.

JF: Wow. Thank you. That would be—thank you! The only problem is I'm not sure the format and the paper of this book are going to be right for photographs.

NEW YORK STATE'S PUBLICIST: Jon, like I said, I'm not trying to tell you how to do your job. But unless you can think of a way to fit the proverbial thousand words on a single page, there's a lot to be said for pictures.

JF: You're absolutely right. And I will check with Ecco Press and—

NEW YORK STATE'S PUBLICIST: Who, what? Echo what?

JF: Ecco Press. They're publishing the book?

NEW YORK STATE'S PUBLICIST: Oh dear. Your book is being published by a small press?

JF: No, no, they're an imprint of HarperCollins. Which is a big press.

NEW YORK STATE'S PUBLICIST: Oh, so HarperCollins, then.

JF: Yes. Big, big press.

NEW YORK STATE'S PUBLICIST: Because, God, you had me worried for a minute.

JF: No, no, huge press. One of the biggest in the world.

NEW YORK STATE'S PUBLICIST: Then let me just go check and see how things are going. In fact, you might as well have your sitdown with Mr. Van Gander now, if you want to follow me back this way. Just, yes, good, bring your bag. This way . . . Rick? Do you have a minute to talk to our, uh. Our "literary writer"?

NEW YORK STATE'S PERSONAL ATTORNEY: Sure! Super! Come in, come in, come in! Hello! Rick Van Gander! Hello! Great to meet you! Big fan of your work! How's life in Brooklyn treating you? You live out in Brooklyn, don't you?

JF: No, Manhattan. I did live in Queens once, a long time ago.

NEW YORK STATE'S PERSONAL ATTORNEY: Huh! How about that? I thought all you literary types were out in Brooklyn these days. All the really hip ones at any rate. Are you trying to tell me you're not hip? Actually, now that you mention it, you don't look very hip. I beg your pardon! I read something in the Times about all the great writers living out in Brooklyn. I just naturally assumed . . .

JF: It's a very beautiful old borough.

NEW YORK STATE'S PERSONAL ATTORNEY: Yes, and wonderful for the arts. My wife and I try to get out to the Brooklyn Academy of Music as often as we can. We saw a play performed entirely in Swedish there not long ago. Bit of a surprise for me, I admit, not being a Swedish speaker. But we enjoyed ourselves very much. Not your typical Manhattan evening, that's for sure! But, now, tell me, what can I do for you today?

JF: I don't actually know. I didn't realize I was going to talk to you. I thought I was supposed to have an interview with the State—

NEW YORK STATE'S PERSONAL ATTORNEY: That's it! There you go! That's why you're talking to me! What I can do for you today is vet your interview questions.

JF: Vet them? Are you kidding?

NEW YORK STATE'S PERSONAL ATTORNEY: Do I look like I'm kidding?

JF: No, it's just, I'm a little stunned. It used to be so easy to see her. And just, you know, hang out, and talk.

NEW YORK STATE'S PERSONAL ATTORNEY: Sure, sure, I hear you.

Everything used to be easy. Used to be easy to buy crack on the corner of 98th and Columbus, too! Used to be easy to pave the bottom of the Hudson River with PCBs and heavy metals. Easy to clear-cut the Adirondacks and watch the rivers choke on topsoil. Rip the heart out of the Bronx and ram an expressway through there. Run sweatshops on lower Broadway with slave Asian labor. Get a rent-controlled apartment so cheap you didn't have to do anything all day except write abusive letters to your landlord. Everything used to be so easy! But eventually a state grows up, starts taking better care of herself, if you know what I mean. Which is what I am here to help her do.

JF: I guess I don't see how having been open and available and exciting and romantic to a kid from the Midwest is equivalent to having let the Hudson River be polluted.

NEW YORK STATE'S PERSONAL ATTORNEY: You're saying you fell in love with her.

JF: Yes! And I had the feeling she loved me, too. Like she was waiting for people like me to come to her. Like she needed us.

NEW YORK STATE'S PERSONAL ATTORNEY: Hmm. When was this?

JF: Late seventies, early eighties.

NEW YORK STATE'S PERSONAL ATTORNEY: Good Lord. Just as I feared. Those were some wild and crazy years, all right! She was not altogether of sound mind. And you would do her a great kindness—do yourself a big favor, too, incidentally—if you would avoid mentioning that entire period to her.

JF: But those are precisely the years I wanted to talk to her about.

NEW YORK STATE'S PERSONAL ATTORNEY: And that is why I'm here to vet your questions! Believe me, you will not find her friendly on the subject. Even now, every once in a while, somebody gets it in his head to print some more pictures of her from those decades. Usually it's malicious—you're always going to find a couple of disgusting paparazzi outside the rehab clinic, waiting for their shot of somebody infinitely classier than they are, at a single regrettable moment in her otherwise brilliant life. But that's not the worst of it. What's unbelievable are the guys who honestly believe she looked *better* back then, because she was so easy. Think they're doing her some kind of favor by showing her dirty as hell, spilling out every which way, spaced out of her mind, mega hygiene issues, not a dime in her purse. Crime, garbage, crap architecture, shuttered mill towns, bankrupt railroads, Love Canal, Son of Sam, riots at Attica, hippies in a muddy farm field: I can't tell you how many deadbeats and failed artists walk in here all smitten and nostalgic and thinking they know the "real" New York State. And then complaining about how she's not the same anymore. Which—damn right she's not! And a good thing it is! Just imagine, if you will, how *mortified* she feels about her behavior in those unfortunate years, now she's got her life back together.

JF: So, what, I guess this puts me in the company of the deadbeats and failed artists?

NEW YORK STATE'S PERSONAL ATTORNEY: Hey, you were young. Let's leave it at that. Tell me what else you got for questions. Did Janelle mention this great new photography project we've started up?

JF: She did, yes.

NEW YORK STATE'S PERSONAL ATTORNEY: You'll want to leave plenty of time for that. And what else?

JF: Well, honestly, I was hoping she and I could have a more personal conversation. Do some reminiscing. She's meant a lot to me over the years. Symbolized a lot. Catalyzed a lot.

NEW YORK STATE'S PERSONAL ATTORNEY: Sure! Of course! For all of us! And "personal" is great—don't get me wrong about that. Up-close and "personal" is great. She's not just about power and wealth, she's about home and family and romance, too. Definitely go there, with my blessing. Just be sure to avoid certain decades. Let's say roughly from '65 to '85. What sort of stuff do you have from before then?

JF: From before then, hardly anything. A couple of charm-bracelet images, basically. You know—the big New Year's Eve ball at Times Square that came down on TV in the Midwest at eleven o'clock. And Niagara Falls, which I was surprised to learn was turned off every night for hydroelectric purposes. And the Statue of Liberty, which we were taught was made out of pennies donated by French school kids. And the Empire State Building. Fifteen miles on the Erie Canal. That's about it.

NEW YORK STATE'S PERSONAL ATTORNEY: "About it"? "About it"? You've just named *five* top-notch, bona-fide American mega-icons. Five of 'em! Not so shabby, I'd say! Is there another state that comes even close?

JF: California?

NEW YORK STATE'S PERSONAL ATTORNEY: Another state besides California?

JF: But it was just kitsch. It didn't mean anything to me. For me, the real introduction to New York was *Harriet the Spy* . . . a kid's book. The first time I ever fell in love with a character in literature, it was a girl from Manhattan. And I didn't just love her—I wanted to *be* her. Trade in my whole pleasant suburban life and move to the Upper East Side and *be* Harriet M. Welch, with her notebook and her flashlight and her hands-off parents. And then, even more intense, a couple of years later, her friend Beth Ellen in the sequel novel. Also from the Upper East Side. Spent her summers in Montauk. Rich, thin, blond. And so deliciously unhappy. I thought I could make Beth Ellen happy. I thought I was the one person in the world who understood her and could make her happy, if I could ever get out of St. Louis.

NEW YORK STATE'S PERSONAL ATTORNEY: Hmm. This is all sounding a tiny bit, ah . . . aberrant. By which I mean the underage aspect. New York, of course, is very proud of her long tradition of diversity and tolerance— come to think of it, give me two seconds here, I've got an idea. (*Dialing*) Jeremy? Yeah, it's Rick. Listen, do you have a minute for a visitor? Yeah, it's our "literary writer," yeah, yeah, doing some kind of travel guide. We're trying to set him up with some angles, and—oh. Oh, great, I didn't realize. Tolerance and diversity? Fantastic! I'll bring him right over. (*Hanging up*) The State Historian's got some stuff for you. Made up a whole packet for you. Things have gotten so crazy, the right hand doesn't know what the left is doing.

JF: That's very kind. But I'm not sure I need a packet.

NEW YORK STATE'S PERSONAL ATTORNEY: Trust me, you'll want this one. Jeremy, heh heh, gives excellent packet. And not to burst your bubble, but you might find it comes in handy when you go to write your book. Just in case the interview isn't everything you'd hoped for. Are we clear on the ground rules, by the way? Can you repeat them back to me?

JF: Steer clear of interesting decades?

NEW YORK STATE'S PERSONAL ATTORNEY: Yes. Good. And also your thing for the little girlies.

JF: But I was just a kid myself!

NEW YORK STATE'S PERSONAL ATTORNEY: I am simply warning you she's not going to be receptive to it. Your passion for her and her exciting new projects? Yes! Absolutely! Your passion for some fictional prepubescent Upper East Side chicklet in the brutish 1960s? Not so much. Please follow me back this way.

JF: Do we have some sort of estimate of when I'm finally going to be able to see her?

NEW YORK STATE'S PERSONAL ATTORNEY: Jeremy? I'd like you to meet our "literary writer." A Manhattanite, interestingly.

THE NEW YORK STATE HISTORIAN: Tolerance. . . . Diversity. . . . And centrality. Are the three watchwords of New York State's preeminence.

NEW YORK STATE'S PERSONAL ATTORNEY: I'll leave the two of you to chat a bit.

THE NEW YORK STATE HISTORIAN: Tolerance. . . . Diversity. . . . Centrality.

JF: Hi, nice to meet you.

THE NEW YORK STATE HISTORIAN: To the north: Puritan New England. To the south: the great chattel-slavery plantation colonies. In between: a splendid deepwater port and system of highly navigable interior waterways, endowed with a wealth of natural resources and settled by the mercantilist and famously tolerant Dutch. They were among the first nations to make explicit the connection between good business and personal freedom—between enrichment and enlightenment; and New Netherland was their brainchild. The Dutch West India Company expressly forbade religious persecution—a stricture against which the autocratic Governor Peter Stuyvesant frequently chafed and inveighed. The first Jews reached New York in 1654, joining Quaker immigrants from England and Puritan renegades from Massachusetts, including Anne Hutchinson and her family. Stuyvesant was reprimanded by his Company for harassing the Jews and Quakers. In his defense, he complained that New Netherland was, quote, "peopled by the scrapings of all sorts of nationalities." Fortunately for all of us, New Netherland's prodigious granddaughter, our dearest Empire State, remains so peopled to this very day. She is the gracious and only conceivable hostess of the United Nations, the ardent champion of equal rights for gays, lesbians, and the transgendered, the ladle of the Melting Pot, the cradle of American feminism. Nearly a hundred and fifty languages are spoken at home by the parents of students in a single school district in Elmhurst, Queens. And yet they all speak the same single universal language of—

JF: Money?

THE NEW YORK STATE HISTORIAN: Of tolerance. But, yes, of money, too, of course. The two go hand in hand. New York's epic wealth is a testament to that proposition.

JF: Right. And this is even somewhat interesting to me, but unfortunately also totally beyond the scope of—

THE NEW YORK STATE HISTORIAN: The Revolutionary War: one long slog of attrition and attenuation. Slippery General Washington forever dodging definitive engagement. In the course of this lengthy never-quite-war, this awkward game of hide-and-seek, of cut-and-run, of bob-and-weave, of peek-and-boo, two battles in particular stand out as crucial turning points. Both of them early in the war. Both of them relatively minor in terms of casualties. And both of them fought where?

JF: This is, wow, this is really—

THE NEW YORK STATE HISTORIAN: Why, in New York, naturally. In centrally located New York. Our first battle of interest: Harlem Heights. Situation dire. Washington and his shaky amateur army perilously bottled up in Manhattan. General William Howe newly arrived in New York Harbor with a veritable armada—upwards of thirty thousand fresh, well-trained troops, including the storied Hessians. Our Continental Army demoralized by heavy losses and available for easy crushing. Critical engagement: Harlem Heights, near present-day Columbia University. Washington's troops fight the British to a draw, allowing the General to escape to New Jersey with his army more or less intact. Terrible lost opportunity for the British, tremendous morale-boosting break for Washington, who lives to fight—or avoid fighting!—another day.

JF: Excuse me—

THE NEW YORK STATE HISTORIAN: Second battle: Bemis Heights, Saratoga. The year: 1777. The British plan for winning the war: simple. Unite Howe's overwhelming southern expeditionary force with eight thousand British troops from Canada, under the leadership of General John Burgoyne—the so-called "Gentleman Johnny." Establish supply lines, control the Hudson and Lake Champlain, sever New England from the southern colonies. Divide and conquer. But it's the boggy northland, the buggy morass. American troops, many of them part-time, dig into Bemis Heights at Saratoga, where, inspired by the heroics of Benedict Arnold, they launch a series of crippling assaults on Gentleman Johnny, who within a week surrenders his entire army. A stirring victory with enormous strategic implications! News of it encourages France to side decisively with the Americans and declare war on England, and through the next six years of war the finest army on the planet proves ever more tentative and ineffectual against the Americans.

JF: Help?

THE NEW YORK STATE GEOLOGIST: Jeremy?

THE NEW YORK STATE HISTORIAN: The lesson? Control New York, control the country. New York is the linchpin. The red-hot center. The crux, if you will.

THE NEW YORK STATE GEOLOGIST: Jeremy, excuse me, I'm just going to take our guest down the hall here for a minute. He's looking a little shell shocked.

THE NEW YORK STATE HISTORIAN: First capital of the newly formed United States of America, as stipulated by its splendid new Constitution? Site of George Washington's inauguration as our republic's first President? Did someone say . . . New York City? And though our infant state may not have hosted the capital for long, she certainly did have another trick or two up her sleeve! Hemming the young republic in against the Atlantic seaboard: a formidable chain of mountains stretching all the way from Georgia up to Maine. Only three viable ways to get past them and tap the vast economic potential of the mid-continent: far south around Florida through the Gulf of Mexico; far north around Nova Scotia through the inhospitably Canadian waters of the St. Lawrence; or, *centrally, centrally,* through a gap in the mountains cut by the Hudson and Mohawk rivers. All that was needed was to dig a *canal* through some swampy lowlands, and an inexhaustible flood of timber, iron, grain, and meat would funnel down through New York City while a counter-flood of manufactured goods went back upriver, enriching its citizens in perpetuity. And lo! Lo!

THE NEW YORK STATE GEOLOGIST: Come on—this way.

THE NEW YORK STATE HISTORIAN: Lo! It came to pass!

JF: Hey, thank you!

THE NEW YORK STATE GEOLOGIST: Who the heck sent you in to Jeremy?

JF: It was Mr. Van Gander.

THE NEW YORK STATE GEOLOGIST: Quite the practical joker, Rick Van Gander. I'm Hal, by the way, I'm the Geologist. We can breathe a little better out here. You want a doughnut?

JF: Thanks, I'm fine. I just want to do my interview. At least, I thought that's what I wanted.

THE NEW YORK STATE GEOLOGIST: Sure thing. (*Dialing*) Janelle? The writer? He's asking about his interview? . . . OK, will do. (*Hanging up*) She's going to come and get you. If she can remember where my office is. Is there something I can help you with in the meantime?

JF: Thanks. I'm feeling somewhat bludgeoned. I had this idea that I could just sit down with New York in a café and tell her how much I've always loved her. Just casually, the two of us. And then I would describe her beauty.

THE NEW YORK STATE GEOLOGIST: Ha, that's not the way it works anymore.

JF: The first time I saw her, I was blown away by how green and lush everything was. The Taconic Parkway, the Palisades Parkway, the Hutchinson River Parkway. It was like a fairy tale, with these beautiful old bridges and mile after mile of forest and parkland on either side. It was so utterly different from the flat asphalt and cornfields out where I came from. The scale of it, the age of it.

THE NEW YORK STATE GEOLOGIST: Sure.

JF: My mom's little sister lived for a long time in Schenectady with my two girl cousins and her husband, who worked for G.E. When I was in high school, they moved him away from manufacturing in Schenectady to their corporate headquarters in Stamford, Connecticut. He spent the last years of his career leading the team that designed the new corporate logo. Which turned out to look almost exactly like the old corporate logo.

THE NEW YORK STATE GEOLOGIST: Schenectady ain't doing so well anymore. None of those old manufacturing towns are.

JF: My aunt and uncle escaped to arty Westport. The summer I turned seventeen, my parents and I drove out to see them there. The first thing that happened was I conceived a huge crush on my cousin Martha. She was eighteen and tall and funny and vivacious and had poor eyesight, and

I could actually talk to her halfway comfortably, because we were cousins. And somehow it got arranged—somehow my parents signed off on it—that Martha and I would drive in to Manhattan and spend a day there by ourselves. It was August 1976. Hot, smelly, polleny, thundery, weedy. Martha was working as the babysitter and driver for three Westport girls whose father had gone to South America for two months with his wife and his mistress. The girls were sixteen, fourteen, and eleven, all of them incredibly tiny and obsessed with body weight. The middle one played the flute and was precocious and constantly bugging Martha to take her to high-school parties where she could meet some older boys. The vehicle Martha chauffeured them in was an enormous black Town Car. By August, she'd already smashed one Town Car and had had to call her employer's office to arrange for another. We sailed down the Merritt Parkway in the left lane at high speed, with all the windows open and furnace-hot air blowing through and the three princesses splayed out across the backseat—the older two of them cute enough and close enough to me in age that I could barely say a word to them. Not that they showed the slightest interest in me anyway. We landed on the Upper East Side, by the art museum, where the girls' grandmother had an apartment. The most impressive thing to me was that the middle girl had come to the city for the day without any shoes. I remember her walking up the hot Fifth Avenue sidewalk barefoot, in her sleeveless top and tiny shorts and carrying her flute. I'd never seen entitlement like this, never even imagined it. It was simultaneously beyond my ken and totally intoxicating. My parents were ur-Midwestern and went through life apologizing and feeling the opposite of entitled. You know, and the hazy blue-gray sky with big white clouds drifting over Central Park. And the buildings of stone and the doormen, and Fifth Avenue like a solid column of yellow cabs receding uptown into this bromine-brown pall of smog. The vast urbanity of it all. And to be there with Martha, my exciting New York cousin, and to spend an afternoon wandering the streets with her, and then have dinner like two adults, and go to a free concert in the Park: the self I felt myself to be that day was a self I recognized only because I'd longed for it for so long. I met, in myself, on my first day in New York City, the person I wanted to become. We picked up the girls from their grandmother's around eleven and went to get the Town Car out of the art museum garage, and that was when we discovered that the rear right tire was flat. A puddle of black rubber. So Martha and I worked shoulder to shoulder, sweating, like a couple, and got the car jacked up and the tire changed while the middle girl sat cross-legged on the trunk of somebody else's car, the soles of her feet all black with the city, and played the flute. And then, after midnight, we drove out of there. The girls asleep in back, like they were the kids I'd had with Martha, and the windows down and the air still sultry but cooler now and smelling of the Sound, and the roads potholed and empty, and the streetlights a mysterious sodium orange, unlike the bluish mercury-vapor lights that were still the standard in St. Louis. And over the Whitestone Bridge we went. And that's when I had the clinching vision. That's when I fell irretrievably for New York: when I saw Co-Op City late at night.

THE NEW YORK STATE GEOLOGIST: Get outta here.

JF: Seriously. I'd already spent the day in Manhattan. I'd already seen the biggest and most city-like city in the world. And now we'd been driving away from it for fifteen or twenty minutes, which in St. Louis would have been enough to get you out into pitch-dark river-bottom cornfields, and suddenly, as far as I could see, there were these huge towers of habitation, and every single one of them was as tall as the tallest building in St. Louis, and there were more of them than I could count. The most distant ones were over by the water and otherworldly in the haze. Tens of thousands of city lives all stacked and packed against each other. The sheer number of apartments that you could see out here in the southeast Bronx: it all seemed unknowably and excitingly vast, the way my own future seemed to me at that moment, with Martha sitting next to me doing seventy.

THE NEW YORK STATE GEOLOGIST: Huh. And did anything ever come of that? You and her?

JF: I crashed for a night on her sofa four years later. Again the Upper East Side. In some anonymous Co-Op City–like tower. Martha had just finished college at Cornell. She was sharing a two-bedroom with two other girls. I was in the city with my brother Tom. We'd had dinner down in Chinatown with the in-laws of my other brother, who'd married his own Manhattan girl a couple of years earlier. Tom went to stay with one of his art-school girl-friends and I went uptown to Martha's. I remember in the morning, the first thing she did was put Robert Palmer's "Sneaking Sally Through the Alley" on the living-room stereo and crank up the volume. We took an unbeliev-ably crowded 6 train down to SoHo, where she had a job selling ad space for the SoHo News. And I thought: Boy, this is the life!

THE NEW YORK STATE GEOLOGIST: Again without irony, presumably.

JF: Totally without irony.

THE NEW YORK STATE GEOLOGIST: "New York is where I'd rather stay! / I get allergic smelling hay!"

JF: What can I tell you? There's a particular connection between the Midwest and New York. Not just that New York created the market for the goods that made the Midwest what it is. And not just that the Midwest, in supplying those goods, made New York what it is. New York's like the beady eye of yang at the center of the Midwest's unentitled, self-effacing plains of yin. And the Midwest is like the dewy, romantic, hopeful eye of yin at the center of New York's brutal, grasping yang. A certain kind of Midwesterner comes east to be completed. Just as a certain kind of New York native goes to the Midwest to be renewed.

THE NEW YORK STATE GEOLOGIST: Huh. Pretty deep stuff there. And, you know, what's genuinely interesting, though, is that there's a connection at the level of geology as well. I mean, think about it: New York is the only state on the East Coast that is also a Great Lakes state. You think it's any accident that the Erie Canal got dug where it did? You ever driven the Thruway west along the Mohawk? Way, way off in the distance on the southern side, miles and miles away, you can see these enormous, sharp river bluffs. Well, you know what? Those bluffs used to be the edge of the river. Back when it was a miles-wide cataclysmic flood of glacial meltwater bursting out of mid-continent and draining down toward the ocean. That's what created your easy route to the Midwest: the last Ice Age.

JF: Which I understand was pretty recent, geologically speaking.

THE NEW YORK STATE GEOLOGIST: Yesterday afternoon, geologically speaking. It's only ten thousand years since you had mastodons and woolly mammoths wandering around Bear Mountain and West Point. All sorts of crazy shit—California condors out Syracuse way, walruses and beluga whales up near the Canadian border. And all recently. Yesterday afternoon, more or less. Twenty thousand years ago, the entire state was under a sheet of ice. As the ice began to recede, all across North America, you got these huge lakes of meltwater with nowhere to go. And it would build up and build up until it found a catastrophic way out. Sometimes it flowed out on the western side, down the Mississippi, but sometimes there were monumental ice dams over there and the water had to find a way out to the east. And when a dam finally broke, it really broke. It was bigger than biblical. It was awe-inspiring. And that's what happened in central New York. There came a time when the way out for all that water was right past present-day Schenectady. It carved the bluffs to the south of the Mohawk, it carved the Hudson Valley, it even carved a canyon in the continental shelf that goes two hundred miles out to sea. Then the ice pulled back farther and farther north until another new exit opened up: over the top of the Adirondacks and around the east side of them and down through what eventually became Lake George and Lake Champlain to the Hudson. So what you see in the Hudson today is in fact a close cousin of the Mississippi. Those two rivers were the two principal southern drainages for a continent's worth of melted ice.

JF: The mind reels.

THE NEW YORK STATE GEOLOGIST: New York City's cosmopolitanism runs pretty deep, too, geologically speaking. We've been entertaining foreign visitors for better than half a billion years. Most notably the continent of Africa, which came over about three hundred million years ago, crashed into America, stuck around long enough to build the Alleghenies, and then headed back east. If you look at a geological map of New York, it looks a lot like a state map of ethnicity. The bedrock geology upstate is fairly white-bread uniform—big deposits of limestone from the time when New York was a shallow subtropical sea. But when you get down toward the lower Hudson and the Manhattan spur, the rock becomes incredibly heterogenous and folded and fragmented. You've got remnants of every kind of crap that's come crashing into the continent tectonically, plus other crap from various magmatic upwellings due to rifting, plus further crap that got pushed down by the glaciers. Downstate looks like a melting pot that needs a good stir. And why? Because New York truly always was very central. It sits at the far southeastern corner of the original North American shield, and at the very top of the Appalachian fold belt, and on the western margin of all the gnarly New England volcanic-island crappy-crap that got appended to the continent, and in a northwest corner of our ever-widening Atlantic Ocean. The fact that it's a conjunction of all these things helps explain why it ended up as the most open and inviting state in the whole seaboard, with its easy routes up to Canada and over to the Midwest. Because, literally, for hundreds of millions of years, New York is where the action's been.

JF: What's funny, listening to you, is how much less ancient this all seems than my own early twenties. Three hundred million years is nothing compared to how long it's been since I was a senior in college. And even college seems relatively recent compared to the years right after. The years when I was married. If you want to talk about a tortured, deep geology.

THE NEW YORK STATE GEOLOGIST: I don't suppose you married your vivacious cousin?

JF: No, no, no. But definitely a New York girl. Just like I'd always dreamed of. Her people on her dad's side had been living in Orange County since the 1600s. And her mom's name was Harriet. And she had two very petite younger sisters who were a whole lot like the girls in the backseat of Martha's Town Car. And she was deliciously unhappy.

THE NEW YORK STATE GEOLOGIST: Unhappy was never my idea of delicious.

JF: Well, for some reason, it was mine. Three hundred million years ago. The first thing we did when we got out of school was sublet an apartment on West 110th Street. By the end of that summer, I was so in love with the city, it was almost an afterthought to propose that she and I get married. Which we did, a year later, on a hillside up in Orange County, near the terminus of the Palisades Parkway. Late in the day, we drove off in our Chevy Nova and crossed the Hudson on the Bear Mountain Bridge, heading back toward Boston. I told the toll-taker that we'd just got married, and he waved us on through. It's hardly an exaggeration to say that we were happy then and happy for the next five years, happy being in Boston, happy visiting New York, happy longing for it from a distance. It was only when we decided to actually live here that our troubles started.

NEW YORK STATE'S PUBLICIST: (*Distantly*) Hal? Hello? Hal?

THE NEW YORK STATE GEOLOGIST: Oops—excuse me. Janelle! Wrong way! Over here! Janelle! She can never find me . . . Janelle!

NEW YORK STATE'S PUBLICIST: Oh, this is terrible, terrible! Jon, she's been ready for you for *five minutes* already, and here I'm wandering around and around and around in this *warren*. I know I promised you a half hour, but I'm afraid you may have to content yourself with fifteen minutes. And, I'm sorry, but, *hiding* back here with Hal, you do bear a certain amount of responsibility yourself. Honestly, Hal, you need to install *escape-path lighting* or something.

THE NEW YORK STATE GEOLOGIST: I feel lucky to be funded at all.

JF: It's been nice talking to you.

NEW YORK STATE'S PUBLICIST: Let's *go*, let's *go*. Run with me! I should have sprinkled some bread crumbs behind me. . . . A person could lie down and die here, and the world might never know it. . . . She hates to be kept waiting even five seconds! And you know who she'll blame, don't you?

JF: Me?

NEW YORK STATE'S PUBLICIST: No! Me! Me! Oh, here we are, here we are, we're coming coming coming coming, here, just go on in, she's waiting for you—go on—and don't forget to ask about the pictures—

JF: Hello!

NEW YORK STATE: Hello. Come in.

JF: I'm really sorry I kept you waiting.

NEW YORK STATE: I'm sorry, too. It cuts into our already very limited time together.

JF: I've been here since eight-thirty this morning, and then, in the last half hour—

NEW YORK STATE: Mm.

JF: Anyway, it's great to see you. You look terrific. Very, ah, put-together.

NEW YORK STATE: Thank you.

JF: It's been so long since we were alone, I don't know where to begin.

NEW YORK STATE: We were alone once?

JF: You don't remember?

NEW YORK STATE: Maybe. Maybe you can remind me. Or not. Some men are more memorable than others. The cheap dates I tend to forget. Would this have been a cheap date?

JF: They were *nice* dates.

NEW YORK STATE: Oh! "Dates" plural. More than one.

JF: I mean, I know I'm not Mort Zuckerman, or Mike Bloomberg, or Donald Trump—

NEW YORK STATE: The Donald! He is cute. (*Giggles*) I think he's cute!

JF: Oh my God.

NEW YORK STATE: Oh, come on, admit it. He really is pretty cute, don't you think? . . . What? You truly don't think so?

JF: I'm sorry, I'm . . . just taking it all in. This whole morning. I mean, I knew things were never going to be the same with us. But, my God. It really is all about money and money only now, isn't it?

NEW YORK STATE: It was always about money. You were just too young to notice.

JF: So you remember me?

NEW YORK STATE: Possibly. Or possibly I'm making an educated guess. The romantic young men never notice. My mother even came to find the Redcoats rather handsome, back in the war years. What else was she supposed to do? Let them burn everything?

JF: I guess it runs in your family, then!

NEW YORK STATE: Oh, please. Grow up. Is this really how you want us to spend our ten minutes?

JF: You know, I was back there last month. The hillside where I got married—her grandparents' house. I was driving up through Orange County and I went back to try to find it. I remembered a green lawn spilling down to a rail fence, and a big overgrown pasture with woods all around it.

NEW YORK STATE: Yes, Orange County. A lovely feature of mine. I hope you took some time to savor the many tracts of spectacular parkland around Bear Mountain and to reflect on what an extraordinary percentage of my total land area is guaranteed public and "forever wild." Of course, a great deal of that land came to me as gifts from very rich men. Perhaps you'd like me to be pure and virtuous and give it all back to them for development?

JF: I wasn't sure I ever actually found it, the land was so altered. It was all hideous sprawl, traffic, Home Depot, Best Buy, Target. Next door to the town's old brick high school there was this brand-new, pink, aircraft-carrier-sized building with signs at the entrance that said PLEASE DRIVE SLOWLY, WE LOVE OUR CHILDREN.

NEW YORK STATE: Our precious freedoms do include the freedom to be tacky and annoying.

JF: The best I could do was narrow it to two hillsides. The same thing was happening on both of them. Building-size pieces of earth-moving equipment were scraping it all bare. Reshaping the very contours of the land—creating these cute little fake dells and fake winkles for hideous houses to be sold to sentimentalists so enraged with the world they had to inform it, in writing, on a road sign, that they love their children. Clouds of diesel exhaust, broken full-grown oak trees piled up like little sticks, birds whizzing around in a panic. I could see the whole gray and lukewarm future. No urban. No rural. The entire country just a wasteland of shittily built neither-nor.

NEW YORK STATE: And yet, in spite of it all, I am still rather beautiful. Isn't it unfair? What money can buy? And trees do have a way of growing back. You think there were oak trees on your hillside in the nineteenth century? There probably weren't a thousand oak trees left standing in the entire county. So let's not talk about the past.

JF: The past was when I loved you.

NEW YORK STATE: All the more reason not to talk about it! Here. Come sit next to me. I have some pictures of myself I want to show you.

NORTH CAROLINA

CAPITAL   Raleigh

ENTERED UNION   1789 (12th)

ORIGIN OF NAME   In honor of Charles I of England

NICKNAME   Tar Heel State

MOTTO   Esse quam videri ("To be rather than to seem")

RESIDENTS   North Carolinian

U.S. REPRESENTATIVES   13

STATE BIRD   cardinal

STATE FLOWER   dogwood

STATE TREE   pine

STATE SONG   "The Old North State"

LAND AREA   48,711 sq. mi.

GEOGRAPHIC CENTER   In Chatham Co., 10 mi. NW of Sanford

POPULATION   8,683,242

WHITE   72.1%

BLACK   21.6%

AMERICAN INDIAN   1.2%

ASIAN   1.4%

HISPANIC/LATINO   4.7%

UNDER 18   24.4%

65 AND OVER   12.0%

MEDIAN AGE   35.3

NORTH CAROLINA
Randall Kenan

"I like pigs. Dogs look up to us. Cats look down on us. Pigs treat us as equals."

—WINSTON CHURCHILL

The rural North Carolina world in which I grew up has largely gone. Farms were small and plentiful, and country boys like me learned so much about life from livestock—especially, in North Carolina, from hogs.

My cousin Norman lived directly across the dirt road from my mother and me. Along with his other farm concerns—tobacco, corn, soybeans, chickens—he raised scores of hogs, killing a number in December for their meat, and selling the prized ones a bit later for cash money. An old man when I was born, he had the air of an Old Testament figure, and seemed to know everything there was to know about coaxing plants from the ground and the feed and care of animals. His grandsons, Harry and Larry, were daily fixtures on his farm, and my best buddies in the whole wide world.

Then in high school, they were a few years older than me, and they were my educators about all those things grown-ups were never going to explain to me. Grown-up things. The birds and the bees sorts of things. Subterranean, hidden things were our major topics, after basketball and comic books. So much of the good stuff about adult human society seemed off-limits to me, which made me even hungrier to know about them. The world was an endlessly fascinating, alluring, deadly, promising place, and they had the vocabulary to describe it all, and the opinions to make it make more sense. They had a knack about making the salacious seem routine, yet still somehow magical. As far as I was concerned they knew everything.

Their grandfather kept his hogs in a two-story barn: It held corn in a great room and had an open cavity where the tractor slept. Above that was the tall, wide room with large double doors in front—the belfry, where the dried tobacco was stored. To the south were stalls for the hogs. Their pens extended from their wooden chambers out into the fenced-in cornfields where they rooted and rutted and went about their hog business.

One early spring afternoon after school we awaited the arrival of a particular hog star the way a crowd of fans awaits the arrival of the UNC basketball team after winning an away game. There was much talk of what would occur between boar and sow—between boar and many sows in fact, one by one. About how that boar was a right lucky fellow: a true stud. I had a vague notion of what was about to happen: a boar hog was to impregnate each sow so that Cousin Norman could have more hogs to raise and butcher or sell. This part made sense. The fuzzy part, in my eight-year-old mind, was the act itself. Thanks to Harry and Larry's impeccable tutelage, as well as the R-rated films they took me to, I had learned about the congress between a man and a woman. But the mechanics of hog sex boggled my mind. I kept trying to figure out how it was done, and I was too proud to ask the right questions: What went where? Does the boar ask permission? This was an event I had to witness to complete my education as a North Carolina farm boy. For my cousins—well, this was basically country-boy porn.

The headliner boar hog arrived in a massive wagon towed by an over-sized truck. The hog itself did not disappoint: When the slats were removed, he lumbered out like a creature from a nightmare. It was huge in every direction, dark brown and much hairier than the workaday porkers I slopped in the twilight after supper. I've never seen a hog that big. It stood taller than me, almost as tall as a grown man. The wideness of him, the heft of him, the length of him . . . he was a real-life monster. His head was the stuff of horror movies: Its giant size was matched with mean eyes and woolly mammoth tusks. (Who knew that domestic hogs grew tusks?) I'd never seen such a thing. His cavernous mouth dripped white, frothing ropes of drool. When he snorted I could see the air, like steam but thicker, heavier: The hog looked like pure evil. And, yes, his testicles were outrageous—mighty: pendulous, bulging, spherical things, clearly potent.

But he did disappoint with his seeming indifference to his first intended. A few attempts were made—now I saw how they did it: The impossibly large beast clambered on top of the female hog, herself no sylph, his hooves insistently drawing his great weight across her back, and then his red business attempted to invade her red business. The entire activity was clumsy yet riveting to behold. Suddenly the word "hump" had an entirely new meaning. Piglets were to be the outcome, by and by, by some mysterious process that I still accorded to magic. How else could you explain it?

We leered. Me, Harry, Larry, Cousin Norman, who had the most interest in seeing that the deed was done, for what seemed several hours, until boredom overtook us, and we retreated to watch something far less titillating: *Charlie's Angels*.

But all that night my curiosity pricked at me like fire ants. Are they doing it? What does it look like?

The next morning, while everyone else chewed their bacon, I slipped outside. I couldn't stand it anymore, I had hog sex on the brain: I had to see. I walked across the road, under the great oak, to Cousin Norman's big barn, past the tractor and corn crib, to the rear stall where the great boar hog entertained his hog lady—wow! He was atop her. Penetration had not only been achieved, but was occurring right before my prepubescent eyes. His sighs and grunts sounded like the air being slowly released from a great engine. And the motions he was making were, frankly, obscene. Like a shot I ran back across the road, into the house, into the dining room—the eight-year-old herald of pig fornication.

"They're doing it!"

I ran back to the barn followed by two horny teenagers whose interest in the matter held different curiosities than my own. We witnessed. Larry made some nasty, Rudy Ray Moore–like observations. Harry told me something then that I did not believe, but have come to learn is true: Male hogs have a corkscrew-shaped penis, and their sex act goes on longer than most mammals'. And for me, something momentous had occurred. My mind had been expanded in some mysterious way. I was seeing through a glass a little less darkly.

We sauntered back across the road to finish breakfast, our eyes and ears satiated by having witnessed something primordial, something that felt even forbidden to have beheld.

My mother stood on the porch. Arms akimbo. A look upon her face: I imagined Jack's mother looked the same when he told her he had sold their only cow for some dad-gummed magic beans.

"Don't you ever—ever—do something like that again!" she said. I had never, nor have I since, seen her so close to apoplectic rage. Her fury seemed to loom above her like a towering phoenix afire, her tone like a pissed-off biblical prophet. "You just don't do things like that! You don't talk about such things! Have you lost your mind?" Her disappointment, her disapproval, bewildered me, and I felt dirty and ashamed. "That's not information you broadcast to people. Polite people don't speak of such things. What kind of person do you want to be?" She retreated into the house to get ready for school. Harry and Larry slapped me on the back and laughed.

"Don't worry about it," Larry said to me, "it's natural."

The business of hogs.

The eminent historian Charles Reagan Wilson has joked that the South began when Hernando DeSoto brought hogs with him on his treks through Georgia, North and South Carolina, Tennessee, Alabama, Mississippi, and Louisiana—the land that would become the heart of the Confederacy a few centuries later. The ease of raising and feeding hogs, and their adaptability, led to their wholesale adoption. Native Americans took to the domesticated meat swiftly.

Pork products of all types came to form a solid core at the center of Southern culture: hams and bacon and sausages and loins, not to mention chitlins and pig feet and neckbones, as well as lard and headcheese, which takes a true connoisseur to appreciate. In North Carolina, passion for pork is a birthright. Smokehouses were ubiquitous, dotting the rural landscape along with the tobacco barns and cotton fields. Most of the pork consumed by North Carolinians was raised and butchered locally by individual farmers, like my Cousin Norman, long after Carl Sandburg declared Chicago "Hog Butcher to the World," long after the invention of refrigerated trucks and train cars. The identity of most North Carolinians was bound up in the homegrown hog.

But in the course of a few decades the entire pork industry has changed more than it has in centuries. And Duplin County has become the epicenter of this new and improved hog husbandry in one of America's most swine happy states thanks largely to Wendell H. Murphy, from Rose Hill, about nineteen miles from where I grew up. *Forbes* magazine once called Murphy "the Ray Kroc of pigsties." Murphy pioneered ways to dramatically increase the numbers and weights and quality of his pigs, thus—like Kroc—changing our eating habits and our landscape.

In 1964, a few years after graduating from North Carolina State University in agriculture, Murphy and his father started a feed manufacturing operation in a town near Raleigh. In 1979 they began what is called sow and farrowing operations, borrowing a practice used by poultry producers: contract other farmers to raise the animals. Murphy would provide them with fences, food, and piglets, and the farmers would receive $1 per hog at fifteen weeks, when Murphy would take the developed pigs. This benefited farmers who were too short on funds to make investments on their own, and allowed Murphy Farms to grow at a meteoric rate.

Eager to increase yield, Murphy Farms discovered that younger hogs easily catch diseases from older hogs. So their pigs were separated by age, over three periods of their brief lives (15 days, 50 days, 21 weeks), reducing the chances of passing on disease, until they reached 250 pounds—the desired weight for slaughter. This methodology increased numbers dramatically. Murphy Farms and its contractors also began to raise hogs in confined areas. Computers monitored practically everything in the pig barns, from temperature to ventilation to when a sow is ready to be mated, and if the mating was successful. The Murphy main feed mill, the largest in the USA, delivered over twenty-one thousand tons of feed each week. That improvement added to disease control and, when coupled with new feed formulations engineered through Murphy-subsidized nutritionists and technicians, helped his hog populations explode. The Murphy operation also discovered a way to goose up the number of piglet births. The average number of piglets a sow bears is less than fifteen. Murphy Farms' specially-cared-for sows (they have separate operations for breeding and birthing) average more than twenty-two piglets.

There are now more hogs than humans in North Carolina, and Murphy Farms has helped make Smithfield Foods, the multinational to which it was sold in 1999, the biggest producer of pork products in the world.

All great changes tend to have great side effects, and the effects of this new super-duper hog production are altering the North Carolina land.

Almost everything about North Carolina seems gentle. Even though the tallest peaks on the East Coast rise in the North Carolina Blue Ridge (Mount Mitchell: 6,684 feet), those mountains seem to comfort, to invite, to soothe, when compared to the Rockies' craggy God-like insistence upon their own majesty, or the Brooks and Alaska Ranges' operatic claim of equality with the sky and Denali divinity. Perhaps this gentility is why George Vanderbilt chose the North Carolina mountains to build the largest private residence in the country—so the mountains wouldn't compete with his ego. Biltmore House: It's not big, it's *large*.

Rattlesnakes can kill you, mountain lions can maim you, bears can scare you out of your wits, but not much threatens the average North Carolinian other than other North Carolinians—and that is usually behind the wheel of an SUV these days, or the point of a gun.

Piedmont, coastal plain, mountains, all are crisscrossed by rivers. Cape Fear, Neuse, Pamlico, Haw, Eno, Pee Dee, Yadkin, Catawba. Not grand rivers, nothing like the Mississippi or the Colorado. Gentle rivers, very like the state.

But those rivers in the East are dying. In 1996, the state's most important newspaper, the *Raleigh News and Observer,* won a Pulitzer Prize for a series of articles, collectively entitled "Boss Hog," on the burgeoning neo-pork industry, its methods, and the effects upon the state's ecology. The largest problem was the millions of gallons of hog waste. The vast lagoons where the waste is stored—some as large as ten acres—were found to be leaking into the ground water, contaminating it with nitrates among other chemicals. The lagoons also were known to spill their contents, in good weather and bad, finding their way to creeks and rivers. The run-offs were found to increase algae blooms in the rivers, along with high levels of ammonia, which resulted in disastrous fish kills. In one case state officials reckoned that between 3,500 to 5,000 fish were killed after a ruptured dike released over twenty-five million gallons of swine sewage into the New River in Onslow County.

I will leave the problems of odor to your imagination, but do imagine living near a multi-acre open hog sewer.

The reporters at the *News and Observer* also pointed toward a troubling relationship between the state legislature, the governor, and Wendell H. Murphy, who served in the state house from 1983 until 1988. He also served as a North Carolina state senator from 1989 to 1992. The articles pointed to political contributions made by the Murphy family and their concerns, to a seeming laxity among the North Carolina General Assembly when it came to enforcing regulations governing hog farming, to favorable legislation made toward them, and to general foot-dragging about the ecological problems such practices were causing, problems that in some cases appeared to be irreversible.

A decade later the situation has not improved. Today North Carolina's hog population is well over ten million (the state's human population is under nine million). Small hog farms decreased from around twenty-four thousand in the mid-1980s to under six thousand by the year 2000. According to the USDA small farms are known to produce less harmful waste, because what happens to pig poop is relatively organic in a small farm, but goes largely untreated when the waste is piled up in such vast quantities. Nitrates, copper, antibiotics, and other chemicals harmful to humans accumulate in these lagoons at alarming rates. Due to the fish kills and algae blooms and other compounded diseases directly related to corporate hog farming, North Carolina's commercial fish populations have dropped by 60 percent in the last decade. Yet enforcement of hog waste management and violations remain stagnant. According to one study, in 1997, 88 percent of all factory hog farms had at least one permit or waste management plan violation. The study suggests those statistics were conservative.

Once upon a time I lived in Memphis, Tennessee. A lovely river town built on high bluffs over the great Mississippi. The food there is good. But, alas, those good people suffer from a serious delusion. For some reason they believe barbecue (and for a Southerner barbecue is a noun not a verb) comes from a pork shoulder and is smothered in some sweet, tomato-based muck. Though we agree on the delectability of short ribs, we part company on practically everything else. My four years in Memphis was akin to living among beautiful barbarians when it came to pork.

North Carolinians are fiercely attached to their barbecue. Whether its name comes from the Taino word for sacred fire pit (*barbicoa*) or from a French joke about how the early sailors cooked the entire beast from beard to tail ("*barbe à queue*")—discounted by many historians—a tradition of cooking the whole pig over an open fire has endured. (The term "buccaneer" comes from the act of slowly curing pork over a smoldering fire—"*boucan*" in French—hence "*boucaniers*.") North Carolina passions run high when getting down to the nitty and the gritty of how BBQ should be done.

I am as partisan as they come and do not apologize to any man, woman, or child. The best barbecue in the world comes from North Carolina. And not just anywhere in North Carolina: from the eastern part of the state.

I make no apologies, therefore, in stating with great emphatic zeal and extreme prejudice that a hog should be cooked over a pit, over choice wood, for at least half a day, preferably twice that long. Whole. The tender meat then should be disarticulated from the bones, skin and all, which, in this case, will be a cakewalk as the flesh has been rendered into a state of tender, moist, near-gelatinous compliance, the smell of which should cause mild hallucinations. Next the cooked meat should be chopped—not pulled, plucked, sliced, or otherwise mishandled—chopped. Then it should be mixed with a vinegar-based solution of such clarity and spiciness as to augment but not detract from the suzerainty of slowly roasted hog flesh: The beast gave up its life for your delectation. That should be honored.

A meal, then: preferably served on the simplest dinnerware available—some choose paper plates, some just paper—to be accompanied by white bread, a mound of slaw or potato salad, corn bread (hush puppies actually, but that's another tale), and copious quantities of sweetened ice tea. Lemons optional. Oh yes, and with plenty of Texas Pete Hot Sauce available. The hot sauce of champions.

My brethren and sisteren in the Piedmont and the Mountains will vehemently disagree with this scenario, I assure you. But they are heathens on such matters and should be attended as one would attend a young child: They know not what they do.

Whatever happens in this humble state, as tobacco slowly becomes a memory with banking and bio-tech taking its place at the center of things, hogs will remain nearest and dearest to our hearts. For better or for worse, pigs are us.

NORTH DAKOTA

CAPITAL Bismarck

ENTERED UNION 1889 (39th)

ORIGIN OF NAME From the Sioux tribe, meaning "allies"

NICKNAME Sioux State, Flickertail State, Peace Garden State, or Rough Rider State

MOTTO "Liberty and union, now and forever, one and inseparable"

RESIDENTS North Dakotan

U.S. REPRESENTATIVES 1

STATE BIRD western meadowlark

STATE FLOWER wild prairie rose

STATE TREE American elm

STATE SONG "North Dakota Hymn"

LAND AREA 68,976 sq. mi.

GEOGRAPHIC CENTER In Sheridan Co., 5 mi. SW of McClusky

POPULATION 636,677

WHITE 92.4%

BLACK 0.6%

AMERICAN INDIAN 4.9%

ASIAN 0.6%

HISPANIC/LATINO 1.2%

UNDER 18 25.0%

65 AND OVER 14.7%

MEDIAN AGE 36.2

NORTH DAKOTA
Louise Erdrich

"Our winters are quite cold in North Dakota. But do we ask
anybody to feel sorry for us?"

—BRENT LLOYD WILLS,
NORTH DAKOTA GEOGRAPHY AND EARLY HISTORY

The rare times North Dakota is referred to in the national media, we are the
coldest, emptiest, loneliest, and most depopulated and abandoned state in
the union. We are never the most hauntingly beautiful, sky-filled, the safest,
the centeredest, most content, decentest, the Germanest, Indianest, windi-
est, the birdiest, the non-complainingest, the funniest, the friendliest, or the
easiest place to get a job—all of which are true, or nearly true. North Dakotans get tired of the end-of-the-earth jokes and of the death knells for their
state, and yet have a strange pride that they live in a place nobody else, it
seems, is capable of understanding. I grew up in Wahpeton, North Dakota,
in the southeastern part of the state, and often visited my grandparents
on the Turtle Mountain reservation, way up north beneath the Canadian
border. These days I am a frequent North Dakota visitor, both to work and
to stay with family. Yet I don't know if I understand North Dakota, either.
I do know that I love the place that was first loved by those indigenous to
it—the Dakota, Mandan, Hidatsa, Arikara, Anishinabe, and Cree, and later
the Metis, French-Chippewa who formed a hunting and gathering culture
more indigenous than white.

The second wave of North Dakota lovers hardly saw those who came
before. Nine of every ten native people were dead of smallpox and other
European illnesses by the time the territory was settled, and to this day over
90 percent of North Dakotans are white. Yet the "Vanishing Americans"
were the first to hear their own death knell and survive it. Today in North
Dakota tribal economies and reservation populations are the fastest growing. The farmers and settlers of the second wave have seen the state change
from being an ICBM capital, the world's third largest nuclear power, to
being the world's third largest producer of durum pasta. They chose Teredo
petrified wood as the state fossil, declared the state age the Paleocene, the
state animal the Nokota horse, and the state bird the western meadowlark.
According to statisticians, Fargo is the fourth best city and North Dakota

the eleventh best state to live in, with the lowest crime rate and the greatest number of neighborhoods supportive of children. The average travel time to work is fifteen minutes. North Dakotans are extremely helpful, patriotic, self-sacrificing—the state has the seventh highest per capita number of casualties in Iraq, and a disproportionate number of those who serve are Native American.

There are actually three North Dakotas to write about—the eastern swath of the Red River Valley, the central Drift Prairie, and the Missouri Plateau. To really get a sense of the third North Dakota, which lies west beyond Jamestown's World's Largest Buffalo, I suggest reading the stories of my sister, Liselotte Erdrich, or the novels and poems of Larry Woiwode, Poet Laureate of the state, who lives and farms in southwestern Hettinger County. As for what I really know about North Dakota, it is very personal and mainly about people. It is about growing up in a state that is still safe enough for children to live freely and spend their time outdoors. It is about appreciating a state that has just the right number of people per square mile.

For many years, my Turtle Mountain Chippewa grandfather danced across the cover of the *North Dakota Travel Guide*. A framed copy hangs on my office wall, and I often contemplate Patrick Gourneau stepping tall and proud toward the drawing of a huge spear point. The spear bears a tiny picture of Teddy Roosevelt, who is waving his hat as he clings to a rearing horse. Grandpa is three times the size of Teddy plus the horse, which makes me proud.

Of course the travel guide has since been updated. The up-to-date title is *North Dakota—Legendary*. There is still an American Indian on the cover, a young fancy dancer, plus a kayaker and a couple of cowboys. The presentation is now focused on well-known trail blazers. Grandpa's travel guide modestly suggested to the traveler, "When You Vacation West, Spend a Day in North Dakota." (Just a day? That's all we ask.) The new guide says: "Now that Lewis and Clark have done all the hard work, charting and exploring the West, you get to have all the fun!"

Thanks Lewis and Clark! I *have* had a lot of fun in North Dakota. Since my fun has not yet become legendary, I'd like to talk first about ditch-skiing, which isn't mentioned by the friendly people at the tourist division.

Invented by my father, who had grown up in Minnesota around steep hills you could ski down in thirteen seconds, ditch skiing involved a rope tied to the rear fender of the family station wagon. A child on a pair of giant wooden skis would hold the end of the rope, give her father the thumbs up, and brace herself as he started the car. Towed along at blinding speeds of six to twelve miles an hour while gulping snirt—half snow, half dirt—was a matchless winter experience. And then there was the mosquito fogger—a truck towing a tank that spewed insecticide. I am glad now to say that I only followed it once to get high on Malthion—others who waited for it every summer night, chased it on their banana seat bikes, and became addicted are now survivalists or raging fundamentalists of various types. We caught bullheads in the Red River. To clean them you nailed their heads to a plank and pulled off their skins like wet pants. There was constant skating, pick-up baseball, fort-building, tree-diving over the river, sledding in cardboard boxes, and nightly kick-the-can. And that was only childhood— when you got to be a teenager there was drinking and sex.

Of all these forms of fun (except the last two, I suppose), ditch skiing is the one that has survived and evolved. Snow kiting is now an eco-sport in North Dakota. Just as it sounds, a giant kite is strapped to the skier and— *whoosh*. No need for hills. Just this year, North Dakota conservationists are making a 390-mile trek to publicize our wind energy potential. This group, To Cross the Moon, plans to traverse the state from the Canadian border to South Dakota, stopping in every town to talk about energy and give lessons in snow kiting.

Besides the activities that were really fun but not mentioned at all by the tourism office, there are a host of attractive sites that nobody would even know about from looking at *North Dakota—Legendary*. There is, for instance, no mention at all of the mysterious and wonderful billboards set along our major highway systems. In simple black letters against a plain white background they offer modest advice. SMILE. BE POLITE. SAY THANKS. BE NICE. The billboard messages are surprising and seem to come out of nowhere, giving you a little nudge from beyond, as if God were a gentle second grade teacher.

I've also referred to the absence of people as one of the state's great attractions. Our world is terrifyingly overpopulated, yet North Dakota's population is roughly the same as it was in 1920. I am not alone in finding this one of the best things about the state. In North Dakota there are between nine and ten people per square mile, and most of those live in Fargo, Bismarck, or Grand Forks. If you avoid the population centers, you can travel in a blissful abeyance of humankind. This paucity of humans is incredibly refreshing—a claustrophobe's paradise.

I am at present drinking a cup of tea into which I've dumped a sugar packet labeled with the Minn-Dak farmers' cooperative logo—the Red River Valley is becoming slightly hybridized by Minnesota. But most towns or cities along the eastern border have their twins—Fargo-Moorhead, Grand Forks-East Grand Forks, Wahpeton-Breckenridge. I hate to say this, and I apologize to those North Dakotans, or Nodaks, who are fond of rampant growth, but the largest cities in North Dakota are surrounded by the same sort of soul-sucking big box store urban sprawl you'll see around any American city. Yet downtown Wahpeton is peaceful and pretty, downtown Jamestown is lovingly kept, and downtown Fargo is a treasure. The Round-Up Bar's giant neon cowgirl and the Pink Pussycat Lounge's huge winking cat have disappeared, but the Empire Tavern still exists and the merchants fight to keep Fargo's fifties Grain Belt charm, while the renovated Hotel Donaldson is a surprising oasis of art and down comforters; its HoDo restaurant the Chez Panisse of Fargo.

I ended up in North Dakota in the first place because my father, Ralph Erdrich, came to teach on the Turtle Mountain reservation and there met Rita Gourneau and fell (it is said) in love at first glance. The two were married by Father George Lyons, a formidable shortstop, who passes his days now at Blue Cloud Abbey in South Dakota. Ralph and Rita moved downstate to the southeast corner, and we lived at the edge of Wahpeton, on the Bureau of Indian Affairs campus. There, I grew up with the sky.

Shattering, spectacular, inescapable. The North Dakota sky is a former tallgrass prairie heaven tarp that stretches down on every side and quiets the mind. In the summer, distance melts off into mirage, a jitter of shaking air on hot dust. When the sun is magnified by a dust storm it can fill the sky like a nuclear dawn. Sounds travel as far as the ear allows. Vision stretches as far as the eye can strain. Pure sky pulls you right out of yourself and yet bears down so close it seems crushing.

I saw more sunrises in North Dakota than anywhere I have lived since. They just aren't worth getting up for in other states. In contrast to the magnificence of heaven, however, there was the earthbound reality of being a mixed-blood nonentity in a world of blazing Scandinavian beauties and gung-ho Valkyries.

Every summer morning beginning at age eight, I went down to the Chahinkapa Park Pool to swim laps behind gorgeous tanned blondes with hard biceps and fluid dolphin kicks. I never won so much as a ribbon at swim meets. I came in last in every heat. I persisted because I had a deadly crush on our swimming coach, and also because there was a certain coolness to being part of the Viking Girl scene—eyes piercing bright over zinc-smeared noses, skin glistening with iodine-laced baby oil, hair streaked lemon-lime from the chlorine bleach, ears stuffed with alcohol-soaked cotton. I kept beating at the freezing water every morning until, eventually, two things happened.

First, my parents thought I was going deaf, and took me to the doctor. He vacuumed out my ears and found two bits of crumpled business letters lodged against my eardrum. I had inserted paper in lieu of cotton, to get that cool swimmer's ear look. Uncrumpled, the bits of letters were still legible. "Dear Ralph Erdrich." In the amazing week that followed it was like I'd gained a super power. I could hear the slightest movement of the leaves. I walked about, charmed by the slap of my bare feet on the cement. My sheets rustled. I heard the wind in the eaves. (North Dakotans, by the way, often become attached to the various sounds of wind and feel the musical absence anywhere else.)

I persisted in losing swim meets until age twelve, when the other thing happened. My new swimming suit, a ploy to ensnare the swimming coach, arrived in the mail. I'd ordered it from the Montgomery Ward catalogue. My one-piece was white, and had a bra-let of molded rubber, which I'd upped several sizes on the order form, out of hope, a certain eye-trap.

The first day I wore the swimming suit, very white against my tan, I walked out on the hot disinfected pool cement, and stood in casual anticipation. I was immediately noticed by my crush. His face twisted in complimentary pain; he wrung his hand as if to say, *she's so hot she's burning me.* Then he climbed onto his chair. His eyes stayed on me, as did other eyes, all eyes! I walked onto the diving board, posed, leaped into the air, and did a scornful swan dive. The impact completely inverted my bra cups. I didn't notice this until I'd mounted the board for a second dive. Then, I looked down at my chest and saw two begging bowls.

Getting out on the shallow end of the pool, where I'd swum underwater—yes, I could swim fifty yards without a breath, after all—I decided that I would quit swim team and take my first job, hoeing sugar beets, a crop that was just then taking over the Red River Valley.

Again, I was up at sunrise. I slipped into an old cotton swimming suit, threw clothes over it, and picked up a lunch that always included a thermos of my mother's vegetable soup. Chopping seven-foot purple thistles, battling the massed mustard and goldenrod and switch grass that wanted to invade our tender new local economy, I sought purifying obscurity. Anyway, I was making the big money—$1.29 per row. I was on an all-girls crew. The only man, our boss Sam Roberts, a Dakota man and friend of the family, sharpened our hoes with a file at the end of every row and treated me with a neutral kindness. I didn't look at boys again until I'd actually grown into the top of my swimming suit.

I suppose the swimming suit hubris could happen anywhere, but only in North Dakota could a girl find salvation and start a new life in the blazing heat of a sugar beet field. After my two rebirths—to sound and self-esteem—I got my Red Cross certificate and began working at the pool. I taught a number of Wahpeton's most upstanding citizens to swim, got another job, and sold Kentucky Fried chicken to a few who now inhabit the town cemetery. I dragged main with kids who are the town's backbone—judges and funeral directors, police officers and state representatives. Later on, I worked the graveyard shift at Country Kitchen, now The Frying Pan restaurant. I cleaned up after the bars closed, and in doing so felt the panicked self-pity of the young, who vow to go to school and get a job that does not involve assembling Mississippi Mud sundaes or swabbing up after amateur drinkers. During college, I came home and worked road construction on the new interstate highway (I–29) bypass. With that money, I bought my first Smith-Corona typewriter, electric, at Globe Gazette in Wahpeton, and I still write in the hardbound green record books I bought at that store's sad close-out.

When I ran out of construction money, the state arts board hired me as a North Dakota Poet in the Schools. I traveled to any place that would have me for a residency, including the Turtle Mountain reservation. There, I could sleep on my grandmother's afghaned sofa. My grandfather's mind had started to wander by then, but he still told good stories. In a café, just off the reservation, eating toward each other over an entire sour cream and raisin pie, which the waitress split down the middle when she saw us enter, I asked my grandfather to tell me about the things he had done.

My grandfather mentioned the time he was brought down to Fargo to name a visiting dignitary, who happened to be Tricia Nixon. Naming is a very sacred event in Chippewa life, so my grandfather, who had, after all, testified in front of Congress and managed to keep our tribe from termination in the early fifties, did a very diplomatic thing. He gave her a name that sounded impressive and melodious in our traditional language, Ojibwemowin. I asked him what the name meant, and he said Woman Getting Off an Airplane.

Since those first years of hoeing sugar beets, the crop has become a mega-success and mega-pollutant in the Red River Valley. The beet is rivaled by sunflowers, which everybody vastly prefers, as the beet is a squat and ugly crop that stinks when processed for sugar. North Dakota grows more sun-flowers than any other state, which is another thing that makes it beautiful. My hope is that pesticide and herbicide use, and the habitat destruction that is killing western meadowlarks, bobolinks, and so many other eastern Red River Valley bird species will stop. Some years ago, I noticed the absence of birdsong in Wahpeton, so I walked to the edge of town, then past the edge of town, then out of town. Finally, I quit. The air was still quiet. The meadowlarks were gone. But western North Dakota is still bird-rich, and with a little cover and more bug-life, they could easily come back.

I began returning to the Turtle Mountains every summer to teach with my sister Heid Erdrich at the ingeniously constructed and energy self-sufficient Turtle Mountain Community College. Our reservation lies near the Missouri Plateau, up so far north it nearly touches the Canadian border, and is a Great Plains anomaly, since it is composed of hills covered with glacial drift. The Turtle Mountains are a lovely, intimate, richly forested and lake-dotted region. Our desperate tribal history includes an absolute re-fusal of the Chippewa to be removed from this homeland to White Earth—members of the Pembina band starved rather than leave. Of the original twenty-three township reservation, only twelve square miles, or two town-ships, still belong to the tribe. Woodticks have now consecrated that area as their homeland, too. Each June, trillions of them come alive and prepare to attach themselves to any animal brushing near. Most of the woodticks die off in late July, and that is why we hold our workshop in August.

Heid and I run the only Ojibwe Writing Workshop that I know of, and every summer it has its own cast of characters, primarily tribal members, but often the sort of people who start a new life in North Dakota. The sort of people, for instance, who start emu farms, and slaughter and process those prehistoric birds for all their healing oil, then hope to get rich selling the miracle substance on the Internet. The sort of people who move from San Francisco to a place along no major geologic fault lines, but who are seismically shocked anyway at the lack of fresh winter produce. One recent winter night at a friend's house in remote North Dakota we turned on the TV and the lead local news story was that a truckload of ripe peaches had entered town. My friend got up without a word, pulled on her jacket, and got her car keys. An hour later, she came back with three crates of peaches, the limit per. People had left their homes at night and stormed the grocery store parking lot.

So in a way my state of origin really is *North Dakota—Legendary*. My grandfather, whose traditional name, Aunishinabay, means Original Man, will dance for all time, bigger than a president. The sky will outdo attractions in any state in the union. Last summer just after dawn, driving toward the Turtle Mountains, I stopped the car because I could not believe what I was seeing. In the cloudless east a sparkling sun rose in lucid air. But directly over me, as though divided with a compass, the sky split. A storm had boiled out of the west, dropping a black curtain. Against it, the rising sun ignited four fierce rainbows. Lightning stepped through rainbow hoops like a circus walker on blazing stilts. There were distant licks of violent rain. A horizon of surging dark. And on the other side of the world, the baby pure sun continued to rise. *Legendary.*

So the next time you hear a late-night comedian do a North Dakota joke, you will know better. North Dakota is the place you can live safely and get hired fast; it is cold, yes, but you will learn not to complain. Its billboards will make you Smile. Think. Say Thank You. With fewer people, you can even Be Polite, or if you wish, eccentric. North Dakota is known for its historical eccentrics—King Whiskers, Tree-tops Klingensmith, The Smallest Pioneer, The Giant of Frog Point, and the World's Champion Miniature Writer, who wrote Lincoln's Gettysburg Address on a single 2 1/4-inch strand of human hair. You can be odd, but not weird—you cannot, for instance, sit naked in your pickup truck. Just this past January, law enforcement agencies from northwestern North Dakota and eastern Montana chased a naked Iowa man, who was caught after nearly nineteen hours. At least by then, said authorities, he'd managed to don bib overalls. So keep your clothes on in public. Other than that, you are free to strap on a kite and see what it's like to fly across the surface of the moon. You can stand in a field of sunflowers. You can eat well at the HoDo. You can attend stirring powwows at United Tribes or the University of North Dakota, or check any reservation calendar. You can hike the Badlands or stay at the Nature Conservancy's Cross Ranch. And if all of these things aren't enough for you, just stay home. Don't bother. Nobody in North Dakota really needs you all that bad, unless you can Be Nice.

OHIO

CAPITAL   Columbus

ENTERED UNION   1803 (17th)

ORIGIN OF NAME   From an Iroquoian word meaning
"great river"

NICKNAME   Buckeye State

MOTTO   "With God all things are possible"

RESIDENTS   Ohioan

U.S. REPRESENTATIVES   18

STATE BIRD   cardinal

STATE FLOWER   scarlet carnation

STATE TREE   buckeye

STATE SONG   "Beautiful Ohio"

LAND AREA   40,948 sq. mi.

GEOGRAPHIC CENTER   In Delaware Co., 25 mi. NNE of
Columbus

POPULATION   11,464,042

WHITE   85.0%

BLACK   11.5%

AMERICAN INDIAN   0.2%

ASIAN   1.2%

HISPANIC/LATINO   1.9%

UNDER 18   25.4%

65 AND OVER   13.3%

MEDIAN AGE   36.2

OHIO
Susan Orlean

The flatness, it turns out, is a myth. There are certainly some long stretches of level land, but there is nothing in Ohio like the endless planed prairies of Iowa or the sheer horizontal Western plateaus: Ohio is actually a bumpy state, with acres and acres of hills and dales, slopes and valleys, banks and basins, rolls and mounds and knolls.

The vast cornfields are also a myth. There are plenty of cornfields—big ones—but if you want to see vastness in Ohio, the cornfields are nothing compared to the General Motors plant in Lordstown, which is truly colossal: almost four million square feet of factory, and that doesn't count the parking lots. It feels like it takes a good seven or eight minutes to pass it on the turnpike, even at sixty miles an hour. The main factory building is so big that the trucks lined up at the loading ramps look like toy trucks hauling toy triple-trailers.

The hard, nasal, cawing accent is mostly a myth, though now and again, as you roam through Ohio, you will certainly hear words shaped without any roundness or melody. Then again, as soon as you head a little south in the state, you will hear a version of an Ohio accent that is as buttery and languid as something straight from Tennessee. Head west and it sounds like North Dakota. Head north and the accent is uninflected—plain American, without any road map implied.

Even the Midwesternness of Ohio is a myth. The Census Bureau reclassifies Ohio every few years—these days it's considered Mid-North-Central rather than Eastern Midwest, and someday it may be officially designated West-of-Eastern/East-of-Western/North-of-Southern/Mid-Rustbelt, which is probably closer to the truth. Hell, northeastern Ohio was part of *Connecticut* to begin with, and even now, 220 years after Connecticut gave it up, this part of Ohio still has more in common temperamentally, sociologically, and culturally, with Pennsylvania and New York than it does with, say, Kansas. Cleveland and Pittsburgh and Buffalo are triplet cities, all clock-punching capitals of industry and enterprise, their rich people scions of the business world, not the agribusiness world, their aspirations to sophistication more Manhattan-like than Chicagoan. Southeastern Ohio is far less Midwestern than it is Appalachian. There is nothing prairie-like, plains-like, or farm-belt about it at all: The landscape is rough, striated, gullied, folded, coal dusted.

Like most mountain places, its economy comes from underground—clay, coal, gravel—rather than above ground in broad daylight, as it is in the true Midwest. And like most mountain places, southeastern Ohio is gripped with an ungentle sense of religion and fate—maybe the imminent possibility of tumbling into a rocky void accounts for this—so it is pocked with churches and roadside crosses and Jesus signage and even at midday you can feel the apprehension of dusk. If anyone had the least bit of sense, they would clip off this corner of Ohio and paste it onto West Virginia, where it clearly belongs. While you have your scissors out, snip the southwestern corner of Ohio and tape it to Kentucky, since Cincinnati and Louisville really should be in the same state. In fact, that strip of land at the southwestern Ohio border is officially denoted, geographically, as "The Bluegrass Region," in case you needed more evidence of where it really belongs.

That leaves the center of Ohio, and that might actually be considered Midwestern, though it has lately made a business out of not being Midwestern, which really is a specific regional personality, but being the American average itself—Columbus and the area around it is marketed as a nearly perfect place to do surveys, test products, homogenize fashion, and study consumers. Even so, let's call the center of the state Midwestern. That means about one-sixth of the Ohio land mass fits the conventional notion of what Ohio is.

A few more things used to describe the state are not quite myths, but no longer accurate, thank goodness: The fouling of its waters, for instance. The Cuyahoga was once such a stew of industrial runoff that it regularly ignited, most famously in 1969, when flames reached five stories high. The fires in the river had occurred regularly over the previous hundred years; while it enjoyed the greatest notoriety of all, the 1969 conflagration was described by the chief of the Cleveland Fire Department as a "strictly run-of-the-mill fire." And now? One still would not choose to skinny-dip in the Cuyahoga River, but the fish are back, they don't have weird tumors, and they even taste like fish and not like steel-plant outflow. Bald eagles live nearby, without needing to line their nests with asbestos. Similarly, Lake Erie, the world's tenth largest lake, a spill of blue so immense that if you grew up in northern Ohio you would gaze at it and find it impossible to imagine that any ocean could be bigger, was for a long time considered, literally, dead. The case of Lake Erie was so well known that it was almost a matter of distinction—who could name the other Great Lakes, anyway? Everyone knew about Lake Erie, though, even if the reason was unfortunate. But then came Earth Day and the Clean Water Act and nowadays the lake is swimmable, boatable, fishable. Ohio with filthy water was an object lesson in industry run amok. Ohio with clean water is a better place by far, but gives you much less to talk about.

That is the character of Ohio—it conveys a certain regularness, a lack of wild distinction, a muting of idiosyncratic extreme. The state is a sampling of nearly every American quality and landscape but it levels out to something quietly and pleasantly featureless rather than creating a crazy quilt of miscellany. It is an excellent place to live and a less excellent place to try to describe, since nothing stands out in that theatrical way that allows for easy description. The cities are abundant and they are all medium-sized. The sports teams are always okay, never great but also never sensationally flawed and tragic. Lots of things are made in Ohio—rubber, machine tools, tractors, matches, pillows, cash registers—but nothing that has sex appeal. It isn't a place that had a grand and dramatic history and then faded into weary, benign irrelevance like, say, Portugal; it has always been a workaday, useful place without airs. In 1940, the *WPA Guide to Ohio* awkwardly praised the solid, utilitarian nature of the state: "The life of practically everyone in the Nation has been touched, and in some degree made more livable, by the products of Buckeye enterprise."

The *WPA Guide to Ohio* is, in fact, line after line of equivocation when it comes to describing the state: "No sudden weather changes. . . ." "Although Ohio is heavily populated and industrialized, it provides excellent upland game hunting. . . ." "The better residential sections of most cities in Ohio show examples of the Cape Cod cottage, English half-timber house, French farmhouse, Italian villa, Colonial houses of both New England and southern prototypes, and of numerous other styles. . . . Ohio has never had a group of writers such as the Hoosier School in Indianapolis . . . Ohio was settled too rapidly by all sorts of people, it was too much exposed to new developments in the turbulent nineteenth century, too busy cutting timber, plowing farms, building canals and railroads, smelting ore, and doing a thousand other things, to cultivate its provincial heritage, like Kentucky, or to bother its head or heart with the unprofitable job of creating a regional literature. Moreover, the State never has had a center . . . Ohio is either cosmopolitan or a group of provinces dominated by the great cities. Its authors have usually followed the custom of escaping to the East as soon as possible. . . ."

In elementary school, when we studied Ohio, we learned that many Presidents had been born here—not good Presidents or memorable ones, but lots of them. This became for me a metaphor for the state—a place with a lot of people, a fair amount of power, considerable wealth, great accomplishment, but an aching lack of charisma, which is something that mattered a lot to me when I was young. Ohio wasn't old-old, like places in the East, and it wasn't swingy new, like the Northwest, and it wasn't gothic and fabulous like Louisiana, and it wasn't really rural, like Missouri, and it wasn't really urban, like New York, and it didn't offset its squareness with a single jazzy event like Indiana does with the Indy 500 and Kentucky with the Derby . . . these things count for a lot when you're young, because you still find your sense of your self by context rather than through any true self-knowledge. So my context—and by extension, my personality—was Ohio, and that made me feel like I was expected to be mild, productive, and utterly normal—so I grasped for anything that would make being an Ohioan seem more dazzling. At summer camp, where the other girls were mostly from Connecticut and New York, I boasted that Sam Sheppard, the osteopath who murdered his wife in the sixties and became the inspiration for *The Fugitive*, was from Ohio. To be honest, I also claimed, quite insanely, that my mother had dated him, and therefore she was almost, sort of, a murder victim herself—an effort to make myself a little more spectacular, I guess. The point is, I thought that having interesting, well-known criminals gave Ohio some panache, which I wanted very badly for it to have. It simply wasn't enough to me to have grown up in a progressive, lovely, friendly place, which was the case; I wanted so much to be from somewhere that had drama. As I got older, I stopped boasting about Dr. Sheppard but still found myself defensively, reflexively boasting about Ohio however I could, making a preemptive strike whenever I was asked where I was from. I would cite things I was indeed very proud of about Ohio, and also plenty of things that I didn't care about, really, or didn't think were socially significant, but if they were memorable or distinctive in any way, they served my purpose. "I'm from Ohio—did you know that the Shah of Iran came to the Cleveland Clinic to have his heart bypass? that Debra Winger, the actress, is from Ohio? that most people think the Cleveland Orchestra is one of the greatest in the world? that Cleveland was the first major American city to have an African-American mayor? that Jacobs Field is one of the most beautiful stadiums in the Major Leagues? that Mike Tyson bought a house on Lake Erie? that John D. Rockefeller was from Ohio? that the last Presidential election really depended on Ohio?" And on and on and on. This is after thirty years of living elsewhere. I am still an Ohioan, though, and always will be, and will always have that need to protest my own regularness. To be honest, I haven't completely given up Dr. Sheppard, either, and still get excited when there is some legitimate excuse to talk about it ("Media circus? Nothing could compare to the Sam Sheppard trial. That took place in Cleveland!"). I no longer claim that my mother dated him, so progress has been made.

The main drag through the Cleveland suburbs, where I grew up, is called Chagrin Boulevard. It is a four-lane thoroughfare, heavily traveled, lined with office buildings, shopping centers, golf courses, gas stations, hair salons, restaurants, car dealerships, and a few stray houses making a valiant stand against the tide of commerce washing down Chagrin. The road is named for the nearby Chagrin River. For a long time, it didn't occur to anyone I knew that these two major features of the area shared a very odd name—it was one of those things that is just a name, not a word, if you grow up hearing it that way, and you don't notice it until an outsider says, as they always did, What a weird name for a road/river! It's like having a main road called Disappointment! Or Frustration!

It was a bit of a sting to realize that a name that was so familiar to us was actually a peculiar name with a negative connotation. The realization compounded my persistent need to explain away my connection to a place that seemed to have no character, even though I knew it had a great and, more importantly, good nature, and that as a place it transcended anything that could have made it superficially more "interesting," because it was so deeply and permanently in my soul as home. My comeback was always the same: Chagrin Boulevard is named for the river, and the river was named Chagrin because an explorer looking for a different, more exciting place ended up in Ohio, to his chagrin. He stayed here, and he prospered, and he ate well, and he made a good living, and he knew it was an excellent place to live, but he never got over his disappointment that it wasn't somewhere else. I thought that was what someone had told me, or maybe it was something I'd learned in school.

Years and years and years later, I found out that was not true at all. The river had been named by the Erie Indians, who called it Sha-ga-rin, which means Clear Water. Maybe so. But I can still see that explorer at the bank of the river, scanning the rolling Ohio landscape, the thick trees, the soft valleys, the middling Presidents, the hardy settlers, the medium-sized cities, the fine sturdy houses, and then swallowing his little nub of disappointment and settling in.

OKLAHOMA

CAPITAL   Oklahoma City

ENTERED UNION   1907 (46th)

ORIGIN OF NAME   From two Choctaw Indian words
   meaning "red people"

NICKNAME   Sooner State

MOTTO   Labor omnia vincit ("Labor conquers all things")

RESIDENTS   Oklahoman

U.S. REPRESENTATIVES   5

STATE BIRD   scissor-tailed flycatcher

STATE FLOWER   mistletoe

STATE TREE   redbud

STATE SONG   "Oklahoma"

LAND AREA   68,667 sq. mi.

GEOGRAPHIC CENTER   In Oklahoma Co., 8 mi. N of
   Oklahoma City

POPULATION   3,547,884

WHITE   76.2%

BLACK   7.6%

AMERICAN INDIAN   7.9%

ASIAN   1.4%

HISPANIC/LATINO   5.2%

UNDER 18   25.9%

65 AND OVER   13.2%

MEDIAN AGE   35.5

OKLAHOMA
S. E. Hinton

People often seem a little surprised to hear I'm from Oklahoma, but they are always downright shocked when I say I live here still. After all, nobody can control the circumstances of her birth, but you can write from anywhere.

It's not like I've never been anywhere else. I've traveled quite a bit, both in the states and other countries, and lived in one of the nicest places in the United States—northern California—for three years. I can't forget the scenery there, or the horse trainer who gave me invaluable help with my green-broke horse. But I never doubted I'd come back to Tulsa.

It's not because Will Rogers said the Oklahomans who moved to California during the Dust Bowl raised the IQs of both states, though I suspect he was right. He ought to know: He was born in Oklahoma and spent nearly half his life in California.

It's hard to explain other than love of home. I drive by the hospital where I was born several times a week, though it has grown from a small brick building into a several-block complex. Will Rogers High School, where I was inspired to write *The Outsiders*—in fact where I wrote a lot of it when I should have been doing other things—remains an art deco beauty, though now, in its seventies, it is getting a little worn around the edges. Well, so am I. The University of Tulsa is booming, expanding, increasing the value of my degree every year. I still hang out with friends I went to high school and college with. None of them is a writer; they're school teachers, truck drivers, bartenders. Which is good, because I never felt it was too healthy for writers to hang out with each other.

I take a class at the university every once in a while, fun now that I don't worry about papers or grades. I took a screenwriting course and was motivated to finish an original screenplay that has been optioned. And I took a course in Jane Austen that remains one of the highlights of my life—and my life has had plenty of highlights.

In the nearly sixty years I've lived here, I've watched my city grow, stagnate, grow, boom, slow down, expand. It's a pretty city; a proper city, not just a large town. We have a symphony, a great ballet, several local theater groups and we get plenty of touring productions. Tulsa sits on the Arkansas River, a beauty of a river now that it's under control. The beauty of the river makes the citizens itchy, makes them want to do something with it besides the miles and miles of biking and walking trails, the bronzes of wildlife, the playgrounds that have already improved it. I can remember when the river banks were weedy marshes and now it is the most used park system in town. I think it exists on its own merit.

Will Rogers also said everybody talks about the weather but nobody does anything about it. Well, we still can't do anything about it but in Oklahoma predicting it has become an art, and we treat the weathermen—uh, *meteorologists*—like demi-gods. We forgive them when we're shoveling five inches of "possible light flurries" off our cars because they can also tell us to the minute where the tornado will come through our neighborhood, and it's time to gather the pets and kids and photo albums and get in the cedar closet.

For this is a place where we have weather, not climate, and extremes of everything—heat, cold, floods, droughts, and of course twisters. Yes, the sky really does turn green and yes it does sound like a train. I've never been directly involved in tornado damage, and it should be easy to get blasé, but viewing the damage first-hand makes a strong impression.

In fact, contrary to popular belief the Dust Bowl was not caused by an unusual drought. It was a regular drought that occurred every dozen years or so, the difference being the tall prairie grass roots that always held the soil down like an immense web net had been sliced and diced by wheat farming. It remains the biggest manmade ecological disaster in American history. So far.

Oklahoma has all kinds of terrain, mountain ranges, flatlands, tall grass prairies where the buffalo still roam, the Great Salt Plains where you can dig up salt crystals. I live in the northeast corner called Green Country, near the Oklahoma Ozarks. It is a pretty country, with scrub oak forests, cottonwoods, a fall that can be breathtaking, and spring heralded by the wild red-buds, dogwood, and plum trees.

Right now I am sitting in a pile of kindling that used to be a yard full of old oaks and magnolias, reflecting on a record-breaking ice storm—the eighth time this year our state has been declared a disaster area, which is a record in itself.

Living with the weather here always keeps you a little on edge, a little lively, knowing the temperature can drop fifty degrees in an hour and a sunny spring day can be followed by a blizzard. In one way, it can play havoc with your nerves, but you learn to expect the unexpected, and you discover that the world is an unkind place but there are ways to deal with it without resorting to unkindness.

I live in midtown Tulsa, which is not downtown, but it's miles and miles away from the suburbs. It's an older neighborhood, full of tall oak trees and decades-old azaleas, red maples, and magnolias. Wildlife adapts here. I've seen (and heard) barred owls, red shouldered hawks, foxes, raccoons, coyotes, possums, an abundance of rabbits and squirrels, and once a flock of wild turkeys in my own yard. Before this latest ice storm I used to look out my office window to see blue jays quarreling with the squirrels in one of my magnolia trees, cardinals in the azaleas right outside my window, the flowers in the spring so white and heavy it is like I am looking out on snowdrifts.

I probably will again when spring planting gets here. Meanwhile the people who do have power are sheltering those who don't, people with trucks and chainsaws are clearing the neighbors' driveways. But there's no point claiming that virtue just for Oklahomans. Americans everywhere are resilient. That's what most people will do—plant again once the power comes back on and the mess gets cleaned up. Oklahomans are just very representative of Americans.

Tulsa is a surprisingly (to non-Tulsans) tolerant city. Sure, there are churches on practically every street corner, from Greek Orthodox to one of the largest Unitarian congregations in the United States, every kind of Baptist and fundamentalist sect imaginable—but there are also mosques and temples and places for Buddhists to meditate and you can go to one, all, or none and nobody will think any differently of you.

If you move into a new neighborhood the chances are you will be invited to join a prayer group or a poker game, but no one is offended if you say no.

There is a freedom of thought here that results in diverse opinions. I asked my son, who went to college on the East Coast and is now settled on the West, what he appreciated most about growing up in Oklahoma. After a moment, he said, "the cultural ignorance."

I was puzzled. We have access to the same Internet, the same publications, the same cable television, several of our movie theaters play the offbeat, art-house, and foreign movies that the big coastal cities get. He went on to explain, "When I was living in Hartford, everyone seemed to think whatever was emanating from New York City. In San Francisco, what San Francisco thinks is what everyone thinks. But in Tulsa, I could use my own brain to form my own opinions."

He's right. But that's not cultural ignorance, it's cultural independence. In other places, you can count on a uniformity of thought and opinions. Here nobody thinks alike. Sometimes that makes it hard to get things done, but it also makes it easy to hear all sides of an issue. You've got rough trees to scratch your thinking antlers on. You are free to use your imagination, intellect, and rationalization. No one expects anyone to think alike—in fact we take great pleasure in thinking differently.

Oklahoma is famous for its Indians, outlaws, and politicians, and a lot of the time they can be all three at once. No state is prouder of its Native American heritage, no state had a wilder frontier when there was no law west of Fort Smith, Arkansas. There was a judge there named Isaac Parker, who was fond of hanging people who needed it; naturally those who needed it preferred to get away from his jurisdiction. We have a funny way of electing officials here. Whoever can stand up and say the most goofball thing with the straightest face gets elected. Then we roll on the floor howling with laughter when the rest of the country looks at us aghast.

All of this makes Oklahoma a great place for a writer. A free place for a writer.

In 1995 a whack-job named Timothy McVeigh with a chip on his shoulder and, according to him, one planted in his butt by the Army, came to Oklahoma to strike a blow at the federal government. He murdered 168 innocent men, women, and children instead; the federal government remained unscathed.

In the aftermath of that tragedy, Oklahoma was on the news 24/7. The whole world saw people of every race, age, and economic status helping each other without hesitation. Caring for their fellow humans, setting an example for conduct during a disaster with simple, noble grace.

I was in Europe that spring, and as I watched the rest of the world watching my home state, I thought "Well, at least this will keep those fools from asking me why I still live in Oklahoma."

But it hasn't.

OREGON

CAPITAL   Salem

ENTERED UNION   1859 (33rd)

ORIGIN OF NAME   Unknown

NICKNAME   Beaver State

MOTTO   Alis volat Propriis ("She flies with her own wings")

RESIDENTS   Oregonian

U.S. REPRESENTATIVES   5

STATE BIRD   western meadowlark

STATE FLOWER   Oregon grape

STATE TREE   douglas fir

STATE SONG   "Oregon, My Oregon"

LAND AREA   95,997 sq mi.

GEOGRAPHIC CENTER   In Crook Co., 25 mi. SSE of Prineville

POPULATION   3,641,056

WHITE   86.6%

BLACK   1.6%

AMERICAN INDIAN   1.3%

ASIAN   3.0%

HISPANIC/LATINO   8.0%

UNDER 18   24.7%

65 AND OVER   12.8%

MEDIAN AGE   36.3

374

PORTLAND, 2007

My friend Mike is a painter, mainly of Oregon landscapes.

I LOVE THE LIGHT IN THIS ONE.

He works on large canvases and often chronicles the beautifully ugly confluence of man and nature.

He's the sort of guy who knows local history and can tell you what Native American tribes used to live here. For inspiration he drives to Eastern Oregon and camps in the desert for days.

For the longest time, I didn't even know Oregon had a desert.

Sometimes I look into his paintings and I feel I don't belong here.

Not because I'm not attached to Oregon—I am, and there's no place I'd rather live—but because I feel superfluous, like I'm only taking up sacred space.

J. SACCO 1-08

375

376

PENNSYLVANIA

CAPITAL Harrisburg

ENTERED UNION 1787 (2nd)

ORIGIN OF NAME "Penn's Woodland" in honor of Adm.
   Sir William Penn, father of William Penn

NICKNAME Keystone State

MOTTO "Virtue, liberty, and independence"

RESIDENTS Pennsylvanian

U.S. REPRESENTATIVES 19

STATE BIRD ruffed grouse

STATE FLOWER mountain laurel

STATE TREE hemlock

STATE SONG "Pennsylvania"

LAND AREA 44,817 sq. mi.

GEOGRAPHIC CENTER In Centre Co., 2 1/2 mi. SW of
   Bellefonte

POPULATION 12,429,616

WHITE 85.4%

BLACK 10.0%

AMERICAN INDIAN 0.1%

ASIAN 1.8%

HISPANIC/LATINO 3.2%

UNDER 18 23.8%

65 AND OVER 15.6%

MEDIAN AGE 38.0

PENNSYLVANIA
Andrea Lee

GREEN

I suddenly get Pennsylvania back in my life, when I hear the children hollering between hillsides. Hey you guys! Hey! Late one May afternoon, my son stands in the garden of our house outside Turin and yells over to the American kids who have moved in across the valley. Three anarchic towheads, whose family comes—it seems significant to me—from my home state. Their voices, ringing across woods and vineyards where Roman legions and Napoleonic troops once passed, widen the tight, civilized European landscape. The sound brings back my own childhood spring evenings in a Philadelphia suburb where our shouts have an edge of arcadian freedom, and as we scramble through the bushes, and the earth leaks shadow into the sky, we always have a sense of territory behind us, all that leaf-colored outback.

Pennsylvania, my birthplace, is green. Not because of forestage, or ecological virtue or the pastels on elementary school maps. Just in terms of the colors with which my synesthesiac mind defines alphabet letters, and states of the union. To me, Maine and Virginia are also green, but the former is a dour nordic spruce and the latter suggests pea soup. Only the Keystone State—that charmless architectural nickname that yet has a certain heavy whimsy—is the proper pastoral shade. I recognize it at once, when in a history text I first read William Penn's dreamy yet transpicuous instructions for the first layout of Philadelphia:

> Let every house be placed in the middle of its plat . . . so that
> there may be ground on each side for gardens or orchards or
> fields, that it may be a greene country towne which will never
> be burnt and always wholesome . . .

His green suggests both utopian ambition, and the kind of nostalgia for a nonexistent perfect past that Gatsby feels, gazing at Daisy's green light. It is the green of hope, that Benjamin West captures in his iconic painting of the glade beside the Delaware, where Penn and other tricorned Quakers strike their treaty with the Lenape Indians. It's the shade that European philosophers see as they first gaze over the Atlantic and envision Eden in the virgin New World forests, the same woods that inhabit Pennsylvania's name. No doubt it hovers in Voltaire's mind as he eulogizes Penn: "[He] might glory in bringing down upon earth the so much boasted golden age, which in all probability never existed but in Pennsylvania. . . ."

Golden ages are so often green.

Of course Pennsylvania has other colors: fieldstone gray; mousebrown pastures; the black of slagheaps, of shadowy faces under the El; red city bricks striped with graffiti; the blued bronze of Penn himself, enchanted into the statue whose tyrannical Quaker hat-brim for so long stunts Philadelphia skyscrapers. Yet at the same time, the green is always there: inexhaustible, ineluctable bequest of Penn the proto-suburbanite, who dies bankrupt—sucked dry by his greedy new colony—yet, one imagines, still expectant, envisioning those verdant mansions, each on its wholesome plat.

Writing about my state brings with it a rush of energy that feels almost like love. I'm not sure I love it, but all the same it's mine.

COLORED MAN'S GARDEN

In fact, my idea since childhood has been that Pennsylvania is a nursery place, to be outgrown and left behind as soon as possible. I do this early, moving from college in New England to New York to Europe, traveling to Asia and Africa. My rare trips home from what I think of as the great world, the world worth exploring and conquering, show me a Philadelphia as unbearably eroded by the passing years as my mother's face, and in the background the rest of the state—still green, but worn and disposable as an old bath mat. I marry an Italian, settle in northern Italy, and begin exploring in art and in life what it means to be a foreigner.

I'm good at being foreign—I learn it as a child. In the sixties, my parents, an elementary schoolmistress and a Baptist minister, are part of a group of black Philadelphians from the middle-class brick neighborhoods of Christian and Ringgold Streets, who advance into the suburbs with the wary determination of earlier settlers pressing back the frontier. That is: timorously proud of lawns and colonial houses; stockaded in the country clubs they've had to create; ambitious in pushing their children, like small, reluctant Indian scouts, into the new territory of white schools. Good works are part of the deal: with Quaker and Jewish friends, they march in Washington, Birmingham; boycott in Philadelphia; run fellowship weekends, work camps, youth clubs.

All this with—we kids feel it—a light but unceasing wind of fear whistling at the back of the neck. Fear of the South, its charred nooses and cattle prods such a short drive away, down Baltimore Pike, just past the shopping center;

fear, also, of the poor black masses—our brothers, but oh so removed—slowly combusting in the inner city. We kids, riding bikes, calling our faithful dogs like kids on TV, feel only half in possession of our domain. There is always a distant murmur telling us that this fat life is not our birthright. Always the possibility of running into the bad Catholic kids who throw bottles and shout nigger from cars. Always the possibility that a traveling salesman may assume that one's mother, opening the door of the big fieldstone house in her June Cleaver apron is not June Cleaver but the maid—Hattie McDaniel. My father, the civil rights leader, the broad-minded ecumenical Baptist, laughs scornfully when I asked him to plant roses in our front yard.

"And have it look like a colored man's garden?" he sneers.

So we are immigrants, but we often revisit the old country: the row houses of North and South Philadelphia. Where, in earlier years, my mother and her sisters scrub their marble steps before tripping off to Girls High; where my father trudges home from days among hostile white seminarians at Eastern Baptist; where my grandfather the insurance man has his family photographed reading in a prim Edwardian group; where an ancient cousin has crowded her what-not shelves with Moroccan brass and Navaho pottery from her travels with the Negro Women Globetrotters Association. By the time we children visit, the streets of our parents' narrow past are furnished with trash and scary nodding men with do-rags and dead eyes. Still, all the institutions—the doctor, the dentist, the hairdresser, the caterer, the undertaker—remain in the city. Not to mention my father's church, First African Baptist, its centennial gray bulk rising on Christian Street, its roots extending deep, with the bones of slaves and free blacks, into Philadelphia history. When I am very young, that name, First African, carries to me shameful savage echoes. It's not in any history books. It has little to do with the brick Georgian hall where powdered aristocrats have left a piece of parchment inscribed with freedom. In my father's church, as his baritone oratory echoes on the gilt ceiling, as the choir alternates Bach and spirituals, we hear only about burdens to be lifted, liberty still to be achieved.

Later, I'm one of the first blacks to enter a rich girls' school in a Main Line suburb. Here, as a teenager, I learn how to drug myself with literature. And spring after spring, I watch girls with cornsilk hair soar off campus in open cars, bound, I imagine, for supernal debutante parties, nymph dances in rolling pastures beyond the last commuter stop, in some mystic arch-suburb that is the real Pennsylvania. Which is for girls like them, not me.

For them, not me. This is a basic belief, a motive, that sends me away from home and across the Atlantic to a place where, for a long time, I try to shrug off my piece of America.

NOTHING

Mom, tell us some more of those weird stories about when you were a social worker back in Pennsylvania!

A car with a passel of sunburnt kids, and two women—me and my new friend, the neighbor from across the valley. Mother of the boys who shout across to my son. We're driving back through the Ligurian highlands from the beaches of the Cinque Terri.

My friend downshifts, pushes up her swimsuit strap, and launches into a series of tales of herself at twenty-one, a fresh-faced college graduate with a cape of Goldilocks hair, venturing with her new degree into the drug- and incest-ridden desolation in the country towns of southeastern Pennsylvania.

"Tell us," her boys clamor. "Tell us about the crazy Mennonite farmer and where he locked up his daughter. About that gross trailer full of roaches, like moving wallpaper. About the guy who stuck doorknobs up his butt."

The tales are startling in their grotesque humor, the light they shed on the draggled hinterland between civility and monstrosity. The fact that they come from the lips of a small, blonde, beautiful woman with an overwhelming air of health and normalcy at first makes the facts she recounts seem obscene, like toads dropping from the lips of a comely television housewife. I'm briefly shocked that she'd tell this stuff to our kids, but I see that she's in control of her narrative; that the stories are dark, but pruned of complete horror; that even the most bizarre are softened by a luminous compassion. Delivered in her clear voice, with that flat, familiar, mid-Atlantic intonation, the stories take on the exalted dimensions, the eerie pedagogic grandeur of fairy tales. And I get caught up too, guffawing in amazement. Staring out of the window at the passing landscape where plummeting valleys succeed ruined castles like illustrations from a gothic novel, I'm startled to find that my cast-off state, Pennsylvania, has become romantic as well.

My new neighbors have been transferred to Italy for two years. My friend and her husband are both from Altoona, a crumbling red-brick railroad city, set above the Juniata River almost at the center of the state, and their rambunctious family forms a traveling homeland with roots still magically connected to this land-locked region, where there are school friends, parents, cousins, acres that hold their name. They are the best American travelers I have ever seen—adventurous, courteous, without pretensions. They impress even my traditionalist Italian husband, who is shocked by the barefoot wildness of the boys, but won over by their supremely elegant confidence, the core of identity they carry with them.

"We come from nothing," my friend once jokes to me, over coffee. "Nothing" meaning: "not much money." But her half smile means that she knows how much they actually come from. What inherited wealth they've brought to the Old World. And how, as I'm beginning to understand, nothing is the beginning of everything. A starting point for stories. Another word for home.

NIGGER LIPS

I don't realize it is a mob until later. The girls of Lenape Division cluster around me under the weak bug-yellow light bulb. It's a kind of light I associate with cabins, with the image of settlers huddled in a frail carapace of logs chinked with mud, wilderness pressing in, the sighing darkness of trees punctuated with panther screams. Of course the first Europeans have no electricity, no smelly spruce-brown toilets, no stretched-out screens with girls' initials painted on them in nail polish. This is camp, a Petit Trianon exercise in bushwhacking, somewhere out in the Pennsylvania boondocks. But it's a pioneer expedition for me, because through some lapse in my parents' sensitive racial radar, I'm the only black camper in all of Camp Sunnybrook.

A Baptist institution: fairly open minded, with only a few campfire hymns. But the kids in this session are all white, and not white like my schoolmates, whose parents in sensible shoes drop by our house for tea, carrying mimeographed sheets about rallies and charity square dances. No, these kids are the white unknown, like the teenagers lounging on car hoods outside the Bazaar, our local dingy proto-mall. Kids from blue-collar suburbs where Northerners act like Southerners—burning crosses on Negro lawns. My parents sometimes slip, and call them trash. These campers aren't from Philadelphia but from far corners of the state, outside Pittsburgh, outside the pious German farm territory; from anthracite towns and half-civilized hollows on the West Virginia border. My mother has gone off with my aunt to explore ten-dollar-a-day Paris. My father is at a religious conference in Denver. And I'm abandoned to a wilderness sinkhole of unreconstructed Caucasians.

And I love them. At least I try to suck up to them, particularly my bunkmates, a big-breasted blonde from Williamsport, and an evil-tongued will-o'-the-wisp with a pixie cut, from some hamlet called Beaver. I try hard, from an animal sense of self-preservation, but also because I've always imagined winning the hearts of hateful people. I picture the cross-burners, the baying homicidal crowds in Alabama—and myself, parting the human mass like the Red Sea, sending everyone into a trance of goodwill with my courage, my good looks, my compelling speech on why all men are brothers. However, the real me is a small, bony, light-skinned girl with unkempt hair exploding out of its maternal braids into a jungle of frizz. A natural victim, I have no saving charisma, or gift for sports or for anything except scribbling poetry, a talent worthless at any camp.

Yes, I seek to impress my cohorts with tales of school, travels, my cool brothers. But here I am, under the yellow light, in the free hour before dinner when the counselors disappear with illicit cigarettes, and the killing fields are open for business.

One girl asks me where my father is.

"In Colorado. At a meeting for Baptist ministers."

"African Baptists," comes a whisper from the crowd, and everyone giggles but me.

"Where's your brothers?" demands another girl, known for her phenomenal number of scabby bug bites.

"At home with my aunt. One is working for a newspaper, the other—"

"Where's your mother?"

"In France."

A hush falls, and then my pixie bunkmate says: "I hear they like people like you there. Does your mother look like you?"

"Yes, she does, she—"

"She must be pretty," says my blonde bunkmate, who is big and bossy enough to stop this if she wants to, but she doesn't.

"Does she look like you, does she have your same mouth? Your mouth is really cute, isn't it? Your mouth—"

"Nigger lips," hisses the pixie. Something has locked my eyes to my sneakers; I can't stop staring down.

The others crack up, and break into a chant I've heard them whispering before. "Two little niggerboys sleeping in a bed / One fell out and the other one said / I see your hiney, all black and shiny!"

"To think they let these things happen in a BAPTIST camp!" rages my mother, weeks later, when she is back from Europe with souvenir cameos and kid gloves. As if religion has something to do with it.

And when my parents come to get me, I run to them, melting into them, but for days say nothing true about my two weeks in the woods.

The afternoon they pick me up, my jolly reunited family wants to picnic, to visit local beauty spots. We tour a famous cave nearby, and nobody remarks on my unusual silence as I walk through chambers of shining underground fortresses and cathedrals. Mutely I observe cascades of crystals, stalactites like frozen ghosts, mineral rainbows shining under the mountain. A photo taken that afternoon shows me perched on a log outside the cave, still in my Camp Sunnybrook T-shirt. I'm very skinny, almost transparent, and my eyes are fixed on the dark entrance with a wary yet resigned look, as if I already know what monster will peer out at me.

THE ONE WHO STAYS

My middle brother is the one who stays.

Of the three kids in our family, my oldest brother, and I, the youngest, leap in opposite directions, far from Philadelphia. Our brother, the second son, is curiously content to live where he was born. He travels around the world, visits me in Italy and his older brother in California, but is immune to the malady that gnaws his siblings: the idea that life could be better over there somewhere, out of sight.

Some facts about this brother:

Always our mother's favorite. When I am in college, I walk into the living room one day and find him and our mother chatting together like an old married couple, and realize suddenly that he has been raised by a completely different woman from the one I know. That our mother, too beautiful and eccentric to relish a Baptist helpmeet's role in the shade of her charismatic husband, has made her second son her distraction, and her great love. And who can say how much being your mother's great love has to do with a lifelong passion for your home, your city, your state?

My brother is a historian. At Penn, he runs a famous institute for urban teachers. And he gives me a rousing tour every time I come back to Philadelphia. Driving along with crunchy Philly folk-rock on the radio, pointing out new skyscrapers lifting razor-edged muzzles over streets that still carry wistful Arcadian tree names. Chatting about his good-looking wife, whom he's known since high school. Reminding me how cheese steaks still gladden the heart. Showing me how the blocks around First African have mutated into condominium sleekness; how, farther away, black men still sit dead-eyed in the morning sun.

He's not religious, but he keeps up with First African. He stops by sometimes to check on the bell tower fund. And when the oldest parishioners see him, so much like our father, they don't so much embrace him, as lay hands on him with a wondering pleasure, like Catholics touching a relic.

When I think of my brother, the question in my mind is: How is it that somebody remains? For the shiftless, shifting population of the States, staying put is unusual. In an oblique way, more of a virtue.

All through the years he stays; he busts his ass staying. He stays to help his flesh and blood through the mysteries of decrepitude, and final salutations. And we, the self-styled adventurers, the voluntary exiles, are the ones who, with a pang, receive the 2 a.m. phone calls; jump trembling onto planes; walk like timid children into the arrival zone where our brother is always there to pick us up. With his face so like ours, but transformed by a certain look, a blend of privileged sadness, and a knowledge we don't possess. Standing there waiting, of course, with his feet planted firmly on the ground.

MEETING

We, proud members of the Landsdowne Friends fifth grade, practice the words of Psalm 19 after lunch, every day for a week. We're mostly ten years old, lords of this small Quaker elementary school, just lower than the sixth-grade royalty. This psalm is for performance in Thursday morning meeting, before the elders and the rest of the school, and our anticipation gives a satisfying gravitas to those orotund King James verses about the firmament showing God's handiwork. Excited, the eighteen of us boom so loud that Teacher—all teachers at our school are called Teacher—has to regulate us like a blaring television.

We recite some verses together, and then some lucky show-offs get solos. I've been chosen to chime in with a spectacular line: "More to be desired are they than gold, yea, than much fine gold . . ." And my deskmate, her slanted black eyes gleaming through pink plastic glasses, will complete the phrase: "Sweeter also than honey and the honeycomb."

We're excited, but not in a stomach-churning way. Since second grade we've attended weekly meeting: an island in time, a morning half hour suspended in the beeswax smell of the old meeting house, set beside the school in a golf-green lawn shaded by a fat copper beech. Silence seems like the natural element for the Quaker elders who sit ranged like a tall, dusty row of idols up in the benches facing the rows where we sat. These sere figures never dress up in suits and floral hats like the solemn old deacons and church mothers of the First African Baptist church. Instead they wear sweaters and skirts and trousers in faint colors that match their gray hair and their placid faces, faces that have something historical about them. Like their last names: Penn, Bacon, Watt. They are all rich, it is rumored, but they don't care about such things. I've seen the oldest and tallest of them, his long springy legs like stilts, carrying an A&P grocery bag stiffly down Landsdowne Avenue. Because, it's said, he doesn't believe in cars.

Most of us kids aren't Quakers. We're a motley flock: black, white, Asian, gentile, and Jewish, and the school runs special assemblies featuring reform rabbis, freethinking bishops, Eastern Orthodox clergy, and even—to my embarrassment—my own Baptist father, who rambles on, as always, about love. Attending meeting is school tradition, and we memorize King James verses, they tell us, because it's English literature.

Certainly, our psalm recitations bring worldly turmoil into the meeting house. When it's not our week to recite, we listen to other classes, with the exacting scorn of opera critics. And our hearts pound during our own performances, and afterwards our faces glow with smugness.

For years things go without a hitch, but on the morning of Psalm 19, our class fails. First the short, deep-voiced boy who is our bellwether, stumbles over his verse, and, purple-faced, shudders to a halt. And I, with gold ready to pour from my lips, simply freeze. At Teacher's frenzied prompting, we burst into the chorus, about errors and secret faults. But the words are a trip wire: Somebody's helpless giggle becomes a rout. We double over, choking with uncontrollable laughter.

The beams of the meeting house ring with echoes of our debacle, and we wither under the sidelong smirks of the sixth grade. Still, in a minute a curious transformation occurs. One by one we are able to look up at the faces of the elders, which are not severe and condemning, nor yet smiling with the kind of amused indulgence with which grown-ups greet endearing childish mishaps. Nor do they display any desire to make this a character-building experience. Those old faces are simply present: alert. Regarding us and the rest of the hall with a boundless, patient comprehension that raises us to their own dignified level. Letting the silence flow back. And gradually something becomes clear: a kind of radiant indifference to words, mistaken or correct. What the elders, the Friends, pass on to us this morning is an inkling as to how strong silence is. Essential; eternal. But common, in the best sense. Always present, if we just listen for it. Inside or outside meeting.

OUT THERE

I am nineteen, and when I get home, over twenty-four hours later, there'll be a pair of detectives in my bedroom, rifling my childhood desk. My mother presiding with a bloodless terrified look that morphs into towering maternal rage, as I, clearly unchaste and impenitent, walk in with my lame excuse.

But before all this, I'm on the train to somewhere in Pennsylvania I've never been. And nobody knows, except me and one other person. Home for the summer from college, caged among the worn-out stuffed animals on my single bed, determined to cuckold my devoted boyfriend, I'm pursuing an old dream with the ferocious single-mindedness known only to sentimental young girls.

I've had white boys—had made sure, early on, to leap over that risky threshold—but L. is the first one I want and can't get. An instructor at a summer canoeing program, where at fourteen I run category three rapids on the Lehigh, and twist my guts into knots as L. flirts with older cuties in damp football jerseys. A college student, he has hair the color of a new broom, and he wears—get this—an Amish hat. Wears it irreverently, allusively, because he and his people, though not of the faith, are from one of the little allegorical towns out there in Pennsylvania German land. And he's a tormented country dreamer, a bit of a poet, who quotes Berryman and knows about Indian curses. Who ignores me and my crush except to write, for an end-of-summer skit, a sardonic verse about me losing my retainer on the trail. But after camp, we begin exchanging letters. And sensing a more-than-indulgent embryo writer, he pours out his artistic soul in a Donleavyesque stream that makes my heart beat fast. Though I sort of hate Donleavy.

Five years of high-minded correspondence, written with very few capital letters. And now I'm on my way to transform all those figments into accomplished desire. Virgin no longer, sans retainer, and with a body that I've discovered can make boys do what I want. "Take the train to Lancaster," L. writes—we've never talked on a phone   and so, informing no one at home, I grab a dawn local into Thirtieth Street Station, and from there step onto one of the old, rocking Penn Central coaches.

Past the Main Line, with its lacrosse fields and faux chateaux; past Valley Forge; past Wyeth-brown hills; into a fat, prosperous land of sappy-leaved sweetgum forest humming with cicadas, and high midsummer corn glistening like shook cellophane. It's the space of it that gets me. The fact that I, with my heart pointed like the prow of a ship toward Boston, then New York, then Europe, have all this unexplored territory outside my back door. I scan a map before leaving, and the names tickle me: White Horse. Compass. Ercildoun. Brandywine. Modena. Unicorn. Octoraro. And of course the sweetly obvious: Intercourse. Blue Ball. Paradise—an actual train stop, where across rows of soy I catch a glimpse of a gaunt black Amish carriage, poised like a scarab against the dazzling midday sun.

Content ↓

And in Lancaster, down-at-heel colonial city, with urban graffiti and a faint smell of manure, I meet my rustic poet, now deep in the writing of a history dissertation. He looks impressed by how I've grown up. In fact I'm irresistible, in tight jeans and cheap, musky perfume. How ruthless girls are! I set my sights with the brisk efficiency of a sportsman going after wild turkey. An awkward stroll through the brick downtown, and I know I can sleep with him. At the same time, I tried to ignore other, drearier, realizations. That L., the subject of years of riverine fantasies, won't be joining me in a mystic union of hearts. That I can't quite recall what it was about him that left me, at fourteen, dizzy and speechless. That presently, instead of confessing a sudden kindling of eternal love, he's lecturing me, with pedantic relish, on how the Paxton Boys exterminated the innocent remnants of the Conestoga Indian tribe right where we're standing. His Amish hat has floated away somewhere on the currents of the past, and he's got that unmistakable graduate student look of having climbed out of a root cellar.

Still, I've yearned too long to bend to simple reality. So there is the arrival at his daguerreotype-brown apartment, the smoking of the obligatory joint, and the tumble into bed. Afterwards I keep myself from despair on a strange mattress, an unknown man wheezing beside me, by imagining the huge summer night over the old brick provincial city, the countryside spreading out in dark generosity.

Early the next day, after L. leaves to teach his class, I dash down the staircase and out of the building, and run through the hot summer morning streets to the Lancaster train station as if the Paxton Boys were after me.

Of course I keep the whole thing secret. And, as secrets do, this one transforms itself in memory. By the time I've graduated, and left for a semester in France, L. and even I myself, the silly heroine, are only tiny figures: the kind landscape artists use to show scale. The lasting vision is of the countryside I dive into, with such careless glee. A landscape that doesn't start out as foreign and then slowly grow familiar, like the Europe that will absorb my future; but a familiar territory that, in a sudden act of possession grows mysterious, even precious.

But riding home that day, I salve my bruised vanity by imagining myself an intrepid adventuress.

By the time I walk through the front door, the power is so much upon me that my hysterical parents have no choice but to accept my offhand lies. Only the detectives—one black, one white, suave enough to be in a TV series—look at me with cold eyes. Their faces tell me that in their world vanished girls are mostly dead ones. And that wherever the hell I've been, I hardly deserve my luck.

IN UMBRIA

"Di dove sei?" asks the director, helping himself to more ricotta. "Where are you from in America?"

We're at lunch in Casteluccio, in an inn made of brown seventies tiles, perched high on the sweeping Umbrian mountainside, me and my husband and the director, who is an old friend of his from the time in Rome when they were both starving dolce vita boys working with Visconti. There's the director's girlfriend, too, a starlet gnawed by resentment, because he hasn't married her. It is the first time I've met the director, who is famous for only one film about flesh-eating zombies, but more famous as a womanizer. I like him more than I thought I would. White-haired and blue-eyed, shrunken and gentled by age, he turns his flirtatious attention to me with an air so dutiful that even his girlfriend doesn't mind.

"Pennsylvania," I tell him, "Philadelphia." Ready, as always in talking to Italians, to add the qualifying description: not far from New York.

But the director's eyes light up, and his girlfriend glowers as he exclaims: "Ah, Pennsylvania, my favorite place in the world!"

I look at him in disbelief.

The director is sincere. There is, of course, a woman involved. Thirty years ago, strolling in tight seventies trousers on a dock in Antigua, he met a blonde, who called from a yacht that she liked his watch, and then loaded him on board like a rent boy. She was a divorcée with two famous Philadelphia last names, and found it a lovely indulgence to sail round the world with a filmmaker whose tough Trastevere accent sounded like Italian music to her. He liked her money, her monograms, her rangy equestrian figure, but what he liked most of all was her fieldstone Montgomery County house with its rolling pastures and stalls of thoroughbreds. There was a natural gentleness about the countryside there, he says, his blue eyes opaque with regret.

I'm amused, and for one clairvoyant moment see Pennsylvania as the director does, as a bungled dream, the perfect life that got away. Hearing someone rhapsodize about your birthplace gives you a disoriented feeling, like talking to a man who long ago had a passion for your mother. Beyond this—and perhaps it is simply an old tombeur's easy charm with women—I have the odd feeling that he is speaking to me not as an Italian to a foreigner, but as he might to someone who was born and bred understanding his emotional idiom. Someone who can stare, as he does, across land and sea toward a shimmering mirage of America. It's a sly claiming of intimacy, both flattering and unsettling, and I suddenly believe all the stories I've heard about him.

"So what happened ? Why didn't you stay?" I ask.

The director starts to reply, but his girlfriend breaks in with a laugh. She says: "It's simple—the Pennsylvania bitch threw him out!"

RHODE ISLAND

CAPITAL Providence

ENTERED UNION 1790 (13th)

ORIGIN OF NAME From the Greek Island of Rhodes

NICKNAME Ocean State

MOTTO "Hope"

RESIDENTS Rhode Islander

U.S. REPRESENTATIVES 2

STATE BIRD Rhode Island red hen

STATE FLOWER violet

STATE TREE red maple

STATE SONG "Rhode Island, It's for Me"

LAND AREA 1,045 sq. mi.

GEOGRAPHIC CENTER In Kent Co., 1 mi. SSW of
Crompton

POPULATION 1,076,189

WHITE 85.0%

BLACK 4.5%

AMERICAN INDIAN 0.5%

ASIAN 2.3%

HISPANIC/LATINO 8.7%

UNDER 18 23.6%

65 AND OVER 14.5%

MEDIAN AGE 36.7

RHODE ISLAND
Jhumpa Lahiri

Rhode Island is not an island. Most of it is attached to the continental United States, tucked into a perfect-looking corner formed by the boundaries of Connecticut to the west and Massachusetts above. The rest is a jagged confusion of shoreline: delicate slivers of barrier beach, numerous inlets and peninsulas, and a cluster of stray puzzle pieces, created by the movement of glaciers, nestled in the Narragansett Bay. The tip of Watch Hill, in the extreme southwest, extends like a curving rib bone into the Atlantic Ocean. The salt ponds lining the edge of South Kingstown, where I grew up, resemble the stealthy work of insects who have come into contact with nutritious, antiquated paper.

In 1524, Giovanni Verrazzano thought that the pear-shaped contours of Block Island, nine miles off the southern coast, resembled the Greek island of Rhodes. In 1644, subsequent explorers, mistaking one of Rhode Island's many attendant islands—there are over thirty of them—for another, gave the same name to Aquidneck Island, famous for Newport, and it has now come to represent the state as a whole. Though the name is misleading it is also apt, for despite Rhode Island's physical connection to the mainland, a sense of insularity prevails. Typical to many island communities, there is a combination of those who come only in the warm months, for the swimming and the clamcakes, and those full-time residents who seem never to go anywhere else. Jacqueline Kennedy Onassis and Cornelius Vanderbilt were among Rhode Island's summer people. Given its diminutive proportions there is a third category: those who pass through without stopping. Forty-eight miles long and thirty-seven wide, it is a brief, unavoidable part of the journey by train between Boston and New York and also, if one chooses to take I–95, by car.

Historically it has harbored the radical and the seditious, misfits and minorities. Roger Williams, the liberal theologian who is credited with founding Rhode Island in 1636, was banished from the Massachusetts Bay Colony by, among others, Nathaniel Hawthorne's great grandfather. Williams's unorthodox views on matters religious and otherwise made him an enemy of the Puritans. He eventually became and remained until his death a Seeker, rejecting any single body of doctrine and respecting the good in all branches of faith. Rhode Island, the thirteenth of the original thirteen colonies, had the greatest degree of self-rule, and was the first to renounce allegiance to King George in 1776. The Rhode Island Charter of 1663 guaranteed "full liberty in religious concernments," and, to its credit, the state accommodated the nation's first Baptists, its first Quakers, and is the site of its oldest synagogue, dedicated in 1763. A different attitude greeted the indigenous population, effectively decimated by 1676 in the course of King Philip's War. Rhode Island is the only state that continues to celebrate, the second Monday of every August, VJ Day, which commemorates the surrender of Japan after the bombings of Hiroshima and Nagasaki. On a lesser but also disturbing note, it has not managed to pass the bottle bill, which means that all those plastic containers of Autocrat Coffee Syrup, used to make coffee milk (Rhode Island's official beverage), are destined for the purgatory of landfills.

Though I was born in London and have Indian parents, Rhode Island is the reply I give when people ask me where I am from. My family came in the summer of 1970, from Cambridge, Massachusetts, so that my father could begin work as a librarian at the University of Rhode Island. I had just turned three years old. URI is located in the village of Kingston, a place originally called Little Rest. The name possibly stems from accounts of Colonial troops pausing on their way to fight the Narragansett tribe on the western banks of Worden Pond, an event known as the Great Swamp Massacre. We lived on Kingston's main historic tree-lined drag, in a white house with a portico and black shutters. It had been built in 1829 (a fact stated by a plaque next to the front door) to contain the law office of Asa Potter, who was at one point Rhode Island's secretary of state, and whose main residence was the larger, more spectacular house next door. After Asa Potter left Rhode Island to work in a bank in New York, the house became the site of a general store, with a tailor's shop at the front. By 1970 it was an apartment house owned by a fellow Indian, a professor of mathematics named Dr. Suryanarayan.

My family was a hybrid; year-rounders who, like the summer people, didn't fundamentally belong. We rented the first floor of the house; an elderly American woman named Miss Tay lived above us, alone, and her vulnerable, solitary presence was a constant reminder, to my parents, of America's harsh ways. A thick iron chain threaded through wooden posts separated us from our neighbors, the Fishers. A narrow path at the back led to a brown shingled shed I never entered. Hanging from one of the outbuildings on the

Fisher's property was an oxen yoke, an icon of old New England agriculture, at once elegant and menacing, that both intrigued and scared me as a child. Its bowed shape caused me to think it was a weapon, not merely a restraint. Until I was an adult, I never knew exactly what it was for.

Kingston in those days was a mixture of hippies and Yankees and professors and students. The students arrived every autumn, taking up all the parking spaces, crowding the tables in the Memorial Union with their trays of Cokes and French fries, one year famously streaking on the lawn outside a fraternity building. After commencement in May, things were quiet again, to the point of feeling deserted. I imagine this perpetual ebb and flow, segments of the population ritually coming and going, made it easier for my foreign-born parents to feel that they, too, were rooted to the community in some way. Apart from the Suryanarayans, there were a few other Indian families, women other than my mother in saris walking now and then across the quad. My parents sought them out, invited them over for Bengali dinners, and consider a few of these people among their closest friends today.

The gravitational center of Kingston was, and remains, the Kingston Congregational Church ("King Kong" to locals), where my family did not worship but where I went for Girl Scout meetings once a week, and where my younger sister eventually had her high-school graduation party. Across the street from the church, just six houses down from ours, was the Kingston Free Library. It was constructed as a courthouse, and also served as the state house between 1776 and 1791. The building's staid Colonial bones later incorporated Victorian flourishes, including a belfry and a mansard roof. If you stand outside and look up at a window to the right on the third floor, three stern white life-sized busts will stare down at you through the glass. They are thought to be likenesses of Abraham Lincoln, Oliver Wendell Holmes, and John Greenleaf Whittier. For many years now, the bust of Lincoln has worn a long red-and-white striped hat, *Cat in the Hat*–style, on its head.

From my earliest memories I was obsessed with the library, with its creaky, cramped atmosphere and all the things it contained. The books used to live on varnished wooden shelves, the modest card catalog contained in two bureau-sized units, sometimes arranged back to back. Phyllis Goodwin, then and for decades afterward the children's librarian, conducted the story hours I faithfully attended when I was little, held upstairs in a vaulted space called Potter Hall. Light poured in through enormous windows on three sides, and Asa Potter's portrait, predominantly black apart from the pale shade of his face, presided over the fireplace. Along with Phyllis there were two other women in charge of the library—Charlotte Schoonover, the director, and Pam Stoddard. Charlotte and Pam, roughly my mother's generation, were friends, and they both had sons about my age. For many years, Charlotte, Pam, and Phyllis represented the three graces to me, guardians of a sacred place that seemed both to represent the heart of Kingston and also the means of escaping it. They liked to play Corelli or Chopin on the little tape recorder behind the desk, but ordered Patti Smith's *Horses* for the circulating album collection.

When I was sixteen I was hired to work as a page at the library, which meant shelving books, working at the circulation desk, and putting plastic wrappers on the jackets of new arrivals. A lot of older people visited daily, to sit at a table with an arrangement of forsythia or cattails at the center, and read the newspaper. I remember a tall, slightly harried mother with wire-rimmed glasses who would come every two weeks with many children behind her and a large canvas tote bag over her shoulder, which she would dump out and then fill up again with more volumes of *The Borrowers* and Laura Ingalls Wilder for the next round of collective reading. Jane Austen was popular with the patrons, enough for me to remember that the books had red cloth covers. I was an unhappy adolescent, lacking confidence, boyfriends, a proper sense of myself. When I was in the library it didn't matter. I took my cue from the readers who came and went and understood that books were what mattered, that they were above high school, above an adolescent's petty trials, above life itself.

By this time we no longer lived in Kingston. We had moved, when I was eight and my sister was one, to a house of our own. I would have preferred to stay in Kingston and live in an enclave called Biscuit City, not only because of the name but because it was full of professors and their families and had a laid-back, intellectual feel. Instead we moved to a town called Peace Dale, exactly one mile away. Peace Dale was a former mill town, an area where the university didn't hold sway. Our housing development, called Rolling Acres, was a leafy loop of roads without sidewalks. The turn into the neighborhood, off the main road, is between a John Deere showroom and a bingo hall. Our house, a style called Colonial Garrison according to the developer's brochure, was historical in name only. In 1975 it was built before our eyes—the foundation dug, concrete poured, pale yellow vinyl siding stapled to the exterior.

After we moved into that house, something changed; whether it was my growing older or the place itself, I was aware that the world immediately outside our door, with its red-flagged mailboxes and children's bicycles left overnight on well-seeded grass, was alien to my parents. Some of our neighbors were friendly. Others pretended we were not there. I remember hot days when the mothers of my American friends in the neighborhood would lie in their bikinis on reclining chairs, chatting over wine coolers as my friends and I ran through a sprinkler, while my fully dressed mother was alone in our house, deep-frying a carp or listening to Bengali folk songs. In Rolling Acres we became car-bound. We couldn't walk, as we had been able to do in Kingston, to see a movie on campus, or buy milk and bread at Evan's Market, or get stamps at the post office. While one could walk (or run or bike) endlessly around the looping roads of Rolling Acres, without a car we were cut off from the rest of the world. When my parents first moved to Rhode Island, I think they both assumed that it was an experiment, just another port of call on their unfolding immigrant journey. The fact that they now owned a house, along with my father getting tenure, brought the journey to a halt. Thirty-seven years later, my parents still live there. The Little Rest they took in 1970 has effectively become the rest of their lives.

The sense of the environment radically shifting from mile to mile holds true throughout Rhode Island, almost the way life can vary block by block in certain cities. In South Kingstown alone there is a startling mixture of the lovely and the ugly—of resort, rural, and run-of-the-mill. There are strip malls, most of them radiating from a frenetic intersection called Dale Carlia corner, and no one who lives in my town can avoid negotiating its many traffic lights and lanes on a regular basis. There are countless housing developments, filled with energy-efficient split-levels when I was growing up, these days with McMansions. There are several Dunkin' Donut shops (Rhode Island has more per capita than any other state). There are also quiet farms where horses graze, and remote, winding roads through woods, flanked by low stone walls. There are places to buy antiques and handmade pottery. Along South Road is a sloping, empty field that resembles the one where Wyeth painted Helga. There is a house on Route 108, just after the traffic light on 138, with the most extraordinary show of azaleas I have ever seen. And then, of course, there are the beaches.

We did not live on the ocean proper, but it was close enough, about five miles away. The ocean was where we took all our visitors from Massachusetts (which was where the majority of my parents' Bengali friends lived), either to Scarborough, which is the state beach, or to Point Judith Light. They used to sit on the grassy hill speaking a foreign tongue, sometimes bringing a picnic of packaged white bread and a pot of *aloo dum*. On the way back they liked to stop in the fishing village of Galilee, where the parking lots of the shops and restaurants were covered with broken seashells. They did not go to eat stuffies, a local delicacy made from quahogs and bread crumbs, but to see if the daily catch included any butterfish or mackerel, to turn into a mustard curry at home. Occasionally my mother's best friend from Massachusetts, Koely Das, wanted to get lobsters or crabs, but these, too, received the curry treatment, a far, fiery cry from a side of melted butter.

The Atlantic I grew up with lacks the color and warmth of the Caribbean, the grandeur of the Pacific, the romance of the Mediterranean. It is generally cold, and full of rust-colored seaweed. Still, I prefer it. The waters of Rhode Island, as much a part of the state's character, if not more, as the land, never asked us questions, never raised a brow. Thanks to its very lack of welcome, its unwavering indifference, the ocean always made me feel accepted, and to my dying day, the seaside is the only place where I can feel truly and recklessly happy.

My father, a global traveler, considers Rhode Island paradise. For nearly four decades he has dedicated himself there to a job he loves, rising through the ranks in the library's cataloging department to become its head. But in addition to the job, he loves the place. He loves that it is quiet, and moderate, and is, in the great scheme of things, uneventful. He loves that he lives close to his work, and that he does not have to spend a significant portion of his life sitting in a car on the highway, or on a crowded subway, commuting. (Lately, because my parents have downsized to one car, he has begun to take a bus, on which he is frequently the sole passenger.) Though Rhode Island is a place of four proper seasons, he loves that both winters and summers, tempered by the ocean breezes, are relatively mild. He loves working in his small garden, and going once a week to buy groceries, coupons in hand, at Super Stop&Shop. In many ways he is a spiritual descendant of America's earliest Puritan settlers: thrifty, hard-working, plain in his habits. Like Roger Williams, he is something of a Seeker, aloof from organized religions but appreciating their philosophical worth. He also embodies the values of two of New England's greatest thinkers, demonstrating a profound lack of materialism and self-reliance that would have made Thoreau and Emerson proud. "The great man is he who in the midst of the crowd keeps with perfect sweetness the independence of solitude," Emerson wrote. This is the man who raised me.

My mother, a gregarious and hard-wired urbanite, has struggled; to hear her recall the first time she was driven down from Massachusetts, along I–95 and then a remote, lightless stretch of Route 138, is to understand that Rhode Island was and in many ways remains the heart of darkness for her. She stayed at home to raise me and my sister, frequently taking in other children as well, but apart from a stint as an Avon Lady she had no job. In 1987, when my sister was a teenager, my mother finally ventured out, directing a day care and also working as a classroom assistant at South Road Elementary School, which both my sister and I had attended. One day, after she'd been working at the school for a decade, she started to receive anonymous hate mail. It came in the form of notes placed in her mailbox at school, and eventually in her coat pocket. There were nine notes in total. The handwriting was meant to look like a child's awkward scrawl. The content was humiliating, painful to recount. "Go back to India," one of them said. "Many people here do not like to see your face," read another. By then my mother had been a resident of Rhode Island for twenty-seven years. In Rhode Island she had raised two daughters, given birth to one. She had set up a home and potted geraniums year after year and thrown hundreds of dinner parties for her ever-expanding circle of Bengali friends. In Rhode Island she had renounced her Indian passport for an American one, pledged allegiance to the flag. My mother was ashamed of the notes, and for a while, hoping they would stop, she kept them to herself.

The incident might make a good start to a mystery novel, the type that always flew out of the Kingston Free Library: poison-pen letters appearing in a quaint, sleepy town. But there was nothing cozily intriguing about the cold-blooded correspondence my mother received. After finding the note in her coat pocket (it was February, recess time, and she had been expecting to pull out a glove), she told the school principal, and she also told my family what was going on. In the wake of this incident, many kind people reached out to my mother to express their outrage on her behalf, and for each of those nine notes, she received many sympathetic ones, including words of support from the former president of the university, Francis Horn. The majority of these people were Americans; one of the things that continues to upset my mother was that very few members of Rhode Island's Indian community, not insignificant by then, were willing to stand by her side. Some resented my mother for creating controversy, for drawing attention to their being foreign, a fact they worked to neutralize. Others told her that she might not have been targeted if she had worn skirts and trousers instead of saris and bindis. Meetings were held at the elementary school, calling for increased tolerance and sensitivity. The story was covered by the *Providence*

Journal-Bulletin and the local television news. Montel Williams called our house, wanting my mother to appear on his show (she declined). A detective was put on the case, but the writer of the notes never came forward, was never found. Over ten years have passed. South Road School has shut down, for reasons having nothing to do with what happened to my mother. She worked for another school, part of the same system, in West Kingston, and has recently retired.

I left Rhode Island at eighteen to attend college in New York City, which is where, following a detour up to Boston, I continue to live. Because my parents still live in Rhode Island I still visit, though the logistics of having two small children mean they come to me these days more often than I go to them. I was there in August 2007. My parents, children, sister, and I had just been to Vermont, renting a cabin on a lake. There was a screened-in porch, a Modern Library first edition of *To the Lighthouse* in the bookcase, and a severe mouse problem in the kitchen. In the end the mice drove us away, and during the long drive back to my parents' house, I was aware how little Vermont and Rhode Island, both New England states, have in common. Vermont is dramatically northern, rural, mountainous, landlocked. Rhode Island is flat, briny, more densely populated. Vermont is liberal enough to sanction gay marriage but feels homogenous, lacking Rhode Island's deep pockets of immigration from Ireland, Portugal, and Italy. Rhode Island's capital, Providence, was run for years by a Republican Italian, Buddy Cianci. In 1984 he was convicted of kidnapping his then-estranged wife's boyfriend, beating him with a fire log, and burning him with a lighted cigarette. In 1991 he ran again for mayor, and the citizens of Rhode Island handed him 97 percent of the vote.

It was hotter in Rhode Island than it had been in Vermont. The Ghiorse Beach Factor, courtesy of John Ghiorse, the meteorologist on Channel 10, was a perfect 10 for the weekend we were there. On my way to buy sunscreen at the CVS pharmacy in Kingston, I stopped by the library, excited to see the sign outside indicating that the summer book sale was still going on. The library has been expanded and renovated since I worked there, the circulation desk much larger now and facing the entering visitor, with a computer system instead of the clunky machine that stamped due date cards. The only familiar thing, apart from the books, was Pam. "Just the dregs," she warned me about the book sale. As we were catching up, an elderly couple with British accents approached. "Excuse me," the woman interrupted. "Can you recommend something decent? I'm tired of murder mysteries and people being killed. I just want to hear a decent family story." Pam led her away to the books on tape section, and I went upstairs to Potter Hall to look at the sale. It was just the dregs, as Pam had said, but I managed to find a few things I'd always meant to read—a paperback copy of Donna Tartt's *The Secret History*, and *Monkeys* by Susan Minot. The curtained stage that used to be at one end of the room, on which I had performed, among other things, the role of the Queen of Hearts in *Alice in Wonderland*, was gone, so that the space seemed even bigger. The grand piano was still there, but Asa Potter's portrait was at the Museum of Fine Arts in Boston, Pam later explained, for repairs. She told me she was thinking of retiring soon, and that Phyllis, who had retired long before, had discovered a late-blooming talent for portrait painting. "It's a quirky place," Pam reflected when I asked her about Rhode Island, complaining, "There's no zoning. No united front." And practically in the same breath, proudly: "Kingston is the melting pot of the state."

In the afternoon I took my children, along with my mother and sister, to Scarborough. The beach was packed, the tide high and rough. As soon as we set down our things, a wave hit us, forcing us to pick up a drenched blanket and move. Scarborough is a large beach with a paved parking lot that feels even larger. The parking lot itself is also useful in the off-season, for learning how to drive. Scarborough lacks the steep, dramatic dunes and isolated aura of lower Cape Cod, a stretch of New England coastline I have come, in my adult life, to love more than the beach of my childhood. The sand at Scarborough is extremely fine and gray and, when moist, resembles wet ash. A large tide pool had formed that day, and it was thick with young muddied children lying on their bellies, pretending to swim. My son darted off to chase England gulls. The breeze blew impressively in spite of the sultry weather, justifying Ghiorse's ten out of ten. In the distance I could see Point Judith Light. The giant billboard for Coppertone, the Dr. T. J. Eckleburg of my youth, has vanished, but I imagined it was still there—the model's toasted bikini-clad seventies body sprawled regally, indifferently, above the masses.

An announcement on the loudspeaker informed us that a little girl was lost, asking her to meet her mother under the flag on the boardwalk. Another announcement followed: The men's hot water showers were temporarily out of service. The population was democratic, unpretentious, inclusive: ordinary bodies of various sizes and shades, the shades both genetic and cultivated, reading paperback bestsellers and reaching into big bags of chips. I saw no *New Yorker* magazines being read, no heirloom tomato sandwiches or organic peaches being consumed. A trio of deeply tanned adolescent boys tripped past, collectively courting, one could imagine, the same elusive girl. The sun began to set, and within an hour the crowd had thinned to the point where a man started to drag his metal detector through the sand, and the only kids in the tide pool were my own. As we were getting up to go, our bodies sticky with salt, it occurred to me that Scarborough Beach on a summer day is one of the few places that is not a city but still manages, reassuringly, to feel like one. Two days later, I headed home with my sister and my children to Brooklyn. On our way through West Kingston to catch the highway, a lone green truck selling Dell's, Rhode Island's beloved frozen lemonade, beckoned at an otherwise desolate intersection, but my sister and I drove on, accepting the fact that we would not taste Dell's for another year.

As long as my mother and father live, I will continue to visit Rhode Island. They are, respectively, in their late sixties and seventies now, and each time I drive by the local funeral home in Wakefield, I try to prepare myself. Just after I'd finished a draft of this essay, early one November morning, my mother had a heart attack at home. An Indian doctor at Rhode Island Hospital, Arun Singh, performed the bypass operation that has saved her life. When I was a child, I remember my mother often wondering who, in the event of an emergency or other crisis, would come running to help us. During the weeks when I feared she might slip away, everyone did. Our mailbox was stuffed with get-well cards from my mother's students, the refrigerator stuffed with food from her friends. My father's colleagues at the library took up a collection to buy my family Thanksgiving dinner. Our next door neighbor, Mrs. Hyde, who had seen the ambulance pulling up to our house, crossed over to our yard as I was heading to the hospital one day, and told me she'd said a special prayer for my mother at her church.

Due to my parents' beliefs, whenever and wherever they do die, they will not be buried in Rhode Island soil. The house in Rolling Acres will belong to other people; there will be no place there to pay my respects. At the risk of predicting the future, I can see myself, many years from now, driving up I–95, on my way to another vacation on the Cape. We will cross the border after Connecticut, turn off at exit 3A for Kingston, and then continue along an alternative, prettier route that will take us across Jamestown and over the Newport Bridge, where the sapphire bay spreads out on either side, a breathtaking sight that will never grow old. There will no longer be a reason to break the journey in Little Rest. Like many others, we will pass through without stopping.

SOUTH CAROLINA

CAPITAL Columbia

ENTERED UNION 1788 (8th)

ORIGIN OF NAME In honor of Charles I of England

NICKNAME Palmetto State

MOTTO Animis opibusque parati ("Prepared in mind and resources") and Dum spiro spero ("While I breathe, I hope")

RESIDENTS South Carolinian

U.S. REPRESENTATIVES 6

STATE BIRD Carolina wren

STATE FLOWER Carolina yellow jessamine

STATE TREE palmetto tree

STATE SONG "Carolina"

LAND AREA 30,109 sq. mi.

GEOGRAPHIC CENTER In Richland Co., 13 mi. SE of Columbia

POPULATION 4,255,083

WHITE 67.2%

BLACK 29.5%

AMERICAN INDIAN 0.3%

ASIAN 0.9%

HISPANIC/LATINO 2.4%

UNDER 18 25.2%

65 AND OVER 12.1%

MEDIAN AGE 35.4

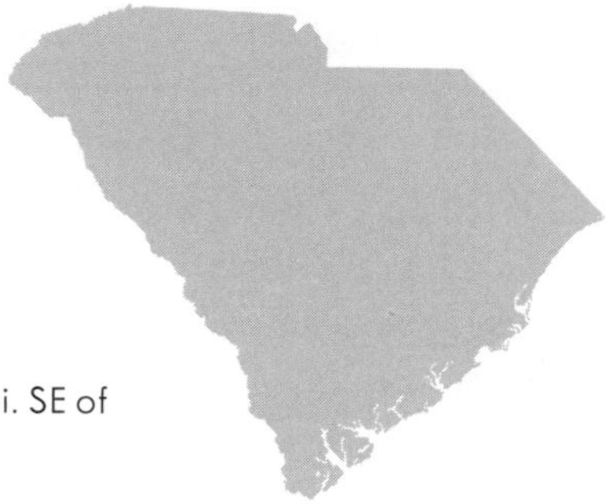

SOUTH CAROLINA
Jack Hitt

When South Carolinians proposed to separate from the United States in December 1860, a state legislator named James Louis Petigru vehemently opposed the idea. As the story goes—and it's a story every South Carolinian can tell you—Petigru rose to his feet and declared that he opposed secession because "South Carolina was too small to be a sovereign nation, and too large to be an insane asylum."

South Carolinians love that story because no other anecdote quite captures our easy rage, china-shop recklessness, and merry eccentricity. That we tell the Petigru story acknowledges that there was something profoundly idiotic about starting the war, but here's the key part: We did it anyway. Other states may be halfway between the East Coast and the West, or halfway between biggest and smaller. Ours is halfway between freedom and insanity.

I was born and raised in South Carolina. At times, I have lived in California and Oregon, Spain, New York, and Connecticut, but none of those places ever quite got its claws in me. I return to the family homestead two or three times a year because it's impossible not to. Like Petigru, I'm fond of the location. There's a lot of "there" there, which is saying something, statewise. Most states aren't *places* as much as they are political compromises or tourism slogans. Most people passionately claim their cities and patriotically claim their country. But their state?

The reason Gertrude Stein's famous insult works—"There is no there there"—is because she said it about a *city*. (Oakland.) Who'd really get upset if she'd said it about a state? Cities are supposed to possess lots of "there" because they are communities where everybody else is just down the street. At the other end of the telescope are nations, defined by Olympian matters of geography—continents, crescent valleys, archipelagos—whose identities were forged long ago, usually in blood.

States were typically born out of a minor occasion that is remembered only by some amateur historian, usually a guy at the public library (or owner of an antiques store) who self-publishes an unreadably earnest account of state lore. States tend to be matters of property law, borders that are either Euclidean lines etched across the landscape by a frontier surveyor whose name escapes me right now (check with the local historian, he'll know).

Or, the border is a squiggly line that follows the bank of a major waterway where, once upon a time, it seemed logical to set a border since all the people who lived across the river were funny looking, and unwashed, and spoke in unpleasantly guttural grunts, and whose women were alluringly promiscuous, and whose menfolk all possessed comically small or terrifyingly large penises, depending.

For the longest time, states made no sense whatsoever, and few could really care. We still don't quite know what state Andrew Jackson can claim as his birthplace—both North and South Carolina have a say in this—because it's not altogether certain just where the line ran through the Waxhaw Settlement when his mother had him in 1767.

Then we had the War Between the States, and suddenly states mattered a great deal. And, in time, each of them accrued a kind of character. Most states can sum up their identity in an official slogan or a bumper sticker. Don't expect to find "I ♥ South Carolina" plastered on too many cars when you're driving through. The feelings run a bit deeper than Chamber of Commerce marketing. The state's identity is a long story—actually a lot of short stories, like the Petigru one. These are mostly old stories that every card-carrying South Carolinian knows how to tell, although a few new disturbing ones have recently been added to the playlist.

Here's another one. It concerns the famous remark made by some distant orator from North Carolina. Apparently he rose to speak (everybody rose to speak back then; they had no talk-show sofas). And he identified himself as a citizen of North Carolina—"that vale of humility located between two mountains of conceit." Anyone reared in the southeast of America knows he was referring to the twin peaks of southern gentry: Virginia and South Carolina.

And this is where it gets interesting because Virginia may be seen as a vast swath of aristocracy, but no one thinks of South Carolina that way. They think of red-necks from Spartanburg, inbreds from the Piedmont, pig-biters from Edgefield County, the redbones of Sumter County, or hillbillies scattered among the hills rotting out their brains on lead-tainted moonshine.

Right. The aristocracy in South Carolina was more confined, to the "Lowcountry" specifically, or more accurately, Charleston, or to get right down to it, downtown Charleston south of Broad Street. Which is where I grew up.

South Carolina is a high-strung place, born of the tension between one arrogant, scornful, haughty, supercilious, snooty, proud, puffed-up, peacock of a town—Charleston—and the rest of the state. This tension defines almost everything in the state and manifests itself in every aspect of life there, even geography. There is the Lowcountry and there is the Piedmont.

If South Carolina often told the rest of the country to get lost, then Charleston just as often had the same message for the rest of South Carolina.

James Louis Petigru? Charlestonian.

Charlestonians feel, in a measure far exceeding any other town except for maybe Rome, that their ancestry and birth is a glorious gift from God. They like to say that the two rivers that shape the peninsula of downtown Charleston—the Ashley and the Cooper—"come together to form *the Atlantic Ocean.*"

Here's another story you always hear. An old man whose parents brought him to Charleston as an infant had spent his entire, long life there. He'd gone to the local school with the other boys. As an adult, he served on the vestry at St. Philip's Episcopal Church and headed a named law firm on Broad Street. He was a member of the Carolina Yacht Club and joined all the right Charleston societies. When he finally died, the town folks buried him among the most prestigious plots at St. Philip's and on his gravestone it listed all his local achievements and then concluded, "We miss him as one of our own."

Charleston always strained to draw a sharp line between the aristocrats and the hicks, or in the old language, the bourbons and the red-necks. The upstate had hoedowns; Charleston had the St. Cecilia Society, a club devoted (technically) to the love of classical music. Charleston hosted sailboat regattas; the upstate held drag races. Charlestonians traveled in Packards, then Cadillacs, then BMWs, while the Piedmont folks drove jacked-up rattletrap trucks to the NASCAR races at the Darlington 500.

When I was growing up, no one ever flew the provocative battle flag of the Confederacy in Charleston. This had nothing to do with anyone's Petigru-esque thoughts on the war; any gentleman downtown could discourse on battlefield valor in the "Late Unpleasantness" until your head exploded. But the battle flag? That was white trash.

I visited an old Charlestonian friend once at his country house and his parents also drove in from downtown for a big cookout. He had the Confederate flag flying off his porch, and he tried out the new "heritage not hate" line. But his mother protested that he should take it down. For her, all that in-your-face Confederate stuff was just too vulgar, too *red-necky.*

Upstate South Carolinians speak in the rural twang made famous by Gomer Pyle and the man-rapers of *Deliverance.* Charlestonians spoke

Charlestonese, which is heavily influenced by the African-American speech known as Gullah—a musical way of talking in which the speaker chews up and swallows most of a word while lingering lyrically over the occasional interesting vowel.

The split falls along religious lines, too. Upstate was Baptist and involved a lot of church-going while the Lowcountry was predominantly Episcopalian and considered attendance at Easter and Christmas just fine. Charlestonians had long ago ceded all the adult responsibility to the upstate. The Baptists wanted all the moral outrage and preachers' fury? Fine. They could have it. And they could have all the political posturing, too. Some 200 years ago, when Charleston was the state capital, they kicked out the politicians and sent them to the geometric center of the state, Columbia, a town ridiculed then as the middle of nowhere and despite the influx of nearly 120,000 people in the intervening two centuries still described that way in Charleston.

The upstate was H. L. Mencken's notorious "Sahara of the Bozart," an endless chain of speedtrap parishes with economies gone bust a century ago. The mills closed down and nothing came to replace them. In the century of desolation to follow, the local Baptist ministers convinced their neighbors that this ruination had nothing to do with themselves, but rather the Jews and "the Negro." Nowadays, the more enlightened preachers are hip enough to pin it on the "Hollywood liberals" and "inner-city welfare queens."

Plus ça change.

As the moral fundamentalists wailed from pulpits all across the upstate, Charlestonians merrily wallowed in being dismissed as Whiskeypalians. They loved it that the blue noses freaked out, learning about our private drinking societies, speakeasy bars, or the annual Rockville Regatta—a boat race so notorious for its decadent onshore parties that the one sure mark of being a naïve outsider was showing up with a sailboat. Yet with all these differences, here is the one truth every Charlestonian knew: Eventually, the most adventurous of those Baptists would find an excuse to come downtown—to drink our liquor, smoke our cigarettes, and dance with our debutantes.

One of those hicks was my father. A beanpole of a kid from a dusty podunk called Bamberg, my father attended The Citadel, the local military college. He mastered cotillion dancing in the arms of a downtown belle who also introduced him into the pleasures of drinking and smoking, and later bore him five children, the last of whom is now telling you this story.

What has kept our peninsula of mutual self-congratulation so splendidly isolated and cocksure is, oddly, architecture. If you've been there, you know that Charleston is a little village of antebellum houses. We don't have mighty mansions of the Newport variety. One of the biggest houses we have—the Calhoun Mansion, as it's called—is hardly impressive by mansion standards. Charleston's physical beauty comes from being an entire collection of modest, lovely things. Street after street of regular residences with side piazzas and old longleaf pine clapboarding painted so many times that south of Broad is a fusion of antique textures, mottled bricks, tilted walls, comfortably settled foundations, sagging shutters, rusting earthquake rods, and shimmering old panes of glass. I always tell visitors to Charleston to skip the tours and the official nonsense. Just fix a cocktail (a traveler, the old folks called them) around 4 p.m. on a sunny afternoon and head off down the streets amid the light of the setting sun angling in and around the warm lived-in-ness of our snug alleys.

The classic Charleston dwelling is called a single house. On the street, it is one room wide and then retreats backward—a series of rooms stacked one after the other like a railroad flat, often an unlikely number of them. The story goes that property taxes were once configured according to how much house fronted the street. So the city quickly became populated by these tall lanky houses that sidled up to the street like a man cocked sideways at a bar. The town possesses a public sense with its privacy tantalizingly just out of view. The houses might face out, acknowledging the exterior world, but keep a strong sense that what is really happening lies hidden behind a blaze of azaleas, ginkgos, and massive live oaks.

The other quality of Charleston's architecture that perpetuated its beauty was disaster. After the American Revolution, Charleston never had enough money to fix the town up, tear the old places down, and build gleaming new ones. Historically, Charleston and Boston were very similar towns, sister towns. In the storied, distant past, they were both port cities that traded visiting debutantes and brides for grooms and otherwise kept an easy exchange of money and goods and ideas. As Charlestonians love to tell you, there was a Charleston Tea Party, too.

Then Boston expanded and eventually luxuriated in the Industrial Revolution and ditched much of its colonial architecture for the next new style until they tore down that one and then on into the present day of gleaming office towers, downtown malls, and Boston's City Hall, a massive concrete puck of eye-averting brutalist density. Charleston was stuck with itself and never really got on her feet. Every time it looked like prosperity might be coming, some new disaster struck. It might be the War of 1812, the Panic of 1819, the Great Fire of 1838, the Civil War blockade of 1862–65, Reconstruction, the Great Earthquake of 1886, the Panic of 1893, World War I, the Depression, World War II, or Hurricane Gracie in 1958. Whatever it was, it seemed as if every generation, circumstances forced us back into our old houses—broke once again but willing to make do with the only claim to greatness always within reach. Ourselves.

Like so much Southern aristocracy, Charleston's was mostly myth. Few families downtown had any money. So we turned that embarrassing detail into a point of pride. My mother would sometimes take note of some Charlestonian who was "wealthy enough to have a maid out front polishing the brass door-knocker but too poor to put food on the table." I was almost out of high school before I realized that my widowed mother and I were pretty much two of those Charlestonians.

The city's arrogance emerged organically long ago as a bulwark against the town's persistent poverty, tough times, and just bad luck. In the days of everyone's great-grandparents, the attitude was, we might not have money, and we might live in these ratty old houses, and we might actually be poor and we might live next door to a black person (or secretly *be* a black person), but we are Charlestonians, okay? And you're not.

I say ratty old houses because the pride Charlestonians take in that old architecture downtown is of fairly recent vintage. Most of our history we shamefully patched up the old places after the latest fire/hurricane/earthquake/depression/war. The preservationist surge that developed in Charleston occurred in the mid-twentieth century. And what saved a great deal of the beautiful antebellum architecture from destruction was—I am proud to report—the vulgarity of my great-grandfather, Walter Pringle. He lived in one of the premier houses downtown in those days, the Col. John Stuart house on the corner of Tradd and Orange. It is the house where, it is said, the revolutionary war hero Francis Marion ("The Swamp Fox") escaped a British raid by leaping out a second-floor window, breaking his ankle on the ground, and running off anyway.

Walter, or Fardee, as the family called him, lost most of his wealth in the Depression. His wife never again left the house for a social occasion—paralyzed by the shame of not being able to reciprocate the invitation. Then, one day, a Yankee museum of American "interiors" offered him a dollop of money for the drawing room of his house—the floor boards, the moldings, the fireplace, etc. It was enough that he could rebuild the room with suitable reproductions and have a comfortable sum left over, so he took the deal.

One day, in came the Yankees to pry up the floorboards and take down the walls to the structural foundations. When the elegant ladies downtown found out that crazy Walter (he looked like a bantam-sized version of Colonel Sanders) was selling off the city's treasures and doing so by practically reenacting a kind of Shermanesque violation of the town, they freaked out. According to family lore, the group founded by these ladies—the Society for the Preservation of Old Dwellings—pushed for a zoning ordinance (which passed) declaring some 4,800 houses and 138 acres of the Charleston's peninsula to be forever afterward an "Old and Historic District."

I went hunting for this room, and sure enough, you can visit my great-grandfather's notorious drawing room online nowadays. It's funny because when I was growing up the aunt of many of my friends, Francis Edmunds, ran a similar outfit, the Historic Charleston Foundation. (The city is clotted with such 501(c)(3)s these days.) She always treated me with a kind of cautious distance, and it wasn't until I was much older that I wondered if Francis probably didn't see me as irredeemably tainted by my great-grandfather's original sin. This is how Charleston works. As the great man said, the past is not even past.

But the past is not what it used to be, either. Two leveling forces—Republican politics and Hurricane Hugo—have recently managed to homogenize the state and, I fear, relieve the fundamental tension of South Carolina.

Throughout most of the South in the eighties, the old-line Southern Democrats were being driven from office by a wave of new Reagan Republicans. The populist presentation of this new Republican was very working class, very pickup truck, very red-neck, very *upstate*. It was the Moral Majority and Baptist preachers. It was NASCAR and trucks, guns and dogs, lots of church-going. There was not a lot of party-indulging or looking the other way for a bit of pot-smoking. While there was some cotillion-attending and society dancing, not so much since the new Republican was trying to shed the country-club image. The appeal of the new blue-collar hard-working Republican red-neck became so engaging a symbol that I started seeing him far outside the South. In the early 1990s, I began to see the Confederate flag on pickup trucks in *Connecticut*. Young Republicans everywhere saw in the red-neck a pure emblem of the American rebel in political revolt against all that Democrats had come to symbolize—deficit spending, bureaucratic incompetence, internationalism.

The appealing character of the Southern red-neck became attractive to everyone. Lewis Grizzard was the first to work Tobacco Road for jokes, doing for red-necks what Erma Bombeck was doing for housewives.

Now we live in a world of red-necks—Johnny Knoxville, Jeff Foxworthy, King of the Hill, Larry the Cable Guy, Bill Engvall. One of SIRIUS Radio's most popular business moves was wrangling the "Blue Collar Comedy" Channel. After this kind of comedy's stunning success in movies, concerts, books, and DVDs, SIRIUS issued a press release when it happened in 2006, boasting, "Blue Collar brand expands to satellite radio." Red-neck is a brand now, like shampoo.

And people adopted that brand, especially politicians. George Allen was a fake Southerner who served as the senator from Virginia, but grew up in California. As a young man, he moved to Virginia, developed a twang, and got so far into character he publicly ridiculed a dark-skinned man as "macaca" and lost his job.

The most famous fake Southerner, of course, is George W. Bush, born in New Haven, Connecticut; reared amid the breezy glades of Kennebunkport, Maine; schooled at Andover, Yale, and Harvard—as Yankee a pedigree as one could possibly imagine. Yet as a young adult he moved to Texas, learned to speak cowboy, got hisself a pickup truck, found a hat, and just a few months before he began his presidential campaign, he bought that Crawford ranch.

Red-neck chic happened all over the South. For a lot of us, it was amazing throughout the 1980s to watch the diverse South suddenly get so quickly homogenized and then encased in the tacky amber of RC Colas, squirrel pie, and mayonnaise Jell-O molds. I grew up eating and doing none of this stuff, and yet, everywhere I went, I was suddenly expected to share my presumed expertise on Coca-Cola as birth control, the recipe for roadkill gumbo, and the pleasures of incest.

Outfits like the Center for the Study of Southern Culture opened for business and it seemed that one side effect of their existence was to stamp one popular version of the South across the land. There was no room for an Elvis-dissenter anymore. We were all hound dogs now.

In Charleston, I just assumed that our native arrogance would serve as a bulletproof shield to this change. But these flattening forces proved inexorable. Sure, the bachelor balls are still held, but the pickup trucks are everywhere. The emphasis is on the good old boy. Friends I used to sail with and who never got anywhere close to a NASCAR race when we were little now insist to my face that they've always *loved* the Darlington 500. The Charleston accents of my generation now ring with an unconsciously Bushian twang. Folks who used to tell me belittling jokes about hicks now send me emails headed, "You may be a red-neck if . . ."

These delicate differences that defined South Carolina (and the rest of the South, too) have been composted into a giant steaming mulch pile of faux Republican red-neckism. And yet, Charleston could easily have pulled out of even this sweeping cultural shift, except that in the middle of it all came the most powerful hurricane in decades: Hugo. Late one evening, in September 1989, I watched it come ashore on *Nightline* in my apartment in New York City. Ted Koppel had on some goofy professor of meteorology who was standing in a wind tunnel to show us the effect of hurricane winds. They turned on the machine and ratcheted up the speed to simulate what Hugo was doing right then to my hometown. I watched as the professor's cheeks melted into rubber and started beating the back of his head.

I got worried.

I called my sister on the telephone at about quarter of midnight. She was in her house with her family and my mother. I had called earlier that day and my mother had insisted that hurricanes weren't really that big a deal. Now, this is all I heard: "Can't talk now, brother, trees have fallen on the house, opened up the roof. Hugo is in the house. We're retreating to the back rooms. Pray for us." Click.

I ran around my New York apartment in total despair. I called my friend, Gus, another Charlestonian across town. He was already talking to another Charlestonian, John, and they were gassing up a car to drive home and save their parents. They picked me up and a few minutes later, we were on I–95, traveling near twice the speed limit. Driving through the night, we arrived in Charleston, miraculously, at lunchtime the next day.

Part of the way, we took a back highway we thought might be less clotted with fallen-over trees and on that drive we saw true Lowcountry horror. Entire swaths of longleaf pine trees laid over uniformly on their sides, as if some vengeful giant had decided to sit down on the Francis Marion Forest. Everywhere, images of powerful destruction. Those big interstate signs? Balled up like green tissue on the side of the road. Ancient live oaks, half a millennium old, lifted right out of the ground, lying unnaturally on their sides. In curiously cleared-out areas, we saw eerie orange fluff snagged in the nearby trees—baffling for a moment until we realized we were looking at insulation and all that was left of a mobile home.

For Charlestonians, it is safe to say, Hugo was taken in stride. After all, Charlestonians were used to it. We all grew up looking at Matthew Brady's famous pictures of the collapsed heaps on Meeting Street, the rubble left by so much Civil War cannonade. We all grew up looking at pictures of the charred houses after the Great Fire. We all grew up looking at snapped church spires from earlier storms, or the hideous Depression-era photos of Market Street, populated only by man-sized buzzards snacking on dead cats.

What was Hugo but another in a long line of these? Wouldn't we weather this? Rebuild? Hold on as our ancestors did? I stayed in Charleston for two weeks, helping my sister's family clear a half dozen trees off her house. And when my mom and I finally got downtown, her house's first floor was filled with water, the ancient family rug buried under five inches of mud. We shoveled it out and set to fix things. Everyone in town was up to the same work. It's what Charlestonians did—start the slow journey back to normal life.

Only one thing was different now. It wasn't slow this time. This time there was massive amounts of insurance money (over $2 billion) to rebuild houses and lots of FEMA funds to fix everything else (roughly $300 million). The Federal Emergency Management Association. For years, we'd always derided it as the *Florida* Emergency Management Association.

Now Charleston was suddenly on the receiving end of all that insurance and federal money. Within a year, the town was more spruced up than it has been since Ben Franklin started a newspaper there. Everybody had a new paint job, the bricks got repointed, every house was refurbished pretty much at the exact same time. This had never happened and suddenly the architectural jewel of the South was photographed everywhere, written about everywhere, seen by everyone. A slow trend of noticing Charleston that had begun with the Spoleto Festival and a PR campaign delicately drawing the upstate/Lowcountry distinction ("South Carolina's Best Preserved Secret") now picked up galloping momentum. Outsiders, really rich outsiders, looked at these old beautiful houses and started bidding up the prices.

Poverty, which had long protected the city from outside markets, was gone. The city was all gussied up for the first time, and the sales started to click. I remember hearing that my cousin Ashmead's house was up for sale and, sitting in New York, I flipped to the back of the *New York Times Magazine* to see one of those quarter page ads. His house was selling for close to a million, an unheard of sum of money. I called friends to marvel at it without realizing this was no anomaly to celebrate but a bull market starting to stampede. Within the decade, Charlestonians sold their city right out from under themselves. (In 2003, Ashmead's house went for $6.9 million.)

The number of super-wealthy software jockeys and corporate chieftains who wanted to own a "Charleston house" overwhelmed downtown. (Confession: My family talked my mom into selling her modest place and moving across the Cooper River.) The exodus began and my regular visits home often had me bypassing the very part of town where I grew up. Instead, I found myself in Mount Pleasant or out on Wadmalaw Island or renting a house on the beach.

Now when I go downtown, it's like taking a walk on a Hollywood set. The houses are all, still, extremely well maintained. They are painted every year after a hot summer of salty wind. The slate roofs are perfectly set. And the new immigrants in Charleston have a name: house collectors. These words are uttered with withering disdain (in Mount Pleasant and Wadmalaw). The phrase refers to those itinerant plutocrats who bought the houses and maybe show up in the spring, when the air is still cool enough to sit out on the porch. Their friends fly in aboard their private jets, they hold a big party, and then they are gone. The emptiness they leave behind is palpable. The city I grew up in pedaling my bike everywhere has almost no bikes, kids, or people—other than organized tours—walking the streets. We used to make fun of the John D. Rockefeller–built Potemkin village of a colonial town called Williamsburg, Virginia. But increasingly—and it pains me to say this—the new Charleston with its swarm of tour guides in tri-corner hats or hoop skirts looks a whole lot like it.

The loathing of these outsiders has even wormed its way into the law. One of the great ladies of historic Charleston, Phyllis Walker, helped to create a new kind of property covenant called a "primary resident easement." It attempts to insure that homes will only be sold to locals or at least to people who intend to live in them for most of the year. But it's probably too late.

With the Great Charleston Diaspora, the old city feels scattered around itself, out on those islands and smaller towns where the older folks (like my mom) now live, as if in waiting. I get the sense that the old Charlestonians believe that the house collectors will eventually feel the local disdain for their drive-by love of our architecture and eventually sell their places at a tremendous loss back to the people who have always lived there and then go away.

I'm not sure that's going to happen. The free market has ended a very long reign and, with it, has alleviated the tension that defined the state of

South Carolina. Charleston is no longer a place. As the real estate ads put it so brutally, Charleston now is a "lifestyle." Anybody with enough money can live it. For the first time in a long run, Charlestonians and South Carolinians have to wonder just what "there" can be salvaged now amid the exploding Floridian sprawl of generic golf courses, cookie-cutter marinas, and gated communities with cotton-candy names like Reverie on the Ashley, The Preserve at Fenwick Plantation, Sable on the Marsh, and, my favorite for sheer naïveté: Rivertowne.

A while back, I was interviewing the former CEO of PepsiCo. In the opening chat of the conversation, he detected a bit of a Charleston accent come out of my mouth and asked me where I grew up. I told him.

"Oh, I love Charleston," he said. Yes, I replied, it is unquestionably a beautiful place.

"I have a house there," he told me. Oh, I said, where? What street? He seemed surprised.

"You would know the street?" he asked. I told him that everyone downtown knows every street, every house. I could draw the entire downtown tomorrow from memory with as much precision as James Joyce could draw Dublin.

"Meeting Street," he said.

"Ah! Where? What number?" I replied.

"Oh, come on," he laughed. "You'd know the number?"

Pretty much, I insisted. My friend Parker lived at 76 Meeting and Canty was 40-something. Charlotte was in the 30s probably, and the Bennetts, too. The Hawks were at number 1—

He stopped me, apparently in awe. I explained to him that this was nothing to anybody who grew up there. The place just isn't that big and we all grew up running in and out of each other's houses.

"I don't know the number," he confessed. "I haven't yet visited the house in Charleston. I've never been there."

SOUTH DAKOTA

CAPITAL   Pierre

ENTERED UNION   1889 (40th)

ORIGIN OF NAME   From the name of a Sioux tribe
meaning "allies"

NICKNAMES   Mount Rushmore State or Coyote State

MOTTO   "Under God the people rule"

RESIDENTS   South Dakotan

U.S. REPRESENTATIVES   1

STATE BIRD   ring-necked pheasant

STATE FLOWER   American pasqueflower

STATE TREE   black hills spruce

STATE SONG   "Hail! South Dakota"

LAND AREA   75,885 sq. mi.

GEOGRAPHIC CENTER   In Hughes Co., 8 mi. NE of Pierre

POPULATION   775,933

WHITE   88.7%

BLACK   0.6%

AMERICAN INDIAN   8.3%

ASIAN   0.6%

HISPANIC/LATINO   1.4%

UNDER 18   26.8%

65 AND OVER   14.3%

MEDIAN AGE   35.6

SOUTH DAKOTA
Saïd Sayrafiezadeh

The idea of traveling to South Dakota for vacation had been all mine. I hit upon it one night in my apartment on the Lower East Side of Manhattan. I was casually flipping through a glossy travel magazine with my wife, Karen, when I spotted a photograph of a bighorn sheep standing in the middle of the Badlands and gazing seductively at the camera.

"Let's go there!" I said.

South Dakota had an exotic quality to me, despite the fact that it was located in the center of the United States. It would be like going to another country: Finland, maybe. The Lower East Side, after all, was the epitome of East Coast urban living, concrete and steel and so many orthodox Jews that the elevator in my apartment building had been programmed to stop on every floor during the Sabbath to avoid the proscription on work.

After that, Karen did the research and made the phone calls, occasionally presenting various options about things to do and places to visit—none of which I had any real opinion about. The Badlands: Sure. The Black Hills: Why not? Mount Rushmore: Might as well.

"Do you want to go trout fishing?" she'd ask.

"Sure," I'd say. "What the hell?"

I'd never been trout fishing before—I'd never been *fishing* before—but it didn't matter. The whole trip felt like an adventure and I was up for anything. None of my friends had ever traveled to South Dakota or had ever even considered traveling there—and I liked that. I believed that it revealed in me a certain pioneering spirit.

"South Dakota!" friends would say with alarm when I told them where we were going. "What's there to do in South Dakota?"

"Trout fishing," I'd say casually.

When we arrived at the Rapid City Regional Airport, it seemed so minuscule and empty that it reminded me of an elementary school after hours. I took that to mean that South Dakota is also minuscule and uninhabited. To judge by the airport, there were also no black people living in South Dakota. There were, however, American Indians. I knew this because of an enormous exhibit of black-and-white archival portraits that had been donated by the Farm Bureau of Western South Dakota and which took up an entire wall next to the bathroom.

I studied the display. "Dedicated to the good will and better understanding of all people," a plaque read. The giant photos were of a reunion that had been held some sixty years ago in Custer State Park for the survivors of the Battle of the Little Bighorn in 1876. Nine elderly Indian men with grim faces and names like Dewey Beard and Iron Hawk sat in a grassy field, both singularly and then as a group, staring off into the distance toward their childhood selves caught in the midst of slaughter. The Indians were dressed traditionally in long-sleeved shirts with modest zigzag patterns, and on their heads they wore enormous fluffy feathered headdresses. It was billed as a reunion but it didn't appear to be a festive one. It looked dismal and disheartening, and it led me to wonder if the Indians had been costumed by a Farm Bureau publicist. The whole thing looked more like an unfortunate picnic in which many invitations had been sent but only nine had bothered to show up. Those nine now lamented their decision.

The plan in South Dakota was for us to spend four days in the Badlands and then four days in the Black Hills. Our first order of business, however, was to go grocery shopping. This was no small matter. Karen and I are both vegetarians, or as close to being vegetarians as one can be while occasionally eating chicken or beef, and we had paid extra to have a cabin with a kitchen. Our diet was comprised not just of organic fruits and vegetables, but also of a complicated mixture of whole grains and beans and nuts and oils and rice milk and small wild fish, all of which my nutritionist had patiently counseled me on, and all of which Karen had cautioned me might not be easily available in South Dakota. "All they eat is beef," she said, "and not just beef but bison beef." In preparation for our trip, we had briefly considered bringing along with us a week's worth of brown rice and black beans and agave nectar and other staples, but as the list grew longer we soon saw the impracticality of this. Instead, Karen had discovered online a health food store in Rapid City, apparently one of two in the entire state. So instead of packing our suitcase with beans, we packed it with our eight-quart Fagor pressure cooker, which we then stuffed with our underwear and socks.

So the first thing we did the morning after arriving in Rapid City was to drive ten minutes through wide vacant streets to Staple & Spice Market located on Mt. Rushmore Road. It was a nice store, clean and airy, but it was a far cry from Integral Yoga Natural Foods in Manhattan, where I shopped once or twice a week.

"They don't carry teff," I let Karen know.

"Who cares?" Karen said.

"I'm disappointed."

"Would you rather eat bison burgers for the next eight days?"

We spent the greater part of an hour carefully choosing all that we thought we'd need to survive our week. In a burst of inspiration I recommended buying a bottle of toasted sesame oil as a quick and easy way to add zest to our salads and sautés. In the end our total came to $126.69. This, unfortunately, did not include any fruits and vegetables, which Staple & Spice Market for some reason did not carry.

"You can try Albertsons," the cashier offered.

Albertsons was on Omaha Street. It took us fifteen minutes to get there. It should have taken us five but I read the map wrong and we got lost.

"Look how gigantic it is," Karen said as we pulled into the parking lot.

Whereas the airport in Rapid City was the size of an elementary school, the grocery store was the size of an airport. Upon entering it we were immediately dwarfed by the brightly colored boxes and bottles and bags that towered above us, running aisle after aisle. We meandered slowly through the near empty store. Where was everyone?

"Is it a holiday?" I said to Karen.

"Oh, no," Karen exclaimed. "The rice milk is cheaper here!"

For a moment we debated returning to Staple & Spice, but the day was getting on, and the Badlands were waiting, and so we quickly loaded up on romaine lettuce and cucumbers and tomatoes and mustard greens and bottled water and bananas and oranges. I felt guilty about the bottled water. I recalled how Mayor Bloomberg had just recently informed New York that not only was New York tap water the best in the country, but that the trillion discarded plastic water bottles were doing irreparable harm to the environment. I wasn't sure if South Dakota could make a similar claim regarding its tap water, and who knows what had happened to the generations of South Dakotans who had consumed it, and so rather than take a chance I bought eight gallons.

After that, we were hungry.

So we got back in the car and drove another fifteen minutes until we happened upon Main Street, which looked to be the city's premier shopping district. The street was exceptionally wide and exceptionally spotless, and it was fronted by little restaurants and shops, most of them not yet open for the day, even though it was almost noon. It just so happened that the Central States Fair annual parade was taking place that morning, and Karen and I watched as burly men in cowboy hats rode past on horses, followed by little girls on horses, followed by municipal garbage trucks, followed by Shriners wearing maroon fezzes and riding mopeds, followed by Bozo the Clown, followed by a silver Mustang Convertible carrying Lynae Tucker, National American Miss South Dakota Junior Teen, waving cheerfully to the smattering of onlookers that lined the sidewalks. Karen and I waved back.

Across from us was a place called B&L Bagels, which, despite being shiny and new, made me think fondly of Kossar's Bialys on the Lower East Side that's been making bagels for something like sixty-five years.

"Let's eat bagels," I said enthusiastically to Karen.

As we were waiting for our bagels to be toasted, I happened to overhear a woman behind me talking about yoga, and after some hushed discussion with Karen I got up the nerve to ask the woman if there was a yoga studio in the area.

"Oh, yes," the woman said, smiling warmly at me. In fact, she was the teacher. But it turned out that the class was only held once a week. She gave me the information anyway and I wrote it down and I promised that if we ever happened to be in Rapid City on a Tuesday night at seven o'clock we'd definitely come by and take her class. Then we chatted for a little while. She was about thirty-five years old, and she was lean and lithe like a yoga teacher, with blond hair and clear skin. She said that she was originally from Fort Lauderdale, but had moved to Rapid City ten years ago because she "didn't feel safe in Fort Lauderdale."

"I love it here," she said. "I feel completely safe."

I told her we were visiting from New York.

"I love New York," she said. "I've been there a few times. I would never feel safe enough to live there, though."

Safety was obviously paramount for her.

"I think New York's pretty safe," I said.

"In Rapid City," she said, "you can stand on the sidewalk and talk to someone without getting mugged."

This seemed to be an outlandish child-like view of the danger of urban life and I wanted to say so. I also started to suspect that the word "safe" was really a euphemism for "no blacks or Hispanics," and that the two of us had been speaking in code. Then again, it was possible that "safe" meant "safe," and I was guilty of my own outlandish child-like view of the inherent racism of middle-American life. This was troubling.

"In the wintertime," Laura continued, "old ladies will go shopping at Albertsons and they'll leave their car doors unlocked with the keys right in the ignition so they can keep the heat running. That's how safe it is here."

"That does sound safe," I said reluctantly.

Laura smiled at me as if she had won.

Then the guy behind the counter was telling us our bagels were ready.

We took the scenic route to the Badlands, driving east on Route 44. We passed wide tracts of empty field that were dotted with silos and water towers and a billboard of an adorable little baby telling us, "I have the right to life." We arrived at the Badlands just before sunset. Karen parked at an overlook so we could get out to watch as the light shifted over the tall white buttes that rose and fell around us like teeth in a mouth. Beyond the buttes, stretching as far as the horizon, was the soft yellow prairie of the Great Plains. I reconsidered my observation that South Dakota was minuscule.

"It's beautiful," Karen whispered.

"It's stunning," I whispered back.

We stood for a while as a breeze gently blew around us. A deep silence encompassed everything. How could it be so vast and yet so silent? I thought of the barking dog in Apartment 1303. A small black bird with a white stomach fluttered past. Slowly the prairie began to change from yellow to orange and then to red and then to utter darkness.

We got back into the car without saying anything and drove to our cabin where we were instantly dismayed with what we discovered. The cabin looked less like a cabin and more like a rundown one-bedroom apartment owned by an absentee landlord. It reminded me of an illegal sublet I had lived in for two years on East Eighty-third Street when I was broke and single. Everything about the cabin was worn and shabby, including the stack of towels that had been left for us. Had the towels been washed? A dozen flies buzzed and swirled around giving the impression that something was rotting beneath the floor. Another dozen flies could be found here and there smashed against the walls, murdered by a previous tenant who had been so demoralized they had not bothered to wipe away the carcasses. There was carpeting in the bedroom but it was worn and matted and I resolved to keep my shoes on at all times. A basket of plastic red roses had been placed on the nightstand in what looked to be a last-ditch effort by the absentee landlord to give the appearance of care and consideration.

"This place is disgusting," Karen said.

As I began unloading our groceries and eight gallons of bottled water from the car, Karen set about washing the mismatched dishes and silverware that had been supplied. But when she turned on the faucet and began to scrub a long trail of ants appeared on the countertop, marching their way somewhere. To combat the ants, Karen sprayed Off!, which eliminated the ants but also rendered the countertop unusable. That evening, while the pressure cooker screamed with steam, I bent over an unsteady plastic table sawing away at our Albertson vegetables with a butter knife as I recalled my former troubled life on East Eighty-third Street.

We had not come to the Badlands for the cabin, though: We had come to the Badlands for the Badlands. Nearly 250,000 acres of moody wilderness, mythic and theatrical, with weather ranging from blizzards to violent thunderstorms, and where deer, coyote, and bison could still be found roaming free.

So the next morning, with four bottles of water and our fanny packs stuffed with as many snacks as we could fit, we set off. We began with the shortest trail, the Window Trail, just a quarter of a mile, and gradually worked our way up until, by the fourth and last day, we had done them all except the longest, the Castle Trail, ten miles round-trip. It sounded daunting but we both felt that we had satisfactorily conditioned ourselves for the challenge.

The trail wound through the prairie and was almost completely flat, happily requiring little exertion. It was also incredibly narrow, and Karen and I had to walk single file most of the time. In the beginning I took the lead because I was male and Karen said she was afraid of being attacked by the rattlesnakes that the park signs had warned us about. The prospect of snakes, however, frightened me just as much, maybe more, and I kept my eyes glued to the ground, proceeding with great caution and flinching at any sign of rustling. Eventually, Karen complained that I wasn't walking briskly enough and that what should take three hours was going to take six, and so we switched places. The pace increased. Our footsteps sounded in unison. I felt lulled. A gentle breeze blew from time to time bending the tall grass. This time of year it was supposed to be a hundred degrees, but a heavy rain had cooled the region. It was eighty maybe. It was cloudless. In the near distance, rising out of the prairie, were buttes that looked less like pointy teeth and more like small delectable slices of cake.

"Don't they look like slices of cake?" I said to Karen.

"They're crumbling," Karen said.

"What's that?"

"The buttes—they're crumbling. They're really just sand and clay. I read about it. Every time it rains a little more gets washed away. In 500,000 years the Badlands will be completely gone."

The thought was sobering. We walked on. I brooded.

Soon the trail veered sharply to the left and took us off the grassy plain and out onto what looked like the surface of the moon, white bubbly earth surrounded by giant craters. The soft rocky terrain crunched under our feet.

"Look!" Karen cried out, stopping suddenly.

I lurched at the sound of her voice. "What is it? What do you see?"

"Look."

"Where?"

"There!"

I looked in the direction she was pointing, not down where a snake would be, but out and over, many hundreds of yards away, maybe a mile away, and sure enough there was the tiny white shape of a bighorn sheep moving slowly along the prairie, and then, as if it knew it was being watched, pausing and looking toward us.

The next morning we repacked our groceries and our bottled water and our pressure cooker and departed for the Black Hills. Part mountain range, part forest, the Black Hills cover the western edge of South Dakota and some of Wyoming. The discovery of gold in 1874 prompted a mad head-long rush into the region. A fly followed us into the car and accompanied us on our drive west along Route 240, as we passed silos and water towers and billboards advertising homemade donuts. It was with great apprehension that we arrived two hours later at our destination in Hill City—population 780—and pulled up to our cabin.

"I'm going to scream if it's gross," Karen said.

"We'll find a hotel," I said.

We need not have worried. The cabin was large and spacious with a comfortable couch and a loft space that held our bed. Above all, it was pristine. We could very well have been the first tenants. It had been built out of logs so it had a quaint authentic feel to it, but the bathroom and appliances were entirely modern so it had none of the drawbacks that come with quaint authenticity. Nor were there any ants or flies. There were deer, though. And as evening approached, Karen and I sat on the porch watching them come out of the woods to graze in the wide grassy field in front of us. The mother, or perhaps the father, would lead the way, bouncing over the grass, barely landing before it rose again, followed by the young children who floated with even less effort. Then they would all pause to nibble.

"They move like ballerinas," Karen said.

That evening, as I chopped our vegetables for dinner—using a chef's knife—I had a thought. Perhaps we might consider moving out here one day. A summer home perhaps. Or a winter home. It might be a nice place to get away to, a nice reprieve from the Lower East Side. We could watch the deer in the snow.

"I wonder how much a cabin like this would cost," I said aloud.

"It's $180 a night," Karen said.

"No, how much it would cost, you know, to buy. To own."

"I have no idea."

We were in the Black Hills, which is forest, as opposed to the Badlands, which is prairie and teeth and lunar surface. The landscape, therefore, was gravely anticlimactic, and after one brief hike huffing and puffing up a muddy path in the woods, where our fear of deer ticks outstripped our fear of rattlesnakes, we decided that we would spend our remaining days pursuing other interests.

No trip to South Dakota would be complete, after all, without visiting Mount Rushmore. So on day six of our vacation we got back in our car and drove a mere fifteen minutes to one of the world's most famous attractions. I realized I was excited to finally experience in person those four presidents' heads I had been seeing since I was in first grade. Roosevelt, Lincoln, Jefferson, Washington. I also realized once we arrived that I had been operating my entire life under the false assumption that a visit to Mount Rushmore entailed parking your car on the side of the road and strolling around on the tops of the heads. I had even gone so far as to picture a staircase leading down into an ear. Perhaps I had extrapolated it from my experience at age five of entering the Statue of Liberty and ascending toward her crown.

The reality was much more regimented and mundane. It involved first parking in the underground parking garage for eight dollars, and then walking with a crowd of sightseers with gift bags through a gauntlet of flags, billed as the Avenue of Flags—a flag for every state and territory—as if this construction in itself were some sort of major achievement, and then finally coming out onto the Grand View Terrace where 500 feet in front of me—maybe a thousand feet—were those familiar heads rising out of the mountain, each staring off in a different direction. The heads looked exactly the same as any photo I'd ever seen of them, and considering we could barely get any closer I wondered if the fifteen-minute drive had been ill spent. I watched with irritation as a young couple took a grinning picture of themselves with the heads as backdrop.

"I'm disappointed," I said softly.

There was an audio tour "wand" that you could rent at the Audio Tour Building for five dollars. An organization called the Association of Partners for Public Lands had apparently selected it as the winner of the 2007 Media and Partnership Award in the audio/visual division. Karen and I rented it.

"They gaze over the landscape as if sentinels," a man's voice intoned in my ear as soft music played in the background. *"A living memorial that speaks to us, listens to us, and challenges us."*

The voice was firm, gentle, and wholly optimistic.

There was a concrete path that ran around the base of the mountain and we were instructed by the voice to follow the path, which we did, stopping when it told us to stop and pressing the next number on the wand when it told us to press it.

"To learn about the transformation of Mount Rushmore from a roadside attraction to a national memorial, press the pound key."

This was how five minutes of viewing Mount Rushmore became three hours. This was also how I learned almost everything there was to know about the sculpture, the mountain, the Indians from whom the mountain had been stolen, the artist—Gutzon Borglum—whose idea it had been to carve the mountain in the first place, his son—Lincoln Borglum—who took over after his father's death just months before it was finally completed in 1941. A lot also seemed to be made of the fact that, while the heads were already gigantic—each the size of a six-story building—they were actually scaled to a figure who would stand 465 feet tall, and that that figure, if it had ever been sculpted, would then be taller than the Statue of Liberty.

By the time we reached the end of the audio tour, number twenty-eight on the wand, Karen and I were more exhausted than when we had walked through the prairie. We lay down on a bench and listened numbly as recordings of everyday people described what Mount Rushmore meant to them.

"Symbolism."

"Awesome."

"Provocation."

"Understanding."

"They're not eroding," Karen said.

"What's that?"

"The heads—they were carved in granite so they're not eroding. I read about it. One inch every ten thousand years. That means even a million years after the Badlands are gone they'll still be here."

On our last day in South Dakota we went trout fishing. I had never fished before, of course, but Karen said her father had taken her fishing as a little girl and she thought that her early childhood experiences would see us through. We planned to grill what we caught along with the remaining vegetables as a fitting final dinner of our trip.

The owner of our cabin was kind enough to lend us two poles and a plastic bag full of gear. The nonresident fishing licenses we had to buy ourselves for fourteen dollars each at a minimart. Then we drove twenty minutes to Sylvan Lake in Custer State Park. The very park where the reunion had been held for the nine living survivors of the Battle of the Little Bighorn!

I had hoped for a small secluded lake somewhere deep in the woods, more pond than lake, some approximation of Huck Finn, where Karen and I could recline on the bank with our poles in the water, maybe even nap. Sylvan Lake, instead, was big and public and so well maintained that it looked manmade. There was a parking lot about twenty-five feet away and as we were pulling in a tour bus was pulling out.

"I'm disappointed," I said.

We gathered our bags and fishing poles and bottled water, and walked along a paved path until we came to a contrived little clearing along the bank. Stones were conveniently placed so there would be a place to sit.

"Hey, this looks like a good spot," Karen said as if she were the first to discover it.

I stood next to her while she fiddled with the various knobs and switches on the reel, trying to recall what it was her father had taught her that you were supposed to do. It was immediately apparent that she had retained nothing from her childhood.

"I thought you said you remembered," I said.

"I can remember how to catch crabs."

"There aren't any crabs here."

"I know," she said, "but it was a lot of fun."

"Let me try," I said. I swung the rod the way I had seen it done on television but the line did not cast. Nothing I did would make it cast. Ducks floated by. "Maybe these poles are broken."

"They're brand new," Karen said.

"Catch anything yet?" a voice called.

Karen and I turned to see a husband and wife walking toward us along the path. They were both about fifty years old and they were holding hands and smiling. The woman was round and the man was burly. They both had gray hair.

"Not yet," I said shamefully. And then I said: "You don't by any chance know how to fish?"

"Know how to fish?" The woman laughed. "My husband's an expert."

"I think our poles might be broken," I said.

"Let's see," the husband said, and he took the fishing pole from me and examined it briefly, and then with a quick flick of his wrist cast the line a hundred feet out into the water.

I giggled in embarrassment. "Could you tell me how you did that?"

The man slowly reeled the line back in. "The first thing you need to do is put some bait on this. Do you have any bait?" The man examined the contents of our plastic bag and withdrew a jar of little orange balls. "These are salmon eggs," he said. And he picked two out and stuck them on the hook. "The next thing you do is hold the rod like this," and he put his beefy hands around my skinny hands, "and you hold that little button down," which I did, "and then you pull your hands back," and he gently pulled my hands back until they were right at my shoulder, "and then as you bring the rod forward you take your finger off the button." I did as he said and the line sailed fifteen feet out into the water.

I stared in astonishment.

"Can you show me?" Karen said.

And so he did. And then he explained to us what the bobbers were for, and what the lures were for, and how far you needed to cast the line, and how to reel it in once we felt a bite, and how to cut the gills so that the fish would bleed quickly and taste better when we grilled it later that night.

"Do you have a knife?" he asked.

"Yes," Karen said, "we have a Swiss Army Knife."

"That'll do," he said.

I kept worrying that I was taking up too much of the man's day, but neither he nor his wife seemed to mind, and when he had finally told us all we needed to know, and there was nothing more I could think to ask him, we said good-bye. I was sorry to see him go.

"Good luck," he said.

We watched them walk off down the path hand in hand. Then I took the Swiss Army Knife out of my pocket.

"Maybe you better hold on to this?" I said.

"Why?" Karen asked.

"You know . . ." I said, "in case, you know . . . you need it."

"What if you need it?" Karen said.

I laid it on the ground between us. We eyed it cautiously. Then we sat down on the rocks and waited. Fifteen minutes passed. The lines remained slack.

"How long does something like this take?" I asked.

"I don't know," Karen said.

Thirty minutes passed. It was getting noticeably cooler. I looked down the path to see if the man and woman might be returning but the path was empty.

"Maybe I should try recasting the line," I said. "Maybe it's not in the right spot."

"I don't think it's going to make a difference," Karen said.

I reeled the line back in anyway. As I did the hook became tangled and in the process of untangling it the salmon egg fell off into the water. I took out the jar of bait and carefully put another one on the hook. I marveled at my mastery of this task. Then with finesse I recast the line thirty feet out into the lake.

"Look at us," I shouted. "We're trout fishing in South Dakota!"

Two hours later, after having recast the line multiple times, after having moved to another manmade clearing farther up the lake, after having added far too many salmon eggs to the hook, there were still no bites on either of our lines. By now Karen and I had both grown hungry and cold and stiff from sitting for so long, and so with a great sense of failure we slowly reeled our lines back in and repacked the bobbers and the sinkers and the lures that the man had so generously taught us about.

"I'm disappointed," I said.

"Don't forget this," Karen said, and she bent down and picked up the unused Swiss Army Knife. I took it from her and put it in my pocket, and as I did a sad and distressing image came into my head of a small fish struggling desperately on the bank of the pond as it slowly bled to death through its gills.

I watched a tour bus pull away, its headlights cutting through the falling dusk.

"Maybe it's good we didn't catch anything," I said.

"Yes," Karen said.

And with the poles slung over our shoulders, the two of us turned and walked hand in hand back the way we had come.

TENNESSEE

CAPITAL   Nashville

ENTERED UNION   1796 (16th)

ORIGIN OF NAME   Of Cherokee origin; meaning unknown

NICKNAME   Volunteer State

MOTTOS   "Agriculture and Commerce" and "Tennessee—America at its best!"

RESIDENTS   Tennessean, Tennesseean

U.S. REPRESENTATIVES   9

STATE BIRD   mockingbird

STATE FLOWER   iris

STATE TREE   tulip poplar

STATE SONGS   "My Homeland, Tennessee"; "When It's Iris Time in Tennessee"; "My Tennessee"; "Tennessee Waltz"; "Rocky Top"; "Tennessee"; "The Pride of Tennessee"

LAND AREA   41,217 sq. mi.

GEOGRAPHIC CENTER   In Rutherford Co., 5 mi. NE of Murfreesboro

POPULATION   5,962,959

WHITE   80.2%

BLACK   16.4%

AMERICAN INDIAN   0.3%

ASIAN   1.0%

HISPANIC/LATINO   2.2%

UNDER 18   24.6%

65 AND OVER   12.4%

MEDIAN AGE: 37.2

TENNESSEE
Ann Patchett

I have on several occasions been told that the secret to making money, big money, is to find that place at the edge of town where the real estate stops being priced by the square foot and begins to be priced by the acre. The idea is then to buy as many of those acres as possible and wait for the town to creep toward you so that you will be there, ready and waiting, when the land is converted down into feet.

I have lived the better part of my life in Nashville, Tennessee, and time and again I have seen this theory put into cash-making practice. Acres that in my youth were so bucolic they were fit only for the laziest of cows and nibbling deer now are the physical underpinnings of sprawling shopping malls and housing developments and golf courses—shimmering expanses of manicured greens where once stood only thickets of blackberries. The cows and the wildlife, not unlike the urban poor, are then forced from their neighborhoods and herded off to distant pastures.

But why should it be different for cows than it is for the rest of us? This is not a city that can take any pride in its urban planning. Lovely old homes are knocked down, appalling condominiums spring up in their stead, traffic multiplies geometrically, Mom and Pop operations issue a mouse-like cry trying to hold back the mighty chains, and then are eaten by those chains in a single bite. This scarcely distinguishes Nashville from any other urban center.

But for every way this city has changed for the worse there is some other way in which it has changed for the better. When I was a little girl the Klan marched down at the square on Music Row on Sunday afternoons. Men in white sheets and white hoods waved at your car with one hand while they held back their enormous German Shepherds with the other. My sister and I pushed the buttons of our door locks down and sunk low in the backseat. Those men are gone now, or at least they aren't out walking the streets in full regalia. If the growth and modernization of a city means you get rid of the Klan but have to endure bad condos, I say so be it.

Nashville used to be one of those places that cared more for your genealogy than your character (in some very limited circles this may still be the case). If your family hadn't been in the state long enough to remember what Lincoln had done to it, then you might be tolerated but you were never truly welcome. I knew this having moved here when I was five. But too many people have moved here in the last decade to keep up with such technicalities, and somewhere in the transition I miraculously came to be regarded as a local. After all, I remember when the Grand Ole Opry was still lodged downtown at the Ryman Auditorium. I sat on the floor backstage every weekend when I was six and watched Roy Acuff absently let his yo-yo slip down its string and then flick it back again while he waited for his turn to go on.

When all the changes are assembled and the good and the bad are averaged out, I still believe this place is more the same than it could ever be different, because while Memphis has changed and Nashville has changed and Knoxville has changed, Tennessee the state has not. To understand this you have to go back to that place where real estate still prices out by the acre. Plenty of people made a killing on those deals, but don't be fooled, many, many more are still holding their land. And yes, the city does push out, but down here the city is an island surrounded by country and the country pushes back hard. There is a powerful root system that reaches far beneath those mall parking lots, and the minute we stop hacking away at it, the plants come back.

This sounds metaphorical. It isn't. For all its urban centers, Tennessee is first and foremost a trough of rich, deep soil sitting beneath hot, humid weather. Its role on earth is less to be the home of country music and more a showcase of dazzling plant life. From the ages of eight to twelve I lived on a farm in Ashland City. We called it a gentleman's farm, which meant that the only thing we did to the land was look at it. We kept a couple of horses that could be ridden only if they could be caught, and a very large pig that fell into the same category. (There is a picture of my sister sitting on top of the pig, her knees demurely together, riding side-saddle.) There were banty chickens named after members of Nixon's cabinet; the dogs had an uncanny knack of eating them one at a time as their namesakes fell before the Watergate committee. Alongside the well-fed dogs there was an endless parade of cats, rabbits, hamsters, and canaries, but the most abundant form of life were the things that grew out of our untended ground—all manner of trees: eastern redbud and tulip poplar, sweet gum, fringe tree, river birch, and blue beech, frothy seas of white dogwoods, all types of maples, red oak and white oak, black locust, red cedar, and enormous black walnuts tall enough to give Jack's beanstalk a run for its money. All through the end of summer and into fall those trees dropped their smelly green-hulled nuts the size of baseballs and we tripped on them and skinned our hands. Once a year in a fit of boredom or optimism we would forget everything we knew about black walnuts and scrape off the filthy husks and dry the nuts on the front porch, thinking we would eat them, but they were impossible to get into, yielding a tiny bit of meat for an enormous amount of work. Before we ever got enough together to make a quart of ice cream, the squirrels would come and carry our burden away.

Mine was a childhood carried out among wild flowers, ferns, and mosses. Days were spent with only the dogs, hacking my way into the thick undergrowth of woods with the single parental admonishment that I should keep an eye out for snakes. I didn't much worry about the snakes. We had thirty-seven acres, so much room, so much leaf and bark and trunk and bloom, that it seemed impossible that any snake and I would arrive at the exact same place at the same time. Since this was the seventies, the Age of Terrariums, I ran a child's business digging up moss and selling it to a flower shop in town. It gave me a reason to go out in the summers. I sunk my tennis shoes into the larkspur and spotted wintergreen, ran my fingers through colonies of mayapples. I counted shooting stars, sweet anise, Virginia bluebell and jewelweed, looked out for trillium. The land was my office, my factory, and I would slip beneath the endless shade of leaves, spade and box in hand, and go to work.

In Nashville we have a Tiffany's now, a J. Crew, countless Starbucks. But drive out to Ashland City sometime, a scant half hour away. Go down the River Road to what used to be Tanglewood Farm and I can promise you that not one thing has changed except perhaps that the roots on all those trees have dug themselves down another twenty feet or so. Every year the country grows thicker. Every year it inches closer to town.

Tennessee, with its subtropical summers and mild winters, is a perfect climate for almost any sort of plant. The non-natives thrive alongside the natives. Consider the kudzu vine, which arrived from Japan in the late 1800s in a little thought-out plan to help slow soil erosion. It has since spread an impenetrable web over the South, draping fields, billboards, barns, and forests. If left unchecked (not that anyone has had much luck keeping it in check) it would easily take out the interstate system. So ripe is this state for the explosive growth of plant life that the species have become extremely competitive. "Think of those plants growing in the California deserts," a botanist friend said to me, and I picture the succulents and flowering cactus that thinly dot the vast stretches of sand. "Those are the plants that can't compete."

Tennessee plants are so competitive that every day is a slug-fest, a deciduous tree blocks off the light to a shrub, a vine crawls out from beneath the shrub to pull down the tree, insects bore into the bark, birds fill out the branches, worms as blind as Homer chew through the soil, crunching the fallen leaves into a thick layer of duff that coats the forest floor. Among the hale and hearty, one of the uncontested kings in the Volunteer State is poison ivy. It sweeps over everything and we leave it alone. We're supposed to leave it alone. The counselors at Camp Sycamore for Girls, not fifteen miles from our farm in Ashland City, made the point so clearly we could not possibly claim to have misunderstood. "This is poison ivy," they said, pointing to what seemed to be an entire field. *"Leaves of three, let it be.* Do not go near it."

Lee Ann Hunter and I talked it over one night in our tent with all the balanced consideration two eleven-year-olds could muster. We had heard about the plant but had never seen it in action. Unhappy at camp, we felt certain we could ride its vine out of those miserable tents and back into our own sweet beds. The next night after dinner we took a detour through the forest, back to the very field we had been warned against. Like virgins to a volcano, we threw ourselves in. We rolled in it. We picked it. We rubbed it in our hair and stuffed it in our shirts and ground it into our eyes. Reader, we ate it. What was so bad about camp? It was boring? We didn't like the food? Some other girl got the better bunk? That part of the story is lost to memory. All I know is that we turned to the plant in our hour of need as much as Juliet had turned to a plant: to transport her out of a difficult situation and into a happier time. Like Juliet, we miscalculated the details. I cannot say the hospital was a better place to spend my summer, but I was out of Sycamore.

Of course even plant life is subject to change: One tree is hit by lightning, another is up-ended in a storm. I remember our Dutch elm succumbing to the blight that wiped out its kind. One tree goes down and the vacancy is filled in a matter of minutes. Even if this endless expanse of green is composed of different members over time, the land is still pumping out plants faster than anyone can count them. The plants, I believe, have shaped this state more than people ever have. When the success of a crop determines where people will live then who is making the choice as to where we settle? The hundreds of little towns that lie between the cities have hardly changed at all in the years I've been driving through them. If a silver oak grew up in the space that the Dutch elm left behind, then maybe a tanning salon took the place of a beauty shop or a hamburger joint became a pizza shack, but as in the forest these changes are negligible in town. For the most part people are poor. The last truly revolutionary thing to come to their homes was electricity.

On one particularly scorching summer afternoon coming home from a trip to Memphis I decided to leave the interstate and take the two-lane highway down to Shiloh to see the famous Civil War battlefield. The insect life joined their voices together in such a high-pitched screed I could hear it over the air conditioning and through the rolled-up windows of my car. The bugs and plants and I were alone on that highway. I did not see another car for ten miles, and then for twenty. The millions of leaves on either side of the road were so dense and bright you could almost feel them growing. And then I saw a man standing in the middle of the road waving his arms in crosses above his head. He looked like he was trying to land a plane. I stopped the car. It must have been 100 degrees out there on the blacktop. To not stop for him would have been to kill him.

There was a woman there on the side of the road, leaning up against the car. They both were in their seventies. When I rolled down the window the man held an artificial voice box against his throat. "Ran-out-of-gas," the machine said. I told them to get in quick before they melted. I would drive them to the station and bring them back.

But the woman didn't want to go. They both got car sick and neither one of them could ride in the back. My car was small. "I'll stay here," she said. "I'll be fine. There's plenty of shade."

So I drove the man fifteen miles to the gas station while he told me the unbearably sad story of his life in the flat monotone of electric speech. Cancer of the larynx. Once he was sick his wife left him and took the kids. He got laid off from the factory. He had to go back to the country, where he'd grown up, see if he could farm some on the land his father had owned. Hard times. This new wife was nice to him though, that was a plus. At the end of every couple of sentences he'd thank me and I had to tell him to stop. He told me I could drop him off at the station and he would hitch a ride back, but we didn't pass a car the whole way there.

"I can take you back," I said. "I'm just out driving around. I don't have anyplace to go." It sounded suspicious but it was the truth.

I waited with him at the station even though he kept trying to shoo me off. He thought he was going to see a car heading back in his direction but no one came; after a while there was no choice but to relent. He said he would only take the ride if I let him pay me. We argued politely about this. I told him were the roles reversed, and they could be reversed, he would never take money from me. Reluctantly he raised the voice box to his throat and agreed with that. I drove him back to where the new wife was waiting. Just as it was over and we had said our good-byes, he leaned back in through the open window of my car and put five dollars on the passenger seat, then he turned quickly away. It broke my heart in a way that was out of all proportion to the greater sadnesses of life.

It was lonely out there on the road after he had gone, lonely when I pulled into Shiloh an hour before the park closed. More than ten thousand men from the Union and Confederate armies had died there in April of 1862. It took very little imagination to see this place the way it would have been that April, dogwoods and cherry trees and apples all blooming in the mighty undergrowth, the energy it would have taken the men to fight their way through the trees in order to come to some sort of opening where surely they would be shot. The Union dead are buried on a hill with a view to the Tennessee River. It is a lovely spot, cooler for the breeze that comes off the water, and each grave has a small white marker. Outside the gates of the graveyard there is a copy of the Gettysburg Address written on a metal plaque. The Confederates are buried in a mass grave in a trench that lies at the bottom of the hill, but they at least were all together, and they were home. I did not pass another soul in the park save the ranger at the gate who told me to leave when it was dark.

If anybody tells you Tennessee has changed much, tell them to come out to Shiloh. Tell them to listen hard to the stories of the men you pick up on the road on your way there.

Had I grown up in the city I might now feel the loss of my early life. I might look at one building and wish for the happier day when it had been something else. But I grew up in Tennessee, by which I mean the country, and out there everything stays exactly as I remember it, good and bad and every bit of it mine.

TEXAS

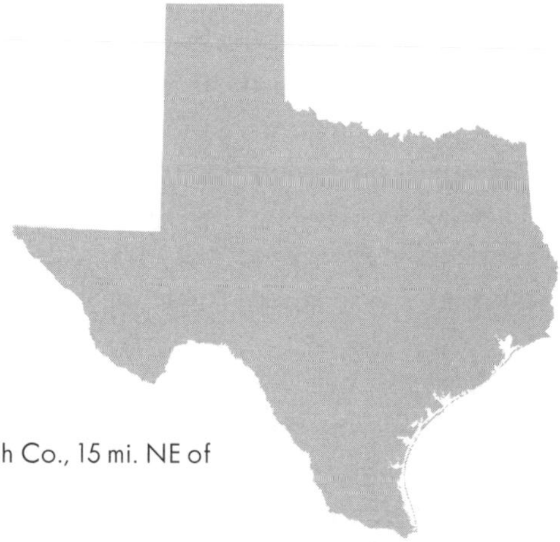

CAPITAL   Austin

ENTERED UNION   1845 (28th)

ORIGIN OF NAME   From an Indian word meaning "friends"

NICKNAME   Lone Star State

MOTTO   "Friendship"

RESIDENTS   Texan

U.S. REPRESENTATIVES   32

STATE BIRD   mockingbird

STATE FLOWER   bluebonnet

STATE TREE   pecan

STATE SONG   "Texas, Our Texas"

LAND AREA   261,797 sq. mi.

GEOGRAPHIC CENTER   In McCulloch Co., 15 mi. NE of Brady

POPULATION   22,859,968

WHITE   71.0%

BLACK   11.5%

AMERICAN INDIAN   0.6%

ASIAN   2.7%

HISPANIC/LATINO   32.0%

UNDER 18   28.2%

65 AND OVER   9.9%

MEDIAN AGE   32.3

TEXAS
Cristina Henríquez

This is how a lot of people think of Texas: dusty plains and broad prairies freckled with tumbleweeds and sagebrush; a land with the occasional striated canyon and sweeping basin; a place occupied by ranchers and cowboys and horses; all of this under a huge, open sky. Texas is John Wayne movies and mammoth oil rigs and President George W. Bush and the place where, according to the song, all of George Strait's exes live.

This is all true.

In a way. The sky there does seem vast, mostly because the view of it is uninterrupted by the endless unfolding of flat land. On working ranches, herds of longhorn cattle graze on a carpet of bluebonnets. Almost every other car has a W. THE PRESIDENT sticker on its bumper or back windshield (Texans have come a long way from when State Senator Guy M. Bryan wrote, in 1845, "We are all Democrats in Texas"). And the moment George Strait's song starts playing in any bar in any part of the state I've ever been, people will raise their beers and sing along, no matter what.

Texas, of course, is more than its surface and stereotypes. Every place is. But the lore associated with Texas seems to be piled thicker than for other states. You have to drill down deeper to get to what lies beneath.

Before moving to Texas, I remember sitting in my apartment in Iowa and watching one of those commercials that state tourism boards put together to entice people to visit their magnificent and scenic and family friendly locales. The commercial concluded with the slogan, "Texas. It's like a whole other country." Which felt less like an invitation and more like a finger-wagging threat. As in, "Texas. You Have No Idea What You're Getting Yourself Into." It was full of such braggadocio and inflated pride. Who did these people think they were, anyway? I thought. And in the next second, seriously, what *was* I getting myself into?

I had lived in six states by then—Delaware, Florida, Virginia, Indiana, Illinois, and Iowa—in settings ranging from a mountain town so small that the phone numbers were a mere five digits long, to suburbs filled with street upon street of identical houses, to a city apartment with three deadbolts plus a chain on the door, to laid-back college towns, but not one of them felt like adequate preparation for what I imagined Texas life would be. Not that it really mattered at that point. My husband and I had already committed, because of a job opportunity, to moving there—to the Southwest, to Texas, and to Dallas specifically. For the next three years, we would call it home.

There is a clear division in Texas between those who have spent their entire lives calling the Lone Star State home and those who are transplants. Either you're a Texan or you ain't. Since I wasn't born there, I ain't. I could have lived there for the rest of my life and never made much headway on bridging that divide (although perhaps if I had adopted one of those "I Wasn't Born in Texas, But I Got Here as Fast as I Could" bumper stickers, it would have helped). I was, as my friends there liked to remind me, a Northerner at heart. This, despite my Panamanian heritage and the fact that I grew up in a household where both my parents spoke Spanish. As a half-Panamanian Northerner, I tried my best to resist Texas. The whole time I was there, I complained. But now I'm gone, and I find myself wistfully recalling the state I left behind.

Aside from the television show that bears its name, Dallas may be best known for the famed Dallas Cowboys football team, complete with cheerleaders and aging Texas Stadium (actually in Irving), which has a hole cut out in the top of it so that, as linebacker D. D. Lewis once said, "God can watch his favorite team." It is also home to the Mavericks (the NBA team owned by billionaire Internet entrepreneur Mark Cuban, who bought it from Ross Perot, Jr.), the Stars (winners of the 1999 Stanley Cup—yes, that's hockey), and the Rangers baseball club (co-owned by George W. Bush before he became governor). But most of all, Dallas is a shopping city, featuring everything from the flagship Neiman Marcus (a building that takes up nearly a full downtown block), to the one and only Stanley Korshak, which offers services like closet-editing and vacation-packing, to the self-described oldest mall in America—Highland Park Village—these days full of upscale brands like Escada and Hermès.

Dallas residents dress accordingly. I swear they dress up even to go to the gas station. When friends from New York came to visit one weekend we went out to a neighborhood bar, nothing fancy, and they dressed in what they thought was—and what anywhere else would have been—appropriate: hoodies, jeans, New Balance sneakers. But when we arrived and were confronted with a sea of women dressed in Jimmy Choos, silk tops, and $300 jeans, and men decked out in custom-made button-down shirts, lightweight blazers, and $300 jeans, they felt so conspicuous that we left early. As my friend said, "It felt like we stumbled into some absurd debutante ball." Dallas is the headquarters of Southwest Airlines, Mary Kay Cosmetics, Pizza Hut, Kinko's, and 7-Eleven. Dallas is a place where, when the temperature shot up past 100 degrees for more than thirty days one summer, no one complained. I remember going to restaurants that summer and asking for a table inside, in the air conditioning, while true Dallasites requested seats on the patio, for which there was always a wait. In fact, patio dining was so popular that restaurants that didn't have the space for one would extend a patio into the parking garage, and, still, people flocked to it.

More than anywhere else I've ever lived, in Dallas you must have a car. And everyone in Dallas does their best to drive not a BMW or Mercedes (please, you might as well be driving a Tonka truck) but an Aston Martin or a Maserati as they zoom two blocks to anywhere rather than walk. Walking is so un-Dallas. I learned this in an unusual way. I had been living in Dallas for a few weeks when I snagged an interview to be an assistant at the local glossy city magazine. The magazine offices were exactly 1.7 miles from my apartment, and I had thought I might walk there and back (my husband and I shared one car, which he used to get to work, twenty-five miles away). When I woke up the morning of the interview, though, it was a steamy ninety-seven degrees outside, and because I would be wearing a wool-blend suit, walking was out of the question. I can't remember now whether I even thought about taking a taxi because, as far as I was concerned, having been trained by endless El and bus rides when I had lived in Chicago, my next best option was to take public transportation.

I consulted a few maps and learned that I would have to take one trolley and two buses to get there. The trolley was a restored, old-fashioned streetcar that ran along a track in the brick-paved street. I stepped aboard in my suit, a portfolio folder tucked under my arm, and was greeted by a conductor wearing a uniform and cap. Cheerfully, he told me the history of the trolley car as he drove. "You're riding car number 186, the Green Dragon. She was once owned by someone in North Dallas who used her as a hay barn." The buses were surprisingly clean and bright and, unlike those in Chicago, they ran on time. Sure, I almost melted waiting at the stops, but everything was going fine.

At the interview, the publisher asked me to sit at a round table in his office. On the wall behind his desk was a rifle attached to a wooden plaque. The first thing he said to me was, "You are totally unqualified for this job." I didn't know how to respond. We got to the bottom of it soon enough:

He meant I was overqualified and wanted instead to have me try my hand at writing for them. It sounded good to me and we ironed out the details. Then, as I was about to leave, he said, "So you made it here OK?"

Oh, sure, I told him, I just took the bus.

He blanched. "What are you doing taking the bus?"

"I don't have a car yet, but I used to live in Chicago and took public transportation all the time."

"You shouldn't be taking the bus," he said. "I don't like the idea of it."

"Really, I don't mind."

He looked alarmed, though, and after another second, called his current assistant into the room. He mumbled something to her, and she left, only to return a few minutes later with a set of keys, which he promptly handed to me.

"Here," he said. "Now you have a car. You can drive it until you get one of your own."

Then he turned to walk out of the room, while I stood there dumbfounded. He looked back, as if it had just occurred to him to ask, "You have insurance, right?"

"You know," I stammered, "I don't really feel comfortable—"

"Don't worry about it. No employee of mine will ride the bus."

"But I don't—"

"Come on. I'll walk you down to the parking garage so we can find it."

I realized that he was not going to let me leave the building without that car. So I nodded and followed him to a teal Mercury Sable parked in the first space by the elevator. He unlocked it and, like a Texas gentleman, opened the door for me. Then he gave me back the keys and told me to keep it for as long as I needed, until I got my own car. As I pulled out of the garage, I could see him in the rearview mirror giving me a double-fisted thumbs-up and smiling so big his cheeks pushed up his glasses.

A ustin, the state capital, is the one place in Texas that everyone who suspects they might not like Texas all that much is willing—and should be willing—to visit anyway. The city's motto is "Keep Austin Weird," which says something about its resistance to homogeny and about its attempt to keep itself creative, environmentally conscious, laid back, progressive, and humble in all the ways that has made it famous.

People come to Austin to go to school at the University of Texas's main campus, which enrolls nearly fifty thousand students each fall. They come for the tech jobs. They come to see one of twenty-one complete and original editions of the Gutenberg Bible at the Harry Ransom Center. And they come to watch hundreds of thousands of Mexican free-tailed bats swarm out from their perch under the Congress Avenue Bridge, just as dusk is falling, all summer long.

But the reason I first went to Austin, and the reason I returned again and again, was for what has to be the best literary offering in the state: the Texas Book Festival. Curiously, there are people in Texas—*writers* in Texas—who have never heard of the Texas Book Festival, although I think that says more about the rest of the state than about the festival. The event is a four-day extravaganza of readings and panel discussions and interviews with some of the best writers working today. Nearly all of it is free. It takes place in late October and early November, when the thermometer in Austin is still spiking at around 100 degrees, and writers and readers descend upon the capital with their programs in hand, trying to map out how they're possibly going to do and see all the things they want to. The first time I went, I think I missed half a morning of readings because I didn't comprehend how rigorous the schedule was. But after I got the hang of things, I spent the whole weekend dashing around to events in a sort of cultural ecstasy. In three years, I saw Barack Obama, Bill Clinton, Salman Rushdie, Augusten Burroughs, Frank McCourt, Gore Vidal, Myla Goldberg, Seymour Hersh, Amy Sedaris, Jonathan Ames, Kevin Brockmeier, Jane Smiley, David Mc-Cullough, and lots of others. And I saw them in a pretty spectacular setting—the state capitol building.

The Texas State Capitol anchors the city of Austin. As the original *WPA Guide to Texas* notes, "Austin's life revolves around the capitol, whose massive red dome dominates the physical scene. . . ." Regardless of whether you agree with either Austin city politics or Texas state politics (the two, hammered out less than a mile from each other, are diametrically opposed), it's pretty impressive to walk into a reading and sit in a high-back leather swivel chair in front of a desk where a state representative usually sits and listen to an author's voice echo through the spaciousness of the house and senate chambers. The first time I did it, I sat in one of those leather chairs and ran my hands over a locked wooden desk with a phone mounted underneath and listened as Joy Williams, wearing a pair of sunglasses, stood in front of the podium—an electronic voting board and oil paintings of historic Texas hung in a line behind her—and spoke about short stories, her words floating up into the roped-off balcony high above my head.

In accordance with the unofficial edict that "Everything is bigger in

Texas," the Texas State Capitol, at 360,000 square feet, is the biggest capitol building in the country. It has 392 rooms and 938 windows. It sits on 2.25 acres of land. While every other capitol building in the country was built by contractors who were paid money for their time and labor, the Texas State Capitol is the only one that was paid for with land—3 million acres of it, to be exact. I heard a rumor once that Texas is the only state allowed to fly its flag at the same height as the United States flag, and although that's false, the fact that people believe it is a testament to Texas's reputation as a state more independent than the rest. In its early history, after all, Texas was a sovereign nation known as the Republic of Texas. When it joined the Union—the only state to do so by treaty—it kept the Lone Star Flag as its state symbol. One of the curious provisions of the treaty gave Texas the right, should it choose to do so, to divide itself into a total of five states. Officially: "New States of convenient size, not exceeding four in number, in addition to said State of Texas, and having sufficient populations, may hereafter, by the consent of said State, be formed out of the territory thereof, which shall be entitled to admission under the provisions of the Federal Constitution." Although, as the *WPA Guide to Texas* says:

> The question, occasionally discussed, as to whether or not, if Texas insisted, the National Government would be obliged to admit the additional States, is academic; no desire has ever been seriously evinced on the part of Texans to split up the "southwestern empire" of which they are so proud, even though by doing so they might have ten United States Senators, instead of two.

Texans have clung fiercely to the notion of independence. When I lived there, I heard more rhetoric about being a Texan than I heard in any of my previous residences about being a Delawarean or a Hoosier or a Chicagoan or even an Iowan. The only other place in the world where I've seen people exhibit such chest-thumping pride is Panama. I grew up hearing my father contend that Panama was not part of Central America or of South America. It was part of the world, certainly, but with an identity that linked it to no other place. When I was younger, there was even a popular T-shirt emblazoned with the words, "My name is Panama." My father, if you ask him where he's from, will invariably respond, "I'm from a small country in Latin America called Panama." Though he explains it that way because he's not sure that people here will recognize it by name only (many people over the years have thought I said "Canada"), you can see the pride shining in his eyes. Texans don't assume any lack of recognition, but the sense of pride is the same. My born-and-bred Texas friend said that when he tells someone he's a Texan, he's thinking of the Alamo and what it represents. He said, "We're tough, we're fighters, but we're polite. We embody the best of the American spirit." For him, and for most everyone else there, saying you're a Texan isn't just telling someone where you're from; it's telling someone who you are.

In San Antonio I visited the Alamo, of course. I had buttermilk pie and the best vodka martini of my life. I went to the McNay Art Museum and stood for a long time in the sun-drenched courtyard. I drove by Sandra Cisneros's bright purple house. I strolled along the River Walk. I toured the galleries at the Blue Star Arts Complex. I went from shop to shop—all with open doors and all selling Mexican art—in Southtown's Art Walk.

All of Texas teems with Mexico's influence. Sit idling in your car at a stoplight and you're likely to hear Mexican music from the Mexican radio station filtering through the window of the pickup truck next to you. Go to the grocery store and the Mexican food is not relegated simply to part of one aisle, but takes up two. I used to visit elementary schools to teach creative writing to the students, and all they wanted to write about—no matter their race—was Mexican soccer heroes and pop stars. The Spanish-speakers among them often assumed, by looking at me, that I spoke their language. Which wasn't a bad assumption, since it often seemed that I couldn't walk more than five feet in any direction without running into someone who knew at least a little Spanish. Certainly, I got the chance to practice my language skills there more than anywhere else I've lived. When I worked tearing tickets at a movie theater, I overheard the cleaning crew joking with each other in Spanish one day and I laughed at something one of them said. After that, they talked to me on every shift, telling me about their kids at home, whom they were working to send money to, and asking me what the movies playing in the theater were about. In my first Texas apartment, the building handyman would hang around even after he'd fixed the light switch or grouted a cracked tile because in me he found someone to speak Spanish with. He was Venezuelan, and as much as he missed his country, he longed to assimilate to America. I remember asking him once whether he ever ate at a Venezuelan restaurant nearby, figuring he would love it. He shook his head and said, "*Me gusto* Red Lobster." It was odd, though, because there were times that some combination of speaking Spanish and meeting people who missed their homeland, who felt that part of themselves had been displaced, reminded me of Panama and of my father and of myself. There were times that I saw in the Latinos and Mexicans there a version of what my father might have looked like when he first came to this country more than thirty years ago—the earnestness and determination, the bewilderment and yearning, the optimism and insecurity. There were times I felt more connected to Texas because of that.

But what made San Antonio come alive to me was meeting a man named Mike, and staying in his house. I was in the city to give a reading. The organization that had invited me arranged my lodging, setting my husband and me up with Mike, who lived in a remarkable house in the King William district (named after Prussia's King Wilhelm I). When we arrived in the late afternoon, Mike was nowhere to be found. We walked up his driveway and around to the back of his house where, in a small yard, a few chickens were roaming around.

The house itself was pure San Antonio: historic, grand without being big, eccentric, unpretentious, and a fantastic amalgam of cultural influences. The walls were covered from floor to ceiling with record album sleeves and contemporary art. The downstairs bathroom was wallpapered in concert and theater ticket stubs that dated back decades. There was a Pee-wee Herman doll perched on the mantel, and an old-fashioned bicycle parked inside the front door. There was a Christmas tree that was actually more of a Christmas bush, full and boxy and with no aspirations whatsoever to triangularity. Underneath it was a full-scale, three-dimensional replica of various Texas scenes, including a rodeo. There were Mexican *papel picado*—filigreed paper banners—hanging from the rafters. There was artwork featuring the Virgin of Guadalupe and Day of the Dead skeletons. There were Tiffany lamps on top of tables made of bamboo. The wingback chairs throughout the house were vintage, upholstered in floral fabrics. And there were scores of tinwork Mexican folk art sconces and chandeliers, the shades hole-punched to cast images of shadow and light against the walls and ceilings, in every corner and alcove and stairwell.

Mike was a slender fellow with glasses and a neat bow tie. I gave him a copy of my book, even though I'm pretty sure he had no idea who I was. He was simply a general supporter of artistic pursuit and, as such, had signed up to host visiting writers in town. He showed us around, told us to make ourselves at home, asked what we liked and didn't like to eat, and then excused himself to a gallery function he had already committed to. Later, he cooked for us, and we ate on the back porch, the chickens milling outside, while Mike explained the German influence on San Antonio, and told us how a shameful number of the details in the movie version of *Brokeback Mountain* were incorrect and how Larry McMurtry, a Texan and the man who wrote the screenplay, should have known better. Mike was hospitable, interesting, and warm—just like San Antonio.

M y fondness for Houston was slow to surface. The first time I was there, I somehow developed neck spasms—second only to childbirth in pain—and spent half of my trip in the emergency room. The other half I spent laid up on the couch while a tropical storm flooded the city.

The second time, I went to meet my then-boyfriend, now-husband, and help him pack up his things and move back to Chicago. We rented a U-Haul trailer, hitched it to his '93 Toyota Corolla, and hit the road. It was raining, and the sideview mirrors on the car were useless. I had to stick my head out of the car window every time he wanted to change lanes.

When I stuck my head out of the window the first time and saw that all was clear, I shouted into the wind-driven rain, "Go!"

My husband, driving along, dry as paper, said, "Did you say no or go?"

"Go!" I yelled.

"No or go?"

I whipped my head back inside the car. "GO!"

We switched to a yes/no system after that.

Houston was 0 for 2 with me.

I didn't think I would ever go back, but it turned out that one of our good college friends lived there, and since we were already in Dallas, it seemed easy enough to drive down and say hello.

By now, every state in the country relies on a web of highways, but I know of no other state that is built quite so much *along* the highways. You can drive in virtually any direction through Texas and see whole towns and the majority of cities from your car. In other states, you zoom down the highway and then, when you near your destination, you take an exit, drive a bit and rumble into town. In Texas, there's no such thing as a town or city offset from the highway, so what you see as you're speeding along are churches and upscale restaurants and bowling alleys and condos and sports stadiums and boutique shops. It's peculiar, but it makes for visually stimulating road trips pretty much anywhere you go. Anywhere, that is, but the drive from Dallas to Houston. That drive is all about desolation.

It's a four-hour trip and for about the first three hours the main attractions lining the road are a Dairy Queen, a drive-in movie theater, and a few adult-video stores. Then, out of the barren landscape rises what is billed The Largest Statue in the World of an American Hero, a towering, gleaming white statue of Sam Houston. It's scary if you don't know it's coming: Sam Houston, standing in a long coat, seemingly stepping out of the forest at his back, about to take one giant step across the highway, his walking stick in hand. The statue is technically in Huntsville, about seventy miles north of Houston and where Sam Houston—two-time president of the Republic of Texas as well as governor of the state—liked to spend his time, but it's how you know you're getting close (seventy miles is close in Texas) to the city that claims his name. When I saw it (I had only flown into Houston previously), it made me like the entire city just a little bit more.

The rest of the trip supported my burgeoning favorable assessment. I ate at the House of Pies, a diner that offers thirty varieties of pie and ten kinds of cake. My husband and I went to a series of Gold Cup soccer matches at Reliant Stadium, where we watched Panama lose to the United States and where I think I nearly lost my hearing from all the horns and whistles that erupted when Mexico's team took the field against Guatemala. (As my husband said later, "It was like being in Mexico.") I shopped for antiques on Westheimer, spending quite a bit of time in a futile search for a three-foot-tall rooster made from spare auto parts that a friend had spotted once and desperately wanted. And I partook in a Texas experience if ever I had one: a Hank Williams III concert. The concert was at a bar called Fitzgerald's, with a sagging porch and a dank interior, and we drank beer from bottles (Lone Star, since we knew we would be laughed out of the establishment if we tried to order anything else). We stood around in a loud, raucous, smoky room until Hank III took the stage and all hell broke loose. People were hanging from the balcony going *crazy* for this man who until that night I had never heard of. His grandfather, Hank Williams, Sr.? Sure. His father, Hank Williams, Jr.? Of course. But Hank III? It quickly became clear to me, though, that this was not so much a problem with him as with me, since everyone else was swooning, screaming the lyrics to his songs, and jumping around in uncontained revelry.

After he finished his "country" set, he went through some sort of transformation and took the stage again as a metal rocker, playing a brand of music that I have since learned is called "hellbilly." I felt, I'll admit, distinctly out of place, but also strangely exhilarated. I wasn't thinking about the rain in Houston, or the humidity, or about how I should have ordered a different kind of pie earlier. I was just thinking, This is it. This is Texas.

Energetic and loyal and proud and rowdy and a world unto itself. Hank III
sang it in his doleful way to a rapt and swaying crowd:

> It's a certain kinda livin',
> It's a certain kinda style.
> Not everybody likes us,
> But we drive some folks wild.

UTAH

CAPITAL   Salt Lake City

ENTERED UNION   1896 (45th)

ORIGIN OF NAME   From the Ute tribe, meaning "people
of the mountains"

NICKNAME   Beehive State

MOTTO   "Industry"

RESIDENTS   Utahan or Utahn

U.S. REPRESENTATIVES   3

STATE BIRD   California gull

STATE FLOWER   sego lily

STATE TREE   blue spruce

STATE SONG   "Utah, We Love Thee"

LAND AREA   82,144 sq. mi.

GEOGRAPHIC CENTER   In Sanpete Co.,
3 mi. N. of Manti

POPULATION   2,469,585

WHITE   89.2%

BLACK   0.8%

AMERICAN INDIAN   1.3%

ASIAN   1.7%

HISPANIC/LATINO   9.0%

UNDER 18   32.2%

65 AND OVER   8.5%

MEDIAN AGE   27.1

UTAH
David Rakoff

"Great swarms of bees will arise. Are you ignoring the signs?" This fortune cookie is nothing more than a canny History Channel promotion for a special about Nostradamus, but it seems an eerie message to receive mere days before my departure for Utah. After all, the forty-fifth state owes much of its history to fiery-eyed revelation and prophecy, and Deseret—the original pioneer name for the territory—was a neologism Joseph Smith coined in *The Book of Mormon* to mean "honeybee." The beehive is even the state's symbol. Perhaps it is folly to ascribe wisdom to a cookie, but with just over a week to visit and explore a state with an area of almost 85,000 square miles, I can use all the *ju-ju* I can get.

If the lobby of the Salt Lake Plaza is any indication, the end of October is an auspicious time to visit, with the air abuzz with omen and augury. Arriving past midnight, I am greeted by an elaborate Halloween display of a dry-ice fountain, skeins of cobweb, and cutouts of Dracula and Frankenstein, made all the more ghoulish by overhead fluorescent lighting, like the nurses' station in a state hospital. Turning on the television in my room, cheerfully located between the sixth-floor elevators, I note that the public access channel is showing a late-night program of a group of local Franciscans playing touch football in their brown cassocks, their rope belts swinging. The springs of my bed wheeze. The elevator dings. The ice machine right outside my door rumbles forth its icy bounty, a steady tattoo that beats "Stay up! Stay up!" I am in a canvas Edward Hopper never felt bummed-out enough to paint.

Morning banishes the gloom. The air is sun washed and pristine, carrying only a veil of haze from the California wildfires that have been raging for weeks. The lobby is full of genealogy tourists who have come to trace their family histories at the extensive Mormon archives. Utah, it seems, is where one comes to be found.

I join their happy ranks and follow them the few short blocks up to Temple Square, the spiritual and geographic heart of the city. A bride and groom hop up onto the stone ledge of a planter for the photographer, the better to capture the shining gold statue of the angel Moroni in the background. Moroni is the archangel of the faith, the prophet-warrior who gave Joseph Smith the golden plates that would eventually become *The Book of*

Mormon. There are numerous couples in white dresses and tuxedoes marking their big day, but the walkways of Temple Square are filled with an excitement that dwarfs anything matrimonial. Some back-up dancers from the *Hannah Montana Live* show have been spotted, identifiable by their tour jackets, scrubbed faces, and natural turnout. Children and elders alike swarm like bees and approach repeatedly to ask, "Is She here?"

She is not, alas, and we must console ourselves with naught but the opulent glories of these world headquarters of the Latter Day Saints. I begin in the South Visitors' Center, a sparsely furnished, carpeted space as hushed as a high-end rehab facility. The bulk of the displays are about the extraordinary and arduous efforts of the early Mormon pioneers in building the Temple. Huge, rough granite blocks were hewn by hand, transported one at a time over miles in wagons that often broke under the weight of the stone.

"The Latter Day Saints labored with faith for forty years to build the temple," reads one display. "A flawed initial foundation [and] the arrival of federal troops in 1858 caused major delays." This is an oblique reference to a skirmish known as the Utah War, when the federal government, alarmed at the subversive and un-American practice of polygamy, sent soldiers in and replaced Mormon leader Brigham Young with Alfred Cumming as territorial governor. Meanwhile, the chief mason had his leg amputated and still managed to hobble the twenty-two miles to Temple Square and then climb the scaffold in order to carve the final, consecrating declaration "Holiness to the Lord" in the stone façade.

In his 1873 novel *Around the World in Eighty Days,* Jules Verne sends Phileas Fogg and his valet, Passepartout, through Utah by train. There they encounter a man, dressed in the severe dark clothes of a clergyman, pasting flyers up and down the train. "Passepartout approached and read one of these notices, which stated that Elder William Hitch, Mormon missionary, taking advantage of his presence on train No. 48, would deliver a lecture on Mormonism in car No. 117, from eleven to twelve o'clock; and that he invited all who were desirous of being instructed concerning the mysteries of the religion of the 'Latter Day Saints' to attend." Passepartout takes a seat among thirty listeners. The Elder William Hitch begins his heated oration "in a rather irritated voice, as if he had been contradicted in advance: 'I tell you that Joe Smith is a martyr, that his brother Hiram is a martyr, and that the persecutions of the United States Government against the prophets will also make a martyr of Brigham Young. Who dares to say the contrary?'"

Hitch's outrage is understandable. Verne was writing in 1872, less than fif-teen years after the Utah War. Brigham Young had been imprisoned by the United States government for polygamy just the previous October. But by the end of the jeremiad, Passepartout is the only one left listening.

Nearly a century and a half later, the Mormons remain objects of suspi-cious scrutiny, a reputation stoked by the likes of lunatic fringe polygamist leader, convicted rapist (and, it should be noted, non-Utahan) Warren Jeffs. Or by the fact that blacks were only admitted into the Mormon Church in 1978 (a divine revelation of racial inclusion that coincided a little too tidily with the recruitment needs of the Brigham Young University football team, I am told). A sampling of some of the other things about the Latter Day Saints mentioned to me over the course of my time in Utah includes:

- Polygamous houses are identifiable by the screening stands of cedars out front.
- Mormon housewives will "accidentally" throw a red item of clothing into the washing machine thus changing their Garments—the ritual underclothing that comes in standard-issue white—pink.
- There is a growing social problem in polygamous families where the patriarch—also known as the father—like a silver-back gorilla whose sexual dominance is threatened, casts out the male children upon reaching puberty. This is particularly common in households where some of the wives are young teenagers themselves. Facing homelessness, these adolescents fall under the care of the state or live in group homes, eking out livings as carpenters and cabinet-makers, part of the tra-ditional LDS skills set.
- The usual proscriptions against caffeine do not apply to Coca-Cola, since BYU's board of trustees has a financial interest in the beverage company.
- There is a higher-than-average incidence of homosexuality among Mormon men. (This tidbit was always accompanied by a hyperlink to a calendar of shirtless missionaries and, like many theories in the "who's gay?" phylum, was almost in-variably followed up with the super-scientific assessment that "Mormon boys are the hottest.")
- The best place to see polygamous families is at Costco, where the competitive pricing and mayonnaise in jars the size of fire

hydrants makes it the obvious choice for a household with eighteen children. (Perhaps I went to the wrong one. I see nobody resembling sister-wives. But far more miraculous are the free eats. Unlike the eagle-eyed young foodies who dole out the samples in New York where they memorize your face, thus making going back for seconds nigh on impossible, the Costco I went to in Salt Lake City employs a veritable army of the geriatric, the halt, and the mentally not all-entirely-there, who man stations in their red uniforms and hand out free pizza, *chile relleno*, penne with chicken in "a quattro formaggio sauce," and never once give you the fish-eye, even if you return in under a minute for another pleated paper cup of those canned Indian River grapefruit segments.)

Some of this is demonstrably true (Warren Jeffs *was* a polygamist and he *is* in jail; if social services is taking case histories from boys being thrown out of their homes, then Q.E.D.), some of it is essentially unverifiable (without proper LDS identification, you cannot even see the Garments for sale in a Salt Lake City department store). But it is the tenacity of—and the pleasure taken in disseminating—the whispered chatter that is remarkable. Prior to my trip, I did not fail to receive a joking "Don't let them get you!" warning from everyone I spoke to, as if I were marching into the waiting jaws of a cult.

To understand why the Mormon faith might be routinely tarred with the Weird brush—and also why it should not be—one need but visit the North Visitors' Center. The lower level is an unassailable and impressive testament to present-day Mormon initiatives, both local and global, for fighting hunger and other good works. There are the requisite photographs of beautiful Third World children enjoying some all-too-rare nutrition or inoculation, although it is an unassuming pallet of canned food labeled "Deseret Industries," stretch-wrapped and ready for air-lift that packs the poignant punch.

Then, not twenty feet away, are interactive dioramas of scenes from *The Book of Mormon*, dealing with the prophet Nephi, a sojourn by the Nazarene Himself to the New World (there he is, blessing the Indians), and the Golden Book of runes revealed to and translated by Joseph Smith. In spirit, the particulars of the narrative are no more preposterous than the sagas that make up the cornerstones of Western society. This is not Scientology. Still, given this added liturgy and its narrative, found nowhere in the New Testament, it can be difficult to remember that Mormonism is a Jesus-based, Christian religion. (Over dinner, Morris Rosenzweig, a twenty-year resident, composer, and professor of music at the University of Utah in Salt Lake City, tells me of the time he was teaching a seminar on Bach, and mentioned in passing the *kyrie eleison* only to be met by blank stares. A fairly observant Jewish man, late of New Orleans and New York City, he then had to stop and teach the components of the Christian mass to his Mormon students.) But Christ remains the fulcrum, as evidenced when one walks the circular ramp to the upper level of the Visitors' Center. There a *tall*—18 feet?—statue of Jesus stands in the center of a domed atrium. The walls and ceiling have been painted in a hallucinatory rendering of the universe, all lurid planets and surging nebulae. In the words of anyone who has ever been sixteen, attended a laser rock show at their local planetarium, gazed longingly at an air-brushed van, or used *Dark Side of the Moon* to pick out stems and seeds, it is *fucking awesome.*

Of the original, pioneer-era buildings of Temple Square—the Tabernacle, Assembly Hall, and Temple itself—the worst architectural accusation one might level at them is that they are festooned with Gold Rush frippery. With their Gilded Age flourishes and frontier striver opulence of faux marble columns and polychrome plaster flowers, they are reminiscent of the Opera House in Aspen, Colorado. At the northern extreme of Temple Square, on the other hand, are two buildings that call up less benign associations. One is an imposing structure of white stone with square columns that would not be out of place in Fascist Italy. Diagonally across from this Mussolini edifice is another huge LDS headquarters, this one a near-parody of Cold War–era brutalism, with huge relief maps of the globe on either side of the massive doors. The building broadcasts an agenda of world domination, like some Strangelove-vintage United Nations of Really, Really Bad Guys. Neither does the church any public relations favors.

A shame, and not really true. For decades, Mormon boys (and some girls) have spent two years overseas on mission as a matter of course. The late unpleasantness of delayed black membership notwithstanding, there is a cultural value placed on learning other languages and encountering other people, a concomitant lack of xenophobia, and a focus on the often forgotten Christian notion of welcoming strangers in one's midst. On my way to the library—an impressive Moshe Safdie–designed multistory atrium with glass elevators for which the taxpayers dropped some serious coin—I am approached by an African-American man. He wonders if there wasn't once a building at a now-empty corner. He hasn't lived here for twelve years. He is back in town to find work as a cook, and off to the library to work on their computers.

"Oh, you've moved back," I say.

"Not really *moved* back. Washington state didn't work out. California didn't work out. I'm back at Square One." And Salt Lake City is about the best Square One he can think of. That's a bit of a surprise, given the church's only recent admission of blacks into its ranks. "That's *why*," he says, as an explanation for the kindness. He has Mormon friends all over the country. The Mormons are vigilant about treating people of color very well, he tells me.

If they are so friendly and benevolent, has he himself become LDS? "No way," he says. "That would be like joining the Klan."

According to Mary Jane Ciccarello, a lawyer who deals with the elderly, Salt Lake City was once known as a welcoming city all over the West, to the point where other towns would give vagrants the bus fare and send them here. We are sitting in one of the hearing rooms of the Mathison Courthouse. We play peekaboo with a Hispanic boy seated in the row in front of us, a beautiful child of about seven, nestled in the crook of his affectionate father's arms, a man of twenty-five at the oldest. The boy smiles at us throughout the hearings and fixes us with his enormous chocolate eyes. His father's left eye, by contrast, is occluded and milky with a neglected condition.

A very large young woman with a Polynesian name is called to the front (Salt Lake City boasts a sizable population of Mormon converts from Tonga). The public prosecutor is willing to lessen the disorderly conduct charge against her. He tantalizes us with just a hint of the actual story. "She was more the one who aided and encouraged, rather than actually the one who cut the hair."

A fellow in a tan county jail jumpsuit with greasy Wolfman Jack hair comes out from the holding area. Mouthing "I love you" to his elderly mother, he faces the judge. He has meth and domestic violence violations. He has failed to show up for court-ordered counseling or treatment. "Any reason we shouldn't revoke his probation and send him to jail?" asks the judge. The public defender mentions that his father is in ill health and it's not certain how much longer he will be alive. The defendant wants to "straighten up his life and fly right." But it seems he had ample opportunity to do so on many occasions, the judge counters. His case manager stands up to address the judge. But even this Angel of Mercy is over it. She has tried everything.

"He said he couldn't urinate in front of other people, so we did hair follicles and it was off the charts. It was nine times the limit. He should stay in jail and do the program there," she advises. The judge agrees.

"Put some money on my books," the man tells his mother as he is escorted out.

There is a cultivated dignity to the courtroom. The walls are decorated with framed artwork by children. The judge is respectful to all the defendants who come before him, almost particularly so to those who jangle in, their progress hindered by leg irons. No one here is getting rich from doing this work, but there is none of the exhaustion, squalor, or apathy one generally associates with the court system. The proceedings are run efficiently by the clerks, two blond women who tap away at their computers throughout, scheduling hearings and return appearances, etc. Mary Jane pegs them as LDS.

"No doubt about it," she says. "They probably have a ton of kids. The myth is that Mormon women don't work, that they're home being mothers. They all work. They have to."

In *Around the World in Eighty Days*, when Phileas Fogg and Passepartout venture out into the City of the Saints, they find that they cannot "escape from the taste for symmetry which distinguishes the Anglo-Saxons." The grid might have been noteworthy for a Frenchman like Verne, but it's a wonder that he makes no mention of the width of the streets of Salt Lake City, which are a steppe-like 132 feet across. This breadth was decreed by Brigham Young so that a team of oxen and a covered wagon might be able to turn around in a full circle unimpeded. (A similar pronouncement was attributed to Cecil Rhodes when he was overseeing the layout of the city of Buluwayo in Rhodesia. Perhaps this bit of hypertrophic urban planning was one of the Seven Habits of Highly Effective Nineteenth-Century Men with Big Ideas). The avenues yawn open, human proximity is vanquished, and the nearest people seem alienatingly distant. Perhaps such space between souls, such an uninterrupted vista of sky, imbues a populace with a sense of possibility; in its most literal sense, "room to grow."

Landscape shapes character, after all. This is never more clear than when I encounter the closest thing resembling a crowd at the Gateway Mall, a bi-level outdoor shopping center constructed to look like an Umbrian hill town (if Umbrian hill towns had California Pizza Kitchens). People, many of them in Halloween costumes, stroll eight abreast like one of Young's mythic team of oxen, never moving faster than the speed of cold honey. I have never been in a public space in America where a sense of how to walk among others was so completely and confoundingly absent. People stop abruptly, cut across lanes, and generally meander as blissfully unaware as cows in Delhi.

Perhaps it's not just space that informs this entitlement, but the idea behind it. Human history has always been subject to the random and anarchic interactions of rock and water. Settlement succeeds or fails according to an unwritten checklist: Is there a felicitous dearth of malaria-bearing insects and wild animals? A convenient absence of marauding locals? Does that vengeful and quick-to-ire volcano god routinely incinerate our children and bury our homes beneath an infernal slurry of lava? No? Let's stay a while.

What makes Utah unique is not just that those who settled it felt they *could* live here, but that they *should* live here. It was upon receiving the reports from his advance men of this paradoxical region of arable land hard by an inhospitable desert and a crop-killing inland sea that Brigham Young then received the divine revelation that this was the true land of the Saints. Topography as God-given destiny.

And what topography! My friend Wyatt Seipp drives down from Idaho, and we head out of the city. Barely an hour out of town, all is harsh and huge. We drive past the flaming smoke stacks of oil refineries, past small towns in the foothills. For the nonalpine dweller, "foothills" seems an oddly reductive term for such incline and sky-blocking mass. The tiny houses nestle toy-like against the slopes, and highest of all, by design, the local LDS Temple, the golden pin dot of its Moroni statue gleaming.

We're heading for Promontory Point, home of the Golden Spike historical site, about a hundred miles northwest of the city. It was there, on May 10, 1869, that the tracks of the Central Pacific met those of the Union Pacific and were joined to form the first transcontinental rail system. The landscape is as large and unprepossessing as the museum/restroom/gift shop is small and inconspicuous. It can be hard to fathom that we are at one of the most important places in the United States, but it was here at the Golden Spike that the country turned into, well, a country. The first transnational telegraph had been completed eight years earlier (in Salt Lake City, in fact) in October of 1861. The effect was felt immediately. This is not metaphoric. The Pony Express ceased operations literally two days later. You can still tap-tap-tap "Mother ill. Come soonest. Stop" all you like, but if you're relying on the stage coach to get you to the deathbed in question, I'm afraid I have some bad news. With the railroads, the trickle of settlers coming by wagon trains was suddenly upgraded to a flood of terrifyingly efficient westward expansion. Manifest destiny was transformed from the merely notional into reality at a speed never known theretofore. Just ask the Indians.

Scrub plain stretches in all directions to the suede brown hills in the distance. Even seen from above, the satellite images on Google Earth reveal an expanse as beige and unvaried as a slice of bologna. One has a sense of how delayed the gratification of congress must have been for the Central and Union Pacific teams. No doubt, they must have had one another in their sights for weeks before they could consider the job done. Then again, the sight of anyone new, even if only in the distance, must have been a welcome tonic after months of laying track out in the middle of nowhere. F. Scott Fitzgerald stopped too soon when he wrote about the fresh green breast of the New World (affectionately known as Long Island) that bloomed before Dutch sailors' eyes as being the last time mankind came face to face with something commensurate with his capacity for wonder. There was a whole continent beyond the eastern seaboard to slake the thirst of those seeking such adventure.

Standing at the squat commemorative obelisk, I try to conjure the mind-set that beheld this vast, sere pan of brown dirt—with the bare foot-hills rising in the distance, and the far more forbidding gray, snow-capped mountains rising farther beyond, all under a sky whose unbounded immensity proclaims one's insignificance with an irrefutable and terrifying truth— but I cannot do it. How does one take all this in and *still* think, *Yes, I will go ever gaily forward. I will endure a preindustrialized trek over hundreds of miles on a rocking, hard-slatted wagon bench or in a saddle, or on foot. I will leave my children behind, or watch them succumb to scarlet fever, rickets, or infection. On those special occasions when I do wipe my ass, it will be with leaves. I will have an abscessed molar extracted by some half-blind chuck-wagon drunkard wielding a pair of rusty pliers, and I will employ my own just-past-neolithic tools to make this railroad, this house, this town. And one fine day, with my remaining teeth, I will bite down on a leather strap while they amputate my leg without benefit of anesthetic and then I will hobble twenty-two miles on foot—one foot!—so that I might then climb a scaffold in order to carve a tribute to His glory into the unyielding granite escutcheon of a cathedral.* How did they do it? The monks and abbots who hauled the rocks to build their monasteries on craggy Himalayan peaks and kept at it until the job was done? Ditto the conquistadors who, even fueled with the promise of gold, saw those jagged, stratospheric peaks of the Andes and didn't just say *Oh fuck this, I'm going back to Spain.* It seems frankly remarkable that anyone anywhere ever attempted anything.

Clearly—and history thanks them for it—people did. And they have not stopped trying, either. We get back in the car and drive about thirty miles south to Rozel Point on the northeast shore of the Great Salt Lake proper, to the *Spiral Jetty*: Robert Smithson's 1970 earthwork, arguably the most significant piece of environmental art in the country, along with Walter De Maria's *Lightning Field* in New Mexico. The directions, downloaded from the Dia Art Foundation website, are exhaustively chatty. Instead of telling us to turn right, we read, ". . . drive 1.3 miles south. Here you should see a corral on the west side of the road. Here too, the road again forks. One fork continues south along the west side of the Promontory Mountains. This road leads to a locked gate. The other fork goes southwest toward the bottom of the valley and Rozel Point. Turn right onto the southwest fork . . ." They also warn us that the quality of the roads diminishes precipitously after the Golden Spike, and they're not kidding. It is rutted and dusty and cratered with potholes, and Wyatt has to serpentine the jeep, slowing down to such an extent that we eventually give up, get out, and walk the last bit.

The hills are littered with black basalt boulders. Below us to our left the jetty projects out into the lake. Cue the screeching brakes of dashed expectations. It's still an impressively huge project, but the thirty-eight years since its construction have not been kind. Its shape is barely discernible, certainly not the pristine fiddlehead fern the photographs would have one believe. Whatever whorl Smithson constructed is now largely lost; we think we make out a counterclockwise swoop but it stops well before another arc doubles back. And the whole is further diffused with errant rocks and old wood pilings. Picking our way down the hillside, we resolve to make the most of it and walk along whatever portion of the earthwork we can still find.

The jetty's decay is a bit of a surprise. Given the meticulous stewardship of the Dia Art Foundation—to say nothing of their website that documents essentially every pebble that might fly up to the undercarriage of our vehicle—one might think there would have been some warning or indication of the depredation of this, one of their jewels. The ingredients are all present and accounted for: the setting, the Salt Lake, black basalt. But it's like the Internet date who didn't lie, exactly; he *is* an underwear model, but for a prosthetics catalog.

We mask our disappointment with Pollyanna chatter about how fine the day, the relief to be out of the car, and similar platitudes. At one point stepping along the makeshift path, my feet sink down into the sucking mud. I pull my boots out with a terrestrial fart and soldier on with forced *Smell that air!* cheer. In the end, Wyatt's odometer will measure our journey at 250 miles round trip, and for what? A walk over crushed water bottles on sodden, uneven ground.

We turn back from a good quarter of a mile out on this ruin and survey the shore. There, parked on the hillside, 500 yards to our left, we see an SUV that had passed us earlier. And there down below, also 500 yards over, two small figures quietly standing in awed silence beside Robert Smithson's perfect, sublime *Spiral Jetty*.

Oh. I once knew a Swedish piano student at Juilliard who spent his first six weeks in New York thinking that Americans were a bunch of delusional blowhards before he understood that the Statue of Liberty that was underwhelming him daily was a one-tenth-size replica on top of a carpet store on the West Side of Manhattan.

There have, in the past, been years-long stretches when the jetty was submerged and largely invisible, but the water level has gone down, leaving in its place a hard-packed, blinding white tundra of salt. The gyre of ebony basalt couldn't be more beautifully visible, a black curl as pristinely contrasted on the salt sheet as a hair on a bar of soap. We are able to walk over and all around the 1,500-foot work on the surface of the lake, hard as solid ground in places, pleasingly slushy in others. In the distance, the roseate glow of the salt-loving algae makes a pink ribbon on the horizon. Smithson had likened the lake to a red Martian sea. The boulders of the spiral exposed to the windward side of the lake have taken on a tufted rime of salt, covered in small blunted protrusions; a stubby, thick fringe of sausage curls that make the rock resemble a line of sleeping lambs. Unyielding mineral rendered suckling-sweet. Like at the Golden Spike, the wind is a constant, cleansing hum on the ears.

The other couple move silently about the jetty, taking long-exposure close-up photos of rock, puddle, and the super-saturated lake's crystalline progress that has built up in places to a cubic zirconium size and brilliance. They don't say a word to Wyatt or me or to one another during the entire time we are there, although they occasionally bestow on us the almost drowsy half-smile of the devotional pilgrim. The notion of pilgrimage was central to Smithson's vision of the work's impact. He chose Rozel Point because of its remoteness. As for the jetty's shape—a snapshot in stone of an unfurling galaxy—it spoke to his interest in notions of entropy. "I am for an art that takes into account the direct effect of the elements as they exist from day to day," he wrote. "Parks are idealizations of nature, but nature in fact is not a condition of the ideal. . . . Nature is never finished."

Nor are we. All around us are odd bits of industrial detritus—a barely standing, low concrete structure where we left the car, the decoy jetty we mistook for the real thing—remnants of human effort, spinning out in ever-wider circles. Smithson saw it all as "evidence of a succession of man-made systems mired in abandoned hopes." Smithson is right about everything except for that penultimate word, "abandoned." Maybe it's the unwavering brown that greets the eye, or the parching airborne salt one can taste on the breeze that jump-starts some atavistic impulse to defy such inhospitality and to shape this intractable land to our will. Aspiration may be the only thing that has not pulled up stakes here. The pioneers who founded Zion are long dead. The dust that was once those railroad barons has little need of the personal fortunes they amassed, but hope remains as green and tender as a lily stem. Even Smithson himself, devotee of atomizing dissipation, dead in a plane crash before the age of forty and gone from this earth for over thirty years, constructed what might as well be a diorama of this unyielding faith. Newly emerged from decades of underwater obscurity, it is now visible from space.

VERMONT

CAPITAL Montpelier

ENTERED UNION 1791 (14th)

ORIGIN OF NAME From the French vert mont, meaning "green mountain"

NICKNAME Green Mountain State

MOTTO "Vermont, Freedom and Unity"

RESIDENTS Vermonter

U.S. REPRESENTATIVES 1

STATE BIRD hermit thrush

STATE FLOWER red clover

STATE TREE sugar maple

STATE SONG "These Green Mountains"

LAND AREA 9,250 sq. mi.

GEOGRAPHIC CENTER In Washington Co., 3 mi. E of Roxbury

POPULATION 623,050

WHITE 96.8%

BLACK 0.5%

AMERICAN INDIAN 0.4%

ASIAN 0.9%

HISPANIC/LATINO 0.9%

UNDER 18 24.2%

65 AND OVER 12.7%

MEDIAN AGE 37.7

THINGS MIGHT NEVER HAVE COME TO SUCH A PASS IF ON MY FIRST VISIT WE HAD NOT PROCEEDED DIRECTLY FROM THE AIRPORT TO THE SUMMIT OF A MOUNTAIN CALLED CAMEL'S HUMP.

I LOVE YOU.

HEIGHT OF FOLIAGE SEASON

SILVERY LAKE

KEEP OFF THE SEDGE

I WAS CONFUSED, OF COURSE. I'D FALLEN IN LOVE NOT WITH THIS PERSON, BUT WITH THIS PLACE.

SEVERAL MONTHS LATER, WITH NO MORE THAN THE USUAL DIFFICULTY...

U-HAUL

GENTLE RIDE

...I LEFT HER ISLAND AND SETTLED IN THE FOOTHILLS OF THE GREEN MOUNTAINS.

0   10

LAKE CHAMPLAIN

GREEN MOUNTAINS

Camel's Hump

WHAT'S SO COMPELLING TO ME ABOUT THE MOUNTAINS? IS IT THAT THERE'S ALWAYS SOMEWHERE TO GO?

New York

4000
3000
2000
1000 ft

UP ↑

← CAMEL'S HUMP

DOWN ↓

MILES   16   32   48

VERMONT in profile

New Hampshire

IS IT THE SUPRAMUNDANE PERSPECTIVE AFFORDED BY A SUMMIT?

TH' INSIGNIFICANCE OF IT ALL....

IS IT GENETIC? MY GRANDFATHER HERDED GOATS AS A BOY IN THE AUSTRIAN ALPS.

HE TOOK ME TO SEE *THE SOUND OF MUSIC* WHEN I WAS FOUR. IT MOVED US BOTH PROFOUNDLY.

WHILE IT EVOKED MEMORIES FOR HIM OF HIS TYROLEAN CHILDHOOD, IT BECAME A MEMORY FOR ME—MY EARLIEST EROTIC EXPERIENCE.

...BLESS MY HOME-LAND FOREVER...

THOSE VERTIGINOUS MOUNTAINSCAPES ARE FOREVER FUSED WITH THE STRANGE FEELING THAT THE ANDROGYNOUS EX-NUN INDUCED IN ME.

...TILL...YOU...FIND...YOUR...DREAM!

The End

UPON ESCAPING THE NAZIS, THE REAL VON TRAPP FAMILY SINGERS MOVED TO VERMONT AND OPENED A TOURIST LODGE IN A ROLLING VALLEY OUTSIDE OF STOWE THAT REMINDED THEM OF HOME.

MINUS THE HIGH PEAKS, BUT ALSO MINUS THE NAZIS

THE LODGE IS STILL HERE, AND BOASTS AN EXCELLENT CROSS-COUNTRY SKI AREA.

NORDIC CENTER

ABSENCE OF NAZIS, PRESENCE OF HILLS.

THE SAME REASONS I MOVED TO VERMONT.

MARIA PLAZA

LODGE ▶

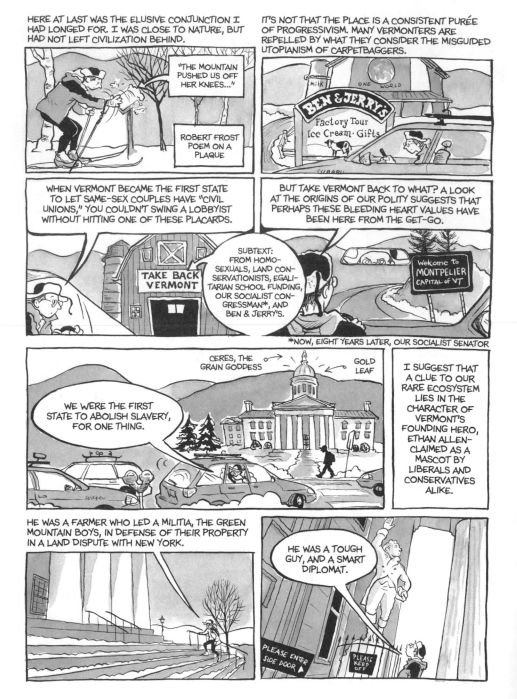

HERE AT LAST WAS THE ELUSIVE CONJUNCTION I HAD LONGED FOR. I WAS CLOSE TO NATURE, BUT HAD NOT LEFT CIVILIZATION BEHIND.

"THE MOUNTAIN PUSHED US OFF HER KNEES..."

ROBERT FROST POEM ON A PLAQUE

IT'S NOT THAT THE PLACE IS A CONSISTENT PURÉE OF PROGRESSIVISM. MANY VERMONTERS ARE REPELLED BY WHAT THEY CONSIDER THE MISGUIDED UTOPIANISM OF CARPETBAGGERS.

milk ONE WORLD
BEN & JERRY'S
Factory Tour
Ice Cream · Gifts

WHEN VERMONT BECAME THE FIRST STATE TO LET SAME-SEX COUPLES HAVE "CIVIL UNIONS," YOU COULDN'T SWING A LOBBYIST WITHOUT HITTING ONE OF THESE PLACARDS.

TAKE BACK VERMONT

SUBTEXT: FROM HOMO-SEXUALS, LAND CON-SERVATIONISTS, EGALI-TARIAN SCHOOL FUNDING, OUR SOCIALIST CON-GRESSMAN*, AND BEN & JERRY'S.

BUT TAKE VERMONT BACK TO WHAT? A LOOK AT THE ORIGINS OF OUR POLITY SUGGESTS THAT PERHAPS THESE BLEEDING HEART VALUES HAVE BEEN HERE FROM THE GET-GO.

Welcome to MONTPELIER CAPITAL of VT

*NOW, EIGHT YEARS LATER, OUR SOCIALIST SENATOR

CERES, THE GRAIN GODDESS

GOLD LEAF

WE WERE THE FIRST STATE TO ABOLISH SLAVERY, FOR ONE THING.

I SUGGEST THAT A CLUE TO OUR RARE ECOSYSTEM LIES IN THE CHARACTER OF VERMONT'S FOUNDING HERO, ETHAN ALLEN—CLAIMED AS A MASCOT BY LIBERALS AND CONSERVATIVES ALIKE.

HE WAS A FARMER WHO LED A MILITIA, THE GREEN MOUNTAIN BOYS, IN DEFENSE OF THEIR PROPERTY IN A LAND DISPUTE WITH NEW YORK.

HE WAS A TOUGH GUY, AND A SMART DIPLOMAT.

PLEASE ENTER SIDE DOOR ▲

PLEASE KEEP OFF

AFTER RUNNING YOUR NON-CHAIN STORE ERRANDS IN MONTPELIER, YOU CAN GO TO A NON-CHAIN THEATRE FOR A THREE-HOUR FOREIGN FILM.

7 PM LADY CHATTERLEY

I SAW ONE HERE LAST MONTH. I LIKED THE AUDIENCE BEST.

...SHE CUT DOWN A SMALL SUGAR BUSH TO GET THE VIEW.

I TOOK EXCEPTION TO HIS TERM "TERRORIST SUSPECTS" IN MY LAST BLOG POST. DID YOU SEE IT?

UH... NO.

GRAYING, ERUDITE BACK-TO-THE-LANDERS.

I HAD ENOUGH CLUES TO TRACK DOWN THE BLOGGER WHEN I GOT HOME. HE TURNED OUT TO BE POSTING UNDER AN INTERESTING PSEUDONYM...

ETHAN ALLEN'S BLOG

Submitted by Ethan Allen on Sat. 12/01/2007 - 11:04am

The term "terrorist suspects" is turning up i

meeting in Montpelier, in vain, that I want t

...ON A SECESSIONIST WEBSITE.

VT Commons

Vermonters should peaceably secede from the United States Empire and govern themselves as a more sustainable independent republic once again.

TOGETHER? OR APART? MAYBE SECEDING ISN'T AS CRAZY AS IT SOUNDS. AFTER I LEFT THE WOMAN I CAME TO VERMONT FOR, I MET SOMEONE ELSE. WE WERE TOGETHER FOR A LONG TIME.

Foot of snow on April 1927!

BUT THEN WE BROKE UP, TOO. IT'S IMPOSSIBLE TO ISOLATE A SINGLE FACTOR IN THESE MATTERS, OF COURSE, BUT OUR DIFFERENCES BECAME POLARIZED AROUND PLACE.

I CAN'T TAKE ONE MORE WINTER ON THIS HILL.

I CAN'T MOVE TO TOWN. I'D... I'D **DIE**.

WINTERS IN VERMONT ARE LONG. THE ABENAKI PEOPLE WHO LIVED HERE HAD A RULE: IN THEIR CRAMPED WINTER WIGWAMS, EVERYONE GOT A SMALL BUT INVIOLATE SPACE OF THEIR OWN.

THIS COULD NOT BE ENTERED WITHOUT PERMISSION.

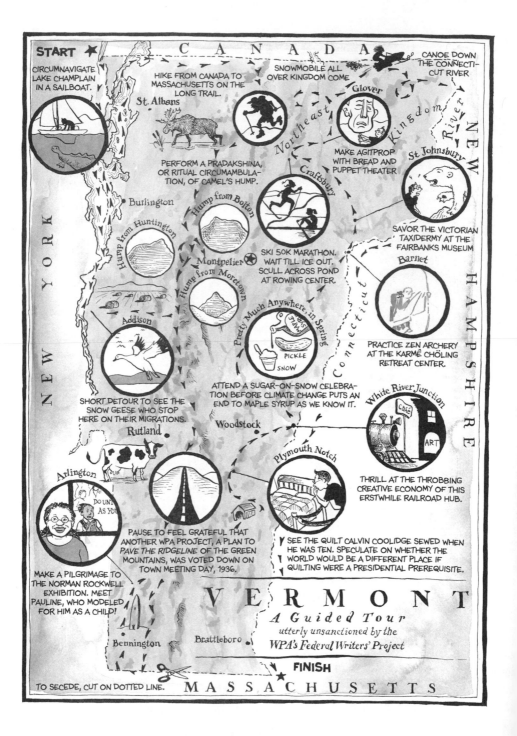

START ★

CANADA

CIRCUMNAVIGATE LAKE CHAMPLAIN IN A SAILBOAT.

HIKE FROM CANADA TO MASSACHUSETTS ON THE LONG TRAIL.

SNOWMOBILE ALL OVER KINGDOM COME

CANOE DOWN THE CONNECTI-CUT RIVER

St. Albans

Glover

MAKE AGITPROP WITH BREAD AND PUPPET THEATER

Northeast Kingdom River

NEW

St Johnsbury

PERFORM A PRADAKSHINA, OR RITUAL CIRCUMAMBULA-TION, OF CAMEL'S HUMP.

Craftsbury

Burlington

SAVOR THE VICTORIAN TAXIDERMY AT THE FAIRBANKS MUSEUM

Hump from Huntington

Hump from Bolton

Montpelier ✪

Barnet

SKI 50K MARATHON. WAIT TILL ICE OUT. SCULL ACROSS POND AT ROWING CENTER.

Hump from Moretown

NEW

YORK

Pretty Much Anywhere, in Spring

Connecticut

PRACTICE ZEN ARCHERY AT THE KARMÉ CHÖLING RETREAT CENTER.

Addison

PICKLE SNOW

HAMPSHIRE

White River Junction

SHORT DETOUR TO SEE THE SNOW GEESE WHO STOP HERE ON THEIR MIGRATIONS.

ATTEND A SUGAR-ON-SNOW CELEBRA-TION BEFORE CLIMATE CHANGE PUTS AN END TO MAPLE SYRUP AS WE KNOW IT.

Woodstock

CAFÉ
ART

Rutland

Plymouth Notch

THRILL AT THE THROBBING CREATIVE ECONOMY OF THIS ERSTWHILE RAILROAD HUB.

Arlington

DO UNTO AS YOU

PAUSE TO FEEL GRATEFUL THAT ANOTHER WPA PROJECT, A PLAN TO PAVE THE RIDGELINE OF THE GREEN MOUNTAINS, WAS VOTED DOWN ON TOWN MEETING DAY, 1936.

SEE THE QUILT CALVIN COOLIDGE SEWED WHEN HE WAS TEN. SPECULATE ON WHETHER THE WORLD WOULD BE A DIFFERENT PLACE IF QUILTING WERE A PRESIDENTIAL PREREQUISITE.

MAKE A PILGRIMAGE TO THE NORMAN ROCKWELL EXHIBITION. MEET PAULINE, WHO MODELED FOR HIM AS A CHILD!

VERMONT
A Guided Tour
utterly unsanctioned by the
WPA's Federal Writers' Project

Bennington

Brattleboro

✂ ➤ FINISH ★

TO SECEDE, CUT ON DOTTED LINE.   MASSACHUSETTS

VIRGINIA

CAPITAL   Richmond

ENTERED UNION   1788 (10th)

ORIGIN OF NAME   In honor of Elizabeth, the "Virgin Queen" of England

NICKNAMES   The Old Dominion or Mother of Presidents

MOTTO   Sic semper tyrannis ("Thus always to tyrants")

RESIDENTS   Virginian

U.S. REPRESENTATIVES   11

STATE BIRD   cardinal

STATE FLOWER   American dogwood

STATE TREE   dogwood

STATE SONG   none

LAND AREA   39,594 sq. mi.

GEOGRAPHIC CENTER   In Buckingham Co., 5 mi. SW of Buckingham

POPULATION   7,567,465

WHITE   72.3%

BLACK   19.6%

AMERICAN INDIAN   0.3%

ASIAN   3.7%

HISPANIC/LATINO   4.7%

UNDER 18   24.6%

65 AND OVER   11.2%

MEDIAN AGE   35.7

VIRGINIA
Tony Horwitz

In fourth grade at Waterford Elementary, my son's teacher came up with a creative assignment called Hotel Virginia. Each student had to research a figure from state history and build a shoebox diorama of that person's room. From the contents, parents would guess whom the rooms belonged to when they toured Hotel Virginia on Parent-Teacher night.

I arrived to find the boxes stacked in rows, a cardboard catacomb. My son's held a pistol, a rebel flag, and other miniature effects of John Mosby, the elusive Confederate guerrilla known as the "Gray Ghost." Two rooms were draped in the bloody uniforms of Rebs who didn't get away, Jeb Stuart and Stonewall Jackson. Fur and beads filled other boxes, for Opechancanough, the Indian chief shot in the back at Jamestown, and his niece, Pocahontas, kidnapped by the English and killed by disease at twenty. A black raven adorned the room of Edgar Allan Poe, nevermore at forty. One chamber was done up like the log inn where Meriwether Lewis shot himself in the head, three years after crossing the continent with Clark.

When I told the teacher her students seemed morbidly inclined, she laughed and said, "At this age, kids don't care about the Declaration of Independence. All they want to know is, 'What was the body count?' " If that's so, then Virginia is a fourth-grader's paradise. Having lived in six states and toured the other forty-four, I've never seen one so steeped in gore. Nor is there another that clings to its dark history so insistently. Hotel Colorado or Hotel Arizona I imagine as sunny, uncluttered places. Hotel Virginia, inescapably, is a charnel house.

Much about Virginia has changed since the WPA published *A Guide to the Old Dominion* in 1940. "Our people," the governor observed in an opening letter, with evident pride, are "largely of Anglo-Saxon blood." Highlights of the state's calendar included "Anniversary of the death of General Robert E. Lee" and "National Tobacco Festival and Pageant." Two thirds of Virginia's 2.5 million inhabitants were rural, and most of those were poor, grossing less than $600 a year. Quite a contrast to today, when the population is three times as large, median household income is $51,000 (well above the national average), and almost a third of Virginians are clustered in the high-tech and largely Latino and Asian suburbs of Washington, D.C.

But one line on the second page of the WPA Guide seemed instantly familiar. "There is a deliberate cult of the past," it reads. "Virginians are Shintoists under the skin."

I first became aware of this fifteen years ago, when my wife and I settled in a village the WPA Guide described as "dozing between low hills that roll down to meadows along a lazy creek." Waterford, population 200, seemed a good place to rot after years of nomadic reporting from history-haunted lands like Bosnia, Sudan, and Iraq.

Then, as soon as we'd moved in, Disney announced plans to build a theme park thirty miles away, beside the Manassas battlefield, where the South scored a surprise rout at the start of the Civil War. Disney's "imagineers" concocted rides and pyrotechnics that would, they claimed, do for history what textbooks and school trips never could. "The idea is to walk out of Disney's America with a smile on your face," the park's manager explained. "It is going to be fun with a capital F." Disney's chairman, Michael Eisner, contrasted this delight to the un-imagineered history he'd ingested as a child, while being "dragged" to the region's sites. "It was," he said, "the worst weekend of my life."

Like the over-confident Union Army that marched on Manassas in 1861, Disney misjudged its foes. The theme park was howled out of the state amidst cries it would desecrate "hallowed ground." Never mind that Manassas had long since been sullied by smog and exurban sprawl. The matter was spiritual. For Virginia, custodian of American history's holiest places, ceding an inch of sacred ground to vulgarians from California would be like Saudi Arabia surrendering Mecca and Medina to pork-eating infidels.

Not long after Disney retreated, I set off from Waterford, at the northern tip of Virginia's tricorn, to tour the state's Civil War sites. Most lie close to Interstate 95, which enters Virginia at the Potomac River and runs through Fredericksburg, Richmond, and Petersburg before crossing into the piney woods of North Carolina. Speeding south from Washington, I noticed something odd. Not until I'd driven fifty miles through Virginia and reached the Rappahannock River did I arrive at the state Welcome Center. Most states plant their tourist facilities right at the state border, and Virginia observes this protocol at all its interstate entry points—except this one.

It's a small but telling bit of symbolism: an internal border post, guarding the state's heartland from the breakaway region of *Northern* Virginia. Like so much about Virginia, this separation is mired in bloody history. For much of the Civil War, the Rappahannock was the conflict's eastern front, a crooked line between vast armies encamped on opposing banks. Four of the War's bloodiest battles were fought by the river, almost within cannon shot of the Welcome Center.

Most of Virginia above the Rappahannock was occupied territory, and in the view of many state residents, it remains so today. Northern Virginia, once the proud name of Robert E. Lee's army, has become a pejorative, denoting a soulless expanse of malls, subdivisions, federal bureaucracy, and liberal politics—the invading edge of BosWash. Below the Rappahannock, accents broaden, the pace slows, the landscape turns rural and the people more religious and conservative. Waitresses address you as "honey" while pouring from pitchers of sweetened iced tea. Grits appear on the menu. Welcome to Virginia. Welcome to the South.

Turning off I–95 at the Rappahannock, I went to see the spot where Thomas "Stonewall" Jackson was shot from his horse while chasing retreating Yankees at Chancellorsville. In 1921, a Marine Corps general named Smedley D. Butler was conducting military exercises in the area when a local told him that Stonewall's arm lay buried on a nearby farm. "Bosh," Butler declared. "I will take a squad of marines and dig up that spot to prove you wrong!"

He did—and found a bone, which he promptly reburied beneath a bronze plaque. The plaque is gone but I found a simple headstone in the middle of a field: "Arm of Stonewall Jackson, May 3 1863." That's the date of the limb's amputation. The rest of the Confederate hero died a week later, at a cottage now known as the Stonewall Jackson Shrine. After a funeral procession so prolonged that his badly embalmed body began to decompose, Jackson was buried in the Shenandoah Valley town of Lexington, where he'd taught artillery tactics and natural philosophy at the Virginia Military Institute.

The story gets more macabre, as it always does in Virginia. Stonewall's mount on the night of his mortal wounding, Little Sorrel, outlived its master by twenty-three years and became a Southern icon, paraded at county fairs and Confederate fetes. Upon its death, a taxidermist mounted the gelding's hide on a plaster of Paris frame. Little Sorrel's skeleton did service in biology classes at VMI.

Then, in 1997, the Institute decided to inter the horse's 147-year-old bones. I went to the "funeral" in Lexington, a pretty town nestled between mountains. Confederate-clad pallbearers lowered a walnut coffin into the VMI parade ground, and women in period mourning attire showered the casket with clods of dirt scooped from the battlefields where Little Sorrel rode. Musket volleys were fired, tears shed, carrot wreaths laid. Then the mourners filed off to pay their respects to Little Sorrel's tattered hide, still on exhibit at VMI's museum, and also to Robert E. Lee's warhorse, Traveller, buried nearby after its own long period of public display.

One reason Virginians can't leave their bones alone is that there are so many of them. Half or more of the Civil War's 620,000 dead perished in Virginia; the toll in the state's camps, prisons, hospitals, and battles is at best a guess, because most of the fallen were unaccounted for. In the spring of 1864, when Grant launched an offensive across the Rappahannock that cost the Union 65,000 casualties in seven weeks, soldiers kept stumbling on the decayed bodies of men killed there the year before. Bones still turn up from time to time. Of the state's countless Confederate monuments, the most apt may be one in Rappahannock County, erected in memory of the "Deathless Dead."

But Virginia, for all its Civil War carnage, shouldn't be viewed only in ambrotype. It was a necropolis from the start. The territory first called Virginia was a royal grant from Elizabeth I to Walter Raleigh, a retainer who repaid the favor by naming his domain in honor of the Virgin Queen. This is the rare shard of state history that's since been dishonored, in favor of the tourist slogan "Virginia Is for Lovers," which first appeared in an issue of *Modern Bride*.

In any event, Raleigh dispatched a party to colonize Virginia, including a young scholar, Thomas Hariot, who wrote that natives "are notably preserved in health, and know not many grievous diseases." Hariot attributed this to the Indians' use of tobacco, a habit he adopted until dying of cancer. However, Hariot also noticed that soon after the English arrived, Indians "began to die very fast, and many in a short space." Natives thought the English were "shooting invisible bullets into them," which was essentially the case. The virgin wilderness of American imagination was a land cleared of its native inhabitants by successive waves of epidemic disease.

Raleigh's colonists didn't fare well, either. When the first group at Roanoke Island failed, Sir Walter sent another, in 1587. The colony's leader quickly sailed home for more supplies, leaving behind 115 settlers, including the first English child born in America, Virginia Dare. They were never seen or heard from by the English again, having vanished into lore: the "lost colonists" of Roanoke.

In 1607, when the English tried to colonize Virginia again, at swampy Jamestown, the story came close to repeating itself. Of the 105 original colonists, two thirds died within a few months, mostly from starvation and disease. Thousands more colonists followed, only to succumb at a similar rate. The English called this "seasoning." Settlers landed, fell ill, and if they recovered, became "seasoned" to their new surrounds. A staggering 80 percent didn't. "Virginia," observes historian Edmund Morgan, "was absorbing England's surplus laborers mainly by killing them."

The colony survived by exporting tobacco (more death, but that's another story) and Jamestown was abandoned for better ground. It became a ghost settlement, and later, the site of a Confederate bulwark. Until recently, there wasn't much to see there, except monuments to John Smith and Pocahontas. Then, digging beneath the Civil War breastworks, archaeologists found remnants of the English fort. Much of it was floored with shallow graves and human remains, not all of them undisturbed. During a long winter known as the Starving Time, when all but sixty of Jamestown's five hundred settlers died, colonist George Percy wrote: "Nothing was spared to maintain life and to do those things which seem incredible, as to dig up dead corpses out of graves and to eat them." History: fun with a capital F!

A mong the more exuberantly absurd ideas for Disney's America was one offered by the park's creative director: "We want to make you feel what it was like to be a slave." He didn't elaborate, but some glimpse of that experience is readily available near Jamestown. In 1619, a year before the Pilgrims landed at Plymouth, "20 and odd Negroes" were unloaded from a ship at the mouth of the James River and sold to the colony in exchange for food. Though little else is known of the "Black *Mayflower*" and its cargo, African slaves soon became the labor force on the great tobacco plantations that sprang up along the James.

The most famous of these is Berkeley Plantation, a Georgian pile with a boxwood garden and lawns rolling down to the river. Hostesses in wide skirts now give tours of Berkeley's "manor house" and tell of its fine furnishings and famous inhabitants, most notably Benjamin Harrison V, one-time governor of Virginia, signer of the Declaration of Independence, and a man extolled in the plantation's literature as "the perfected product of the aristocracy devoted to producing the superior individual."

A small item in Berkeley's basement museum gives a darker portrait. It's a 1791 inventory of Harrison's 110 slaves, each identified by a first name or moniker such as "Old Nanny." Precise monetary values are recorded beside every name, and a third bookkeeping column is headed "remarks," often just a single word: "crippled," "worthless," "infirm." An "Old boye" of sixty-two is described as "mad" and valued at zero. His owner, who died in 1791 of corpulence and gout, passed Old boye and Old Nanny to his heirs, one of them his son, William Henry Harrison, who became America's ninth president after campaigning as a humble "log cabin" candidate.

While the Virginia of tourist imagination is crowded with wigged gentry and baronial estates, the state's plantation aristocracy barely outlasted Benjamin V and his gout. In the early 1800s, Virginia entered a long decline, due to the wasting of its soil by tobacco and the out-migration of its people to better lands. The state's principal remaining asset was its surplus of slaves, which Virginians turned into an export commodity, selling over 10,000 a year, mostly into the burgeoning cotton fields of the Deep South. By the Civil War, just five percent of white Virginians owned slaves and there were only 114 who owned as many as Benjamin Harrison had seventy years before.

Yet it was antebellum Virginia that spawned by far the bloodiest slave revolt in U.S. history. It occurred due south of Berkeley, in Southampton County, one of the most rural in Virginia. Of the state's many haunted places, Southampton is to me the eeriest. There are no monuments to what happened there, but the setting is little changed: low fields fringed by swampy woods, weatherboard houses set far apart, a route still called Jerusalem Plank Road, though the planks laid on top of mud in the nineteenth century have long since given way to asphalt. And then, beside a peanut field, one of only two road markers in Southampton acknowledging the "servile insurrection" that broke out late one August night in 1831.

Nat Turner, a thirty-year-old slave preacher, led six accomplices out of the woods, armed mainly with farm tools, then marched from farmhouse to farmhouse, hacking or bludgeoning to death every white they found. The band swelled to sixty and rampaged for two days before a hastily assembled militia dispersed the rebels, killing or capturing most of them. Whites then went on a revenge spree of their own, murdering, torturing, and dismembering hundreds of blacks—many times the number Turner's men killed. The heads of some were impaled on stakes along a road still known as Blackhead Signpost.

After a two-month manhunt, "Nat the Contriver"—described in a reward notice as "knock kneed" and scarred "by a blow"—was found hiding in the woods and jailed in Jerusalem, the county seat he'd hoped to seize. In a confession from his cell, Turner spoke of visions and portents he'd seen since boyhood: "white spirits and black spirits engaged in battle," "drops of blood on the corn," "hieroglyphic characters and numbers" imprinted on leaves. All of this convinced him the moment had come "when the first should be last and the last should be first," and that God had commanded him to "arise and prepare myself, and slay my enemies with their own weapons."

Even more chilling to white Virginians was Turner's dispassionate account of the "work of death," beginning with the slaughter of a man "who was to me a kind master," along with his wife and three children, including an infant killed in his cradle. Most of those slain in the revolt were women and children, including a schoolteacher and her ten students. At his trial, Turner pleaded not guilty, "saying to his counsel that he did not feel so."

He was hanged six days later. Since he was "late the property of Putnam Moore, an infant," the child's estate was recompensed by the state for chattel destroyed, as were the owners of other executed slaves. Turner, literate and skilled, brought $375.

Like Stonewall Jackson and Little Sorrel, Nat the Contriver had a long and ghoulish afterlife. His corpse was dismembered, with some of its skin turned into a purse and the head sent to a college for study. Rumors of the body parts' whereabouts circulated well into the twentieth century. And in the 1930s, when the WPA interviewed elderly ex-slaves in Virginia, some spoke of a ghostly figure known as "Ole Nat" or "Prophet Nat" who had fought to free his people.

Though Turner failed, his revolt emboldened abolitionists, including William Lloyd Garrison, who wrote in *The Liberator*: "The first step of the earthquake, which is ultimately to shake down the fabric of oppression, leaving not one stone upon another, has been made." In 1859, John Brown set out to arm slaves, as Turner had done, at the other end of Virginia. He, too, went to the gallows, declaring, "the crimes of this *guilty* land will never be purged *away* but with Blood." John Brown's body, at least, was carried out of Virginia and lies a'mouldering in peace, in upstate New York.

Harpers Ferry, where Brown staged his famous "raid," no longer belongs to Virginia. In fact, like so many of the state's historic figures, Virginia has been cut up and distributed for centuries. The original Elizabethan land of Virginia—which Sir Walter lost upon his conviction for treason, before also losing his head—stretched from Florida to Maine and inland for an indeterminate distance. In those days, the "North Part of Virginia" referred not to Fairfax or the Dulles Corridor, but to the cold, rocky shore of Massachusetts and Maine.

In 1614, Northern Virginia was rechristened New England, by Jamestown's hero, John Smith. The Carolinas were carved out of Virginia's underside in 1629; Maryland broke off three years later. In 1784, Virginia ceded most of its vast interior, which extended beyond the Mississippi and north to Canada, to the newly created United States. Kentucky fell away in 1792, and West Virginia completed the vivisection by joining the Union in 1863. Once almost boundless, Virginia now ranks a lowly thirty-fifth among the states in geographic size. If, as some Virginians only half-jokingly suggest, the state were to lop off its head at the Rappahannock, it would shed another five counties and several million people.

Which raises the question: Will Virginia, now entering its fifth century, ever shed the shackles of its dark and divided history? One baby step in that direction seemed to occur in 1997, when the General Assembly in Richmond voted to retire the state song, "Carry Me Back to Old Virginny," a nineteenth-century minstrel that waxed nostalgic for "massa and missus" and included the refrain, "There's where this old darkey's heart am long'd to go." A song commission was formed and a contest announced to find a new anthem that had "dignity," "singability," and broad appeal to Virginians.

Hundreds of submissions flowed in, and with them came lawsuits, charges of pork-peddling (Jimmy Dean, a songwriter and sausage magnate, contributed to the campaign of one judge), and wrangling over lyrics. "That thing has been a nightmare," one frustrated legislator declared of the sniping. " 'Well, your song didn't have anything about Northern Virginia. Well, your song didn't have anything about Southern Virginia.' "

In 2006, after almost a decade of debate over ditties, the state senate proposed "Shenandoah" as an interim song. Then complaints arose that the lyrics don't mention Virginia; instead, they're about leaving the state and crossing "the wide Missouri." Arguing in the song's defense, a legislator noted, "At one time, Virginia did stretch to Missouri. All the way!"

But those days are long past, and "Shenandoah" was voted down. Virginia retains a state shell (oyster), state insect (tiger swallowtail butterfly), state bat (Virginia Big-Eared Bat), and state fossil (*Chesapecten jeffersonius*). But it is the only state in the nation without a song.

Like the balladeer of "Shenandoah," I've now left Virginia and often long for the state's mountains and rivers. I even miss its gloomy fetish for the past—refreshing, almost, in a country that's relentlessly optimistic and forward-looking. Instead of trying to forget or sanitize Virginia history, the legislature could take a cue from my son's fourth-grade class, and adapt the famous song by the Eagles:

> On a dark Southern highway, hot wind in my hair
> Warm smell of magnolia rising up through the air . . .
> I heard a distant death knell and was thinking to myself,
> This could be Heaven or this could be Hell . . .
> Blood on the ceiling and bloody limbs on ice
> We are all just prisoners here of our own device . . .
> Welcome to the Hotel Virginia.

WASHINGTON

CAPITAL Olympia

ENTERED UNION 1889 (42nd)

ORIGIN OF NAME In honor of George Washington

NICKNAME Evergreen State

MOTTO Al-Ki (an Indian word meaning "by and by")

RESIDENTS Washingtonian

U.S. REPRESENTATIVES 9

STATE BIRD willow goldfinch

STATE FLOWER coast rhododendron

STATE TREE western hemlock

STATE SONG "Washington, My Home"

LAND AREA 66,544 sq. mi.

GEOGRAPHIC CENTER In Chelan Co., 10 mi. WSW of Wenatchee

POPULATION 6,287,759

WHITE 81.8%

BLACK 3.2%

AMERICAN INDIAN 1.6%

ASIAN 5.5%

HISPANIC/LATINO 7.5%

UNDER 18 25.7%

65 AND OVER 11.2

MEDIAN AGE 35.3

WASHINGTON
Carrie Brownstein

Certain 1980s models of the Chrysler LeBaron sedan had pinstriped seats—pencil-thin, black-and-gray lines, so that you and your business attire merged into a single professional unit, at least during the drives to and from work. In a LeBaron such as this, cushioned in the dizzying pattern, I learned how to drive. It was 1989, and my father and I were in a decade-old business park. The business park was a mock city within the real town of Redmond, Washington, across Lake Washington from Seattle. Everything was wider than it should have been: pudgy roads, bright white lines, and broad sidewalks, as though the plans had been drawn in chalk. And it was all pristine. Alongside the grass strips were spindly trees, young saplings spread apart, the space between them bearing the hope of the shade they would cast, of the void they would one day fill.

Before these pubescent trees, of course, this had been a forest of adult trees, great-grandfather and great-great-grandfather trees, evergreens that sometimes fell under the strain of a Northwest winter storm—maybe a so-called Pineapple Express coming in from the tropics. They were trees that sheltered businesses such as U-Fish, where you could throw in a line and catch a salmon, or at least a slippery creature with a mouth, right there in someone's backyard. We rode our bikes through makeshift trails on the floor of the woods, skinning knees and catching splinters.

Redmond, like many cities and towns in Washington State, is part wild, part tame. Even the state's largest city, Seattle, is embedded in trees, with parks and pathways where you can lose your way, or at least your footing. The Washington frontier has been merely subdued. Like a bearskin rug in the living room, or mounted elk antlers above the fireplace, much of the wilderness has been memorialized and moved indoors. But residents of Washington feel the wilderness within them at all times.

When I moved into a development called Country Creek, in second grade, the neighborhood kids told me that there had been a restaurant in the woods behind my house. Not an actual structure, but a clearing in the trees where people ate. This seemed feasible to a child of the Northwest, that people would eat on logs and sweep the dirt. And so I did this, for an entire summer, getting the woods ready to be a restaurant. My friends and I would cook in my parents' house, but we would eat outside under the branches.

In between bites of grilled cheese sandwiches or bagel dogs from Costco we'd make plans for how this could become a money-making venture. Only later, after months of grooming the dirt in the hopes that smoothness was tantamount to hygiene, did I realize my friends had been joking about a restaurant ever having been there.

The concepts of outdoors and indoors in Washington have always been blurry. The ground is damp, and dampness is a cold that creeps in like no other. Rooms, especially basements, are moist, often moldy. Floors are smudged with pine needles, decks are weathered, hands are chapped. To live in Washington is always to be aware that wilderness is just outside the door, partly because it's just inside the door as well. Few people bother to carry umbrellas. (I find myself suspicious of those who do, thinking of the accessory as a handbag for the head—both unnecessary and conspicuous.) So, with dripping GORE-TEX hoods and soaked woolen hats, we enter the indoors with the rain in our clothes—blurring the journey with our destination.

Although Washington has a reputation for being rainy, it's not the wetness that's difficult. Rather, it's the way the light never quite meets the day—in fall and winter, there is a bluish-gray sky that barely appears in the morning; then a faintly perceptible recession of that same muted color signifies night. The whole day is a half-opened eye, and this heavy-lidded weather can last months.

Washington is two states, west and east. The former, founded by fur traders, is verdant rain forest, and the latter, founded by gold diggers, is arid high desert. East and west are split by a mountain range that contains the state's tallest peak, Mount Rainier. The Cascade Mountains sit between two distinct worlds. Most of the population resides in the western half of the state. It has the mountains, the forests, the ocean, as if it were a contest of weight, tilting everything to the left—and incidentally it's one of the most liberal parts of the United States. We western Washingtonians often forget there is an eastern half. We might go tubing along the Yakima or Wenatchee rivers in the summer, head east to Whitman or Gonzaga or the state university in Pullman for a few years, go to the rodeo in Ellensburg, but most of us return to the urban density of the west. Maybe this is why the mountain range through the middle is known as the Cascade Curtain, we can peek through and glimpse our other half, or we can pretend it's not there.

Mount St. Helens, located along the line between east and west, is a reminder that human technological and industrial advancement can't always outpace forces of nature. Take, for instance, a tale of two eruptions: one natural, the other manmade. In May of 1980, the nine-hour eruption of Mount St. Helens changed Washington's landscape forever. The mountain went from an iconic triangular peak to a collapsed soufflé, a symbol both of nature's power and its vulnerability. For days after, ash covered our neighborhood, as it did countless others across the state. We kids rode bikes and played outdoors wearing handkerchiefs, looking like bandits. For months, even years after, everyone had Mason jars of ash on their mantels, little urns, as if a loved one had died.

Twenty years later, Seattle would demolish St. Helens's steel and concrete counterpart, the Kingdome. Nicknamed "The Tomb" by visiting sportswriters because of its gray gloom, the stadium was gone in 16.8 seconds. Built in 1976, it had a roof that weighed 25,000 tons, which was meant to keep out the perpetual winter rain, even though it resembled a permanent, impenetrable cloud cover. Despite the fact that people disliked the Kingdome—it was a loud, echoing ogre—it was still the biggest indoor space in Washington. In 2000, people drove from all over to witness the demise of one of the state's most recognizable structures. The cloud of dust rose 500 feet as onlookers everywhere—from boats on Elliot Bay to the sidewalks below the Jumbotron in New York's Times Square looked on. After twenty minutes the dust settled and the building was gone. I could not watch the Kingdome fall. I stayed home with the TV off, wondering what heavy, earthbound structure would now counter the spindly upward reach of the Space Needle—the two buildings having represented Seattle on every souvenir shop T-shirt, mug, and shot glass. I was not alone in my uneasiness. One onlooker told the *Seattle Post-Intelligencer*, "I look at it as a funeral."

Both the implosion of the Kingdome and the explosion of St. Helens were treated with similar reverence, the same sense of loss, or that something essential had gone missing.

Growing up in Washington, I was aware that getting lost meant more than reaching for the wrong hand on a department store elevator—that odd sensation of looking up and meeting a face that was not my mother's. The idea that one could disappear and end up as remains seemed almost natural, like part of the Washington bargain. But nature wasn't what scared me growing up. It was people who gave the woods their menace, a sound composed of wind and leaves and footsteps.

Ted Bundy and The Green River Killer brought a sense of danger and a sick hunger to the forests of Washington. These men used the wilderness as an accomplice. They haunted landscapes both real and imagined, twisted the notion of discovery, made open roads feel like dead ends, turned the edges of the forest into gaping, eager mouths. At birthday party sleepovers or on multifamily camping trips, with flashlights held up to our faces for effect, my friends and I constantly calculated the degrees of separation between ourselves and the victims. It might have been a cousin of a girl who was on your soccer team, or the lunch lady's niece's friend. It felt far away and up close at the same time—it always felt like a possibility.

Out of lack of skill or tactics or just due to bad luck, plenty of people get lost in the dense woods of the Pacific Northwest. But there are also those who simply vanish. In 1999, a partially mummified body was found about an hour outside of Redmond. The body lay in the Thurston County morgue for nearly a year before being identified. Jeff Sheyphe had disappeared without anyone noticing. His family in Oregon didn't even know he was gone until a few months after he walked into the woods to kill himself. Neither his boss nor his landlord thought to do anything more than pack up his belongings and put them in a box; no one had bothered to call the police.

It was not callousness on the part of his acquaintances. It was that Washington is still a place of drifters and transients: friends park their trailers in your front yard for a few months before heading onward, tree houses crop up in the woods, yurts are built on the far edges of property, tents or tarps are staked on river beds, sleeping bags wash up with the sea foam. It is always in the back of one's mind that there are people living among us in Washington—"off the grid" might be the political term, or even a strangely glamorous one—who simply don't want to be found.

When Nirvana's "Smells Like Teen Spirit" was released, late in 1991, Seattle's mainstream alternative music station, 107.7 The End, played the song all morning. Even though I listened to the station each day on my way to high school, I don't remember a single song they played before that moment. They might have been broadcasting late period Clash, or solo Morrissey, or maybe they played the most mainstream examples of the underachieving genre known as college rock. But the DJ that morning knew that "Smells Like Teen Spirit" would induce a sonic amnesia—everything before it would feel hazy and misshapen. The song was a nascent state anthem that became a national anthem. It was our state battle cry, distorted like the way some of us felt; and through this carved-out-trunk-turned-megaphone message, Washington was going to be found. This moment was more than a local band making good—this was a local band unearthing the grittiness and changing the weather.

Ink and tears, apprentices and imitators have all followed the death of Kurt Cobain. There is little more to say. Maybe grunge is what pop sounds like filtered through Washington, after the tune has been dragged through muddy rivers and covered in moss. Cobain's songs are catchy but not infectious: They are too full of ache to spin incessantly like little twisters in your head. Rather, the songs seize on a moment and wrestle it to the ground; they are intimate and memorable emotional battles, fought and not always won. Cobain wrote shadowy tunes that flirt with but don't always find the light of day. Exposure can be strange and disorienting for people who spend most of the year under cloudy skies. And when you feel exposed the urge is to disappear.

Though Nirvana came from the coastal town of Aberdeen, the state capital of Olympia defined the boundaries the band would stretch and eventually break. Olympia, a town of less than 50,000, is Washington's cultural lens, the place that sizes up the bigger cities, whether they know it or not.

Olympia was co-founded by two men—one a fisherman reportedly scared of the sea, the other a ministerial student with a weak constitution. These two turned out to be prototypes for a city full of talent yet hampered by self-consciousness. They split the area into two parcels, each promising that whoever died first would cede the entirety of the land to the other. When the minister died following an epileptic seizure, the fisherman inherited the rest of the town: a tale of cooperation, sensitivity, unlikely pairings, and simple luck.

Today Olympia is still a strange confluence of inhabitants, from the civil servants filing in and out of state capital buildings and keeping artisan bakeries in business during the legislative sessions, to the students of the liberal Evergreen State College, where I went, and where my progress was measured in a three-inch binder of "qualitative evaluations." The students, state workers, and hipsters mingle with what's left of the logging trade and fishing industry. And the population that can't fall asleep without hearing the words "last call" closes out the bars only a few hours before the longshoremen wade in for morning happy hour and a warm breakfast.

The city is an incubator of music—it hosts the farm team, so to speak. Plenty of bands that expanded well beyond the borders of Washington were informed by or influenced by Olympia bands and labels. From larger independents like Kill Rock Stars and K, to smaller startups such as Chainsaw and Atlas, Olympia put punks behind desks and retro-frock-wearing, knitting-needle-wielding vegans into storefronts. With cheap rent, a penchant for craft and craftsmanship, and the need to stave off small-town boredom, Olympia helped foster the do-it-yourself movement. Those who couldn't or didn't want to play music expressed the Olympia sensibility in other mediums. The result was an art movement based on irreverence and earnestness; it strove for originality and took into consideration place, context, and community. Above all, and likely owing to the town's being outside of the entertainment industry, there was an underlying anti-professionalism—a sense that ambition was anathema to art. This manifested itself as either brave or sophomoric, depending on the execution.

Olympia and its fellow cities west of the Cascades typify an assumption that political minds are of the same shade, if not altogether homogeneous. It's true that from Bellingham, up near the border of Canada, to the island communities on the Puget Sound—Bainbridge, Vashon, Whidbey, the San Juans—west of the Cascades is a bastion of liberalism, environmentalism, and progressive thinking. (This ideology extends to the western part of Oregon as well, and all the way down to California—a coastline where the most liberal voters in the country have settled.) Olympia's biodiesel-converted Mercedes and Subaru Outback driving populace advertises its philosophy in the most concise means possible: the bumper sticker. Whether it's IF ONLY CLOSED MINDS CAME WITH CLOSED MOUTHS, PRACTICE RANDOM ACTS OF KINDNESS AND SENSELESS ACTS OF BEAUTY, or VISUALIZE WHIRLED PEAS, only in a place where the assumption was that the driver behind you would nod their head and say "Right on," would one so unabashedly turn one's means of transportation into a thought bubble on wheels. The sheer number of liberal bumper stickers plastered on the back of a Washington car is also an act of effacement, as if to cover up the shame that one is driving a vehicle at all.

But leave the (semi-)urban environment, and the political and cultural slogans shift toward the right. In Chehalis, thirty miles south of Olympia, is the notorious Uncle Sam billboard, which was originally put up by a farmer named Alfred Hamilton when the freeway was built on his land. Uncle Sam looks like Mr. Potato Head with a George Washington wig on, and his succinct messages have been inflaming lefties for years, inspiring paintball vandalism and momentary road rage before drivers calm themselves with a "free speech for all, free speech for all" meditation. Messages

range from the outrageously offensive—AIDS TURNS FRUITS INTO VEGE-
TABLES—to clever jabs at state officials, such as, BOOTH GARDNER: A MAN
WHO THINKS TWICE BEFORE HE SAYS NOTHING. The looming, anonymous
messages provide a stark reminder that just because we're all drinking the
same coffee doesn't mean we're all here for the same reasons.

Part of any new freedom or discovery is erasing what came before. Washington's titular trend, from city names to housing developments, tells of
what used to be. Evergreen Place—that business park where I went from
digging for first gear as if it were in the bottom of a duffel bag to gliding
between second and third with only the faintest implication of whiplash—
speaks to the felled trees, but place names like Leschi, Alki Point, Lummi,
Tenino, Mukilteo, and Tillicum are signs of loss that speak of a far more
egregious trespass. So numerous were Native Americans on the land that it
would be easier to make a list of Washington cities' etymologies *not* based
on a Native American word or tribe.

Seattle takes its name from Chief Seattle, who on the occasion of Washington's first governor, Isaac Stevens, establishing the first Indian Reservation said simply, presciently: "It matters little where we pass the remnants of
our days. They will not be many. . . . A few more moons, a few more winters,
and not one of the descendants of the mighty hosts that once moved over
this broad land or lived in happy homes, protected by the Great Spirit, will
remain to mourn over the graves of a people once more powerful and hopeful than yours. But why should I mourn at the untimely fate of my people?
Tribe follows tribe, and nation follows nation, like the waves of the sea. It is
the order of nature, and regret is useless. Your time of decay may be distant,
but it will surely come, for even the White Man whose God walked and
talked with him as friend to friend, cannot be exempt from the common
destiny. We may be brothers after all. We will see."

The name Evergreen Place was a half-hearted apology, its woods relegated to the corner of the lot, a ragged green border on a polished drawing.
But even that was short-lived: A computer company moved its headquarters
from California into the Redmond office park. Within a few years, the "Evergreen" on the sign was gone, replaced by "Microsoft." Little did I know
that Microsoft would become a metonym of Redmond. Never again would
I need to clarify that my hometown is a "suburb of Seattle."

Redmond, like Washington State, has been found. But there will always
be wilderness to discover, and wilderness we'll never know.

WEST VIRGINIA

CAPITAL   Charleston

ENTERED UNION   1863 (35th)

ORIGIN OF NAME   In honor of Elizabeth, the "Virgin Queen" of England

NICKNAME   Mountain State

MOTTO   Montani semper liberi ("Mountaineers are always free")

RESIDENTS   West Virginian

U.S. REPRESENTATIVES   3

STATE BIRD   cardinal

STATE FLOWER   rhododendron

STATE TREE   sugar maple

STATE SONGS   "West Virginia, My Home Sweet Home," "The West Virginia Hills," and "This Is My West Virginia"

LAND AREA   24,077 sq. mi.

GEOGRAPHIC CENTER   In Braxton Co., 4 mi. E of Sutton

POPULATION   1,816,856

WHITE   95.0%

BLACK   3.2%

AMERICAN INDIAN   0.2%

ASIAN   0.5%

HISPANIC/LATINO   0.7%

UNDER 18   22.3%

65 AND OVER   15.3%

MEDIAN AGE   38.9

WEST VIRGINIA
Jayne Anne Phillips

First: the land, so mountainous and intransigent, so verdant and densely forested as to be nearly uninhabitable. Here, in the highest average altitude east of the Rockies, the Appalachian Mountains isolated a thousand years of paradise for animals, flora, fauna, all fed by interlacing rivers and countless clear streams that ran from the highest elevations to the deepest valleys. European settlers came to claim and fight over what seemed an untapped frontier, unaware the Indians used the land only for hunting and attendant ceremonies and rituals. Hunting parties of Tuscarora, Mingo, Shawnee, and Delaware fed whole tribes with the spoils of twice or thrice yearly excursions. The mountains were full of game and bear, deer, even bison; rival tribes seldom fought over sustenance. Fish were so plentiful that hunters had only to aim knives or spears at schools of blue pike and trout flashing by in the rapids. They stood downriver of falls and runs, gathering the exhausted fish in their arms and storing them in submerged baskets. Predatory birds scaled peaks that folded and flung ever upward: ten species of hawk, bald eagles, even the rare golden eagle, falcons, ospreys. The tentlike canopy of trees was a form of deciduous jungle, and topography varied so extremely from the heights of the mountains to the shaded valleys that plants from three life zones thrived. As recently as the 1930s there were 3,400 plant species in West Virginia: thirty species of orchid, sixty of fern. Before names and records, there were miles of towering evergreens, mountain glades that suggested northern tundra, acres of rhododendron and the ancient box huckleberry, oldest plant on earth; fields of wild lilies, lobelia, meadow rue, virgin's bower. The trees, unmolested for hundreds of years, were typically so large that two men could not clasp hands around them. George Washington remarked in his 1747 diary that a tree on Three Brother Island was sixty feet in circumference. The land was virgin country marked only by three Indian trails, the Seneca, the Kanawha, and the Monongahela. No tribe claimed the land or lived upon it. The mountains were considered spiritual ground and left to themselves, towering, untamed, bountiful.

The mighty rivers fed paradise and doomed it. The rivers, coursing through valleys sculpted by rushing water, brought the Europeans, the explorers, and speculators, those with a Western vision of ownership and industry. They were oppressors or fled oppression into a frontier that entirely dominated effort at human settlement for two hundred years. White men, fur traders seeking a route to a "western ocean," first saw New River Gorge in 1641; sixty years later, befuddled traders still believed they'd found a source of "ye South Sea" at the Falls of the Great Kanawha. England had secured only a thin strip of New World along the east coast; the English challenged France on her claim to the limitless west bordered by the Mississippi. Morgan ap Morgan, a Welshman who recognized no Crown, settled at Mill Creek in western Virginia by 1726. Settlers of Dutch, Scotch, Irish descent ignored the French/English disputes and filtered in. The frugal Germans, driven from Pennsylvania by Penn's heirs, were 200 strong in Mecklenberg (the name was changed to Shepherdstown as the Germans lost dominion) in 1748. A nephew of Lord Fairfax became the first presiding justice at Romney by 1762, but government was fiction.

The land was territory. Blood flowed in the rivers and along the banks of the burgeoning streams. There are stories of isolated settlements massacred to the last man and woman. Children old enough to walk were sometimes taken. No one to bury the dead; only the snow, the rain, layers and layers of bright leaves. Foraging animals and fertile soil enfolded the bodies where they lay. Marauding Shawnee slaughtered the entire population of Draper's Meadows in the New River Valley, save William Ingles, who fled through the woods, and Mary, his wife. She was kidnapped by the Indians and taken beyond the Ohio, "forced to make salt for her captors . . . the first made by a white person in Western Virginia." The Shawnee taught her other skills, apparently, she escaped later that year and found her way back alone, in the winter of 1755, to "rejoin her husband," but the mountains remained a battleground. The Indians allied with the French. The English hacked roads through the wilderness to supply British forts, but only the French defeat at Fort Duquesne encouraged George III to make a deal with native Americans. Paradise was lost to them, but the King of England proclaimed colonists forbidden in the Trans-Allegheny.

Settlers, walking the road to revolution, ignored the law and marked their squatters claims, slashing the trees with axes, stating boundaries. Drunken whites murdered the family of Logan, a Mingo chief, in Hancock County, and Lord Dunmore used the ensuing uprising as a diversion. Settlers momentarily forgot their resistance to the Crown and united to win the Northwest for the Colonials. Lord Dunmore's War left them a mobilized force and cleared the way for the Revolution, sweeping away Benjamin

Franklin's already approved proposal that western Virginia be declared a fourteenth colony. The colony was to be called Vandalia. *Vandalia*: a name for a paradise, a word Cervantes used to denote an imaginary place in his mythical *Don Quixote*. Had revolution held off another year, western Virginia's secession from Virginia eight decades later need never have happened; Vandalians might have forged a more viable world in the mountains and forests, a world not so easily bought and sold.

The name and the paradise were forgotten. Frontiersmen fought the Revolution from sixty isolated forts in the mountains, deflecting waves of British-led Indian attacks. They helped win the war but lost the peace: Political skirmishes between eastern and western Virginia began in earnest. The banks and the money were in Richmond (and farther southeast), as were most of the slaves. Geography was morality: There were no plantations in the mountains, no acres of fields. Farmers and woodsmen in the still wild western territory sustained themselves, growing what they ate, trapping, hunting. Virginia law decreed property taxed equally, with one exception: slaves. Human property was taxed at lower rates than "beasts of the field." Translation: cheaper to own a human being than to own a horse, cow, pig. Western Virginians paid higher taxes than their eastern brethren to sustain a system with which they largely disagreed. The Virginia Legislature did count slaves as population when they apportioned representation, again slighting the (mostly white) population of the western counties, and it kept funds for public works largely in eastern Virginia. In 1860, as the resisting western counties agitated, Virginia did begin construction of a lunatic asylum at Weston—the first public institution funded. Like all the asylums of that era, it was vast, with city blocks of surrounding lawns: Weston State Hospital was the only state mental institution west of the Alleghenies. It was a hospital for indigents and outcasts, for the odd and insane and homeless. Back then, family took care of family. Only those who were unwanted, sexually profligate (women), or violent (men), were sent away.

Just the previous October, John Brown, mad genius abolitionist, had raided the federal arsenal at Harpers Ferry. His subsequent hanging in Charles Town roused deeper secessionist passions against the slave-holding government in Virginia. South Carolina fired on Fort Sumter and Virginia seceded from the Union; western Virginians immediately declared themselves the "restored" government of Virginia, then New Virginia, and finally, by Abraham Lincoln's proclamation, West Virginia. Paradise was engaged. Families were divided. One of my own ancestors spied for the Confederacy while her sons fought for the Union. Some towns changed hands fifty times.

Stonewall Jackson, who boarded at Thomas Phillips's farm in Coalton as a schoolboy, briefly captured Harpers Ferry for the Confederacy in September of '62, but the spirit of John Brown prevailed and the Union held.

Bitterness continued. West Virginia, that fought and bled for the Union, was forced by the United States Supreme Court to pay over fourteen million dollars of Virginia's public debt. West Virginia passed the Test Act, which required voters to swear they'd never borne arms against the United States, disenfranchising fifteen thousand Confederate veterans. Nearly thirty-seven thousand Union veterans demanded public acknowledgment and first consideration for jobs. There were two sides, two stories, and now that the war was over, the capitalists moved in. They bought timber and mineral rights to the land for almost nothing, and shipped the wealth of paradise to the northern cities.

First came the timber barons, who finished cutting the giant trees and floated the wood to market on the rivers. Then came the coal companies, with their throbbing deep mines and company stores that turned men into indentured labor. Later, strip mines blasted the faces of the mountains to get at the seams of coal. Largely owned by out-of-state concerns, they employed fewer miners and brought in their own men to drive the machines.

Mountaintop mining, a contemporary disaster, began in the 1980s and '90s. Coal companies simply blast off the tops of the mountains and dump tons of soil and rock into the hollows and streams below, destroying watersheds and the checks and balances of weather itself in the Appalachians. They've buried or damaged, to date, over two thousand miles of streams, and cut employment of miners from almost sixty thousand in 1980 to just over fifteen thousand in 2004. Manipulation of the unions in deep mining led to lax safety measures, disasters, and bad publicity; blasting the mountains themselves meant no one had to go underground. Machines and explosives could do the work, and the tight-lipped descendants of Welsh miners, their wood frame houses weakened by the blasting, tended not to complain. Mountaintop mining uses ninety-four metric tons of explosives a year in West Virginia alone. Coal slurry impoundments, towering waste full of toxins and heavy metals, hang over the towns and settlements, waiting to weaken in hundred-year floods that happen more frequently, much more frequently, every other year, it seems: no clear running streams to absorb the storms, the snow melt. The dumped ground that buried the interlacing waters of the mined land (1.4 million acres projected destroyed by 2012) is loose, unstable. The drenched earth turns to rivers of poison mud. The coal companies exhaust the coal, bury the valleys, "restore" the tops of the mountains to level, moon-like landscapes, seeded with grass and little trees, and move on. They pollute the water and air, end hunting and fishing, buy out the disseminated towns, desecrate the cemeteries. Sometimes they're forced to move the dead to create more death.

Though 66 percent of West Virginians polled in 2004 oppose mountain-top mining, the practice continues, creeping farther north from the southern counties. They're destroying the mountains, not just in West Virginia, but in Kentucky, Virginia, and Tennessee. Central Appalachia, one of the most biologically diverse eco-systems in the world, is no longer paradise. Only the rocks, the land and rivers and gorges, the stone faces of the cliffs at Audra and the high glades of Dolly Sods, the towering silent mountains in the still pristine regions of the state, remember, as inchoate, molecular imprint, another world. Almost heaven? Almost. The glorious trees in the protected forests open and bud, impervious, beneficent.

Back in the 1920s, mining was a growing industry strong enough to oppose the unions, but timber was still big business. A few of the wealthy lumbermen were home grown. My mother's father, J. W. Thornhill, owned a mill along a river and a row of houses in which he housed his workers. This was fifty years after the Civil War, in Hampton, West Virginia, in what was just becoming an altered landscape. A widower, J. W. eloped with his second wife, Grace Boyd, a girl younger than his eldest daughter, and brought her home on the train that ran along the river. His workers lined up beside the tracks and cheered. Fourth of July bunting hung in the trees and the families and children waved small American flags made in America. He built her a small mansion with stained-glass windows in Belington; the sidewalk in front of the house is still imprinted with his name, as was every piece of wood in the house.

Years later, after the births of six children and the deaths of three, J. W. moved one of his mill secretaries into a second-floor room. The place was his, he said, to do with as he liked, every stick of it. By then he was drinking heavily. Grace was kind to the girl but moved to Buckhannon, a larger neighboring town. There was no divorce, but she "locked her door against him." He lived in both houses until he became too "eccentric" to live alone. He lost the mill during the Depression, and then he lost his mind. He was like a child, raging or dependent. The mansion was sold to an undertaker and is still a funeral parlor today. J. W. moved "to town." The top floor of the house in Buckhannon became his refuge.

My mother was a youngest child, born after the deaths of the three children between herself and a much older brother and sister. At fourteen, the only child at home, she was helping her mother run the Buckhannon house as a business, boarding college students from Wesleyan, the local Methodist college. They kept a cow and chickens, sold dairy goods, raised a garden, canned food to get them through the long winters, and managed to keep the house. One fall, they'd painstakingly raked the yard and back lot by the barn (in the late 1930s, there were still countless canopied trees in Buckhannon). J. W. picked up a pitchfork of blazing leaves and chased them around the fire. Grace called the Weston State Asylum, the same institution so beneficently granted Western Virginia just before secession. It was all she could afford. The day they came to get him, J. W. famously turned at the door and asked, "But Gracie, aren't you coming with me?"

The women in my family all had two names: Jocasta Andora, Margaret Lee, Jessie May, Martha Jane, Mary Price, Maud Ellen, Mary Lee, Amy Jo, Molly Jean. Both branches of the family had emigrated to America before the Revolutionary War. The Phillips family, in receipt of a land grant from the King of England, came from England and Wales to what is now Randolph County in the early 1700s. Sons, including my great uncle, my father, my brother, were called Randolph. The town that grew up around the farm, originally settled by Germans, was called Womelsdorf, but subsequent Anglo-Saxon settlers changed the name to Coalton. The family lived there for 200 years as the land was deeded to generations of sons, then sold, and so lost.

In the 1870s, the family gave land for a church and graveyard still in existence: Phillips Chapel is a small wood frame sanctuary, rebuilt on the footprint of the original structure, minus the steeple it once possessed. The cemetery is beautiful and small, an enclosed level ground of lush grass and gravestones. The wooden fencing is white and the metal gates are silver, scrolled with ironwork, and wide enough to admit an automobile. Tall iron spires on either side bear the arched legend PHILLIPS CEMETERY. The silver letters, mounted on wire, seem to float in midair. I remember going to funerals there as a child, always in the snow, driving what seemed a long way from Buckhannon into the country, and standing with my father and his people as one of the old aunts, all of whom lived into their late nineties, was "rested." Rough men in work gloves lowered the casket on hand-held ropes. The rectangular hole of the grave and the piled earth beside it were already white with snow. Snow fell on the oiled wood of the casket and slid away into the dark below. The flat graveyard was still, ringed with trees and the low fence. The only sound was snow brushing snow. The snowflakes touched their ice to the monuments and humped stones with the shushing whisper of sleet cushioned in air. Snow fell, constant, breathing its way.

There was a secret at the farm in Randolph County, but family was family. They kept the secret, even from me, and from my father, whose life it blighted. The story was that Warwick, one of the four brothers, showed up at the farm with his wife, a woman no one knew. Her name is written as Icie Hoffman or Huffman on a framed family document from the 1920s; she stayed at the farm during her confinement, then "went back to her people," leaving the baby with his father's sisters. The aunts raised him, lovingly, on the farm until he was school age, then, as they married and the farm was sold, took him into their families, each for a few years; he was intensely loyal to them. Born in 1910, he went to high school in Buckhannon, then to work, learning construction, road building, paving streets for the city. He said of his father that he "never knew him," but in fact, Warwick Phillips moved a town away, married again, and had a son. An obscure Internet site concerning Coalton, West Virginia, and Phillips Cemetery features old photographs of Randolph and Mary Phillips, parents of Warwick, his four brothers, and the four aunts. Photographs show Warwick and his second wife, and Warwick's (second) son, Warwick Maurice Phillips, in WWII uniform. My father was nearly forty when he became a soldier; his half brother is ten or fifteen years younger. The pictures were posted in 2003 by a friend of Sarah Phillips, a young blonde who must be a granddaughter of Maurice Phillips. My father's cousin, in her seventies now, remembers hearing that when Warwick died, my father, surprisingly, was asked to attend the reading of the will. He drove hours from a work site in the southern part of the state to find that his father had left him a cheap watch. Warwick's other son was never in contact with the aunts, with the family; I never knew his name until I read it on the Internet. Was he my father's brother? Why Warwick's bitterness toward a child he left as a baby? On infrequent visits to the farm in my father's childhood, he "paid not a damn bit of attention" to the son his sisters enjoyed and coddled as the only child among them. My father left the farm at six or seven. His early memories were hazy, but he remembered hiding in the field once as Warwick stood on the broad porch of the big house, firing a rifle repeatedly into the tall grass. The child crouched low, hearing the bullets zing well past him, over his head. I have one or two photographs of my father as a child in blousy clothes, blond, with one or another of the smiling aunts, and I think of him, holding very still in the summer field, sweating in the buzzing grass, the bullets whining over him.

My father grew up rejected by his father, thinking his mother abandoned him. My parents divorced in the mid-1970s, and my father moved back in with the great-aunts. Retired, living on a small pension and veteran's benefits, he stayed, driving them to the store and the doctor's office, doing grocery shopping and errands. One died at home at 102. The other, the youngest of the nine children, lived on with my father. "We take care of each other," she told me. Visits home, I stayed with my mother, and visited my father most days. In good weather we sat out back, on the porch with my great-aunt. Once, I asked if he'd ever tried to find his mother. Yes, he said, he'd asked after the family when he was down in that part of the state. No one had ever heard of them. My great-aunt, still vigorous at ninety, said nothing, her eyes magnified behind the thick lenses of her glasses. "Strange you never heard from her again," I said, "in all that time." "Why," my aunt interrupted, "we did hear from her. She came and tried to take Russell, but we wouldn't let her have him. By then he was used to us." My father, hearing this for the first time at seventy, only raised his brows, tilted his head inquiringly. I asked how old he was then, when Icie came for him. "Two or three. Little. He didn't know her." I wanted to press her. I wanted the whole story, and the truth, but the weight of the secret, some sense of its nature, stopped me. "She saw you were taking good care of him," I told my aunt. She nodded affirmatively, dismissively, in her red sweater. She wore it even in the summer. Like all of the aunts, she was tall and bone thin in old age. I never once heard her raise her voice in irritation or anger. She treated the men in the family with deference, but shook her head at human nature, at folly, at the stories that made the rounds in town. "Did you ever?" she'd marvel. "Well! The Lord bless us and keep us."

If all stories are fiction, fiction can be true—not in detail or fact, but in some transformed version of feeling. If there is a memory of paradise, paradise can exist, in some other place or country dimensionally reminiscent of our own. The sad stories live there too, but in that country, we know what they mean and why they happened. We make our way back from them, finding the way through a bountiful wilderness we begin to understand. Years are nothing: Story conquers all distance.

In West Virginia, you are your people, your home place. Your town, your county. People have one home, and home is where you come from. West Virginians are a less mobile population than almost any other in the country.

It's beginning to change, but the bulk of those living in West Virginia are descended from generations who've stayed in place, stayed home, made a living despite the vagaries of economy, history, politics.

The Thornhills and Boyds, my mother's people, emigrated from the "thorny hills" of Derbyshire, in England. They were blue eyed, fair skinned. Nevertheless, my mother, her mother, my Boyd grandfather, were olive skinned and brown eyed, Black Irish, most likely, descended from the survivors of the Spanish Armada sunk off the coast of Ireland during the reign of Queen Elizabeth. A stranger, an elderly man, once appraised me knowingly in a Chicago elevator. "Black Irish," he said. "Excuse me?" "Oh yes, with that jawline and chin. Was your mother darker than you?" I shrugged and he smiled, pointed to his own face. "Black Irish," he said, as though words settled the matter.

On both sides, there was unacknowledged Native American blood, faces with pronounced high cheekbones, narrow, almost Asiatic eyes, children who looked like changelings. My Boyd grandmother, a DAR member who resigned when the organization prohibited Marian Anderson from singing at Constitution Hall in 1939, traced her line back to the Revolutionary War through one John Goodwin, born 1762, who served as "Indian Spy in Captains William Lowther and Joseph Gregory's Companies in the Virginia Troops" from Harrison County, "six months of each year," 1776 to 1782. Goodwin would have been an adult fourteen-year-old, moving in woods he knew, in the county adjacent to that occupied by his descendants three hundred years later. He ended his service at twenty, and filed for a pension fifty years later, perhaps to benefit the nine children who survived him. The frontier was another country then, in 1832, firmly governed by a colonial power, the Indians vanquished, the settlers themselves doubly oppressed by England and Virginia.

A hundred years hence, at the beginning of World War II, my mother fell in love with a high-school classmate. He was the youngest of five brothers and a sister; there are photographs of them all dressed in morning coats at their mother's garden party, the mother and sister in long black-lace dresses. His father was a minister and college professor whose heart had failed when the boy was twelve; the older brothers all became doctors, helped the mother manage until she, too, died. The boy was sixteen then, another adult child. His sister still at home turned the house into a girl's dorm for the local college; he moved into a rooming house with his best friend. The summer after high-school graduation, he complained of chest pain as he walked my mother home from a date. The doctor said he had heartburn; he was eighteen years old, take some Tums. My mother was worried and phoned one of the doctor brothers, who set off, driving from Chapel Hill. Tell him to keep still until I get there, the brother said. The boy died in the bathroom of the rooming house, having gotten out of bed to wash his face. The brother stayed for the funeral. All the brothers came in, too late. Their sister asked my mother to plan the service. The boy's name? William Goodwin, a descendant of that same long-lived Goodwin who linked my mother's family to Revolutionary-era western Virginia. Somehow, the line had weakened: the Goodwin men, all the boy's stalwart doctor brothers, died young, of heart attacks.

My mother married Russell Randolph Phillips five years later. She met him at a Veterans of Foreign Wars dance. He was thirty-eight, a man about town. He took one look at her and said, "I'm going to marry that girl." It sounds like fiction, but all stories are fiction.

In the late 1960s, Buckhannon is a football town. The relatively small high school has claimed the AAA State Championship three times in a decade, and the white wooden scoreboard on the courthouse lawn is kept up to date, Wins and Scores painted on each Saturday morning. Game nights, on Fridays, boyfriends steer their dressed-up girls into the bleachers, touching their shoulders. The girls have hair like pretty dogs, bright brown or blond, shoulder-length silk. A smoke of haze chars the air. The band mills around at field's edge in their blue-and-white uniforms, turning the brass bowls of awkward tubas. The plumed hats nod or swing, carried by their straps like lunch pails. Pep Club mothers open up the soda stands, stacking tiers of waxen red cups printed with the Coca-Cola legend. Hot dogs in the grills are already shiny. The mothers dump ice into coolers from big clear bags, standing with their legs apart, braced to support the heavy bags in their laps. They pound at the plastic covered surfaces to get the ice moving and rake it with their fingers, the flesh of their hands reddening and their platinum rings wet. The majorettes stand for first cokes, casual as off-duty movie stars. Their thighs are gold with pancake makeup and subtle glitter, their white boots spotless, their waists impossibly small in tight blue satin sashes. They dangle silver batons in one hand, occasionally turning them in nonchalant demonstrations of skill. The girls walk away biting ice, sipping carbonated syrup as numbers light up on the broad electric scoreboard above their heads. Their clean hair ripples perfectly, reflecting the illumination of the field in yellow tones. White pom-poms swing at their boot tops with a sound like the swish of long hair against leather. Their taps crunch on the gravel track and their white short-shorts are a white wool called "winter vanilla," identically sewn by a hired seamstress. Their jackets are double breasted, trimmed in gold braid and military buttons, and the long tails of the jackets move in mock tuxedo fashion on the curves of their hips. The majorettes hold their shoulders straight. They are girl gentlemen, unwittingly androgynous, and the boys, the tall broad-chested cream of the town, suiting up in shoulder pads, helmets, knee guards, cleats, and tight laced pants, will be giants.

Small-town pride is a given. There is still a thriving Main Street. Families around town own the men's and women's wear stores, the hardware stores, the restaurants, the bookstore that sells mostly newspapers and magazines. There are two large grocery stores, Krogers and the A&P, and local people work the same jobs in the aisles for thirty years: butcher, manager, check-out clerk. Giant oaks lift their branches over traffic driving up Kanawha Hill, teenagers go to first-run movies at the Colonial on Main Street, or the Kanawha on Kanawha Hill: The marquees are edged in pink and blue streamers of running neon. There are churches, steeples in every quadrant of the town: Presbyterian, First and Second Baptist, Methodist, Episcopalian, and one Catholic church and hospital. Public schools serve fish on Fridays. The town is tamped down; there are no Holy Rollers or snake handlers, no speaking in tongues. Nearly everyone is white.

Buckhannon, a town of six thousand, is the county seat of Upshur County; settlements fanning out along the macadam and gravel or dirt roads are called by the names of streams and runs of water: Brushy Fork, Mud Lick, Sago, Rock Cave, Spall Run, Lost Creek. School buses bring kids in from the runs and hollows, dirt roads, sometimes, places verdant and green in summer, cold in winter, in those houses that heat with coal fires. My friend, a dentist's daughter, has a canopy bed I much admire; I sleep in a high walnut spool bed my mother refinished by hand and fitted with pink gingham shams, skirt, coverlet. Kids out in the deep country roads sleep together to stay warm. Some of them eat their main meal of the day in the school cafeteria: corn bread and kidney beans, spinach from cans, cling peaches. The elementary school children arrive at school hungry, their skin pale as porcelain, their fingers tinged blue. Their hair is uncombed; their wrists and ankles ringed with old dirt, and it's nobody's business. Many of them, held back year after year, drop out before high school. The town kids are one world; they're another. My mother, a first-grade teacher when I was growing up, gave her students our outgrown coats and boots, and bought gloves and hats at half price every spring, for the next winter. Some kids from the rural hollows are bright; they persist; they stay in school. They sit together at football games, girls mostly, and boys too small in stature to be wooed away by the military, or sent to the mines. The athletes and cheerleaders are mostly kids from town, kids whose parents can pick them up after practices, cheer them on, supervise the cheerleaders' routines, sell drinks and concessions at home games.

My mother wouldn't let my brothers play football, and she didn't attend the games. She said she'd seen a boy die on the field once, hit too hard. The story may have been fiction. She'd seen a boy die: That was true. Or she'd seen it in her mind, over and over, the boy on the bathroom floor, in the rooming house. My older brother, thin and rangy, became a high-school pool shark and loved fast cars. The younger one took up spelunking, ski instructing, and spent his twenties at the beach, sailing South Carolina tourists on catamarans. Both left West Virginia and moved South, to the Carolinas and Tennessee, while I moved North.

In the popular imagination, West Virginia—when it's considered at all—is a place so exotic, so foreign, so dark and dense with myth as to be unreadable from the outside, just as the primeval, virgin expanse of the mountains was once unknown, unimaginable, to Western eyes cast into its depth and majesty and threat. It's why Batboy, protagonist of a recent hit musical, was supposedly born in a cave in West Virginia. It's why the late and lamented X Files, the popular TV series starring FBI agents Mulder and Scully, set its darkest, most primal segments in West Virginia. There was one about a man with a tail, and another about a peculiar inbred family who were actually monsters—all doubtless filmed in LA.

Celebrities don't hang out much in West Virginia. In the West Virginia I know, we don't much hold with celebrity. If you don't work, and work hard, then who are you? Work makes a man a man, and a woman a woman. You work; you don't brag or put on airs. It's day-to-day, the land, the town, the garden, the field, the mine, the family, the business, home. Why leave home if home is here? You don't leave your place because the going is tough any more than you'd leave your child if he was troubled or in trouble. Family is family. Communal art is respected: quilting, woodworking, playing music, and singing the songs. The talent that challenges, stands out, flares against, often leaves home. Home won't always have those kids, and the cities draw them like magnets. They make their lives elsewhere, but they know they've left home. Home is behind them. Maybe they write about home, or dream about it. Maybe they try to forget about home, and can't. Home eludes them. It's the price they pay for leaving.

They're one reason West Virginia is steadily losing population, yet it's somewhere you can find a place to live. The mountains slow global warming somewhat, and the seasons are still inarguable. If you look, you may find an untouched valley, a road along a river, a community. Jobs don't pay well, but you won't need much money. You'd better garden, enjoy good physical health, seldom complain, and have a rich internal life. The 200 present residents of Coalton, West Virginia, where the Phillips Cemetery lies in protected silence, have a median family income of $36,875. The average income for single males is around $28,000; for women, $13,469. The largest percentage of owner-occupied homes falls in the $50,000 to $59,000 range; the largest percentage of renter-occupied dwellings include eight or more rooms. Translation: There's space. And quiet.

Is West Virginia poor? As poor as inner city anywhere, as poor as towns stranded in the Nevada desert? No. It is geographically isolated and relentlessly exploited by outsiders and some insiders, all looking to sell paradise and make a buck. But you just can't buy that kind of pride, a stubborn dignity rooted to the land, and you can't sell it. In our co-opted world, West Virginia remains mysterious, downtrodden, sold short—another country within a celebrity-obsessed American culture that takes no notice.

Understand: Born and raised in West Virginia, you can never truly leave. Those who stay, and those who don't, stand in the middle of the story, wherever they go. They share the feel and smell and mind's eye image of a narrow road in summer, a dirt road or a paved one, bordered by woods and fragrant weeds, overhung with trees, twisting deeper.

WISCONSIN

CAPITAL Madison

ENTERED UNION 1848 (30th)

ORIGIN OF NAME French corruption of an Indian word that may have meant "river that meanders through something red."

NICKNAME Badger State

MOTTO "Forward"

RESIDENTS Wisconsinite

U.S. REPRESENTATIVES 8

STATE BIRD robin

STATE FLOWER wood violet

STATE TREE sugar maple

STATE SONG "On Wisconsin"

LAND AREA 54,310 sq. mi.

GEOGRAPHIC CENTER In Wood Co., 9 mi. SE of Marshfield

POPULATION 5,536,201

WHITE 88.9%

BLACK 5.7%

AMERICAN INDIAN 0.9%

ASIAN 1.7%

HISPANIC/LATINO 3.6%

UNDER 18 25.5%

65 AND OVER 13.1%

MEDIAN AGE 36.0

WISCONSIN
Daphne Beal

There are people I know, people west of where I am sitting right now by about a thousand miles, some of whom I am related to, some who saw me through my adolescent worst, who will smile—genuinely, indulgently, courteously, knowingly, all at once, because this kind of multilayered smile, flickering with contradictory sentiments, is a specialty of my home state— when they learn that I am writing about Wisconsin.

"You? But you left Wisconsin when you were what? Fifteen? Eighteen?" I imagine these people saying in a kind way, because, in most situations, Wisconsinites adhere to a certain unshakeable kindness (distinct from its close cousins, niceness and politeness). "You, who have never even been to a Packers game wearing a gigantic wedge of yellow foam cheese on your head, much less added your name to the list of 74,000 people waiting for season tickets?"

"Yes, *me*," I imagine myself saying, smiling, always smiling because that is the state-determined social contract among us, and perhaps adding that such a wedge (a cheddar-Swiss hybrid, if you've never seen it) took up a precious amount of room in my New York City closet for a long time.

The fact is that not only was I born and raised in Milwaukee, but I am from the state in a way that feels programmed into my DNA, as if one of the double helixes was coded with W-I-S-C. Even though I have chosen in my adulthood to live in a universe far, far away called Manhattan, I still claim Wisconsin as my own and head back several times a year to the state where my maternal ancestors settled in 1874 in the then-bustling town of Racine, poised on Lake Michigan's rocky shore, almost halfway between Milwaukee and Chicago, or as I recently heard the area called for the first time, in this age with its penchant for proper-noun amalgams: the Chiwaukee Corridor.

It is where I return each summer with my husband and children to spend time near the lake that my son, Owen, is named for, nestled in the heart of the Chequamegon (pronounced Shawamagon) National Forest in the northwest corner of the state not far from the Great Lake—Superior—that borders Wisconsin's northernmost edge. (Surrounded by Lakes Michigan and Superior and the Mississippi River on three sides, the state challenges the definition of landlocked.) My parents and sister are there, as is my childhood home and the rolling farmland—rising and falling away from the roadways, interrupted by stands of trees, and met at its perimeter by a mildly domed sky that once seemed to contain everything I knew. After years of driving through this land, seeing it head on from behind the wheel, and, when I was younger, while tumbling from the backseat of a station wagon to the "way back," or looking up from a book, a conversation, a squabble, a game, I realized this terrain is my internal landscape. It's the land that came first and the one that abides.

Because of this, when people ask where I grew up, I say Wisconsin first and Milwaukee second. The memories of my childhood are described by a long, skinny obtuse triangle within the state. The first point is Milwaukee in the southeast corner; the second is Racine, where my grandparents and cousins lived, forty miles farther south; and then Lake Owen in the northwestern corner, some 400 miles away from the other two, where we drove several times a year in a kind of staircase pattern, climbing the state through towns with names like Spooner, Tomahawk, Black River Falls, Waupaca, and Fond du Lac (pronounced Wah-packa and Fondalack, because lack of pretension is another proud Wisconsin trait).

Milwaukee in the 1970s and '80s was—both subjectively and objectively—less a cohesive entity than a series of atomized destinations. The business district downtown was a collection of imposing Germanic-style buildings (neoclassic, Renaissance, Romanesque) that lined wide avenues whose sidewalks were mostly empty. Outside that fifteen- or twenty-block radius, the city, threaded through by highway interchanges, became a series of factories, each with its own signature odor: the sour smell of hops from Schlitz, Blatz, Pabst, Miller (only the latter survives, flanked by a handful of microbreweries); the stomach-turning rankness of paper mills; the acrid scent of tanneries; and blissfully, the one we begged our parents to drive us by, the sweet, Willy-Wonka fantasy smell of the Ambrosia Chocolate Factory.

Claiming the state before the city may also have to do with the fact that I'm not from Milwaukee proper, but from a suburb just north of the city—OK, not just any suburb, but *the* suburb of River Hills, which Milwaukeeans have all sorts of notions about, namely that it is not true Milwaukee. The address is too far north and too posh for the proudly working-class city, whose largely Polish and Germanic heart lies farther south and west. River Hills is not the Milwaukee of beer halls and polkas, Catholic churches and Friday night fish fries. People from "down by the south side," as Milwaukeeans say, look at you skeptically if you say you grew up there, as if you'd just said you grew up in, say, a Fabergé egg. But while my childhood knew nothing like privation, I like to think that if we could have lived in opulence, we would not have. It's not the Wisconsin way.

As children, my brother, sister, and I were ferried from the suburbs to see the Chicago Symphony at the Performing Arts Center, *A Christmas Carol* at the Pabst Theatre, or the Bucks or the Admirals play at the Milwaukee Arena. At County Stadium, each time one of the Brewers hit a home run, a man went down a slide beneath the scoreboard into a giant mug of beer that erupted with helium balloons. School fieldtrips took us to the Domes, which looked like three glass breasts among warehouses and factories—filled with exotic flora. Up until a few years ago, the Milwaukee Art Museum was housed in a serviceable if not dowdy building from the 1950s, but is now a $120-million-dollar white-winged ship-bird, poised to set sail across Lake Michigan, designed by the Spanish architect Santiago Calatrava. (Like Bilbao, the Spanish city that is home to Frank Gehry's titanium-skinned Guggenheim, Milwaukee is a hard-working town that's made good, recessions and Rust Belt economics notwithstanding, and claims itself as a destination in its own right—that is, according to an ongoing PR campaign, "A Great Place on a Great Lake.")

All these cultural institutions were just slightly longer drives from our home than our regular spots—the Bayshore Mall for ballet and piano lessons; Brown Port Mall for bowling; Silver Spring Avenue to shop for party favors at Winkie's or gifts at The Changing Scene (which never did change), or to see a movie at the Fox Bay Theatre; and the Milwaukee Country Club (aka the MCC) for tennis lessons followed by cherry Cokes and patty melts by the pool. But because all these locations were disconnected from each other, nothing in my experience made up a city as I knew them to be from books, movies, or visiting my aunt and cousins in Chicago. There were no sirens at night, no newsstands or subways, no spraying fire hydrants when the hot weather came. And there was nothing shining and sparkling on a hill, no collection of glimmering towers making a jagged skyline in the distance in some approximation of Oz. To judge from reading the WPA's *Guide to the Badger State*, published in 1941, this effect had been true for decades:

> Newcomers and visitors sense a reason for [Milwaukee's low-crime] record in the suburban, rather than the metropolitan face that the city presents: the low buildings of the downtown area, . . . the acres of field and forest in one of the country's outstanding park systems, . . . the neat cottages in the

German and Polish neighborhoods, . . . and a nocturnal quiet that often produces the waggish comment: "You could fire a cannon down Wisconsin Avenue [downtown's main thoroughfare] at midnight and never hit a soul!"

Approaching Milwaukee by car on I–94 was, and remains, something of a nonevent, interrupted by bursts of recognition of far-flung landmarks: First was the large block-lettered sign on a factory roof that said HEIL, the company my Boston-transplant father worked for, selling garbage trucks to municipal governments from Riyadh to Santiago. The German name—which was definitively not emblazoned on trucks sold in Europe—came from its founder, Julius Heil, who started the company when Milwaukee was becoming "the machine shop of the world," and who, ironically, was governor from 1939–43.

Then comes St. Josaphat's gold-domed basilica, known for being "built by the pennies of the workers." We always looked to see if the Koss company had changed its billboard: James Dean in headphones was "Rebel With a Koss," and Whistler's mother sat in her rocking chair wearing a pair beside the reminder to "Phone Your Mother." Downtown Milwaukee is almost invisible from the freeway, except for its lone skyscraper, built in the early '70s for First Wisconsin Bank. After I–94 turns into I–43, the modest two-story A-frames of peeling paint with leaning porches of the North Side line the highway, and a more recent sign notes the exit for America's Black Holocaust Museum, a manifestation of the fact that Milwaukee is now known as the most residentially segregated city in the United States, despite Wisconsin's strong history of abolitionists and Underground Railroad activity. The GOP, in this sometimes-blue–sometimes-red state, was founded in Ripon, Wisconsin, in 1854, on the anti-slavery platform.

Beyond that, just east of the highway, the LED sign for Kopp's Frozen Custard stand announces daily flavors such as cherry amaretto cheesecake, banana walnut chocolate chunk, and German apple streusel, all with twice the amount of butterfat of regular ice cream and squirting, somewhat indecently, in long, thick trails from gleaming stainless steel machines. Finally, we exit at West Good Hope Road, and our first turn north leads us windingly into River Hills.

B ecause my experience of home has always included long stretches of highway, driving to Racine, as we did countless times a year to visit my grandparents, was just an extended version of the two-and-a-half-mile drive to school each day. After the smokestacks and the cabbage fields came my grandparents' house of hushedness—stately Midwestern, elements of Prairie style, not too big, not too little, with a muffling effect on all of us. We always entered through the heavy oak door to the slate-tiled front hall. Beyond it the living room sat untouched except on Christmas or Easter, with wall-to-wall beige carpeting, dusty-rose drapes, and cabinets with mesh-screen faces protecting my grandmother's porcelain Doughty birds. The large plate-glass windows that lined the room faced a rolling lawn, with two large willows (their thick trunks filled with concrete to keep them upright) like sentries at its edge, and then the lake.

Not that we did much more than look at the lake. It was always cold, but more than that, for many years its rocky beaches were lined with windrows of rotting alewives, ocean fish that came in through the St. Lawrence Seaway and were prone to massive seasonal die-offs. Between the stink and the biting flies, we were quick about our lakeside expeditions: hunting for flint rocks to bang together for a spark in the dark of the front-hall closet while the brass hangers clanged above us, stones for my grandfather's polisher, or fossils—coral, trilobites, and brachiopods, we learned in eighth-grade pale-ontology, dating from some 500 million years ago, when Wisconsin was still under a shallow inland sea.

Despite the feeling of limitlessness that came from the lake's distant horizon my memories of Racine as a child take place almost entirely at the house—games of gin rummy at the card table, golf on the TV, drinks at five o'clock for the grown-ups with Planters cheese balls and sodas for the kids (soda *is* soda in Wisconsin, not "pop" like it is in Michigan or Minnesota), holiday dinners where we quietly unbuttoned our waistbands as we became progressively more stuffed, and birthday lunches with Oscar Mayer wieners and angel food cake. There were long days around the kidney-shaped pool, where all boisterousness occurred, and where my grandfather kept watch over us—wearing a straw hat on his pink head and a slightly worried ex-pression on his face—as he tended to his horse chestnut tree, one of whose smooth nuts he always carried with him for luck, a tradition my mother continues to this day. My grandmother labored over her rose garden and would sometimes stand up to shout, "One for the money, two for the show, three to get ready, and four to go!" before we tried a new trick off the diving board. We made the occasional excursion to the Piggly Wiggly for groceries, the Racine Country Club (more subdued behavior required, but they had candlepin bowling in the basement), and to the small zoo, which amazingly included—for a city whose population has increased only from 67,000 to 87,000 since the WPA Guide came out in 1941—a giraffe and an elephant.

I remember only a few of the streets. It was never particularly exciting to leave the compound. But whether I knew the lay of the land or not was irrelevant, because I knew from an early age that this city, all of it, was a part of who I was. My mother, aunt, uncle, grandfather, and great-grandfather were born and raised there. I don't remember how old I was when I learned that *racine* meant root, but it seemed perfectly apt to me. Of course this city was the root of things, of everything, and it had nothing to do with the Root River or the Miami Indian origin of its name. It was where my maternal family started, where this quiet sense of prosperity had been hatched and nurtured. Much the same way the painted signs along the wide, greasy automotive strip of Fourth Avenue in Brooklyn, New York, would not be advertising Walker Mufflers in 2008, if my great-grandfather, Willard Walker, had not helped develop and produce the first "louvered" automotive muffler (which apparently worked, unlike its predecessors) in 1930—if not for the city of Racine, I would not exist.

Last year, my Aunt Mary and Uncle Bill (also Willard Walker) sold their house of more than forty years in Racine to move to the twenty-third floor of one of downtown Milwaukee's few high-rise condominiums overlooking the lake, to be near their children and grandchildren. They were the last Walkers, after 133 years in Racine, to go. It was not a huge surprise, since Walker Forge—the business my grandfather, Gordon, started in 1950, which was passed on to my uncle and now to his son (Willard Walker again, or Young Bill)—moved the last of its plant operations out of Racine in 1992 to a 280,000-square-foot facility in Clintonville, near Green Bay. There, around 275 employees use 850-ton to 4,000-ton mechanical presses to produce such forgings as gear blanks and wheel spindles used by John Deere and Caterpillar.

Before last year, I hadn't seen Racine since a gray day in January, 1996, when I attended my grandmother's funeral at the Episcopal church on a deserted Main Street (the same 142-year-old church made of cream brick where I was baptized, my parents were married, grandparents married, grandfather baptized, and so on and so forth). Determined to fill in some of the missing pieces of the story of both the city and my family, I flew back to Milwaukee, and on a sunny November morning, I headed south with my mother as my guide and my baby daughter in tow. We exited I–94 (the United States's northernmost east-west interstate that runs from Montana to Michigan) at Hwy. 20, a road whose progression in the course of ten miles to downtown Racine tells a story in and of itself. It begins in the heart of farm country; small houses, with old trees beside them, barns, and fields line the divided highway's roadside. A few miles along, a small billboard nestled in leafy branches shows a closeup photograph of a pretty, if weary teenage girl with the words, DEPRESSION HAS MANY FACES. RECOVERY IS POSSIBLE, a resonant slogan in a city that was the second largest manufacturing center in the state and now has its highest unemployment rate, at 10 percent.

The farmland gives way to business parks and car dealerships. Then the inevitable strip malls begin unfurling in a dim parade of Starbucks and Oodles of Noodles and the like. We pass an ur-pawnshop called American Coin, and Washington Park, where my mother learned to play golf, and whose green hills were sculpted over massive, low earthen burial mounds produced by the Indians known simply as the Effigy Mound culture a thousand years ago—among them a 130-foot-long panther. The only undisturbed Indian mounds left in Racine are modest ones among the settlers' and their descendants' graves in Racine's Mound Cemetery, established in 1852, adjacent to the park. After a residential area, we enter West Racine, with its bars and kringle bakeries (kringle is the super-sweet Danish pastry ring that Racine FedExes around the country at Christmastime). My mother points out Schmitt's Music Store, where she used to walk after school to take French horn lessons—still in business, if a little worn at the edges—then we bump over a railroad track to the shining Golden Rondelle Theater that was part of the Johnson Wax Pavilion at the 1964 World's Fair in New York, and where a short documentary called *To Be Alive!* is projected in a curved band around the room.

We have arrived in time for the weekly tour of the Frank Lloyd Wright buildings that were commissioned by H. F. Johnson, known as Hib, the third and most colorful of the five generations to lead the S. C. Johnson Company (makers of such utility closet staples as Off!, Windex, Glade, Raid, and Pledge). As we enter the administration building's carport area, a familiar claustrophobia that I remember from visiting Wright's home, Taliesin, west of Madison, presses down on my head. Then, suddenly, as we step into the "The Great Workroom," the two-storey-high ceiling springs up like the sky itself, supported lightly by tapered, "dendriform" columns (radical in their time for being narrower at the bottom than the top). The still-functional National Historic Landmark is a peaceful, rigorous, and delightful building—delightful for the apparent mania it must have taken to create it. A pizza delivery man appears at the front desk with five boxes, coincidentally in Wright's signature colors of beige and "Cherokee red."

When I was growing up, the Johnsons were peripheral figures—my grandparents' neighbors and fellow denizens of Lake Owen where we all spent holidays. Now "The Wax Company," as it's called locally, and its offshoots dominate Racine. Even a quick drive around town suggests that if the family, with their businesses and philanthropy, were to up and leave (which they seem to be far from doing), it would be the end of the place once and for all. Main Street alone is home to a Johnson Bank, the Johnson Outdoors headquarters, and the Racine Art Museum, a contemporary jewel box housed in a reimagined bank building that is the near single-handed work of Karen Johnson Boyd, a bright-eyed octogenarian and passionate collector, who laughingly told me her friends call her an "art fart."

In the basement archives of the Racine Heritage Museum, between frequent trips to the bubbler (Wisconsin's finest linguistic contribution, meaning drinking fountain), I pore over articles in manila folders labeled "Walker," "Walker Manufacturing," and "Walker Forge." I learn that my great-great-grandfather William Walker was the son of immigrants from Yorkshire, England, who settled in Ohio by way of New Orleans and St. Charles. He met his wife Margaret Goff (also the daughter of immigrants from Yorkshire) at a Universalist Church Convention in Buffalo, and the two of them moved to Racine in 1874—thirty-three years after it became an incorporated village, and twenty-six years after President Polk made Wisconsin the 30th state—when the area was beginning to change from agricultural to industrial, producing threshing machines, baskets, and boots.

William worked in the real estate office of a relative, and as a postal clerk. Later he owned a shoe store where his twin sons Willard and Warren worked. In 1908, he and his grown sons gained a controlling interest in Economy Spring, a wagon spring manufacturing company, changed the name to Walker Manufacturing, and began producing car jacks and, later, mufflers. In 1950, my grandfather, then vice-president of sales (the family lost controlling interest in the late 1930s), started his own company, Walker Forge, with sixteen workers in a neglected factory in West Racine, a company that never saw the success that Walker Manufacturing did, but that has weathered the years, privately held, and even flourished in recent times.

In this fly-by tour, I was looking for a clue to what had once been, an idea I had gleaned less from stories I'd heard (there aren't a lot in circulation) than from time spent at that third point on the long, skinny, obtuse triangle, Lake Owen, where Racine's captains of industry and their descendants have migrated seasonally for the better part of the last hundred years. At first, it was for summer fishing trips; then in the fall for hunting deer and "upland game" such as pheasant, partridge, and ruffed grouse; and finally in the winter for cross-country and even downhill skiing, thanks to an alpine resort called Telemark, built in the 1940s, around an unlikely 350-foot hill.

The Racine decampments started about a century ago when businessmen were regularly invited to the "Horlick fishing camp," located in a small bay where bald eagles like to roost, at the north end of the ninety-foot-deep, nine-mile-long lake, not by the Horlick brothers (among the first internationally known Racinians for inventing malted milk, one of America's first processed foods), but by a subsequent owner from Racine named Al Barnes. An old photo I saw recently shows a group of men on a porch at the camp being shaved by a visiting barber with a straight razor, and that the great Northwoods—the dense and dappled forests of hemlock, fir, pine, aspen, birch, maple, and oak that I've known for nearly the last forty years—were little more than a collection of stumps and scrappy seedlings.

The Rust-Owen Lumber Company had already done its work, cutting down the virgin white pine forests around the lake, starting in 1882, floating the trees down the lake to a dam at the north end, and sending them by sluiceways to the mill pond in Drummond (named for the company treasurer) before the timber was sent out by rail. In 1930, when the operation sent its last tree through the mill, 80,000 acres, and almost 1.3 billion feet of wood, had been cut down in the area. Lake Owen's shores were lumbered out earlier though, and so the company began selling land to private individuals and to the government, which in turn established the Chequamegon National Forest. The first family to build a house after the Owens themselves were the Sturgises from St. Paul, one of whom apparently palled around with F. Scott Fitzgerald. Then came the Racinites (as the Sturgis matriarch supposedly called them, pronouncing it *Rass*inite with a little hiss of irritation): the Johnsons of Johnson Wax, which back then was still about making "any floor a danceable surface"; then the Battens, whose company Twin Disc made clutches that wouldn't "pop the farmer off his tractor," starting in 1918, according to third-generation CEO Michael Batten. The Battens sold to their friends the Erskines (whose Racine Hydraulics manufactured power saws) on one side, and the Modines (of radiator fame) on the other. Last to join the camp in the woods, in 1932, was my great-grandfather, Willard Walker.

In 2004, when I was pregnant with our first child, there were two things I was absolutely certain of. One was that she was a girl, and two was, if by chance I was wrong, there was no way I could name him Owen. But when the boy arrived he was nobody but Owen—the sweet roundness of his head, the lake-blueness of his eyes, even the first sound he made, a nice full, "O!" My husband and I tried out Eamon, but it was too complicated to spell, and our connection to Ireland is tenuous. We flipped through pages of the baby-name book in the hospital room while our checkout time loomed, until I looked up and asked, *"Can* we name him Owen?" When I had ruled it out months before, it was because of an unspoken, seemingly irresolvable rift among the older generation that meant I hadn't been to the lake in thirteen years, since I was twenty-one. Before, I thought naming my son Owen would be a painful reminder of that, but here he was, pure joy, and so Owen he was.

When he heard the name, my uncle readily offered us the house for ten days in August, and five weeks later, my husband, son, and I flew to Minneapolis and drove four hours to the lake to meet my family there. The car trip I've always known is from Milwaukee. The road from Minneapolis is less exciting. We passed a number of depressed Wisconsin towns, ho-hum farmland, and plain-Jane little lakes. But then we got to Hayward, the heart of this "playground of the Middle West," according to the WPA Guide, where:

> Girls in shorts, sun-blacked youths in slacks, women in khaki shirts, and pink-faced men mopping their bald heads, jostle on the streets; occasionally a couple of lanky backwoodsmen slink diffidently along the edge of the sidewalks, thinking perhaps of the days when only Hell, Hurley, and Cumberland could match Hayward for hard-fisted bravado.

There's a Wal-Mart there now, unsurprisingly, but also an organic food store. Turk's Inn Supper Club, with an Aladdin genie on its sign, is still there, as is the National Freshwater Fishing Hall of Fame, with its remarkable two-storey-high fiberglass muskie—you can climb up the interior to a balcony in its mouth. At Cable, the nearest town to Lake Owen, the nearly 100-year-old grocery store, Rondeau's, was unrecognizably modernized, and the crossroads looked different, but soon enough we were on Lake Owen Drive with its nauseating twists and turns through low forested hills surrounding the lake, until we turned onto the familiar crunch of the gravel driveway, and finally there was the house itself. I walked right through it to the porch, which, because of its perch on the hill, looked through the treetops to the setting sun glittering on the lake, as big swipes of orange and pink glowed above the dark treeline. There was Loon Island in the middle, and all the marshmallow-sticky memories of cookouts and skinny dipping, chicken pox and snowstorms, capsized sailboats and marathon swims to neighboring docks, came flooding back.

Swimming through the silky, cool water the next day with little waves lapping at my face, for the first time as a real adult, I was aware more than ever that this place of extraordinary beauty—unpopulated as it is, in an era consumed by development—is inflected by a deep form of privilege, and that it is pure chance that I was born into it. At the same time it is part of who I am. My parents, Robert and Polly Beal, met on a porch here in the summer of 1965, and the story goes that when a few days later my twenty-three-year-old mother navigated the boat home in a thick fog, my Bostonian father thought, "This is the girl for me." Forty-three years later, the young man who was transferred by Pan Am to work in Milwaukee, "knowing only," he confesses now, "that it was one of the Twin Cities," is still there.

When I think about this coming summer, the first where my four-year-old son will truly be able to take in the place, I wonder, Why is it so important that we make terrariums from moss and lichens called British Soldiers, or that we go kayaking in the early morning when the lake is still glassy? Because without the pileated woodpeckers and puffball mushrooms, the boat rides and the Northern Lights, and without this sense that due west of New York is a whole world that grew me up, living at the center of intellectual thought and culture wouldn't mean the same thing to me. My mother's older sister, Suzanne McNear, another ex-pat Wisconsin writer, sent me an email about my family and our state recently:

> When I went away to boarding school in Connecticut people were fascinated to learn where I was from. Wisconsin was never entirely clear to them, as a place. It was the same as or very near Michigan or Minnesota. Yes? And when I asked my father why people made fun of the Midwest he said, "We are the heart of America. The roots. The producers." Later, he wrote, "Once some years ago at a dinner in New York I found myself the only manufacturer in a group of ten, perhaps twelve other men. All of them spoke as though life away

from Wall Street did not exist, and yet, I said to myself, and yet, where would they be without us? Without men such as myself, there would be no Wall Street."

It's not just that there would be no Wall Street. For me, New York without Wisconsin would be like having a head with no heart, and my guess is that some part of this idea is the source of the word "heartland," even if the state is hard to locate for people from the coasts. It's true that I don't live there and even that it's difficult for me to imagine moving back, but I know that without Wisconsin's ballast I'd be lost.

WYOMING

CAPITAL Cheyenne

ENTERED UNION 1890 (44th)

ORIGIN OF NAME From a Delaware Indian word meaning "mountains and valleys alternating"

NICKNAME Equality State

MOTTO "Equal rights"

RESIDENTS Wyomingite

U.S. REPRESENTATIVES 1

STATE BIRD western meadowlark

STATE FLOWER Indian paintbrush

STATE TREE cottonwood

STATE SONG "Wyoming"

LAND AREA 97,100 sq. mi.

GEOGRAPHIC CENTER In Fremont Co., 58 mi. ENE of Lander

POPULATION 509,294

WHITE 92.1%

BLACK 0.8%

AMERICAN INDIAN 2.3%

ASIAN 0.6%

HISPANIC/LATINO 6.4%

UNDER 18 26.1%

65 AND OVER 11.7%

MEDIAN AGE 36.2

WYOMING
Alexandra Fuller

A cowboy I met—well, now he fixes washing machines and installs stoves and has gut-rot and hemorrhoids from all the bad coffee he drinks staying awake to do it, so I don't guess he's much of a cowboy anymore—told me how once he came to see the whole history of Wyoming in the course of a single cattle drive. He told me it was hard to explain exactly how it happened. He said, "It's like how the smell of branding smoke in your nose brings on the taste of whiskey in your mouth. Do you know about that?"

I said that I did, because I do.

He said, "Well, it's something like that." Then he told me if I didn't want my washing machine breaking down anymore I had to check the pants pockets before I did laundry and it was amazing, he said, how few people did because not only was all this loose change clogging up the works of my machine but that was seventy-five bucks right there to have him come all the way out to this cabin in the middle of nowhere to tell me something my mother should have set me straight on a long time ago.

Our cabin, with the washing machine so full of loose change it makes a sound like Las Vegas every time I turn it on, is tucked up here near the western edge of Sublette County, which, in turn, is inclined toward the west middle of Wyoming. Sublette has a population of less than six thousand people and, when I got here, it had no stop light. Until recently, the people of Sublette didn't need a robot to tell them when to stop or go. And they didn't need the government or the cops or just about anyone else to tell them how to live or die. Freedom—like the kind you used to find in Sublette County—isn't the kind you send other men's boys off to die for. It's the kind you die for yourself.

So.

I told the cowboy-turned-washing-machine-repair man that his stories were worth it.

He laughed and said he didn't guess anyone's stories were worth that much, given they came free with any campfire or barstool.

"Tell me about how you came to see the whole history of Wyoming in a flash then," I said. "I bet that's worth a buck or two."

So he shut the washing machine door and sat back on his heels to take the strain off his hemorrhoids. He hung his great ham hands over his knees and squinted at me over the plastic laundry basket like we had put fresh wood in the fire and were waiting for the smoke to die down before he could start.

"This was some few years back," he said, when he was young and crazy and working for an outfit up near here (he waved toward our kitchen where the baby was putting finishing touches on some wall art with her porridge). He said it was their third straight day getting the cows onto the desert allotments and so the cowboys had smoked a little pot and dropped a little acid that morning to make the drive more interesting because there is nothing quite so sweetly boring as watching the rear ends of a thousand cows—manure-smeared and as stupid as mule crap, is about all there is to say about that—sauntering a mile or two in as many hours, even if the mountains were back-lit at dawn in a velvet sky like Elvis was about to be announced on some great celestial stage. And the way they saw it that morning, with the mist coming up off the Green River and hugging on the lower end of the Wind River Range for all the world like baggy underwear with the lace stretched all the hell out of it, it was a raucous old world.

He said, "To tell you the God's honest truth, I was higher than an angel and tripping like a debutante in a hay field by the time we got 'er started."

Then, he told me, just as they were riding along like that waiting for Elvis to appear in the sky and what have you, he saw Wyoming as it had been in the olden days when it was dinosaur-infested and humid with rain forests and swamps. There were beaches.

"It was Mexico with teeth," he said.

It just about scared the living crap outta him although he figured his horse didn't seem to mind too badly about any of it, not even the dinosaurs.

"The horse wasn't on acid," I pointed out.

"True," said the cowboy-turned-washing-machine-repair man.

"Carry on," I said. "I interrupted you."

But then the sea drained and the dinosaurs died and the rain forests rotted. The planet spun around the sun a few thousand million times. The earth crumpled into mountains and rolled out into plains—he saw all this happen right in front of his very eyes, mind you—the land grew purple and beaver-dammed and was fed by rivers and springs, sunk by high alpine lakes and gouged by glaciers the size of battleships. In the meantime the decomposing dinosaurs and rain forests and boggy swamps compressed into oil and the oil bubbled up out of the ground and soaked his horses hooves black as blood.

"Wow," I said.

"I know," he said. "Then people happened." The Indians first, followed (after a longish pause during which time the cowboy-turned-washing-machine-repair man had to get off his horse and hide in some willows until the Indian Wars had died down) by everyone else. And so that was that. Then he said an Indian came out of the ground, like he'd been waiting down a good-sized badger hole all these last one hundred years, and he said that his name was Crazy Horse and that he spoke not only for the Sioux, but for all the high plains nations when he said, "One does not sell the earth upon which the people walk."

"Wow," I said.

"So, that's a lesson to you right there," said the cowboy-turned-washing-machine-repair man

"Don't do drugs?" I guessed.

"Well, sure," he said. "That was one for-sure lesson."

It is true that Wyoming is a very high state, and it gets crazy-feeling, as if there is no end to the place and no end to the secrets of the place. For example, it looks as if there is nowhere to hide but in reality land is furled into land and the sky is bigger than all the land put together and you can hide in plain sight just like Butch Cassidy and the Sundance Kid, who used to exchange a silver dollar for a fresh horse whenever they needed one. The homesteaders thoughtfully kept a couple of mounts tied up at all times. It would have been like listening for Santa. Imagine! The kids waking up in the morning and running outside, their bare feet making damp stains on the blanket of white frost and there's a pair of tired horses, head-hanging at the hitching post, their coats in dreadlocks of freeze-dried sweat, fresh horses gone.

They were here! They came to us! The kids are doing cartwheels with the silver dollar between their teeth. They really came here!

It was early August in the mid-1990s the first time I drove halfway across Wyoming from Jackson Hole, through Pinedale and then up into Hole in the Wall country (as they call it), where a cleft in the sage-dotted red cliffs near the little town of Kaycee made a hiding place for those outlaws.

The scenery on that drive was so rollicking, so sure of itself, so unblemished that I felt as if I was discovering a whole new territory. These days whole wide worlds of Wyoming—even some of the crazy-beautiful parts—

are tamed and saddled with oil or natural gas rigs and housing developments, and there's roadkill in some places the length and breadth of three
football fields and so the beauty of the land has been put in its place, which
is to say it is no longer *everywhere*. But back then it made me feel positively
Lewis-n-Clark, Annie-Get-Your-Gun, Grizzly Adams, and I guess I'll never
leave the state now, addicted as I am to the idea that if I stay here long
enough I'll feel that way again someday.

There were even a dozen horses running back and forth along a buck-
rail fence against a backdrop of snow-covered mountain peaks, which you
never see except in television advertisements, so I stopped the car and got
out and was immediately hit by a wind so strong it knocked my teeth to the
back of my mind and the only thing stronger than the wind were the mosquitoes, which were of such mass-murderous intent that I jogged around for
quite some time trying to shake them out of my clothes before I got back
into the car. Then I spent a good five minutes swatting the windows. The
mosquitoes plus the wind, I supposed, explained both the running horses
and the unpeopled landscape.

But then a man whose elbow had worn a groove in the bar of the
Cowboy Bar in downtown Pinedale told me, "No, it isn't the mosquitoes so
much—although it is true they can stand flat-footed and procreate with a
turkey. And it isn't the wind, although for sure it sucks more than it blows.
It's the nine-month-long winters that keep the population of Wyoming the
lowest in the nation."

The man's name was something I don't remember now, but he said that
everyone called him Captain because once he'd accidentally landed a job on a
fishing vessel in Alaska. It had something to do, inevitably, with a bar and a
bet and maybe a gun. In any case, there he was, scared witless for six weeks on
the throwing, cold sea and after he got off the boat, just glad to be alive, he
came on back to landlocked Wyoming and told everyone about the horror of
his salty, wet experience, and earned the nickname Captain because although
plenty of folks out here have been on rigs and bucking animals and the great
plains in a white out, almost no one has been on open water.

"Nine-month-long winters," I scoffed. "Surely not."

"Just come back tomorrow," Captain said. "This here today, this day
right here, is all we get of summer."

I lifted up my beer to see its Born On Date. Born on the Fourth of July,
it said. "Look at that," I said. "A patriotic beer."

"After all," said Captain, "there's mosquitoes in Florida and you can't
keep the hordes out of there."

"That seems true," I agreed.

"Whereas," said Captain, "there is a pronghorn antelope for every person in Wyoming."

"And how many antelope is that?" I asked.

"Well," said Captain, "hard to tell exactly. The more people there are, the less antelope."

A little over ten years after I met Captain humans finally outnumbered antelope in the state of Wyoming. And in January, 2007, just to tip the balance even farther in that direction, twenty-one pronghorn antelope were killed in a single collision with an oil-field service truck just east of Pinedale and in the photographs I have seen they lie all tangled up in snow and sagebrush like a Damien Hirst sculpture (work that is supposed to raise questions about death and life in a way that reality normally does not).

It's no single thing—this energy boom that has turned great chunks of the open range into a spider web of roads and rigs and frozen animal sculptures—but an accidental coincidence of politics and climate and appetite. A place doesn't just get paved under in little over a decade without all the wrong things happening just right; an advance in drilling techniques, an administration friendly to mineral development, a war, a hurricane. And they say this boom will go on for another seventy years or more, so I don't guess there's any turning back the clock.

M aybe someone told me this, or I read it somewhere:
There was an Indian explaining to a white man about how ghosts were a fairly ordinary experience and a white man explaining to an Indian about how ghosts didn't exist.

The white man said, "We don't believe in ghosts."

"Why not?" asked the Indian (who may or may not have been an Arapahoe or a Shoshone).

"Because ghosts can't be seen," said the white man.

"But you believe in time," asked the Indian, "don't you?"

Our cabin sits at over eight thousand feet and it is always summertime there because we leave for lower elevations before we turn the clocks back and we can't get back into the place until the clocks (everywhere else) have leapt forward again. So all through the slow months of winter when nothing but foxes and the odd coyote are trying to make a living off the scant debris of fall, the clock in the cabin kitchen steadfastly keeps summer time, like winter isn't happening at all.

Of course winter is happening even if the clock doesn't pay attention. To prove it, when I first come back to the mountains at the end of May, there are layers of living and dead flies on every windowsill and there are dead mice dried into the corners of the log walls and mouse droppings wherever the mice have run, which is everywhere. There is a mold of old snow, a white series of receding high tides from the cabin into the forest. The water reeks of sulfur when the faucets are first opened and the laundry smells like rotten eggs for days.

In 1910 (or thereabout), the last group of Indians ever seen in this part of the country came through, right here, looking to hunt elk, and they were like ghosts themselves, astonished at the seasonal pull that had brought them back here twenty or so years after the Indian Wars had ended (or at least the Indian Wars in this part of the country). When the game warden and ranger arrived to read the hunters a list of broken regulations, the Indians locked the law-enforcement officers in a cabin at a bend in the river and nowhere is it written how the game warden or the ranger escaped. When they did they went running about hollering that there was a party of Indians on the warpath. But the Indians weren't on a warpath, they had come to hunt and to skin on their ancestral hunting grounds. So they went, women and children and men, to the Simmons place and I guess Simmons understood about a man's need to hunt because he let them stay there for a month, taking elk and deer and antelope. And all around the camping site the hides were laid out flat while women rubbed brains on them, since brains contain exactly the right kind of emulsified oils needed to cure skin. And did you know that a deer's brain is exactly big enough to tan its own hide? After that, they went back to the Wind River Reservation. No one who saw them ever said if the Indians were Arapahoe or Shoshone or what they were.

I think about those Indians when I catch that clock in the kitchen unawares. Like the one time we skied up to the cabin to spend Valentine's Day far away from tinsel hearts and every time I glanced at that clock my heart sped forward an hour.

The first time I met our neighbor, John Fandek, he told me, "Used to be, you couldn't see a single light when you looked out there at night."

His arm made a sweeping gesture in the general direction of our cabin. Now there are so many lights that the whole sky glows orange all night as if there was a sunrise fighting to burst out of the high plains. The natural gas field east of Pinedale is covered in blazing drilling rigs. The Sublette flats are trampled with trailers and tract housing (and each house's security light searching into the night sky). There are new hotels in town for all the gas-field workers, and they are lit up all the time, because the drilling never stops.

John is a man who tries not to spook animals, so he does everything right the first time. In winter he is paid by the Game and Fish Department to provision one of Wyoming's many so-called wild elk feedgrounds.

I asked John, "Have you always moved like this?"

"Like what?"

"Unhurried," I said.

John thought about it. "Probably just my arthritic knees."

Captain—the drifter from the Cowboy Bar in Pinedale—didn't exaggerate so much. In the mountains it is real winter for about eight months, from late September until early July. In the high plains that make up the world between the mountains, winter lasts from mid-October to May. Every day for those six months of winter, through wind-chills that will freeze your bare skin to a burn, John hooks up two of his four draft horses to a sleigh, loads the sleigh with hay, and then drives out onto fresh snow and throws ninety 100-pound bales to 900 wild elk in a feedground just about three miles, as the crow flies, from our cabin.

It's not as easy as it looks staying upright on a horse-drawn sleigh with alfalfa-sanded boards surfing over snow whales. John moves back and forth over the sleigh like a sailor on a small boat. He snips the twine off the hay and knots it into bundles, then he kicks one flake (a slab of hay is called a flake) onto fresh snow every ten feet or so. Once in a while he tells the horses, conversationally, "Whoa," and "OK," and they stop and go like that. Everyone knows the routine. No need to go any faster than the turn of the earth. No need for raised voices.

About every two weeks or so, wolves come through the feedground. They work the ragged edges of the herd: a hunter-maimed three-legged elk, a diseased animal, an elk whose jaw has been shot away.

There are common bumper stickers in this state: WYOMING WOLVES—SMOKE A PACK A DAY; SAVE A RANCHER, SHOOT A WOLF. Everyone in rural Wyoming has a wolf story it seems, more embellished every time you hear it: A wolf jumped clear over a man on a snowmobile; a pack of wolves tore through a herd of horses and ran them into barbed wire; a wolf was seen eyeing a child. Wolves are what people in Wyoming believe in, instead of the devil.

In the Rocky Mountains there are now a total of 1,264 wolves. Somewhere around 350 of those live in Wyoming. A quarter of the wolves that leave Yellowstone National Park and stray into Wyoming are killed, mostly by federal officials (in Idaho and Montana, only 12 percent of wolf populations are killed). The Wyoming legislature spends days debating "the wolf issue" and Wyoming newspapers feature a wolf controversy almost weekly. In reality, in 2005 (the last year for which total records were available), 42,000 cattle died in Wyoming. Of those, about 4,000 were killed by predators (2,200 by coyotes, 700 by wolves, 500 by mountain lions, 200 by grizzlies, 100 by dogs and black bears, 200 by other predators). The majority of cows (8,700) died from respiratory problems. Calving accounted for another 7,800 deaths and weather killed 7,000. In other words, ten times as many cows died from weather as from wolves. (Ranchers are compensated for predator attacks, but not for the weather, maybe because, although men and women have tried, you can't shoot the wind.)

The way our neighbor John sees it, he'd rather have a pack of wolves run through a herd of elk than a pack of hunters. "At least wolves finish what they start," he says.

One morning in late spring, a big bull with a massive rack comes up to the sleigh and starts ripping hay from the stack. If John puts out his hand, he could touch the elk's nose. He's a six-pointer, a beautiful trophy bull that someone will likely have mounted on their wall by this time next year. The other elk are calling one another, a mewling noise like a goat might make, but shorter and deeper, and trotting to keep up with the sleigh, their heads held up and back in a way that gives them the impression of royalty at a soup kitchen.

John looks at the bull's antlers and gets to thinking that they must feel like loose teeth right about now, all wobbly and ready to come off. He has an urge to tug the antlers and relieve the bull of all that weight. So he leans over and gives the bull's antlers a tug. Nothing happens. He gives the antlers a hard jerk. The bull takes it as a challenge and leaps onto the sleigh sending John flying off the side into the snow.

So this is how things are for a moment: The bull elk is on the sleigh with the hay, his head thrown back, like an actual king. John is off guard, trying to find purchase in the snow and wondering what will happen next. Harley and Sophie stand in their harnesses and do nothing in particular. It's only humans who think it matters that they are in charge. The world moves at the same speed, whether the sleigh is being driven by John or by a bull elk. Either way works for John and when he sees it that way, he starts to laugh and laugh and it's the sound of him laughing that finally startles the horses.

Afterword

WASHINGTON, D.C.

A Conversation with Edward P. Jones

In December, 1999, some pay stubs from the 1790s were discovered in the National Archives. The stubs, found among Treasury Department papers, authorized the commissioners overseeing the development of the nation's new capital to recompense slave owners five dollars a month for the use of their slaves in the construction of the Capitol building and the White House. At least a hundred and twenty slaves and a handful of free blacks worked on the buildings in the years spent preparing the federal district for its politicians. Nothing is known about these men beyond a first name—Peter, Nace, Abram, Charles, Jack—and their designation as Negro hires.

From Washington, D.C.'s earliest days, there has been a second history entwined with its political one—the story of the growth of one of America's most significant cities with a black majority. Slave trading was legal in Washington, D.C., until 1850. Slavery itself was abolished in the capital in April, 1862, several months before Abraham Lincoln issued the Emancipation Proclamation. The city swelled with refugees from neighboring states during the Civil War, and by the early 1870s, a quarter of the city's population was black. Within a hundred years, Washington, D.C., was a majority black city. In 1970, in the wake of the riots of 1968, seventy-one percent of its residents were African-American. Today, the figure is fifty-seven percent.

In recent years, the novelist Edward P. Jones has emerged as one of the most powerful chroniclers of life there. Born in D.C.

General Hospital in 1950, and a resident of the city for much of his life, Jones describes a city hidden to most of the politicians and lobbyists and journalists and civil servants who make D.C. their home, and one seldom seen by the fifteen million tourists who visit each year.

—CRESSIDA LEYSHON

The introduction to the *WPA Guide to Washington, D.C.,* which was published in 1937, states: "In the ream of broad (and somewhat trite) generalities, the most fundamental fact about Washington is that it was created for a definite purpose and has been developed according to a definite plan. Therein lies its unique distinction among American cities, and among all existing capitals in the western world." How aware were you that you were growing up in the capital city?

I lived in neighborhoods that didn't have much to do with the fact of living in the capital of the United States. Neighborhood kids usually stayed in their own neighborhoods; we didn't really venture out. I think once, when I was eleven or twelve, there was an astronaut—I don't recall his name—who came back, and they had a parade. I can remember seeing Lyndon Johnson—it must have been when he was vice president—so there was a big parade and all these schoolkids watching the parade, and there was this astronaut, and there was Johnson. But that was unusual. Usually we went to school and we came back home. We played. We had meals. We had friends in the neighborhood. We never really went to the monuments, to the museums.

How far back does your family's connection to Washington, D.C., go?

My mother was born in 1916, in Virginia. I think she came to Washington sometime in the late 1930s. She worked most all of my childhood at Chez François, a French restaurant on Connecticut Avenue less than a block from Lafayette Square, which is across the street from the White House. The restaurant served a lot of people who were in important positions in the government—because, of course, the White House was there, the Old Executive Office was there, and then there were other government offices around there. My mother worked there as a dishwasher, a cleaner. She got that job sometime in the late fifties and she was there until she was too ill to do anything more, in the early seventies.

She didn't talk about her work much, though. When she got home she was exhausted. I do remember once she said she was cleaning up, because one of her jobs was to vacuum the dining room area, and she found a diamond ring and gave it to her boss. The woman the ring belonged to came in the next day and gave my mother some sort of reward. I don't think it was very much.

Washington was situated on the shores of the Potomac by an agreement between the Northern and Southern states. The WPA Guide says of Washington in the 1930s, "Everywhere in the Capital one hears the indolent cadence of southern speech, and encounters that admirable though often irritating southern characteristic—the innate aversion to hurry and worry." Did you feel as though you were living in a Southern city when you were a boy in the 1950s?

Just about all the adults I knew, starting with my own mother, had been born and raised in the South. I was among the first generation to be born in the North—in Washington, anyway. I guess I was essentially being raised by Southerners; what they knew about life they had learned from the South. So in that sense, it was, for me, a Southern city.

The WPA Guide has a chapter titled "The Negro in Washington." It declares that "the Negro in Washington [has], from the start, exerted a profound influence upon the city's destiny. Aside from the fact that at the present day the Negro population constitutes more than one-fourth of the city's total, the Negro's subtler influences are by far greater than might be apparent on the surface." Growing up, how aware were you of the history of the African-American presence in the city?

I was not aware of it at all. All I knew was that the adults I knew came from Virginia, North Carolina, perhaps South Carolina, that's about it. I had no sense of how a lot of those people came to be in Washington, or when things started. It was only when I got to high school that I had any sort of sense of the role that black people played in history. I can remember I did a report on blacks in World War I for one history teacher, but that was quite unusual, and that particular history teacher was unusual in herself.

Did you study the history of slavery?

I can't remember ever hearing about or learning about anything like that. It was a double standard sort of thing, and it's sort of a whitewash of American history. I can remember one of the things they pressed upon you, which was how the American Revolution started. "No taxation without representation," which is rather ironic now, because people in Washington, D.C., could not vote for the president until 1961 and they still have no representation in Congress, really. There's a so-called Congresswoman. She can vote in the committees but she can't vote on the House floor, and there are no senators. So you talk about the capital of the United States, and all of that, but the people of Washington, D.C., essentially have no rights.

What do you think should be done about that?

Well, those of us who were born and raised in Washington are committed to having full rights. And then there are people who come every two years, every four years, who come to work with politicians who have been elected to Congress. And they don't really care. They were born and raised in Nebraska or wherever, and their plan is to go, if not back to Nebraska, then maybe to New York or something. So they don't care that the people of D.C. have no rights. They don't care about the fact that the country was founded on a certain principle and that every day that principle is set aside.

Over the years there has been a demonstration here, a demonstration there. I can remember when Jesse Jackson first came to Washington to live. He was arrested several times along with Walter Fauntroy, who was Washington's first so-called Congressperson. Every now and then people will rise up and say something, but for the most part we just go on with our lives, because nothing can be done. I don't think anything will be done.

In your fiction, the characters are always keenly aware of geography—they often specify precisely where they are, what street they're crossing, how far out of their neighborhoods they're venturing. In "The Store," for example, a story set in the early sixties that appears in your 1992 collection, *Lost in the City*, the narrator describes a bus trip "all the way down P Street, crossing 16th Street into the land of white people." How segregated was the city when you were growing up?

When I was growing up, the only white people I ever saw were those who had stores. I didn't know any white teachers until I got to high school. When I was eleven or twelve, this kid next door, Jobe, had seen in the newspaper that there was a sale going on at a Peoples Drug store. The closest one to us, amazingly, was in Dupont Circle. To get to Dupont Circle, we had to go fifteen or so blocks, and it was evident as we left 10th Street and went down R and got beyond 15th Street, that things were different. It was around 16th Street that we began to see that the world was changing: There were white people.

For some reason, Jobe had wanted us to skate there, but we only had one pair of skates between us, and they were his, so he had one skate and I had one skate and it was hell going down the street. It took a lot of effort, and so you're taxed in that way, and then there was the very real sense that you may not want to be there. It's not a residential area that we're talking about. It had large office buildings and apartment buildings—it still does—and it's very busy during the day. But I wasn't used to being there. I was used only to the area I lived in.

In April, 1968, there were three days of riots in Washington, D.C., following Martin Luther King's death. Had you already left for college or were you still in the city?

I was there for the riots and everything. I didn't really take part in any destruction. I was living at that time at 1217 N Street. That's essentially downtown, and lots of things were happening around there. Two blocks away there was a Safeway on 11th Street, where a lot was happening. In a lot of places, to prevent people from breaking windows and from looting, the owners would put up a sign that read SOUL BROTHER. There was a Chinese laundry on 14th Street, down from U, where they put SOUL BROTHER in the window.

By that time, I didn't have any friends outside of school. I lived most of my life in Northwest, primarily the downtown area, but by the time I was eighteen I had lived in about eighteen different places. Where I was living, I had my books, I had television, and I didn't really have anything else. I would just go to school and come back. So I was rather alone, I wasn't inclined to be out and doing anything—but I went out of curiosity. At 7th and New York Avenue, there was a Hahn shoe store, right across the street from another Peoples Drug store, which I used in the first story in *Lost in the City*. Some people had already broken into the place, and I came along afterward and got a pair of shoes.

What did your mother say when you came home with the shoes?

I never spoke to her about them. My mother would get home around eight or so from Chez François, so she wasn't home yet. In all the riots the only thing my mother ever got was two or three packets of Kool-Aid, and those were lying outside the Safeway there on 11th Street. She was walking up and she saw them there and she picked them up. Before my mother even married, before she had kids, she had a friend and they went into a five and dime store. And this woman goaded my mother into stealing some crochet thread. I think it was one or two packets, maybe five or ten cents each. And my mother always talked about the fact that she felt such guilt for weeks and weeks after that, for something that was less than a dollar. So she would have never ever have gone into any place. I had the shoes and I just never mentioned them.

I went off to college with them, though. They were just a tad larger than would have been comfortable. But in that Hahn shoe store, it was dark and there was a bit of a stench of tear gas, and I was nervous and afraid and I wasn't with anyone. There were other people in there, but I didn't know any of them and they didn't know me, so my whole thing was to get in there and get something and get out.

Were people you met at college interested in the fact you were from Washington?

No, I would tell them, and they had no idea that Washington was a place of neighborhoods, which was one of the reasons that led me, when I got around to it, to writing *Lost in the City*. I wanted to correct the record, as it were, and talk about people who were not part of the federal government. It's as if you say, "I'm from New York," and someone says, "What was the last play you saw?" Chances are you might never have seen a play. That's why I wrote *Lost in the City*.

Have the neighborhoods you grew up in changed much since your childhood?

When *All Aunt Hagar's Children* came out not too long ago in Germany, a film crew came over from German television and filmed me in various neighborhoods where I had grown up, and where some of the stories take place. At one point we found ourselves on the 400 block of M Street, where I had lived before I started school. The sense I got was that there were just white people on the block now. One of the crew, the cameraman or the soundman, I think, said that he knew a lesbian couple who lived in one house. And I could see the house—it was painted a weird color. He said that the neighbors had gotten together to get it changed, because it didn't fit with the new décor of the neighborhood. One of the women who lived in that house did some research and she found that the color fitted the scheme that the block had had in the early twentieth century, so she was allowed to keep the color. The thought that went through my head was that these are the kind of people who want the neighborhood to look a certain way and to have a certain kind of person living there. And if they had anything that my mother could have afforded when I was a kid, I'm sure they wouldn't have wanted my mother and her kids living there. That's the sense that I get of that whole neighborhood now.

Have you seen that happen in many parts of the city?

You can drive through, and the neighborhoods that I knew as a kid, the people who lived in those places when I was growing up aren't there anymore and I don't know where they're living now. The last two mayors, Anthony Williams and Adrian Fenty, their whole thing has been to try to make the place nice for people who are well off, and poor people don't fit into that sort of scheme.

I read a recent guide called *Frommer's Irreverent Guide to Washington, D.C.* It has a section telling visitors where they shouldn't go, explaining how to "redline out the scary parts of Washington." Is it odd to see whole parts of the city treated this way?

That's for all of those tourists. And that's for all of those people who come to work in government. *Over there are all those niggers*, you know, *make sure you don't go into those areas*. When I was growing up there were a good number of middle class, working class black people. You won't find them these days.

Do you feel proud about living in one of the great majority black cities in the United States?

I think that no matter what the color of the people I'd feel better if I thought everyone, especially the people who don't have enough, were taken care of; if I felt that the government, the city government, the federal government were doing all that they could to help them.

When I go to readings around the country, people have been asking me about the baseball team. "Aren't you excited about the Washington Nationals?" they say. Well, no, I'm not. I have a friend who's been teaching elementary school for the last five or so years. I tell them that every year, she has to buy 500 dollars of school supplies for her kids, because she doesn't have enough. She and I spoke last week, and she said actually it's 2,000 dollars' worth. I had been using the 500-dollar figure, because she and I had once gone into an Office Depot and that's how much she spent. My problem is that you can be excited about the Redskins, excited about the Nationals, but the school system is going to pot.

But I do miss Washington when I'm away. When I was at graduate school, in Charlottesville, Virginia, in the early eighties, I remember I was at a friend's house, and he had cable. We were watching a news report about Washington, and there was just a shot of a street and I was overwhelmed with homesickness. . . . Despite the fact that I didn't grow up in one particular neighborhood, there is a sense that it's home.

Do you ever wish that you belonged to a state?

No, I think I've just wished that we had the same rights that everyone else has. I think that feeds into my pessimism. How can you march around the world and talk about how wonderful democracy is, when the people in the very capital of the so-called free world don't have representation? I think it may have been ten years ago when this started, but D.C. license plates now have the phrase, "Taxation without representation." I don't have a car, but I think one of these days I'm going to find out a way to get one of those license plates just for myself.

THE 50 STATES IN NUMBERS

TABLE 1.
POPULATION

1.	California	36,132,147	26.	Kentucky	4,173,405
2.	Texas	22,859,968	27.	Oregon	3,641,056
3.	New York	19,254,630	28.	Oklahoma	3,547,884
4.	Florida	17,789,864	29.	Connecticut	3,510,297
5.	Illinois	12,763,371	30.	Iowa	2,966,334
6.	Pennsylvania	12,429,616	31.	Mississippi	2,921,088
7.	Ohio	11,464,042	32.	Arkansas	2,779,154
8.	Michigan	10,120,860	33.	Kansas	2,744,687
9.	Georgia	9,072,576	34.	Utah	2,469,585
10.	New Jersey	8,717,925	35.	Nevada	2,414,807
11.	North Carolina	8,683,242	36.	New Mexico	1,928,384
12.	Virginia	7,567,465	37.	West Virginia	1,816,856
13.	Massachusetts	6,398,743	38.	Nebraska	1,758,787
14.	Washington	6,207,759	39.	Idaho	1,429,096
15.	Indiana	6,271,973	40.	Maine	1,321,505
16.	Tennessee	5,962,959	41.	New Hampshire	1,309,940
17.	Arizona	5,939,292	42.	Hawaii	1,275,194
18.	Missouri	5,800,310	43.	Rhode Island	1,076,189
19.	Maryland	5,600,388	44.	Montana	935,670
20.	Wisconsin	5,536,201	45.	Delaware	843,524
21.	Minnesota	5,132,799	46.	South Dakota	775,933
22.	Colorado	4,665,177	47.	Alaska	663,661
23.	Alabama	4,557,808	48.	North Dakota	636,677
24.	Louisiana	4,523,628	49.	Vermont	623,050
25.	South Carolina	4,255,083	50.	Wyoming	509,294

SOURCE: U.S. Census Bureau, 2005

TABLE 2.
POPULATION INCREASE 1950–2000

1.	Nevada	1,148.3%	26.	Minnesota	64.9%
2.	Arizona	584.5%	27.	Vermont	61.2%
3.	Florida	476.7%	28.	Wisconsin	56.2%
4.	Alaska	387.3%	29.	Michigan	56.0%
5.	Colorado	224.6%	30.	Indiana	54.6%
6.	Utah	224.2%	31.	Oklahoma	54.5%
7.	California	220.0%	32.	Montana	52.6%
8.	Texas	170.4%	33.	Alabama	45.2%
9.	New Mexico	167.0%	34.	Ohio	42.9%
10.	Washington	147.8%	35.	Illinois	42.6%
11.	Delaware	146.3%	36.	Missouri	41.5%
12.	Hawaii	142.4%	37.	Kansas	41.1%
13.	Georgia	137.7%	38.	Arkansas	40.0%
14.	New Hampshire	131.7%	39.	Maine	39.5%
15.	Maryland	126.1%	40.	Kentucky	37.3%
16.	Oregon	124.9%	41.	Massachusetts	35.4%
17.	Idaho	119.8%	42.	Rhode Island	32.4%
18.	Virginia	113.3%	43.	Mississippi	30.6%
19.	North Carolina	98.2%	44.	Nebraska	29.1%
20.	South Carolina	89.5%	45.	New York	28.0%
21.	New Jersey	74.0%	46.	Pennsylvania	17.0%
22.	Tennessee	72.8%	47.	South Dakota	15.6%
23.	Wyoming	70.0%	48.	Iowa	11.6%
24.	Connecticut	69.7%	49.	North Dakota	3.6%
25.	Louisiana	66.5%	50.	West Virginia	−9.8%

SOURCE: U.S. Census Bureau

TABLE 3.
FOREIGN-BORN POPULATION

1.	California	27.2%	26.	Michigan	5.9%
2.	New York	21.6%	27.	Idaho	5.6%
3.	New Jersey	20.1%	28.	Nebraska	5.6%
4.	Nevada	19.1%	29.	New Hampshire	5.4%
5.	Florida	18.9%	30.	Pennsylvania	5.1%
6.	Hawaii	16.3%	31.	Oklahoma	4.9%
7.	Texas	15.9%	32.	Wisconsin	4.4%
8.	Arizona	15.1%	33.	Indiana	4.2%
9.	Massachusetts	14.1%	34.	South Carolina	4.1%
10.	Illinois	13.8%	35.	Tennessee	3.9%
11.	Connecticut	12.9%	36.	Vermont	3.9%
12.	Rhode Island	12.6%	37.	Arkansas	3.8%
13.	Washington	12.4%	38.	Iowa	3.8%
14.	Maryland	12.2%	39.	Ohio	3.6%
15.	Colorado	10.3%	40.	Missouri	3.3%
16.	New Mexico	10.1%	41.	Maine	3.2%
17.	Virginia	10.1%	42.	Louisiana	2.9%
18.	Oregon	9.7%	43.	Alabama	2.8%
19.	Georgia	9.2%	44.	Kentucky	2.7%
20.	Utah	8.3%	45.	Wyoming	2.7%
21.	Delaware	8.1%	46.	South Dakota	2.2%
22.	Alaska	7.0%	47.	North Dakota	2.1%
23.	North Carolina	6.9%	48.	Montana	1.9%
24.	Minnesota	6.6%	49.	Mississippi	1.8%
25.	Kansas	6.3%	50.	West Virginia	1.2%

SOURCE: U.S. Census Bureau, 2006 American Community Survey

TABLE 4.
POPULATION BORN ELSEWHERE IN U.S.

1.	Nevada	71.5%	26.	Hawaii	34.1%
2.	Florida	58.5%	27.	South Dakota	33.4%
3.	Alaska	58.2%	28.	Maine	32.9%
4.	Arizona	58.0%	29.	Rhode Island	32.3%
5.	Wyoming	56.2%	30.	Missouri	31.4%
6.	New Hampshire	55.8%	31.	Utah	31.3%
7.	Colorado	53.1%	32.	Nebraska	30.6%
8.	Idaho	52.2%	33.	Indiana	28.4%
9.	Oregon	50.1%	34.	California	28.1%
10.	Delaware	48.9%	35.	Texas	27.6%
11.	Washington	46.1%	36.	North Dakota	27.4%
12.	Maryland	45.6%	37.	Alabama	27.0%
13.	Montana	45.5%	38.	West Virginia	27.0%
14.	Vermont	45.2%	39.	Kentucky	26.2%
15.	Virginia	43.5%	40.	Minnesota	26.0%
16.	New Mexico	43.4%	41.	Mississippi	26.0%
17.	Georgia	38.9%	42.	Massachusetts	25.4%
18.	Kansas	36.9%	43.	Iowa	24.9%
19.	South Carolina	36.6%	44.	Wisconsin	24.5%
20.	Arkansas	36.3%	45.	Illinois	22.4%
21.	Connecticut	36.0%	46.	Ohio	22.1%
22.	North Carolina	35.9%	47.	Pennsylvania	20.4%
23.	Oklahoma	35.1%	48.	Michigan	19.6%
24.	Tennessee	34.8%	49.	Louisiana	17.8%
25.	New Jersey	34.4%	50.	New York	17.7%

SOURCE: U.S. Census Bureau. Percentage of native-born Americans in each state who were born in another U.S. state.

TABLE 5.
BIRTH RATE

1.	Utah	21.2		26.	Missouri	13.5
2.	Texas	17.1		27.	New Jersey	13.5
3.	Arizona	16.3		28.	Tennessee	13.5
4.	Idaho	16.0		29.	South Carolina	13.4
5.	Georgia	15.7		30.	Wyoming	13.4
6.	Alaska	15.5		31.	Kentucky	13.4
7.	California	15.2		32.	Alabama	13.2
8.	Colorado	15.2		33.	New York	13.2
9.	Nevada	15.0		34.	Ohio	13.1
10.	Nebraska	14.9		35.	Washington	13.1
11.	New Mexico	14.8		36.	Iowa	13.0
12.	Mississippi	14.7		37.	Michigan	13.0
13.	Kansas	14.5		38.	Oregon	12.9
14.	Louisiana	14.5		39.	Wisconsin	12.8
15.	Oklahoma	14.5		40.	North Dakota	12.6
16.	Hawaii	14.4		41.	Florida	12.5
17.	Illinois	14.4		42.	Massachusetts	12.5
18.	South Dakota	14.4		43.	Montana	12.4
19.	North Carolina	14.1		44.	Connecticut	12.3
20.	Indiana	14.0		45.	Rhode Island	12.3
21.	Arkansas	13.9		46.	Pennsylvania	11.8
22.	Delaware	13.9		47.	West Virginia	11.6
23.	Minnesota	13.8		48.	New Hampshire	11.2
24.	Virginia	13.7		49.	Maine	10.6
25.	Maryland	13.6		50.	Vermont	10.6

SOURCE: statehealthfacts.org, 2003. Number of births per 1,000 population.

TABLE 6.
MEDIAN AGE

1.	Maine	41.0		26.	Tennessee	37.2
2.	West Virginia	40.7		27.	Arkansas	37.1
3.	Vermont	40.6		28	North Dakota	37.1
4.	Florida	39.8		29.	South Carolina	37.1
5.	Pennsylvania	39.6		30.	Virginia	36.9
6.	Montana	39.5		31.	Minnesota	36.8
7.	New Hampshire	39.3		32.	Washington	36.7
8.	Connecticut	39.1		33.	North Carolina	36.6
9.	Rhode Island	38.4		34.	Indiana	36.3
10.	Massachusetts	38.3		35.	Kansas	36.3
11.	New Jersey	38.2		36.	Oklahoma	36.2
12.	Iowa	37.8		37.	Nebraska	36.0
13.	Ohio	37.6		38.	Illinois	35.7
14.	Oregon	37.6		39.	Louisiana	35.6
15.	Wisconsin	37.6		40.	Nevada	35.6
16.	Delaware	37.5		41.	Colorado	35.4
17.	Wyoming	37.5		42.	Mississippi	35.4
18.	New York	37.4		43.	New Mexico	35.2
19.	Kentucky	37.3		44.	Arizona	34.6
20.	Maryland	37.3		45.	Georgia	34.6
21.	Michigan	37.3		46.	California	34.4
22.	South Dakota	37.3		47.	Idaho	34.3
23.	Alabama	37.2		48.	Alaska	33.5
24.	Hawaii	37.2		49.	Texas	33.1
25.	Missouri	37.2		50.	Utah	28.4

SOURCE: U.S. Census Bureau, 2006 American Community Survey

TABLE 7.
GROSS STATE PRODUCT PER CAPITA

1.	Delaware	$64,609	26.	Georgia	$37,554
2.	Connecticut	$53,296	27.	North Dakota	$37,037
3.	Alaska	$51,044	28.	Michigan	$36,830
4.	Massachusetts	$49,647	29.	Ohio	$36,484
5.	Wyoming	$47,728	30.	Tennessee	$36,381
6.	New Jersey	$47,705	31.	Indiana	$36,235
7.	New York	$46,724	32.	Kansas	$36,102
8.	Minnesota	$43,957	33.	Vermont	$35,493
9.	Virginia	$43,162	34.	Oregon	$35,189
10.	Colorado	$42,860	35.	Missouri	$35,033
11.	California	$42,727	36.	Arizona	$33,616
12.	Illinois	$41,439	37.	Louisiana	$33,599
13.	Washington	$41,313	38.	Florida	$33,419
14.	Nevada	$41,151	39.	Utah	$33,346
15.	Maryland	$40,445	40.	Maine	$32,749
16.	New Hampshire	$39,770	41.	Kentucky	$32,446
17.	Hawaii	$39,314	42.	South Carolina	$31,786
18.	Rhode Island	$38,953	43.	New Mexico	$31,601
19.	North Carolina	$38,625	44.	Alabama	$30,394
20.	Nebraska	$38,601	45.	Idaho	$30,334
21.	Texas	$38,536	46.	Oklahoma	$30,225
22.	Iowa	$38,521	47.	Montana	$29,605
23.	Wisconsin	$38,244	48.	Arkansas	$28,805
24.	South Dakota	$37,914	49.	West Virginia	$27,395
25.	Pennsylvania	$37,719	50.	Mississippi	$26,087

SOURCE: U.S. Census Bureau, 2004

TABLE 8.
BANKRUPTCY FILING RATE

1.	Tennessee	109.9		26.	Oklahoma	34.9
2.	Georgia	95.3		27.	Virginia	34.3
3.	Alabama	80.9		28.	New Jersey	32.5
4.	Michigan	66.1		29.	Colorado	31.8
5.	Arkansas	64.3		30.	South Carolina	31.7
6.	Indiana	60.9		31.	Texas	31.6
7.	Kentucky	54.2		32.	West Virginia	30.6
8.	Mississippi	53.8		33.	Iowa	28.4
9.	Missouri	53.4		34.	Rhode Island	28.0
10.	Ohio	51.2		35.	New York	27.3
11.	Illinois	48.2		36.	Florida	27.2
12.	Louisiana	45.5		37.	New Mexico	26.5
13.	North Carolina	44.3		38.	Minnesota	25.8
14.	Utah	43.4		39.	Arizona	25.2
15.	Oregon	43.1		40.	New Hampshire	24.6
16.	Montana	43.1		41.	Wyoming	24.0
17.	Nebraska	42.6		42.	Connecticut	22.4
18.	Pennsylvania	39.2		43.	Massachusetts	21.7
19.	Kansas	39.0		44.	Vermont	21.3
20.	Delaware	38.5		45.	North Dakota	20.1
21.	Washington	37.7		46.	South Dakota	19.8
22.	Idaho	36.8		47.	California	18.1
23.	Nevada	36.8		48.	Maine	17.2
24.	Wisconsin	35.5		49.	Alaska	14.3
25.	Maryland	35.0		50.	Hawaii	14.2

SOURCE: American Bankruptcy Institute. Bankruptcy filings per capita for the first quarter, 2006, expressed per 100,000 population.

TABLE 9.
MEAN TRAVEL TIME TO WORK

1.	North Dakota	15.5	26.	North Carolina	23.4
2.	South Dakota	15.9	27.	Tennessee	23.5
3.	Montana	17.6	28.	Alabama	23.6
4.	Alaska	17.7	29.	Delaware	23.6
5.	Nebraska	17.7	30.	Colorado	23.9
6.	Wyoming	17.9	31.	Mississippi	24.0
7.	Iowa	18.2	32.	Connecticut	24.1
8.	Kansas	18.5	33.	Nevada	24.2
9.	Oklahoma	20.0	34.	New Hampshire	24.6
10.	Idaho	20.1	35.	Texas	24.6
11.	Arkansas	20.7	36.	Arizona	25.0
12.	Utah	20.8	37.	Pennsylvania	25.0
13.	Wisconsin	20.8	38.	Louisiana	25.1
14.	New Mexico	20.9	39.	Washington	25.2
15.	Vermont	21.2	40.	Hawaii	25.5
16.	Oregon	21.8	41.	West Virginia	25.6
17.	Minnesota	22.0	42.	Florida	25.9
18.	Ohio	22.1	43.	Massachusetts	26.6
19.	Indiana	22.3	44.	California	26.8
20.	Maine	22.3	45.	Virginia	26.9
21.	Rhode Island	22.3	46.	Georgia	27.3
22.	Kentucky	22.4	47.	Illinois	27.9
23.	Missouri	22.9	48.	New Jersey	29.1
24.	South Carolina	22.9	49.	Maryland	30.6
25.	Michigan	23.4	50.	New York	30.9

SOURCE: U.S. Census Bureau, 2006 American Community Survey. Time in minutes for workers 16 years and over who do not work at home.

TABLE 10.
UNEMPLOYMENT RATE

1.	South Dakota	2.6%	26.	West Virginia	4.6%
2.	Wyoming	2.7%	27.	Minnesota	4.6%
3.	Idaho	2.8%	28.	Indiana	4.6%
4.	Nebraska	2.8%	29.	Florida	4.6%
5.	North Dakota	3.0%	30.	Maine	4.8%
6.	Utah	3.0%	31.	New Jersey	4.8%
7.	Oklahoma	3.1%	32.	Wisconsin	4.9%
8.	New Mexico	3.2%	33.	Pennsylvania	4.9%
9.	Hawaii	3.2%	34.	North Carolina	5.0%
10.	Montana	3.3%	35.	Connecticut	5.0%
11.	Maryland	3.4%	36.	Arkansas	5.0%
12.	Iowa	3.5%	37.	Georgia	5.2%
13.	Virginia	3.5%	38.	Kentucky	5.2%
14.	Kansas	3.7%	39.	Ohio	5.3%
15.	Alabama	3.7%	40.	Missouri	5.3%
16.	Delaware	3.7%	41.	Tennessee	5.3%
17.	Louisiana	3.7%	42.	South Carolina	5.5%
18.	New Hampshire	3.7%	43.	Oregon	5.5%
19.	Arizona	4.0%	44.	Nevada	5.5%
20.	Texas	4.1%	45.	Illinois	5.5%
21.	Vermont	4.3%	46.	California	5.7%
22.	Colorado	4.4%	47.	Rhode Island	5.8%
23.	New York	4.5%	48.	Mississippi	5.9%
24.	Massachusetts	4.5%	49.	Alaska	6.6%
25.	Washington	4.5%	50.	Michigan	7.2%

SOURCES: Bureau of Labor Statistics. Figures are for February 2008.

TABLE 11.
MILITARY RECRUITMENT RATE

1.	Montana	8.5		26.	Maryland	5.2
2.	Oklahoma	7.4		27.	Iowa	5.2
3.	Hawaii	7.2		28.	North Dakota	5.1
4.	Alabama	7.0		29.	Kentucky	5.1
5.	Texas	6.8		30.	Tennessee	4.9
6.	Louisiana	6.7		31.	New Hampshire	4.8
7.	Kansas	6.6		32.	Wisconsin	4.7
8.	Virginia	6.6		33.	Nevada	4.7
9.	Nebraska	6.4		34.	Pennsylvania	4.6
10.	Washington	6.3		35.	Illinois	4.5
11.	Alaska	6.1		36.	Delaware	4.2
12.	Missouri	6.1		37.	Minnesota	3.9
13.	Wyoming	6.0		38.	New York	3.9
14.	Maine	6.0		39.	Vermont	3.6
15.	Colorado	5.9		40.	New Jersey	3.2
16.	Idaho	5.9		41.	Massachusetts	3.1
17.	Georgia	5.7		42.	Connecticut	2.9
18.	Arkansas	5.7		43.	Rhode Island	2.9
19.	New Mexico	5.7		44.	South Carolina	0.7
20.	Arizona	5.7		45.	North Carolina	0.6
21.	South Dakota	5.6		46.	Mississippi	0.6
22.	West Virginia	5.6		47.	Ohio	0.5
23.	Indiana	5.4		48.	Utah	0.5
24.	Oregon	5.4		49.	California	0.5
25.	Florida	5.4		50.	Michigan	0.4

SOURCE: National Priorities Project Database. The number of total military recruits in 2004 from the Army, Army Reserves, Navy, Navy Reserves and the Air Force. Per capita figures per 10,000 population.

TABLE 12.
POPULATION CLAIMING NO RELIGION

1.	Washington	25%	26.	Oklahoma	14%
2.	Vermont	22%	27.	Wisconsin	14%
3.	Oregon	21%	28.	New York	13%
4.	Colorado	21%	29.	Maryland	13%
5.	Wyoming	20%	30.	Kentucky	13%
6.	Nevada	20%	31.	Iowa	13%
7.	Idaho	20%	32.	Arkansas	13%
8.	California	20%	33.	West Virginia	13%
9.	New Mexico	18%	34.	Connecticut	12%
10.	Utah	17%	35.	Florida	12%
11.	Arizona	17%	36.	Georgia	12%
12.	Montana	17%	37.	Virginia	12%
13.	New Hampshire	17%	38.	Pennsylvania	12%
14.	Delaware	17%	39.	Texas	11%
15.	Maine	16%	40.	North Carolina	10%
16.	Indiana	16%	41.	Tennessee	9%
17.	Massachusetts	16%	42.	Nebraska	9%
18.	Rhode Island	15%	43.	Louisiana	9%
19.	Ohio	15%	44.	South Dakota	8%
20.	Michigan	15%	45.	South Carolina	7%
21.	Missouri	15%	46.	Mississippi	7%
22.	New Jersey	15%	47.	Alabama	6%
23.	Illinois	15%	48.	North Dakota	3%
24.	Kansas	15%	49.	Alaska	NA
25.	Minnesota	14%	50.	Hawaii	NA

SOURCE: American Religious Identification Survey, 2001

TABLE 13.
PUBLIC EDUCATION EXPENDITURE PER PUPIL

1.	New York	$14,119	26.	California	$8,067
2.	New Jersey	$13,800	27.	Montana	$8,058
3.	Vermont	$11,835	28.	Georgia	$8,028
4.	Connecticut	$11,572	29.	Iowa	$7,972
5.	Massachusetts	$11,267	30.	Colorado	$7,730
6.	Delaware	$10,910	31.	Missouri	$7,717
7.	Alaska	$10,830	32.	Kansas	$7,706
8.	Pennsylvania	$10,552	33.	Louisiana	$7,605
9.	Rhode Island	$10,371	34.	New Mexico	$7,580
10.	Wyoming	$10,255	35.	Washington	$7,560
11.	Maine	$10,106	36.	South Carolina	$7,555
12.	Maryland	$9,815	37.	Arkansas	$7,504
13.	Wisconsin	$9,744	38.	Texas	$7,267
14.	New Hampshire	$9,448	39.	Florida	$7,207
15.	Michigan	$9,329	40.	South Dakota	$7,197
16.	Ohio	$9,260	41.	North Carolina	$7,159
17.	West Virginia	$9,005	42.	Kentucky	$7,118
18.	Hawaii	$8,997	43.	Alabama	$7,066
19.	Illinois	$8,944	44.	Tennessee	$6,729
20.	Virginia	$8,891	45.	Nevada	$6,722
21.	Indiana	$8,798	46.	Oklahoma	$6,613
22.	Minnesota	$8,662	47.	Mississippi	$6,575
23.	Nebraska	$8,282	48.	Idaho	$6,283
24.	North Dakota	$8,159	49.	Arizona	$6,261
25.	Oregon	$8,115	50.	Utah	$5,257

SOURCE: National Center for Educational Statistics. Does not include expenditure for adult education, community services, and other nonelementary-secondary programs.

TABLE 14.
VOTER PARTICIPATION RATE

1.	Minnesota	79.2%	26.	Pennsylvania	64.5%
2.	Wisconsin	76.6%	27.	New Mexico	64.4%
3.	Oregon	74.0%	28.	Florida	64.3%
4.	Maine	73.1%	29.	Kansas	64.2%
5.	New Hampshire	71.5%	30.	Louisiana	64.2%
6.	North Dakota	71.5%	31.	Arizona	63.8%
7.	Iowa	71.3%	32.	Rhode Island	63.7%
8.	Montana	70.2%	33.	Alabama	63.2%
9.	Massachusetts	68.6%	34.	Connecticut	63.2%
10.	Missouri	68.5%	35.	South Carolina	63.2%
11.	South Dakota	68.3%	36.	Virginia	63.1%
12.	Utah	67.8%	37.	Oklahoma	62.3%
13.	Alaska	67.6%	38.	California	61.9%
14.	Washington	67.6%	39.	Mississippi	61.7%
15.	Colorado	67.5%	40.	Idaho	61.6%
16.	Vermont	67.3%	41.	North Carolina	61.4%
17.	Michigan	67.1%	42.	New York	60.2%
18.	Wyoming	66.9%	43.	Nevada	58.9%
19.	Delaware	66.4%	44.	Arkansas	58.7%
20.	Ohio	66.1%	45.	Indiana	58.6%
21.	New Jersey	66.0%	46.	West Virginia	57.2%
22.	Illinois	65.6%	47.	Texas	57.1%
23.	Maryland	65.6%	48.	Georgia	56.8%
24.	Nebraska	65.3%	49.	Tennessee	54.6%
25.	Kentucky	65.0%	50.	Hawaii	50.8%

SOURCE: U.S. Census Bureau, Current Population Survey, November 2004. Voter participation in 2004 Presidential election.

TABLE 15.
OIL CONSUMPTION PER CAPITA

1.	Alaska	77.0	26.	Tennessee	21.8
2.	Louisiana	63.8	27.	West Virginia	21.7
3.	Wyoming	55.1	28.	Massachusetts	21.5
4.	Texas	49.4	29.	Pennsylvania	21.2
5.	North Dakota	41.5	30.	Ohio	20.9
6.	Montana	32.4	31.	North Carolina	20.6
7.	Kentucky	31.4	32.	Florida	20.2
8.	Delaware	31.0	33.	Idaho	20.0
9.	Mississippi	30.5	34.	Michigan	19.6
10.	Oklahoma	30.1	35.	Utah	19.4
11.	Vermont	27.3	36.	Illinois	19.0
12.	South Dakota	27.0	37.	Nevada	19.0
13.	Kansas	26.9	38.	Colorado	18.6
14.	Iowa	26.5	39.	Maryland	18.6
15.	New Jersey	25.9	40.	Oregon	18.4
16.	Arkansas	25.6	41.	California	18.2
17.	New Hampshire	25.4	42.	Rhode Island	17.0
18.	Indiana	24.5	43.	Arizona	16.3
19.	New Mexico	24.4	44.	New York	16.0
20.	Washington	24.3	45.	Hawaii	3.3
21.	Minnesota	24.3	46.	Maine	3.2
22.	Missouri	23.3	47.	Nebraska	2.3
23.	Wisconsin	22.5	48.	Georgia	2.1
24.	Alabama	22.1	49.	South Carolina	2.0
25.	Virginia	22.1	50.	Connecticut	0.2

SOURCE: National Priorities Project Database, 2001. Number of barrels of petroleum consumed per capita per year.

TABLE 16.
GASOLINE CONSUMPTION PER CAPITA

#	State	Value	#	State	Value
1.	Wyoming	15.9	26.	Maine	10.8
2.	North Dakota	13.3	27.	New Jersey	10.8
3.	South Dakota	13.1	28.	Colorado	10.6
4.	Alabama	12.7	29.	Wisconsin	10.6
5.	South Carolina	12.6	30.	Maryland	10.6
6.	Mississippi	12.5	31.	Idaho	10.6
7.	Montana	12.4	32.	Massachusetts	10.2
8.	Iowa	12.4	33.	Florida	10.2
9.	New Hampshire	12.3	34.	Washington	10.1
10.	Kentucky	12.3	35.	Connecticut	10.1
11.	Oklahoma	12.1	36.	Oregon	9.9
12.	Minnesota	12.1	37.	Arizona	9.9
13.	Virginia	12.0	38.	Pennsylvania	9.7
14.	Indiana	12.0	39.	Alaska	9.6
15.	Arkansas	12.0	40.	Illinois	9.5
16.	Louisiana	11.8	41.	Nevada	9.5
17.	Michigan	11.8	42.	Utah	9.3
18.	Nebraska	11.6	43.	Rhode Island	8.9
19.	Tennessee	11.5	44.	Hawaii	7.6
20.	North Carolina	11.4	45.	New York	6.9
21.	New Mexico	11.2	46.	Vermont	1.3
22.	Texas	11.2	47.	Georgia	1.3
23.	Kansas	11.0	48.	Missouri	1.3
24.	Delaware	11.0	49.	Ohio	1.1
25.	West Virginia	10.9	50.	California	1.0

SOURCE: National Priorities Project Database, 2001. Number of barrels of motor gasoline consumed per capita, per year.

TABLE 17.
CLASSIC MOVIE THEATERS AND DRIVE-INS PER CAPITA

1.	Rhode Island	143.1		26.	Alaska	36.2
2.	North Dakota	111.5		27.	Washington	35.8
3.	Oklahoma	108.2		28.	Indiana	35.2
4.	Missouri	102.1		29.	Vermont	33.7
5.	Illinois	83.1		30.	Alabama	33.3
6.	Wyoming	80.5		31.	New Mexico	32.7
7.	New York	74.0		32.	Maryland	30.4
8.	Montana	66.3		33.	Oregon	29.4
9.	Idaho	65.8		34.	Minnesota	28.2
10.	Massachusetts	65.5		35.	Iowa	28.0
11.	Connecticut	64.7		36.	Virginia	25.1
12.	New Jersey	63.8		37.	Texas	25.0
13.	South Dakota	59.3		38.	Georgia	24.7
14.	Utah	54.7		39.	West Virginia	22.0
15.	Tennessee	54.2		40.	Nevada	19.9
16.	Hawaii	52.5		41.	Kentucky	19.6
17.	Michigan	50.9		42.	Delaware	19.0
18.	Pennsylvania	50.7		43.	South Carolina	18.6
19.	Nebraska	45.5		44.	Colorado	15.9
20.	Wisconsin	42.3		45.	North Carolina	15.3
21.	New Hampshire	42.0		46.	Arkansas	15.1
22.	Maine	41.6		47.	Mississippi	13.7
23.	Kansas	41.5		48.	Florida	13.0
24.	California	41.3		49.	Louisiana	10.4
25.	Ohio	38.9		50.	Arizona	10.1

SOURCE: Cinema Treasures. Movie theaters considered classic theaters or drive-ins as of July 2006, per 1 million population.

TABLE 18.
ROLLER COASTERS PER CAPITA

1.	New Hampshire	5.3		26.	Arkansas	1.8
2.	New Jersey	4.7		27.	Connecticut	1.7
3.	Ohio	4.0		28.	Oregon	1.6
4.	Missouri	4.0		29.	South Carolina	1.6
5.	Pennsylvania	3.8		30.	Illinois	1.6
6.	Nevada	3.3		31.	Massachusetts	1.4
7.	Utah	3.2		32.	Texas	1.4
8.	Colorado	3.2		33.	Alabama	1.3
9.	Maryland	3.2		34.	South Dakota	1.3
10.	Maine	3.0		35.	West Virginia	1.1
11.	Idaho	2.8		36.	New Mexico	1.0
12.	Georgia	2.8		37.	Tennessee	1.0
13.	Wisconsin	2.7		38.	Michigan	0.9
14.	Kentucky	2.4		39.	Arizona	0.8
15.	Delaware	2.4		40.	Louisiana	0.7
16.	Minnesota	2.1		41.	Nebraska	0.6
17.	New York	2.1		42.	Kansas	0.4
18.	Florida	2.1		43.	Mississippi	0.3
19.	Iowa	2.0		44.	Alaska	NA
20.	California	2.0		45.	Hawaii	NA
21.	Virginia	2.0		46.	Montana	NA
22.	Oklahoma	2.0		47.	North Dakota	NA
23.	North Carolina	2.0		48.	Rhode Island	NA
24.	Indiana	1.9		49.	Vermont	NA
25.	Washington	1.9		50.	Wyoming	NA

SOURCE: The Roller Coaster Database, 2006. Number of steel and wooden roller coasters per capita, expressed per 1 million population.

TABLE 19.
VIOLENT CRIME RATE

1.	South Carolina	765.5		26.	New Jersey	351.6
2.	Tennessee	760.2		27.	Ohio	350.3
3.	Nevada	741.6		28.	Washington	345.9
4.	Florida	712.0		29.	Indiana	314.8
5.	Louisiana	697.8		30.	Minnesota	312.0
6.	Alaska	688.0		31.	Mississippi	298.6
7.	Delaware	681.6		32.	Wisconsin	284.0
8.	Maryland	678.6		33.	Iowa	283.5
9.	New Mexico	643.2		34.	Virginia	282.2
10.	Michigan	562.4		35.	Nebraska	281.8
11.	Arkansas	551.6		36.	Hawaii	281.2
12.	Missouri	545.6		37.	Connecticut	280.8
13.	Illinois	541.6		38.	Oregon	280.3
14.	California	532.5		39.	West Virginia	279.7
15.	Texas	516.3		40.	Kentucky	263.0
16.	Arizona	501.4		41.	Montana	253.7
17.	Oklahoma	497.4		42.	Idaho	247.2
18.	North Carolina	475.6		43.	Wyoming	239.6
19.	Georgia	471.0		44.	Rhode Island	227.5
20.	Massachusetts	447.0		45.	Utah	224.4
21.	Pennsylvania	439.4		46.	South Dakota	171.4
22.	New York	434.9		47.	New Hampshire	138.7
23.	Alabama	425.2		48.	Vermont	136.6
24.	Kansas	425.0		49.	North Dakota	127.9
25.	Colorado	391.6		50.	Maine	115.5

SOURCE: U.S. Bureau of Justice Statistics, 2006. Number of violent crime cases per 100,000 population.

TABLE 20.
INCARCERATION RATE

1.	Louisiana	736	26.	Colorado	357
2.	Texas	724	27.	Wisconsin	336
3.	Oklahoma	622	28.	Idaho	330
4.	Mississippi	574	29.	South Dakota	327
5.	South Carolina	550	30.	Wyoming	327
6.	Nevada	542	31.	Tennessee	325
7.	Alabama	509	32.	Indiana	321
8.	Arizona	507	33.	Kansas	310
9.	Georgia	502	34.	Montana	310
10.	California	478	35.	Hawaii	307
11.	Michigan	466	36.	Pennsylvania	303
12.	Missouri	457	37.	New Mexico	271
13.	Florida	447	38.	Oregon	260
14.	Ohio	432	39.	Iowa	258
15.	Delaware	429	40.	Washington	247
16.	Virginia	420	41.	Rhode Island	220
17.	Maryland	418	42.	Nebraska	215
18.	Arkansas	415	43.	Utah	208
19.	Alaska	413	44.	West Virginia	192
20.	New York	385	45.	New Hampshire	182
21.	New Jersey	382	46.	Massachusetts	174
22.	Kentucky	379	47.	Vermont	162
23.	Connecticut	372	48.	Maine	139
24.	North Carolina	358	49.	North Dakota	131
25.	Illinois	357	50.	Minnesota	117

SOURCE: U.S. Department of Justice. Incarceration rates for inmates sentenced to more than one year, expressed per 100,000 residents.

TABLE 21.
BREASTFEEDING RATE

1.	Montana	88%	26.	North Dakota	73%
2.	Oregon	88%	27.	Illinois	72%
3.	Washington	88%	28.	Massachusetts	72%
4.	Colorado	86%	29.	North Carolina	72%
5.	Idaho	86%	30.	Wisconsin	72%
6.	Alaska	85%	31.	Maryland	71%
7.	Vermont	85%	32.	South Dakota	71%
8.	Arizona	84%	33.	Tennessee	71%
9.	California	84%	34.	New Jersey	70%
10.	Utah	84%	35.	Rhode Island	69%
11.	Hawaii	81%	36.	Georgia	68%
12.	Minnesota	81%	37.	Missouri	67%
13.	New Mexico	81%	38.	Oklahoma	67%
14.	Connecticut	80%	39.	Pennsylvania	67%
15.	Nevada	80%	40.	South Carolina	67%
16.	Wyoming	80%	41.	Indiana	65%
17.	Nebraska	79%	42.	Delaware	64%
18.	Virginia	79%	43.	Michigan	63%
19.	Florida	78%	44.	Ohio	60%
20.	Maine	76%	45.	Arkansas	59%
21.	Texas	75%	46.	Kentucky	59%
22.	Iowa	74%	47.	West Virginia	59%
23.	Kansas	74%	48.	Alabama	52%
24.	New Hampshire	74%	49.	Louisiana	51%
25.	New York	74%	50.	Mississippi	50%

SOURCE: Centers for Disease Control and Prevention. Percentage of children ever breastfed.

TABLE 22.
POPULATION WITHOUT HEALTH INSURANCE

1.	Texas	24%	26.	Maryland	14%
2.	New Mexico	22%	27.	Tennessee	14%
3.	Florida	21%	28.	New York	14%
4.	Arizona	20%	29.	Virginia	13%
5.	Louisiana	20%	30.	Indiana	13%
6.	Mississippi	19%	31.	Washington	13%
7.	California	19%	32.	Missouri	13%
8.	Oklahoma	19%	33.	Delaware	12%
9.	Nevada	18%	34.	South Dakota	12%
10.	Arkansas	18%	35.	North Dakota	12%
11.	Georgia	18%	36.	Nebraska	11%
12.	Alaska	17%	37.	Kansas	11%
13.	Colorado	17%	38.	Vermont	11%
14.	Utah	17%	39.	Ohio	11%
15.	Oregon	17%	40.	New Hampshire	11%
16.	North Carolina	17%	41.	Michigan	10%
17.	South Carolina	17%	42.	Connecticut	10%
18.	Montana	16%	43.	Rhode Island	10%
19.	West Virginia	15%	44.	Pennsylvania	10%
20.	Idaho	15%	45.	Maine	10%
21.	New Jersey	15%	46.	Massachusetts	10%
22.	Alabama	15%	47.	Iowa	9%
23.	Wyoming	15%	48.	Wisconsin	9%
24.	Kentucky	14%	49.	Hawaii	9%
25.	Illinois	14%	50.	Minnesota	9%

SOURCE: Urban Institute and Kaiser Commission on Medicaid and the Uninsured. Estimates based on the Census Bureau's March 2006 and 2007 Current Population Survey.

TABLE 23.
TOOTHLESSNESS RATE

1.	West Virginia	40.5%		26.	Kansas	19.1%
2.	Kentucky	38.9%		27.	New Hampshire	18.6%
3.	Tennessee	34.9%		28.	Nebraska	18.6%
4.	Mississippi	31.5%		29.	Minnesota	18.6%
5.	Louisiana	28.9%		30.	Texas	18.6%
6.	Oklahoma	28.3%		31.	Nevada	18.4%
7.	Alabama	27.2%		32.	Montana	18.2%
8.	Maine	26.2%		33.	New Jersey	18.2%
9.	Missouri	24.1%		34.	Rhode Island	17.9%
10.	Pennsylvania	23.9%		35.	Delaware	17.8%
11.	New Mexico	23.8%		36.	New York	17.5%
12.	Alaska	23.6%		37.	Florida	17.4%
13.	South Carolina	23.0%		38.	Michigan	17.3%
14.	North Dakota	22.9%		39.	Massachusetts	17.2%
15.	Arkansas	22.7%		40.	Wisconsin	16.9%
16.	North Carolina	22.6%		41.	Maryland	16.2%
17.	Ohio	21.6%		42.	Oregon	15.9%
18.	Georgia	21.5%		43.	Washington	15.4%
19.	South Dakota	21.4%		44.	Utah	14.8%
20.	Indiana	21.2%		45.	Virginia	14.4%
21.	Wyoming	20.1%		46.	Arizona	14.3%
22.	Iowa	19.8%		47.	California	14.0%
23.	Idaho	19.7%		48.	Colorado	12.9%
24.	Vermont	19.7%		49.	Connecticut	12.8%
25.	Illinois	19.3%		50.	Hawaii	9.6%

SOURCE: Center for Disease Control and Prevention. Percentage of adults aged 65 and over who have had all of their natural teeth extracted.

TABLE 24.
OBESITY RATE

1.	West Virginia	61.2%		26.	Illinois	55.8%
2.	Alabama	61.0%		27.	Delaware	55.6%
3.	Mississippi	60.8%		28.	Ohio	55.6%
4.	Michigan	60.2%		29.	Wisconsin	55.5%
5.	Alaska	59.5%		30.	Maryland	55.2%
6.	Kentucky	59.4%		31.	Idaho	55.0%
7.	North Dakota	59.3%		32.	Nevada	54.8%
8.	South Carolina	59.3%		33.	California	54.6%
9.	Tennessee	59.0%		34.	North Carolina	54.5%
10.	Arkansas	58.9%		35.	Wyoming	54.5%
11.	Iowa	58.8%		36.	New Mexico	54.4%
12.	Texas	58.8%		37.	New York	54.4%
13.	Indiana	58.7%		38.	Oregon	54.4%
14.	Louisiana	58.4%		39.	Arizona	54.1%
15.	Missouri	58.4%		40.	Montana	54.1%
16.	South Dakota	58.2%		41.	Florida	53.9%
17.	Minnesota	57.6%		42.	New Hampshire	53.5%
18.	Kansas	57.5%		43.	New Jersey	52.9%
19.	Nebraska	57.0%		44.	Rhode Island	52.9%
20.	Pennsylvania	57.0%		45.	Utah	52.1%
21.	Washington	56.7%		46.	Vermont	52.1%
22.	Virginia	56.4%		47.	Hawaii	51.6%
23.	Oklahoma	56.2%		48.	Colorado	51.5%
24.	Georgia	56.1%		49.	Connecticut	51.4%
25.	Maine	55.9%		50.	Massachusetts	51.3%

SOURCE: Kaiser Family Foundation, statehealthfacts.org, 2003.

TABLE 25.
ALCOHOL CONSUMPTION

1.	Wisconsin	21.8%	26.	Connecticut	14.8%
2.	North Dakota	20.4%	27.	California	14.7%
3.	Minnesota	19.8%	28.	Indiana	14.4%
4.	Iowa	18.9%	29.	New Jersey	14.4%
5.	Rhode Island	18.2%	30.	Washington	14.2%
6.	Nevada	18.0%	31.	Louisiana	14.2%
7.	Nebraska	17.6%	32.	Virginia	13.7%
8.	Pennsylvania	17.6%	33.	South Carolina	13.5%
9.	Illinois	17.5%	34.	Oregon	13.1%
10.	Delaware	17.4%	35.	New Mexico	13.0%
11.	Colorado	17.2%	36.	Oklahoma	13.0%
12.	Montana	17.0%	37.	Maryland	12.8%
13.	South Dakota	16.9%	38.	Kansas	12.8%
14.	Massachusetts	16.9%	39.	Alabama	12.7%
15.	Ohio	16.9%	40.	Idaho	12.6%
16.	Alaska	16.3%	41.	Florida	12.4%
17.	Missouri	16.2%	42.	Georgia	12.1%
18.	Vermont	16.1%	43.	Arkansas	11.2%
19.	Wyoming	16.1%	44.	Mississippi	10.4%
20.	Michigan	16.1%	45.	West Virginia	9.7%
21.	New Hampshire	16.0%	46.	Kentucky	9.6%
22.	Texas	15.6%	47.	North Carolina	9.5%
23.	Arizona	15.5%	48.	Utah	9.2%
24.	New York	15.2%	49.	Tennessee	8.2%
25.	Maine	14.9%	50.	Hawaii	NA

SOURCE: Centers for Disease Control and Prevention (2004). Percentage of adults who have five or more drinks on one occasion, which the CDC defines as "binge drinking."

TABLE 26.
CIGARETTE CONSUMPTION

1.	Kentucky	33.3%	26.	Rhode Island	26.1%
2.	West Virginia	32.1%	27.	Georgia	25.9%
3.	Oklahoma	30.8%	28.	Wisconsin	25.8%
4.	Missouri	30.6%	29.	Wyoming	25.5%
5.	South Dakota	30.2%	30.	Alaska	25.5%
6.	Arkansas	30.0%	31.	Virginia	25.4%
7.	Ohio	29.3%	32.	Vermont	25.3%
8.	Louisiana	28.6%	33.	Minnesota	25.0%
9.	Mississippi	28.0%	34.	Delaware	24.9%
10.	Tennessee	28.0%	35.	New York	24.9%
11.	Kansas	27.9%	36.	Arizona	24.8%
12.	Michigan	27.8%	37.	New Hampshire	24.6%
13.	Alabama	27.7%	38.	Oregon	24.4%
14.	North Dakota	27.5%	39.	Nebraska	24.2%
15.	Indiana	27.4%	40.	Florida	24.0%
16.	Iowa	27.1%	41.	Washington	23.8%
17.	North Carolina	27.1%	42.	New Mexico	23.6%
18.	Pennsylvania	27.1%	43.	Connecticut	23.6%
19.	Illinois	27.1%	44.	Maryland	23.1%
20.	South Carolina	26.9%	45.	New Jersey	22.7%
21.	Maine	26.6%	46.	Idaho	22.6%
22.	Nevada	26.6%	47.	Massachusetts	21.9%
23.	Colorado	26.5%	48.	Hawaii	20.3%
24.	Texas	26.2%	49.	California	17.8%
25.	Montana	26.1%	50.	Utah	17.6%

SOURCE: Office of Applied Studies. Percentage of adult residents who have used cigarettes in the past month.

TABLE 27.
DIVORCE RATE

1.	Oklahoma	6.6		26.	Missouri	3.8
2.	Nevada	6.4		27.	Hawaii	3.7
3.	Arkansas	6.1		28.	Delaware	3.7
4.	Wyoming	5.2		29.	Ohio	3.6
5.	Idaho	5.0		30.	Texas	3.6
6.	West Virginia	5.0		31.	Louisiana	3.4
7.	Alabama	4.9		32.	Michigan	3.4
8.	Kentucky	4.9		33.	Nebraska	3.4
9.	Tennessee	4.9		34.	Kansas	3.3
10.	Florida	4.8		35.	Maryland	3.2
11.	New Mexico	4.6		36.	South Carolina	3.2
12.	Mississippi	4.5		37.	Georgia	3.2
13.	Colorado	4.4		38.	North Dakota	3.1
14.	Maine	4.3		39.	South Dakota	3.1
15.	Washington	4.3		40.	Connecticut	3.1
16.	Alaska	4.3		41.	New York	3.0
17.	California	4.3		42.	New Jersey	3.0
18.	North Carolina	4.2		43.	Rhode Island	3.0
19.	Arizona	4.2		44.	Pennsylvania	3.0
20.	Oregon	4.1		45.	Wisconsin	3.0
21.	Utah	4.1		46.	Iowa	2.8
22.	New Hampshire	3.9		47.	Minnesota	2.8
23.	Virginia	3.9		48.	Illinois	2.6
24.	Vermont	3.9		49.	Massachusetts	2.2
25.	Montana	3.8		50.	Indiana	NA

SOURCE: Division of Vital Statistics, National Center for Health Statistics, Centers for Disease Control. Number of divorces per year by state of occurrence per 1,000 residents.

TABLE 28.
SUICIDE RATE

1. Alaska	23.6	26. Alabama	12.0
2. Montana	18.9	27. Louisiana	11.9
3. Nevada	18.9	28. Iowa	11.6
4. New Mexico	18.7	29. Ohio	11.5
5. Wyoming	17.4	30. South Carolina	11.5
6. Colorado	17.3	31. North Dakota	11.5
7. Idaho	16.9	32. Pennsylvania	11.4
8. West Virginia	15.7	33. Indiana	11.3
9. Utah	15.6	34. Delaware	11.2
10. Oregon	15.5	35. Virginia	11.1
11. Arizona	15.3	36. Georgia	10.9
12. Vermont	15.0	37. Michigan	10.9
13. South Dakota	14.5	38. Minnesota	10.3
14. Oklahoma	14.4	39. New Hampshire	10.2
15. Florida	13.7	40. Texas	10.2
16. Kansas	13.5	41. Nebraska	9.5
17. Kentucky	13.5	42. California	9.4
18. Tennessee	13.4	43. Hawaii	9.2
19. Washington	13.4	44. Maryland	9.0
20. Arkansas	13.1	45. Connecticut	8.4
21. Maine	13.0	46. Illinois	8.1
22. Missouri	12.4	47. Rhode Island	7.9
23. Mississippi	12.1	48. New Jersey	6.9
24. North Carolina	12.0	49. Massachusetts	6.6
25. Wisconsin	12.0	50. New York	6.2

SOURCE: CDC, "Fatal Injury Reports," American Association of Suicidology. Number of suicides per 100,000 residents.

TABLE 29.
HIGHEST MONTHLY TEMPERATURE

1.	Arizona	105.0°		26.	Illinois	87.1°
2.	Nevada	104.5°		27.	Maryland	87.1°
3.	California	98.8°		28.	Wyoming	87.1°
4.	Texas	98.5°		29.	Montana	86.6°
5.	Oklahoma	93.9°		30.	South Dakota	86.5°
6.	Arkansas	93.6°		31.	Iowa	86.2°
7.	Louisiana	93.3°		32.	Pennsylvania	86.2°
8.	Utah	93.2°		33.	Ohio	85.8°
9.	Kansas	92.9°		34.	Delaware	85.6°
10.	New Mexico	92.8°		35.	New Jersey	85.6°
11.	Mississippi	92.5°		36.	West Virginia	85.6°
12.	Colorado	92.2°		37.	New York	85.3°
13.	Georgia	92.2°		38.	Connecticut	84.8°
14.	South Carolina	91.9°		39.	North Dakota	84.4°
15.	Florida	91.7°		40.	Washington	84.0°
16.	Alabama	91.5°		41.	Minnesota	83.4°
17.	Tennessee	91.5°		42.	Michigan	83.1°
18.	Idaho	90.6°		43.	Wisconsin	82.8°
19.	Missouri	90.5°		44.	New Hampshire	82.6°
20.	Nebraska	89.5°		45.	Oregon	82.6°
21.	Indiana	88.8°		46.	Massachusetts	81.8°
22.	Virginia	88.4°		47.	Rhode Island	81.7°
23.	North Carolina	88.3°		48.	Vermont	80.5°
24.	Kentucky	87.6°		49.	Maine	78.9°
25.	Hawaii	87.1°		50.	Alaska	71.8°

SOURCE: National Climatic Data Center

TABLE 30.
LOWEST MONTHLY TEMPERATURE

1.	Alaska	−21.6°	26.	Utah	19.7°
2.	North Dakota	−5.1°	27.	Rhode Island	20.0°
3.	Minnesota	−2.9°	28.	Washington	20.0°
4.	South Dakota	1.9°	29.	Texas	21.7°
5.	Wisconsin	5.4°	30.	New Mexico	22.3°
6.	Iowa	6.3°	31.	Kentucky	23.1°
7.	Vermont	7.7°	32.	Delaware	23.2°
8.	Montana	8.1°	33.	West Virginia	23.9°
9.	Nebraska	8.9°	34.	New Jersey	24.2°
10.	New Hampshire	9.0°	35.	Maryland	24.3°
11.	Illinois	9.8°	36.	Oklahoma	24.8°
12.	Maine	11.9°	37.	Virginia	26.2°
13.	New York	11.9°	38.	Arkansas	26.6°
14.	Wyoming	11.9°	39.	North Carolina	27.3°
15.	Michigan	14.0°	40.	Tennessee	27.8°
16.	Colorado	14.3°	41.	Alabama	31.0°
17.	Idaho	15.1°	42.	South Carolina	31.2°
18.	Ohio	15.5°	43.	Georgia	32.6°
19.	Massachusetts	15.6°	44.	Oregon	32.8°
20.	Kansas	15.7°	45.	Mississippi	34.9°
21.	Indiana	15.8°	46.	Louisiana	36.2°
22.	Connecticut	16.7°	47.	California	36.8°
23.	Pennsylvania	18.0°	48.	Arizona	38.1°
24.	Missouri	19.4°	49.	Florida	39.9°
25.	Nevada	19.5°	50.	Hawaii	65.3°

SOURCE: National Climatic Data Center

Acknowledgments

David Hirshey, our editor for *The Thinking Fan's Guide to the World Cup*, asked us to consider doing another anthology together—we're grateful to him for providing the initial spark. His colleague Daniel Halpern and everyone at Ecco—Rachel Bressler, Abigail Holstein, Carrie Kania, Sunil Manchikanti, Michael McKenzie, Greg Mortimer, and Allison Saltzman—made it a real fire. They have been a pleasure to work with, and they have improved *State by State* at every turn.

If and when the federal government decides to organize some future Federal Writers Project, we know who should represent it: David McCormick and Zoë Pagnamenta. In the meantime, we thank them for all their work on our behalf. For encouragement and support of our efforts on *State by State* and much else besides, we also thank Tim Adams, John Bennet, Carin Besser, Kimberly Burns, Elizabeth Byrne, Linda Byrne, Willing Davidson, Tom Davis, Jeff Frank, Ann Godoff, Philip Gourevitch, Horacio Herrera-Richmond, Brent Hoff, Ian Jack, Miranda July, Jonathan Karp, Jed Lipinski, Michael Meredith, Anna Musso, Deborah Treisman, Simon Trewin, Alice Truax, Henry Wessells, and Daniel Zalewski.

We are grateful, too, to the photographers and artists who generously donated their work for the book: Christopher P. Bills, Michael Brophy, Maureen Gallace, Tom Gralish, Ertana Kolenovic, Ride Hamilton, Susan Z. Hitt, Chris P. Johnson, Douglas N. King, Lisa Klausner, Erin Kunkel, Jim Lewis, Rachel Mason, Andrew L. McFarlane, Joseph J. McGovern, Jr., Peter Miller, Pepper Pepper, Jon Rowley, Mark Seeman, Robert L. Segal, Wyatt Seipp, John C. Spence, Thomas Struth, Debbie Taylor, and Holly Rae Taylor.

Finally—first, really—we thank our families: Daphne Beal and Owen and Mira Wilsey; and Eugenia Bell and Enzo Weiland. Now that we're done with the book: *road trip!*

About the Contributors

A native of Ghana, MOHAMMED NASEEHU ALI is a writer and musician. His fiction and essays have been published in *The New Yorker*, the *New York Times*, and *Essence*, and he is the author of the story collection *The Prophet of Zongo Street*. Ali is a graduate of Interlochen Arts Academy in Michigan and lives in Brooklyn, New York.

DAPHNE BEAL'S work has appeared in *Vogue, McSweeney's*, and *The London Review of Books*. Her novel, *In the Land of No Right Angles*, has just been published by Vintage/Anchor Books.

ALISON BECHDEL is the creator of the long-running comic strip *Dykes to Watch Out For*. Her graphic memoir *Fun Home*, published by Houghton Mifflin in 2006, was nominated for a National Book Critics Circle Award. She lives in northern Vermont, where she's working on another memoir.

WILL BLYTHE grew up in North Carolina, spent part of every summer in Massachusetts, and lives in New York City. He is the author of *To Hate Like This Is to Be Happy Forever*.

CHARLES BOCK is a Las Vegas native, and the author of the novel *Beautiful Children*. He lives in New York with his wife and pets.

ANTHONY BOURDAIN is the host of the television series "No Reservations" and the author of eight books, including the bestselling *Kitchen Confidential*, *The Nasty Bits*, and *A Cook's Tour*. A thirty-one-year veteran of professional kitchens, he is the executive chef at Les Halles in Manhattan. He lives in New York City.

KEVIN BROCKMEIER is the author of the novels *The Brief History of the Dead* and *The Truth About Celia,* the story collections *Things That Fall from the Sky* and *The View from the Seventh Layer,* and the children's novels *City of Names* and *Grooves: A Kind of Mystery.* Recently he was awarded a Guggenheim Fellowship and named one of *Granta* magazine's Best Young American Novelists. He lives in Little Rock, Arkansas, where he was raised.

CARRIE BROWNSTEIN was a member of the critically acclaimed rock band Sleater-Kinney. Her writing has appeared in *The Believer, Slate,* and various anthologies on music and culture. She writes a blog for NPR and is a contributor to public radio's *Day to Day.* Brownstein is at work on her first book of nonfiction.

SUSAN CHOI was born in 1969 in South Bend, Indiana. She is the author of three novels: *The Foreign Student* (1998), recipient of the Asian-American Literary Award; *American Woman* (2003), a finalist for the Pulitzer Prize; and *A Person of Interest* (2008). She lives in Brooklyn with her husband, Pete Wells, and their sons Dexter and Elliot.

JOSHUA CLARK is the author of *Heart Like Water: Surviving Katrina and Life in its Disaster Zone.* He runs the KARES writers relief fund and covered New Orleans in the hurricane's aftermath for Salon.com and National Public Radio. He is the founder of Light of New Orleans Publishing, and serves on the executive board of the Tennessee Williams/New Orleans Literary Festival. He lives in New Orleans.

PHILIP CONNORS is editor of the *New West Reader: Essays on an Ever-Evolving Frontier.* His work has appeared in the *Paris Review, Salon, The London Review of Books,* the *Virginia Quarterly Review,* and *n+1.* He lives in New Mexico.

ANTHONY DOERR is the author of *The Shell Collector, About Grace,* and *Four Seasons in Rome.* Doerr's short fiction has won three O. Henry Prizes and has been anthologized in *Best American Short Stories, The Anchor Book of New American Short Stories,* and *The Scribner Anthology of Contemporary Fiction. Granta* named Doerr one of its Best Young American Novelists in 2007. Doerr lives in Boise, Idaho, with his wife and two sons. From 2007 to 2010, he will be the Writer-in-Residence for the State of Idaho.

DAVE EGGERS is the editor of *McSweeney's* and the author of four books.

LOUISE ERDRICH is the author of eleven novels, volumes of poetry, children's books, and a memoir of early motherhood. She lives in Minnesota with her daughters and is the owner of Birchbark Books, a small independent bookstore.

JOSHUA FERRIS grew up in Florida and Illinois. His first novel, *Then We Came to the End*, was published in 2007. He currently lives in Brooklyn.

JONATHAN FRANZEN is the author of *The Twenty-Seventh City*, *Strong Motion*, *The Corrections*, *How to Be Alone*, and, most recently, *The Discomfort Zone*. He lives in New York City and Boulder Creek, California.

ALEXANDRA FULLER lives in Wyoming with her husband and three children. Her most recent book is *The Legend of Colton H. Bryant*.

DAGOBERTO GILB is the author of the novel, *The Flowers*, as well as *The Magic of Blood*, *The Last Known Residence of Mickey Acuña*, *Woodcuts of Women*, and *Gritos*.

MYLA GOLDBERG is the author of the novels *Bee Season* and *Wickett's Remedy* and, most recently, an illustrated children's book called *Catching the Moon*. She is almost entirely ignorant of the state capitals, but can recite all fifty states in alphabetical order.

PAUL GREENBERG is the author of the novel *Leaving Katya* and a frequent contributor to *The New York Times Magazine*, writing on ocean issues. His forthcoming book on the future of seafood will be published by the Penguin Press.

BARRY HANNAH was born and raised in Mississippi. He is the author of more than a dozen novels and story collections, including *Geronimo Rex*, *Airships* and, most recently, *Yonder Stands Your Orphan*.

CRISTINA HENRÍQUEZ is the author of *Come Together, Fall Apart*, a collection of stories and a novella. Her work has appeared in *The New Yorker*, *Ploughshares*, *Glimmer Train*, and other journals, and she was featured in the *Virginia Quarterly Review* as one of "Fiction's New Luminaries." She lives in Chicago.

Born in Tulsa, Oklahoma, S. E. HINTON is one of the most popular and best-known writers of young adult fiction. Her first novel, *The Outsiders*, was published in 1967. Since then she has published *That Was Then, This Is Now*, *Rumble Fish*, *Tex*, and other novels. Her books have been taught in some schools, and banned from others. Hinton lives in Tulsa with her husband David.

JACK HITT is a contributing writer for *The New York Times Magazine*, *Harper's* and the radio program *This American Life*. Most recently his work can be found in *Best American Travel Writing*, *Best American Science Writing*, and the *Oxford American Anthology of Great Music Writing*. He is currently at work on a book, *Bunch of Amateurs: Searching for the American Character*.

JOHN HODGMAN, a Massachusettsean, is the author of *The Areas of My Expertise*, a book of made-up trivia that led to his current position as Resident Expert on *The Daily Show with Jon Stewart*. His writing has appeared in *The Paris Review*, *McSweeney's*, and *The New York Times Magazine*. He also portrays a "PC" in a series of television commercials for Macintosh computers. His new book is called *More Information Than You Require*.

TONY HORWITZ has been a union organizer in rural Mississippi, a staff writer for *The New Yorker*, and a war correspondent covering conflicts in the Persian Gulf, Sudan, Lebanon, Bosnia, and Northern Ireland. He was awarded the Pulitzer Prize in Journalism in 1995 for a series on working conditions in low-wage America. His books include *One for the Road*, *Baghdad Without a Map*, *Confederates in the Attic*, and, most recently, *A Voyage Long and Strange*.

HA JIN has published three books of short stories, three volumes of poetry, and five novels. His most recent book is a novel, *A Free Life*. His work has garnered the National Book Award and two PEN\Faulkner Awards. He teaches at Boston University and lives outside Boston.

EDWARD P. JONES was born and raised in Washington, D.C. He is the author of two collections of stories, *Lost in the City* and *All Aunt Hagar's Children*, and the novel *The Known World*.

HEIDI JULAVITS is the author of three novels, most recently *The Uses of Enchantment*. She is a founding editor of *The Believer*.

RANDALL KENAN is the author of several books, including *A Visitation of Spirits, Walking on Water: Black American Lives at the Turn of the Twenty-First Century*, and *Let the Dead Bury Their Dead*, which was a finalist for the National Book Critics Circle Award. He is an associate professor of English at the University of North Carolina at Chapel Hill.

BENJAMIN KUNKEL is a founding editor of *n+1* magazine and author of the novel *Indecision*.

JHUMPA LAHIRI is the author of *Interpreter of Maladies* and *The Namesake*. Her new book, *Unaccustomed Earth*, was published in the spring of 2008. She lives in Brooklyn, New York.

ANDREA LEE was born in Philadelphia. She is a former staff writer for *The New Yorker*, and the author of *Russian Journal*, the novels *Sarah Phillips* and *Lost Hearts in Italy*, and the short story collection *Interesting Women*. She lives with her husband and two children in Turin, Italy.

JIM LEWIS is the author of three novels, most recently, *The King Is Dead*.

CRESSIDA LEYSHON is the deputy fiction editor of *The New Yorker*.

JACKI LYDEN is an award-winning journalist for National Public Radio, serving as host and senior correspondent, who has worked frequently in the Middle East but began in the Middle West. A native of Wisconsin, she is the author of *Daughter of the Queen of Sheba*, a memoir. Her forthcoming book, *Vox Babylonia*, chronicles the lives of an intimate circle of Iraqis and their passions across the divide of both wars in Iraq. She lives in Brooklyn, New York, and Silver Spring, Maryland.

LYDIA MILLET is the author of six novels, most recently *How the Dead Dream* (Counterpoint). Her fifth, *Oh Pure and Radiant Heart*, was shortlisted for Britain's Arthur C. Clarke Prize, and an earlier novel, *My Happy Life*, won the 2003 PEN/USA Award for Fiction. Also an essayist and critic, Millet lives in the desert outside Tucson, Arizona, where she works as a writer and editor at the nonprofit Center for Biological Diversity.

RICK MOODY is the author of four novels, three collections of stories, and a memoir, *The Black Veil*. His most recent publication is *Right Livelihoods: Three Novellas* (Little, Brown).

SUSAN ORLEAN was born and raised in Shaker Heights, Ohio. Since then, she has lived in Ann Arbor, Michigan; Portland, Oregon; Boston, Massachusetts; New York, New York; Boston (again); and Pine Plains, New York. She has been a staff writer for *The New Yorker* since 1992 and has written five books, including *The Orchid Thief* and *The Bullfighter Checks Her Makeup*.

GEORGE PACKER is a staff writer for *The New Yorker* and the author, most recently, of *The Assassins' Gate: America in Iraq*, a finalist for the Pulitzer Prize. He has published four other books, *The Village of Waiting, Blood of the Liberals, The Half Man*, and *Central Square*. His first play, *Betrayed*, opened in New York in February 2008. He lives in Brooklyn.

ANN PATCHETT is the author of five novels including *Bel Canto* and *Run*, and two works of nonfiction, *Truth & Beauty* and *What Now?* She lives in Tennessee.

Originally from Omaha, Nebraska, ALEXANDER PAYNE was educated by Jesuits and later studied History and Spanish Literature at Stanford before earning an MFA in Filmmaking from UCLA. His four feature films so far are *Citizen Ruth, Election, About Schmidt*, and *Sideways*. He is currently at work on his next film.

JAYNE ANNE PHILLIPS was born and raised in West Virginia. Her books, including the novel *Machine Dreams* and the story collection *Black Tickets*, have been translated and published in twelve foreign languages. She is the recipient of a Guggenheim Fellowship and two National Endowment for the Arts Fellowships. She is Professor of English and Director of a new MFA Program at Rutgers-Newark, the State University of New Jersey.

DAVID RAKOFF is the author of the books *Fraud* and *Don't Get Too Comfortable*. He is a regular contributor to Public Radio International's *This American Life*, and his writing has been featured in *Best American Non-Required Reading* and *Best American Travel Writing*. He lives in New York.

JOE SACCO is the author of *Palestine* and *Safe Area Gorazde*. He is currently working on a book about the Gaza Strip.

SAÏD SAYRAFIEZADEH's essays and stories have appeared in *The Paris Review, Granta, Open City*, and elsewhere. His memoir about growing up communist in the United States will be published by Dial Press in 2009. He lives in New York.

TARA BRAY SMITH was born and raised in Hawaii. She is the author of *West of Then*, a memoir, and is currently at work on a trilogy of young adult sci-fi novels set in Portland, Oregon. She lives in Germany and New York City with her husband, the artist Thomas Struth.

JOHN JEREMIAH SULLIVAN was born in Louisville, Kentucky, and now lives in Wilmington, North Carolina, with his wife and daughter. He was an editor at *Harper's* for four years before becoming a correspondent with *GQ*. His first book is *Blood Horses* (Farrar Straus & Giroux), and he's finishing another, about the recovery of a long-lost eighteenth-century utopian manifesto.

CRAIG TAYLOR is the author of *Return to Akenfield*, an oral history of a rural village in England. His next book, *One Million Tiny Plays About Britain* (Vol. 1), will be published by Bloomsbury next spring. He lives in London.

SARAH VOWELL is the author of five books, including *Assassination Vacation, The Partly Cloudy Patriot*, and the forthcoming *The Wordy Shipmates*.

ELLERY WASHINGTON's writing has appeared in the French publication *Nouvelles Frontières, Out Magazine, The Berkeley Fiction Review* and various literary anthologies. Born in Albuquerque, New Mexico, he has spent the past ten years living in Europe, working as a script consultant for international film companies and, for two of those years, teaching at a French public high school. He now resides in Berlin.

WILLIAM T. VOLLMANN is the author of seven novels; three collections of stories; *Rising Up and Rising Down*, a seven-volume critique of violence; Poor People, an examination of poverty across the globe; and *Riding Toward Everywhere*, an immersive study of the hobo lifestyle. His most recent novel, *Europe Central*, won the National Book Award in 2005. Vollmann lives in Sacramento.

About the Editors

MATT WEILAND is the Deputy Editor of *The Paris Review*. He has been an editor at *Granta*, *The Baffler*, and the New Press, and he worked on a documentary radio unit at NPR. His writing has appeared in the *New York Times Book Review*, the *New York Observer*, *The Nation*, and *The New Republic*. He is the co-editor, with Sean Wilsey, of *The Thinking Fan's Guide to the World Cup* and, with Thomas Frank, of *Commodify Your Dissent: The Business of Culture in the New Gilded Age*. He lives in Brooklyn with his wife and son.

SEAN WILSEY is the author of *Oh the Glory of It All*, a memoir. He is also the co-editor, with Matt Weiland, of *The Thinking Fan's Guide to the World Cup*.